AN INFINITE HISTORY

AN INFINITE HISTORY

THE STORY OF A FAMILY IN FRANCE
OVER THREE CENTURIES

EMMA ROTHSCHILD

PRINCETON UNIVERSITY PRESS

PRINCETON & OXFORD

Published by Princeton University Press
41 William Street, Princeton, New Jersey 08540
6 Oxford Street, Woodstock, Oxfordshire OX20 1TR

press.princeton.edu

Library of Congress Cataloging-in-Publication Data

Names: Rothschild, Emma, 1948– author.
Title: An infinite history : the story of a family in France over three centuries / Emma Rothschild.
Other titles: Story of a family in France over three centuries
Description: Princeton : Princeton University Press, [2021] | Includes bibliographical references and index.
Identifiers: LCCN 2020017235 (print) | LCCN 2020017236 (ebook) | ISBN 9780691200309 (hardback) | ISBN 9780691208176 (ebook)
Subjects: LCSH: Farrand family. | Aymard, Marie, 1713-1790. | Aymard, Marie, 1713–1790—Family. | France—Genealogy. | Angoulême (France)—History.
Classification: LCC CS599 .F314 2021 (print) | LCC CS599 (ebook) | DDC 929.20944—dc23
LC record available at https://lccn.loc.gov/2020017235
LC ebook record available at https://lccn.loc.gov/2020017236

British Library Cataloging-in-Publication Data is available

Editorial: Priya Nelson and Thalia Leaf
Production Editorial: Lauren Lepow
Text Design: Leslie Flis
Jacket Design: Karl Spurzem
Production: Danielle Amatucci
Publicity: Alyssa Sanford and Kate Farquhar-Thomson

Jacket illustration by Sean O'Rourke

This book has been composed in Arno Pro text with Avenir display

Printed on acid-free paper. ∞

Printed in the United States of America

10 9 8 7 6 5 4 3 2 1

To Kate and to the memory of Iris

CONTENTS

AN INFINITE HISTORY

INTRODUCTION

The Ebb and Flow of Existence

This is a history of three or four thousand people, who lived in agitated times. It is a story—or ninety-eight stories—about a small town, and an inquisitive, illiterate woman, Marie Aymard, who lived there throughout her life. It is the story, too, of an extended family over space, and over the historical time of the eighteenth and nineteenth centuries: Marie Aymard's family, over five generations, and over the course of their unlikely lives, ending with the death of her great-great-granddaughter in 1906. It is an inquiry into the changing possibilities of historical investigation in our own times, and into the infinity of sources or evidence about past lives.

The small town is Angoulême, in southwest France, and in Marie Aymard's lifetime it was known as a place of "disquiet," introversion, and endless legal-financial "affairs."[1] Two generations later, it was a society, still, of "the most fatal immobility," as Honoré de Balzac wrote in the sequence of novels that he described as a "drama with three or four thousand personalities." To become unprovincial, in Balzac's novel of paper and printing, *Les illusions perdues*, was to "se désangoulêmer," or to "de-Angoulêmize oneself."[2]

The history begins in the winter of 1764, with two pieces of paper. One was a power of attorney to which Marie Aymard attested, as part of her "researches"—in her own expression—into the fate of her late husband, a carpenter who emigrated to the island of Grenada, and who had become the owner, or so she had heard, of "a certain quantity of Negroes." The other was a prenuptial contract that was signed a few weeks later by eighty-three people in Angoulême, on the occasion of the marriage of Marie Aymard's daughter to the son of a tailor.[3] These two acts or agreements, drawn up by a notary in the town, were the point of departure for a history that proceeds from an individual to her own connections, and to their connections, and to a very large historical inquiry: a history by contiguity of modern times. There was a seamstress living in poverty in Montmartre in Paris, in the generation of Marie Aymard's grandchildren's grandchildren, and her sister, a street seller; a naval pharmacist in Tahiti; the widow of a disgraced banker in Le Mans; and the cardinal-archbishop of Carthage.[4]

The family's lives take unanticipated turns, and so do the stories of their acquaintances and neighbors; this is a history in the spirit of the *gazza ladra*, the thieving magpie who flies away with teaspoons and plates and shiny new coins.[5] It is infinite, or incipiently infinite, in that there is no end to the information, diversions, and episodes of ordinary life. It is about contiguity in space, and in the space of social relationships; the inquiry starts with Marie Aymard's family, with the larger social network of the eighty-three signatories of the marriage contract of 1764, and with the even larger society of the 4,089 individuals who were there in the parish registers of the town in the same year. It is also about contiguity in time, and the overlapping generations of family life, as the story continues into the eventful historical time of the French Revolution, and of the economic changes of the nineteenth century. It is inspired by an interest in other people's lives—in what happened next, and what it meant—and by an exhilarated, exhausted sense of the possibilities of historical inquiry.

The history of Marie Aymard and her family is a journey in space and time, and it is also my own journey. I happened to go into a bookshop in Florence in the summer of 1980, and happened to see a history journal, *Quaderni Storici*, with an article—Carlo Ginzburg and Carlo Poni's manifesto of a prosopography from below, or of a history that is full of individuals and stories, and is not of necessity a history of the great and the celebrated—that made me wish I could be a historian.[6] Fifteen years later—in Angoulême, near the railway station, in the unromantic setting of the Archives départementales de la Charente—I was captivated by archives, and have never wanted for a moment to lose the spell.

The technology of doing history has changed almost beyond recognition over the forty years since 1980, and that, too, is part of the story of this book. I have been lingering in the virtual space of the website of the Archives municipales d'Angoulême, or being distracted, on 795 different days since the spring of 2012, and have 1,348 pages of images of my hand-written notes. But the sense of touching the history of individual lives is still there, and the sense of infinite possibilities. It is joyous to lose oneself in such a sea; "e il naufragar m'è dolce in questo mare."[7]

This is a history that has been an encounter, throughout, with novel-ists and the novel. It is a sequence of incomplete stories, like *A Sentimen-tal Journey*, Laurence Sterne's novel without an ending; one of the ninety-eight stories is about the little spotted dog of Sterne's daughter Lydia, which was stolen on a quiet street in Angoulême in 1769.[8] The most poi-gnant events of *Les illusions perdues* were set on the corner of the same street, where six of Marie Aymard's granddaughters were living in 1837. The lives of the nineteenth-century family are a history, like Emile Zola's own great human comedy, the *Rougon-Macquart*, of the children and grandchildren of a matriarch in an apparently isolated provincial town, who made their way, over five generations, to the distant corners of France.

But *An Infinite History* is a story that is without a sense of destiny, or of the development of character over time. It is "flat" and "positivist," as in the naturalist novel, in Zola's description; an "exact study of facts and things."[9] It starts with an observation of the present and an assumption about individuals in the past, that everyone, without exception, exists amidst relationships or networks of exchange, news, and information. "It is impossible to understand the past" without being interested in the present, Marc Bloch wrote in 1940, and for the historian of the medieval countryside, to look at the shape of the fields was as important as to be able to read old records.[10] It is important, in our own times, to observe the conversations and silences in the streets: to look around, now, and to see everyone, essentially without exception, telling stories and look-ing at images and sending messages, and to ask, How would it be if everything had always been like this?

It was the marriage contract of Marie Aymard's daughter in 1764, even more than the power of attorney, that was the point of no return for the historical journey, and for the book. There has been something endlessly distracting about the occasion and the names. Over the two pages of the signatures, there are different inks and different flourishes, children's names ("Rosemarin") and imposing names ("Marchais de la Chapelle"), names that are crowded together and names that are impossible to read; it is as though the eighty-three signatures arise from their place on the page. "Every single piece has a principle of motion of its own," as Adam Smith wrote of the "game of human society."[11]

So the initial expansion of the story of Marie Aymard into a larger history of modern times was an inquiry into the signatories of the marriage contract, and their own social relationships. Who were all these people, and why were they there, on a dark afternoon in December 1764? The history of the signatories has been an alarmingly inconsistent enterprise, in which the process of looking for individuals by name is one of error, repetition, chance, and reading the same pages of registers over and over again. It is a sort of detection, with an unseemly interest in other people's lives, a multiplicity of confused identities, and relationships of which it is possible to make sense only by going far back and far forward in time. It led on, in turn, to a larger inquiry into the social relationships of Angoulême, or to what seemed, at first, to be a detour into orderliness. This became a list, and a social network visualization, of everyone who was present, or was mentioned, in the registers of the Catholic parishes of Angoulême in 1764: the virtual society of 4,089 people. It was an effort to arrive at some sense, or any sense, of completeness—of the population in which the histories of Marie Aymard and the eighty-three signatories were situated.[12]

The subsequent expansion—together with most of the book—has been an extension of the historical inquiry, not in space or in the social space of connections, but in time. To find out who all these individuals were, in the end, was to find out what happened next. So the story has become a history of the years preceding the French Revolution in Angoulême, and the legal affairs of the 1760s, 1770s, and 1780s; of the French Revolution in the town; of the changing destinies of Marie Aymard's grandchildren over the revolutionary and Napoleonic period; and of the nineteenth-century economy of credit, taxes, the colonies, and the church, from the perspective of an obscure place and an unknown family. It is a story, like so many nineteenth-century histories, of revolutionary politics, of migration, social change, and economic opportunity, and at the same time a story of immobility. It is a history, through the lives of these individuals and of others connected to them, of the transformations of modern times.

A Story about Information

"Everything is grave, serious, and important" in the records of civil registration, Marie Aymard's grandson declared in 1826, in a marginal annotation of the register of births of the Atlantic port city of Bayonne; "all the enunciations they contain should be in conformity with the most exact truth."[13] It is these universal archives, over the course of two centuries—the records and registers of ordinary life—that are at the heart of this inquiry. They are no more, on occasion, than lists of names and dates.[14] But they are also full of stories. They are archives that can be read as literature, and as history. They can be reduced to numbers, and they can be adorned with the apparatus of historical scholarship, of the footnote, and of the critique of sources.[15]

The registers of births, marriages, divorces and deaths have led to other, even more austere archives, or to the records of economic life— the incipiently universal records of taxes, of who lived next to whom, in the old tax islands of Angoulême; the "registers," "bundles," and "sacks" of the reports of subaltern jurisdictions that one of the archivists of the Charente found in an attic in 1858, covered with an "extremely inconvenient dust;" the notarial acts, records of entitlements and expectations; the registers of revolutionary property and of who bought who else's house—and to the census, cadastral, mortgage, and succession records of the nineteenth century.[16]

This history has been an encounter, from the outset, with the domineering technologies of the contemporary information society. It is about "personal connections," or "friends, family, and groups," as in the social networks of modern times: "bringing people closer together—whether it's with family and friends, or around important moments in the world."[17] The universal archives of eighteenth- and nineteenth-century life are also the record of connections, and even of moments in the world. But they are evidence of the occasions for conversation or exchange, rather than of the content of the exchanges: of the possibility of "personal influence" and "opinion"—or the conditions that have been the object of the sociology of social networks—rather than of opinions and ideas.[18]

In the economics of social networks, which is one of the inspirations of the book, there are resources available on a scale that is unimaginable in historical inquiry: a survey, in a recent study, in which the investigators "asked every adult in each of 35 villages to name the person in their village best suited to initiate the spread of information."[19] There is nothing of this in the history of Marie Aymard and her family, amidst a continuing exchange of news and information that extended over time and space and the Atlantic Ocean.

The records of the town were full of "informations," in the legal sense of the expression: reports of insults and injuries and atrocious calumnious songs. But there were no published sources of news, amidst the printers and papermakers of mid-eighteenth-century Angoulême, and very few books.[20] Even the nineteenth-century family of Marie Aymard—with the exception of the cardinal, and of his second cousin once removed, who kept an inexpensive restaurant in Paris with her two sons—left very few traces.[21] There are only a handful of personal letters that I have been able to find, written in the 1880s by the cardinal's sister, Louise Lavigerie—with whom the book ends—and conserved in his archives in Rome. It is the multitude of very small histories, in these circumstances, that is an approximation to the endless, inexorable evidence of modern exchanges.

The history of Marie Aymard's family has been an encounter with a different dominating technology, as well, or the search for genealogy: a lineage from the individual in the present to ancestors in the past, or a "chain of histories of unions."[22] This, too, is one of the oceanic industries of modern times, with "billions" of records and "millions of family trees," "bringing together science and self-discovery" to help "everyone, everywhere discover the story of what led to them."[23] It is a product, in its modern form, of the period since the 1990s; which is a form, or an archive, that changes continuously over time.[24]

The technologies of ancestry have been a continuing presence in this inquiry, even though the story, which is essentially matrilineal, is only in part a history of unions. The central figure in the financial history of the nineteenth-century family, as it turned out, was the oldest daughter of the couple in the marriage contract, Jeanne Allemand Lavigerie, who lived with her four sisters, was never married, and died in 1860 at the age of ninety-one, a few minutes' walk from where she was born. The history of the family has been a story about time, in the sense that it has followed (or tried to follow) the children and grandchildren as they moved forward in historical time, and over the course of their own lives, into an imagined and unknown future, one step at a time. It is told, at least to some extent, from their own perspective, or from the perspective of the individuals amidst whom they lived. But this is very different from the view of their eventual posterity, after ten or more generations. It is horizontal and historical, and not vertical or genealogical; it is about how it really was, and not "who I really am" (the unknown "I" in an unimagined future).

There are other respects, all the same, in which the historian's and the family historian's inquiries are not always so distinct. The sources are similar, or identical; the story of Marie Aymard and her children is a history of other people's ancestors. The family historian asks, "Who am I, really?" (or "What led to me?"), and she also asks, "Who were they, really?" those distant forefathers and foremothers, in their different, distant world. This, too, is a kind of historical insight. It is a way of imagining the past, to discover the streets in which the ancestors grew up, and the individuals amidst whom they lived. Connections are a matter of historical circumstance, and elective affinity, as well as of descent. Marie Aymard's youngest grandson, when he was married in 1839 to a lemonade seller, in a small industrial town at the confluence of the Seine and the Yonne, declared that all his grandparents were dead, and that he did not know where they lived, or when they had died.[25] The five unmarried sisters were so important in the story, as will be seen, because of their own economic circumstances, and their connections to their nieces and great-nieces.

The book has been a process of discovery, and also of "search": of searching in the sense of the distracted, iterated, inconsequential process of looking (or finding) that is as much a part of the vista of modern times as seeing images or sending messages. This is a family history that has been the story (a romantic story) of provincial archives, in Angoulême and elsewhere. It is filled with descriptions of pieces of paper that are faint and unphotographed. But there are other sources, especially in relation to the nineteenth-century history: newspaper reports of tragedies at railway stations; histories of Mesopotamia and studies of the color-giving properties of plants; commercial directories and judgments about the jurisprudence of banking supervision— sources, or texts, that can be read and searched online. There are many of the parish records, too, and most of the civil registers, that can be read online, of which some—a proportion that is increasing over time— have been indexed or transcribed.

These are familiar sources that pose unfamiliar questions. The oldest of Marie Aymard's sons to survive infancy, Gabriel Ferrand, was for a time, in the 1790s, the archivist of the Charente. The page of the parish register on which his baptism was recorded is missing in the online images of the register.[26] He was married in Angoulême in 1763; a large inkblot obscures the name of the bride.[27] In 1793, amidst the turmoil of the revolutionary market in religious property, he purchased a lease on a "former church"; the page on which the transaction was recorded is missing in the online register of leases.[28] There was once a picture of him (or a picture of a picture); it has not been seen since 1910.[29]

Even in the (continuously changing) universe of printed sources, the limits of the inquiry—into one family, in a small provincial town—are elusive.[30] So the circumstantial history is itself a vista or an image of modern times. There are so many historical journeys that are now possible, virtual and otherwise, and so many possibilities, too, for being distracted, or for following long, circuitous diversions. This is a history that is local, and micro in size, and that has become larger by contiguity—by following individuals into the settings of their families, friends, and neighbors, and in their own journeys in space and time. It is a flat and positivist history, in the sense of being adorned, or overadorned, with endnote references (many of them to the municipal archives of Angoulême). But it is also an opportunistic story, of individuals glimpsed out of the corner of the eye, or at the edge of the screen. It is a history, as so often in the online universe, of both solitude—"forever voyaging through strange seas of thought, alone"—and agoraphobia.[31]

A Historical Story

The history of Marie Aymard and her family is a vast story, of the long French Revolution and of the economic revolution of the nineteenth century. It is in the spirit, like so much in twentieth-century historical inquiry, of a history seen "from below," and in particular of histories that seek to tell a large or important story through the history of an individual, or a place, or a family, or a profession.[32] This is an established, capacious genre, in respect of different times and places; one of the inspirations of the book is the microhistory of early modern Italy, and another is the "history of the world of San José," with its parish registers and "tiny facts," its gaze "in all directions."[33] The inspiration in the realism (and naturalism) of the novel is even vaster, from Shanghai to Montmartre.[34] The changes in access to information that have been the condition of the inquiry, including information about individual lives, are literally worldwide.

The story is idiosyncratically French, in that it is inspired by the amazing abundance of records and registers in France. There were nineteen notaries practicing—or being indolent, according to a royal edict of the following year—in Angoulême in 1764, and they produced at least a thousand notarized acts over the course of the year; "archives are infinitely precious," as a minister of the interior wrote in 1829, in a circular received in the departmental archives of the Charente.[35] The story is inspired, too, by a generation (or more) of histories of unexceptional lives in the French provinces—of the idyll of "certain, verifiable facts," and of the conviction that a thousand pages about an individual "who existed" can be a journey, in the end, into the history of modern times.[36] It is in the lineage of microhistories that are variable in scale, as well as in exemplarity (or representativity), and it is an attempt to make sense out of "the trajectories of thousands of people," in an inquiry that is intermediate, or "meso-," between the micro and the macro.[37] It is a "social history of individuals," and of the multiplicity of sources in respect of family life.[38] It draws on efforts to connect micro- and macro-histories by the individuals' own connections, including networks of friendship, place, and family.[39]

The ninety-eight stories in the book are inspired, at the same time, by a different and more dispersed historiography, in histories of economic life. The story started with an exceptional (illiterate) individual, and ended in an entirely unforeseen destination, in nineteenth-century finance and the nineteenth-century church. It is in the spirit of the new economic history to which Marc Bloch once looked forward, in which the "political," the "economic," and the "religious" would be intertwined, in contrast to a ("bloodless") history of "a world without individuals."[40] Bloch's new history, with its "marvelously disparate character" of materials, is now a flourishing, eclectic, and worldwide subdiscipline, in which economists use "many . . . kinds of evidence," economic historians use "uneconomic" sources, and historians of economic life use legal, visual, and economic sources in a multiplicity of different inquiries.[41]

The history by contiguity in which this book is an experiment—the story of three or four thousand people—is an effort to put together the individual and the collective, the economic and the political, a history from below and a history of the largest events of modern times. It is an inquiry into the circumstances of individual lives, and into the "why," as well as the "how," of economic changes and political events.[42] Causal histories are a repudiation of the most profound condition of historical inquiry, which is to try to understand the lives of individuals in the past, and to be a history, always, of "human consciousnesses."[43] But we think in whys as well as hows. So the book is about a multitude of very small histories, and about the possibility of edging toward understanding and explanation (as in the children's game of Grandmother's Footsteps) in very small steps.

The choice of historical scale or size is poignant, and it is ideological in the sense that it distributes the immense cemeteries of the dead into two classes, of the important (individuals with ideas and sentiments) and the unimportant (individuals of whom there are no records, or nothing very much, and who can be counted, but cannot be understood). In choosing the history of individuals, which is small, the historian chooses to understand small and unimportant changes (except in the circumstance that the individuals are themselves important, like Marie Aymard's grandson's grandson, the cardinal). In choosing the history of the social economy, the historian chooses to live in a world of the past without ideas or hopes or friendships, and to understand important changes, like the causes of revolutions, or the rise of the modern economy. But these are not the only possibilities, and there are times—like our own times—when it is important, and even urgent, to try to understand political and economic transformation from the perspective of individuals and families: of ordinary life.

The individuals in this story—this history of economic life—lived in a period of change, the long French Revolution, that was a political event, with economic consequences and economic origins, and in a period of economic revolution over the course of the nineteenth century that had political consequences and political conditions.[44] But the view from below, which is the view from the perspective of a particular (obscure) family, is disconcerting in relation to some of the established distinctions of large-scale history. The lives of individuals do not divide themselves, effortlessly, into the economic and the personal and the political. Everyone's inner life is a jumble of high and low ideas. Religion is a faith, a practice, and an economic institution. Economic exchanges are interested and disinterested, public and private and intimate. Individuals are mobile or immobile in life, and also in imagination—in the information or misinformation they have about distant places and long-lost friends.

Angoulême was a place where very little happened, over the course of the French Revolution—or at least in the historiography of the revolution—and the family of Marie Aymard were invisible (with one, marginal exception) in the entire historiography. But the history of the revolutionary years from the perspective of an obscure place and an unknown family is itself, as will be seen, a large story. There is a revolutionary hero, of sorts, who grew up around the corner from the family, and a heroine of the counterrevolution. The journeys of Marie Aymard's grandchildren were a history, in their own way, of the transformation of the conditions of life, over the revolutionary period.

The history recounted in this book is disconcerting, too, in relation to large presumptions about modern times.[45] Marie Aymard's nineteenth-century family were enterprising and industrious, or some of them were, in the vast economy of the state (and the church) more than in the market, and in a sequence of economic relationships that were indistinctly of the market and of the state. They were "uneconomic," in that they found advancement in the public and private services that loomed so large, then as now, in economic life. Their economic fortunes were determined, from time to time, by the choices of calculating, industrious women who never went anywhere at all—like Marie Aymard's granddaughters, whose lives (and savings) were at the center of the nineteenth-century story. The only person in the family who became important, in the history of the extended French economy, was Marie Aymard's grandson's grandson in Carthage: Charles Martial Allemand Lavigerie, visionary of humanitarian information, campaigner against the trans-Saharan slave trade, and a "marvelously adroit businessman," in the opinion of his critics, "a millionaire, a multimillionaire."[46]

The stories of Marie Aymard and her family are disconcerting, most of all, in the extent to which they subvert the asymmetry of time, or the affliction of knowing what happened next. To have almost no evidence other than the most ordinary of archives is to be obliged to follow the rhythms of ordinary life; to live in the present (of the individuals in the past) and in their (approximately) remembered past; to know nothing of their future, or of the large revolutions of which they were a part. It is to know almost nothing other than what they knew, or anticipated, or who it was amidst whom they lived. But this is itself a history of information, and of change over time.

The history of Marie Aymard and her family has been an experiment in thinking with numbers—in a world swimming in information—and an experiment in thinking with stories, in a world of endless storytelling. It has been inspired, throughout, by a sense of the incompleteness and the immensity of historical sources: of the possibility of finding everyone (in the generation of the grandchildren's grandchildren, or in the parish records of Angoulême in 1764) and of the limits of even the most universal evidence. It is an infinite history in this respect as well. The only solace, along the way, is to try to be as obvious as possible about the sources and the statistics, and to hope that others will find more connections, more sources, and more hypotheses to be explored.[47] This is a good time for a story of living with uncertainty, and a story with no end in sight. It is a story of changing times from the perspective of a single, large, unequal family. It is a history, above all, of what it is like to live amidst events that are beyond one's control.

Chapter One

THE WORLD OF MARIE AYMARD

The Historical Record

Marie Aymard was born in Angoulême in 1713 and died there in 1790.[1] She was an only child. Her parents, when they married in 1711, stated that they were unable to sign their names. Her mother was the daughter of a shoemaker who had moved to Angoulême from a small community to the southwest of the town; her father was described as a shopkeeper or merchant, a *marchand*.[2] He died when she was a little girl, and her mother married again, when Marie was five, to a widower, a master carpenter.[3] In 1735, Marie was married to Louis Ferrand, an apprentice joiner or furniture-maker. She declared on their marriage, as on so many subsequent occasions, that she was unable to sign her name. Her husband, who signed the register, was an immigrant to the town, the son of a clogmaker from the diocese of Tours, some two hundred kilometers or several days' walk to the north of Angoulême.[4]

Over the next fourteen years, Marie Aymard had eight children, of whom two died in infancy. It is possible, but unlikely, that she ever left Angoulême. She and her husband moved frequently, within the small parishes of the town; over the six-year period from 1738 to 1744, she gave birth to six children in four different parishes of the old center of the town.[5] Louis remained an outsider; he was described as "Ferrand dit tourangeau," the man from Tours, in the record of the baptism of Jean or Jean-Baptiste, his youngest child.[6] But he became a master joiner, and by 1744 he was a "sindic" or elected official of the community (the small corporation or guild) of joiners in Angoulême.[7] The acquaintances or relatives whom he and Marie chose as godparents for their eight children belonged to the same milieu of the town: a carpenter, a hatmaker, three different locksmiths, the wife of a cooper, and the wife of yet another locksmith.[8]

In June 1753, there was a great event in the family's life. Angoulême was a town with a celebrated college, at the time a Jesuit foundation, which provided free instruction to local boys. In 1753, the couple's oldest son, Gabriel, took the first step—becoming a tonsured clerk or cleric— toward ordination as a Catholic priest; he was fifteen.[9] It was in December of the same year that Louis Ferrand set off to make the family's fortune. He and another man, a carpenter, signed a contract to work for two years on the island of Grenada, for the sum of five hundred livres a year, plus all their expenses of food, lodging, and laundry, "in sickness and in health." Their engagement was with an aspiring planter, Jean-Alexandre Cazaud, who was born in Guadeloupe and settled in Angoulême, where he married the daughter of a local silk merchant; the contract was signed on Cazaud's behalf by his father-in-law, who was later one of the protagonists—the principal "capitalist"—in the most notorious of the legal-financial affairs in the town, or the "revolution" in commerce that began in 1769.[10]

Marie Aymard, at the time her husband left, had six young children, aged from four to fifteen. Her stepfather died two years later, in 1755, and her mother died in 1759; the carpenter who had gone with Louis to Grenada also died.[11] Then, at some point before May 1760, Marie received the terrible news of her husband's death. In an agreement with her son Gabriel, drawn up with a notary who was known for his "bad character," in a town in which the number of practicing notaries was "so excessive" as to become the subject of royal regulation, she was described as the widow of Louis Ferrand.[12]

Gabriel was no longer a priest, or on the route to ordination. But the agreement began with a story about his intentions, which were imposing; "the said Ferrand having formed the plan of becoming a master of arts in order to provide instruction to youth, had, as a result, decided to establish a home . . . where he now lived, and which he had furnished at his own expense." Gabriel then told a history of sentiments. He knew the "strict obligations of children toward those to whom they owed their existence," and he wished to demonstrate to his mother that "his sentiments are to comfort her, as much as is in his power, and to make her life less harsh." "Seeing his mother in a situation where she was no longer able to live, and to support herself without his help," he had therefore entreated her to come and live with him.[13]

Marie Aymard's reply—the words that she or her son dictated, or that the notary drafted—was cool. "Wishing to profit from the good heart of her son," she said, and "assuming that his benevolence toward her will continue, and that he will not abandon her to the destiny in which a sad distress would place her," she had decided to accept his offer, and to move to his home. She brought her furniture with her, and it was described in the notarial act. There were two old wooden beds, garnished with very worn green serge; two half-cabinets or wardrobes in poplar wood; a "worn-out" square table with "ten old bad chairs"; twelve plates, six spoons of ordinary tin, six iron forks, and six sheets. The "two parties"—Marie Aymard and her son—agreed that the value of the property was 130 livres, and that they "did not constitute directly or indirectly any sort of society or community, either tacit or customary."[14]

Life continued to be hard, for the new household that was not a society, and when Gabriel was about to be married in October 1763—to Marie Adelaide Devuailly, from a family of cloth-dyers in Amiens, who had recently settled in Angoulême—he declared that his mother "at the present time has no property, furniture, or real estate in her possession."[15] A few weeks later, Marie Aymard's furniture was again the object of a notarial act. In January 1764, she and Gabriel appeared before a different notary, Jean Bernard, who was known to have "made many instruments for the small people." Gabriel was identified, now, as a "master writer."[16] This time, too, Gabriel Ferrand and Marie Aymard told a story. Over the period since 1760, they recounted, Gabriel had been obliged to make payments, "out of his own funds," to a number of his mother's creditors, who wanted to seize the "said furniture." She owed money to a shoemaker, a maker of potash for washing clothes, someone who sold cooking fat, and a cloth merchant; the total of her debts was 290 livres.[17]

In order to be reimbursed for at least part of his expenditure, Gabriel said, he had considered taking out an order against his mother, for the seizure and judicial sale of the furniture. But she explained to him that the costs of a forced sale would consume almost the entire value of the furniture. She proposed that she sell it to him, "a la miable," or in a friendly manner; he had bought everything from her, in 1763, for 130 livres.[18] The following day, before yet a different notary, Marie Aymard acknowledged that her late husband's employer, too, had paid a debt of 150 livres on her behalf, plus 606 livres—a substantial sum, more than her husband's yearly salary—to two families of bakers in the town.[19]

The Power of Attorney

In October 1764, Marie Aymard appeared before the notary Jean Bernard, and identified herself as the widow of Louis Ferrand, "master carpenter," and the mother of five minor children. "She said to us [that] her husband had left the said town of Angoulême and had gone with M. Cazaud to Martinique in the year 1753," the notary wrote; "he then went to establish his residence in the island of Grenada." Over the next several years, Marie Aymard "learned that her said husband had bought a certain quantity of Negroes and several mules, that he earned twenty-four livres per day, in addition to the fifteen livres that his Negroes brought him, also per day." He had made "a small fortune during the four or five years he lived in Grenada," and "returned to Martinique with the idea of leaving from there to return to his family." But "he was attacked by an illness, of which he died on the third day," in the care of a religious hospital, the "Pères de la Charité."[20]

The purpose of Marie Aymard's declaration, and of the power of attorney she requested, was to find out what had happened to the small possible fortune. Her husband, before he died, had "deposited his fortune in the hands of M. Vandax, shipowner or merchant living on the Promenade du Mouillage [in Martinique] or in Fort Saint-Pierre." Or so she had been told; "these are the facts about which the party has been instructed at different times by certain persons in the town of Angoulême." The informants had "at the same time reported to her that the said M. Vandax had replied obscurely to the inquiries they had made to him verbally on this subject, leading her nevertheless to hope that she would have satisfaction once her children had reached their majority."[21]

It was here that matters rested, for some time. "This hope, her indigence, and the distance," Marie Aymard declared, "had forced her to defer, until now, her researches," as well as the effort to recover her inheritance, "without which she could no longer subsist." But she had now learned that a sublieutenant in the merchant navy, called Pascal Chauvin, was on the point of leaving for Martinique. The power of attorney was to him, as her "general and special" representative, and the document ended in a profusion of legalisms. Chauvin was empowered to represent her before "all judges, notaries, clerks, and other public persons"; to "formulate all demands against the said M. Vandax and all others, as he sees fit"; to "request, plead, appeal, oppose, defend, and contradict." "Promising to approve and approving" whatever he did, she indemnified him against any losses in the future, for which she "entered into obligation and mortgaged all and each of her goods and those of her said children."[22]

Marie Aymard could not write: "the party declared that she did not know how to sign her name." But she lived in a cloud of news. There were the facts about which she had been instructed, and the reports about the obscure inquiries in Martinique; there were her researches and what she had learned. She had letters written for her, and she and her husband exchanged information slowly across the ocean; she knew that he had made a "particular acquaintance" with a M. de Flavigné in the parish of "Marquis a la Cabeste" in Grenada, and with a M. Herbert du Jardin, a merchant in Saint-Pierre in Martinique, to whom she addressed her letters. She had two possible places of residence for M. Vandax. She knew names and addresses and calculations: "the fifteen livres that his Negroes brought him, also per day."[23]

So this was the power of attorney, a single folded page. The story of Marie Aymard was so intriguing, at first, because it seemed to offer a vista of the busy, buzzing sources of information or misinformation about the outside world that existed in the eighteenth century, even in the deep interior of France. It was of interest, that is to say, in relation to the traditional historical question of "how it really was." Marie Aymard was describing, in the formal language of the notaries, the unwritten exchanges, the facts and news and obscure inquiries, that were the media of information in early modern times, and that are so transient in the archives and digital repositories of historical scholarship.

The story was intriguing, too, in relation to a different historical question, or "what really happened." Marie Aymard told a story with a beginning, in 1753, when her husband left the town of Angoulême, and a very obscure end. So what did the sublieutenant find out, if he ever went to Martinique? Who was M. Cazaud, her husband's employer, who paid her debts to local bakers, and who turned out to be a figure of "cruelty," "violence," "relentlessness," "avarice," and "atrocity," according to an unrelated lawsuit of 1779, and the son-in-law of the principal "capitalist" or creditor in the financial crisis of 1769?[24] Who was M. Vandax? Who were her husband's Negroes, if they were ever his? And who was she, this indigent and exigent Marie Aymard?

There is evidence, of a sort, of her economic circumstances: her worldly wealth, in 1764, was valued, with unusual precision, as amounting to minus 160 livres. There is a description of the things amidst which she lived, the old bad chairs and the six iron forks, and of the individuals with whom she had relationships of exchange, or of credit and indebtedness. There is an evocation, in the power of attorney, of her sources of information (and misinformation): "the facts" about which she had been "instructed," her "researches," the people who had "reported" to her that the merchant on the promenade in Martinique had "replied obscurely" to their inquiries, the reports of letters that had been read to her and letters that had been written for her. There is a list of her acquaintances, or of the eighty-three people who signed the prenuptial contract of her daughter, on a December day in 1764. But this, in sum, is the historical record of Marie Aymard. She had twenty-two grandchildren who were born in Angoulême during her lifetime; one of them—the grandfather of Louise Lavigerie and the future cardinal Lavigerie—was already married when she died. Marie Aymard lived through the first nine months of the French Revolution; she died in the parish of Petit St. Cybard at the age of seventy-seven, and was buried in yet another parish, of Notre Dame de Beaulieu.[25]

Eight Children

Even the lives of Marie Aymard's children, or of most of them, are lost in time. Her first child, *Anne Ferrand*, was born in 1736, and died at the age of nineteen months, in March 1738.[26] *Gabriel Ferrand*, her second child, and the first to survive infancy, was born a few days later, in April 1738; he was the only one of her children whose life was for a time profusely, even obsessively documented.[27] Gabriel lived throughout his life in the world of the word, and he fulfilled his early intention of providing "instruction to youth." He married a woman called Marie Adelaide Devuailly, and they had six sons, all of whom were born in Angoulême; by the time his youngest son was baptized in 1775, he was a "master writer and master of a boarding school." When he died in Angoulême in 1816, he was described as "head of the Bureau of Archives of the Prefecture of the Department of the Charente."[28]

The third of Marie Aymard and Louis Ferrand's children, *Léonard Ferrand*, also died in infancy; he was born in 1739 and died shortly after his second birthday.[29] *Françoise Ferrand*, the bride in the sociable prenuptial contract, was the fourth child, and the second to survive infancy. She was born in November 1740, and she, like Gabriel, led a documented life.[30] She was the godmother, at the age of fifteen, of the daughter of a master carpenter in the parish of St. Martial, and signed the register in a large and confident hand, "Françoige Ferant."[31] She married Etienne Allemand Lavigerie and had thirteen children, all baptized in Angoulême; she was a witness at the marriage of her oldest son, Martial, in 1790; at his divorce, by mutual consent, in 1796; at his second marriage, in 1801, to Bonne or Bonnite, a young woman from Saint-Domingue; and at his own prenuptial contract, in which Bonnite, too, promised all her "goods and rights," and any "other things," to be "appropriated, researched, and recovered."[32] Françoise Ferrand died in Angoulême in 1805. It is her children, grandchildren, and great-grandchildren—the posterity of Marie Aymard in the matrilineal descent—who are at the center of the nineteenth-century history in this book.

There is almost no evidence of the existence of Marie Aymard's third surviving child, *François Ferrand*. He was baptized in 1742, and he was listed in the power of attorney about the missing fortune as one of her

five minor children; he signed his brother Gabriel's marriage contract
in 1763, but was not a signatory of his sister's marriage contract the following year.[33] He was still in Angoulême in 1766, when he was present
at the baptism of Gabriel and Marie Adelaide's third son; the godfather,
who was absent, was the child's maternal uncle, and François was listed
as his representative, "François Ferrand, also an uncle."[34] This is where
the record ends (or the records that I have so far been able to find). It is
possible that François is the same person as "François Ferand," who
lived fairly near the Allemands and the Ferrands, and who was listed in
a tax roll for 1763 as a "domestic servant" of the innkeeper of the Cheval
Blanc; the innkeeper, together with his wife, were among the signatories
of Françoise's marriage contract.[35] But there are some nineteen thousand entries or family trees for persons called "François Ferrand" on
family history websites, and none of them correspond to the domestic
servant at the Cheval Blanc, or to Marie Aymard's son.[36]

Marie Aymard's fourth surviving child, *Mathurin Ferrand*, has vanished with even less trace. He was baptized in 1743, and listed in the
power of attorney about the fortune; that is all there is.[37] He too signed
his brother's marriage contract in 1763—in an uncertain hand—and not
his sister's, the following year.[38] He is not in the parish records, not in
the tax rolls, and not (as of the infinitesimal present) in the family history websites. In two of the lists of "fugitive boys," at the time of the
lottery for the militia in Angoulême in 1758, there is a "Tourangeau," the
apprentice of a knife-maker. "Tourangeau" was the name by which
Marie Aymard's husband was known; it is possible that Mathurin Ferrand was also called "Tourangeau," and was a fugitive from the historical
record because he wished, himself, to flee.[39] He is in any case at one
extreme of the fragmentariness of historical existence in Angoulême,
and his oldest brother, the archivist, is at the other.

Marguerite Ferrand, Marie Aymard's fifth surviving child, is almost as
invisible. She was baptized in 1744, and listed in the power of attorney
about the fortune (as an afterthought, in the margin).[40] She was the
godmother in 1767 of Françoise's oldest son, and again, in 1768, of
Gabriel's fourth son; she was the only witness of the burial of Françoise's infant daughter, in 1767; she signed the registers, in an uncertain
hand, "Margerite Ferrante" or "Ferrainte."[41] But that, again, is all there

is. In the online world of ancestry and genealogy, there are almost as many family trees for "Marguerite Ferrand" as for "François Ferrand," and none of them, so far, have anything to do with Marie Aymard's family. There were many ways to vanish from the historical record of the eighteenth and nineteenth centuries: to be a domestic servant, to be indigent, to be a fugitive, to lead an uneventful life, to be unable to write one's own name in registers, to be unmarried (or to have no children, in whose ancestries and genealogies to find enduring life). There is no evidence, so far, as to which, if any, were the destinies of Marie Aymard's three middle children, François, Mathurin, and Marguerite. "It is always disagreeable to say, 'I do not know, I cannot know,'" Marc Bloch wrote, and it is disconcerting, in a different way, to know that one could eventually know.[42]

Marie Aymard's youngest child, *Jean-Baptiste Ferrand* or *Jean Ferrand*, was the only one of the six children whose life was overturned by the large revolutions of the times, and the only one of whom there is any evidence that he ever left France. He was baptized in 1749, and he signed his sister Françoise's marriage contract, in an ornate hand, at the age of fifteen.[43] In 1774 he married Elizabeth Boutoute, the daughter of a saucepan-maker, who came from a family, like his own, with connections to the far-off world of the French colonies; he was described as a watchmaker.[44] He and Elizabeth had four children, of whom one died in infancy.[45] At some point after the death of their son, in 1777, the family left for Saint-Domingue, where they lived until the dramatic days of the Haitian Revolution. Jean-Baptiste had a shop in Cap-Français (Le Cap, or the modern Cap-Haitien), selling coffeepots and oil cruets; in his later recollection, he owned fifteen Negroes.[46] By 1795, the family had returned to Angoulême as destitute refugees; Jean-Baptiste died in Paris in "deprivation," in 1831.[47]

On the Island of Grenada

These are the stories, in brief, of Marie Aymard and her children. But the question with which she was herself so preoccupied—of what really happened to her husband—is still obscure. It is a question, in turn, in which the asymmetry of information as between the historical subject and the historian—the possibility of knowing something that Marie Aymard wanted to know, and could not herself find out—is imposing.[48]

There is no evidence, in any case, or none that I have been able to find, that there ever was a fortune, or, if it existed, that it was restored to the family in France. There was no one, among Marie Aymard's children and grandchildren, who lived in any kind of opulence (the story is different in the next generation, but that is part of the nineteenth-century history). Louis Ferrand, if he completed the two years of indentured work on the island of Grenada for which he was engaged, would have been free of his engagement in early 1756. His employer had at this point returned to Angoulême; Jean-Alexandre Cazaud signed the record of the baptism of his own son in the parish church of St. Jean in April 1756.[49] Louis Ferrand's new life of industry and ownership would therefore have begun, in Grenada, at a moment when the universe of the Caribbean colonies was about to be transformed by the long conflict of the Seven Years' War.

Grenada was in the 1750s a society entirely dominated by its slave population. There were 12,608 enslaved Africans on the island in 1755, together with 347 free blacks and mulattos, and 1,077 whites: a society, or a prison, in which 90 percent of all "souls," in the expression used in the French censuses, were enslaved. Louis Ferrand, if he was in Grenada in 1755, was one of 247 (white) "men bearing arms," as listed in the census.[50] The regime of slave production was itself expanding rapidly. There was approximately the same number of whites on the island in 1740, in 1755, and in 1782; the population of slaves increased more than 350 percent over the same years, from 7,107 in 1742 to 12,608 in 1755 and 26,147 in 1782.[51]

The Seven Years' War began in May 1756, so the period in which Louis Ferrand was supposed to have made his small fortune, and to have set off for Martinique "with the idea of leaving from there to return to his family," was a time of naval, economic, and existential conflict. He lived in Grenada for "four or five years," according to Marie Aymard's power of attorney of 1764. If this were so, he would have left in 1758 or 1759: years of extraordinary warfare, in which the blockade of ports, the seizure of slave ships, and the starvation of the enslaved were the naval techniques of choice. French officials reported from Grenada, in July 1758, on the capture of a ship carrying flour from Cádiz to Bermuda, another ship carrying butter from Dublin to Antigua, and a "little ship with three masts" from the coast of Angola, "with 414 Negroes on board." There was a report from Martinique, in March 1758, of the capture of a ship with elephant teeth, gold, and "1,007 slaves," of whom 364 died "during the passage."[52] The British invaded Martinique, unsuccessfully, in January 1759, and Guadeloupe, with more success, in May 1759; they captured Grenada; they invaded Martinique, again, in 1762.

The information that Marie Aymard described in her power of attorney of 1764, in the aftermath of the chaos of war, was an amalgamation of true and partial news. The two individuals whom Louis mentioned in his letters as his "particular acquaintances"—M. de Flavigné in the parish of "Marquis a la Cabeste" in Grenada, and M. Herbert du Jardin, merchant in Saint-Pierre in Martinique—really existed. After the British capture of Grenada, in 1762, the initial census listed a M. de Flavigny in the parish of Marquis, with 167 slaves "on whom tax is paid"; Cazaud was listed in the neighboring parish, with 50 slaves.[53] Léon Marie Herbert du Jardin was a merchant in Martinique. He died there, in September 1764, only a few weeks before Marie Aymard took out the power of attorney in Angoulême; his infant daughter became the central figure, a few weeks later, in one of the interminable legal cases of the times, over the contested inheritance of slave plantations in Grenada, in French and English jurisprudence.[54]

The obscure M. Vandax, the "shipowner or merchant" in whose hands Louis Ferrand had deposited his fortune, and who had responded in such an unsatisfactory way to the verbal inquiries, also existed. There were two brothers, Bernard Vandas—also known as Vanda, Wanda, Vvanda, or Uranda—and Pierre Vandas, who appeared from time to time in the records of the parish of Saint-Pierre du Mouillage in Martinique. Both were described as merchants; they came from the Landes, where Bernard ("Vanda") was baptized in Mont-de-Marsan in 1707 and Pierre ("Ouanda" or "Wanda") in 1709.[55]

Pascal Chauvin, the sublieutenant to whom Marie Aymard entrusted her search for the truth, was a more shadowy figure. He was not present at the little ceremony of the signing of the power of attorney, in which Marie Aymard mortgaged all her goods and the goods of her children; he "was going to live in Martinique," but there is no evidence that he ever arrived there. "Jean Pascal Yrvoix Chauvin" was the son of a grocer in Angoulême, whose mother sold cooking fat in the parish of St. André, a few minutes' walk away from the Allemands and the Ferrands. He was baptized there on Easter Sunday of 1738, and was almost exactly the same age as Gabriel Ferrand.[56] He did go to live in the West Indies, and died in the island of Sainte-Lucie, described as a merchant, a lieutenant in the artillery, and a captain in the militia.[57]

The establishment of the Dominican mission, the Pères (or Frères) of Charity, in which Louis Ferrand was supposed to have died on the third day of his illness, was really there, near the waterfront in Saint-Pierre de Martinique. It was a hospital for "seafolk and workers": "people passing through or artisans arriving in or domiciled in the colonies, who are treated without cost by the religious order."[58] But Saint-Pierre was also the site, over the months and centuries after Louis Ferrand's death, of an unimaginable sequence of natural disasters. The "Mouillage" on which M. Vandax or Vandas may or may not have lived was burned to the ground in a terrible fire in September 1759. It was devastated again in the "great hurricane" of October 1780, in which a thousand people died in Saint-Pierre alone. A century later, Saint-Pierre was at the center of the most cataclysmic natural disaster in French history, following the volcanic eruption of Mount Pelée in May 1902, in which the Dominican hospital, the archives, the population of some thirty thousand people, and the entire cosmopolitan universe of the town were destroyed.[59] Saint-Pierre is no more than a city of specters, now, in which the destiny of Louis Ferrand is submerged, with so many other lives, in the ashes of time.

The Atrocious Employer

Even the history of Jean-Alexandre Cazaud, to whom Louis Ferrand was indentured, can offer no insight into the last years of the life of his former employee. Or rather, it provides insight only into the phantasmagorical elusiveness of personal identity, amidst the exchangeable empires of the eighteenth century. Cazaud was born in the parish of Basse-Terre, Guadeloupe, in September 1727.[60] His father was a lawyer in Bordeaux, who had married the daughter of a plantation owner called Bologne or Boulogne, a commander of the militia in Guadeloupe. The older Cazaud had traveled to Guadeloupe in the course of an intractable dispute with his father-in-law over the payment of his wife's dowry. In the eventual view of the administrators of the island, asked to intercede in the matter, Cazaud "did not have as much reason to complain about Sr. Bologne as he had led [them] to believe," and "Sr. Bologne wished even more fervently to see his son-in-law in France, than Sr. Cazeaud wished to be there."[61]

At some point in the early 1730s, the family returned to France, and to Angoulême. At least one of their slaves, or their domestic servants, came with them. In July 1733, a large number of spectators, "attracted by the unusual nature of the ceremony," were present in the parish church of St. André on the occasion of the baptism of Jean-François-Auguste, a "Negro of the nation of the coast of Juda" (Ouidah in modern Benin). Jean-François-Auguste had been brought "from the islands" by the older Cazaud, the father of Louis Ferrand's employer, "with the intention of taking him back there," according to the parish register; his employer, or owner, declared that he "could be aged around sixteen or seventeen." The godparents were Jean Cazaud, canon of the cathedral of Angoulême, and Marie Cazaud; the baptism was performed by yet another Cazaud, the curé of the parish of Notre Dame de Beaulieu. The sight of the "young proselyte," wearing a surplice and with a wax taper on his head, was so "edifying," Cazaud, the curé, wrote in the parish register, that many of the congregation asked to be remembered in his prayers.[62]

Jean-Alexandre Cazaud, Louis Ferrand's employer and the son of the owner of Jean-François-Auguste, entered military service in a mounted infantry regiment serving in Bohemia; he identified himself, for the rest of his life, as "a former officer of the dragoons."[63] He returned to Angoulême fairly often, and in 1752 he married the daughter of a rich silk merchant and money changer in the town, Silvie Calixte Benoit des Essarts. She was seventeen.[64] A little over a year later he engaged the two carpenters, of whom one was Louis Ferrand, on the security of his father-in-law, and left for Grenada.[65]

Over the next few years, Cazaud went back and forth between his new venture in Grenada and Angoulême, where his son and daughter were baptized in 1756 and 1757; he started to use a new and impressive name, "Cazaud de Roumillac."[66] In the wartime year of 1759, he moved definitively to Grenada, where in 1761 he "made some considerable acquisitions"—this was according to his own historical narrative, in a lawsuit some years later, about the terms of his wife Silvie's will—and he subsequently took Silvie to the island, "to place her at the head of his establishments."[67] It was at this point that he was listed as the owner of fifty slaves.[68] After the conquest of Grenada by the British, Silvie returned to Angoulême, where she gave birth, in 1764, to another daughter.[69] Cazaud was naturalized as a British subject. He then again took Silvie back to Grenada, but "feeling herself to be French by inclination and affection, she used the pretext of her health to return to France in 1770," where she remained until her death in 1781. Her real reason for returning home, Cazaud's lawyers said in the lawsuit over her will, "was to satisfy her taste for dissipation and pleasure."[70]

Cazaud was over the ensuing decades either British or French, or both at the same time. He took the Oaths of Allegiance and Supremacy to the British crown in 1767; this was according to a melancholy petition sent by his son to a British official in 1811 ("so deplorably afflicted have I been through life by nervous disorders, that I have been compelled very frequently to change my residence").[71] Cazaud also subscribed to the Test Act, affirming his allegiance to the Church of England and the repudiation of his Catholic faith, although this was a matter of some dispute. It had been inadvertent, he declared when the French reconquered Grenada in 1780. "I was by inattention given one piece of paper instead of another, and I signed it without paying any more attention than the person who presented it to me," he wrote to the new French governor of the island. The conclusion of the official investigation by the new French administration was cool; "if this inscription is no more than the outcome of a lack of attention, it is an error even more unfortunate than it is implausible."[72]

"The whole island was in the utmost state of violence & distraction," one of the new British proprietors wrote of Grenada in the early period of British government, and Cazaud was fully engaged in the turbulent Anglo-French politics of the times.[73] At one point, in the course of a dispute over elections to the new general assembly of Grenada, Cazaud was charged with "scorn and contempt of the dignity, authority and justice" of "his majesty's council"; there was a "great *uproar*," in which he "began in a tumultuous manner to read a French paper which he called a protest." He was imprisoned in the town jail of St. George's, Grenada, "with the run-away negroes and malefactors of every class, kept close in a small room, where there were several prisoners, one of whom was in irons"; there was an "offensive smell," and he was "obliged continually to burn tobacco and paper and to sprinkle vinegar." Cazaud then, having signed a submission in which he recognized the "justice and moderation of the council," departed for England.[74]

In 1770, Cazaud was described in a complaint by British proprietors to the Privy Council in London, as a "gentleman of fortune and credit," who had been committed, in a "most tyrannical, confused, and illegal series of proceedings," to the "most loathsome prison." He had meanwhile been "appointed by the new adopted subjects," or the French proprietors who had taken British subjecthood, "to represent [in London] the state of their grievances."[75] Over the next few years—this is again according to Cazaud's later lawsuit over Silvie's will—he "came and went, sometimes in France, sometimes in Grenada, and sometimes in Italy, or elsewhere, according to the affairs of his business." He maintained a continuing domicile in Grenada, the "seat of his fortune"—or, in his lawyers' description, of the "immense fortune that he was acquiring every day."[76]

By 1779, Cazaud was in Paris, living in a rented house with his older daughter, Marie Marthe, and a slave, known as Jean-Alexandre James. Jean-Alexandre, identified variously as a "native of the Gold Coast, near the trading post of Juda in Africa," and a "Negro from the Kingdom of Timor," had been transported to Grenada as a child, and "delivered to M. Cazeau"; he was in his early twenties.[77] Cazaud brought him first to London and then to Paris, as his valet de chambre. In June 1779, Jean-

Alexandre, after a long period of "the most inhumane treatment" by Cazaud and his daughter, found his way to the Admiralty Court in Paris, where he claimed his freedom. "The harsh and overbearing character of this young lady, who dominated her father in a strange way, often exposed this unfortunate servant to unheard-of excesses," Jean-Alexandre's lawyers wrote; he was "treated with atrocity," pulled from his sickbed in wintertime, and imprisoned in a dark and unhealthy cellar with no food. Cazaud's other servants were horrified by the spectacle, in the lawyers' account, and left his employment.[78]

The court agreed to hear the case; Jean-Alexandre had in the meantime been seized and imprisoned, on the basis of "secret and calumnious memoranda" prepared for Cazaud. In September 1779, the Admiralty Court granted Jean-Alexandre his freedom, and awarded him five hundred livres in damages; much as the Somerset case in London, six years earlier, had invoked French legal precedent, Jean-Alexandre's case invoked the precedent of English law.[79] Cazaud appealed against the sentence, and against Jean-Alexandre's freedom. In April 1780, Jean-Alexandre was severely beaten in the street, in an attempted kidnapping, and escaped only because of a "sort of riot"; two other Africans were attacked by Cazaud's "satellites" in Paris on the same day, "by mistake." In a memorandum for Jean-Alexandre, which turned on the highest principles of the jurisprudence of slavery in the British and French Empires, the advocate general of France described the conduct of Cazaud as "odious" and "revolting." To accept Cazaud's arguments would be to say that "it is sufficient in France to be an African, and to be claimed by someone, to be a slave"; "it was time for justice to avenge this servant who had taken refuge in its sanctuary."[80]

Over the same period—at exactly the same time, in fact—Cazaud had once again reinvented himself, in an entirely new identity. In February 1779, a "Mr Cazaud" of the island of Grenada read a long and technical paper to the Royal Society of London, *Account of a New Method of Cultivating the Sugar Cane*. The paper, which was concerned inter alia with the "four sets" of the roots of the sugarcane—"the second order of roots, composed of its first set, *aa*, of its second, *bb*, of its third, *cc*, of its fourth, *dd*"—was published in the same year, in both English and

French.[81] In April 1780, Cazaud was elected a fellow of the Royal Society.[82] By 1785, he had acquired a new name, as well as a new philosophical existence. His *Considérations sur quelques parties du méchanisme des sociétés*—a study composed of fourteen "hypotheses," together with quantitative illustrations along the lines of "How would you extract from the territorial capitalist the sum of £3,333,333: 13: & 4: of the portion that *he was obliged* to keep free in order to pay taxes on his consumption?"—was identified as the work of "le Marquis de Casaux, de la Société Royale de Londres."[83]

One of Hundreds of People

This was the figure to whom Louis Ferrand indentured himself in December 1753, and whom he set out to meet in Bordeaux, for the long and eventually fatal journey to the Americas. Cazaud/Casaux encountered thousands of people in the course of his lamentable life, and had hundreds of servants and slaves; it is unsurprising that the destiny of a solitary joiner from Angoulême should have left so little trace in his existence. Although Cazaud was in Angoulême at the time of Marie Aymard's power of attorney of October 1764 (according to the lawsuit over Silvie's right to make a will), he is mentioned in it only in connection with the initial engagement of 1753.[84] There were no members of Cazaud's large extended family among the signatories of Marie Aymard and Louis Ferrand's daughter's marriage contract, even though Silvie was a resident, at the time, of the same small "island" of houses in Angoulême as the bridegroom's father, the notary who drew up the contract, and sixteen of the signatories.[85] Louis Ferrand was no more than an incidental figure, over the last years of his life, in Cazaud's tumultuous universe.

Chapter Two

THE MARRIAGE CONTRACT

Eighty-Three Individuals

The marriage contract of Marie Aymard's and Louis Ferrand's daughter—to return to the more tranquil social relationships of Angoulême—was drawn up a few weeks after the power of attorney, in December 1764. Françoise Ferrand, who was twenty-four, was engaged to Etienne Allemand, the son of a tailor in the town; he was also twenty-four, and a "master of arts." In the contract, the betrothed couple constituted themselves as a "society and community" under customary law. They each contributed an advance of fifty livres. Etienne's promise was simple: "all his goods and rights, present and to come." Françoise's promise was a tissue of expectations. She included "all the goods and rights that have come to her by the death of her father, in whatever they might consist, and wherever they might be found, and those that might come to her in the future by the death of her mother, or otherwise, and by whatever title." The missing fortune, that is to say, and the possible slaves.[1]

Françoise also included a sum of money that was owed to her, she said, by her brother, Gabriel Ferrand. She presented—or "represented"—a piece of paper to her future husband and future father-in-law, and to the other relatives who were there, in the presence of the notary: a promissory note for one thousand livres, from Gabriel and his wife, dated March 26, 1764, and payable in full in July 1765. (This was a large sum; about a tenth of the price of a "bourgeois house," according to an engineer who lived in the same parish as the bridegroom.)[2] It was her own money, Françoise declared, the product of her industry and savings, and she constituted it as her dowry.[3]

The oddest part of the contract is the conclusion. For the document was signed, on a December afternoon in Gabriel Ferrand's home, by eighty-three people. It was a sort of winter charivari; a procession of relatives and neighbors, young girls and grandfathers, bakers and trinket sellers and seamstresses. It was also an unusually large assembly.[4] Marie Aymard did not sign the marriage contract, and she declared, as on so many occasions, that she did not how to.[5] But the eighty-three people were her own social milieu, at least for a time. She was the mother of the bride, and the ceremony was in her own home, or in the house in which she lived with her son.

The eighty-three signatures are the picture of a moment in time; of a Sunday afternoon in December 1764. They are evidence of eighty-three lives that began long before December 9, 1764, that continued afterward, and that were connected to each other, if only for a time. They are a depiction, too, of conversation or exchange. The eighty-three signatories—and the other individuals who were there and did not sign, including the mother of the bride—were talking to each other, in Gabriel Ferrand's house, and exchanging information. This was not a procession of soundless figures, waiting silently in a line to inscribe their names.

The history of Marie Aymard, so far, has been an investigation in time and in space, like her own inquiry into what happened to her husband and his fortune. In the perspective of the marriage contract, it is an investigation in the space of social relationships; from Marie Aymard to her acquaintances, friends, and neighbors, in the small parishes of Angoulême. One of the points of departure has been the social networks of our own times, and the visualizations (and explanations) that are possible with modern technologies. The signatures on the marriage contract are only an approximate and momentary depiction of Marie Aymard's social network, or of the intersecting social networks of the bride and the groom.[6] But they are the evidence that is there, and that can be visualized, and understood, as the picture of a network.

The eighty-three signatories—or the eighty-one whom I have been able to identify, so far, with any sense of confidence—had fairly little in common, other than their presence in the same house on the same Sunday in 1764. The oldest, a tailor and the grandfather of the groom, was seventy-nine; the youngest, "Rosemarin," was the ten-year-old daughter of a trinket seller, a close neighbor of the groom's father.[7] There were forty-three women and girls, more women than men. There were three tailors; two hatmakers; two bakers; a butcher; a candle-maker; two seamstresses and a dressmaker; a button-maker; a musician; two sisters who sold cooking fat and crockery; a widow who sold tobacco; two clerks; an innkeeper; a saddler; a woman who sold trinkets and her brother-in-law, also a trinket seller; a salt merchant; the two daughters of an official of the town police; a retired goldsmith; two boarding school students; two teachers and two master writers; a tax collector and his wife.[8] The goldsmith, who was one of the richest men in the town, died a few months later, in 1765; a boy who signed the marriage contract at the age of twelve, the son of another tax collector, died in the village of Aigre in 1839.[9]

The inquiry into who these individuals were has been recursive, to say the least; a combination of reading parish registers (and then reading the same registers again, to look for someone else); looking for other events (the records of other marriages, and of baptisms, with the signatures of godmothers and godfathers); finding out when particular individuals died and at what age; and finding their children in the postrevolutionary world, with the innovation of detailed civil registration, including inquiries into the lives of long-lost grandparents. The only way to find out who the signatories of the marriage contract were, and why they were there, was to find their connections in time and space and family life: when they were born and when they died, who their parents were, and their children, whom they chose as the godparents for their children, and to whom they were themselves godparents.

So the process of inquiry has led, along the way—or in the course of all the unanticipated lingering in the virtual universe of the Archives municipales d'Angoulême—to information about a larger group of individuals, consisting of the eighty-three signatories, and their own close relations and friends. It is this larger group that has been the basis for a social network visualization of the marriage contract. Eighty-three people are too many, together with their own social relationships, to imagine as a network, to keep straight in one's mind. But the network, and the connections of the individuals of whom it is composed, the "nodes" and the "edges" that connected them, were the point of departure, in turn, for an investigation of economic life in eighteenth-century Angoulême, of the political and economic revolutions of the long nineteenth century, and of the influence of the outside world in the deep interior of France.

Only one of the eighty-three signatories—the youngest, "Rosemarin"—was a political figure, in the minimal sense that she had her own police dossier, over the course of the French Revolution, in which she was described as being "of a known patriotism," on the evidence of a representative of the Committee of Public Safety whom she had seen "almost every day."[10] The signatories of the marriage contract, of whom at least thirty-six lived into revolutionary times, were part of the ordinary life of the revolution, all the same; they were still there, as will be seen, or several of them were, together with their own connections, in the historical record of the French Revolution in Angoulême.

Who Were the Signatories?

The eighty-three signatories can be grouped into five categories: the family of the bride; the extended family of the groom; the near neighbors of the bride's brother, in whose house the marriage contract was signed; the near neighbors of the groom's father; and "others." (There is a list of all the signatories in appendix 2, including the one name—"Racom"—of whom there is almost nothing to be said, or that I have so far managed to say.)[11]

On the bride's side of the ceremony, the signatures were exiguous. Her brother Gabriel signed, and so did her youngest brother, Jean or Jean-Baptiste; her two other brothers and her sister, who were listed a few weeks earlier in the power of attorney about the missing fortune, did not sign (or were not present). Marie Aymard was identified as an important figure in the agreement, together with the widowed father of the groom; when the ceremonial of the signing started, she "declared that she did not know it" (the world of signing one's name).[12] The only members of the bride's extended family were a hatmaker from the suburban parish of St. Ausone, Marie Aymard's second cousin, with his father and his wife; and Gabriel's wife, Marie Adelaide Devuailly, together with her sister, Dorothée, and her brother-in-law, Gabriel Lemaitre, a painter, and the grandson of a cook called Klotz (or Clod or Kloche).

The other side in the ceremony, the second group of signatories, was much more prolific. At least thirty-five of the individuals who signed were members of the extended family of the groom, Etienne Allemand. Etienne, the son of a master tailor, was a precocious student. His first appearance in the parish registers of Angoulême, following his own baptism, was at the age of eleven, when he signed the record of the baptism of one of his cousins, in a careful, confident hand.[13] He was described as a "master of arts," in his marriage contract; he had become what his brother-in-law Gabriel hoped to be. In the record of Etienne's marriage to Françoise, a few weeks after the marriage contract was signed, he was described as the master of a boarding school; he was a "schoolmaster" in the record of the baptism of their first child.[14]

Etienne's father, Marc Allemand, the tailor, was the grandson of "Guillaume Allemand dit Lavigerie," also a tailor, who was born around 1630; he was an immigrant to the town from the small village of Lavigerie, ten kilometers to the west of Angoulême, according to the naming conventions of the town.[15] (There was an Allemand family in Lavigerie, still, more than two centuries later; a Marguerite Allemand, daughter of another Guillaume Allemand, died there in 1808, and Pierre Allemand, a farmer, was among the seventy-one individuals listed in Lavigerie in the census of 1841.)[16] Marc Allemand himself signed his name as "Lavigerie," on occasion; in the tax roll for 1763 he was listed as "~~Lavigerie~~ allemand dit lavigerie."[17]

Marc Allemand had eight children, and in these times of high maternal mortality, he was widowed twice.[18] His first wife died in the aftermath of childbirth, and so did his second wife, Etienne's mother, when Etienne was five. Etienne's maternal grandfather, also a tailor, had sixteen children, with two wives; he was one of the signatories of the marriage contract, together with his second wife, Etienne's step-grandmother.[19]

The relationships within the extended family went far back in time. Twenty-eight of the signatories were the descendants of Etienne's paternal great-grandparents, whose children were impressively exogamous, across the artisanal occupations of the town. One of their daughters (Madeleine) married a baker, and another (also called Madeleine) married a salt merchant; their daughter Marguerite married a draper. Of the younger Madeleine's daughters, one married a butcher and one married a saddlemaker. It is these two families, in the matrilineal descent—the Godinauds, bakers; the Glaumonts, salt merchants; the Jouberts, drapers; the Yrvoix, butchers and candle-makers; and the Dumergues, saddlemakers—who accounted for most of the cousins among the signatories of the marriage contract.[20]

The third group of signatories, the near neighbors of the bride's brother, Gabriel Ferrand, were very different. There were two detailed tax rolls, or lists of individuals who were subject to (or exempt from) royal taxes, that were prepared in Angoulême in 1763 and 1766; they were part of a sustained and elusive effort to increase tax revenues in the aftermath of the Seven Years' War, and are one of the principal sources for this history. The rolls (of 1,319 households in the town, in 1766, and a further 1,229 in the surrounding suburbs) listed the residents of the town by the "islands" in which they lived—the "isle de maisons," in eighteenth-century town design, was a cluster of contiguous houses— and it is possible to see, from the lists, who lived near to whom.[21] It is possible, too, to see changes over (a short period of) time; and to see who was still there during the French Revolution, when the residents were listed again in another register of tax contributions and households, also in the Archives municipales d'Angoulême.[22]

The "pension" or boarding school in which Gabriel lived with his mother, and in which the marriage contract was signed—where boys studying at the collège d'Angoulême, a Jesuit establishment until 1762, had lodgings—was in a prosperous, studious part of the town.[23] The small parish of Notre Dame de la Peine was a place of "narrow streets and houses crowded together," according to a study of the old parishes of Angoulême by a nineteenth-century archivist of the Charente, in which magistrates, clerks, lawyers, and tax officials were "encamped," together with the "little people they needed": watchmakers, "masters of arts," and the printers of the town, clustered around the episcopal palace that provided so much of their business.[24] These were Gabriel's neighbors. Five of the signatories were near neighbors of Gabriel Ferrand in the Isle de la Place du Collège and the Isle du Collège: the widow of a lawyer, who lived in the adjacent house; the daughter of the director of the post; her father; her husband, who was a lawyer; and the daughter of a printer.[25]

The near neighbors of Marc Allemand, the father of the groom, who are the fourth category of signatories, were a more disparate group. They lived only a few minutes away, immediately to the east of the Place du Mûrier (now the Place Francis-Louvel), in the center of the town. Gabriel and his mother's house was to the south of the Place du Mûrier, which was, and is, more of a triangle than a square, and the scene, later, of revolutionary spectacle, of domestic tragedy, and of an extended bonanza of transactions in expropriated property. The great landlords, in and around the Place du Mûrier, were the nuns of the Tiercelettes (the Sisters of Saint Francis) and the Dominicans (the Jacobin Fathers). The bridegroom's family, to the east of the Place, lived in a different parish, St. Antonin, that was also clustered around a palatial building—in this case, the château of Angoulême, with its invalid soldiers and its prisoners of war, and the tradesmen who were their purveyors of goods and services.

Eighteen of the signatories, or their close relatives, were listed in the same island as Marc Allemand, known in 1766 as the Isle de la Cloche Verte. There was the wife of a cloth merchant and former shoemaker, who signed with three of her daughters; the daughter of the police official, who signed together with her sister and niece; a seller of cooking fat; a trinket seller, who signed with his two daughters, both called Rose Marin; a teacher or "regent"; Rose Rezé, also a seller of trinkets; a registry clerk, who signed with his sister and his eleven-year-old son. Jean Bernard, the notary who drew up the marriage contract, lived in the same island.[26]

Then there was the fifth, residual category, of everyone else: eighteen signatories. There were the two boarding school students, who also signed the parish register of Notre Dame de la Peine as witnesses of Etienne and Françoise's marriage a few weeks later.[27] There were six members of the extended family of Jean-Baptiste Marchais, the retired goldsmith.[28] There was the widow who sold tobacco, who was a couple of years older than Marie Aymard, and connected, like her, to the prison administration of the town; her father, like Marie Aymard's maternal grandfather, was a "concierge" of the royal prisons.[29] There was another high official, a receiver of the *aides* imposition, together with his wife and sister, signing with the notables at the end of the contract.[30] There was a merchant called Yrvoix, unrelated to the Allemands; a dressmaker; and the fourteen-year-old granddaughter of another lawyer. There was "St Mexant De Crevecoeur," the twelve-year-old boy who died in 1839, and who signed Gabriel's marriage contract, in 1763, under the name "F. Crevecoeur"; he was from a family of tax collectors and army officers in Aigre (and Guadeloupe).[31] Then there was one of the six individuals in Angoulême in 1764 who were called "Jean Roy"; and "Racom," or "Racomp."

A Social Network Visualization

These are the individuals who constituted the transitory network of Marie Aymard. They had their own, continuing relationships of friendship, family, employment, and proximity: "those close to them, relatives and friends," in the language of the parish clerks of the town, and the approximation, in eighteenth-century Angoulême, of the social networks of modern times, the signatories' "primary conduits of information, opinions, and behaviors."[32] It is this larger set of individuals—the signatories and their own connections—who can be visualized as a social network; the Eighty-Three.

The Eighty-Three network consists of the signatories and a subset of all these other, related individuals: those who had a "close" relationship to one of the signatories, as recorded in the parish records and civil registers of Angoulême (and elsewhere).[33] The signatories were connected to each other, and they also had their own connections in the town and the outside world. They can be described as the "Aymard-network," in the sense that they were the individuals who surrounded Marie Aymard, on an afternoon in December 1764. The other, close individuals can be considered, in the spirit of the history of mathematics, as having an "Aymard number" of 1; like the twentieth-century mathematicians who had an "Erdös number" of 1, because they were coauthors of a scientific paper with the Hungarian mathematician Paul Erdös, they were proximate to the "Aymard-network."[34]

The network is historical or diachronic, a representation of relationships over the entire lifetimes of the eighty-three individuals who were all together only once, fleetingly, on December 9, 1764. But it is limited, in the visualization, to only those of these related individuals who were alive, and who did not die in childhood, during the lifetime of Marie Aymard, from 1713 to 1790. It is a network, to put the matter differently, and more sentimentally, of individuals who were alive on earth at the same time as Marie Aymard. This book is not a history of Marie Aymard, and the network was not her network in any enduring sense. In its extended version, of the eighty-three and the others, it was not at all her network. But the inquiry started with Marie Aymard, and the network was a society of which she was once at the center, on a December afternoon in the parish of Notre Dame de la Peine in Angoulême.

Networks are "a simple tool" in historical research, as Claire Lemercier and Paul-André Rosental have written: a way of thinking, in particular, about the lives of individuals in networks as "bridging the micro-macro link."[35] This has been the preoccupation, for almost half a century, of the sociology of networks, and it is the promise, still, of the economics of social networks and information.[36] The Eighty-Three network is a tool, in this spirit. It is a way, among others, of locating Marie Aymard and her family within the larger society of Angoulême (and elsewhere). It provides some indication, here, of the overseas connections of the signatories of the marriage contract, and of how these connections were diffused in a larger network. It can provide an overview, eventually, of the next generation within the network, as their lives unfolded in historical time: their connections, if any, to the events of the French Revolution, and their (prodigious) mobility in the revolutionary period. It is incomplete, like so much else in this history; there are other possibilities.

Why Were They All There?

So what can be said, with all these stories and all this visualization, about who the eighty-three people were, and why they were there? The question of why is easier to answer than the question of who, in a history that is even incipiently (as Marc Bloch said that all history should be) a history of human consciousness.[37] The eighty-three were there because they were inquisitive; they were curious about the entire, obscure business. They were interested (as Adam Smith said that everyone is) in "the characters, designs, and actions of one another," and the story of the possible long-lost inheritance—the rights that were pledged in the marriage contract, "in whatever they might consist, and wherever they might be found," and the "certain quantity of Negroes" identified in the power of attorney—was unquestionably interesting.[38]

More than half of the signatories were either relatives or close neighbors of Marc Allemand, the father of the bridegroom, and it is implausible that they would have heard no version at all, in the narrow, crowded streets of the central parishes of Angoulême, of the odd story of his daughter-in-law-to-be. There is an economistic explanation, that the signatories, all these second cousins and step-grandmothers, were there because they hoped that they, too, might eventually inherit a part of the distant fortune. The other and far more obvious explanation is that they were there because they wanted to know what had really happened.

The Eighty-Three network is an approximation, in this sense, to the exchanges of information in eighteenth-century Angoulême. Who is best suited to initiate the spread of information? the modern theorists of social networks asked in India, and there were individuals in the network who had multiple opportunities for the exchange of news, opinions, and information.[39] Marc Allemand, the tailor, is a central figure in the story so far, because it is a relationship to him, of family or propinquity, that has explained the presence of so many of the signatories. He is central to the network of the Eighty-Three in a formal sense as well; of the "nodes" in the visualization, or the individuals depicted, the signatories and their own connected individuals, Marc Allemand has by far the most "edges," or connections to other people. He was a sociable figure, in a profession that was of necessity sociable, and his house was a local landmark.[40] He signed the registers of nine different parishes in Angoulême on forty-four different occasions, over a fifty-five-year period from 1715 to 1770.[41]

The Economic Life of the Provinces

The signatories of the marriage contract were not very poor, in general, and not very rich. They were a subset of the acquaintances of the bride and the groom, a self-selected subset, to the extent that they were the relatives and friends who were able to write their names. Only one out of Etienne's five siblings, and two out of Françoise's siblings signed, and the individuals who participated in the ceremony of signing the contract had done better in the world, in general, than those who were not able to write (or "did not know it").[42] Even Marie Aymard, who was so alarmed, after the death of her husband, by the prospect of "the destiny in which a sad distress would place her," and who described herself as living in "indigence," was not poor. Her debts, in the year of her daughter's marriage, were larger than the value of her assets (the forks and the chairs). But she lived with her son; she was not one of the individuals, most of them women, whose households were listed as "poor" in the tax roll for 1766.

There were several of the signatories whose lives were harsh, in the sparse narration of the tax rolls: the widower of Etienne's aunt, a retired musician, living with his sister-in-law and his daughters, all of them seamstresses; his sister-in-law and daughter, after his death; Rose Rezé, the trinket seller, who was the poorest person listed in the tax island of the Cloche Verte, where she was Marc Allemand's neighbor, according to the assessments for the *taille* in 1766.[43] The richest person, in the assessment for the little cluster of houses, was the notary, Jean Bernard, who drew up the marriage contract; the next richest was the cloth merchant and former shoemaker whose wife and three daughters were signatories.[44]

There were no signatories who were really rich, even by the standards of Angoulême. None of them were listed as "noble," in the registers, and only two them were exempt from taxation because of their official positions: Brillet, the receiver of the *aides* imposition, in 1763, and Gralhat, Gabriel's neighbor and the director of the post, in 1766.[45] The richest of the signatories were the family of the retired goldsmith, Jean-Baptiste Marchais, and his younger brother, Pierre Marchais, the innkeeper of the Cheval Blanc. The older Marchais died in 1765; his son, seven years later, was in a position to buy the office of mayor of Angoulême, for fifteen thousand livres, and to be reinvented, thereby, as a member of the nobility.[46]

The lives of the signatories were insecure, in multiple respects. Of the five young married women of Françoise's age who signed the contract, two died within a few years, in the aftermath of childbirth.[47] The wife of the innkeeper of the Cheval Blanc, Magdelaine Dumergue, was one of the well-connected individuals in the network, and signed multiple parish registers over the course of half a century, in a large confident hand.[48] She had thirteen children over the period from 1728 to 1750, of whom seven died in infancy or childhood; a mortality rate, in one family, of over 50 percent.[49] The summer months, in the town, were particularly precarious. In the deadly summer of 1740, fifteen infants died in the parish of St. André alone, in the months of August and September; they included the sister of one of the signatories, two of the brothers of another signatory, and one of the sons of Magdelaine Dumergue.[50]

The occupations that individuals declared in the parish registers, or that were assigned to them in the tax rolls, were approximate, in many cases, or aspirational. In the notarial acts, there was particular scope for invention. Etienne Allemand described himself as a "bourgeois," in the inventory made in advance of his future brother-in-law's marriage, in October 1763; Gabriel described himself as the son of a "merchant."[51] But almost all the signatories came from families in three clusters of occupations. The largest group were from the restrictive "communities" or "corporations" of the town. The bridegroom's father, like the late father of the bride, had been a participant, over many years, in the little societies that the economist A.R.J. Turgot, at the time the intendant of the generality of which Angoulême was a part, later denounced as vexatious residues of the age of ignorance: the organizations of tailors, furniture-makers, bakers, and others, regulated by the state to pursue "contraventions" of their own rules.[52] At least thirty-five of the signatories were from the families of artisans in the town, many of them insecure; "most of the artisans in Angoulême are in the greatest indigence," in the lamentation of the notables of the town, in 1789, "barely able to buy the tools they needed for their professions."[53]

Then there were the signatories who worked in the small commerce of the town, interconnected, in many cases, with the extended families of the artisanal communities: the candle merchant who lived with his wife, who sold cooking oil, and her sister, also a shopkeeper; a button-maker, whose wife was a *fripière*, or seller of old clothes; two sisters who were seamstresses; the signatories identified only as "shopkeepers"; a trinket seller with his two daughters and his sister-in-law, who was the trinket seller Rose Rezé. There was a grocer and a draper, with his wife who was the daughter of a wigmaker. There was the daughter of a different wigmaker, the daughter of a cooper, and the daughter of a hide-bleacher.

The third cluster of signatories, including the neighbors of Marie Aymard and her son, were lawyers, clerks, and government officials. There was the director of the post, with his son-in-law, a lawyer, who became director after his death, and his daughter, who became director of the post, in turn, after her husband's death.[54] There was the widow of another lawyer; the two daughters and granddaughter of the official of the police; the clerk of the town registry, with his sister and son. There was the collector of the *aides* imposition, with his wife and someone who may have been his sister. These were individuals with power, on an occasion that was also a ceremony of social connections—eventual patrons of the families of the Allemands and the Ferrands.[55]

Mobility and Immobility

The signatories belonged to the immobile society of the town, in the sense that (at least) sixty-two of the eighty-three were born in Angoulême, and baptized in the Catholic parishes of the town.[56] But their lives were also a scene of continuing social and economic change. The church, which was the great employer and proprietor in the town, and the reliable customer of the tailors and candlemakers, was itself a source of mobility in the lives of the signatories and their families. Four of the signatories were teachers, and the church was an impressive route to improvement through education.[57] It was the college of Angoulême, established in 1516, and a Jesuit foundation from 1622 to 1762, that so transformed the life of Marie Aymard's own family. The positions of "regents," or teachers, were not well paid. But the opportunity of education reached across the parishes of the town. A list of the boys from Angoulême, like Gabriel Ferrand, who took the first step toward ordination in the middle decades of the eighteenth century included seventeen individuals from the extended families of the signatories.[58]

The royal administration was another source of mobility, from time to time. The registry clerk, who was Marc Allemand's near neighbor in the Isle de la Cloche Verte, was the son of a joiner, and married the daughter of a saucepan-maker.[59] Marie Aymard's maternal grandfather, Pierre Queil, came to Angoulême from La Couronne, to the south. In 1676, he married the fifteen-year-old daughter of a tailor in the parish of St. Antonin: a literate, resilient child, who went on to have fifteen children over a seventeen-year period. He was described as a master shoemaker in 1682; in 1687 he was "concierge of the prisons of the château"; in 1688 he was a shopkeeper; in 1695 he was again "concierge of the château"; he was a shopkeeper, once more, in 1696, 1697, and 1699.[60] When he died in 1702, he was identified as "Sr. La Couronne, concierge of the royal château." His widow paid thirty livres for the costs of his funeral, including the fees of the sacristan, deacon, and subdeacons, and the expense of twenty masses; she described herself as "Madame de La Couronne."[61] Their son, Marie Aymard's maternal uncle, took over his father's position as "concierge of the château" in 1708; he was a shopkeeper in 1716; in 1718 he was a clerk in the tax office, a *commis aux aides*.[62]

The two brothers of Jean-Baptiste Marchais, the goldsmith, were, respectively, a wigmaker, who later became a brandy merchant, and a pâtissier, who became an innkeeper. Jean-Baptiste himself married the daughter of the official who licensed the printing of playing cards in the generality of Limoges; his second son, Pierre, was the one who purchased nobility, and the office of mayor of Angoulême, for fifteen thousand livres.[63] His oldest son, also called Jean-Baptiste Marchais, the husband of one of the signatories of the marriage contract, was a brandy merchant who went bankrupt three times, and settled with his creditors, in 1765, for debts of more than sixty-seven thousand livres.[64]

The family of the signatory Rose Rezé was similarly mobile, across the occupations and destinies of the town. The Rezés were one of the families of printers that were "grouped around the episcopal palace, under the aegis of the bishop and in the neighborhood of the Jesuits."[65] They were the printers and publishers, starting in 1633, of the *Proprium SS. Ecclesiae et diocesis Engolismensis*, the *Arte rhetorica* of the Jesuit college, and other works of devotion and the law, including, in 1741, a volume of poetry dedicated to the son of Louis XV by "Monsieur de Boulogne de l'Amérique," the uncle of the employer of Marie Aymard's husband, the itinerant Jean-Alexandre Cazaud.[66]

The history of the Rezés in the eighteenth century, as it unfolded in the parish records, was a more disparate scene. Rose Rezé was one of thirteen children of the grandson of the first Rezé to establish himself in Angoulême. Her father sold playing cards, and her mother was the sister-in-law of the signatory Jean-Baptiste Marchais. One of Rose's brothers continued in the printing business; she had two brothers called Pierre, of whom one was a pastry cook and the other a musician (and later a cloth merchant); both she and her sister, also called Rose Rezé, were trinket sellers, as was her sister's husband, another of the signatories.[67] Her nephew, Claude, was a printer, the official supplier of the Jesuit college, and printer of municipal ordinances, passports, and tickets for the lodging of troops.[68] Rose had two nieces, both, again, called Rose Rezé, of whom one married a "writer to the navy" in the port of Rochefort.[69] A nephew called Simon sold "fashions," and another nephew, also called Simon, was an army commissary, in "the regiment of the queen."[70]

The Rezés had a distinctive propensity for domestic disputes. Rose's nephew, Claude Rezé, the printer of municipal ordinances, sued his parents when they tried to prevent his marriage to his first cousin, another of Rose's nieces, Rose Marin, who was one of the signatories of the marriage contract (and the older sister of "Rosemarin," who was so patriotic in 1793); she was eighteen, when she and Claude eventually married, and he was forty-two.[71] Claude was then sued by a neighbor in 1769 for threatening to kill him, in "criminal and mysterious terms," waylaying him on the threshold of a bakery, and hitting him on the head with a stick.[72] One of the younger Rose Rezés was the plaintiff, also in 1769, in a criminal case about a miserable afternoon when she was walking with her sister-in-law—the signatory Rose Marin—and the son of the neighbor insulted her "outside the house of M. Lavigerie the tailor," called her "garce," "putain," "chienne," and tried to break her thumb.[73]

The Influence of the Outside World

The connections of the signatories extended far beyond Angoulême. Only one of the eighty-three signatories, Jean-Baptiste Ferrand, eventually made his way outside the geographical or metropolitan France, on the unfortunate journey to the jewelry shop in Cap-Français, Saint-Domingue. But there was a larger group of individuals, among the eighty-three signatories and the other individuals who were close to them, who were connected in different ways to overseas exchanges. They were linked to the outside world by flows of individuals, of commodities, and also of credit, contracts, information, inheritance, and expectations.[74]

It was these invisible exchanges with which the social network of the Allemands and the Ferrands was so dense. There were those, like Jean-Baptiste's brothers and sisters, who had a close relative who traveled outside France; those who were involved in the war economy of the times, or were caught up in the ceremony of the lottery for the militia, with the (distant) possibility of encountering foreign enemies; those who bought or sold colonial (or pseudo-colonial) commodities; those who were immediate neighbors of individuals from overseas; those who had expectations of an inheritance. This was the world of information that Marie Aymard evoked in her power of attorney about the missing fortune—the letters she had written for her and the reports of obscure inquiries in Martinique—and it was diffused across the entire network of the signatories of the marriage contract, their families, and their friends.

The War Economy

The consequences of almost worldwide war—the Seven Years' War of 1756–1763—extended deep into the daily life of Angoulême. There were barracks for invalid soldiers in the parish of St. Antonin, in which Marc Allemand lived in the Isle de la Cloche Verte, and English prisoners of war from the early months of hostilities.[75] Two of the bakers in the town—relatives of several of the signatories—made a "treaty" or "verbal market," in 1757, with the naval lieutenant of the port of Rochefort, to "furnish all the foodstuffs necessary for the English prisoners detained in the castle." But the bread they supplied turned out to be horrible: "brown," full of "defectuosity," probably adulterated with cold water. So the treaty ended in arbitration, and a professional "inspection of the bread," a "visitte du pain," in which the offending provisions were weighed, tasted, and eventually exonerated (by two of the other baking families of the town).[76]

The presence of the army and the navy was evident in Angoulême before, during, and after the war.[77] Angoulême was a port of entry to the hinterland of the naval base at Rochefort and the naval depot of Saint-Jean-d'Angély, with its supplies of timber, brandy, and artillery. It was a riverine port, at the point where the Charente became navigable; there were officials of the navy in the town, assigned to the quayside parish of St. Jacques de l'Houmeau. The brother of one of the signatories filed a formal protest, in 1765, against a person "calling himself the commissioner of the navy in the said port," over an instruction to load "cannons and wood" instead of brandy for overseas customers.[78] Another signatory, a saddlemaker, was involved in a complex dispute in 1766, over two cabriolets or carriages that had been rented to the "inspector of the navy to take him to Nantes," and damaged in the course of "some contestations" along the way."[79]

Early in 1758, the war came to Angoulême in a violent and immediate sense. The elaborate ceremonial of the lottery for the militia—of which Turgot wrote that "there is nothing that makes the people feel more strongly their degradation and their servitude"—took place in the royal palace of the town in February and again in October 1758.[80] Claude Rezé, printer of tickets for the lodging of troops, and of "tickets of invitation" for "public ceremonies," took the opportunity to request an increase in his fees, on the grounds of an unanticipated increase in the paper required, and in the number of the "assemblies."[81]

In the initial procedure, in February, ninety-one of the young men of the town were listed, by the "sergeants" of each neighborhood, as subject to the lottery. Seventy-four of them, or more than 80 percent, were identified as "absent" and thereby "fugitive"; of the seventeen who appeared, seven drew tickets marked with the deadly "M," and were ordered to report for service in the militia. In October, the ceremony was repeated; 185 individuals were identified as eligible for the lottery, 103 were absent and deemed deserters, and 26 drew the tickets marked "M." An additional 33 inhabitants were chosen to contribute to the costs of marching the new militia from Angoulême to Limoges; and toward the European theater of war.[82] In one of the violent rituals of the procedure—Turgot described it as "a sort of civil war"—the new conscripts were allowed a period in which to "search for and arrest" the fugitives, and to present them to serve in their place; they were permitted to "use force," while observing "good order."[83]

The uncertainty of the lottery for the militia, in the midst of a long-distance war, reached into almost all the households and families of Angoulême. Their sons and apprentices were forced, in Turgot's romantic expression, to "expose themselves to a destiny the very idea of which plunges them into despair."[84] The nobility were exempted, and so were their servants; students were exempt "if there was no presumption that they had been made scholars in order to exempt them from drawing lots"; the masters of the collège d'Angoulême were exempt.[85] But the law and the practice of exemptions were part of the uncertainty; in the October 1758 procedure, one of the young men on the list was excluded because "he could be considered to be bourgeois";

another, a gardener aged eighteen, was "sent away by the intendant," on the grounds that he had been found to be "the domestic servant of Madame the Abbess."[86]

"Lavigerie" appeared one of the October lists, with two children, "one in the service of the king, and the other a student"; the one who was a student provided a certificate from a teacher, and was declared exempt. Gilles Yrvoix, a butcher, who was one of the signatories and a cousin of the bridegroom, appeared twice in the records of the militia in 1758; his domestic servant was included in the list of fugitive boys, and he was required to contribute to the costs of the (uphill) march to Limoges. So was the widowed mother of Marie Bonnard, a signatory and a baker.[87] The nephew of a signatory, Elizabeth Glaumont, was one of the young men selected in the lottery; he presented an immigrant to the town, from a village in the Jura, to serve in his place.[88] A list of "those present on whom the lot was drawn" (the "sort," or the destiny) included another signatory, the son of Gilles Yrvoix, and one of the Glaumonts, a saddlemaker. Another Glaumont, a salt merchant, was on the list of "names of those absent."[89] There was the fugitive "Tourangeau," who may or may not have been Marie Aymard's son Mathurin, and who left so little trace in the parish records of the town.[90]

There was even a figure identified as "la veuve Tourangeau," who may have been Marie Aymard, and who appeared in the records of the lottery of 1758, with the confusing identities so characteristic of the procedure. In the power of attorney, in 1764, Marie Aymard recounted that her husband had left for the island of Grenada in (December) 1753 and lived there for "four or five years," before setting out to return home.[91] It is possible, if he stayed only four years, and made his way to Martinique amidst the naval warfare of 1758, that she was already a widow by the time of the lottery for the militia in Angoulême. "La veuve Tourangeau" was described in October 1758 as having three sons, of whom one was a preceptor or tutor, and two were aged "thirteen to fourteen"; there was a marginal note, "check the condition and age," and then an annotation, in another document, that the oldest son, the preceptor, was living in a village to the east of Angoulême, and that the other sons were "all young."[92]

The Color of Life

Marie Aymard and her family were at a distance, with all their anxieties, from the other local economy of worldwide exchange, or the commerce in colonial commodities. The diffusion of unfamiliar commodities has been seen, convincingly, as one of the principal ways in which the new world of commerce influenced the interior life of France (and elsewhere in Europe).[93] Among the signatories of the marriage contract, there were several whose daily life unfolded amidst exotic commodities. Jean Dumergue, the saddlemaker who quarreled with the inspector of the navy, was involved in a further dispute, in 1768, with a carter who lost two of his horses, while transporting "forty-two bales of cotton" and "thirty-one other pieces of merchandise, coffee, oranges, and other," from Bordeaux to Orléans.[94] There was Catherine Bonvallet, who sold tobacco.[95] When Paul Faveraud, whose mother, aunt, and sister were signatories of the marriage contract, was married in 1775, the inventory of his wife's apothecary shop on the Place du Mûrier included Brazil wood from Pernambuco, Smyrna alum, Carolina rice, 9 livres of chocolate, 18 livres of tea, 45 pounds of Martinique coffee, and 68 pounds of coffee from Saint-Domingue.[96]

The textiles called *indiennes* and *siamoises*, with their evocation of distant lands, were for sale in Angoulême in the 1760s, and they were even fabricated within the generality. The proliferation of fake Indian cotton was a continuing preoccupation, at least in respect of exports from the Atlantic ports.[97] Two merchants in the parish of St. André returned a bale of *indiennes* to a supplier in Limoges, in 1760, on the grounds that the pieces were of neither the "color" nor the "quality" (*demi-fin*) that they had ordered.[98] But the consumers of brightly colored clothing—two generations before Jules Michelet's "great and capital revolution," the *révolution d'indienne*—were in many cases the prosperous official families of Angoulême.[99] The widow of a naval officer in Saint-Domingue, who lived in St. Antonin and whose daughter was the immediate neighbor of one of the signatories of the marriage contract, owned a dress of Indian batiste lined in pink taffeta and a skirt of embroidered *siamoise*, according to the inventory of her estate. The wife of the mayor of Angoulême who presided over the lottery for the militia, and who was herself an heiress from Martinique, owned 124 shirts in different fabrics, a dress made of Indian satin, and an embroidered Indian *mousseline*.[100]

The parish and civil records that are at the heart of this story are full of stories, evasions, and lies. But they are colorless, in a literal sense, and so are the tax registers of the town. It is the notarial acts, with their inventories, that show something of *siamoises* and pink taffetas, and they tell a history of enduring inequality in the color of life. There are very few inventories of the Allemands and the Ferrands, until the nineteenth century; they owned very little property and had no shops filled with commodities. There were Marie Aymard's two beds, garnished with very worn green serge; Elizabeth Boutoute, the daughter of the saucepan-maker, owned a bed with "an Indian counterpane" when she married Jean-Baptiste in 1774.[101] Gabriel, before his own marriage, requested an elaborate inventory of the house he shared with his mother and sister, which was also his place of work, the *pension* for the students in the nearby college. His property consisted of beds and (fifty-eight) sheets; there was a bed garnished with "little pieces of *siamoise*" and a "yellow ribbon," a bed with a blue ribbon, and a bed with a "quilted cover in *indienne*."[102]

Sojourners and Visitors

The most visible overseas presence, in eighteenth-century Angoulême, was in the form of sojourners from distant colonies. The eighteen of the signatories who were near neighbors of Marc Allemand, in the Isle de la Cloche Verte, were also near neighbors of Jean-Alexandre Cazaud, with his many journeys to and from the island of Grenada, whose house in Angoulême was in the same tax island.[103] Jean-François-Auguste, the "Negro of the nation of the coast of Juda" whom Cazaud's father had brought with him "from the islands," was baptized in the town in 1733. There were other individuals from Africa as well, in the parishes of Angoulême. In 1758, the bishop of Angoulême presided over the baptism, also in the parish church of St. André, of "a Negro of the nation of Capélaou in Guinea [Cap Lahou, in Côte d'Ivoire], aged about fifteen." The child was named Claude, and his godfather was Claude Benoit des

Essarts, "to whom he belongs."[104] Benoit des Essarts lived in the same tax island as four of the signatories (the musician, the seamstresses, and Godinaud the baker); he was the brother-in-law both of Jean-Alexandre Cazaud and of the mayor of Angoulême who presided over the lottery for the militia in 1758.[105]

There was François Martin Aliquain, aged "around twelve," and the son of "unknown parents" in "laguinne en affrique," who had been living in the parish of St. Jean for three months, in 1775, when "of his own free will and without any constraint," he "abjured paganism at the door of the parish church"; his godfather, François Martin de Bourgon, was a former army officer, one of whose sons was a major in a regiment in Martinique, and another was in the army in Guadeloupe, and later governor of French Guyana.[106] Thomas Toussaint Bracher, described as a native of Guadeloupe, the servant of a "M. de Rouffignac," was living with his wife, "Marie Anne," in the parish of Petit St. Cybard in the 1770s; two of his children were baptized there in 1773 and 1775.[107]

Anne Faure, one of the signatories of the marriage contract, and the daughter of a shoemaker, signed the baptism record, in 1775, of yet another child who had been brought from Africa to Angoulême. He was "Jean L'Accajou," "a native of Africa," "aged fifteen," who was baptized in the parish of Petit St. Cybard; he was described as having "arrived in France on the ship La Cicogne, Captain Delage, or so it appears, and declared at the admiralty in La Rochelle," in 1773.[108] La Cigogne was a slaving ship that undertook five voyages between 1769 and 1778. It left La Rochelle in June 1771, and embarked 495 slaves in Ouidah, in the modern Benin; 430 slaves were disembarked in Cap-Français, Saint-Domingue (Haiti) in April 1772, and the ship returned to La Rochelle in September 1772. The captain was Michel Delage; he left three months later on another slaving voyage, and died in Africa in March 1773.[109]

Inheritance

The family relationships of the eighty-three signatories provide an intimate view of the occasions—the disputes over inheritance, the powers of attorney, the misdirected letters—of long-distance exchanges. Elizabeth Boutoute, who married Jean-Baptiste Ferrand and moved to Saint-Domingue, had her own family history of loss and expectation, entangled with the organization of entitlements in the town.[110] Her uncle was a party, in 1772, to an elaborate case involving the inheritance of his late brother-in-law, Louis Deschamps, a wigmaker from Angoulême. Louis Deschamps was one of the nine thousand men, women, and children who emigrated to "la France Equinoxiale," or French Guyana, in 1764–1765, in the aftermath of the Seven Years' War, and died there in the tragic expedition to Cayenne.[111] The inheritance involved Louis's brother, a merchant in Bordeaux, his two sisters, and their husbands, a blacksmith and a saucepan-maker, who was Elizabeth's uncle; the estate, on which the case turned, consisted of the right to "farm," or lease, the office of wigmaker in Angoulême for the sum of fifty livres.[112]

The signatory Jean Dumergue, the disputatious supplier of carriages to the intendant of the navy, was one of twelve sons of a saddlemaker, and the bridegroom's second cousin.[113] He was deeply involved, in the 1760s, in a family dispute over his late parents' inheritance, and he, too, had a brother in the colonies. François Dumergue, who was born in Angoulême in 1732, was at the time a merchant in Fort-Dauphin, Saint-Domingue (the modern Fort-Liberté, on the Atlantic coast of Haiti, near the border with the then Spanish colony of Santo Domingo).[114] The two brothers were in correspondence, in a discursive, familial sort of way; in a letter of 1769, which Jean deposited with the notary Caillaud, François wrote about the inheritance, the "good character" of one of their brothers, the generosity (or otherwise) of the others, the tax burden of military expenditure, and the impending revolution in the island: "two-thirds of this island are already in great trouble," with only a small chance "of avoiding a civil war." He also offered to find an opportunity for one of his nephews as a clerk in the colony, if the boy knew how to write. But he was not yet in a position to return to France, he wrote in February 1769, given that "commercial affairs were going very badly."[115]

A few months later, in September 1769, François Dumergue appeared in the *Affiches Américaines*, the commercial journal of the colony, advertising for the capture of a runaway Creole slave called Nannette, who spoke "very good Spanish and French." She was "branded on her two breasts, DUMERGUE," and on her shoulders with his initials, "FD."[116] In April 1770, he advertised again, with further details, for a "Creole negress, branded DUMERGUE above her two breasts, a dressmaker, about to give birth if she has not already done so."[117] His own "commercial affairs," in the meantime, had continued to go badly, and by July 1770, François Dumergue was no more than a "former merchant." His inventory—handkerchiefs, hats, stockings, the fabric for the clothing of slaves that the French called "ginga"—was advertised for sale, "by requisition of his creditors."[118]

The history of the (possible) inheritance of the children of a dancing master in the town, Marc René Lefort Latour, provides an even closer view of the exchanges of information between Angoulême and the outside world, from Berlin to Saint-Domingue. Marc René was a close friend of two of the signatories, Jean Joubert, a cloth merchant (another Allemand cousin) and his wife, Marguerite Durousot (the daughter of a wigmaker).[119] Marc René and his wife had twelve children over the period from 1730 to 1751. Some years after her death in 1763, it transpired that their surviving children were among the heirs of her brother, a merchant in Angoulême. Marc René, who at that point was sixty-nine, took upon himself the enterprise of finding all the documents and papers of the eventual heirs. It was a demanding procedure: three of his children, who were living in Paris, provided powers of attorney drawn up by a notary there; one of his brothers-in-law, who was a wigmaker in Berlin, sent an elaborate power of attorney certified by an official of the French embassy.[120] His fifth son, Louis Gabriel, was in Saint-Domingue, and it is his exchanges with Marc René that provide so much detail about the media of information involved in these elaborate procedures, over (in this case) extremely small inheritances.

Louis Gabriel Lefort Latour was semiliterate and highly discursive. He was a surgeon on a slave plantation in Artibonite, Saint-Domingue, and corresponded with his father; the letter about the inheritance survives, having been deposited with the notary Caillaud. It is a litany of misfortune and missing information. Marc René's own letter had been misdirected; Louis Gabriel's letters were delayed, and the letter from his father had been opened by another surgeon on the island, who was also called "Latour"; the correct address was "maître en chirurgie demeurant sur les Biens de messieurs les héritiers de Laville a la plaine de l'Artibonite cartier de St Marc ille St Domaingeue."

Louis Gabriel was himself in difficult circumstances. He needed a horse for his work; he too had brothers who had failed to keep their promises, and all he could send his father was a consignment of coffee, to be sold on his behalf by a merchant in La Rochelle. Louis Gabriel was an intermediary in the exchange of long-distance information, but he had been unable to find answers to a sequence of questions that his father had sent him on behalf of others in the town. He sent his best wishes to "Mlle de Boisnoble"; he had been able to find out that "her brother's plantation consists of a coffee estate with some Negroes and some animals," of which he had sent further details to a "M. Deraix"; the plantation would take five years to liquidate; he had not yet received an answer to a letter requesting further details; he had not seen "M. Leconte," who was in Port-au-Prince, to give him the letter from "David"; he had written to Cap-Français to get information about a person named Dusouchet, but it had been impossible to find.[121]

In the matter of his own possible inheritance, and the power of attorney, circumstances were no less difficult. Louis Gabriel had talked to a notary in Saint-Domingue, who "asked me for 72 livres." So he decided to do nothing, on the reasonable grounds that the power of attorney would cost more, in the end, than the succession was worth: "Je ne puis vous Envoyer ma procuration atandu que Sela me couteroit plus que La Sucsaitions ne vos."[122] The eventual proceeds, in the inheritance, amounted to 7 livres, 14 sols, 3 deniers per person.[123]

Information and Expectations

This was the world of incomplete information that Marie Aymard evoked in her power of attorney—of the exchanges that take place when one signs a parish register, or delivers bread to prisoners of war, or inquires about letters from Saint-Domingue, or decides to run away from the lottery ("a destiny the very idea of which plunges [one] into despair").

It was the world, too, of the signatories of the marriage contract and their connections.

To see the eighty-three signatories, together with their own immediate networks and friends, as a single social network, is to be able to visualize some of these exchanges. Even the most conventional indications of overseas influence—of emigrants (as a share of the population) or of foreign commerce (as a share of consumption, or production)—are elusive, within the statistical and archival sources of eighteenth-century colonial empires. The invisible exchanges of the times, of information and expectations, are more fugitive still. But their history is complementary, in principle, to the larger history of overseas influence; it tells a similar story.[124]

The Eighty-Three network, like so much else in this history, is incomplete. It is composed of a well-defined universe (eighty-three individuals, together with other individuals connected to them by specified relationships) and a process, of looking for the other individuals, that is potentially endless. It provides a tool, all the same, for visualizing the influence of the outside world—the probability that an individual had some sort of information or misinformation about distant events—as it was diffused across the social relationships in the network. In one iteration of the social network, individuals who had traveled outside France—Jean-Baptiste Ferrand, among the signatories, and other individuals among their connections—were thus shaded deeply in the visualization, and those with a family member who had lived outside France were shaded more lightly. The individuals who were palely shaded had one or more of the following connections to distant events: they or a relative had been contractors to the army or navy; they or a member of their household had been registered in the lottery for the militia in Angoulême in 1758; they were a neighbor of or signatory to one of the sojourners from Africa in the town; or they were immediate neighbors, in the same "island" or cluster of houses, of someone who had lived outside France. The influence of the outside world is invisible, in the sense that it is not material in the exchange of individuals and commodities; it is visible, or depicted, in the connections across the network.

The information in the Eighty-Three network can be used, in other iterations, to show the extent of mobility within France, within the society of a small provincial town: the probability, for example, that individuals had connections to the villages surrounding Angoulême, or to Paris, through family relationships. The eighty-three signatories and their connections will recur, on many occasions, as this history moves forward, with Marie Aymard's own children and grandchildren, into the historical time of the French Revolution; the Eighty-Three network can be a tool to show the diffusion of revolutionary (or counterrevolutionary) sentiments across families and friendships.

The connections between Marie Aymard's family and the individuals who signed the marriage contract were disparate and unequal, in the intensity or the continuity of the relationships, and also in the power of the different participants. The relationships changed, too, over historical time. The patronage of the family of the rich goldsmith continued into the lives of Marie Aymard's grandchildren. The most important source of capital for her grandson Martial, in 1790, was the savings of the two seamstresses who signed the marriage contract, living in poverty with their aunt and their widowed father. So the story of these eighty-three individuals is itself a large history. The signatories of the marriage contract were surrounded by news and information; they were the society, or one of the societies, amidst which Marie Aymard and her family lived.

Chapter Three

A BIRD'S-EYE VIEW

1764

The history of Marie Aymard and her family has been a sequence of stories: a connected history of individual and family lives. It is not a typical story, or a case study. It has been orderly, or systematic, in the sense that it started with the history of an individual: it moved outward to her family; and further outward to the social network, or the approximation to a social network (on a single afternoon in December 1764) that was evoked in the marriage contract of her daughter; and to the connections of the signatories of the contract.

But there are other historical points of view, and they are more orderly, or less incomplete. So the largest extension, in this history of the social universe of Marie Aymard, is vast. It inverts the entire procedure, in that it is an overview of (approximately) everyone in Angoulême in 1764; it proceeds, not from the individual to the family to the social network, but from the "society" to the individual or individuals, and to their stories. It has inverted the process or practice, as well. The restless pursuit of the eighty-three individuals is the sort of inquiry that is well suited to solitude (to the procedures of a solo private investigator, the sort of unseemly detective who specializes in the events of family life). The transcription and visualization of information about 4,089 individuals—for that is the population or society in question—is a different and collective undertaking.[1]

The 4,089 individuals consist of everyone who is mentioned in all the registers of the Catholic parishes of Angoulême in the course of 1764.[2] This is an adventitious population, in the sense that there were far more people (some twelve thousand, including around eight thousand in the central parishes) who were living in Angoulême at the time.[3] The individuals who are mentioned in the registers were there because of some event, or something that happened; they were baptized or married or had children or died, or were named in the records of these events. There are godparents and signatories in the registers, some of whom were no more than passing visitors in the town; the list of 4,089 individuals includes everyone who is mentioned in the registers, even those who were dead or far away.

The shorter list of individuals who were actually there, in Angoulême in 1764, is itself incomplete, as a depiction of the population of the town. There are all the other people who were there, and to whom nothing happened in the course of the year, or nothing to be recorded in the parish registers. There were the individuals who were not Catholics, and who appear only fleetingly in the parish registers; this was a town with a long history of religious conflict, where the parish register for St. Antonin, in 1731–1735, was enclosed in a parchment, dated 1680, enjoining the mothers, fathers, and masters of the town to restrain their children and servants from throwing mud and stones at persons of "the supposed reformed religion."[4] There were also the individuals who were present at these events, and were not mentioned, even to note that they could not sign. The newly married are overrepresented, with their families and friends; children are mentioned, for the most part, when they are born, and the old are mentioned when they die.

The priests in the different parishes had highly diverse practices in respect of how much information they provided, and the small, prosperous, literate parishes are also overrepresented in the list of everyone who was mentioned. There were so many individuals, there, who could sign their names, and so much space in the registers for signatures and flourishes, life histories, and the recitation of the achievements of the long-departed ("chevalier de St Louis et chef des escadres et armées navalles," in the case of a naval officer whose widow was buried in St. Antonin in 1764).[5] These are sources, like all sources, with their own idiosyncrasies, and their own omissions. But they are all there is, for the universality of the Catholic population of Angoulême in the year of the marriage contract of Marie Aymard's daughter.

4,089 Individuals

The list of the 4,089 individuals is an overview of Angoulême in 1764: a bird's-eye view, as though from far above the roofs of the houses. It is a picture of the lives of individuals in the town. It is also a source, like the much smaller list of the signatories of the marriage contract, together with their friends and relations, of the sort of information or data that can be depicted in a social network visualization. In the visualization, it is possible to see who, of all these individuals who happened to be there in the parish registers for 1764, was connected to whom, and who was particularly sociable, or connected, in the sense of a "node," or individual, with particularly many "edges," or connections to other individuals. (They were the people who were married in the course of the year, for the most part, who had many literate relations, or who participated in several different events.)

The overview of the 4,089 individuals is complementary to other evidence in respect of the history of eighteenth-century Angoulême. There are the two tax rolls, in 1763 and 1766, and the lists prepared in connection with the lottery in 1758. There were three competing lists of debtors and creditors in the town compiled in connection with the financial-legal affair that began in 1769. There were the thousand or so "acts" or records drawn up in 1764 alone by the nineteen notaries practicing in the town; there were also the registers of the criminal jurisdiction of the town. Individuals appear and vanish in the records, becoming fugitives or claiming exemptions or dividing inheritances or suing their neighbors—in the case of the criminal jurisdiction—for calumny, attempted murder, and singing atrocious songs. The list of the 4,089 individuals provides an overview, of sorts, for locating these other, intermittent figures.

The list makes it possible, too, to zoom inward from the bird's-eye view, or the vista of the "society," to the individual, and outward, again, to the view from the society or the data. The individuals in the list of 4,089 are real, or historical, in the sense that their existence is something that was recorded and can be verified.[6] There were events in their lives that really happened. There were also falsifications, and entries to be

"rectified," often many years later. (It was in connection with the rectification of an earlier lapse of memory that Marie Aymard's grandson had
occasion, in Bayonne in 1826, to describe the records of civil registration
as "grave, serious and important.")[7] But the registers are "poor, dry, and
formal," in general, in comparison to the richer and "more loquacious
sources" of the notarial and judicial archives.[8]

The individuals in the notarial acts were describing themselves as
they wished to be described, in the episodic discourse of contracts or
complaints or declarations. So were the plaintiffs in the criminal jurisdiction, telling stories, like that of Rose Rezé (one of the Rose Rezés)
about walking down the street with her sister-in-law. The individuals
who are described in the tax rolls, too, can be seen as figments of the
imagination, or the estimation, of the weary clerks who drew up the lists,
their handwriting deteriorating as they made their way through the
streets and the registers of the town.[9] In the militia lists there are detailed visual descriptions—the only depictions that exist, or that I have
been able to find, of any of the thousands of women and men in mid-
eighteenth-century Angoulême who are the subject of this book—and
they are there because the people described were fugitives, or were expected to become so.[10]

The possibility of zooming from the 4,089 "nodes" to an individual
life, and from an isolated notarial act to a social network of 5,329 "edges,"
is in this sense disconcerting. It is a variation in scale that is also a variation in kinds of history, and kinds of relationship to historical individuals, or to individuals who once existed. There have always been different
kinds of reality in historical inquiry, and different historical sources for
different kinds of individuals: the quantitative or macro or social for
"the mass of families who live almost entirely from their labor," as the
philosopher Condorcet anticipated in the 1790s—"the most obscure,
the most neglected, and for which monuments offer us so little
material"—and the qualitative or the micro for individuals who had
lives in history, or interesting lives.[11] There are individuals who can be
described in stories, and individuals who can only be counted. The parish records make it possible to traverse at least some of these different
kinds of history. They are universal (for the Catholic population), in a

cursory equality of destiny, or of the events of birth, marriage, and death; everyone is there, the low and the high and the obscure.

Endless Counting

Even to look at the parish registers of eighteenth-century France, as the historian Pierre Goubert wrote in 1954, is to be seduced by quantities; "Should we, like so many others, set ourselves to counting furiously, interminably?"[12] So these are the numbers. To start with births: 505 infants were baptized in the twelve parishes of Angoulême in the course of 1764.[13] There were no baptisms of heretics or pagans or Anglicans in the course of the year, although in July a two-year-old girl called Marie was baptized in the parish of St. Martin; she was "born of a Protestant marriage," and her mother had "for some time been a vagabond."[14] One young woman in the parish of St. André—she was the younger sister of the Pascal Chauvin to whom Marie Aymard entrusted her investigations in Martinique—gave birth to a son, who was baptized "Pierre," in January 1764, and gave birth again, in December 1764, to another son, who was also baptized "Pierre."[15]

Of the 505 infants who were born and baptized in 1764, 50 were buried in the same year. [16] There were more boys born than girls; 36 of the 271 boys baptized died within the year, and 14 of the 234 girls. The infant mortality rate for children born in Angoulême in 1764—the proportion who died before their first birthdays—was 9 percent for girls, and 15 percent for boys.[17] Life was most precarious for the 31 infants, 13 girls and 18 boys, who were described as "unknown," "bastard," "illegitimate," or "exposed": placed in the "box," a sort of enclosure in the wall, where newborn babies were left in the care of the parish, the town, or the state. It was in general a relatively healthy year in the town.[18]

The summer months were the most dangerous, in this little town with no reliable water supply, and in which the prosperous made their own arrangements for water to be carried up the hill. (The widow of a weaver, in one of the notary Jean Bernard's transactions, entered into an agreement with a merchant in the town over the occasional use of a black goat, and the obligation to deliver water to his house.)[19] In August, September, and October 1764, "only" 48 children aged five or under were buried in the town. In the same months of 1765, 205 children were buried, in a year of terrible mortality, especially in St. André, St. Jacques, and St. Martial.[20] Of the 505 children who had been born in Angoulême in 1764, 54 died in the course of 1765, almost all of them in the three deadly summer months.

There were 122 marriages in the parishes of Angoulême in 1764; nine of the couples who were married had a child in the course of the year. Of the 122 couples, the age at marriage was declared for fewer than a third; the average age of the women was 29, and the average age of the men was 31. The oldest was a widower of 60, from Agen, who married a widow of 55 from La Rochefoucauld. The youngest was described as 15, and was the son of a cooper; he was in fact 12 years and 6 months old, and married a woman of 20.[21] Of those who were married, 14 of the women and 37 of the men, came from outside Angoulême. Most of them were in the semirural parishes of St. Martial and St. Jacques, and almost all of them came from nearby provinces; one man was described as a native of Turin. Only 39 of the women and 56 of the men signed their names in the registers, although only 22 declared that they did not know how to.

Only 2 out of the 122 women who were married in the course of the year declared their occupations; both were domestic servants. Of the 122 men, there were 66 who declared occupations: 16 day laborers, 4 coopers, 4 shoemakers, 4 tailors, 3 farm laborers, 3 weavers, 2 fishmongers, 2 carpenters, 2 hatmakers, 2 joiners, 2 men describing themselves as "squires," an army officer, a former army surgeon, a baker, a blacksmith, a bookbinder, a chair-carrier, a clothmaker, a comb-maker, a *commis* or clerk, an innkeeper, a "knight," a lawyer, a legal intermediary or *praticien*, a locksmith, a merchant, a painter, a papermaker, a sergeant, a shopkeeper, a stonecutter, a master writer. There was only a single person from the metal industries of the incipient industrial revolution, a "worker in iron wires," from the suburban parish of St. Yrieix.

The individuals who died in Angoulême in the course of the year were for the most part children and the elderly. Of the 327 burials, 122 were of children aged 15 or under, and 71 were of people aged 50 or over; there were 93 people whose ages were not known, or not recorded. The children who died were mostly in the poorest parts of the town, 27 percent of them in St. Martial, compared to only 15 percent of the elderly who died. More men died than women; but of the 41 individuals who died as young or fairly young adults—in the years of childbearing—25 were women and 16 were men. There were a few people who lived for a very long time. The oldest person in the parish registers was called "Marguerite Cassaud." She died in the hospital of the Hôtel-Dieu, and was buried in the parish of Notre Dame de Beaulieu; she was aged "around 100."[22]

Economic Circumstances

These 1,026 people—the infants who were baptized, the men and women who were married, and the people who were buried—are the principal figures in the overview of 4,089 individuals in and around Angoulême in 1764. There are then the 3,062 other individuals who were there in the parish records in the course of the year: the mothers, and most of the fathers, of the infants who were baptized; the godparents who were present at the baptisms and signed the registers; the other signatories and witnesses who were there at the various events; and a few people, like Marie Aymard at the baptism of her first grandchild, the son of Gabriel and Marie Adelaide, who were noted as being present, and who did not sign.

These other individuals were no more than mentioned in the registers. But they were significant in the lives of the 1,026 protagonists; that is why they were there. The overview of Angoulême in 1764 is a depiction of a point in time. (It is a long point, as in so much of the social science of time series: a sequence of winter and spring and autumn, in which individuals, like Jeanne Nouel, the wife of an innkeeper, was married in January 1764, mourned the death of a child in February, and gave birth in October.)[23] It is also, fleetingly, diachronic; a view, or a shadow, of the parents who were remembered at the marriages of their children, or the late husband of the widow who died in St. Antonin, described by the acquaintances who organized her solitary funeral.

The large inquiry into these 4,089 individuals is an overview of the economic circumstances of the times. Angoulême was a place of trades-men, day laborers, lawyers, and domestic servants, according to the oc-cupations that are declared in the parish records. Shoemakers, of whom there were 39, were the largest group among the 671 individuals whose occupations were listed; there were also 34 day laborers and 23 domestic servants. Then there were 21 individuals who described themselves as "procureurs"—lawyers, or associated with the law—and 8 advocates. There were 12 traders and 32 "shopkeepers" of various sorts; shopkeeper-butchers, shopkeeper–saucepan makers, shopkeeper-spurriers. There were 11 carpenters, 8 joiners, and 7 stonemasons, together with two in-dividuals described as "entrepreneurs" (in the contemporary sense of building contractors).

The parish records that are the basis of the inquiry—and particularly the records in respect of the "other individuals" who were not them-selves born or married or who died, the signatories and witnesses—are biased toward the literate and the self-describing. (It was in the parishes filled with lawyers and clergymen, for the most part, that there were long entries in the registers, and long lists of signatories.) There were 9 master writers, among the individuals in the records for 1764; 6 nota-ries; 2 masters of arts; 2 schoolboys and 3 students; and 3 schoolteachers (of whom one was "interim professor of humanities," in the college from which the Jesuits had been expelled). There was also an array of oc-cupations associated with the great local enterprise of the diocese of Angoulême: acolyte, almoner, archpriest, canon, choirboy, chorister, curé, deacon, monk, prior, sacristan, treasurer of the cathedral church.

But the records of the 4,089 individuals are also an overview of the variety of provincial life. The two large and semirural parishes of St. Martial and St. Jacques, together with the suburban parishes, ac-counted for more than half the population of the town. There were 29 farm laborers, 7 stonemasons, and 17 coopers, most of them in the river port of St. Jacques. Even the inner parishes, where almost all the signa-tories of the marriage contract lived, were partly agricultural. The parish of St. Martial, in which Françoise Ferrand was born, extended outside the walls of the town to fields and quarries. It was a place of "day laborers, beggars, and the inhabitants of caverns," the inhabitants complained in September 1782: a "rendezvous for all the victims of misery and indigence, not only from the province of Angoulême but from the neighboring provinces."[24]

The armed forces were important in the town—there were 8 officers, 7 sergeants, and 15 soldiers, of whom 11 were invalids. There was a contingent of clerks and officials, mostly from the administration of taxes: a *commis* or clerk, 2 *commis* in charge of tax receipts, 5 officials of the *greffe* or registry, 6 *huissiers* or government ushers, an employee of the imposition called the *aide*, and a receiver of taxes. The manufacturing industries of the generality were marginal in the parish registers: 5 young men in the records who were apprentice papermakers, 14 men and 2 women who were weavers or spinners or wool-sorters, and another 10 who were clothmakers; a man in St. Jacques who worked with the hemp fibers that were used for packaging. In the distinction that was beginning to become familiar to the economists of the time—in which to be productive was to be employed in agriculture, or in manufacturing—the life of the town was "unproductive."[25] There were 13 innkeepers and tavern-keepers, 12 wigmakers, and 8 surgeons; this was the world of work in Angoulême in 1764, in which the Allemands and the Ferrands were making their own economic lives.

Women's Work

Among all the 4,089 individuals in the parish registers for 1764, there were only 22 women for whom an occupation was declared: 9 were domestic servants; there were also 2 dressmakers, a shopkeeper, a cook, a wet nurse, a midwife, a nun, a fishmonger, 2 tailors, a seamstress, a wool-sorter, and a spinning woman. Half of these 22 women were there in the registers in a single role: as godmothers—twice in the course of the year, in the case of Jeanne Chenaud, a dressmaker—to the infants who had been deposited in the "box" in the parish of St. Paul. Only 4 were protagonists, in the sense of being people to whom something happened in the course of the year (or something that was recorded in the parish registers). Hypolite Binet, a servant, was married in July 1764

to a cooper; Elizabeth Coste, also a servant, was married to a day laborer; Marie Julie Laroque, who was described as a tailor when she was
a godmother in August, was married to a cooper, six days later; Anne
Tabuteau, a nun, died in October.[26]

The records of these 22 women are only a tiny piece—a wisp of cloth,
like the ribbons that were tied, a generation later, to the wrists of the
infants abandoned in the town—of the economic history of women in
Angoulême. The two tax rolls for the period, in particular, provide a
complementary overview of the economic life of the inner parishes and
the surrounding suburbs—and another systematic part of the historical
inquiry. There were 119 households, of the 2,548 that are listed in the tax
roll for 1766, that either were headed by women whose occupations
were specified, or included women with occupations: 128 women in all,
since there were several households, like that of "Marguerite et Geneviève Courlit loueuses de chaises," in which there were two or three
women with occupations listed. In the tax roll for 1763 there were 120
households that included women with occupations: in all, 135 women,
of whom 40 were still there in the tax roll two years later.

Only two of the women with listed occupations, among the 4,089
individuals in the parish registers, were also there in the tax records.
Jacquette Couprie, the shopkeeper or "marchande," appears in 1763 and
again in 1766, in one of the crowded tax islands of St. André, as the
widow L'Esparvin, lemonade seller. She was the widow of a clothmaker,
and was fairly prosperous, with an estimated taxable value, in 1763, of
400 livres. (The uncle of the bridegroom, in the marriage contract, who
lived in the same island, was taxed at 150 livres.)[27] The dressmaker who
was godmother to two of the infants from the "box" was also in the tax
roll for 1763: "la Chenaude couturière," with a taxable value of 15 livres.[28]

The description of the entire society of occupied women in
Angoulême—the 223 individuals who were listed in the registers for
1763 or 1766 or both—shows a much more diverse scene. The women
listed in the tax rolls were relatively prosperous, even though the rolls
included several individuals with "nothing." There was only one female
domestic servant in the list for 1766, "Marie Charité." There is no allusion
at all, in the tax rolls, to the unpaid work that dominated the economic

lives of so many of the women in Angoulême: the sort of work that was evoked in the list of Marie Aymard's debts, in January 1764: 74 livres for potash for washing clothes, 49 livres 11 sols for cloth, 94 livres for cooking fat.[29]

The women with identified occupations in the tax lists were for the most part either single or widowed; fewer than a quarter were described as living with husbands. There were households full of women: the Courlit sisters who rented chairs; three sisters who were tailors; a widow and her daughters, dressmakers; the family of the retired musician, a signatory of the marriage contract, who lived with his daughters and his sister-in-law, all of them seamstresses.[30] There were parts of the town in which industrious women settled together. In the little tax island where the dressmaker Jeanne Chenaud lived, there was also a laundress, a wool-sorter, a spinner, and a woman described as "servante en ville"; 13 out of 27 households in the island were headed by women.[31] In the island of the Petit Maure, there was the innkeeper, "la veuve Croiset," 3 women who were used-clothes sellers, 3 who were shopkeepers, a tailor or *tailleuse*, and a seller of cooking fat—she was the mother of Pascal Chauvin, who was leaving for Martinique—all within an island of 14 households.[32]

There was a concentration of women in the sociable, discursive occupations of the central parishes of the town: the lemonade seller, the two sisters who rented chairs, the innkeeper, and eight tavern-keepers. The largest occupations were clustered around the domestic work of women: 17 tailors, 15 seamstresses; 10 women selling cooking fat; 8 laundresses; 4 midwives. There were 11 women bakers, all of them widows; 9 fruit sellers and a grape merchant; 4 *cocassières*, or chicken merchants; a fishmonger and a sardine seller; a seller of herbs. There were retailers of household goods: 13 *fripières*, or sellers of used clothes; 3 sellers of trinkets or *clincaillerie*, of whom one was the signatory of the marriage contract Rose Rezé. There was a *marchande colporteuse* or peddler, a farm laborer with her own oxen, a papermaker and 2 paper merchants, an iron merchant, a butcher, 2 sisters selling forage, and 2 schoolmistresses. In the vast, undescriptive society of the parish records, there are no more than glimpses of these industrious women; they were there, in 1764, in the economic life of Angoulême.[33]

The Signatories and the Population

So these are the 4,089 individuals in the parish records of Angoulême, in a bird's-eye view. There are 33 of the signatories of the marriage contract—to look, now, inside the families of the town—who are there in the parish records. Two of the signatories, Gabriel Ferrand's sister-in-law, Dorothée Devuailly, and Gabriel Lemaitre, the painter, were married in September 1764 in the parish of Notre Dame de Beaulieu: an elaborate occasion with 16 signatories in the parish register, including 5 of the 83 signatories of the marriage contract of Françoise Ferrand and Etienne Allemand.[34] Marguerite Godinaud, a signatory and the daughter of a baker, was also married in 1764, in June, in the parish of St. André: another large occasion, with 18 signatories, of whom 4 were among the signatories of the marriage contract.[35] But the marriage was ill-fated. Marguerite died in the immediate aftermath of childbirth in 1769; her widower remarried, and died soon after, in 1771; his widow—Marguerite's widower's widow—then married Jean Abraham Rodriguez Sarzedas, a merchant from Bordeaux who had abjured Judaism in 1773, in the parish of St. Jean; she died in 1776, and Sarzedas in turn remarried the following year; Sarzedas died seven years later, in 1783.[36]

The signatories of the marriage contract, even within the large population of the town, were sociable individuals: signatories and witnesses, godparents and friends. Marie Aymard is there, as the godmother of her first grandchild, and one of the few individuals, among the 4,089, of whom it is noted that "she did not know how to sign."[37] Marc Allemand, the father of the bridegroom, signed the record of the marriage of a shoemaker and the widow of a tailor, in January 1764; Louis Dupard, the button-maker, signed a marriage record in May, and was a godfather in October.[38] Marie Chaumont Gautier, Gabriel Ferrand's neighbor, was the godmother of a baby baptized in Notre Dame de la Peine in July, the son of a domestic servant, who was married to another domestic servant.[39] Rose Marin was the godmother of an infant baptized in St. André in November, the posthumous daughter of the domestic servant of one of the local theologians.[40]

The eighty-three signatories were relatively prosperous, within the larger population, in the sense that there were no day laborers, or farm laborers, or domestic servants among their family connections (with the possible exception of the bride's brother, who may or may not have been the domestic servant of the innkeeper of the Cheval Blanc). They were tailors and seamstresses, like so many others in the records. Five of the signatories were the daughters of shoemakers, or of former shoemakers, or married to shoemakers; Marie Aymard was the granddaughter and great-granddaughter of shoemakers. They were industrious, in the sense of living in the multigenerational and multioccupational households that recur in the tax rolls: Louis Dupard, the button-maker, living with his father-in-law, his wife, who was a used-clothes seller, his sister, who was a tailor, and his wife's brother; Jean Faure, the musician, with his daughters and his sister-in-law, seamstresses; Jean Yrvoix, the candle seller, who lived with his wife, Jeanne Chabot, a shopkeeper selling cooking fat and pottery, and his sister-in-law, also a shopkeeper, all three of them signatories of the marriage contract.[41]

Other People's Connections: Magdelaine Faure

The signatories of the marriage contract were unexceptional, too, in their discursiveness and in the multiplicity of their sources of information. There are other stories to be found in the vista of 4,089 individuals: other streets, houses, and the individuals within them, making plans for their future lives. The most connected person among the 4,089 individuals in the parish records—in the formal sense of the node with the most edges, or the most connections in the course of the year—was a twenty-one-year-old woman from the quayside parish of St. Jacques, Magdelaine Faure. She was married in October 1764 to Jean Roy, who identified himself as a bookbinder in the parish register, and as a day laborer in his marriage contract, the previous day. Nineteen people signed the record of their marriage, and twenty-eight people signed the marriage contract.[42] Magdelaine Faure was the godmother of the daughter of a stonecutter in September 1764, also in St. Jacques; she signed the record of the baptism of the daughter of an oven-keeper in the central parish of St. Paul in October; in November she signed the record of another baptism, in St. Martial.[43]

Magdelaine Faure lived in a milieu of exchanges of information that was distant from the connections of the signatories of the marriage contract. Her father was a messenger, traveling between Angoulême and Bergerac, in the Dordogne; he had earlier been a letter carrier in the messenger service between Bordeaux and Angoulême. One of her sisters, Luce Faure, was a carpet-maker. Her husband was a toolmaker before he became a bookbinder; her brother-in-law (who was the husband of her sister Marguerite, as well as the brother of her husband) was successively a cooper, a packer, and a bookbinder. She and her sisters were sociable, literate figures, and frequent signatories in the different parishes of the town. In 1760, when she was sixteen, she and her future husband were godparents in the parish of St. Paul; Luce Faure also signed the record, at the age of twelve. All three sisters signed the baptism record of the son of an apprentice messenger in May 1765, in St. Jacques.[44]

The tax island in which Magdelaine Faure and her husband lived was a neighborhood of multiple occupations, like so many others in the town; there was a bonnet-maker, a cooper, a painter of pottery, a shoe-maker, a toolmaker, and one rich merchant, a former wigmaker (who was the father of one of the eighty-three signatories of the marriage contract, and the brother of Jean-Baptiste Marchais, the goldsmith). Magdelaine Faure's father, the messenger, was listed with a taxable income of 300 livres in 1763; her future husband was listed as "poor."[45]

With all her connections and all her sociability, Magdelaine Faure was part of the history of the "low" Enlightenment in Angoulême, and of the milieu of printers and bookbinders that was so susceptible, in the view of the Enlightenment's enemies, to the seduction of modern times.[46] She was also part of the social history of insecurity. Her daughter Marguerite Roy was born on August 14, 1765, and baptized the same day, in the parish of St. Jacques; she died four days later. Magdelaine Faure survived her daughter by nine days. She was buried in St. Jacques on August 27, 1765, a week after her twenty-second birthday: a victim, with her daughter, of the deadly summer months. Her husband, Jean Roy, remarried in 1767, in the parish of St. André. Magdelaine's mother and sister signed the record. He had nine more children, and founded a dynasty of printers, paper merchants, and lithographers in Angoulême.[47]

Other People's Marriages: Jacques Thinon

Marie Aymard's family were unexceptional, in turn, in their propensity for marriage contracts and other notarial acts. The ceremony of the registration of the marriage contract of Françoise Ferrand and Etienne Allemand was extraordinary in the number of participants (the eighty-three signatories, and the others who were there, including the mother of the bride). But there were marriage contracts for most of the 122 couples who were married in the town in 1764.[48] Jean Bernard, who drew up the contract, and who made so "many instruments for the small people," prepared contracts for eleven of the couples. There were two laborers or farmers, from the nearby communities of Magnac and Dirac; the son of an oven-keeper who married the daughter of a stonecutter; a weaver who married the daughter of a day laborer; a *commis* or clerk from the naval port of Rochefort, who was the son of a carpet-maker in Boulogne-sur-mer; and Jacques Thinon, a beggar, who married the daughter of a beggar.[49]

Jacques Thinon and Marie Leger were married in St. Martial in July 1764.[50] Jacques Thinon was identified as coming from the small parish of Coulonges—it had thirty-seven households—to the north of Angoulême.[51] In the marriage contract, Jacques and Marie constituted themselves as a "society in community" in accordance with the customary law of the province of the Angoumois; they each contributed the sum of five livres. The agreement also included provisions for future debts, charges, and the bride's personal privileges in respect of her "clothes, rings, jewels, and underwear"; the cost of the contract was thirty-nine sols, which was marked "reimbursed."[52]

Over the next sixteen years, Jacques Thinon and Marie Leger had two daughters and five sons, all of whom were baptized in the parish church of St. Jacques. Of the fourteen godparents of their children, only two could sign their names.[53] Then, in February 1776, the family were parties to a different contract, again with Jean Bernard. This was the resolution of a dispute that had begun in 1748 in the parish of Balzac to the north of Angoulême, over the property of Marie Leger's maternal grandparents, and involving her great-uncle and her mother's first cousin.[54] By 1776, the parties involved were the grandson of the great-uncle, a laborer in Balzac; Marie and Jacques; and the two daughters of the first cousin, both called Marie Godinaud, who were living in two different villages, and of whom the younger sister was the domestic servant of a man called Godard. Jacques Thinon was described as "without profession in that he is blind."[55]

The objects to be inherited, in this dispute over the course of twenty-eight years, were small; "their low value and their bad condition reduced them to not very much." Fifteen members of the family were identified in the agreement, together with the employer of the younger Marie Godinaud, and a judge in Balzac.[56] Four years later, Marie Leger died in Angoulême at the age of forty, following the birth of her seventh child. Three months after that, in February 1781, Jacques Thinon remarried. His wife had been living for twenty years in the parish of St. Paul as a domestic servant; she too was aged forty. They had a daughter, born in April 1783; in the record of the baptism, Jacques was identified, again, as a beggar.[57] Jacques Thinon and Marie Leger's older daughter was married in 1790, to a sailor; she died in Angoulême in 1850, at the age of eighty-five.[58]

Pascal Chauvin and Others

The signatories of the marriage contract were like others among the 4,089 individuals in the parish records, even, in their connections to distant opportunities. Pascal Chauvin or Jean Pascal Yrvoix Chauvin, who was going to live in Martinique, and became the repository of Marie Aymard's power of attorney, was not there in the parish records for 1764. But his family were present, in the ordinary events of life. His grandmother, the widow of a baker, died in May at the age of "around eighty-three," in the parish of St. Jean.[59] His mother was one of the nine enterprising women in the tax island of the Petit Maure, listed in the tax roll as a seller of cooking fat.[60] Marie Yrvoix Chauvin, who had two children in the parish of St. André in the course of 1764, was his younger sister; his brother-in-law, who was heavily indebted, was identified variously as a candlemaker, a shopkeeper, and a grocer. [61]

Pascal Chauvin died on the island of Sainte-Lucie, about eighty kilometers to the south of Martinique. He was a merchant and a captain in the militia, who left his estate—consisting largely of uncollected debts on the island—to his brother and sister in Angoulême. But the estate could not be realized, in part because one of the largest of the sixty-two debtors was the local official in charge of law enforcement, and the bailiffs "did not dare" to pursue the case. In one of the stories of tangled successions with which the history of the French colonies is so amply adorned, Marie Yrvoix Chauvin and her husband sought the protection of the military governor of Angoulême; he wrote on behalf of "these unfortunate people" that the principal heirs "live in Angoulême and are truly in need."[62]

There were others of the 4,089 individuals in the parish records with their own histories of expectation and loss; and their own family connections to the slave economies of the colonies. Two of the daughters of the dancing master, the sisters of the surgeon on the slave plantation in Artibonite, Saint-Domingue, were there in the records, on the occasion of a baptism in St. Martial in August 1764.[63] There was the sister of the wigmaker who emigrated to French Guyana, whose daughter was baptized in June in St. André.[64] Rose Civadier, one of the 4,089 in the parish records, who signed the record of a marriage in St. Paul, was married herself, in 1766, to a "master surgeon" certified by the "sovereign council of Cap-Français."[65] The daughter of the patron of François Martin Aliquain, who abjured paganism aged "around twelve," was a godmother in October in Notre Dame de la Peine.[66] The captain of the slaving ship on which Aliquain arrived in La Rochelle was not in the parish records for Angoulême in 1764 (he was preparing for a slaving voyage, of a different ship, the *Constant*, that left La Rochelle in February 1765); fourteen other people called "Delage" were present, in four different events.[67]

Even the world of prison ships impinged in 1764 on the parishes of Angoulême. One of the 4,089 individuals was Marc Gestraud, a blacksmith, who was the godfather of a boy baptized in the parish of St. Yrieix in November 1764. On September 16, 1764, Marc Gestraud signed a marriage contract with Mathurine Rippe, the widow of a messenger.[68] Six days later, on September 22, Gestraud's mother appeared before the notary Jean Bernard, and registered an "act of opposition" to the proposed marriage. She gave no reason for her opposition to the marriage (and she referred to her prospective daughter-in-law as "Rose Ripe"); she noted that her husband, Jean Gestraud, also a blacksmith, had been "absent from the province for more than fifteen years."[69]

At this point, Marc Gestraud produced an additional, remarkable document, in the form of a notarial act signed by his absent father, in Toulon, on August 28, 1764, giving his consent to his son Marc to "establish himself in marriage with any single woman or widow as he pleases." Jean Gestraud was a prisoner in the galleys, "for the crime of desertion," detained at the time in the "bagne," or the forced-labor prison, in the naval port of Toulon. He had been brought in iron chains to the office of one of the notaries of the town, by the *pertuisanier* of the prison, the warden who was chained, during the working day, to ten of the prisoners. At the critical moment in the proceedings, the warden "removed the irons and freed the said Gestraud," "constituting him with a hat upon his head." Gestraud was then reimprisoned in the irons, and "reestablished in the same condition as he was before the passing of the present act."[70] In February 1765, Marc Gestraud and Mathurine Rippe were married at last, in the parish church of St. Yrieix.[71]

Klotz or Clod or Kloche

The connections of the 4,089 individuals in the parish records extended to the east, into the German lands, as well as to the sea. There were three sisters, called Marie Anne, Marie, and Françoise Klotz, relatives by marriage of Gabriel Ferrand, who appear in the records for 1764. Marie Anne and Marie signed the record of the elaborate marriage of two of the signatories, Gabriel's sister-in-law and the painter Gabriel Lemaitre.[72] Gabriel Lemaitre was their nephew, and the godson of Marie Anne; he was the son of their older sister, also called Marie Anne Klotz, who had died in 1748.[73]

The Klotz sisters were the daughters of an elusive figure called Johann Georg Klotz, who first appeared in the parish records of Angoulême on the occasion of his marriage, in November 1717, to a local woman, Moricette Bourdage. He was described as the cook of "M. De Torsac"; he married with the consent of his employer. Johann and Moricette's first child, the older Marie Anne, was baptized a few months later; Johann was again described as a cook. The godmother was Marie Anne Janssen de Torsac, the wife of his employer.[74] She was the heiress of a Dutch paper merchant, one of the founders of the modern paper industry in the town, who had moved to Angoulême in the mid-seventeenth century. Marie Anne Janssen's brother, born in Angoulême in 1654, was the notorious "Sir Theodore Janssen M.P." who emigrated to Wimbledon, became a founder of the Bank of England and the East India Company, and was disgraced spectacularly in 1721, following the famous South Sea Bubble fraud, as a director of the South Sea Company, established to trade slaves to the Spanish colonies in America.[75]

Johann Georg Klotz appeared frequently in the Angoulême records in the years following his marriage, as a godfather, a signatory, and on the occasion of the baptisms of his children. He was described as an innkeeper, starting in 1719. He, or his unfamiliar name, was also a source of mystification to the clerks of the parish registries. His own signature was large and elaborate, and changed very little over time. It was transcribed in wildly different ways, recorded successively, in the records of the parishes of Notre Dame de Beaulieu and St. Jean, as Klocq, Blocq, Clod, Bloch, Bloth, Kloche, Kloz, Klotz, Cloth, Cloche, Klots, Kloss, and Kloste.[76]

At some point after the mid-1720s, Johann disappeared for a time from the registries of the town. At least three of his children were baptized elsewhere; his daughter Marie, who signed the records of two elaborate marriages in 1764, was described on her death in 1813 as having been born in a village in the Dordogne, close to the estate of Marie Anne Janssen's sister-in-law.[77] When his oldest daughter, Marie Anne, was married in 1737, he was described, again, as a cook, living in Angoulême. By the time of the marriage of the younger Marie Anne, in 1751, he was no longer alive.[78]

Amidst all these vicissitudes, Johann Georg Klotz became the founder of a large and imposing dynasty in Angoulême. He had twenty-two grandchildren who were baptized in the town, and a further six born outside Paris, to his son Jacques. Jacques Klotz, who was born in Angoulême in 1723, was described on the occasion of his marriage in 1755 as a "bourgeois de Paris." He was the "valet de chambre" of a high army officer, "Prince Casimir Pignatelli, Comte d'Egmont," and he spent much of the period of the Seven Years' War "on campaign"; Egmont and his sister, lady-in-waiting to the wife of Louis XV, were the godparents of Jacques's first child.[79] Egmont was a member of the revolutionary constituent assembly, and emigrated in 1792. Jacques Klotz returned to Angoulême, together with one of his daughters, Elizabeth Sophie; Elizabeth became the proprietor of a large house on the Rue du Minage that had once belonged to a family of army officers, "Klootz fille majeure acquéreur."[80]

The Trials of Silvie Cazaud

These were the ventures of the "small people," among the 4,089 individuals in the parish records, and of the families into which Marie Aymard's children married. The adventures of the bourgeoisie of Angoulême were spectacular in their own way. Silvie Calixte Benoit des Essarts, the estranged wife of the atrocious employer of Marie Aymard's husband, Jean-Alexandre Cazaud, was one of the 4,089. Her daughter Mélanie Gabrielle was baptized in September 1764, in the parish of St. André; Cazaud was not present. Mélanie's godfather was her maternal uncle, Claude Benoit des Essarts, the owner of "Claude," "of the nation of Capélaou," who had been baptized in the same church six years earlier; her godmother was "Dame Appollonie Usson femme de Mr de Bologne."[81]

Over the next few years, Silvie returned to Grenada, and then to France in 1770; she was imprisoned by order of her husband; she died in Paris in May 1781. She was known by then as "Madame la Marquise de Cazot," and she was living at the time in a rented apartment on the Rue des Petits Augustins. Her death was followed by one of the extended procedures of metropolitan life, the placing of seals on the residence of the deceased (to prevent the removal of property from the estate). At 4:30 in the morning of May 22, 1781, commissioners of the judicial administration of Paris were instructed to make their way to the apartment, where they found the "body of a female," and proceeded to "appose" their seals. Over the next nine months—for the seals were removed only in February 1782—there ensued a procession of creditors, porters, maids, relatives, visiting lawyers (from Angoulême), and generous friends, sufficient to populate an entire human comedy of Parisian life. Silvie's name was noted consecutively, in the course of the procedure, as Cazot, Cazeau, Caseau, Casseau, Cazaud, Decazeaux, and De Cazeauld.[82]

There were forty-one separate requests registered by individuals who wished to assert their own rights in respect of the removal of the seals; they included a locksmith, two perfumers, a jeweler, two tapestry-makers, two caterers, a joiner, three dressmakers, an apothecary, two tailors, a nurse, a doctor of medicine, a painter, a blacksmith, a supplier of fashions to the queen, a papermaker, a shoemaker, a domestic servant, a merchant, a draper, a wine merchant, the person who had guarded the seals, a wigmaker, and Silvie's personal maid, who had lent money to her in the last days of her life, and who had also, out of her own funds, paid the priest, the gravedigger, and the porter, and covered the cost of "food for the parrot."[83]

Silvie's landlord, a wine merchant, together with the personal maid, notified the commissioners in August 1781 that Cazaud, or "the Marquis de Casseau, the husband of the deceased," had been written to, but that there had been no reply, "for more than three months." In September, Silvie's brother arrived with a lawyer from Angoulême (who was the uncle of one of the signatories of the marriage contract of 1764), staying in the "Grand Hôtel de Toulouse."[84] Cazaud appeared, at last, in

November, and was identified as "Jean Alexandre de Cazeau Ecuyer, former deputy of the French inhabitants of Grenada to the Court of St. James, and former officer of dragoons." He was the fortieth person to register rights in opposition to the lifting of the seals, on behalf of himself and his three children; he too was staying in a hotel nearby (the "Hôtel de l'Espagne garni").

At this point, another figure entered the scene, with a new legal history: a cavalry officer called the "Comte de Gamaches," in the form of his legal representative. M. de Gamaches, according to his lawyer, had been assisting Silvie out of his own purse and with guarantees of credit, since February 28, 1779. This was the "day of the revocation of the *lettre de cachet* that M. de Cazeau had obtained against her," the lawyer recounted: the date, that is to say, when Silvie was released from the arbitrary imprisonment that was within the power, with royal sanction, of the husbands and fathers of the ancien régime. While Cazaud was reading his paper about sugarcane to the Royal Society in London, and his slave Jean-Alexandre James was languishing in a cellar, Silvie, too, was coming to the end of her own prison sentence.[85]

M. de Gamaches was himself, by now, a creditor of Silvie's estate. His expenditures, as listed in the accounts of various purveyors, included the costs of 155 meters of white damask (with a "rose-colored design"), and of 8,500 gilded nails. But there were also memories of happier times. The personal maid, when she was examined about Silvie's jewelry, said that Silvie had very little, except for "two gold rings containing locks of hair," which "she imagined that the said late Mme. De Cazeau must have returned to the Comte de Gamaches." The porter of the building, also examined about Silvie's jewelry, said that he had no particular knowledge of what was in her apartment; all he knew was that "on one of the days of the Longchamps Races, he had seen her going out in a carriage with the Comte de Gamaches, and that she was wearing diamond earrings, which seemed to him to be extremely beautiful."[86]

Cazaud's lawsuit about Silvie's estate followed the removal of the seals on the apartment. In the summer before her death, Silvie had made a will in which she left the sum of fifty thousand livres to one of her elderly legal advisers, from whom she had borrowed money, with the

provision that in addition to reimbursing himself, he should make bequests to her two daughters, and to her maid.[87] It was this will that
Cazaud sought to have declared invalid, in the case that produced all the
elaborate arguments about when exactly he was living in Grenada, when
he had brought Silvie to preside over his plantations, and when he was
traveling on business, "sometimes in Italy, or elsewhere," together with
equally elaborate opposing arguments, about how deeply French Silvie
had always felt herself to be.[88]

The case was concerned—like so much else in Cazaud's existence,
and in the universe of captured islands into which Marie Aymard was
conducting her researches—with the intersection of French and English laws. "Can a French woman, by the sole fact that her husband
moved his domicile to a foreign country, have lost her domicile in
France, which she never had the intention of leaving?" the *Gazette des
Tribunaux* asked, in its report on Cazaud's lawsuit. Silvie had never intended to leave France, it was argued on behalf of the elderly lawyer
(who had by now conveyed his unconvincing legacy to a new party,
known as the "Dlle. Lucie"). Silvie's visits to Grenada had "never been
more than momentary and determined only by the will of her husband"; "her husband had not been able to force her to follow him to a
foreign country and to abdicate her fatherland." Cazaud himself, in any
case, had never become English, having returned to Angoulême within
the eighteen months of legal interlude during which French subjects
(by the terms of the Treaty of Paris that ended the Seven Years' War)
were permitted to leave the English colonies, or to "retire with all safety
and freedom."[89]

But the case was decided, in the end, on even more momentous
grounds. It was transposed, on Cazaud's behalf, into a cause about—or
in opposition to—the rights of women, and about the nature of marriage. Silvie's will should be declared invalid, Cazaud argued, on the
grounds that "according to English law, the law of their shared domicile,
no woman, being in the power of her husband, can make a will without
his permission and authorization." It was to this argument that Cazaud's
opponents responded that he had never become domiciled in England,
and that even if he were, Silvie was not. Cazaud responded, in turn, that

this, too, was a right that married women did not possess; "he established that a wife, within the power of her husband, could not have a domicile different from that of her husband." The case was decided, on appeal, in favor of Cazaud.[90]

Marie Marthe in Rome

By the time the case over Silvie's will was determined, in September 1783, Cazaud had moved on, to yet another jurisdiction. He was living, at this point, with his older daughter, Marie Marthe, the "harsh and overbearing . . . young lady," born in Angoulême in 1757, whom Jean-Alexandre James had described in his petition of 1779.[91] In October 1782, Cazaud and Marie Marthe settled in the papal enclave of Avignon. Two months later, she was married to a local figure, the Marquis de Roux. The marriage lasted no more than a few weeks, and in March 1783, Marie Marthe, who was pregnant, was granted a provisional separation. She said that her husband was violent and jealous; he said that she was cold; she asked, "Was it love that you required? Sir, did I ever promise that to you? I said to you before our marriage that it was something I was incapable of." Marie Marthe was supposed to have a dowry of six hundred thousand livres; her husband, or his agents, said that when they married, she was already pregnant, by someone else. These events were narrated by Cazaud himself, in a 245-page history that he published in London in 1784 under his new name: *Mémoire justificatif du Marquis de Casaux, de la Société Royale de Londres.*[92]

In April 1783, according to the *Mémoire justificatif*, Cazaud and Marie Marthe fled from Avignon, to the nearby home of a cousin from Guadeloupe.[93] In May, Marie Marthe's husband filed criminal charges against Cazaud, charging him with kidnapping and with having failed to make dowry payments. In August, Cazaud and the by now heavily pregnant Marie Marthe fled again, to Rome, the highest jurisdiction of the Avignon courts. In September, "nine months and three days after her marriage," Marie Marthe died in childbirth, in Rome.[94]

The *Mémoire* was a dire story of witnesses to domestic violence (Cazaud's banker and his wigmaker); of the law of domicile, once again (for Cazaud insisted, to his son-in-law, that he was a subject of "the island of Grenada," which was French in 1782, when the narrative began, and English when it ended in 1783); and of the rights of women to make wills (under the papal law of Avignon). It ended in scenes of horror. "If I die, will he not lose everything?" Marie Marthe was reported to have asked, and was told, "You are deceiving yourself; if you die at a time when your pregnancy is viable, then they will cut you open and a single movement of your child's finger will be enough to ensure that his succession goes to your husband."[95]

Cazaud settled comfortably, on his return from Rome, into his new life as a philosopher, economist, and figure of the Enlightenment. Even the *Mémoire justificatif* about his daughter's marriage, in all its craziness, veers from time to time into large reflections on the "invisible hand" of destiny, the possibility of a "universal, maritime Police" in respect of property rights in the American colonies, and the future of the Atlantic empires; within "eighty or one hundred years," Cazaud wrote, Great Britain would in all likelihood "be obliged to transport the seat of its empire to *America,* and the old metropolis would be no more than an *American* province" (a paraphrase of a celebrated observation in *The Wealth of Nations*).[96] His treatise *Thoughts on the Mechanism of Societies. By the Marquis de Casaux, F.R.S.*, with its inconsequential inquiries (into "whether imports and exports be not a mere sport, as innocent as the game of tennis") was described by the *Critical Review* as "excentric," with "the appearance of calculation, and the semblance of reason."[97] It was followed, over the period from 1786 to 1792, by eighteen further publications, on subjects from public debt to the French constitution to the advantages of colonial commerce.

In the first years of the French Revolution, Cazaud was once again in France. He was a prolific figure of the conservative Enlightenment; a man of "great spirit," who supported the monarchy and "defend[ed] slavery, the slave trade, and the aristocracy of the color of one's skin."[98] One of his pamphlets was described by Mirabeau as "the work of genius that has produced the revolution," and "an inexhaustible source of sound and profound ideas."[99] He became an auxiliary, in the controversies over the costs of the colonies of 1791–1792, of the theorist of slavery Pierre-Victor Malouet (from whom he had been able to elicit a character reference, ten years earlier, in his interminable disputes over whether he was really English or really French).[100] "The civil and political existence of Europe" was dependent on colonial commerce, Cazaud wrote in 1791, and a "false measure, in this regard, would be followed inexorably by a scene of universal devastation, the very idea of which makes one tremble." It was the economic exchanges—the supposed "extravagances"—of the colonies, he asserted, that provided employment to nine or ten million people in Europe, and "DISTRACT FROM THE IDEA OF TERROR."[101] Jean-Alexandre Cazaud died in England in 1796, and was buried in Woodford in Essex, under the name "The Marquis de Cassaux, Jean Alexandre."[102]

The Long Life of Mélanie Gabriele Sophie

Mélanie Gabriele Sophie, Silvie's youngest child—the daughter whose birth was later invoked as evidence of her parents' fluctuating residence, domicile, and national identity—was one of the "protagonists" in the parish records, the 454 children who were baptized in Angoulême (and who survived the year). Amidst all her family's disputes, she lived a long and uncherished life. She appeared fleetingly in the report, in 1783, of the lawsuit over her mother's estate: in the contested will, which her father succeeding in overturning, her mother had left bequests of ten thousand livres to her older daughter, one thousand livres to her younger daughter (Mélanie), and four hundred livres to her maid.[103] Mélanie was left behind when her father and her sister, Marie Marthe, departed for Avignon and Rome; the only reference to her, at any point in the 245-page work that her father wrote about the troubles of his older daughter—"alone in the midst of tigers and panthers"—was when Marie Marthe, in Rome, was described as "pretending" to reply to a "letter from her sister."[104]

Cazaud provided Marie Marthe with a dowry of six hundred thousand livres, by his own account. To Mélanie, he provided "the annual sum of eighty pounds"; this was according to the will of their brother, Jean-François (who was born in Angoulême in 1756, and was so "deplorably afflicted . . . through life by nervous disorders").[105] Jean-François inherited the family sugar plantation in Grenada, now augmented by a cotton plantation on the island of St. Vincent; he also acquired an additional family name, "John Francis Dugout, Marquis de Casaux, of River Sallee in the British West India island of Grenada." In his will, which was proved in London in March 1832, he left two hundred pounds a year to his sister, "Mélanie Gabriele Sophie." (He also directed that his heart should be buried in the coffin of his "friend Ann Smith," in a burial ground in Bruges in Belgium, and that the "other parts of [his] mortal remains" should be "deposited at the feet" of his late father, in Woodford in Essex.)[106]

Time passed; Mélanie survived the French Revolution, the July Revolution of 1830, the French Revolution of 1848, and the end of slavery in the island of Grenada. In the will of her niece, Henriette, the daughter of the afflicted Jean-François, which was registered in Nantes in January 1852, there is another bequest: an annuity of thirty pounds to "our dear good aunt Sophie Mélanie Gabriele Dugout de Casaux." This, too, was an eccentric will, by the standards of this eccentric family. Henriette was subject to "fainting fits," so—fearing being taken for dead—she provided for an incision to be made in her left or right heel, no less than eight hours "after I am believed to be dead." Her estate was mostly "invested in Russian bonds"; her executor went bankrupt, which required a codicil to the will; in another codicil, in Nantes, she declared that "as I no longer live in England I annul all the gifts that I have made to the Catholic chapels of that country." She then invested in a "Russian stock deposit"; she endowed "one thousand low masses for the repose of my soul."[107]

Mélanie Cazaud died in 1852, at the age of eighty-seven. She described herself as "Sophie de Casaux," "late of Paris in France, but now of George Street, Portman Square," in London. Her will, at least, was straightforward. She left everything to the "Reverend Pierre Wailly," of the French Chapel, Little George Street, Portman Square.

The Lady with the Little Dog

Mélanie's godmother, who was listed in the parish register of St. André as "Dame Appollonie Usson," was a link, finally, between the provincial world of the 4,089 individuals in the records for 1764, and the eternity of literary fame. Her name was Bénédictine Husson, and she had been married, since 1737, to a poet from Guadeloupe called Pierre de Bologne. Pierre de Bologne was Jean-Alexandre Cazaud's uncle, the son of the plantation owner and commander of the militia in Guadeloupe.[108]

It was Bénédictine Husson, "la dame de Bologne," who was the landlady of Elizabeth and Lydia Sterne in Angoulême. Laurence Sterne died in London in 1768, and his widow and daughter then set off for France, in search of a sunnier climate and a more economical way of life. They ended up in Angoulême, where they rented rooms from the "Sieur et dame de Bologne," in their house on the Rue des Cordeliers (now the Rue de Beaulieu) near the center of the town. The Bolognes, too, were in straightened circumstances; it was a debt of eighty-six hundred livres that they owed to an innkeeper and his son (relatives of the Klotz sisters) that precipitated the legal-financial crisis of the 1760s and 1770s in Angoulême.[109]

The history of the little dog began on the morning of October 4, 1769, when Lydia Sterne's dog was discovered to be missing; it was a white water dog, completely "shaved with the exception of its head," with "a large black spot on its back and small black spots all over its body."[110] A servant of Elizabeth Sterne was sent out to make inquiries; later in the day, the town crier went through the center of Angoulême, beating his drum and asking for information about the dog.[111]

On October 9, 1769, Elizabeth Sterne filed a complaint in the criminal jurisdiction of the town. The dog was "one of the rarest in its species," she said, and had been the "object of covetousness on the part of certain persons." It had been stolen at around eleven in the morning of October 4, and despite her best efforts, she had been unable to find it; the dog had no doubt been transported out of Angoulême by "the author of the theft, his associates, and accomplices." She asked that a criminal investigation—an "information"—be initiated into the facts and circumstances of the case. Her daughter was extremely fond of the dog, she said; it had a yellow copper flowered collar, lined in red morocco leather, marked "Mlle Sterne anglaise."[112]

The "information" began the following day, on October 10. It was a busy week in the subaltern jurisdictions of Angoulême, as the legal-financial crisis of the "usurers of Angoulême" began to unfold in the town. But a culprit in the case of the missing dog was readily identified, and he was the servant of Silvie Benoit des Essarts, "la dame Cazaud." There was an oven-keeper who testified that when he was crossing the bridge into town, he had seen a tall, blond man, unknown to him, carrying something under his left arm, wrapped up in a dirty cloth; it was wriggling, and he "took it to be a dog or a cat." A wigmaker saw someone he knew, the servant of "la dame Cazeaud," picking up a dog that was passing in the street, between the Rue des Cordeliers and the corn market (the Minage), and taking it away; he recognized the dog, which was a "chien barbet" or water dog, recently shaved, and which he had often seen walking with the English lady in the Champs de Beaulieu.[113]

There was a knife-maker who was at the door of his house, opposite the corn market, when he saw a man whom he took to be a domestic servant, wearing an overcoat and carrying a dog under his left arm. He recognized the dog by its (unshaved) head, which was protruding from under the coat; he had seen the English lady out for a walk a few days earlier, with the dog walking ahead of her. The fourteen-year-old son of a lawyer was outside his father's house, and saw the servant of "la dame Cazeaud" walking away from the corn market carrying a dog under his left arm, which he recognized, and whose head was protruding from under the overcoat; he had seen the dog on many occasions, walking with the English lady in the vicinity of the prison. A merchant was at the door of his shop opposite the corn market, and saw a man across the street, unknown to him, carrying a dog, which he recognized, under his left arm; he too had seen the dog many times with the English lady. Later that day, when the town crier went through the town beating his drum for the little dog, the merchant recounted what he had seen; a young girl, whom he did not know, told him that the man was the servant of "la dame Cazeaud."[114]

The evidence seemed compelling, and Alexandre Prevaut, described as the servant of la dame Cazaud, "living in her house, Rue des Cordeliers," was arrested and imprisoned. He had joined the household in the Rue des Cordeliers only recently. In June 1769, when he was married to a woman from Brive named Liberalle Langlade, he was described as a joiner or carpenter, from a village in the Dordogne. In October 1769, when their daughter Jeanne was baptized in the parish of St. Jean, a few days after his arrest, he was described as the "valet domestique" of "Mme Cazeaud."[115] He appealed his imprisonment; the case was remitted to the Parliament in Paris, on December 9, 1769.[116]

So this is the end of the story of Laurence Sterne's daughter's little dog, and of the 4,089 individuals in the parish registers of Angoulême—as in the end of *A Sentimental Journey*, "So that when I stretch'd out my hand I caught hold of the *fille de chambre's*—"[117] In March 1770, Lydia Sterne wrote to her cousin in England, from the house on the Rue des Cordeliers in Angoulême, that "the town tho' ill built is situated most agreeably, the prospects fine, the walks beautiful.—but as to the inhabitants except a small number.—n'en disons rien.—yet thus far I must speak in their praise, they understand eating, & play better than any people in the world . . . we have 59 traiteurs [or caterers] in this little town, that wear laced coats, & couteaux de chasse [hunting knives] and but one Bookseller, & he poor man is in want, & looks like Shakespear's starved apothecary.—this gluttony renders the market very dear [and] therefore we intend going a little further south where we may live cheaper, civil as the people are to us."[118]

Chapter Four

THE FIRST REVOLUTION

Historical Time and Family Time

The history of Marie Aymard and her connections has been an inquiry, so far, into relationships of contiguity in space (the small neighborhoods of Angoulême) and in the social space of family networks (the signatories of the marriage contract and the parish registers of 1764). It has also been a history of episodes, and thereby a story in time—of the trinket seller and her sister-in-law, or the dancing master's son in Saint-Domingue, or the long, uncherished life of Mélanie Cazaud. This was the only way, in the end, to find out who the individuals in the networks were, and it has become a journey with no end in sight.

The rest of the history is an inquiry into relationships over time: the historical time of the long French revolution, and eventually of nineteenth-century modernity. It is about the contiguity in time of family (and other) relationships, and about what happened next to Marie Aymard's children and their own families. It is as though the individuals in the story make a ninety-degree turn, and walk away into a different dimension, which is the dimension of historical time. This is a movement, in turn, into a different sort of history. Everyone lives in time (although no one, in the story so far, has been a historical figure, in the sense of someone who was important in the history of France or of the world). There is the time of family life, the time of work and romance, the time of credit and expectation. Everyone in Angoulême in 1764—all the signatories and all the 4,089 individuals in the parish records—also existed in the time of political history, and this is the subject of the next part of the book.

Marie Aymard died in Angoulême in April 1790. She was born in wartime and lived through two almost worldwide wars; she was in Angoulême during the first year of the French Revolution. Mathurin, her third son, who may or may not have been a fugitive from the militia, was born in Angoulême in 1743: the same year as Jean-Paul Marat, M.J.A.N. Condorcet, and Toussaint Louverture. Her daughter-in-law Elizabeth, the daughter of the saucepan-maker with the relative who died in Cayenne, was born in 1755, the same year as Marie Antoinette. Marie Aymard belonged, like so many of the people amidst whom she lived, to the generation of the long French revolution.

The political story starts in the year of the marriage contract, and with the period of transformation, over the course of the 1760s, 1770s, and 1780s, that Tocqueville described in *L'ancien régime et la révolution*, in part on the basis of the administrative records of the generality of Limoges, as the beginning of the "long revolution."[1] It continues into the (exiguous) history of the French Revolution in Angoulême, and to the period of the revolutionary wars (in the lives, for the most part, of Marie Aymard's grandchildren). Angoulême was a place in which nothing much happened over these years of turbulence, according to an enduring local history; even the website of the modern prefecture, in 2019, recounted that "during the revolution, the Charente experienced the backlash of the great events that were unfolding in Paris and on the frontiers, while avoiding the abuses and the disorders."[2]

The Allemands and the Ferrands were almost entirely invisible within this apparently unexceptional history. There was no one in the extended family who was important in the events of the times, and only a single, cryptic reference, to Gabriel's second son, in the historiography of the revolution.[3] Even within the social networks of the eighty-three signatories of the marriage contract, only three people were even minor political figures over the course of the revolution. But the history of the revolution, from the point of view of the families and their connections, is itself a political history. It is a history of what really happened, and of the events in daily life—the opportunities and losses and encounters— that were the outcome of revolutionary change. It is the story of a time when almost everything in public and private existence, including ideas of the public and the private, the economic and the political, was changed by the new circumstances of administration, of the church, and of universal war.

The early period of the French revolution was in Tocqueville's description a time of "inner shuddering," in which individuals were "agitated in [their] condition, and trie[d], to change it."[4] The history of Angoulême in 1764–1789, in what follows, is a story in four scenes, and it, too, is a history of agitated times. The first is the legal-financial affair, or the "revolution" in commerce, that started over the same days in October 1769—and in the same small streets around the Place du Mûrier—as the theft of Eliza Sterne's little dog, and that eventually brought Angoulême into national and even international notoriety. The other scenes are the ones in which Marie Aymard's own family sought to improve their condition: the church and its educational establishments; colonial exchanges; and the administration of taxes, in which Martial Allemand Lavigerie, the oldest son of the couple in the marriage contract of 1764, found employment at the very end of the ancien régime.

Marie Aymard's Grandchildren

The history of the twenty-five years between 1764 and 1789 can be told as a story of family life. Marie Aymard's children were married and had children of their own. Françoise and Etienne, the couple in the marriage contract of 1764, had nine daughters and four sons; Gabriel and Marie Adelaide had six sons; Jean-Baptiste was apprenticed to a watchmaker and emigrated to Saint-Domingue. Etienne found a position teaching humanities in the (formerly Jesuit) college of Angoulême. Françoise and Etienne's oldest son, Martial Allemand Lavigerie, was the first of Marie Aymard's grandchildren to be married, a few days before her death in 1790.[5]

The early lives of the grandchildren unfolded within a restricted space. Gabriel's six sons were all born in the tiny parish of Notre Dame de la Peine, in which his sister's marriage contract had been signed in 1764. Etienne and Françoise lived for a time after their marriage in the nearby parish of St. Antonin, where Etienne's father, Marc Allemand, had his tailor's shop. They then moved to Notre Dame de la Peine, close to Gabriel and his family; by 1783, Marie Aymard was surrounded by at least seventeen grandchildren, all living within a few steps of each other. Gabriel's occupation was listed throughout, in the parish register, as "master writer"; in 1775 he was "master writer and master of a pension," or boarding school. Etienne was listed as "master of arts," as "schoolmaster," as "regent", and as "master of pensioners."[6]

The two young families were closely, even introvertedly, involved. Of the thirty-eight individuals whom Gabriel, Marie Adelaide, Etienne, and Françoise chose as godparents for their children, twenty-eight were immediate family members: brothers, sisters, cousins. The others were schoolchildren, and patrons of various sorts: "Sieur Pierre Louis Martin Grand de Luxollière," a schoolboy, in 1778, or, in 1779, the widow of a plantation owner recently arrived from Saint-Domingue, "Dame Marie Catherine Mandrou veuve Berthoumieu delamerique."[7] It was as though Gabriel, Françoise, and Etienne had left behind, forever, the sociable world of their parents: the carpenters and hatmakers and locksmiths' wives who had been godparents to the children of their own generation, in the old Angoulême.[8] Etienne adopted the compound surname "Allemand Lavigerie," starting in 1771; he was known to the administrators of the college as "Lavigerie."[9]

The families were also strikingly resilient. Françoise had thirteen children, of whom seven were born over a six-year period in 1765–1771, and at least eleven of whom survived infancy. So did at least five of the six children of Gabriel and Marie Adelaide, and three of the four children of Jean-Baptiste and Elizabeth.[10] Of Françoise's nine daughters, five were still living in Angoulême in the 1850s. Her oldest daughter, who called herself "Jeanne *ainée*," and who became the most important source of capital for the nineteenth-century family, died in Angoulême in 1860, at the age of ninety-one. Her youngest daughter, Louise Mélanie, died in 1865, near Le Mans, while she was on a visit to her great-niece in the Sarthe. Françoise's oldest son, Martial, the grandfather of Cardinal Allemand Lavigerie, died in Angoulême in 1856, at the age of eighty-eight.[11] Marie Aymard's youngest grandchild died in a small town in

Normandy in 1873, in the aftermath of the Franco-Prussian War.[12] It is these children and grandchildren, and their own eventual families, who are the central figures in the rest of this inquiry.

The Capitalists and the Cabalists

The episode of the alarming commercial crisis, which was eventually so momentous, began in Angoulême in 1769, and continued, in two phases, until 1789. Angoulême was an uneconomic town, in A.R.J. Turgot's description, in the memorandum he wrote about the episode, or the "revolution"; it should have been "commercial," but it never was. Even the families who did well, Turgot lamented, sought to retire from commerce as soon as they could, and to buy their way (like the son of the signatory of the marriage contract Jean-Baptiste Marchais) into the minor nobility of public office.[13] Commerce was in the hands of people with very little capital, and of the three main industries in and around Angoulême—the manufacture of paper, the trade in brandy, and the metal foundry and forge industry for naval procurement—both the brandy and the forge industries were subject to very great risks. It was in this economic milieu that the "affair of Angoulême," or the "affair of the usurers," unfolded.[14]

The legal proceedings began, in October 1769, when a "cabal" of debtors—in Turgot's expression—denounced their creditors, or the "capitalistes," for having charged usurious rates of interest. One of the minor figures in the social network of the signatories of the marriage contract—Marie Anne Klotz, the godmother of Gabriel's brother-in-law, and the daughter of Johann Klotz—was married to the leader of the cabal. Turgot happened to be in Angoulême a few weeks later, having come to "make his department," or inspection of the generality. He found the town in a state of "terror" and a "sort of vertigo." The cabal, with the assistance of a local lawyer, and the tacit support of the principal prosecutor, had demanded restitution from the capitalists, invoking long-unenforced prohibitions on usury. One of the capitalists ran away, on the basis of "imprudent" advice from his lawyer, who was also his first cousin; the son of another capitalist, a paper merchant called Abraham-François

Robin, was accused of attempted murder; there was "total interruption of all commercial speculation."[15]

The case was the subject of eight successive decrees of the royal Conseil d'Etat, from 1770 to 1776, and ended (for a time) in the vindication of the capitalists. It was also the subject of competing historical narratives. There was an official version, recounted by Turgot, in the memorandum, eventually published in 1789, of which the object was to tell "the story of what has happened in Angoulême," and to outline a theory of risk, expectations, and the freedom of financial markets: the theory that was the foundation, in the view of later economists, of the entire subsequent reform of financial institutions.[16] There was the capitalists' version—a story of "trouble, fear, and dread [in] the spirits of the bankers"—recounted by Abraham-François Robin in a "secret history" of the "revolution that took place in the commerce of Angoulême" that he wrote for his children.[17] There was the cabalists' version, in which they complained of an impending "most fatal revolution," and which was suppressed by the Conseil d'Etat, in 1776, as "reckless, injurious, and contrary to the respect due to His Majesty."[18] The stories were adorned, in turn, with lists of individuals involved in capital transactions in the town: competing enumerations of debt and credit in Angoulême.

There were five principal capitalists in the case; they used the fairly new word "capitaliste" in their own description of themselves.[19] The two most prominent were the father of Silvie Cazaud, who had signed the indenture of Marie Aymard's husband in 1753 on behalf of his son-in-law, and her brother Claude Benoit des Essarts, who was the owner of "Claude." The capitalist who ran away was their cousin by marriage; there was also the receiver of the *taille* imposition, Pierre Marot, and the paper merchant Abraham-François Robin. Robin was a former alderman and "grand judge" in the merchants' consular court in the town, "who did a little banking with his own funds."[20] Claude Benoit des Essarts was the only one of the five among the 4,089 individuals who appeared in the parish records for 1764—as the godfather of his niece, Mélanie Cazaud.[21]

The two principal conspirators in the crisis—the "cabalistes," in Abraham-François Robin's description—were there in the parish records for 1764: an innkeeper called Pierre Nouel and his son Jean-Louis, to-gether with Pierre's grandson and another son, Guillaume.[22] Pierre Nouel was a central figure in all the histories. In Turgot's story, he was "a former innkeeper in Angoulême, who after having cast himself into a mass of badly planned enterprises, is like an animal at bay."[23] Nouel's son Jean-Louis was a brandy merchant, in Robin's history, and a "leader of the cabal." Pierre and Jean-Louis were judged by the Conseil d'Etat, in 1770, to owe 18,314 livres in restitution to the capitalists; they were the plaintiffs, and ostensible authors, together with their lawyer, in the memoir suppressed by the Conseil d'Etat in 1776, *P.-J.-L. Nouel, l'aîné & fils, & Drou, Au roi, et à nosseigneurs de son conseil.*[24]

In the parish records, Pierre Nouel appears as the patriarch, on the occasion of the marriage of his younger son, Guillaume, in the parish of St. Jean; Jean-Louis Nouel was present, together with his wife, Marie Anne Klotz—an "Aymard-1," in the extended network of the marriage contract—at his brother's marriage, and their own son, Pierre, was bap-tized in Notre Dame de Beaulieu.[25] His new sister-in-law—in one of the family connections with which the entire episode was so entangled—was the sister of the lawyer who was at the heart of the subsequent con-spiracy, chosen, in the description of Abraham-François Robin, because he was "a hard and pitiless man, without faith and without honor."[26]

Several of the minor figures in the story—shopkeepers who appeared in the competing lists of debtors—were there in the larger society of the 4,089. The husband of Marie Yvroix Chauvin—who had two sons called Pierre in the course of the year, and was the sister of Pascal Chauvin, who was supposed to have set out for Martinique—was listed as having borrowed money from all five of the capitalists, and judged by the Con-seil d'Etat to owe sixty livres in restitution, for the money he had been given as compensation, under duress, for past interest paid.[27] Jean-Pierre David, a cloth merchant and occasional financial intermediary who lived on the Place du Mûrier, and who was the godparent, together with one of the Rose Rezés, of a girl born in St. Jean in November 1764, was listed by the cabalists as having declined to seek restitution of inter-est paid, and as having then been obliged, by one of the capitalists, to sign an indemnity against future claims.[28]

The episode of the capitalists and the cabalists was of consuming interest in and around Angoulême, in the description of all the competing histories. It was a time of universal "anxiety and discredit," in Turgot's account, and of an "absolute shortage of money."[29] One of the capitalists, the receiver of the *taille*, complained of "muffled voices," "clamors," and false "sounds."[30] There was "atrocious desolation" among the creditors, in Robin's description, and the cabalists "spread across the public places and crossroads of Angoulême, in nearby towns and in the countryside, all manner of libels and songs, in which each of the bankers was named with the most dreadful epithets."[31] Another of the figures in the parish records for 1764, a jeweler whose son was baptized in St. André, sued another of the capitalists for having made injurious comments; the eventual judgment in his favor was "posted and plastered in Angoulême."[32]

Marie Aymard and her immediate family were invisible, in the competing accounts of the crisis, and in the competing lists of the debtors and creditors. They lived in a different, segmented economic society in the town: a society with very little capital, and with only the most limited, domestic property. Even Marie Aymard's own creditors, the sellers of potash and cooking fat who had threatened to seize her furniture in 1764, and the intermediaries whom they employed, were too modest, or too unenterprising, to appear in the enumerations of debtors and creditors.[33] Within the larger network of the signatories of the marriage contract, there were three who were involved in the history, all on the side of the cabal. Gabriel Lemaitre, who was Gabriel Ferrand's brother-in-law, was the nephew by marriage of Jean-Louis Nouel. Jean Dumergue, the saddlemaker with the brother in Saint-Domingue, was included by Abraham-François Robin in his list of the thirty-four principal merchants who made "extortions," described as "bankrupt and separated from his wife."[34] The husband of the signatory Marie Durand, who was the son of the rich goldsmith Jean-Baptiste Marchais, was listed as among "the other merchants who had gone bankrupt before their extortions from the bankers in 1769."[35]

In the crowded spaces of Angoulême in which Marie Aymard and her family lived, the "vertigo" was far more present. The sounds and the spectacle of the credit crisis were all around. Claude Benoit des Essarts lived on the Place du Mûrier, and Abraham-François Robin lived nearby, a few steps away from Etienne Allemand and Françoise Ferrand. The older Benoit des Essarts and the imprudent lawyer lived in the same small tax island—the Isle de la Cloche Verte—as Marc Allemand and so many of the signatories of the marriage contract.[36] One of the cabalists was a forgemaster from the Dordogne, who stayed when he was in Angoulême with his brother-in-law in the Rue du Collège, almost next to Gabriel Ferrand's house.[37]

The house on the Rue du Collège was even the scene, in October 1769, of a frightening confrontation. Jean-Louis Nouel suggested that he and Robin should meet there, early in the crisis; Robin went alone, and was confronted by Nouel, his brother, and his brother's brother-in-law (the hard and pitiless lawyer). No one would have heard had he cried out, Robin recalled in his secret history; the forgemaster's room was "at the back of a house in the most isolated part of town; this was chosen on purpose, and it was nine o'clock at night, in the month of October."[38] A few days later, the house was the venue for a complaint in the criminal jurisdiction of the town, when Robin's son was accused by the forgemaster of attempted murder: the young man was in a state of fury, according to the deposition, with an object in his pocket that the plaintiff "presumed to be a pistol"; according to the deposition of the forgemaster's brother-in-law, Robin's son was followed a little later the same day by his sister, who was weeping profusely ("fort espleurée"), lamenting that "it is too painful for children to see their father denounced."[39]

Agitated Times in the Diocese

The economic milieu in which Marie Aymard's oldest son Gabriel set out to pursue his vocation in 1760—the "instruction of youth"—was at the time a far more peaceful scene.[40] The church, with its schools, seminaries, and colleges, was then the dominant economic enterprise of Angoulême: an uneconomic local economy, in the classification of Turgot and other economists, or a set of institutions that provided employment, and opportunities for profit, without producing commodities. The Jesuit college in the 1750s was a flourishing enterprise with some 280 students and fifteen to twenty instructors. There was a building surrounded by summer and winter gardens, a courtyard with linden trees, and a vast library. The college put on theatrical performances for the town, and held public celebrations for the distribution of prizes.[41] Only twenty-five of the students (of whom a few had foundation scholarships) were residents, living within the college, with their own servants and apartments. The others were local children who lived at home, or children who lived in one of the "pensions" or boarding schools that clustered around the college; the masters or "preceptors" of the pensions, such as Gabriel became, helped them with their lessons, and were allowed to teach the elements of French and Latin.[42]

This was a large population of teenage boys, in the middle of Angoulême, and an impressive microeconomy. The students, with their professors, servants, chaplains, and gardeners, constituted a resilient market for services and goods. The college bought candles, books, wine, and butter; it had a laundry and a tailor's shop and purchased the services of apothecaries, notaries, and surgeons. It had its own suppliers, like the nephew of the trinket seller Rose Rezé, official printer to the college. The students in the college, who appeared only infrequently in the parish records of the town—as godparents at the baptisms of their schoolmasters' children, or as witnesses to lonely deaths—were central to the town's economy.[43]

The expulsion of the Jesuits, in 1762, and the period of "disorganization," "anarchy," and "decadence" that followed—the "miserable agony" of the college, in the description of its nineteenth-century historians— was a time of opportunity for the young men of the town. The Jesuit professors left (they were allowed to take their beds with them, and eighteen shirts) and were replaced by the "regents," or the secular masters of boarding schools, who described themselves as masters of arts; two petitions in 1766 spoke of the "extraordinary weakness of the instruction," and the "inadequacy and incapacity of many of the masters." The regents were in turn replaced, or augmented, by new masters of pensions.[44]

It was in these years of change that Gabriel Ferrand became the master of a pension or boarding school, and Etienne Allemand, the bridegroom in 1764, was successively a master of arts, a regent, and "professor of humanities." The positions were not well paid. The regents were among the poorest individuals in the tax rolls, and Etienne's life was a long sequence, as will be seen, of petitions for increases in remuneration, and for the payment of stipends that had never been disbursed. Of the fourteen men and one woman who were listed in the tax rolls as regents, "pedants," or boarding school teachers, only one was fairly prosperous, and he was also a retired "man of business."[45] There was still security, of a sort; there was position, and social improvement.

In the continuing reorganizations of the college, following the departure of the Jesuits, even the architecture of the old establishment began to fail. In January 1774, the "bureau" or management of the college, composed of local notables, were told about missing casements and rotting shutters; in June, they learned that several of the walls had collapsed in the spring rains; in September, the walls of the garden fell down; on November 11, the teacher of the third class in the college (who was himself the son of a tailor in the town, and the son-in-law of Johann Georg Klotz) died suddenly at the age of forty; on November 25, the bureau invited Etienne, "Sieur Lavigerie, teacher of humanities in this town," to be his replacement.[46]

A few years later, the last of the resident students left the college, and the foundation scholars were sent to live with Etienne and his family; one of Etienne's sons was himself selected for a scholarship.[47] One of Gabriel's sons, too, took the first steps, like his father thirty years before, toward ordination.[48] There had been a "revolution," Etienne Allemand and one of the other teachers wrote to the administration in 1786, that had started around twelve years earlier. It was an economic revolution, in the form of a sudden increase in the price of necessities; "this revolution considerably reduced the relative value of our honoraria," and the teachers had been promised, or so they believed, that if prices remained high, they would receive some sort of compensation. Nothing had been forthcoming, they wrote, and "this same revolution is becoming stronger and stronger."[49] Prices had continued to increase, Etienne wrote four years later, requesting a cost-of-living increase in the pensions of the foundation scholars; he had devoted his time and efforts to the scholars, and he was now obliged to sacrifice even the "little products" of his own "industry."[50] Of the 280 students in the college at the time of the expulsion of the Jesuits, there were by 1790 only fifteen students left.[51]

The traumatic destiny of the old college was meanwhile only one manifestation of larger troubles in the local economy of religious instruction. The other substantial educational establishment in Angoulême was a seminary for the instruction of future clergy, in the parish of St. Martial, which had been managed since 1704 by a different congregation, the priests of the mission of St. Lazare (or "Lazaristes").[52] The Lazarists, like the Jesuits, had been caught up, over the course of the century, in the multiple conflicts of royal reform, municipal authority, and the local industries of ecclesiastical renovation and property valuation (the landholdings of the church). These disputes were entangled, in turn, with the conflict of capitalists and cabalists that began in the commercial "revolution" of 1769.

Abraham-François Robin, the author of the secret history of the crisis of 1769, was successively printer of parliamentary decrees about the college, inventorist of the Jesuits' possessions, and delegate of the town to the bureau of the college.[53] Robin's archvillain, the principal prosecutor in the case of 1769, was another delegate; so was the imprudent lawyer, or "lawyer and relation," of the capitalist who ran away.[54] The delegates were preoccupied, over the 1760s, 1770s, and 1780s, with an extraordinary proliferation of religious disputes. In the years following the departure of the Jesuits, the priests of a different educational order, the Dominicans, proposed to fill the void, by providing instruction in philosophy and theology. The bishop was opposed, suspecting the Dominicans of reformist tendencies; the municipality approached the Benedictines, followed by the Lazarists, who agreed to teach philosophy and mathematics (and theology, eventually); the parliament in Paris was opposed to the Lazarists; the municipality went back to the Benedictines, and finally to a small Italian order, the Teatini, best known for their missions in Borneo and Armenia.[55]

It was the seminary of Angoulême, in turn, that became the scene, in 1779, of a new and alarming conflict. The Lazarists who administered the seminary had been caught up, like the other orders, in the royal reforms of the times (which included an early and tentative abolition of certain kinds of church property, in 1768). [56] The seminary provided training for the young men of the diocese before they were ordained as priests; over the period of the "decadence" of the college, the seminary also instituted courses in philosophy, in which day students could participate.[57] Then, on a warm evening in the summer of 1779, some boys or men were throwing stones at the windows of the seminary building in the parish of St. Martial. The priests inside the seminary discharged a firearm into the street, and a boy was killed. Five of the Lazarists were charged with murder; the person who had fired the shot was the seminary's cook, the "frère cuisinier."[58]

The young man or boy who died was known as the "abbé Mioulle." He was twenty-one, and he was also—in the complex ecclesiastical economy of the times—the holder of a fairly senior religious office, as a canon of the cathedral of Angoulême. He lived, like so many of the signatories of the marriage contract of 1764, in the Isle de la Cloche Verte in the parish of St. Antonin.[59] The story, as it emerged, was that one of his friends, also a canon, had been bathing in the river on the evening of July 18, 1779, and encountered another friend, a lawyer; they decided to call on Mioulle, who was at home with his brother, and yet another young lawyer, playing the flute. They ordered beer and almond syrup from a neighboring hostelry, and at around 11:00 p.m. they decided to go out for a walk. They walked past Marc Allemand's house, past the prison, and toward the ramparts. At some point, the abbé Mioulle fell a few steps behind the others, having stopped "for some needs" outside the house of a "M. Ogerdias." A few minutes later, the young men were outside the seminary, and the shot was fired.[60]

The judicial "information," ordered by the principal prosecutor, began on July 21, involved ninety-eight witnesses, and lasted until September. Ten witnesses described disturbances over the course of the summer, in which the windows of the seminary were broken repeatedly by groups of young men, shouting "f . . . gueux [beggars]," "go back to your f . . . country," "send these b . . . Lazarists to Rochefort." There was a tailor who testified that two nights before the murder, she had heard stones being thrown at the windows of the seminary, the windows breaking, and four people shouting "f . . . Lazaristes," "f . . . mitron," "f . . . poufit," "f . . . gueux, go to Bordeaux." The night of the murder, she again heard shouting, "f . . . gueux! f . . . la guenille [rags]!" and breaking glass, but was frightened and "woke up her sister for reassurance"; she then went to bed. A cotton spinner said that she had met some people going toward the seminary, whom she thought, from their hairstyles, were clergymen; according to another witness, the wife of the town executioner, the spinner was not to be trusted, and "says that things are sometimes white and sometimes yellow." The son of an innkeeper had heard a young man saying that he wanted to go and eat some onion soup; five different innkeepers or caterers appeared in the story.[61]

Five of the so-called Lazarists were eventually accused of murder. Only two of them, as it turned out, were priests of the order; the others were a visiting "professor of philosophy," the cook, and the sacristan of the parish of St. Martial. They were pardoned by the king the following year.[62] The visiting professor, who was reported to have said that the young men throwing stones were "from good families" and wore clerical waistcoats, was also the almoner of the formerly Jesuit college of Angoulême; he reappeared, twenty years later, as Jacques Roux, the "red priest" of the French Revolution.[63]

A few days after the disturbances of July 1779, the mayor of Angoulême—he was Pierre Marchais, or Marchais Delaberge, the son of the rich goldsmith and signatory of the marriage contract in 1764, who had purchased the office for fifteen thousand livres—and the aldermen, including Abraham-François Robin, the paper merchant, determined that "in response to the violence," the town was in need of a night watch.[64] Some months later, according to a report by the captain of the watch, a group of young men "approached the night watch" near the churchyard of St. André, called them "f . . . gueux f . . . manan [*manant*, or buffoon] . . . f. b. soldats de mon cul," and started throwing stones at them. The mayor then appeared and observed the group "near the house of M. Desessard" (the brother of Silvie Cazaud, and one of the "capitalists," who lived on the corner of the Place du Mûrier). The young men threw some more stones, which "fell at his feet and hit the soldiers."[65]

At this point "the mayor cried, it is better to fire than to be assassinated," and a shot was fired; one of the men was "lightly wounded," and two were arrested. One of the group returned and said, "Two of my comrades are inside, I want them to be released, I will have them willingly or by force." Another young man was described as approaching the mayor with a bottle in one hand, and in the other "a saber or a hunting knife"; he dropped the bottle and stooped to pick up some stones. The mayor then "cried, I am wounded, fire!" The soldiers fired again, and the man with the bottle and the hunting knife was killed; some of the group ran away toward the Place du Mûrier, and others toward the church of the Jacobins (or Dominicans); the night watch accompanied the mayor to his home, where an "inspection of his wounds," the following day, revealed "two considerable bruises," on two fingers of his right hand."[66] The young man who died was Jean Yrvoix, the son of a local lawyer, and the nephew of one of the signatories of the marriage contract. He was buried the following day, a few steps away, in the church of St. André.[67]

Colonial Exchanges

The opportunities of colonial commerce, in which Marie Aymard's youngest son, Jean-Baptiste, set out to make his fortune, were at first sight far more promising. The year 1764 had been the beginning of a postwar expansion in the American islands, and the period of the early French revolution of the 1770s and 1780s was the most "brilliant" epoch of French colonization.[68] "Oh prodigy of industry! A space of earth equal to that enclosed in the park at Versailles, produces more riches than half the Russian Empire!" a former intendant of Cayenne (and patron of Jean-Alexandre Cazaud) wrote of his own arrival in Saint-Domingue in 1776.[69] The slave trade in French ships increased from 17,400 slaves in 1764 to 54,400 in 1790; there were more than 260,000 slaves disembarked in Saint-Domingue alone in the economic expansion of 1784–1792, within a population of a little over 500,000, of whom around 450,000 were enslaved.[70] These were years of prosperity, war, and violence, of which the consequences extended deep into the interior of France, including into the families of Angoulême.

Jean-Baptiste Ferrand married in Angoulême in 1774, and emigrated with his family to Saint-Domingue in 1779.[71] He was far more fortunate, at least at first, than his father, who died in Martinique, or his uncle by marriage, who died in Cayenne. He flourished in his profession as a watchmaker, in his own recollection, many years later, and he owned a "considerable shop" in Cap-Français, with "gold plate, jewelry, clocks." After fifteen years on the island, he wrote in 1822, he was considered "rather as a Creole than as a European."[72] His shop was on a busy commercial corner in Cap-Français, and by the end of the economic expansion of the 1780s, it was a fixed point in the town, and an exhibition space for visiting entrepreneurs. In 1789, Jean-Baptiste announced that he had become a "merchant jeweler" as well as a watchmaker, and was selling coffeepots, oil cruets, and gold chains. One of his tenants was a hairdresser, recently arrived from Paris with the "newest fashions," and another was a musician, providing guitar lessons, singing lessons, and instruction in "the principles of the harp."[73] Jean-Baptiste's shop was the venue, even, for a waxworks museum, or "a cabinet of figures," mounted in May 1789 by an impresario from Massachusetts with a collection of life-size wax figures of George Washington, Admiral Keppel, and George III, the last clad in a suit that "his Britannic Majesty had given to the artist."[74]

At home in Angoulême, the economy of the American colonies was increasingly conspicuous. The commercial crisis of 1769 was itself a drama, in part, of naval and colonial administration. It began with the "long war of 1740" (the War of the Austrian Succession), as recounted in Abraham-François Robin's history. The immediate crisis was precipitated in 1759, when "the government, exhausted by a ruinous war," suspended payment on its debts to the arms suppliers. Several of the cabalists, co-conspirators of the Nouels, were from the periphery of long-distance commerce. They had taken out risky loans; they were dependent on government contracts. One was a "supplier of artillery" to the military, from a village in the Dordogne; another was a forgemaster who supplied cannons to the French and Spanish armies, and "died bankrupt and destitute," in Robin's retrospect.[75] Another member of the cabal, the son-in-law of the goldsmith who signed the marriage contract, was by 1773 "bankrupt and exiled to Martinique."[76] "Some vile and low spirit" had spread rumors of his debts, the cannon supplier wrote from Paris in 1770; he expected imminent payment of "120,000 livres that Spain owes me, for the supply of artillery furnished to the port of Rochefort"; he would be able to return home "as soon as I have arranged something with Spain, which should happen once the artillery is delivered to Cartagena and Cadiz."[77]

The capitalists in the commercial crisis, too, were connected to distant events. Two of the principal bankers or capitalists—together with the parents of the ill-fated abbé Mioulle—were protagonists in a long dispute over an inheritance in Martinique, involving twenty-one of the descendants of a hatmaker in Angoulême, neighbors of Gabriel Ferrand and Marie Aymard in the parish of Notre Dame de la Peine.[78] The dispute began with the death, in 1760, of François Tremeau, one of the hatmaker's sons, who had emigrated to Martinique and returned home to die; it ended with a family concordat in 1768. The two capitalists, and the older Mioulle, had married granddaughters of the founder, who had emigrated from the Loire to the suburban parish of St. Ausone, where he was married, in 1674, to the twelve-year-old daughter of a local hatmaker.[79] His descendants, by 1768, were merchants or high officials: lawyers, "counselors to the king," and judges in the consular jurisdiction.[80]

Of the twenty-one heirs, and their adult children, only one actually went to live in Martinique, where he inherited his uncle's clothes, a horse, and a newly acquired plantation, with its slaves. The rest of the fortune was to be divided among the brothers and sister in Angoulême, and it included an extraordinary array of obligations, commodities, and instruments. At the center of the case was a debt, of 5,333 livres, that François Tremeau owed to a woman known only as "Henriette mulatresse." Or rather, it was her own money, the proceeds of "a sum received on her behalf" from another merchant in Martinique (as it happened, the father of the heiress with the 124 shirts).[81] The money belonging to

Henriette was to be paid "out of the clearest property in the inheritance"; she received it only after a sequence of court orders, and the seizure by bailiffs of the furniture and effects of one of the recalcitrant heirs. Four of the litigants died in the course of the dispute.[82]

The forty-seven-page settlement in the case is a panorama of economic relationships within the prosperous families of the town—the families who lived amidst Indian satin—and within the new universe of long-distance commerce. There were wartime obligations, drawn in 1758 for the "extraordinary expenditure of the colonies," on which some of the coupons were payable only on the basis of a lottery, and on others of which payment had been suspended, in a situation of the "most entire discredit." There was an elaborate accounting of the distinctions among "capital, income, interest, and sums advanced." There were commodities—bales of rice and barrels of oil, boxes of shellfish or shells, olives from Marseille, trunks and cases sent overland from Cadiz—and the promise of other commodities in the future, to be remitted from Martinique.

There were also family debts, like the 146 livres, 2 sols, that the deceased's sister spent on medicine for her brother, over the eleven years before his death; or 6 livres for washing; or the final payment on one of the last transactions that François made before his death, to buy an apprenticeship for a young man from Angoulême, Noel Virol, the son of a wigmaker.[83] There were the proceeds of the sale of a plantation and slaves, for 4,000 livres, and the coins that François had in his possession in Martinique in 1755; four pagodas (or Chinese coins), a Venetian gold coin, five louis d'or from Malta, piasters and doubloons and Portuguese coins. The heirs assured themselves, at the end of the process, that they were "related persons who are well born and who know each other." The very last words, on the last page of the document signed in the house of the principal capitalist's mother-in-law, was a fragment of an afterthought, on the part of one or other of the signatories: "and in like manner, the four boxes of shells."[84]

Abraham-François Robin, the historian of the revolution of 1769, had his own relatives in the colonies. There was a younger Abraham-François Robin who became "surgeon major of the island of St. Vincent" (one of the territories of the West Indies exchanged between the French and the British in 1763, 1779, and again in 1783). He married an English woman from the island, Elizabeth Stubbs, and became the manager of her family's heavily indebted slave plantation. He then absconded—according to the irate Flemish creditor of his in-laws—with "forty or fifty of the best Negroes," "generally all the animals," and "even the copper pots and cauldrons used in the manufacture of sugar and rum." He was imprisoned in Martinique in 1783, and was fortunate enough to find his way back to Angoulême by 1785 with his English wife, where he lived in the same neighborhood as Gabriel and the Tremeau family, identified as "M. Robin the American."[85]

Exchanges with overseas were a continuing part of the daily life of Angoulême, over the twenty-five years of the early French revolution. One of the notary Caillaud's cases in 1765–1766 involved a victim of the tragedy in Cayenne, a little boy of eight (who was the great-great-nephew of the Dutch heiress, the employer of Johann Georg Klotz). He was represented by five of his uncles: his father had died in Canada, his mother and grandmother died in the expedition to Cayenne, and he was a party in the case of a "packet containing letters of exchange," which had been sent from Cayenne to the "store keeper of the navy" in Rochefort; the "succession of his late mother."[86] There was a young woman from Saint-Domingue—her late father had been a "plantation owner and commander of the Port-au-Prince quarter," and her mother had retired to the convent of the Tiercelettes on the Place du Mûrier—who married in St. André in April 1765. Later in the same year, the widow of a surgeon from St. Marc in Saint-Domingue was married in Notre Dame de Beaulieu; she and her spouse declared that they could not sign.[87] In 1766, a day laborer was hit by the runaway horses of a passing carriage, and broke his leg; the owner of the carriage was identified as "the former surgeon major in chief of the army of the Ottoman emperor."[88]

There was a woman living in the parish of St. Antonin who came to an agreement with her husband, in 1770, that he would travel to Saint-Domingue, where he would oversee the division, "by recourse to justice or in an amiable manner," of the property she owned together with her brother; "goods, movable and immovable property, Negroes, animals, credits, and any other objects."[89] She was also the owner, as it turned out, of half of a plantation that was mortgaged to her grandson by her first marriage, and of half of the "Negroes who had devolved to her in the division."[90] Her husband stayed in Cap-Français for two years. Their eventual settlement, signed in their house in St. Antonin in 1772, was that he owed her 170,159 livres, plus an additional 60,000 livres of income, after the "deduction of travel costs and living expenses."[91]

In 1780, in the parish of St. Martial, there was a woman from Saint-Domingue, living in temporary accommodation, who came to an elaborate agreement with a "bourgeois" from Fort-Dauphin, Emery Chaloupin, who was living in an inn in the parish of St. Jacques, over the sum of seventy thousand livres that he had lent her, in "gold, silver, and money"; she agreed to repay the money in three installments, respectively one year, two years, and three years following "the peace of the present war." (The Chaloupin family were merchants in Fort-Dauphin, selling patent medicines and slaves, including, in 1779, a "negress of thirty-six," together with her two-year-old daughter, an older daughter, and an eight-month-old granddaughter).[92] Sir Thomas Sutton, a director of the French East India Company, proprietor in Saint-Domingue, and entrepreneur of the slave trade in the Indian Ocean, died in Angoulême in 1782 at the age of sixty, while staying at the Hôtel de la Table Royale.[93] A young woman of twenty-seven, Marie Lenoir, died in 1786 "at the house of M. Merilhon, master surgeon, at her passage in this town"; she was the widow of an official who "died in Senegal about two years ago."[94]

The family history of Rose Civadier, who appeared in the parish records for 1764, and was married in 1766 to a surgeon from Cap-Français, Saint-Domingue, turned into a drama of marital and economic exchange over more than thirty years. She was from a dynasty of police clerks, lawyers, and clergymen in the parish of St. Paul; in 1770, her brother moved to Saint-Domingue, as a secretary to the governor, and died there in 1771, leaving his mother as his heir. Her younger brother, Louis Michel Civadier, born in the parish of St. Paul in 1741, was by then also in Saint-Domingue, and was delegated as the agent of their mother in "all contestations that have arisen and may arise."[95] He later became a "receiver of confiscated goods" in Jacmel, Saint-Domingue ("nineteen heads of Negroes, of which four are very good sailors"), and eventually a proprietor, also in Jacmel.[96]

In the early months of the French Revolution, Louis Michel Civadier returned to Angoulême from Saint-Domingue. Soon after his return—in the village of Balzac, and with a special dispensation from the pope, expedited by a firm of bankers in Paris—he was married to his young niece, Marie Charlotte, the daughter of his sister Rose and her late husband, the master surgeon from Cap-Français.[97] He and Marie Charlotte then returned to Saint-Domingue, where she died in childbirth, in Jacmel, in July 1790; in 1796 he was married again, also in Jacmel, to his sister-in-law and niece, Rose's other daughter, described as a "minor" and a "native of Angoulême." He was fifty-four, and she was eighteen.[98]

There was even a figure from the East Indies who settled in Angoulême, as an official of the local administration. "M. Ogerdias," outside whose house the abbé Mioulle paused on the fateful night in July 1779, was the "master of water and forests" in the district, a position he had purchased in 1773.[99] Claude Ogerdias arrived in France in 1772, on a ship from Bengal, preceded, a few weeks earlier, by his wife, their two children, and five "black servants."[100] In Bengal, he had been the "inspector of buildings and fortifications" for the Dutch East India Company, and an expert on ditches, living in the Dutch settlement of Chinsurah (the modern Chuchura), on the Hooghly River north of Calcutta. In 1762, he was in the French East India Company's colony of Chandernagor (Chandannagar), five kilometers to the south, where he married Michel Guenois, the eighteen-year-old daughter of a "supercargo," or supervisor of merchandise, in the company's vessels.[101]

In Chandernagor, Ogerdias became a business associate of the governor of the colony in "diverse cargoes or Adventures," especially in the slave trade to the East Indies; when his son was baptized in Chandernagor in 1768, he described himself as a "merchant in this colony."[102] Ogerdias was a litigant, some years later, in the Chancery Court in London, against two officials of the English East India Company whom he believed to have cheated him out of the insurance payments on an ill-fated voyage carrying slaves to "the coast of Mallay, the straits of Malacca and Borneo." The sums involved were large, "computing the bills drawn on England at 190,000 pounds sterling." There was an additional associate, "Mr Mizzapour"; the English officials denied all knowledge of the transactions.[103]

On his arrival in France in 1772, in the French East India Company's port of Lorient, Ogerdias was sought by and eluded agents of the French government (who set off in error in pursuit of another returning official, the former cashier of the island of Mauritius).[104] In the spring of 1773, he purchased the office of "counselor to the king and special master of water and forests" in the Angoumois for forty thousand livres—the seller was the principal prosecutor in the case against the capitalists that began in 1769—and by the summer he was presiding, in Angoulême, over the public audiences of the mastership.[105] In 1775, he agreed to take over the lease of one of the largest houses in town, the residence of Pierre Marot, the "capitalist" and collector of the *taille* imposition. The house, which faced the ramparts and the prison, was owned by the Carmélite sisters; it was later the Hôtel de France.[106] Michel Guenois stayed in Angoulême for the rest of her life, and died there in 1830, at the age of eighty-five.[107]

Agitated Times in the Tax Office

The first of Marie Aymard's grandchildren to find an established position in Angoulême was Martial Allemand Lavigerie, the oldest son of the couple in the marriage contract of 1764. He was described, when he was married in April 1790 to the daughter of an apothecary, as a *commis à la recette des tailles*. He was a *commis à la recette des tailles*, again, at the baptism of his first child in 1791.[108] In the same year—and as the "shameful expression" of the *taille* (a tax on the common people) was eventually suppressed in the legislation of the French Revolution—Martial rented a house across the street from his grandfather's old employer, Jean-Alexandre Cazaud, and was identified as a *commis à la recette du district*; when his second child was baptized in 1792, he had risen to the position of *caissier à la recette du district*.[109] By 1795, his career in financial administration was over, and he described himself as a *marchand*, or merchant.[110]

The administration of taxes was at the heart of Tocqueville's history of the "details" of the old regime.[111] It was also the venue, in Angoulême, for the longest-lasting of the financial affairs of the times. The commercial crisis that began in 1769 came to an end, in the summer of 1776, with the vindication of the capitalists. The king's highest council prohibited the "cabalists" from pursuing any further lawsuits in the case, and ordered the suppression of the "printed brief" signed by the Nouels and their lawyer; a seventy-two-page pamphlet in which, "under the pretext of respectful representations" about the earlier decision, the plaintiffs had publicized the entire story of the case, and said of the royal decision that it was the "consecration of usury, deceit, and bad faith." The Nouels' lawyer was forbidden, on pain of disbarment, to sign "any similar briefs" in the future.[112]

So this was where the matter rested, in the summer of 1776. But all was not as it seemed, as so often in the minor revolutions of life in Angoulême. The "capitalists" and their children continued to live with the possibility that the decisions in their favor would be overturned, once again, in the continuing transformation of public law and public policy. In 1777, Abraham-François Robin was sent a series of anonymous letters about a different crisis over usury, in the town of Orléans, in which another group of bankers had been condemned for the same sort of loans of which the Angoulême bankers were accused. "In the affair of Orléans," Robin's son wrote to him from Paris, "I must tell you that it is more or less the resentment of the Angoulême affair that has led to the rigorous decision."[113] Then, in the summer of 1778, a new affair began to unfold, with many of the same protagonists, in the tax office of Angoulême.

Of the five capitalists who were vindicated in 1776, all but one were respectable figures, established merchants with extensive connections to overseas commerce. There were the two merchants, father-in-law and brother-in-law of Louis Ferrand's employer in Grenada, of whom one was the owner of "Claude," and their cousin by marriage, the protagonist in the case of the contested inheritance in Martinique.[114] There was

Robin himself, the alderman.[115] Only one of the five, Pierre Marot, was less established, and it was in his office that the new affair began. Marot's parents were "cabaretiers" or wineshop-keepers in a small town to the south of Angoulême, and he started his career in finance as an office boy; it "was from the depths of a *tavern* that he launched himself into business," his critics wrote.[116] In 1749, when his son was baptized in Angoulême, Marot was described as a clerk or *commis: commis à la recette des tailles*.[117] By 1771, he had purchased the office of counselor to the king, and was one of two collectors of taxes for the entire region.[118]

Marot was the capitalist who had complained to his lawyer about "muffled voices," "clamors," and false "sounds."[119] He was described in 1784 as "the richest man in the province of the Angoumois," "perhaps the richest capitalist in the Angoumois."[120] Over the course of a genera-tion, he had made a fortune in the administration of taxes, and in a loan business with the traders of the province—his opponents listed eighty separate transactions, involving sixty-one local borrowers, at rates of interest from 7 to 72 percent—that was estimated, in total, at between 1.5 and 1.8 million livres.[121]

The origins of the new affair started in 1771, when François Laplanche, a young man of nineteen, was appointed by Marot as an assistant clerk in the office—like Marot himself, twenty-two years before, and Martial Allemand Lavigerie, eighteen years later—or a *commis à la recette des tailles*.[122] Laplanche, too, was from what he described as a "subaltern" family, the son of an innkeeper in Angoulême.[123] He was one of the 4,089 in the parish records of 1764, signing the record of a baptism, in St. Jacques, at the age of twelve.[124] In the tax office, he was paid very little: no wages at all in his first three years of employment, increasing to three hundred livres per year in 1778.[125] But he flourished in the posi-tion, and seemed to Marot to be assiduous and honest; in 1772 he served as godfather to the daughter of Marot's cook.[126] In 1775 he was married to the daughter of a shoemaker, and later in the year his own daughter was born.[127] Then, in 1776, according to Marot's story, everything began to change. While Marot was away in Paris—it was the summer of the last, tumultuous litigation in the Conseil d'Etat over the usurious loans—Laplanche began to steal small sums of money.[128]

In August 1778, Marot discovered, or so he recounted, that there was a deficit of 15,830 livres in the accounts of the tax office. He and his son, together with the other, more senior clerk in the office, who was also the cashier, determined that Laplanche was the culprit. They confronted him, assisted by two lawyers, a notary, and three local officers of the court in full judicial robes.[129] In Laplanche's account, Marot kept him imprisoned in the tax office for three days and two nights; he was assaulted, in an inner office, by Marot's son, the cashier, and the notary; his wife was imprisoned in their home, and all their possessions, including his wife's underwear, were valued for sale; he signed a confession, which he later retracted. Laplanche then left for Paris, where he sought legal advice, from the lawyer for the cabalists in the earlier case (the one whose brief had been suppressed in 1776). He returned to Angoulême and charged Marot and his son with calumny and unjust imprisonment; Marot in turn charged Laplanche with theft and falsification of registers. The legal case made its way through seven different court systems, from Angoulême to Paris, and back to Angoulême; Laplanche was sentenced to death (twice). It ended only in 1789, after eleven years of litigation, with Laplanche's vindication.[130]

The affair of the tax clerk of Angoulême, or the continuation of the crisis of 1769, became one of the last famous causes of the old regime. Everyone knew about it in the town; "toute la ville instruite," in Marot's account.[131] Events unfolded in public, starting with the procession of the officials in their judicial robes to Marot's house. The used-clothes seller who made an inventory of Laplanche's possessions was part of the busy, industrious society of the town; she was married to Louis Dupard, the button-maker who signed the marriage contract.[132] Laplanche's wife was "young and pretty," in Marot's description, and two of her sisters were involved in the drama; when she was imprisoned in her home, one sister was seen throwing a bundle of the confiscated underwear out of the window of the house, to another sister in the street.[133] There were onlookers everywhere; one of Marot's servants reported that Laplanche had eaten "a cutlet and a biscuit" on the second day of his imprisonment, and the officers of the court, according to Laplanche's lawyers, had been served "a cake, fruit, and wine."[134] In the legal procedure of

1779, Marot called forty-three witnesses.[135] Laplanche was hanged in effigy in Paris; in Angoulême he was sentenced to be "attached to a gallows to be erected in the public square of Angoulême, with placards in front and behind, reading *commis faussaire et infidèle*" (forger and faithless clerk), whipped, branded, and sent to the galleys for life.[136]

Even outside Angoulême, the case was described as "having made an astounding noise."[137] There were at least twenty-eight lawyers involved. Six of the legal briefs were published as quarto volumes in Paris; even the records of a single procedure in November 1778—the initial "information" or witness testimony in Laplanche's countersuit against Marot for imprisonment—extend over eighteen legal notebooks.[138] The story was an "amphigouri of equivocal and inconsequential depositions," in the description of the journal *Mémoires historiques*, and it was widely reported in the periodicals or correspondences of the times; in the *Mémoires secrets* it was described as "astounding" in the "contradictions" that had been revealed between diverse judgments and decrees.[139] The case of Laplanche versus Marot was invoked, almost a century later, as one of the strangest episodes of the criminal law of the old regime, with its "frightening anachronisms," "complicated, arbitrary, almost barbaric."[140]

The story of the clerk in the tax office was of such obsessive interest, in part, because of characters in the events. Laplanche was described by his own lawyers as "a miserable individual, mistreated by nature," "at most four foot eight inches in height, and a hunchback both in front and behind."[141] He was also a figure with many friends and "protectors." One of Marot's charges, in the legal case, was that Laplanche was living in unseemly comfort, in "a house of a certain tone."[142] Laplanche's not entirely convincing explanation for his prosperity was that he had been attached, as a young boy, to a rich Englishman in Bordeaux (or at least to someone who was "like an Englishman"), whom he refused to name, and who had given him "a fine wardrobe, much money, and jewels." The other explanation was that he had a rich uncle in Guadeloupe, with connections in Nantes, who had sent him large sums of money. The case even turned, at one point, on whether the uncle was poor (as he had claimed in a letter found by Marot) or rich; in Laplanche's account, "my uncle had a large number of poor relations, who were burdening him

with demands. To free himself of their importunities, he wrote me ostensible letters, where he said that he was poor. He wrote to me in particular to show these letters to his other relations: but he was poor only
for them; in relation to me, he was rich and benevolent."[143]

Over the course of the three days that he was imprisoned in Marot's
house, Laplanche was able to borrow large sums of money from two
additional friends: a merchant from Bordeaux, and a former army officer, who had once rented an apartment from Laplanche. It so happened,
the officer recounted, that he had been getting out of a carriage in
Angoulême, on the way back from having taken the waters at a spa in
the Pyrénées, at the very moment in August 1778 when Laplanche was
taken prisoner by Marot and his son. Out of compassion and "lack of
experience," he provided money to Marot in order to secure Laplanche's
freedom; he also bought Laplanche's wife's underwear from Marot, for
six hundred livres. He later filed a countersuit against the Marots, father
and son, for defamation and calumny; the Marots retaliated with "de-
famatory digressions concerning the birth, the person, the fortune, the
morals," and the late mother of the officer.[144] In the *Mémoires historiques*,
the officer was described as the "protector of Laplanche's wife," and in
the *Mémoires secrets* as her "supposed lover."[145]

The case was of interest, too, because it turned at every point on registers and writing. The first thing Marot did, when Laplanche was imprisoned in the inner office, was to "take all his papers": in Laplanche's
description, "this sacred property, which almost always encloses the
most important and most inviolable secrets."[146] There were commissioners of the court of the *aides* imposition in Paris who traveled to
Angoulême in search of documents; Marot invoked Laplanche's marriage contract and the probate record on his father's death. The army
officer had his own agents roaming around the province, who found
Marot's birth certificate, the death record of his father, and two certificates from itinerant tax inspectors, in respect of whether Marot's parents
were wine merchants, who sold bottles of wine, or tavern-keepers, who
sold wine from open bottles.[147]

Laplanche was in his own description a writer of official records, a
commis aux écritures.[148] One of Marot's charges was that Laplanche had
concealed his thefts by falsifying the numbers at the bottoms of the

pages in the tax registers; Laplanche charged that Marot had falsified the falsifications over the course of the three years while the registers were in his possession. There were handwriting experts and "two hieroglyphic notes." The legal briefs in the case included disquisitions on the practice of monthly recapitulations of tax registries, on the "grammatical identity" of nouns, and on the essential nature of letters and digits. "A body of writing," Laplanche's lawyers wrote, "contains relationships and multiple connections"; "numbers, by contrast, are composed of no more than ten figures, isolated and unconnected."[149]

The most obsessive interest of the affair had to do with the daily life of taxes. "These registers, these recapitulations, and these accounts shed the most vivid light on the work of an office for the collection of taxes," Laplanche's last lawyer wrote, and it was as though all the inner routines of the fiscal system were revealed in the case. At the age of nineteen, Laplanche had been "introduced into a house where gold and silver circulated all the time," Marot wrote in his historical introduction to the story. "A tax office is open to the entire world," in the description of Laplanche's lawyers; "some three hundred collectors come to deposit the coins from their receipts in the office of M. Marot," and "these coins, which they bring in little installments, multiply to an infinity their approaches and their deposits."[150]

There were only two clerks, for all these deposits, Laplanche and the cashier. They were constantly being interrupted; the countryside and the town were crowded together. The first time Laplanche opened the drawer in the tax office that contained silver coins, Marot recounted, was when he had happened to leave the key in the lock, having rushed down into the courtyard, distracted by the arrival of a cattle merchant with some calves that he was hoping to buy for his country estate. There were piles of money everywhere; "the silver is counted on a table covered in papers." There were bags of money in "red cloth," other bags that Laplanche was supposed to have hidden behind the safe (or behind the cupboard), and an elaborate office code. Laplanche was at one point accused of having sought to set himself up in the grain trade; when he noted something on a scrap of paper about "nine bags of oats," this was an evident reference, Marot wrote, to "nine bags of twelve hundred livres," which had been "taken from the safe."[151]

Even the arrangement of the furniture in the tax office was a cause of anxiety, by the end of the case. Much of the evidence had turned on the ways in which Laplanche might have concealed the sequestered bags of coins (or "bags of oats"): behind the safe, or behind the desk. But by 1783, the Marot household had moved, and there was a new occupant, who was the former investor in the slave trade to the straits of Malacca; "the sieur Ogerdias was the tenant: everything had taken on a new form. No more chest, no more safe, no more desk. Where then could one go to find the vestiges of the supposed crime?"[152]

There was a sense, most of all, of endless disquiet. The collectors were "always in debt to Marot, always afraid of liability and imprisonment," Laplanche's lawyers wrote. The cashier was afraid that he would be accused of the theft; Marot's son was afraid that his father would discover the extent of his debts; the office was lost in an "abyss of secrets."[153] There were figures of authority, whose roles changed from one moment to the next. The notary who was the first person to summon the officials in their robes, and who assaulted Laplanche in the inner office, was the brother-in-law of the cashier; he was "the most vindictive of all the inhabitants of Angoulême," in Laplanche's description.[154]

Laplanche and his friends used the imposing language of political justice in their pleas. The financiers had made themselves into "despots," in the army officer's account of 1785. Laplanche had been assaulted in respect of "the most sacred rights of man and of the citizen," his own lawyers wrote in the same year.[155] But the tax office was at the same time a world of economic opportunity. In August 1778, when the crisis began, Laplanche enjoyed the esteem of his fellow citizens, his lawyers recalled in their last brief, and he anticipated further advancement; "he saw himself in a position similar to that of the older Marot, when Marot, after a long period of hard work, had succeeded in lifting himself, from a subaltern estate, to a more lucrative condition."[156]

The affair of the clerk in the tax office in Angoulême is a view, in intimate detail, of the anxious administrative power that Tocqueville described in the provinces of the old regime. The "some three hundred collectors" who appeared in Marot's office with their bags of coins were also the figures of Tocqueville's history: reduced to "'despair and almost always ruin,'" "armed with immense arbitrary power," "almost as much tyrant as martyr." The scene of apprehension described by Laplanche's lawyers was also Tocqueville's universe of clerks and collectors, made "pitiless" by their own terror, and of the receiver of the *taille*, "'a tyrant whose cupidity made use of all means to vex the poor people.'"[157] Laplanche's story was at the same time a vista of Tocqueville's other vast theme in *L'ancien régime et la révolution*, or of individual disquiet and economic advancement. It was a universe of advancement in which "perhaps the richest capitalist in the Angoumois"—and the inspirational figure to whose destiny Laplanche aspired—had made his fortune (or was believed to have made his fortune) in small loans and in the administration of taxes.

A Family in Unquiet Times

Tocqueville's evocation of a revolution in sentiments—that preceded and made possible the political revolution—was a reflection of innumerable contemporary observations. Turgot described the events of 1769 in Angoulême as a "revolution," and so did the paper merchant Abraham-Francois Robin. Marie Aymard's son-in-law Etienne Allemand lamented the "revolution" in prices of the 1780s. Even the Nouels, father and son, complained in 1776, in the idiom of their Paris lawyer, of a chaos of "modern and destructive systems," in an impending "epoch of a most fatal revolution in the laws and morality of the French nation."[158] The word "revolution," like the observation of changes in ways of thinking, was a part of ordinary life.

In the vast historiography of *L'ancien régime et la révolution*, the early or antecedent revolution has been understood, ever since, as a cultural or intellectual transformation, in which the ideas of the philosophers of Enlightenment were diffused into the deepest provinces.[159] Tocqueville's own insistence on change within the social economy, and on the details of financial history, has been seen, for the most part, as no more than a distraction. "On the economic, [Tocqueville] remains always superficial and vague," in François Furet's account; "he never used the strictly economic sources on the ancien régime," and "the economic evolution of

French society [was] ignored in itself."[160] The episodes with which this history has been concerned—the agitation of the credit crisis, the affair of the tax office, and the end of the Jesuit college—were in this sense uneconomic, or "strictly" uneconomic. They were unrelated to the "economic meteorology" that was so prominent in mid-twentieth-century histories of the economic origins of the French Revolution: a "revolution of misery or of prosperity."[161] But in a different and more modern sense, the history of the first French revolution in Angoulême can be seen as a hypereconomic story, and even as a history of the vicissitudes of economic choice.

The individuals in the episodes were "disquieted" in their condition, like Tocqueville's economic men, and tried, untiringly, to change it.[162] They described their intentions, like Gabriel Ferrand seeking to become an instructor of youth, or François Laplanche imagining himself in a "more lucrative condition." But they did so, in these stories, within the "unproductive" or uneconomic economies that so dominated their daily life, of the church and the collection of taxes. They sought advancement, too, by being uneconomic in the sense of violating what had become, or were becoming, the (implicit) rules of economic exchange: by seeking patronage, or rents, or by doing well out of changes in regulation, or, in the case of the credit crisis of 1769, by violating the laws as well as the norms of exchange. The lists of creditors and debtors, in the course of the crisis, are the description of an economic society of small shopkeepers and owners of capital, in which the largest opportunities, in exports to the colonies and in naval contracts, were also the most insecure.

The microhistory of Angoulême, in these stories, is complementary to the large conclusions of recent economic history. It is consistent, in particular, with the history of the remarkable expansion in financial activity—in "dark" or notarial credit—that Hoffman, Postel-Vinay, and Rosenthal describe in the last decades of the old regime.[163] It is complementary to histories of the late eighteenth-century economic expansion—in "public prosperity," or in "roads, canals, manufactures, commerce," in Tocqueville's account—that emphasize the essential role of overseas exchanges.[164] It is complementary, in turn, to the recent history of the economic origins of the French Revolution in the "political economy of taxation," and the "monarchy's inability to raise taxes."[165] It is the other side of the same sequence (or the same balance sheet): a history of the public expenditure, on naval contracts and colonies and jurisdictions, to which corresponded, or failed to correspond, the public revenues of the crown.

The stories can be seen, most of all, as a history of volatility. There was endless variation in interest rates, prices, and overseas opportunities, and in the probability of obligations being suspended. The inhabitants of Châlus, a village some eighty kilometers to the east of Angoulême, used a striking metaphor, at the outset of the French Revolution, to describe the maladies of the old regime. They belonged to an "audacious race," they wrote, who had extended "into the far distance, our communications and our glory." But they were disturbed by what they described as the sickness of the "economy of health" and the "public economy": the "*décroissances et bouffissures*," or the comings-down and puffings-up, of public life.[166] This was the history, too, of Angoulême in the years from 1764 to 1789.

The episodes in Angoulême can be understood, from this perspective—which is the perspective of histories of economic life—as incidents in the history of the early French Revolution, and of its eventual economic origins. It is a history not of the economy "in itself," as in Furet's taxonomy, but of the events of ordinary economic existence. The events in this history were public, in the streets and places of Angoulême, and they were of social consequence. They were visible, as in the sight of the Jesuits leaving the college with their beds, or the placards that were posted about the crimes of the capitalists, or the officers of the court progressing in their robes to the tax office. They were also audible: the secret historian's daughter who was weeping on the Rue du Collège, near Marie Aymard's home, or the shooting and shouting outside the seminary, or the young men throwing stones at the mayor on the Place du Mûrier. It is a history of change in the social economy, and it is a microcosm—a way of making sense—of Tocqueville's universal story.

Chapter Five

THE FRENCH REVOLUTION IN ANGOULÊME

An Uneventful Revolution

Angoulême was a backwater in revolutionary politics, as in so much else. It "is never cited in the chronicles of the events of the revolution," in the summary of the only substantial history of the French Revolution in the town; it "traversed the revolutionary period in a manner that was less dramatic and less bloody than its neighbors." It was the capital of "a department that had no exceptional events or personalities who should figure in the revolutionary pantheon," and it was insignificant, even, in the pantheon of the counterrevolution.[1]

There were only two individuals from Angoulême—one of the sons of the paper merchant and secret historian of the commercial crisis, and the niece of the apprentice wigmaker in the case of the inheritance in Martinique—who were in any way important in the larger political history of the French Revolution, and they had left for Paris years before. Rosemarin, the patriotic signatory of the marriage contract, moved to Tours in 1792. But the revolutionary period was a time of transformation for everyone in Angoulême, as for everyone elsewhere in France: in the ownership of property, in the destiny of the church, in the organization of military force, in taxation, and in the registration of births, marriages, and deaths. This was the history of ordinary life within which Marie Aymard's children and grandchildren lived, survived, and died.[2]

A Multitude of Clerks

The revolution began in Angoulême, in a provincial sort of manner, in February 1789. The lamentations against the established order, or the summaries of grievances, the *cahiers de doléances*, that were prepared in advance of the convocation of the first national assembly of the revolutionary period, were concerned, to a striking extent, with the administrative institutions in which the Allemands and the Ferrands had sought their fortunes.[3] These were the institutions, in turn, of Tocqueville's early French revolution, and of the multiple "affairs" of the 1760s, 1770s and 1780s in Angoulême, in the credit crisis of the capitalists and the cabalists, the dramas of the college and the seminary, and the affair of the tax office.

The earliest meetings were organized by the little communities or corporations of the town on February 24, 1789: the carpenters, hatmakers, locksmiths, saddlers, and clothmakers. Then there were the bakers and tailors and notaries (including the vindictive brother-in-law in the tax office, in the case of Laplanche versus Marot). Gabriel Ferrand and Etienne Allemand were among the 468 individuals, all relatively respectable subjects, "born French" and "included in the tax rolls," who participated in the first large assembly of the town of Angoulême. They were among the 182 of the participants, too, who "knew how to write," and who signed the record of the proceeedings.[4]

It was only the saddlers, in these early meetings, who were conspicuously revolutionary. They were the victims, they declared in their *cahier*, of the provincial officials who searched their workshops and seized loans that the officials had themselves made; "if we want to defend ourselves, we are drawn into the disaster of the most abominable trickery . . . we have among us the sad victims of these horrible tyrants." One of the signatories of the marriage contract of 1764, Etienne's second cousin—the brother of the bankrupt merchant in Saint-Domingue who advertised for the capture of his pregnant slave—signed the record of the meeting, together with his son; the *taille* was "unjust," the saddlers wrote, "distributive justice" was lost in "turns and tricks," and "in our municipal administration, everything is illegal."[5] The locksmiths, meeting the same day, complained of "the excess of the *taille* and of taxes of all varieties." They described a frightening landscape of insecurity that would be revealed, if their profession were to be opened "to persons of all sorts": "the locksmiths have at their disposition the keys of all the houses, of all the cupboards, and of everything that is kept under lock and key, in all the towns and all the country places where they work."[6]

The *cahiers* of Angoulême and the Angoumois, as everywhere in France, were a compromise, a juxtaposition of proximate grievances and philosophical reflections, on royal and municipal and universal authority. The college, the diocese, and the office of the *taille* were the object of continuing dissension, as they had been over the course of the first French revolution in Angoulême. The tailors of the town—Etienne's brother-in-law was one of the signatories—demanded that the officials of the municipal administration should be chosen openly and not "clandestinely," and that "the college, which was so flourishing thirty years ago, should be restored to its original condition."[7] The shoemakers, including the uncle of the young wife of Laplanche, the unfortunate clerk in the tax office, demanded that the number of curés be reduced, and that the revenues of defunct abbeys be distributed "to the profit of the colleges" of the town.[8] "The number of young students sent to the different pensions of Angoulême was a resource for the inhabitants," in the expression of the collective *doléance*; the most elaborate revision of the draft, according to the early twentieth-century editor, concerned the paragraphs about the revenues of the seminary and the administration of the diocese.[9]

The "vice of the financial regime," and in particular of the *taille* imposition, was everywhere in the *cahiers* of the Angoumois, as it was in other provinces. The language was portentous: the *taille* was an "unjust and murderous system," "imposed despotically," and the receivers of the *taille* were an object of "horror in all parishes." The locksmiths complained of the "excess of the *taille* and of taxes of all descriptions." The "communes of the town" demanded the abolition of sixteen different taxes, of which the collection had become "arbitrary," as well as the "suppression of the intendants": "one less charge for the state, and one branch of despotic authority destroyed; this is the general will."[10]

The *doléances* were preoccupied, in an immediate way, with the local and individual administration of taxes. The figure of the clerk or *commis*—the subaltern official, like Laplanche in the case of the missing bags of silver, or Martial Allemand Lavigerie, in 1790—became a universal enemy. The inhabitants of one village to the south of Angoulême described "the enormous legend of *commis*": enough "to make one shudder." There was "an establishment of *commis* [of] supernatural exactitude and vigilance," for the inhabitants of a nearby village; in another village to the south, the inhabitants demanded the suppression of all *commis*. In Angoulême, the tailors complained of the "vexations" and "injustice" of the *commis*; the shoemakers were disturbed "daily" by the *commis*; the saddlers demanded "the suppression of all *commis* and other employees"; the main *doléance* of the town observed the "continual vexations" of a "multitude of *commis*," and told a dire story of the rapacious *commis*, looking down "from the top of ramparts" at the farmers cutting hay in the fields below.[11]

There was a *cahier de doléances des femmes*, in 1790, written by a young widow from a village outside Angoulême, Marie Sauvo, with the "delegated powers of all the ladies of my canton." The text, like the *cahiers* elsewhere, was a lightly revised version of earlier lamentations: a combination of philosophical sentiments from the pamphlets of the times, and detailed complaints about "unjust impositions" and the "sinuosities" and "defectuosities" of the law, which "every day lead astray the officials charged with executing them." Marie Sauvo's model was a pamphlet printed in 1789, by a "Madame B* B*" from the Pays de Caux in Normandy. In the centuries of ignorance, Marie Sauvo and Madame B* B* wrote, "the motto of women is to work, obey, and be silent"; in a "time of general revolution," it was permissible for "every individual to make claims, to communicate ideas, to consider, to discuss by means of the press."[12]

Marie Sauvo made about seventy changes, mostly minor, to the text of Madame B*B*. The published pamphlet said: "There is a question, so it is said, of emancipating the Negroes; the people, who are almost as enslaved as they, will be restored to their rights." Marie Sauvo—whose family home in Angoulême was immediately next to the house of "M. Robin the American," the absconding owner of slaves and copper pots—had a different version: "The Negroes *have been emancipated*, so it is said; the people, *who are as enslaved as they, have been* restored to their rights."[13] She also added her address, her own plea for widows, a call for fraternity—"no marks of distinction"—and an imposing peroration: "It should be permitted to us to form a troop of vigilantes; we have enough ardor for arms, as for all other work, to demand to be admitted."[14]

Scenes of Revolutionary Life: Administration

The earliest revolutionary changes, in Angoulême, were in the local economy of public administration. "Our town of Angoulême, as the seat of a large new jurisdiction, and many other towns in the same situation, are going to profit greatly from the revolution," Abraham-François Robin's son Léonard—who had warned him so many years before about the "resentment of the Angoulême affair"—predicted to his father, in a letter from Paris as early as May 1788.[15] The reorganization that began in December 1789, and culminated in the creation of eighty-three new departments in March 1790, each divided into districts, cantons, and municipalities or communes, was to be the basis of a "vast government mechanism [combining] diverse administrative, military, ecclesiastical, judicial, and financial powers."[16] Angoulême, as the capital of the new Department of the Charente, was endowed with an elected assembly, a council, and a permanent directory: opportunity after opportunity for the lawyers and writers and registry clerks of the town.

There was a new municipal administration, with new committees and commissioners, new celebrations, and new certificates of "civisme," or civic duty. An immense map, a "Plan Directeur," was drawn of all the streets and houses in Angoulême, numbered according to a system of numerals established in 1769 (in connection with the lodging of the militia).[17] There was a "matrix of property contributions" listing every house, with the names of the proprietors and tenants, the size and "content" of the property, and an estimate of net taxable income in 1791[18] There was a census of donkeys (there were 268).[19] There was also a "general census of horses," with an assembly in the Place du Mûrier, between Etienne Allemand's family home in the Isle de la Cloche Verte and the Isle de la Place du Collège, where his marriage contract was signed in 1764.[20] In the "inventory" of registers of the year 4, there was a list of "sacks," a "census of wool," and a "list of the fish oil existing in the district."[21] There was a register of "personal, property, and sumptuary contributions," with declarations of rent, carriages, and domestic servants.[22] There were also patriotic gifts to be counted, from the town to the nation: in March 1793, 198 pairs of shoes, 181 pairs of gaiters, 27 pairs of stockings, 8 shirts and 1 hat.[23] There were gifts, in turn, from the nation to the town: a cod for every head of household, in March 1795.[24]

The Department of the Charente, created in 1790, had an imposing appetite for "fixed and regular procedure." "Letters and packages sent to the directory," according to an undated and heavily annotated draft in the earliest file about the administration of the department's archives, "will be placed on the desk [bureau], opened by the president, read to the assembled directory, registered, and distributed without delay to the offices [bureaux]."[25] There was a subdepartment of the secretariat of the department, within a few years, together with four other departments [bureaux], a bureau of émigrés, an accounting department, a commissariat, and a department of archives.[26]

The revolutionary period was a time, too, of the public events that the new officials described as "joy." In a dawn celebration of political abstractions, in 1793, "four hundred female citizens" dressed in white paraded in support of "unity and indivisibility," with a banner on which a "colossal statue, representing the French people, crushed federalism."[27] There was a cortege of "administrators," a few weeks later, who paraded to the house of a young girl of eighteen "whom public opinion had designated to represent Reason."[28] In a festival of "sovereignty," there was a statue that crushed the "monster of despotism," together with "capitularies, decrees, maxims of royal law, pamphlets by Burke"; it was accompanied by professors in the formerly Jesuit college, who marched to the Place du Mûrier together with the commissioners of police, "cursing ancient slavery" to the sound of military music.[29]

The new administrative procedure that had the most evident consequences for the events of ordinary life—or for the records that have been the principal source of the inquiry, so far—was the most universal. It was the institution, implemented in Angoulême in November 1792, of civil registration: a transition, over the course of a few hours, from the system of parish registration of baptisms, marriages, and burial to the registration by public officials of births, marriages, deaths, and divorces. Divorce was made legal in France in September 1792, and the new time of republican government came to Angoulême in 1793.[30] The first infant to be declared under a version of the new calendar—on "the 28th day of the first month of year 2 of the French republic," or October 19, 1793—was the granddaughter of Pierre Nouel, the cabaliste, and of Johann Georg Klotz, the pastry cook; the younger Pierre Nouel, one of the 4,089 in the parish records for 1764, born in the parish of Notre Dame de Beaulieu, was the principal witness.[31]

The registers of the parishes of Angoulême were subsumed almost effortlessly, in November 1792, into the new rhetoric of civil life.[32] Even the same volumes were used.[33] Ten of the twelve old parishes of the town had been abolished in 1791 in a process organized by the new, constitutional bishop of the diocese; he was the nephew by marriage of the dancing master Marc René Lefort Latour, and the first cousin of the discursive surgeon on the slave plantation in Artibonite, Saint-Domingue.[34] In the new parish of St. Pierre, the record of a baptism, on November 5, 1792, was followed by the registration of a birth, on the same page, by the "public officer of this municipality"; one of the signatories of the marriage contract of 1764, Jean Godinaud, was a witness on the same day, together with his brother.[35] A few days later, on November 14, the "parish register" recorded the first divorce in Angoulême; the nephew of the signatory of the marriage contract Rose Rezé was a witness.[36]

The new civil registers began a few weeks later, on January 1, 1793, kept by the public officers of the town. The revolutionary names of the months were used—hesitantly—starting in November 1793; for births and deaths in Brumaire (November), and for marriages and deaths in Frimaire (November/December).[37] The expressions were unfamiliar; *brumaire* appeared as *brumere*, and *decès* (death) as *deceais* or *dessert*.[38] The second divorce in the town appeared in the civil register of marriages, on Valentine's Day of 1793; it involved two of the 4,089 individuals from the parish registers of 1764, the son of a tailor, baptized in January 1764, and the daughter of a policeman, baptized in August 1764.[39]

There were ninety-six divorces in Angoulême over the twenty-four years that divorce was legal in France, of which a quarter were on grounds of the emigration of one of the parties (in each case, the husband).[40] The other divorces were the outcome, for the most part, of the ordinary misfortunes of life. There were four farmers who were divorced, two wigmakers, a horse trader, and a grocer (a *marchande epicière*) who was divorced from a candlemaker and remarried, a few days later, to another grocer.[41] The brother-in-law of Françoise Klotz was divorced in 1793, after eighteen years of marriage; he refused to sign the register, on the grounds that "he did not want to."[42] Two sisters, the daughters of a laborer, married two brothers, the sons of a farmer, in year 2 of the revolution; they divorced in the year 9, on the grounds that the brothers had "been absent" for around eight years, without providing "any news" of themselves; the sisters then married two other brothers, the sons of a stonemason, of whom one had been among the 4,089 in the records for 1764.[43]

The daughter of a clothworker in St. Ausone, Jeanne David, was married in 1795, at the age of fourteen, to Bartélemi Raimond, described as a "deserter from Spain," whose parents were living in Switzerland.[44] A little over a year later, when she was fifteen, she petitioned for divorce, on grounds of "incompatibility of temperament and character." In the record of the preliminary arbitration—inserted "by error" in the civil register of marriages—the friends of the parties determined that Bartélemi had been "not far from reuniting with his wife, but [she] never wanted to reach out to him," and postponed the procedure for two months; after three further requests, she was divorced in June 1797.[45] Jeanne David, described as a shopkeeper, died three months later, in September 1797, at the age of sixteen.[46]

The most demanding task of the new public officers was the duty, when someone arrived to declare a death, of hastening to inspect the deceased; "I transported myself, immediately, to the said hospice," or to the place of the said domicile.[47] There was also the registration of "abandoned" children. A midwife from St. Jacques "presented me with a girl aged around eight days," one of the officers wrote on March 1, 1793; she had been found the previous night and "inscribed on the register of the said abandoned children under the number 365"; "I gave the girl in question the first name 'Catherine' (the said Catherine is marked on the head with a pink ribbon on the right side, three inches long and two and a quarter inches wide, and cut at one end)." Jean Glaumont, one of the signatories of the marriage contract of 1764, was the witness of the infant, and the ribbon.[48]

The destiny of illegitimate or natural children was brutal in Angoulême, by the end of the old regime. The parish register for the suburban parish of St. Martin for April 1789 contained an eight-page petition to the bishop from an apprentice carpenter who needed a certificate of baptism in order to get married. He had never known who his parents were, or where he was born; he remembered that at the age of five or six he was living with a woman in a village in Périgord, but that when he was seven or eight the woman chased him out, with "nothing but blows from a stick to get him to go through the door." He then wandered from parish to parish, trying to earn his living, until he had a chance encounter with a building contractor from Angoulême who recognized the young boy, and took him on as an apprentice. In February 1789, the apprentice traveled back to Périgord, found the woman with whom he had lived, and in the presence of witnesses "called on her to declare who he was." She refused; two other construction workers testified that they also had known him as a child, and had no idea who he was. He was baptized in the parish of St. Martin in May 1789, and married there three days later.[49]

The administration, or misadministration, of the "children of the nation" was on a different and industrial scale in the revolutionary years. The public officers of the commune recorded 689 deaths of abandoned or natural children in Angoulême in 1793–1802; many hundreds more died unregistered, or in the villages surrounding the town.[50] The desolation continued into the Napoleonic period. Ursule, aged one day, was inscribed on the register as number 1,340, in 1804, and identified as "marked with a piece of black velvet twenty-four centimeters long by one centimeter wide, attached to her neck." Denis, number 1,341, the following day, had a piece of yellow striped silk attached to his right wrist; Laure, number 1,342, had a red ribbon attached to her left arm. Ursule with the black velvet, number 1,340, died at the age of eight days, in the "depot of abandoned children."[51] Even the names given to the infants were brutal, by the end of the period: Christine Desolée, Cyprien Almanach, Ischyrion Vert, Olympiade Lunette, Omer Papier, Onésine Perdrix, Privat Privé, Rustique Coq.[52]

Scenes of Revolutionary Life: The Church

The church and its institutions were the dominating economic power in eighteenth-century Angoulême—landowners in the old parishes, employers of the acolytes who appeared in the parish registers for 1764—and their destruction was the great public spectacle of the revolution. The little islands of houses in which the Allemands and the Ferrands lived, in the center of the old town, were clustered around religious institutions. The Isle de la Cloche Verte, where the notary Jean Bernard, the abbé Mioulle, and eighteen of the signatories of the marriage contract all lived, was bounded on one side by the convent of the Jacobins. The Isle de la Place du Collège, where the marriage contract was signed in December 1764, was surrounded by the formerly Jesuit college, the cathedral, and the convent of the Filles de la Foi.[53]

The order of the Tiercelettes (the Sisters of Saint Francis) were among the principal landlords of the town, and their convent dominated the Place du Mûrier. Abraham-François Robin lived in the Isle des Tiercelettes, as did the capitalist Claude Benoit des Essarts and Etienne Allemand's uncle the musician, with his seamstress daughters. The notarial archives of the town were stored in a space leased from the Tiercelettes.[54] The Rue des Cordeliers—renamed the Rue de Beaulieu—where Elizabeth and Lydia Sterne lived with their little dog in the house of the "dame de Bologne," was crowded with the residences of the canons and chapter of the cathedral. Even the ill-fated tax office where the bags of coins may or may not have been hidden behind the cupboard, the house of the tax receiver Marot and later of Ogerdias, the engineer from Chandernagor, belonged to the religious order of the Carmélites, in the Isle de la Grande Maison des Carmélites.[55]

The transactions and tragedies of reform unfolded, over the revolutionary years, in the public spaces of Angoulême. The nuns and monks of the town were informed, early in 1790, that they were free to leave their orders. In May 1790, three municipal officers visited the convent of the Tiercelettes to measure the premises, and make an inventory of the property; of the twenty-one sisters who were present, all declared that it was "their most ardent desire" to "continue to live together under the rule of their order."[56] There were further inspections and further inventories, lists of the properties the sisters owned, and of their capital, "interest," and "revenue"; a survey of the exact dimensions of the church of the Tiercelettes was signed on behalf of the order, in July 1791, by "Sister Rosalie," the superior, and "Sister Félicité," the order's business manager, or *économe*.[57]

The sale of convent property and possessions began in 1791, with the auction of parcels of land and parts of chapels, silver ornaments, and kitchen furniture. In September 1792, the nuns were expelled from their convents, with a "little linen" (like the Jesuits thirty years before) and the promise, if they swore an oath of loyalty to freedom and equality, of an eventual pension.[58] The property of the Tiercelettes was sold over several days in 1793, including ornaments, plates, furniture, and textiles: a "package of bonnets," a "package of violet damask," and a "package of old crimson damask and velvet, suitable for lining a bed." It was as though all the neighborhood wanted a souvenir: a purchaser identified as "Robin" bought a chair for five livres; "la citoyenne Mimi" bought a "pulpit," and a "large pair of kitchen irons."[59] The libraries of the religious orders were carted to the old monastery of the Capucins, and the bells from the convent chapels were sent down the hill to the river, to be transported by barge to Rochefort and La Rochelle.[60]

There was a continuing flux of things and people. The silver from the convent of the Dominicans, which dominated the Place du Mûrier, was carried along the Rue de Beaulieu, to be stored in the archives of the convent of the Cordeliers.[61] The papers and deeds of the diocese were carried to the convent of the Filles de la Foi.[62] The seminary in St. Martial, scene of the shooting of the abbé Mioulle, was sold to Henry, a paper manufacturer from St. Jacques and the brother-in-law of the new bishop.[63] The seminarists moved to the former Jesuit college. The oldest of the unconstitutional or nonjuring priests of the diocese—who had refused to sign the oath of loyalty to the republic—were imprisoned in the convent of the Carmélites.[64] The offices of the new Directory moved to the old monastery of the Dominicans or Jacobins. The convent of the Ursulines became a prison, and the monastery of the Capucins a depot for prisoners of war. The convent of the Tiercelettes was noted for the "facility" that it offered for "retail trade."[65]

Biens Nationaux

It was the sale of the real property of the church, amidst all this turmoil, that had the most enduring consequences for economic life in Angoulême. The new market in *biens nationaux*, or "national goods," extended across the Department of the Charente, as everywhere in France.[66] In the old center of Angoulême, it was immediate and unavoidable. The new "matrix of property contributions" included a column "to indicate the mutations in the names of the proprietors that will take place in 1791," extensively annotated over the succeeding years, and the revolutionary period brought a frenzy of transactions in urban land. There were about eighty properties listed as belonging to church institutions in the immediate vicinity of the Place du Mûrier, and multiple enthusiastic "acquirers," many of them officials of the new administration. The "Plan Directeur" can be shaded to show all the properties that were deemed to belong to the nation in the early years of the revolution; there are very few streets, in the old neighborhood of the Allemands and the Ferrands, the capitalists and the cabalists, that were at any distance from the new regime of private and public property.[67]

The destiny of the *biens nationaux* was recorded in discursive detail— there were lists of the submissions or offers to purchase, of the auctions with their multiple bids, and of the eventual settlement of the purchases that were completed—and the signatories of the marriage contract, together with their connections, were present in the lists. Even Etienne

Allemand Lavigerie, the bridegroom, who complained so bitterly of the cost of living, was able to buy a house in the former parish of Notre Dame de la Peine, the property of the former chapter of canons of the diocese of Angoulême. The house was "adjudicated" to him in September 1791, for the sum of 4,625 livres, to be paid in twelfths, over twelve years. He made successive payments—initially in assignats, the paper currency issued by the revolutionary legislatures—and the transaction was completed in 1812. The house close to the cathedral was an essential security, by then, in the family's fortune.[68]

The largest single purchase, for 446,000 livres, was of a house owned by the former Jesuit college, facing the Place du Mûrier; the new proprietor was the "Dlle Marchais," of the family of the goldsmith and signatory of the marriage contract.[69] The goldsmith's grandson bought the famous mansion of the Carmélites, subject to the tenancy of the widow of Claude Ogerdias, the daughter of the supercargo from Chandernagor.[70] Another of his grandsons bought a different house belonging to the college, with the life tenancy of "la demoiselle Caliche amériquaine," also known as "la citoyenne Caliche St. Mimi," the neighbor who had bought a pulpit in the sale of the property of the Tiercelettes: she was Catherine Saint-Mesmy, "born in America," and she died in Angoulême in 1827, at the age of ninety-nine.[71]

Barthélemi Thibaud, the son of the registry clerk, and a signatory of the marriage contract at the age of eleven, bought a house that had belonged to the Filles de la Foi; and then, when a new set of properties were put up for sale—confiscated from émigré owners—he bought a house near the ramparts.[72] Dupard, of the family of the button-maker, bought a meadow that had belonged to the Abbey of Beaulieu, and a house on the Rue de Genève (whose owner had been the royal prosecutor in the case of the clerk in the tax office).[73] The "heirs of Pierre Nouel," the principal cabalist of 1769, bought the "Chapelle de St. Augustin."[74] The absconding slave owner from the island of St. Vincent—"M. Robin the American"—bought a house that, like Etienne's, had been part of the former chapter of canons.[75]

The very first of all the offers to purchase in the Charente was submitted by Abraham-François Robin, the capitalist and historian of the crisis of 1769 (who was seventy-four at the time); he announced his intention to buy a riverside estate called Chantoiseau, the former property of the Cordeliers of Angoulême.[76] Henry *l'aîné*, who became the new proprietor of the seminary, announced that he would buy another riverside estate and its mills, the property of the Abbey of La Couronne.[77] There were other exuberant occasions. A garden in the precincts of the former château—which Etienne Allemand Lavigerie had been leasing since 1782—was declared at auction, in the year 3, for 3,375 livres; the price was bid up by six consecutive purchasers, and the garden was sold, eventually, for 30,200 livres.[78]

Gabriel Ferrand, Marie Aymard's oldest son, was involved, for a time, in one of the relatively inexpensive markets in confiscated property. This was the sale of short-term leases of the *biens nationaux*. Early in 1793, the premises of the Abbey of Beaulieu became available as a rental property: on February 26 Gabriel bought a three-year lease of "part of a building" (for 170 livres); on March 5 he bought another lease, for another part of a building, for 26 livres; and the following year (for 90 livres), a third part, "a building giving on to the place." The security for the first lease was his brother-in-law, Etienne Allemand Lavigerie, and for the second lease, "citizen Raby, merchant."[79] Gabriel was even a participant, in a modest way, in the collective frenzy for the property of the Tiercelettes, on the Place du Mûrier. He bought a lease for part of one of the lots of the convent, also on March 5, 1793, for 26 livres; it was "the former church."[80]

Reason and Loneliness

Marguerite Aubert, of the extended network of the marriage contract of 1764, was the unlikely heroine, amidst all these exchanges of church property, in the most picturesque spectacle of deconsecration. She was the goddaughter (and granddaughter) of one of the signatories, the granddaughter of another, and the young girl "whom public opinion had designated to represent Reason," in November 1793; she was welcomed at her home in Angoulême by a cortege of "administrators."[81] The cavalcade, led by a representative of the revolutionary Convention in Paris, and accompanied by female citizens dressed in white, then proceeded to the cathedral or former cathedral of St. Pierre: "Reason set off for her temple." The cathedral or temple had been redecorated for the occasion with vases, torches, and statues. Marguerite was instructed to clamber onto the altar, where she and the women of Angoulême were addressed by the representative of the Convention "in the sacred name of nature": "Do as you would be done by."[82] Marguerite Aubert was described as ravishingly beautiful. In 1807, she was married to a tax officer; she became a draper, like her grandfather, and had a shop near the Place du Mûrier.[83]

The festival of November 1793 was the occasion, as in the celebrations of the old regime, for an exuberant display of local enterprise. The representative of the revolutionary Convention authorized the payment of 690 livres to one contractor for "expenses and works at the Temple of Reason," including the efforts of three carpenters, five stonemasons, two plasterers, two locksmiths, a painter, a sculptor, a seller of candles, and a seller of candlewax or tallow. There were the costs of laborers ("two days and two nights at thirty sous per day"), for "dismantling the grilles of the Temple of Reason" and "supplying a Dome" (described as work "pour la nassiont"), and for "having closed the doors of the elected representatives." There was a separate appropriation for the expenses of the ball held in the comedy theater of the town, to celebrate the celebration; including the costs of four musicians, nails "to hang up tapestries," more candles and candlewax, the rental of chairs, "refreshments" for the musicians, a carpenter to repair the chairs that were broken, and "a man who spent the night." The Yrvoix family from the marriage contract of 1764 were among the contractors, merchants in tallow and illuminations.[84]

There was another figure from the network of the marriage contract, of the younger generation, who was one of the invigilators of desecration. Jean Lecler dit Larose, also known as Lecler-Raby, was a minor, resilient figure in the municipal politics of Angoulême. His father was a wool-bleacher; his aunt (who was also his godmother), his uncle, his grandmother, and his grandfather (who was his godfather) were all among the eighty-three signatories of the marriage contract in 1764.[85] His revolutionary career began, as so often, as a "public official" recording declarations of births, marriages, and divorces, and inspecting the corpses of the deceased.[86] He soon became a specialist in "domiciliary visits," and in what he described as the "painful operations" of visiting suspicious schools. There was a schoolmistress whom he visited in the year 7, a former nun, who announced "in a firm and positive tone" that she was taking her students to vespers; her classroom was filled with "books consecrated to fanaticism," he reported; "the nouns *citizen* and *citizeness* were so foreign, in this house, that it was not possible for us, in spite of our reiterated invitations, to tear them, so to speak, from the mouths of this schoolmistress and these students." Another teacher was providing instruction in nothing other than Latin, mathematics, and biology; "O depths of perfidy!"[87] Lecler-Raby was still in public office in 1805. He survived the empire and the restoration, and was a municipal official, once again, following the July Revolution of 1830; he died in Angoulême in 1848.[88]

The daughter of the dame de Bologne, the landlady of Lydia and Elizabeth Sterne, was a Benedictine nun, called Bénédictine, who was expelled from the Abbey of Notre Dame de Beaulieu. She was fortunate in that she found lodging, by April 1795, in a part of the house in the Isle de la Cloche Verte that belonged to her relative Jean-Alexandre Cazaud, the theorist of slavery and employer of Marie Aymard's husband. She identified him, rather approximately, as "Jean-François Cazaud" (which was the name of his son), and as an inhabitant of and having lived for many years in the "island of" (with the name left blank). Cazaud was by then living in exile in England, where he died a few months later.[89] The immediate circumstances were not encouraging: in the bedroom, the floor was rotten, many planks were broken, and the walls were demolished; there was only a moldy wooden lock for the room she was to occupy. But Bénédictine was still there, four years later, living by then with a maidservant; she kept a boarding school, in 1801, with nine students; she died in Angoulême, still on the Rue de la Cloche Verte, in 1841.[90]

A house around the corner in the Place du Mûrier was the scene, also in April 1795, of a more somber destiny. The house was one of the largest in the square, immediately opposite the entrance to the former convent of the Tiercelettes—it was "the house forming the corner of the Place du Mûrier," formerly the property of the Dominicans—and it was owned by a cloth merchant, Jean-Pierre David, who was the father-in-law of one of the signatories of the marriage contract, the younger Jean-Baptiste Marchais.[91] In the evening of April 13, David and his own father-in-law, a retired baker, appeared at the municipal office to recount that a woman described as "citizen Marie Billiard a former nun Tiercelette aged around fifty-seven or fifty-eight had been removed, drowned, from the well belonging to the said David." They had sought out a local judge, who wrote a report; the public officer of the municipality came to make his own inspection; the dead woman was described as the daughter of the late director of the post in the town of Saintes. She was Marie Eustelle Billard, and she had entered the convent of the Tiercelettes in the summer of 1762. She lived there for thirty years, and died a few steps away, in the year 3 of the revolution.[92]

Scenes of Revolutionary Life: The Military

The military, like the church and the administration of taxes, was a resilient local economy in Angoulême. The preparations for civil war began as early as the summer of 1789, when the "great fear" of the first months of the revolution, with its rumors of an approaching army of 1,000 or 2,000 or 18,000 brigands, reached Angoulême, from Ruffec to the north. "Some say that they are the English, others that they are Pandours [Croatian soldiers], Moors, people escaped from the galleys," the curé of a village to the east of Angoulême wrote in the parish register.[93] Shortly before, the newly established "permanent committee" of the municipality of Angoulême, having heard the alarming news, ordered the immediate formation of a national ("patriotic") guard and a "military council"; the commander of the guard was an intemperate army officer, who had been wounded (in the Austrian Foreign Legion) in the Seven Years' War.[94]

The patriotic guard were concerned, from the outset, with public ceremony. They presided in early August 1789 over a festival to celebrate the destruction of "the privileges of the clergy and nobility," and then, in April 1790, over a larger ceremony involving a "federation" of cavalry, infantry, artillery, and military bands who paraded through the town to an island in the Charente, where they swore allegiance on a newly erected "Altar of Unity." The eventual mobilization for the total war that began in 1792 was an even more public scene. "What a spectacle for those who still remember the profound consternation that followed the news of war, under a corrupt regime," the dignitaries of the town wrote to the commander of the patriotic guard, by now a member of the National Assembly in Paris; "now it is the people who make [war] themselves, for themselves."[95]

The prospect of war, and the revolutionary tricolor, were a matter of enthusiastic anticipation for the shopkeepers of Angoulême. "We had the pleasure of having supper with your traveling salesmen on Friday night," a merchant called Marguerite Allemand wrote in October 1791, to the firm of Baignoux and Quesnel, merchants in Bordeaux who specialized in wine, cloth, paper, and "colonial products," with a side interest in slave voyages to Mozambique. Would it be possible, she asked, to send us "six dozen cockades made of goat's wool—the color should be fine and very bright in three colors"; she also wanted "twelve feathers in the three colors, which should be very beautiful," "twelve dozen buttons for uniforms," "twelve dozen red epaulettes with ornamental knots," and "four dozen dolls in the form of grenadiers."[96]

Of the nineteen deputies who represented the new Department of the Charente in the revolutionary assemblies of 1789–1799, only four were from Angoulême.[97] Two made no interventions at all, as listed in the *Archives parlementaires*; the intemperate army officer was notable mostly for the announcement in the assembly, in April 1792, of the "patriotic gifts" of his wife and young sons: "(*Applause*) . . . 'our tender youth does not permit us to listen to the voice of our courage [but] we have resolved to send you the twelve livres that our papa gives us every month for our little pleasures.'"[98] In the revolutionary Convention, three of the four deputies from Angoulême voted for the execution of Louis XVI, and one voted both for and against. "Louis deserves death," the army officer pronounced; "anathema to the slave who is vile enough to doubt it."[99] One of the deputies, a lawyer called Guimberteau, was sent as a representative to Tours, where there had been a "great assault on liberty" in November 1793. Some "villains," probably bought by English gold, "had the audacity to shout out, in the theater, *Down with the red bonnets.*" "Two of the suspects have been arrested," Guimberteau reported to the Convention, and "I have just established a military commission to judge the guilty on the spot, tomorrow the guillotine will be working nonstop"; "terror is here the order of the day and *ça ira.*"[100]

The formal beginning of hostilities in 1792 brought conscription in Angoulême, a flight from conscription, and new crowds of volunteers seeking to "fly to the frontiers" to defend the nation. There were requisitions of shirts (in excess of six per person), beef suet, ashes for washing powder, and of a large consignment of beans, discovered in a warehouse in St. Jacques. There was also a "requisition of young men from eighteen to twenty-five."[101] The large bell of the church of St. André was "brought down from the bell tower" (or "more accurately, thrown from the top, without actually breaking," in the description of the mayor), and hauled by cart to the warehouse of a paper manufacturer in the port of L'Houmeau, "with the design of being taken to the cannon foundries."[102] The town became a "depot for the cavalry horses of the armies of the republic," who were "lodged in the convent of the Capucins and the church of the ci-devant Jacobins."[103]

There were prisoners of war in the town, as in the earlier worldwide wars of the eighteenth century. The old prisons, just across the street from the mansion of the tax collector, were by the summer of 1792 "no more than a pestilent sewer."[104] The convent of the Carmélites, the Abbey of Beaulieu, and the convent of the Ursulines were all turned into prisons; the prisoners of war, like the cavalry horses, were lodged in the convent of the Capucins, as well as in the old Jesuit college, the church of St. André, and the church of St. Jean.[105] A little girl of two called Louise Robertson died in the town in February 1795; she was described as the daughter of two "English prisoners," and a "native of North Leith."[106] There were Spanish prisoners employed at a foundry just outside the town, in the same year; there were also Portuguese prisoners, "insubordinate" Austrians, "marauding by night," and, by 1807, an auxiliary corps of a reported twelve thousand Spanish soldiers, dressed in dirty white uniforms.[107]

The prisoners of war, and the soldiers accompanying them, needed food and lodging, forage and clothing. A sequence of letters from various "commissioners of war," in the revolutionary summer of 1794, convey the challenges and opportunities of the new economy of war. A citizen Flotte wrote from Bordeaux to the mayor and municipal authorities, to acknowledge a letter about the recent arrival of 345 Spanish prisoners in the depot of "your commune," and to announce the arrival of another 53 prisoners. A month later, another commissioner informed them that an additional 423 prisoners would be arriving within days, and advised the municipality to find "a locale sufficient to contain them," given that the convent of the Capucins "was already occupied by 400 others of these prisoners." Another few days passed, and on 5 fructidor 2, a different group of officials announced the arrival of 900 Spanish prisoners, who will "stay on the 8 and leave on the 9."[108]

These were very large numbers of newcomers to the town: a municipality, still, of no more than around twelve thousand people. There were also immediate exigencies. The same commissioner wrote again, two days later, with a specific request: a Swiss captain had been captured with the Spanish prisoners, all his clothes had been taken, and the authorities were invited to provide him, most exceptionally, with a shirt and a pair of stockings; he had "nothing left on his body except a shirt full of vermin."[109] One of the official responsibilities of the municipal official Lecler-Raby, the relative of so many of the signatories of the marriage contract of 1764, was the inspection of prisons, where in the year 8 he found more than a quarter of the detainees ravaged by a "morbific" disease of the pharynx and the maxiliary glands; "our first concern was to reassure the imagination."[110]

Even the Place du Mûrier was the scene of military conflict, or at least of a military riot. In the crisis over the civil war in the Vendée, in 1793, cannons were installed to protect the town, the same that had been brought out in the "great fear" of 1789.[111] There was also a "Comedy" in the square, a theater that had been constructed in the premises of the old convent of the Tiercelettes. On a summer evening in 1797, the year 5, some soldiers went into a café on the square (the "Café des Electeurs") and searched the premises for counterrevolutionaries; they left, saying that "there are no Chouans [or royalists] here." At that point the theater performance ended. The spectators came out into the square and were assaulted by a large group of soldiers, armed with sabers and sticks, and singing the "Marseillaise"; there was a particular "affectation," according to a passerby, in "the passage of the song, *Aux armes citoyens, Aux armes.*"[112]

All the inhabitants of the neighborhood shut their doors and closed their shops; the fear spread across the entire town. The theatergoers then fought back; some gendarmes appeared from the barracks nearby, making a lot of noise and firing guns; the soldiers accused the commander of the gendarmes of having described his troops as "brave royalists." The record of the events was sent to the Ministry of Justice in Paris, including the testimony of the sister-in-law of the cloth merchant Jean-Pierre David that a young man, a locksmith, had "presented a piece of paper in a mysterious way"; "he seemed very anxious."[113] There was also a long anonymous letter to the minister about the recent history of military riots in Angoulême, and the changing roles of individuals in the town: "But having been denounced before, they have ended up as denouncers," or the denouncers denounced.[114]

Rosemarin

Rosemarin, or Rose Marin, or Rose Marin du Rozier, who signed the marriage contract at the age of ten, was the niece of the signatory Rose Rezé, and the first cousin of the younger Rose Rezé (who had been insulted "outside the house of M. Lavigerie the tailor"). She was thirty-five at the beginning of the revolution, and she owned a small house in the "new quarter" of the town.[115] In the summer of 1792, she sold her house to an officer in the revolutionary *gendarmes*, and left Angoulême for Tours. She then had the misfortune to be denounced for being an "émigré," or having left France. It was her attempt to be removed from the "accursed list" of émigrés ("cette modite licite")—which began the following year, and ended only in the summer of 1798—that is recorded in her police dossier.[116] There are petitions, certificates of residence, certificates of nonemigration, certificates of the impossibility of travel, and testimonials as to her political opinions; there are multiple descriptions ("black hair," "black eyes," "dark brown hair and eyebrows, five feet, an aquiline nose," "a large and open forehead"); her signature, "Rosemarin," was eerily close to her signature as a child, in the ancien régime of 1764.[117]

The dossier is a sequence of misunderstandings and suspicions, a journey through the procedures of revolutionary paper. There were "pieces," or documents, that were "defective," pieces that had the wrong dates, certificates that were "vitiated" by "irregularities," and pieces that "did not have the character of authenticity." Her property was "sequestered"; there was a "citoyenne Labatud," by whom Rosemarin was owed money.[118] At one point, Rosemarin wrote from Tours, she was "close to dying of hunger" ("à la veuille de mourir de fin").[119] Guimberteau, the revolutionary deputy, who played an essential role in the denouement of the case, surmised that Rosemarin had been inscribed on the list of émigrés by the people who owed her money, in order to avoid repaying the loan.[120]

Guimberteau was a family friend, or so it seemed; in the letters in which she requested his help, Rosemarin, who referred to herself as "Rozede," sent wishes from "your dear brother," and signed, "I embrace you with all my heart."[121] She was living in Tours at the time of Guimberteau's military commission of November 1793, in which terror was "the order of the day." It was a busy period for the envoy: "I have removed a dictatorial cabal," he wrote to the Committee of Public Safety in Paris; he had "purified" the popular society and "recomposed the revolutionary government." The "public spirit" had "today reached revolutionary heights," he reported in February 1794, and he was "leaving tomorrow morning" for Cherbourg (to turn his attention to the supply of horses for the revolutionary army).[122] In the midst of these exertions, in December 1793, he sent a letter to the municipal officers of Angoulême in support of Rosemarin's case: "You can have faith in this declaration, because it is sincere." "During the four months I lived" in Tours, he wrote later, "I saw her almost every day."[123] His testimony, as summarized by the municipal bureau of Angoulême, was that "this citizen is of a known patriotism." Rosemarin was removed from the list of émigrés in the summer of 1798; she was living, by then, near the Palais Royal in Paris.[124]

Louis Félix

The figure from the extended network of the signatories of the marriage contract who became prominent in the revolution in Angoulême— Louis Félix—was baptized in the parish of Saint Marc, Saint-Domingue, in November 1765. He was identified as "Louis mulatre," son of an unknown father and of Elizabeth, a black slave; his mother's owner freed him at birth.[125] By the age of fifteen, he was in Angoulême, and living in a pension in the parish of Petit St. Cybard, where he was confirmed in April 1780.[126] In 1785, he was an apprentice goldsmith, living in St. André; his first child was baptized in the same year.[127] In November 1789, he was married, described as the natural son of "Sieur Jacques Orillac and of Marie Elizabeth."[128] His wife died in 1798, and later the same year he married the daughter of two of the signatories of the marriage contract of 1764: Marthe Dumergue, cousin of Etienne Allemand, and daughter of the saddlemaker and cabaliste with the brother in Saint-Domingue, who was also the radical of 1789 ("in our municipal administration, everything is illegal").[129]

Over the course of the revolution, Louis Félix became a well-known figure in the political life of the town. He, too, had a period of service as "public officer of the commune of Angoulême," signing declarations of birth, marriage, and divorce and hastening to the scenes of recent deaths.[130] He was one of the prominent "patriots," in the summer of 1797, in the affair of the military riot in the Place du Mûrier: in the idiom of the times, of denunciation and counterdenunciation, a witness testified that he had been told by someone from the village of Champniers that three individuals from the town had come to their commune and "told the peasants, *they want to put you in irons and give you priests and nobles. You must be ready to support us at the first news*"; the witness's neighbor had informed him that the men were called "Blandeau, Latreille, and Félix."[131]

In September 1797, the municipal government of Angoulême was replaced (in the aftermath of an "antiroyalist" coup d'état in Paris), and Louis Félix was appointed to the new administration; he declared that he was unrelated to any émigrés, and proclaimed the "oath of hatred to royalty and anarchy."[132] In January 1798, he was appointed to the even more powerful (and well-remunerated) position of "commissioner of the directory to the municipal administration," which he held until well into the Napoleonic period.[133] Louis Félix was particularly preoccupied, over these years, with festivals and songs. He wanted more revolutionary feast days (to replace the celebrations that had been "created by monarchy and fanatism") and a more assiduous observation of the new ten-day week; he organized searches of the town, with "domiciliary visits," for hidden and insubordinate priests; he and his friend the apothecary took on the task, themselves, of the extended domiciliary visit, in 1800, to the former seminary in the former parish of St. Martial, now the property of Henry, the (mildly) revolutionary paper manufacturer from St. Jacques.[134] Under the restoration of the monarchy, Louis Félix returned to bourgeois life, as a merchant goldsmith.[135] He died in Angoulême in 1851, three years after the eventual abolition of slavery in the French Empire; he was eighty-five, and described as a "rentier."[136]

Figures of the French Revolution: Léonard Robin

Léonard Robin, the only person from Angoulême who was even close to being important in the political history of the revolution—or the revolution seen from "on high," as a story of "assemblies and parties"—was the third of thirteen children of the paper merchant and capitalist Abraham-François Robin.[137] He was educated at the Jesuit college in Angoulême, and left for Paris in 1763, at the age of eighteen.[138] He became a successful lawyer, specializing in vexed questions of land titles, banking fraud, the estates of the younger brothers of Louis XVI, and the municipal jurisprudence of marshes; he won a major case for the future

Charles X, in respect of the rights of local communities to the unimproved lands known as "terrains vains et vagues." He also helped his father with the many lingering aftereffects of the "affaire d'Angoulême," or the revolution of the capitalists and cabalists.[139]

Léonard Robin's letters to his parents in Angoulême, over the course of 1788 and 1789, are a story of private and public reinvention. He described the intimations of change—or "public troubles"—as early as January 1788; in May 1788, he wrote to his father, "Here we are, at last, in a revolution." "Have we acquired no rights" since the fourteenth century? he asked in his own "little reflections, personal and particular, on the present revolution"; and then, "What am I going to become? What will become of my brothers?" In December 1788, he expressed a "terrible fear" of what was to come: "The future seems to me even more frightening than the past."[140]

The letters were a juxtaposition, throughout, of family and political news. Léonard sent packages of pamphlets from Paris to Angoulême, and copies of his own legal briefs; he reported, amidst all the public turmoil, on his flourishing practice. A case about banking fraud in Rouen, in 1788, was the "most beautiful triumph of my life." He had a particularly demanding client, about whom he sent news in every letter: a Catholic Ottoman dignitary from Smyrna known as Méhémet-Aly or Boullon Morange, and the proprietor of contested marshlands that had been the object, since 1781, of a succession of vexing affairs involving the king's council.[141]

Léonard's father, in turn, sent packages of food from Angoulême to Paris. There was an alarming discovery in 1788, that had to do, as so often, with the depredations of the *commis*. As Léonard wrote:

> I received the pâté this week . . . it was in good condition and I think it will be very good; but the scoundrels of the *commis* at the dispatch office or others seem to me to have interfered with it; the pastry crust on the top was found broken and I noticed that there was an empty hole in the pâté that could only come from someone having taken out the truffles.[142]

Even in January 1789, the exchanges of ordinary life continued. Léonard requested a "good pâté made out of four partridges with truffles," carefully tied in string and sealed, "to prevent the pâté from being pillaged at the customs or in the offices": "I think the best precaution would be to have the box encased in lead in Angoulême; I would happily cover the costs."[143]

By the time of Léonard's next letter, in August 1789, everything had changed. Since "the morning of the famous July 13," he wrote—the day of the riots in Paris that preceded the storming of the Bastille, and precipitated the formation of a bourgeois militia—he had been fully occupied in the daily life of "revolutions that will be remembered forever." He was "elected lieutenant," and exchanged his lawyer's white collar for "all the paraphernalia of an infantry officer." He was involved in "general assemblies of the district, particular assemblies of the military commissioners, guard duty, particular committees, deputations, I had to be everything and everywhere; drafting minutes for an entire month, delivering extracts, getting the deliberations printed, composing speeches and written motions, receiving a crowd of visits."[144]

Léonard also discovered, within himself, a different sort of person. He had been a lawyer for nineteen years, he wrote to his father, and had always thought he "was incapable of speaking without preparation and without a written text"; "I have just experienced the opposite, a thousand times, and in momentous circumstances in which I have had to arouse emotions, persuade, bring back, bring forward, bring to a decision assemblies of four, five, six hundred people or more; all of this is a bit glorious, but very ruinous."[145]

In September 1789, Léonard was elected as the president of his district, and as representative to the city of Paris.[146] He lived on the Rue de Beaubourg, in the Marais, and his district—later known as the Carmélites—was a busy center of commerce, manufacturing, and municipal politics; the building in which he lived was the venue of a factory making saucepans, cutlery, lamps, and ornamental harnesses.[147] The earliest Declaration of the Rights of the Commune of Paris emanated from the assembly of the district, on a motion by Léonard, in July 1789.[148] The district was later the first in Paris, again on a motion from Léonard, to petition for the rights of Jews to be admitted to citizenship. "Considering that the district of the Carmélites, which has the largest number of Jews in its midst, has been, as it still is, in the best position to be knowledgeable about their public conduct," the motion stated, the district decided unanimously to petition that Jews, "of whom it attests to the good conduct and entire devotion to the public good, should henceforth enjoy the rights of active citizens."[149]

These are "unhappy times of internal troubles, perpetual alarms, horrible executions, dangers of every sort," Léonard wrote to his mother in November 1789, in reply to a letter she had sent from Angoulême; without some sort of providence, "we would all have had our throats cut twenty times over in Paris over the past four months." Her letter, he wrote, had calmed the "contractions of the heart that everything that is happening here reproduces again and again I no longer know where we are or what will become of us."[150]

Léonard Robin, over the following three years, became one of the ubiquitous figures of the revolution. He was a member of the committee of three people, together with Jacques Pierre Brissot and Condorcet—he was "less known than the two others," in the understatement of the late nineteenth-century historian of the Paris Commune—who prepared the more elaborate report on the rights of Jews, in May 1790, that became the basis for the emancipation of the Jews in France.[151] In September 1790, he was selected as one of the "notables" of the city. He prepared a report in November 1790 on the organization of the water supply of the region of Paris and the principles of local government, and another report, in December 1790, on how to organize a gigantic competition for "all the monuments and public works of the city of Paris, in painting, sculpture, engraving, medals, architecture, bridges, riverbanks, roads, [and] all objects having to do with belles lettres, sciences, and arts."[152]

Shortly before Christmas 1790, Léonard was chosen as one of two civil commissioners to be sent by the National Assembly to "restore peace" to the Department of the Lot, to the southwest of Angoulême. The department was in the midst of a series of insurrections, involving the repudiation of feudal rents, attacks on châteaux and the "houses of administrators," a multiplication of maypoles, some with a resemblance to gallows, thirty counterrevolutionary gentlemen on horseback, and a "village army" estimated at more than four thousand people. Léonard and his co-commissioner, together with their two secretaries (of whom one was Léonard's younger brother), traversed the department by carriage in early 1791, unarmed and "without any military or civil escort"; they made speeches, signed copies of government decrees, and sought to restore the "power of persuasion and the law." Their initial intention, they reported, had been to contain the instigators of the insurrection "by terror" and their deluded followers "by reason." They had been surrounded, instead, by "signs of repentance": "We embraced with rapture the idea of a great people, who will be obedient only, henceforth, to the empire of reason."[153]

By the time the report was published, in March 1791, Léonard was on the road again, dispatched, in the aftermath of his success in the Lot, to another recalcitrant department in the south of France: the Gard. The northern frontiers of the Gard had been the scene, Léonard proclaimed in Nîmes, of "thirty to forty thousand Catholics," some of them crying, "*Down with the nation!*" He was traveling with the same two secretaries, and two new co-commissioners, drawn, as before, from the municipal politics of Paris; they described themselves as "organs of the National Assembly and the king." "The tyrannical inequality of the ancien régime," they declared, "required not only reform but total regeneration."[154]

In the summer of 1791, Louis XVI and Marie Antoinette fled from Paris, and were arrested in Varennes. In the aftermath of their flight, Léonard was assigned yet another delicate task. He was one of six commissioners instructed by the municipality of Paris, on June 21, 1791, to rush at once to the Tuileries palace, place their seals on the royal apartments, investigate how the family had escaped, and arrest everyone who was left in the interior of the palace. It was an arduous task; "they spent the whole night placing their seals," and then had to get special permission to sell the "comestibles in the palace," and to allow the two thousand or so people arrested to have access to their clothes (while "assuring themselves that there was nothing hidden in these clothes").[155]

The local judges from the neighborhood of the Tuileries complained about the entire procedure, and asserted their own prerogatives in respect of the placing of the seals; Léonard and his fellow commission-ers were assigned yet another task, of finding "a number of horses that had been diverted from the king's stables and dispersed in different parts of the capital." On June 25, 1791, the royal family were back in the palace of the Tuileries, under heavy guard. Léonard and the other com-missioners were reappointed to remove the seals they had placed four days before, and to search the carriages used in the flight to Varennes; their last task was to supervise the removal of the papers found in the carriages, and the apartments, to the new national archives.[156]

The high point of Léonard's political life came in September 1791, when he was elected by the voters of Paris as a member of the new Na-tional Assembly. He was the twentieth out of twenty-four candidates elected (receiving more votes than Condorcet, who was twenty-second).[157] In the assembly, Léonard was concerned, as in his earlier existence, with processes and procedures. He spoke at length on the organization of parliamentary committees and the classification of par-liamentary papers; he was elected to the committee on domains; he de-fended his constituents, "poor rentiers who are in great indigence," and ill-paid public officials (*commis de bureaux* or *commis d'administration*). He proposed an elaborate procedure to decide on the deportation of unconstitutional priests; he also designed the scheme, which has op-pressed hotel clerks over many generations, whereby it was the respon-sibility of the proprietors of lodgings to declare the presence of foreign-ers staying overnight in their premises.[158]

It was a procedure, in the end, that was Léonard's enduring contribu-tion to the French Revolution. The circumstances were glossed over, for the most part, in the eulogies of his friends, and left out entirely in the poignant biographical notes that his father wrote about him, after his death.[159] For Léonard Robin was the principal author of the famous law of September 20, 1792: the first divorce law of modern times. "Your love of liberty has for some time led you to wish to establish it in the very midst of the family, and you have determined that divorce should exist in France," he declared to the Legislative Assembly, and it was the law he drafted, negotiated, and defended in eight successive debates that was eventually adopted by the assembly. Divorce by mutual consent, divorce because of incompatibility, divorce for specified reasons: these were now the law of France, required because "individual liberty can never be alienated in an indissoluble manner by any convention."[160]

The divorce law proposed by Léonard was adopted in the evening session of the very last day of the Legislative Assembly; its provisions were incorporated in another law of the same date, on the civil registration of births, marriages, and deaths.[161] Léonard's zeal for civil legislation was unexhausted even then. The evening session was suspended at one in the morning of September 21, 1792; a few moments earlier, he had proposed yet another draft law, on the subject of the rights of natural children. It was the most compelling of all his writings, a declaration of the "rights of natural children to the affections and goods of their father and mother," and a defense of the "innocent victims" of the "barbarism of prejudices and the injustice of laws."[162]

The revolutionary Convention that succeeded the Legislative Assembly met for the first time later on the same day, and Léonard's political career was at an end. He returned to the practice of law, as an advocate and a judge. He also prepared another, even longer "Instruction" on divorce, a gloss on his original law, which he addressed to the Convention in February 1793, amidst European war and as the revolutionary Terror descended on Paris. There were flourishes suited to the temper of the times: "For too long, this slavery, the harshest of all when disgust, discord, and hatred are a part of the household, has seemed to have been consecrated by religious solemnities." There was also a philosophical, Smithian stateliness—"On the nature and causes of Divorce"—and a settling of earlier disputes. There was even an intimate etiology of domestic "incompatibility": it was "a continuity of little facts, of little wrongs that are imperceptible for everyone other than the spouse who suffers them."[163]

Léonard was "very well known to Robespierre," according to his father's biographical notes; he had been an early member of the Jacobin Club.[164] He was arrested, like so many of Robespierre's old acquaintances, in the Terror that began in 1793. He was imprisoned, and then released, and then imprisoned again—oscillating, in the narrative of his eulogists, between being a "judge of his fellow citizens" and an "inhabitant of the dungeons of tyranny." He was eventually freed in July 1794.[165] One of the prison memoirs of the time recounted Léonard's arrival in the prison of the Port-Libre, also known as the Maison de Suspicion, on January 4, 1794. Léonard had tales to tell of the outside world, according to the memoir, including that twelve hundred arrest warrants had been signed by the Committee of Public Safety. The other prisoners in the Port-Libre, at the time, included Lamoignon de Malesherbes, who had been Abraham-François Robin's protector in the affair of the capitalists of Angoulême, together with his daughter and her husband, the grandparents of Alexis de Tocqueville.[166]

In a very obscure way, over these years of revolution, Léonard succeeded in becoming a wealthy landowner. In 1788, he had been appointed by his demanding Ottoman client (who lived in a Capucin monastery on the Rue St. Honoré, and was also known as "very holy father") as universal legatee for the contested estates. When Méhémet-Aly died soon after, Léonard reported to his father in Angoulême that "this will be a very large fortune for me, if the affairs turn out well."[167] In August 1789—in the letter about his new political life, and his newly discovered capacity for persuading "assemblies of four, five, six hundred people or more"—he was optimistic, still, about the resolution of the affair; his adversaries "were now in the greatest disarray," and there were "people in the ministry who are most favorable toward me."[168]

At some point in 1793, Léonard returned to the affairs of the late Méhémet-Aly. The case, which was the subject of litigation long after Léonard's own death, turned on the value of an investment in marshlands in Normandy that had been transferred from Méhémet-Aly to a family of minor nobility, and from the family to Louis XVI; Méhémet-Aly maintained that the family owed him an immense sum, at least a million livres.[169] By 1792, Léonard's adversaries had emigrated, and their own property (in the Department of the Yonne, in Burgundy) was on sale, as the *bien national* of an enemy of the state.[170] In 1793, Léonard argued the case, yet again, before the court in Paris to which the outstanding affairs of the old royal council had been remitted; he won.[171]

Over the same months of revolutionary frenzy, Léonard started to buy up the property in the Yonne of his old adversaries: the creditors of the estate of Méhémet-Aly. He bought a windmill near Sens belonging to the family, in November 1793; while he was a prisoner in the Port-Libre, in February 1794, he bought the vineyard attached to the family château; in February 1797, he bought the château and its grounds. He had recently been married for the first time, to his longtime companion Marie Elisabeth Emilie Aubourg, the daughter of a merchant in Fontainebleau; Léonard was now himself a landowner, the proprietor of a "very pretty château" and a vineyard, a family man. As a historian of the French Revolution in the Yonne asked in 1915, "Who was he then, this citizen Robin, so avid for gain?"[172]

In Paris, Léonard resumed his prerevolutionary interest in the jurisprudence of domains, and was appointed in 1799 to the lucrative position, noted in Balzac's scenes of provincial life, of "supervisor of mortgages" for the Department of the Charente.[173] "He returned to Angoulême, his fatherland," Abraham-François Robin wrote; but the registration of mortgages was merged with the registration of domains, and Léonard returned to Paris. There, at last, he found a new political position. He was appointed by the first consul, Napoléon Bonaparte, as "commissioner of the government" to the civil tribunal of the Seine, and then, in February 1802, as one of the hundred "tribunes" of the neo-Roman government.[174] He continued, almost to the end of his life, to think of himself as insecure. There is a single letter to his wife that survives, from August 1801 and on the subject, of all things, of a new horse. Léonard was writing from Paris, to Emilie in Burgundy, and it seems that she had acquired a "Hessen horse":

> I am in no way an esquire, I don't get on a horse, I have neither the habit of nor the desire to do so, and I don't like horses. We have no need for a horse at home, you know that I have always rejected the idea of having one. When I have a different position in the future, with a stipend of ten, twelve, or fifteen thousand livres, I promise you that we will have a carriage, a cabriolet, and a horse, until then I want to continue to go on foot . . . No doubt the horse could provide some pleasure to the brothers [but] I wish them well of it. So I beg you *at once* and as advantageously as you can, to get rid of the said Hessen

horse, all saddled and bridled. No news here. My health is getting better and better. I kiss you with all my heart.[175]

Léonard Robin died a few months later, in July 1802, at his château in the Yonne.[176] He had been an unimportant figure in the center of the French Revolution. He was there, to one side, almost unnoticed, in the great events of the times: in the Paris Commune in 1789; with Condorcet in the liberal declarations of 1790; in the palace of the Tuileries in 1791, after Louis XVI and Marie Antoinette had fled; in the ballot for the Legislative Assembly later in 1791; in the desperate last hours of the assembly in 1792, with his project of divorce; in the prison of Port-Libre with Malesherbes; in the Tribunat of Napoléon's counterrevolution.[177] He was never really important; he was simply present, a part of history, living his life and making his way in the world.

Figures of the French Revolution: Marie Madeleine Virol

The other person from Angoulême who was part of the large history of the times was an enemy of the revolution. Marie Madeleine Virol was baptized in the parish of St. Martial in 1768.[178] She was the daughter of a wigmaker, and the niece of one of the peripheral figures in the earlier history of the town: Noel Virol, the son of a wigmaker, and the young man for whom an apprenticeship had been purchased in the case of the capitalists and the contested inheritance in Martinique.[179] Marie Madeleine's grandfather, also a wigmaker, lived in poverty in a small shop rented from the Jacobin Fathers, immediately behind the Place du Mûrier.[180] Her uncle, Noel Virol, became a surgeon, and moved to Paris.[181]

Some time before the revolution, Marie Madeleine also moved to Paris, where she worked until 1792 as a chambermaid in the family of a military officer, a "ci-devant" count from the countryside to the west of Angoulême, and the son of a royal official in Martinique. She then had various other positions, and, in her own account, "traveled to different places."[182] She worked for another "ci-devant," a marquise, until March or April 1794. At that point, she became a hairdresser, and lived on the Rue Coquillière, near the old Palais Royal in Paris.[183] She was twenty-five years old.

At 11:30 p.m. on the night of May 2, 1794, Marie Madeleine and her friend Félicité Mélanie Hénouf, who was twenty-one, walked into the police station of the section of the former Feuillants monastery, not far from the Tuileries palace and the Palais Royal. They presented what they described as their "card": two texts that they had written the night before. "This is my card of citizenship," Marie Madeleine wrote in her manifesto, a folded sheet of paper:

> The entire Convention is a heap of scoundrels, a heap of beggars. Robespierre is a barking dog; in the tribune he acts as a good republican; but the republic is an infamous thing . . . the deputies have thrown powder in the eyes of the poor people . . . There must be a king, there must be, it is necessary for the security of the people . . . Long live my good king! I have your portrait on my breast, I will keep it until I die! Long live Louis 17! Long live Louis 16! Come, return and take your properties, which are in the hands of scoundrels. This is done by me, myself. You are all buggers [*pla bougre*], donkey's jaws.[184]

On the verso she wrote, "I am not a citizen, I am a royalist."[185]

"People, open your eyes," Félicité Mélanie, who worked in a dress shop, wrote in her own manifesto:

> Do not let yourselves be led into error any longer by the brigands who are at the head of the government, because it is in order to reign, and you will always be unhappy. Those whom you are told are evil are for the good cause. Turn to them and you will be happy. I love my king, I regret him every day, and I want to follow him and throw myself into the hands of these vile saracens. They love victims: let them drink the pure blood of the lambs.[186]

Marie Madeleine and Félicité Mélanie were arrested; in the words of the police report, the officers on duty "having examined the said paper, recognized that the said paper manifested the desire to reestablish the monarchy."[187] They were interrogated over the next two days. Marie Madeleine, who was dressed as a man, gave her name and said that she had been born in Angoulême; asked where she lived, "she replied that she did not know much about where she lived"; "as to her family name, she replied, 'This is my secret.'" Who had written the paper? she was asked; "It was she." Where had she written it? "She had written it in a café." Where was the café? "She did not know." When she was searched, she was found to be carrying a piece of paper containing a square of white satin, with a medallion of the royal family, described by the officials as "the tyrant, his wife, and his son."[188]

Félicité Mélanie, too, was asked who had written the paper she presented; "It was she herself." Why had she written, "Long live Louis 17"? "It was so that he should assume the throne and reign." Had she emigrated? "No." For what reason did she want a king? "Because I love them." Why did she love a king more than the republic? "Because people would be happier." She refused, at first, to give her name and address; she said that her home was in the woods, and that she had been living there for the past two months, on whatever she could find. "What was your intention in writing the paper?" she was asked; "The intention of making my opinion known, and being arrested."[189]

"What was your intention?" Marie Madeleine was asked, again, in the next interrogation; "Our intention was to be arrested, because we cannot bear the present regime," and "the paper shows clearly what the intention was." Why did she "persist in concealing her real condition," when it was inconceivable that a woman of the class she purported to belong to, could wish to have a king? "She persisted in always wanting one, because France would be happier, and there would not be so many people killed." Had she been wandering with her comrade in the woods around Paris? she was asked, which she denied; her last employer had gone away three weeks ago, and since then she had been staying with the person with whom she had been arrested, whom she knew only as "Emilie." "Who were the people who had determined them to produce these incendiary writings?" they were asked again; "They persisted in saying that it was they themselves, and that they had been inspired by no one."[190]

On May 5, 1794, Marie Madeleine and Félicité Mélanie were brought before the revolutionary tribunal (established "for the judgment, without appeal, of CONSPIRATORS").[191] "The sentiments contained in this writing, were they really yours?" Félicité Mélanie was asked, and "were you in full presence of mind when you permitted yourself to criticize the republican government?" "My sentiments have never varied, and I enjoyed full presence of mind when I wrote them down." "What are the disgraces that might have affected you to the point that you became a declared enemy of your country?" "It is true that I have experienced some disgraces, but they have never influenced the opinions that I have of my country, and these disgraces are my own secret with which I will die."[192]

"Who suggested the opinions to you?" the public accuser asked Marie Madeleine: "The opinions are my own, they have always been mine, and I am not beholden to anyone for them." "From whom are you born?" "The person from whom I am born was a wigmaker, and I have no one who is a noble in my family." "What are the subjects you have to complain about with the national Convention?" "I have seen the sacrifice of people who were dear to me, and I cannot look favorably at a revolution that deprived me of them; what is more, I owe no account of my sentiments to anyone other than myself." "How can it be that you have ceased to love your country?" "I have detested Robespierre since the beginning of the revolution; I abhor his principles and I recognize no legitimate authority other than that of a king." "You are surely not unaware of the recompense that is reserved for sentiments of this sort?" "I have made the sacrifice of my existence, it is hateful to me, and I will bless the hand that delivers me from it."[193]

Marie Madeleine and Félicité Mélanie were convicted of "having composed writings tending to the reestablishment of the monarchy," and guillotined on the same day.[194] They were both four foot, six inches in height, according to the official record of the prison of the Conciergerie. Félicité Mélanie had chestnut hair and blue eyes; Marie Madeleine had brown hair and brown eyes.[195]

Noel Virol, Marie Madeleine's uncle from Angoulême, was himself, by then, in prison, in the old convent of the Carmes, where he had been since December 1793.[196] In the course of his practice as a surgeon in Paris, he had the fortune, or misfortune, of becoming Robespierre's doctor; he also had as his patients "many members of the Convention."[197] Over the six months he spent in the Carmes, Virol became the "health officer" for the prison, and passed his days in conversations in the convent gardens; he was considered by his enemies to have paid particular attention to prisoners who were able to pay, while "leaving the indigent to suffer."[198]

In the spring of 1794, while Marie Madeleine and Félicité Mélanie may or may not have been living in the woods, and as Robespierre described a theory of virtue and terror, the revolutionary Committee of Public Safety became obsessed with the so-called conspiracy of the prisons. A group of prisoners in the Carmes were planning to leap over the convent walls, it was reported, using a rope from which bells had been suspended in the old church tower, and another rope that had been used to tie mattresses. Three police officers were sent to the prison by the Committee of Public Safety, "to hear the denunciations"; they identified Noel Virol as one of the leaders of the conspiracy.[199]

Various witnesses testified, of whom one said that Virol, while walking in the garden, had declared that "Robespierre was a scoundrel who always imagined new conspiracies," that "Saint-Just & Collot d'Herbois were dirty beggars [*foutus gueux*], and that he had cured the syphilis of one of these idiots [*coquins*], who had not yet paid him." The witness, "to the best of his recollection, believed that he named Saint-Just."[200]A second witness, who said that he knew Virol from Angoulême, declared that he, too, had talked in the garden to Virol, who "at the word *Robespierre* made injurious remarks"; Virol had also said that "the Convention had exceeded its powers," and that "because of the ambition of the Convention, the same thing was going to happen as happened to Rome."[201] A third witness described Virol as a "leader of the counterrevolutionaries," with an "aristocratic way of behaving," who had "said publicly, in the prison, that those who led the government were scoundrels; this was his favorite word." A fourth witness recounted that Virol "said nothing less every day than that *Robespierre was a scoundrel*," thereby "provoking all the hatred of the prisoners against the committees of public safety and general security."[202]

In his own interrogation, Virol denied almost everything. He said that he had "treated several people from the Convention, but he could no longer remember whether they were members of the Committee of Public Safety"; that he was not prepared to say what kind of illness he had treated them for; that "they had not yet paid him"; that he thought Robespierre was "a very honest citizen"; that "he had treated [a deputy from Angoulême] who had not paid him," and "many others, whose names he did not remember." "Who were the people he normally talked to?" he was asked; "He talked to all the prisoners without distinction, and someone had poisoned what he had said."[203]

A moment after the interrogation, Virol jumped out of a window in the prison, and died immediately.[204] Forty-six of the other prisoners were guillotined five days later, convicted of having participated in the conspiracy. After a further four days, Robespierre was himself overthrown, in the Convention of 9 thermidor 2. The Carmes, in the summer of 1794, like the prison of the Port-Libre in which Léonard Robin was incarcerated with Tocqueville's grandparents, had been a mixture of high and low society, of admirals and princes and chambermaids and old soldiers from Cayenne. One of the participants in the supposed conspiracy of the Carmes who died on the guillotine, that summer, was Alexandre de Beauharnais, president of the National Assembly at the time of the king's flight; his wife, later the empress Joséphine, was released from the prison of the Carmes in August 1794.[205]

Chapter Six

A FAMILY IN CHANGING TIMES

The Allemands and the Ferrands

The Allemands and the Ferrands—to return to the story of Marie Aymard's family—were not revolutionary figures in the 1790s, like Léonard Robin, or figures of the counterrevolution, like Marie Madeleine Virol; they continued with their lives, like so many millions of other individuals in France. They were almost invisible in the world of the printed word, in the sense that there was very little that they did, or that happened to them, that was important enough to be recorded in newspapers or books or the bulletins of tribunals. Even in the ocean of paper that the revolution invented—the wave upon wave of declarations of income, registers of property, registers of luxuries, lists of inhabitants, lists of patriotic gifts, certificates of civism—they were visible (or some of them were visible) only from time to time.

The Archivist

There was one of Marie Aymard's children whose revolutionary existence was recorded, for a short period, in the most plethoric and minuscule detail. Gabriel Ferrand was still living in the old parish of Notre Dame de la Peine, in the shadow of the cathedral, when the parish was abolished in 1791. He was present, with four of his sons, in the lists of persons with "certificates of civism" that were drawn up in 1793. His oldest son, Gabriel, was listed as a "captain of grenadiers"; Etienne and Pierre Alexandre were also listed, and "Ferrand jeune instituteur"; his fifth son, Joseph, died in Angoulême in August 1793.[1] Gabriel's own circumstances were comfortable. In the register of properties in Angoulême that was prepared in 1791, the house in which he lived, rented from a surgeon, was the largest and most valuable in the neighborhood.[2] He ventured, for a time, into short-term rentals of the *biens nationaux*: the house on the Place de Beaulieu, and the "church" on the Place du Mûrier.[3] He was an "assessor," in 1794, assisting one of the justices of the peace in the subaltern jurisdiction of the town.[4] When conscription came to Angoulême, Gabriel, who had so many patriotic sons, served on the "jury for the choice of conscripts": new soldiers leaving for the front, "happy children" in the struggle between slavery and liberty.[5]

It was in 1797, at the age of fifty-nine, that Gabriel came to his life's vocation. The new Department of the Charente had an imposing appetite for paper and for "fixed and regular procedure."[6] It was also besieged by citizens wanting records from its own new depositories, which were stores of papers, parchments, land deeds, and a church bell.[7] Gabriel was employed in the new division of the archives, and his name started to appear on receipts and notes; "the citizen Ferrand, employed in looking after the archives of the Department of the Charente," was authorized to provide a transcript to a local notary, or to deliver documents relating to a transfer of land, "while retaining an inventory," and "with a receipt for the pieces."[8] Even in the record of the episode of the almost-unclothed Swiss captain, in 1794, there was a scribbled note, "have authorized Ferrand [to deliver] a shirt and a pair of stockings."[9] In December 1797, Gabriel was described as "Ferrand archivist." In November 1799, he was "head of the bureau of archives."[10]

The short period in which Gabriel's own life was so well documented came in the spring of 1799. On 12 germinal of the year 7 (April Fool's Day, in the old calendar) the department introduced a new procedure, a "register destined to demonstrate the presence of [its] employees." Thirty-nine officials were listed, and signed on the first day, at 8:00 a.m. and again at 3:00 p.m.; Gabriel was there, at the foot of the page. The procedure continued for a little over three months, with the signatures becoming sparser and sparser each day. On the last page of the register, there were only six officials who signed. Gabriel had signed every single page.[11] Later in 1799, in the register related to luxury taxes, he declared that he had no property, that he lived in a house for which he paid 240 livres in rent, and that he had no income other than his "stipend as archivist," "of which one-tenth is retained at source."[12] When he died in 1816, at the age of seventy-eight, he was described as "head of the Bureau of Archives of the prefecture of the Department of the Charente."[13]

The Constitutional Priest

Gabriel and Marie Adelaide's second son, Etienne Ferrand, was the only member of the extended family who came close to being a revolutionary figure, or at least a figure of obloquy for the enemies of the revolution. He started to prepare for holy orders, as his father had thirty years before, and unlike his father he was ordained, in the early months of the revolution. In 1790, he became the vicar, or substitute for the curé, of the parish of Jauldes, a small community to the north of Angoulême. He signed the parish register of Jauldes thirty-nine times between July 1790 and April 1791: records, for the most part, of the baptisms, marriages, and burials of individuals from the even smaller villages in the surroundings of Jauldes.[14]

In the tumultuous months following the civil constitution of the clergy in December 1790, Etienne's life changed once more. He was a juring or constitutional priest, like three-quarters of the priests in the Angoumois, and he was chosen, very soon, for higher office.[15] The parishes of the diocese with recalcitrant or "refractory" priests began a process of choosing constitutional clergy to replace them: "intruders," as they were described by the faithful. This was the festival of new appointments and new ordinations that the bishop of Angoulême, Pierre-Matthieu Joubert, the nephew of the dancing master, began in the weeks following his election.[16]

Of the twelve curés of the old parishes of Angoulême, only one, the curé of St. Martial, refused to take the oath.[17] Etienne Ferrand was chosen in May 1791 as his successor. He became curé of the new, expanded parish, and priest in charge of the seminary of Angoulême, the scene of so much agitation over the course of the first French revolution, and of the shooting of the abbé Mioulle. Etienne was twenty-five, and had been a clergyman for two years. The elderly recalcitrant curé left in late May, followed by the last of the professors from the seminary on June 12; Etienne took his first service in the parish later on the same day.[18] "The intruder who replaced them was the former vicar of Jauldes, named Ferrand," in the narrative of the nineteenth-century historian of the seminary. The historian of the clergy of the Charente was even more succinct: "S.-Martial . . . *Etienne Ferrand*, tr. du vic. de Jauldes. c.i. 12 juin 91.—TSS. *Séc.*" He was an intruder (a *curé intrus*), he had sworn all the constitutional oaths required, and he was later secularized; this is the only reference to Etienne, so far as I know, or to any member of his family, in the immense historiography of the French Revolution.[19]

Over the following months, Etienne signed every entry in the parish register of St. Martial, and hundreds more in the ensuing year of revolutionary transformation: the record, as in Jauldes, of births, marriages, and deaths, and of many of the same families who had been there in the register of the parish in 1764.[20] He signed for the last time on November 15, 1792, in the record of the burial of a girl of seven, "Rosalie, fille illegitimate." The register was closed by the Municipal Bureau of the town later that day; it resumed, on the same page, with the registration, in the new revolutionary form, of the death of another girl, the daughter of two immigrants to the town.[21]

Jean-Baptiste, the American

Jean-Baptiste Ferrand, Marie Aymard's youngest son, is also present in the archives of the revolution in Angoulême, as a pensioner of the revolutionary state, obliged over many vicissitudes to record the details of his own economic life. Jean-Baptiste and his wife, Elizabeth Boutoute, had lived on the island of Saint-Domingue for fifteen years—the epoch of the "considerable shop" in Cap-Français, the "fifteen Negroes," and the waxworks museum.[22] The family lost everything in the great fire of Cap-Français in June 1793, in the aftermath of one of the most devastating battles of the civil war in Saint-Domingue. All the buildings on the corner of the Rue Vaudreuil and the Rue Saint-Joseph, where his shop was located, were destroyed; they are shaded in a map of the town in which "the ravages of the first fire [of June 20] are marked in black ink."[23] Jean-Baptiste and Elizabeth's eighteen-year-old son Martial, born in Angoulême in 1775, "died in the service of the colony."[24]

A few months later, Jean-Baptiste, Elizabeth, and their daughter, Françoise, returned to Angoulême as destitute refugees. They were admitted to emergency relief on April 27, 1795, together with "Rosalie, a woman of color."[25] Jean-Baptiste was described as a "watchmaker unable to work, because of weakness of sight." In January 1796, their son Jean-Baptiste, Marie Aymard's youngest grandchild, and the only one to be born after her death, was born in Angoulême; the registrar was Louis Félix, thirty years after his own birth, as a slave, in Saint-Domingue.[26] The older Jean-Baptiste then found employment, of a sort, in the "depot for the Portuguese prisoners of war," in the former Jesuit college; in 1798, "he had not been paid for eighteen months." He, Elizabeth, Françoise, and their son were issued "certificates of indigence" in September 1798, together with Rosalie and her son, Alsindor. They were among sixteen refugees from Saint-Domingue living in Angoulême and supported by the revolutionary state; there were also nine refugees from Martinique, six from Guadeloupe, and four from the island of Sainte-Lucie, all of them indigent and most of them children.[27]

In the summer of 1799, Jean-Baptiste's circumstances took a turn for the better. On July 7, 1799, the "register destined to demonstrate the presence" of the employees of the Department of the Charente—which Gabriel had signed so diligently at the foot of every page—included a new signature, Jean-Baptiste's, among the personnel of the "Third Bureau." This was the capacious administrative division charged with "religion, the remuneration of the clergy, the sale of national goods, surveillance, commerce, agriculture, the surveillance of forests, and all particular and contentious affairs relative to the above"; Jean-Baptiste signed "Ferrand jeune."[28]

Two days later, he signed the new tax register, as required by the law related to luxuries. He described himself as an "American," "Ferrand américain." "I am employed by the department, and I have no idea what my remuneration will be," he wrote; "I have no servant, and I pay for a woman of color and her child. I receive none of the relief that is due to me as a refugee from Saint-Domingue. I am living in the College of Angoulême."[29] By 1805, he was in Paris, living on the Rue de la Ferron-nerie near the market of the Halles, with Elizabeth and their young son Jean-Baptiste; six of his neighbors—a painter of miniatures and theorist of masonic numbers, a teacher, two employees, the mayor of the ar-rondissement, and the deputy mayor—certified that he had "no prop-erty situated in France," and "no lucrative employment"; "he is living in indigence."[30]

Françoise and Her Family

Françoise Ferrand, the bride in the marriage contract of 1764, was al-most invisible in the records of the revolution. She appeared three times in the registers of the *état civil* over the revolutionary period: when she reported the death of one of the signatories of the marriage contract, her half sister-in-law, Marie Allemand, in 1797; on the occasion of the marriage of one of her sons in 1801; and as a witness to the birth of her granddaughter, also in 1801.[31] Etienne Allemand Lavigerie, her husband, was listed in 1790 among those who pledged patriotic gifts as a contribu-tion to the "needs of the state"; it was a modest gift, in his case, of 6 livres, to be paid in three instalments. Louis Félix, the same year, pledged 12 livres, and Jean-Baptiste Brillet, one the signatories of Etienne and Françoise's marriage contract, pledged 225 livres; Françoise's nephew, the curé Etienne Ferrand, pledged 50 livres, in one installment.[32]

Etienne Allemand received a certificate of civism in 1793, and again in 1794; so did his son Martial, identified as a *commis* in the tax office. His third son, Antoine, who had been one of the last scholars in the old college, was also certified, identified as a *commis*, together with another son, a volunteer in the army.[33] In October 1791, Etienne acquired a part of the physical fabric of the diocese, or of the cathedral surroundings in which he and his family had lived for so long: the *bien national* consist-ing of "the house and courtyard of the ci-devant chapter," which he paid for over the ensuing twenty-one years.[34]

Etienne's lamentations over the working conditions of the professors in the formerly Jesuit college continued, as the "revolution" in "the relative value of our honoraria" of 1786 turned into the revolutionary death throes of the college itself. In 1791, he and two other professors complained to the "second bureau" of the new department, "as Frenchmen and as professors," about the contradictory orders they had received. They had been forbidden to teach by the district of Angoulême, they recounted, and instructed to teach by the National Assembly. "In a conflict of this sort, they believe only that it is for the department to judge," they wrote; "they are bold enough to flatter themselves that [the department] will order the continuation of their honoraria, which the prohibition on fulfilling their functions cannot make any less necessary. It is also no more than a very slight compensation for the sacrifice, which the professors have made to the public good, of a much more lucrative condition."[35] In 1795, Etienne still had five students in his care.[36] But he was living, by then, in what the nineteenth-century historian of the college described as the "blackest misery."[37]

Over the revolutionary years, Etienne and his son Antoine received payments, intermittently, as *commis* or clerks in the Department of the Charente. They were employed, for the most part, in the vast enterprise of the production of lists and certificates; Etienne, or "Lavigerie père," appears in the registers of disbursements as a *commis*, a *commis aux écritures* (or copyist), a *commis expeditionnaire* (or shipping clerk), and a "supernumerary," employed to prepare the registers or rolls for the "forced loan," payable in assignats, of the year 4.[38] Antoine was a *commis* in the administration of "domains," or property, of the district of Angoulême; he was employed in the *bureau de correspondance*, which was "suppressed," and he was then transferred—as Rose Marin's case languished in Tours—to the *bureau des émigrés*.[39] These were not secure positions. Etienne signed another petition, in the year 4, when the supernumeraries, who were supposed to have been paid in assignats, received no stipend at all.[40] A few days earlier, the directorate of the department had decided that employees could be paid in the low-denomination coins, or pieces of one or two sous, that had been depos-

ited in the offices, up to the value of ten francs, in exchange for the assignats in which there was now "so little confidence."[41]

His circumstances, Etienne wrote in December 1795, in a letter to the
minister of war—it was about an involuted affair involving the retro-
gression of his second son, Pierre, from captain to sublieutenant, on the
basis of the unfounded denunciation that he had stolen the uniform of
a wounded friend, that was eventually discovered in a trunk that had
been misdirected somewhere between Nantes and Angoulême—
presented an "afflicting scene." He had "no goods, no fortune, no position, having lost his own in the college of Angoulême"; he was responsible for "eleven children, a granddaughter, and an American girl, of
whose pension he had received almost nothing since 1784."[42]

Etienne was eventually obliged, like others in Angoulême, to return
to the rural universe that his great-grandparents had left behind more
than a hundred years before.[43] He identified himself in the letter to the
minister of war as the "farm manager of the Terre de Gondeville near
Jarnac": a country estate that had been bought in 1793 by the son and
grandson of the goldsmith Jean-Baptiste Marchais, who had signed the
marriage contract in 1764.[44] When Etienne's own son Pierre was married in 1796—he had meanwhile been restored to the rank of captain—
Etienne was described as "ci-devant professor in the College of Angoulême,
currently a farmer."[45] In the tax register of 1799, he declared a house with
a rental value of one hundred livres, and added, "I have no object of
luxury and no one whose wages I pay, wish to observe moreover that I
am supported by my family."[46]

Lavigerie *Ainée*

The register of 1799 was an overview of the economic life of Angoulême,
after ten years of revolution: a compilation of declarations by 522 more
or less prosperous heads of household, the subjects, or potential subjects, of sumptuary taxes. Pierre Marchais Delaberge, the son of the
goldsmith, former mayor, and the owner of so many *biens nationaux*,
was the most opulent figure in the list. He signed next to Etienne, and

declared a house with a rental value of 500 livres, a carriage, two carriage horses, and four servants. Louis Félix, "commissioner of the directory," declared a house with a rental value of 430 livres, and a female servant. Abraham-François Robin declared a house worth 200 livres, and one female servant. Michel Guenois, the "widow Ogerdias," declared one female servant, and a house—or a portion of a house, since she had rented out most of the mansion across the street from the prison, the former tax office—with a rental value of 200 livres.[47]

There was only one of Marie Aymard's twenty-three grandchildren who was present in the register of 1799. In the (annotated) property matrix of 1791, Françoise and Etienne's daughters, the "citoyennes Lavigerie," were listed as living in a house on the corner of the Place du Mûrier, owned by the son of Pierre Marchais Laberge (and the grandson of the signatory of their parents' marriage contract); the other tenants were a caterer, a hairdresser, and a goldsmith.[48] The grandchild who appeared in the tax register, eight years later, was the oldest of the seven surviving daughters, Jeanne Lavigerie. She signed her name, in a bold hand, as "Lavigerie *ainée*," and she was described in the register as "marchande," or shopkeeper. She was the richest person in the family: "The rental value of my personal accommodation is 250, from which 50 should be deducted for the rent of my shop."[49]

Nuptiality

These were no more than passing references, flotsam and jetsam in the ocean of revolutionary evidence. For Marie Aymard's other children and grandchildren, there is even less. They are there, if at all, in the day-to-day records that have been the most important source for this history: the records of births, baptisms, marriages, divorces, deaths, and burials. They belong, thereby, to a different and at first sight unhistorical kind of history. Life goes on; the old and the young fall in love; there are pregnancies and losses and death. This is the sort of history, or story, that is repeated in the reminiscences of grandparents, or in memoirs (in the case of families, unlike the Allemands and the Ferrands, with letters and diaries saved for posterity), or in the genealogies of family history.

It is apart from the political course of events, and from the revolutionary history of the 1790s; it belongs, if at all, to the historical time of vast human conditions, of fertility, nuptiality, and mortality, changing almost unseen over the generations of human existence.

But the "nuptiality" of the family—their marriages over the revolutionary period—is also, as will be seen, a history of modern times. For it is a story of transformation in all the conditions of social life: of transgression, exogamy, social mobility, and mobility across France, Europe, and the Americas. It is a history, like the larger political history of Angoulême, of change in religious institutions and change in the organization of war.

Of Marie Aymard's twenty-three grandchildren, at least twenty survived infancy. Twenty-two of them were born in Angoulême between 1764 and 1781—the exception was Jean-Baptiste and Elizabeth's youngest child, born in 1796, nine months after his parents were admitted to emergency relief as refugees from Saint-Domingue—and they were not particularly nuptial, or disposed to marriage.[50] They belonged to the generation for whom the revolutionary and wartime years of mass mobilization were unpropitious for romance, as they had been for the heroine of another of Balzac's novels of provincial life, *La vieille fille*.[51] Only three out of Marie Aymard's eight surviving granddaughters were married, and seven out of her twelve grandsons. Their marriages, as it turned out, were seriously unprovincial.

Martial's First Marriage

The first of Marie Aymard's grandchildren to marry, and the only one who married in her lifetime, was Martial Allemand Lavigerie, the clerk in the tax office. The marriage took place in April 1790 in the parish church of St. André, just across the street from the convent of the Tiercelettes, which the nuns had been "invited" to leave in January; Marie Aymard died less than two weeks later.[52] Martial was twenty-two, and his bride, Louise Vaslin, the daughter of an apothecary in the town, and granddaughter of a wigmaker, was twenty.[53] It was an endogamous marriage within the social space of Angoulême, the last such marriage in the extended family of the Allemands and the Ferrands. Like his parents, and his uncles and aunts, Martial married someone who lived around the corner, in the center of the old town.[54] Louise's mother lived on the Rue de Genève, and her grandmother in the Isle des Tiercelettes; her grandfather was the godfather of Louis Deschamps, the wigmaker from Angoulême who died in the expedition to Cayenne, and the uncle by marriage of Marie Aymard's daughter-in-law, Elizabeth Boutoute.[55]

It was an advantageous marriage, within the economic world of the small trades of Angoulême. Louise had an elaborate array of expectations as described in the marriage contract (which was signed by sixty-seven people, including five of Martial's sisters and brothers, and his employer, the receiver of the *taille*). She owned a share in the value of her paternal grandparents' house in the parish of St. Jacques; half of her mother's furniture; a sixth of her grandmother's furniture; a quarter of a house in the Rue de Genève; a share of the contents of the house (after deducting the cost of the wine consumed); and a share in the value of her late father's commerce as an apothecary, as agreed with her sister and brother-in-law. There were allusions, in the contract, to the "adjudication" of her grandparents' trade, the marriage contract of her sister and brother-in-law, a notarized agreement about her mother's furniture, and the inventory of her late father's household.[56]

Martial's own expectations were very different. He had a promising position, even in the last months of the fiscal system of the old regime. But his expectation of capital was limited. The source was two unmarried sisters in their sixties, both signatories of the marriage contract of his parents, in 1764: "Jeanne and Marguerite Faure, seamstresses," his first cousins once removed. The sisters signed Martial's marriage contract next to Louise's mother, and declared that on the basis of the "friendship" they bore to the bridegroom, they would each give him 500 livres; to be paid following the death of the surviving sister. The promises of his parents, Françoise Ferrand and Etienne Allemand Lavigerie, were less substantial; they expected to provide a gift of 400 livres as part of their eventual estates, and they also, in this spring of the French Revolution, promised "equality with his other brothers and sisters in their future succession." [57] Martial was entitled, in prospect, to a capital of

1,400 livres, of which 1,000 livres was to come from his cousins; and Louise to "different sums and objects," amounting in value to 9,885 livres.[58]

The Ex-curé of St. Martial

The next of the marriages of Marie Aymard's grandchildren took place four years later, in a transformed social universe. The bridegroom was Etienne Ferrand, the ex-vicar of Jauldes and ex-curé of St. Martial. He was married in Angoulême in June 1794, as the revolutionary Terror eddied toward destruction, to one of his former parishioners, Marie Chausse Lunesse. She was twenty-nine, and lived with her family in the suburban part of the parish of St. Martial.[59] The ceremony followed the procedures of republican marriage—Etienne and Marie "declared aloud that they mutually took each other as spouses"—and there was no one there from the bridegroom's family, or at least no one who signed the register. Three of the bride's sisters signed the register. Etienne was accompanied by one of the other priests from St. Martial, who had himself married earlier in the year, and by a figure of the revolutionary administration of the times, described as a "member of the committee of surveillance."[60]

Etienne's marriage was exogamous as well as transgressive. His new father-in-law described himself in 1790, in the record of the marriage of Marie's sister Françoise, as "counselor of the king, judge, magistrate."[61] In the record of the marriage of Etienne and Marie, he was described as an "agriculteur" or farmer (a denomination widely used at the time by the bourgeoisie of Angoulême). By marrying into the family of the "Chausse de Lunesse," Etienne had married into the privileged classes of Angoulême, on the insecure frontier between the impecunious nobility and the landed bourgeoisie.[62]

A little more than a year after his marriage, Etienne became the owner, or the ostensible owner, of part of a large estate, the domain of Courances, in Marsac to the north of Angoulême. This was the property of his wife's family, or at least the portion of the property that belonged to her brothers, who had been designated as émigrés. Etienne bought the estate for the large sum of 445,000 livres in September 1795, and completed the purchase, in assignats, by December of the same year. There is no evidence that he lived there; he was described in the register of *biens nationaux* as "Ferrand fils, ci-devant curé of St. Martial."[63]

Etienne's new brothers-in-law, meanwhile, were wandering around the French countryside, as they recounted later. Jean Chausse Lunesse, like Rose Marin, had an extensive police dossier, in connection with his efforts (which were unsuccessful) to be removed from the "accursed list" of émigrés. He was a gentle, modest, and peace-loving person, various citizens of Angoulême testified on his behalf in the year 9; and "having no fortune, or prospect," he established himself in a "small commerce." He produced a certificate of residence in Fontenay, to the east of Paris, from 1792 to 1797; he had business interests in Frankfurt and Hamburg; he and his brother (also called Jean Chausse Lunesse) had left the Charente "to seek instruction in the great commercial towns," he recounted, where the "difficulties they experienced in finding employment" led them to become peddlers, "carrying merchandise from one place to another, in order to subsist."[64]

Etienne had married, too, into the extended family of the colonial military administration. Another new brother-in-law, Joseph Martin de Bourgon, who had married Françoise Chausse Lunesse in 1790, was a "former major in the regiment of Martinique," and a chevalier of the order of St. Louis (a military or quasi-military decoration much prized in the French colonies).[65] The family of the Martin de Bourgon were among the old nobility of the central parishes of Angoulême; Joseph's parents had been the godparents, in 1775, of François Martin Aliquain, the twelve-year-old boy from "laguinne en affrique" who abjured paganism at the door of the parish church of St. Jean.[66] Joseph's brother, Jacques Martin de Bourgon, was the proprietor of a sugar plantation in Guadeloupe, and military governor of Cayenne in 1789–1791, in which capacity he presided over an insurrection of the army, succeeded (in his own account) in preventing a slave insurrection, was depicted in a monumental bust in the public gardens, quarreled with the colonial assembly, and was obliged, "in order to suspend the progress of evil," to commission "excessively complicated writings," for which he sought reimbursement from the revolutionary government in Paris.[67]

The marriage of Françoise Chausse Lunesse and Joseph Martin de Bourgon, Etienne's new in-laws, was itself a history of changing times. Not long before the revolution, in October 1787, an infant was baptized with the name "Jacques de Bourgon," in the parish church of St. Paul. He was described as the son of Françoise Chausse and of Joseph Martin de Bourgon, "declared to be the father by sentence of the jurisdiction of the presidial sénéchaussée of the Angoumois"; in the words of the parish register, "the sentence in question is said to have been appealed."[68] Two years later, in January 1790, Françoise and Joseph were married in what was soon to be Etienne Ferrand's own parish church of St. Martial; they declared that "the child baptized in October 1787" was their own, "made and created by them," and that "they have recognized him today as their legitimate child."[69] Françoise and Joseph then lived happily ever after, or at least had five more children. All their sons, Etienne Ferrand's nephews by marriage, became military officers; Jacques de Bourgon was a naval officer, his younger brother was a general, serving in North Africa, and his youngest brother, also a general, died in Paris in the military assault on the 1848 revolution.[70]

A Romance in the Sarthe

The third of Marie Aymard's grandchildren to be married was Etienne Ferrand's first cousin, Pierre Allemand Lavigerie, and here the scene shifts 350 kilometers to the north, to the new Department of the Sarthe. Pierre was the son about whom Etienne Allemand had written so plaintively to the minister of war, in the affair of the missing uniform and the misdirected trunk, and he was married on February 1, 1796, in the little commune of Sillé-le-Guillaume, to the north of Le Mans.[71] He had joined the revolutionary army as a volunteer, and in 1796 was a captain in the first battalion of the Chasseurs of the Charente, stationed at the time, in the vast movement of troops toward the Atlantic provinces, in Sillé-le-Guillaume. At some point in the previous year, Pierre had met a young woman called Adelaide Charlotte Maslin, the daughter of a retired notary and tax collector. Charlotte's parents were enthusiasts of the new times, and their son, born in 1794, was named "Décadi Montagnard Maslin."[72] Her mother was in correspondence with Etienne's father (or so Etienne informed the minister of war); she assured him that his son, whose education she greatly admired, was to her as one of her own children.[73]

The marriage ceremony, so far from home, was a microcosm of Angoulême at war. There were twenty-five signatories of the register, of whom five were relatives of the bride, and at least nine were soldiers in Pierre's battalion of the regiment of the Charente. They included B. G. Nouel, from the extended family of the Nouels and the Klotzes, pastry-makers and cabalists of Angoulême, identified as the quartermaster of the battalion; a young printer, the nephew of one of the signatories of Pierre's parents' marriage contract in 1764; a paper manufacturer, Pierre Auguste Henry, the nephew of the new owner of the seminary, and the merchant to whose warehouse the church bell of St. André was carted in 1795.[74] The essential document in the ceremony was a power of attorney to the commanding officer of the battalion, drawn up in Angoulême by Françoise and Etienne, and giving their permission for the marriage; the officer was the same local dignitary, then a "member of the committee of surveillance," who had been the witness, two years before, in the transgressive marriage of Pierre's first cousin, the former priest Etienne Ferrand.[75]

The Sands of War

Marie Aymard's oldest grandchild—Gabriel Ferrand (the younger), born in November 1764—was listed in a register prepared for the national guard in Angoulême in 1790 as a former watchmaker, and received a certificate of civism in the town in 1793, as a "captain of grenadiers."[76] He too, like his cousin Pierre Allemand Lavigerie, was among the volunteers who had been sent from the Charente toward the successive civil wars in the Vendée. In 1796, he was living in the small Atlantic port of Les Sables d'Olonne, the scene of "horrible butchery," in the description of one of the commissioners of the revolutionary army, and the garrison town of the troops from Angoulême.[77] Les Sables was a town of some two thousand households that became a site of slaughter.[78] Even the civil registers of the town are a narrative of destruction: an "alphabetical table of burials and deaths," which is transposed, in the revolutionary years, into page upon page of destruction, divided into categories for the population of the town and for "military and refugees." The names of the massacred are "indicated by an x."[79]

Gabriel Ferrand was married in Les Sables d'Olonne, on May 14, 1796, to a local woman, Florence Scholastique Borgnet, from a family of pulley-makers and blacksmiths.[80] He was described as a watchmaker who had been living there for more than six months, and he and his family remained in Les Sables for several more years, living on the Rue de la République (in this newly patriotic town, with its Rue du Peuple, Rue de l'Humanité, and Rue de la Révolution).[81] He then moved far inland, to Beaugency in the Loiret, near Orléans, and died there in 1816, at the age of fifty-two.[82] His daughter, Stéphanie Ferrand, kept a wine merchant's shop—eventually the subject of a spectacular bankruptcy in 1871—on a street of dubious renown in the ninth arrondissement of Paris. She was the connection, in the end, between the family in Angoulême and the literary and artistic demimonde of the Second Empire.

Martial's Divorce and Second Marriage

The next occasion in the nuptial history of Marie Aymard's grandchildren was not a marriage but a divorce: the dissolution of the union of Martial Allemand Lavigerie and Louise Vaslin, by mutual consent, in October 1796.[83] The institution of divorce had come to Angoulême within a few weeks of Léonard Robin's peroration of September 1792 ("individual liberty can never be alienated in an indissoluble manner by any convention").[84] Martial and Louise were the fifty-fifth couple to seek a divorce in Angoulême, and the first to divorce "by mutual consent."[85] They had followed the requisite procedures—a meeting with family arbitrators, an "act of nonconciliation"—and the ceremony was uneventful. The presiding officer, as so often, was Louis Félix, born in Saint-Domingue, and son-in-law of two of the signatories of the marriage contract of 1764. Martial described himself as a merchant (a *négociant*). There were no members of his family among the witnesses, and only one relative of Louise's (her young cousin, a student in pharmacy). Martial and Louise had been married for six years, and had three young children; their youngest son, Léon-Philippe, was one year old.[86]

The next marriage in the family came almost five years later, and it was the most elaborate. Martial Allemand Lavigerie was married for the second time, on June 17, 1801, to a young woman from Saint-Domingue, who had made her way, after the death of her mother (in Saint-Domingue) and her father (in Philadelphia), to Bordeaux and then to Angoulême. Her name (although this was later a subject of dispute) was Marie Louise Bonnite Raymond Saint Germain.[87]

The ceremony, on this occasion, was full of contingency. Martial described himself, now, as a merchant's clerk, a *commis négociant*; Bonnite's late father was described as a "proprietor." She was twenty-five, and had been born in Saint-Domingue in January 1776. She had no record of her birth, as a refugee far from home, or of her parents' deaths; all she could provide was an "act of notoriety," signed in Bordeaux in 1797, by "eight citizens" who had known her parents in Jérémie, in the west of the colony. Martial's mother signed the record of the marriage, and so did his oldest sister—"Lavigerie *ainée*," the prosperous sister with the shop—and his youngest brother, Antoine, the former clerk in the *bureau des émigrés*, now also described as a *commis négociant*. There were three witnesses: a notary; the paper manufacturer from Angoulême, Pierre Auguste Henry, who had signed the record of Pierre Allemand Lavigerie's marriage in Sillé-le-Guillaume, five years before; and a newcomer with a romantic signature, "Laurent Silvestre Topin, professor of design at the Ecole Centrale of the Department of the Charente."[88]

In 1801, as in the marriage of Martial's own parents in 1764, Martial and Bonnite had signed a prenuptial contract, a few days before the wedding. It was a sentimental document. The couple constituted a community of goods, present and future, "whatever might be the statutes or the customary law of the countries in which they might live." There were

elaborate procedures in respect of mortgages to come, and of children
yet to be born, including in the event of their deaths in the lifetime of
their father. Bonnite described her hopes and fears:

> Wishing at this time to demonstrate her attachment to her future
> husband, in a certain and absolutely irrevocable manner, and foresee-
> ing the case in which he might survive her, without there being any
> children of their union, [she] declares that she is giving him—and he
> formally accepts, with gratitude—the universality of the goods and
> rights, movable and immovable, credits, fruits, revenues, gold, silver,
> effects, and other things generally whatsoever, of which her inheri-
> tance might be composed, to possess them, search for them and re-
> cover them, enjoy them, use them and dispose of them as his own
> property, as the donee will judge suitable, as soon as the death of the
> donor has come about.[89]

There was another missing fortune, that is to say, and another possible inheritance of rights and slaves, thirty-six years after Bonnite's new
mother-in-law had described her own future rights, in her own marriage contract: "in whatever they might consist, and wherever they
might be found." Martial's parents, Etienne Allemand and Françoise
Ferrand, signed on the last page of the document, and so did his uncle
and aunt, Gabriel and Marie Adelaide; seven of his sisters signed the
contract, and two of his brothers; his cousin Gabriel was there, with his
bride from Les Sables d'Olonne ("Borgnet femme Ferrand"); there was
also "Marchais Delaberge," one of the richest men in Angoulême, the
landlord of Etienne' sisters, and the grandson of the signatory of the
contract of December 1764.[90]

Bonnite Raymond Saint Germain was about four months pregnant
when she signed the marriage contract, and her dismal forebodings
were not borne out. Their first child was born in Angoulême in December 1801, and they, too, lived happily ever after (or for some years to
come).[91] By 1803, the family had moved to the Atlantic port of Bayonne, where they had five more children. Martial, who had been successively, over the revolutionary period, a *commis à la recette des tailles*,
a *caissier à la recette du district*, a *marchand*, a *négotiant*, and a *commis*

négotiant, was now, once more, a public official: "receiver of the lottery of Bayonne."[92]

An Obscure Proprietor

The first of Marie Aymard's granddaughters to be married was Françoise Ferrand, the daughter of Jean-Baptiste Ferrand and Elizabeth Boutoute, who was born in Angoulême in 1777. She emigrated with her parents as an infant, and returned in 1795; in September 1798, she received a certificate of indigence in Angoulême as a refugee from Saint-Domingue.[93] By 1800, she was in Paris, where she married a man named Joseph Brébion. He was a soldier: a "chef d'escadron," or squadron leader. In 1804, she was in New York, where her daughter Clara Brébion was born.[94] By 1814, Françoise was a widow, living in Paris with three young children. She was in a condition of "distress," according to a statement by the mayor of the (old) seventh arrondissement, with no property in France, no employment, and no means of supporting herself "by her own industry."[95]

Françoise, like her father, applied to the Ministry of the Navy and Colonies to be recognized as a "proprietor in Saint-Domingue, a refugee in France." Her petition was sent on to the "committee of notable colonists," established to evaluate the claims of refugees to have owned land or slaves in the island, who determined that she was indeed a proprietor. She was admitted to the "first class of assistance," in August 1814.[96] She received a pension every year for the next forty-five years, until her death in 1860; and for a time after her death, as well, although that is part of the nineteenth-century history of the Allemands and the Ferrands.[97]

The marriage of Françoise and Joseph is in other respects a mystery. It is possible that Joseph Brébion was himself a proprietor in Saint-Domingue; Jean-Baptiste Ferrand, Françoise's father, tried repeatedly, without success, to be recognized as a proprietor by the committee of notables. Joseph was in the armed forces, he owned property, and he had children and grandchildren: three of the conditions that make it relatively likely that individuals can be found, somewhere, in the immense records of family history. But he died in wartime, and the records of existence in Saint-Domingue were (in the description of one of the many officials who sought to reform the arbitrary system of relief to refugees) vanishingly scarce: "The excess of disorders, the pillage, the massacres, and the fires have led to the disappearance in the colony of everything that could serve to provide an acknowledgment of [property] values," of births, marriages, and deaths, and of the "recognition" of individual existence.[98]

A Woman of "Great Art and Address"

The universal war of the 1790s and 1800s was the setting for Françoise Ferrand's marriage to the soldier from Saint-Domingue, and for the marriages of her cousins Pierre, in the Sarthe, and Gabriel, in the Vendée. The military history of her cousin Pierre Alexandre Ferrand was far more painful. Pierre Alexandre was the youngest of Gabriel Ferrand and Marie Adelaide Devuailly's six sons, and he too was married in the midst of wartime dislocation, and in even more obscure circumstances. He appeared in the registers of Angoulême on three occasions: when he was baptized in 1775, when his wife died in 1839, and when he himself died in 1841.[99] His life, in the intervening years, was a sequence of misfortunes, one more awful than the next.

Pierre Alexandre received a certificate of civism in Angoulême in 1793.[100] At some point before then, according to a biographical dictionary of the Napoleonic armies, he had joined the Eleventh Reserve Battalion of the Regiment of the Charente. He was made sergeant major in September 1792, and captain in 1794. He fought in the Army of the North, and then in the Army of Italy. During the passage of the Mincio, in 1800—the ferocious battle in Bonaparte's second Italian campaign, on Christmas Day 1800, when French troops crossed the river Mincio and opened the way to Venice—he "was wounded by a shot to the upper jaw." He was no longer "able to masticate," and left the army as an invalid.[101]

By 1810, Pierre Alexandre had returned to Angoulême, where he settled "with an Italian woman whom he had married in Venice." He had very little money, and he lived on the outskirts of the town; he "fell into dementia because of the wound to his head." In 1831, he was "considered to be an 'alienated' officer."[102] Pierre Alexandre Ferrand died in Angoulême in December 1841, at the age of 66.[103]

Pierre Alexandre's wife was called "Auguste Siva de Villeneuve Solard," and she died in Angoulême in 1839. She was described only as a "native of Venice," "aged around sixty-five."[104] She was also the almost namesake of a picaresque figure of the 1780s: "Clara Sophia Augusta de Ceve de Villeneuve Solar," who had sued an itinerant English baronet, in London in 1787, for breach of a contract entered into in the "Hotel of Europe" in Marseille in September 1784. Auguste or Augusta testified that she was a native of Naples, the widow of a count from the kingdom of Sardinia, and had given the Englishman seventy-five thousand livres in exchange for an annuity. The itinerant baronet responded, in a statement sworn in St. Petersburg, that she was a "courtesan" with whom he had been "intimately acquainted" in Paris. She was a woman of "great art and address," in his description, and he had entered into a sham transaction in order to help her to return to her husband and "several children" in a town called "Oneille" (Oneglia), on "the seacoast between Marseille and Genoa."[105] If "Auguste Siva de Villeneuve Solard" were "Augusta de Ceve de Villeneuve Solar," she would have been in her seventies when she died in Angoulême in 1838—an elderly lady, far from Naples.

An Artist in Angoulême

The only one of Marie Aymard's granddaughters to be married in Angoulême was Jeanne Allemand Lavigerie, known as Mariette, and the sixth of Etienne and Françoise's nine daughters. She was married in July 1801, and her husband was the newcomer with the romantic signature, Laurent Silvestre Topin. Silvestre had arrived in Angoulême in 1796. In 1792, he was an architecture student in Paris, who won a competition—implausibly enough, in the revolutionary summer of the fall of the monarchy—to design a "mansion for a rich private individual."[106] He was taken on as a pupil by the architect David Le Roi, celebrated for his project of a "naupotame," a boat designed to navigate rivers and seas. He then moved, when the Royal Academy of Architecture was closed in 1793, to the patronage of the great painter of the revolu-

tion, Jacques Louis David. Silvestre's drawing of the elevation of a
"house of education" was exhibited in the architecture section of the
Salon of 1795.[107]

Silvestre Topin applied in 1796 for the new position of "professor of
design," in the newly created Ecole Centrale of the Charente, the secular
replacement for the Jesuit college in which Etienne Allemand had la-
bored for so long and so unhappily. He was elected to the chair at the
age of twenty-five, having submitted a "plan of a façade with columns,"
a "geometrical plan of an edifice," and the sketch of an academy in "black
pencil." His classes started later that year, and he was formally confirmed
in his post in 1797.[108] The course in design was an immediate success,
with an enrollment of more than half of all the students in the college.
Silvestre assembled a collection of 545 drawings for the college, and
hoped to "inspire a taste for art in the workers"; his students produced
drawings of a port and a stock exchange, and copied the paintings of
Greuze and Vanloo.[109]

In the summer of 1798, Silvestre's destiny changed once more. As the
armies of the revolution traversed Italy, he was appointed as an official
cartographer to the military. "General Leclerc, charged with drawing up
the map of the campaigns of the army in Italy, has a pressing need for
citizen Silvestre Topin, professor of design in your Ecole Centrale, to
participate in this important work," the minister of the interior wrote to
the administrators of the Department of the Charente in June 1798, and
Silvestre set off for Italy.[110] His adventure across the Alps lasted for a
little over a year—he fulfilled the "functions of a geographer," as well
as designing battle plans—and in the summer of 1799, he was back in
Angoulême, with a decree exempting him, as a matter of "absolute leave,"
from any future military service. Silvestre was by now a cartographer
with important friends. When the administrators of the department delayed his return to his professorship, on the grounds that he might be
called upon, again, for military duties, they received letters, within a few
days, from the minister of war and the minister of the interior: Silvestre
Topin "cannot be troubled [inquiété] to rejoin the armies."[111]

The course in design, on Silvestre's return, was an even greater success. He wrote from Lyon, on his way back, that "I am bringing with me

from Italy precious engravings," "made to inspire young people in the art of design."[112] He was particularly engaged in the choice of prizes to be awarded to deserving students: "the seven sacraments of Poussin," as first prize for figurative drawing in the autumn of 1799, and "antique fragments," as first prize for "ornamentation."[113] The Ecole Centrale was established, now, in the former Abbey of Beaulieu. There were new accoutrements, in the flux of things that was so familiar in Angoulême in the revolutionary period: a botanical garden, elaborate carpentry, and an ornamental iron grille, transported to the new Ecole from the convent of the (former) Tiercelettes, on the Place du Mûrier. The courses in design were taught in a large, sun-filled room, the laundry of the former Benedictines.[114]

Silvestre and Jeanne Allemand Lavigerie were married in Angoulême in 1801. It was a modest occasion, by the standards of the family ceremonies of the times; Jeanne's mother, Françoise Ferrand, did not sign the register, and neither did any of her sisters (six of whom had signed the marriage contract of Martial and Bonnite, only a few weeks before). Her father, Etienne, and her brothers Martial and Antoine Lavigerie were witnesses, together with Pierre Auguste Henry, the faithful paper manufacturer; and the head of the Department of Public Instruction, a former priest, printer of revolutionary decrees, and one of the many possible heirs in the dispute of the 1760s over the hatmaker's son and the estate in Martinique.[115]

Silvestre was described in the record of the marriage as the son of the late Nicolas Topin and of Marie Catherine Lacorne, of Paris, and it was his mother, even more than his military patrons, who was his connection—and the unlikely connection, in turn, of the Allemands and the Ferrands—to the high political history of the French Revolution. Nicolas Topin had been a "painter to the king": in particular, a painter of gilded chairs and trompe l'oeil marble. He was also an inventor, with a "secret" method for producing lightweight military helmets.[116] Marie Catherine Lacorne was a geography teacher, and the daughter of a dancing master (to the pages of a cousin of the king). She was a liberal figure, and she was selected, early in the revolution, to be the "undergoverness" to one of the last royal princesses in France:

Louise-Eugénie-Adelaide, daughter of the revolutionary duke "Philippe Egalité," or Philippe d'Orléans, and sister of the future king Louis Philippe. She lived with the Orléans family in the Palais Royal (the "Maison Egalité").[117]

"Madame Topin" had the serious misfortune, in March 1793, of being sent by the duc d'Orléans to Tournay in Belgium, where his daughter was living in exile, to pay her bills, and bring her back, if necessary, to France. When she arrived, Silvestre's mother found herself in the midst of a military invasion and a political counterrevolution. There was her pupil, now sixteen; the princess's nineteen-year-old brother, the future king; a much grander governess, the novelist Madame de Genlis; and the military hero of the first months of the revolutionary war, and subsequent enemy of the revolution, General Dumouriez.

In the course of "heated" political conversations, as she recounted on her return, Madame Topin "noticed that [the young prince] was shaken," and determined "to warn him about Dumouriez's scheme to entice him into the [counterrevolutionary] party, and thereby to destroy him"; she also hoped to "find a way out of the trap" for the young princess. But one evening a "large number of hussars" arrived and took the princess away, together with Madame de Genlis. Madame Topin returned to Paris, and at once, as a matter of "duty" and "civisme," made her way to a police station. She recounted the events of her Belgian adventure, described the subversive conversations, and reported that she had heard the young prince, in quiet moments, "singing that which is sung at mass and at vespers."[118] Her evidence was published as a pamphlet by the Imprimerie du républicain, in April 1793, and Philippe Egalité was guillotined in November 1793; Madame Lacorne Topin was an emblem, thereafter, of the perfidy of the revolution.[119]

This is the political history from which Silvestre escaped, to the provincial tranquillity of Angoulême. His relationships with his new family were cordial. Jeanne, like her sister-in-law Bonnite, was pregnant when she married in July 1801. Her first child was born in October 1801; her mother, Françoise Ferrand, was now the principal witness. She and Silvestre had another daughter, Françoise Méloé, in January 1803, and a son in August 1804; the witness of their son's birth record was the former surgeon on the island of St. Vincent.[120] But the idyll of the Ecole Centrale of Angoulême, and of the courses in figurative drawing in the laundry of the former convent, had by then come to an end. The new secular colleges, with their departmental autonomy and their revolutionary reputation, were abolished in the Napoleonic educational reforms of 1802; courses ended in Angoulême in September 1804.[121]

Silvestre and Jeanne returned to Paris, where they had two more children, born in 1807 and 1813.[122] Marie Catherine Lacorne Topin, Silvestre's mother, was also in Paris, where she died in 1810. She was living in retirement, in a room on the third floor of the lodgings for artists in the Musée des Artistes, on the Rue de Sorbonne. Her estate, valued at forty-eight francs, was declared by one of the other residents, who had also been a teacher of the painting of historical tableaux for the former royal children; she was said to have "no known heirs."[123]

In the Pyrénées

The twelfth of Françoise Ferrand's thirteen children, Etienne, was a child when the French Revolution began. He signed the record of his brother's (first) marriage in 1790, at the age of nine.[124] At some point during the revolutionary years, he became a goldsmith. In 1806, he was in Pau, more than three hundred kilometers to the south of Angoulême, near the Spanish frontier. On January 1, 1807, he was married there to a fifteen-year-old girl, Marie Montesquieu, whose mother was a grocer in the town.[125] Three years later, in 1810, Etienne was living in the port city of Bayonne, one hundred kilometers to the west.[126] Marie Montesquieu died in Pau in 1837.[127]

Etienne was alive when Marie died; they had no children (or none that were born in Pau or Bayonne, or that I have been able to find, so far, in the continuously changing websites of family history). Marie Aymard's grandchildren had unequal destinies, and there is a blatant inequality of information, too, about their marriages and their lives. There are none of the twenty-three of whom there are letters that survive (or, again, that I have so far been able to find); only one of the grandchildren, Martial Allemand Lavigerie, ever appeared, fleetingly, in a newspaper. But even the records of civil registration are unequally accessible, and all the more so for those, like Etienne, whose early lives were shaped by the migration and mobility of the revolutionary period. At least twenty of the grandchildren survived infancy; of these there are two—both of them boys—of whom there is almost no history.[128]

A Pension in Bayonne

The last of Marie Aymard's granddaughters to be married, over the course of the long French Revolution, was Joséphine Lavigerie, the eighth of the nine daughters of Françoise Ferrand and Etienne Allemand. She was born in Angoulême in 1779 and was christened "Josephe"; her godmother was the widow of a plantation owner in Saint-Domingue. Like many young women in the early years of the nineteenth century, she was later known, like Napoléon's first empress, as "Joséphine."[129]

At some point between 1803 and 1807, Joséphine moved to Bayonne, to join her older brother, Martial, and his new family. In September 1807, she was married to Joseph Alexandre César Ponsard, a teacher from Marseille. She was described as living with her brother, the "director of the imperial lottery." The witnesses to the marriage were from the administrative milieu of wartime Bayonne: a colonel, a merchant, the "principal controller of duties," the "paymaster of the imperial navy." Joséphine and Alexandre's son was born in April 1809, and by then another of her brothers had arrived in Bayonne; the two witnesses to the registration of the birth were Martial Allemand Lavigerie and Pierre Allemand Lavigerie, who had left the army, become an employee of the Department of the Sarthe, and was identified, now, as an "employee in the Treasury."[130]

Joséphine had returned, far from Angoulême, to the way of life of her father and her uncle. Her husband, described as an "instituteur," was a witness, in 1810, of the birth of Martial and Bonnite's daughter Charlotte Ursule; the other witness was Pierre Allemand Lavigerie, by now "adjunct to the paymaster of war."[131] Alexandre Ponsard became a "maître de pension," like his father-in-law and his wife's uncle, and a "member of the university"; he was the witness, in October 1824, of the marriage of Léon Philippe Allemand Lavigerie, the youngest child of Martial and his first wife, Louise Vaslin, born in Angoulême in 1795, and "receiver of declarations in the royal customs office of Bayonne."[132] Joséphine, unlike her brother, never returned to Angoulême. Her husband died in 1847 in their home in the old center of Bayonne, and she died there in 1855, at the age of seventy-five.[133]

The Last Grandchild

Marie Aymard's youngest grandchild, Jean-Baptiste Ferrand, who was born after his parents returned as refugees from Saint-Domingue, was a soldier at the very end of the revolutionary-Napoleonic wars. He was conscripted into the infantry of the Imperial Guard in February 1814, was a lancer in the French campaign, and was discharged five months later, in July 1814. He is the only one of the grandchildren of whom there is a description, of sorts. It is from his military record: one meter seventy-three centimeters, a long oval face, brown eyes, a small mouth, dark chestnut hair.[134]

Jean-Baptiste Ferrand was a painter. He was married to or lived with a woman called Elisa Collet, and they had a daughter, Rose Calista Ferrand, who was born in Paris in 1833; Elisa Collet died in Paris in 1836. Jean-Baptiste married again in 1839, to a merchant and lemonade seller, Anne Thiriot. They lived in the small town of Montereau, a river port like Angoulême, at the confluence of the Seine and the Yonne, and a manufacturing center for painted and printed porcelain. He was forty-three, and described himself as a widower. His parents had died in Paris a few years earlier, he recounted to the registrar of marriages; he was unable to recall the date or place of his grandparents' deaths. Anne Thiriot, too, was a widow; Jean Baptiste was described as an artist and painter.[135] He was still in Montereau twenty-five years later, and still an artist; he became a widower, again, in 1861.[136] Jean-Baptiste Ferrand died in the aftermath of the Franco-Prussian War, in 1873, in the home of his son-in-law, Rose Calista's husband, a tinsmith in the town of Vimoutiers in Normandy.[137]

A Family Revolution

These have been the events of ordinary life, in the extended network of Marie Aymard's grandchildren; the circumstances of love and friendship and death. But the story of the Allemands and the Ferrands is also a history of the French Revolution. It is a story of what really happened, in revolutionary times, and a history of endless change.

The Allemands and the Ferrands were a revolutionary family, in a capacious sense. Two of Marie Aymard's children, her son-in-law, and two of her grandsons were employed by the new, revolutionary administration in Angoulême; another grandson worked for the Department of the Sarthe; six of her grandsons (and grandsons-in-law) served in the revolutionary-Napoleonic armed forces, and two were officials of the imperial government; one was an ex-priest.[138] Etienne and Françoise lived in the *bien national* that Etienne had bought in 1791, the property of the former cathedral chapter.[139] Gabriel owned a three-year lease of the church of the Tiercelettes, and his son was the owner (or ostensible owner) of the *bien national* of his wife's brothers.

The social networks of the grandchildren, as recorded in the registers of their marriages, were full of the friends of revolutionary change: a "municipal revolutionary officer," a member of the "committee of surveillance," the new father-in-law in the Sarthe with the son called Décadi, the paper manufacturer and revolutionary Pierre Auguste Henry.[140] Even the individuals in the larger network of the marriage contract of 1764—the eighty-three and their connections—lived in equanimity with the changes of the times. There were no émigrés, among the network of the eighty-three, or refractory priests, or enemies of the revolution; there were the three local revolutionaries, Louis Félix, Marguerite Aubert, and Lecler-Raby.

There is no one, in the history so far, of whose political sentiments there is any record, or any evidence (with the exception of the itinerant Rose Marin). Only Léonard Robin, the legislator, and Marie Madeleine Virol, the counterrevolutionary, who have been minor figures in the story that started with Marie Aymard, were in any way important in the course of revolutionary events, or the sort of individuals who could have been included in a history of the revolution as biography or proso-pography. Marie Madeleine Virol was a subject of the cursory inquiry into causes that was characteristic of the revolutionary tribunals of 1794: an investigation of why was it that she, as a daughter of the working classes, should have become a counterrevolutionary. Léonard Robin described his own journey of revolutionary discovery in indulgent de-tail; he had feared earlier, he wrote, that he was incapable of speaking without preparation, and "I have just experienced the opposite, a thou-sand times."[141]

The history of the Allemands and the Ferrands is even less a political history in the sense of the largest question of revolutionary history, or of why the revolution happened. It is a history from below, and its sources, for the most part, have been the traditional sources of social history. They are sources about economic life, in the sense of the records of employment, taxes, and property, over the twenty-five years of the "first French revolution," from 1764 to 1789, and the ensuing twenty-five years of revolutionary transformation. These are the sorts of sources that are well-suited, in principle, to the inquiries of a large-scale history in which "factors pile up on top of each other," and political events are the outcome of "forces long established and beyond [political] con-trol."[142] But the history that started with Marie Aymard has turned out to be a story of individual lives—almost the opposite sort of history.

It has been impossible, in the end, to fit the individuals in the story—people with names and addresses and prenuptial contracts—into a his-tory of forces and factors. The evidence of their lives has been too abun-dant; it is as though they are by now too familiar. It is uncomfortable to think of one's own life as being subsumed within a "force"—to intro-spect about the influence of changes in prices, for example, or of the rise of nationalism, on the collective sentiments of which one's own political ideas are a part—and the exercise is uncomfortable in respect of other people as well. This is not even a question of the scale of the historical investigation, in that an inquiry into individual lives can be as small or as large as the endurance of the (exhausted) historians involved. It is reasonably easy to imagine that the history of a few hundred or thou-sand individuals in Angoulême could be extended (assuming limitless resources) to the neighboring countryside, to contiguous provinces, and to the whole of France. But to do so would not help. The vast history would still be a story of individuals, and the sort of history that is not a history of causes.

This has been a history, all the same, of the great events of modern times. The promise of a history by contiguity, in which the story proceeds from an individual, or a family, to the friends and relations to whom they were connected, and to the places in which they lived, is that it can be a history, thereby, of the social spaces in which ideas and opinions were exchanged. There has been something of this in the history of the Allemands and the Ferrands over the course of the French Revolution. They were invisible in the historiography of the revolution. But they are there in the history from below, and in the archives—sometimes the most evanescent of archives, like the receipts that they signed, on little pieces of paper, for their stipends from the revolutionary administration—of ordinary economic life. They and their friends and neighbors are there, too, in the lists of leases and purchases of the *biens nationaux*. Their story is also the history of the economic life of the revolution.

The Social Economy

The Allemands and the Ferrands were figures of the first French revolution, to return to Tocqueville's causal history of the "social economy"; they were agitated, like the "people," by a "burning desire to change one's position."[143] Even the three of Marie Aymard's children who were alive in 1764, and who vanished from this history, because they are not to be found (or have so far not been found) in parish and civil records, sought change of a sort; they all abandoned Angoulême, and went somewhere else to die. The details of the family's social networks are Tocquevillian, too, in their evocation of exchanges of ideas, opinions, and influence.

Tocqueville's hypothesis about the origins of the French Revolution, in the 1850s, was both familiar and obscure. It was obvious in that it was a recapitulation of innumerable reminiscences in the aftermath of the political revolution of 1789, and of a generational effort—within the generation of Tocqueville's own grandparents, who were imprisoned in the Port-Libre with Léonard Robin—to see, or to remember, the deepest causes of the French Revolution in an antecedent change in "the condition and the sentiments" of large numbers of people. It was as though the revolution were too immense to have been no more than the outcome of political circumstance. There must have been an earlier "revolution of ideas," before the "revolution of laws": a time, still remembered or imagined, in which "industry was great, but disquiet was greater still," and "there was nothing constant except the perpetual change in everything."[144]

The hypothesis of antecedent change in sentiments was obscure, at the same time, because it was so difficult to see, or to look for. Tocqueville's journey into the tomb of the ancien régime was in part a search, as in the counterrevolutionary writings of the 1790s, for the influence of philosophical ideas, or of the "books that have made revolutions."[145] But it was also—in Tocqueville's own account—an investigation of the details of the administrative and financial history of the ancien régime.[146] It was a history, for Georges Lefebvre, of the "social influence of the economy," and of the "social consequences of economic change."[147] It was incomplete, in the sense that there was so little evidence of ideas and sentiments, or of the mechanisms of social influence by which ideas were exchanged. But there was a "constitution" of collective ways of thinking, in Lefebvre's description of 1934—of disquiet and burning desires—that was intermediate to, or "intercalated" between, the "conditions of economic, social, and political life," conceived of as causes, and political "events," conceived of as effects.[148]

The history of the Allemands and the Ferrands—which is itself intermediate in scale, between the micro and the vast—is a history of the social economy, in Tocqueville's sense, and it is also a history intercalated between (economic and social) conditions of life and (public or private) events. The children and grandchildren were economic individuals in the sense of buying and selling, borrowing and lending, calculating and advancing (or trying to advance) their own interests. They were industrious, and they were not, for the most part, figures in the modern industry of canals, manufactures, and commerce. The distinction between the market and the state, which has been so essential, since the time of Turgot's own writings about the credit crisis in Angoulême, to the definition of an "economy," was elusive, in their lives; so too was the distinction between the national and the international economy, in a provincial society of continuous exchanges of obligations and expectations between the colonies and home. The property of the family and their friends—their "capital"—was in the form of household goods (Marie Aymard's tin forks, and Gabriel Ferrand's many beds) and of the inherited entitlements that the reformers of the times considered to be so unrespectable, or so baroque.[149]

The economy of the church, the administration of taxes, and the overseas colonies, which was indistinctly political and economic, was the setting for the family's advancement, as it was for so many others within the social network of the signatories of the marriage contract. It was the scene of the multiple "affairs" that transfixed the town over the course of the 1760s, 1770s and 1780s, from the crisis over credit and the jurisprudence of usury, to the possible murder of the teenage abbé outside the walls of the seminary, and the affair of the clerk in the office of the collector of the *taille*. If the economic life of Angoulême was a place of information, expectations, and insecurity, then it was also, over the period of the early French Revolution, the milieu in which the revolution began.

"All centuries, more or less, have been and will be centuries of transition," in the description of the poet Giacomo Leopardi, in 1832, and all ages, more or less, are ages of agitation.[150] The decades preceding the French Revolution, in Angoulême, were agitated, above all, in relationships between political and economic interests. There were political (or social) consequences of economic change, and economic consequences of political change; there were events, or sequences of events, that were "conditions of life." These were changes in the exterior world, and changes in the interior world of ideas and sentiments: of ways of thinking that were collective, or shared, within the social spaces of the town.

Cutting Time in Two

It was an illusion of the French in 1789, in Tocqueville's account, to have sought to "cut in two their destiny," and to separate "by an abyss" what they were to become from what they once had been.[151] His largest venture, in *L'ancien régime et la révolution*, was to demonstrate the continuity of the institutions and sentiments of the old regime, in revolutionary and postrevolutionary France. The history of Angoulême, too, has been a history of continuity. Five of Françoise Ferrand's daughters lived in the same narrow streets in the old center of Angoulême over their entire lifetimes, from the 1760s to the 1860s. (Louise Mélanie was on a visit to her great-niece in the Sarthe when she died in 1865, but that is part of the nineteenth-century history.) "Our town" is going to profit greatly from the revolution, Léonard Robin predicted to his father in May 1788, and the economic life of Angoulême was filled, before, during, and after the revolution, with bureaux, clerks, and *commis*.[152] The small enterprises of the town continued to flourish, from the orders for military ornaments (red epaulettes and dolls in the form of grenadiers) to the iron grilles and candles ("pour la nassiont") in the once and future cathedral.[153]

But the revolution also changed almost everything for the Allemands and the Ferrands, and in this sense their lives were profoundly un-Tocquevillian. For it is in the ordinary course of life, in the end—in the "nuptiality" of the family—that the history of the Allemands and the Ferrands has been most evidently a history of revolution. It was the mobility of the revolutionary period, in space and social condition, that was the setting for all the family marriages. Only Martial's first marriage, to Louise, who lived around the corner, was in any way provincial. Three of Marie Aymard's grandsons married women they encountered far from home, as soldiers in the social transformation of the revolutionary armed forces; her granddaughter married a squadron leader from Saint-Domingue. Etienne Ferrand married his former parishioner, and Martial was divorced. Martial's second wife arrived in Angoulême from Saint-Domingue via Bordeaux and Philadelphia; Laurent Silvestre Topin came in search of employment as a professor of design, from Paris via the cartography of the Italian armies; Joséphine made her way to Bayonne to join her brother in his new career in the imperial administration, and met her husband, the teacher from Marseille.

The history of family life has been thought of as slow or natural or biological—as demographic. Economic life, too, has been seen as changing over the relatively stately pace of moving averages and statistical means.[154] In the family history of Marie Aymard's grandchildren, over the decades of the 1790s and the 1800s, everything was different. To see the events of the revolution in the records of births, marriages, and deaths (or from the "below" of the evidence of daily life) is to see rituals sliced through as though with a knife: in the parish register of St. Pierre, in November 1792; in the first divorce in Angoulême, recorded in the same register; and in the register of the parish of St. Martial, of which Etienne Ferrand was the priest in charge. It is also to see, in the nuptiality of the family, the transformation of space, time, and social condition.

The Revolution in the Place du Mûrier

Even for the five of Marie Aymard's granddaughters who never married, and who lived throughout the revolution in the same streets where their parents had grown up, clustered around the Place du Mûrier, the events of the revolution were a continuing spectacle, impossible not to see. This was the spatial network of the signatories of the marriage contract: the little universe of the streets in which so many bystanders saw the tall, blond servant of Silvie Cazaud absconding with the little dog of Lydia Sterne wriggling under his left arm. It was the site, too, of the imagined history of revolutionary Angoulême in *Les illusions perdues*; "the printing works was situated at the location where the Rue de Beaulieu meets the Place du Mûrier," and the old printer, in "the disastrous epoch of 1793," was awarded the contract, like the witness at Jeanne (Mariette) Allemand Lavigerie's marriage in 1801, to print the decrees of the revolutionary government.[155]

As one entered the Place du Mûrier, from the street where Etienne Allemand grew up, the house of Silvie Cazaud's brother was on the corner, according to the annotated property register of 1791; then there was the entrance to the convent of the Tiercelettes; the church that Gabriel Ferrand leased, in 1793; and then, at the beginning of the Rue de Beaulieu, the house of Léonard Robin's father, the printer Abraham-François Robin. On the south side of the square, there was the house of the apothecary whose mother, aunt, and sister had signed the marriage contract of 1764; then the house rented by Louis Félix; then the property of the cloth merchant Jean-Pierre David, whose daughter was married to another of the signatories, and in whose garden Marie Eustelle Billard died in 1795. As one left the square, in the direction of the childhood home of Françoise Ferrand, there was the property of Marchais Delaberge, occupied, at the time of the register, by the caterer, the hairdresser, and Marie Aymard's granddaughters, the "citizenesses Lavigerie."[156]

Revolutionary Terror was a spectacle in the neighborhood. There was the festival of sovereignty, on the square, with the professors of the college "cursing ancient slavery"; the census of horses, also on the square; the departure of conscripts to the frontiers; a riot in the year 4, on the anniversary of the fall of Robespierre, which led to the closing of the café of the "Citizeness Rezé"; and, a year later, the riot or "rixe" of the year 5.[157] The Place du Mûrier had been the scene of public executions in the ancien régime, and it was there, too, that the guillotine was brought in 1793. "The guillotine, as soon as it was put in place, cut off the evil at its root, and the very sight of it made them return to their duty," a representative of the revolutionary Convention reported from Angoulême, of the millers and bakers of the town; when they caught sight of the guillotine, "they became as amenable and as honest as it is possible for millers to be."[158]

The market in expropriated property was itself a spectacle. The inspection and the eventual auction of the property of the Tiercelettes on the Place du Mûrier—with the "facility" that it offered for "retail trade"—was a public event.[159] So were the journeys back and forth along the Rue de Beaulieu, carting the iron grilles and libraries and church ornaments of the old proprietors. The annotations, in the property register of 1791, are the record of transactions that involved furniture and movers and departures—changes, again, that were impossible not to see.[160] The house numbered 1000, on the south side of the square immediately next to the house of the cloth merchant David, was listed as the property of "the heirs of the late . . ." (so heavily crossed out as to be illegible), "the older Marchais, proprietor" (also crossed out), "occupied by the widow Rezé, merchant" (crossed out), "David, proprietor," and "Félix, tenant." This was the home of Louis Félix, goldsmith, revolutionary, and the son of "Elizabeth negresse esclave."[161]

The streets of Angoulême were the subjects, in turn, of revolutionary reconstruction. There was an inventory of streets in 1792, supposed to be "fixative" of the "alignments" of the town: an elaborate procedure over a two-month period, involving commissioners sitting around a large map and referring, from time to time, to article 17 of the Declaration of the Rights of Man (about the inviolable rights of property). The changes proposed were peremptory—the revision was indicated "by a line drawn in black pencil on the map"—and the properties to be revised or retrenched included those of the sisters-in-law of the clerk from the affair of the tax office in 1778, who had thrown his wife's confiscated underwear out of the window; Silvie Cazaud's brother, who lived on the corner of the Place du Mûrier; and the absconding slave owner, the ubiquitous "M. Robin the American."[162]

These were changes, too, in the lives of known, familiar individuals. Bénédictine de Bologne, who was a girl of sixteen when Elizabeth and Lydia Sterne were lodgers in the house of her parents on the Rue des Cordeliers, later the Rue de Beaulieu, was expelled from the convent of Notre Dame de Beaulieu, a few steps away on the same street; she found lodging a short distance from the Place du Mûrier. Jeanne Françoise Ogerdias, the daughter of the itinerant Claude Ogerdias, who was born in Chandernagor in India and brought to Angoulême at the age of five, became a nun in the nursing order of Sainte-Marthe. She, too, was expelled from a hospital on the Rue de Beaulieu; her mother was living, still, in the former tax office, a few steps away to the north, where the abbé Mioulle had paused on the fateful night in 1779.[163]

There was no possibility of not being seen, in the crowded streets of the neighborhood, and no possibility of not seeing the revolution. There were new façades, new alignments of streets, and new owners. The noise of daily life was different, and the cavalcade outside the doors of Marie Aymard's granddaughters. There was also the cavalcade of family relationships, or nuptiality. Their grandfather, long dead before they were born, had an obscure fortune in the slave islands of America, and so did their new sister-in-law, in the year 9. They had a brother-in-law from a family of dancing masters in Versailles, and a first cousin by marriage from Venice (or Naples, or Nice). Their nephews and nieces were in Bayonne and Le Mans, and their great-nephews, eventually, in Beirut and Carthage, Tahiti and Morocco and Mexico. This is part of their nineteenth-century history, and of the long history of the French Revolution.

Chapter Seven

MODERN LIVES

The Grandchildren's Grandchildren

So what happened next, and how does the story end? Or is it a story, and does it end? This has been a history, so far, of a family in the French provinces, and of the networks of information, friendship, and proximity amidst which they lived. Their existence was suffused with news and misinformation from overseas, like the existence of so many of their friends and neighbors. They flourished (and failed) in the old economy of administration, instruction, and the church. Their lives were transformed by the French Revolution, and by the exogamous, exogenous marriages of the revolutionary years.

The children and grandchildren of Marie Aymard, or most of them, lived on into the modern times of the nineteenth century. They belonged, like the philosopher Brillat-Savarin, in Balzac's description, to the generation of "these old men sitting astride the centuries."[1] Jean-Baptiste Ferrand was born in Angoulême in 1749, and died in Paris in 1831; his son, Marie Aymard's youngest grandchild, died in Normandy in 1873. Jeanne Allemand Lavigerie, the shopkeeper who appeared in the property register for 1799, was born in 1768, and died in 1860. The last large gathering of the grandchildren and their extended families, in Angoulême in 1855, was on the occasion of the signature of yet another marriage contract, between Marie Aymard's grandson's granddaughter, Louise Lavigerie, and a young man from Paris, "inspector of accounts of the Orléans Railway."

It was only the five unmarried daughters of Etienne Allemand and Françoise Ferrand, the couple in the marriage contract of 1764, who remained in Angoulême, and the girls' school in which they taught—in a house on the Rempart du Midi, at the end of the Rue de Beaulieu—was at the heart of the family's exchanges. It is their household that is at the center of the last part of this book. Their brother Martial, whose sons became officials of the customs and tax administration, returned there at the end of his life; so did their sister and her husband, the itinerant architect and former cartographer; Pierre Allemand Lavigerie's son, who founded a new family enterprise of banking in the Sarthe, moved to the Rempart du Midi in 1848; their great-nephew Charles Martial, who was ordained as a priest in 1849, was a frequent visitor. Charles Martial's sister Louise, who was married from the school in 1855, was eventually the principal source, until her death in 1906, of news and information about family relationships: the invigilator of kinship, inheritance, and memory.

The history of the family, over the half century from 1764 to the end of the Napoleonic Empire, was a story of what really happened over the course of the long revolution. The Allemands and the Ferrands made their way, over these years, into the (restless) time of political history. In the remaining part of the book, they move on into the time of economic history, or of the history of economic life—the slow, interminable transition of modern times.

There was no one, within the extended family, who was part of the modern economy of the nineteenth century in the sense of the "leading" industries of cotton, coal, steel, and textiles.[2] But they were economic figures, in the even more modern, or universal, sense of the "desire of bettering our condition."[3] The story of their economic lives is a history, seen from the perspective of a large, obscure family, of the economic revolutions of the nineteenth century. The principal sources are once again the obvious, accessible records of civil registration, notarial archives, and registers of inheritance, taxes and property. These sources have led, in turn, to the unindustrial industries—the administration of taxes, banking, and the church—that were the sources of opportunity, on so many occasions, in the family's nineteenth-century history.

The decorative genealogical trees that are given as gifts, sometimes painted in sky blue, are planted in the present, the "I," and ascend into the ever-wispier branches of parents, grandparents, great-grandparents, and great-great-grandparents. It would be possible, with infinite patience—and in the bad infinity (or Hegel's "uninterrupted flitting over limits") of information that changes continuously over time—to invert the perspective, and to search for all the descendants of Marie Aymard, even into the (infinitesimal) present.[4] But this is a history with a family at its center, and not a family history. It is about the family as one network among many: a network of information over time, just as relationships to friends and neighbors are networks of information in space. So it will end with the generation of the grandchildren's grandchildren—the children who were connected, by the immediate relationships of family memory, to their own grandparents, who were in turn connected, by the same relationships, to Marie Aymard.[5]

The history of the "nuptiality" of Marie Aymard's grandchildren was a story, in part, of family information, and how it changed over the course of the French Revolution. The history of the grandchildren's own grandchildren is a different and less eventful story. It is a less complete story, too, in part because of the unending mobility—in space and class and social condition—that was characteristic, over so many years, of the Allemands and the Ferrands. It is an unequal story, and a history of inequality, because of the divergent destinies, within the family, of upward and downward mobility.

The story of the grandchildren's grandchildren is unequal, too, because of the disparity in the sources or evidence of their different lives. There is more evidence of everyone, in general, in the nineteenth-century age of newspapers, printed law reports, and commercial directories. One of Martial's daughters was listed as a music teacher in a directory of 1832 for Bayonne, and one of Pierre's sons was listed as a merchant in "all varieties of sacks," in 1842, in a directory for Le Mans; the pension on the Rempart du Midi appeared in the commercial directory for Angoulême, in 1857.[6] Gabriel Ferrand's granddaughter was listed as a wine merchant in Paris.[7] But of Françoise Ferrand Brébion's daughters and granddaughters in Paris, there are no more than petitions for relief, and the long, tragic narrative of civil registration: birth, marriage, childbirth, the deaths of children, and death.

The inequality of evidence is most glaring in respect of Martial's grandchildren by his first marriage, to the daughter of the apothecary in Angoulême. This is a history from below that has turned at many points on the "obscurity" of distant events, and on the sorts of lives that were in Condorcet's description "the most neglected, and for which monuments offer us so little material."[8] But there is a figure in the nineteenth-century history who was the object, for a time, of a universal, luminous gaze. Louise Lavigerie's brother Charles Martial was a participant, like so many others, in the ordinary life of the family: he was a signatory of her own marriage contract in Angoulême in 1855, together with the great aunts and cousins; he had been there for the marriage of his second cousin in 1851; and he was there again in 1858, for the marriage of his first cousin. He was also, eventually, one of the most famous individuals of the entire nineteenth century, and of whom there is the most surviving evidence. He was prolific, written about, photographed, and sculpted in marble monuments. He "deployed splendor and magnificence all around him," in the description of an early biographer; "his popularity is immense, universal. His name is glorified in all languages; his image is familiar to all."[9] Cardinal Charles Martial Allemand Lavigerie, too, is a part—a large and disproportionate part—of this family history.

Angoulême Restored

The nineteenth-century history of the family starts amidst the enterprise of restoration, in the most material sense. The first prefect of the Department of the Charente, appointed in 1800 as the representative of the forces of order, was accommodated in the old episcopal residence of Angoulême, adjacent to the *bien national* in which Etienne Allemand and Françoise Ferrand had lived since 1791.[10] The former Jesuit college, where Etienne taught for so many years, and in whose premises Jean-Baptiste Ferrand lived as a refugee from Saint-Domingue, was moved to another national property, the abbey at the end of the Rue de Beaulieu; the new college was restored in 1799–1803, and transformed, by the 1840s, into an imposing neoclassical monument to public instruction.[11]

The restoration of the monarchy, in Angoulême as elsewhere, was a triumph of municipal and diocesan architecture. The effacement of historical memory, in the town council, was well under way in the spring of 1815.[12] The daughter of Louis XVI and Marie Antoinette, by then known as the duchess of Angoulême, visited the town for a few hours in August 1815; her passage was celebrated with a general illumination, and an Ionic column erected below the Rempart du Midi.[13] The designer of the column, Paul Abadie, was the son of a plasterer from Bordeaux, and over the coming decades Abadie and his son, also called Paul Abadie, or "Paul Mallard surnommé Abadie," were the architects of a monumental reconstruction of the town. The Abadies' lives were in turn intertwined, until the 1880s, with the lives of the Allemand Lavigeries.[14]

Over the half century of the restoration monarchy of Louis XVIII and Charles X (the younger brothers of Louis XVI), the "July" monarchy of Louis Philippe (the young prince who had been denounced by the mother-in-law of Jeanne Lavigerie Topin for singing quiet hymns in Belgium, and who became king of France in 1830), and the Second Empire of Napoléon III, the Abadies, together with their patrons and contractors, changed Angoulême into a place of pale façades, neoclassical public buildings, and eventually of neo-Gothic historicism. It was "an almost total transformation," in the expression of one of the older Abadie's biographers, in a "fortunate monumental character."[15]

Angoulême was a spectacle of the new architecture of order. The construction began in the First Empire, with an elaborate project for a departmental *dépôt de mendicité*, or place of confinement for beggars—it was estimated that space would be needed for nine hundred men, women, and children—to be built adjacent to the hospital (on land that was owned, in part, by the family of a signatory of the marriage contract of 1764, Jean-Baptiste Marchais).[16] The first substantial project of the older Abadie, who became the departmental architect in 1818, was a renovation of the municipal prison, at the time a complex of spaces for criminals, debtors, women, and the "condemned."[17] There was a new Palais de Justice that dominated the Place du Mûrier, designed in the inexpensive, luminous local stone.[18] Abadie designed a severe neoclassical palace, in 1828, for the prefect of the department, with accommodation for visiting members of the royal family, a short walk along the ramparts from the old episcopal palace.[19] The projected *dépôt de mendicité* became the venue—transiently—of a new Royal Naval College, with its own neoclassical premises, also designed by Abadie; it was later the railway station of the Orléans Railway. (The professor of hydrography in the college was reported to have purchased a copy of Géricault's celebrated vista of a shipwreck, *The Raft of the Medusa*, "in order to give his pupils an idea of the sea"; the institution was transferred, in 1826, to a naval vessel off the coast of Brest.)[20]

The narrow streets and crowded houses of the center of Angoulême had been an object of horror for the reformers of the late ancien régime and the revolution. The audience rooms of the criminal jurisdiction, across the street from Etienne Allemand's childhood home, were found to be "in a state of absolute dilapidation," by the inspectors sent in 1774 by the future Charles X; in the "Plan Directeur" of 1792, the streets to be "augmented" were shaded in red, and the streets that were "shaded in yellow indicate reduction or parts to be destroyed."[21] There were pavements, starting in 1806, illumination, starting in 1843, and a water supply.[22] The "wide streets," "unified pavement," light "distributed by underground canals," and water "forced to rise to the very summit of the hill" were meanwhile only one component, as the bishop of Angoulême recalled in 1852, in a much vaster reconstruction.[23]

The new architecture of the town was a restoration, above all, of religious order. In 1825, there was a neoclassical façade, designed by the older Abadie, for the twelfth-century parish church of St. André, where Marie Aymard's three youngest children were baptized. There was a newly constructed neoclassical church of St. Jacques de l'Houmeau, with four Attic columns and a zinc roof, also designed by Abadie, starting in 1840.[24] The church of St. Martial, where Françoise Ferrand was baptized in 1740, and of which her nephew was the revolutionary curé, was demolished in 1851. It was rebuilt under the direction of the younger Abadie, in dazzling white stone, in the neo-Roman style of the times.[25] There was a neo-Gothic church of St. Ausone, also designed by the younger Abadie, and constructed on the foundation of "three thousand meters of old stones," piled in "indestructible cement."[26] In 1852, as the bishop of Angoulême lamented in a letter to the future Emperor Louis Napoléon, the façade of the cathedral of St. Pierre still bore the "trace of revolutionary impieties," or "the shameful inscription: Temple of Reason." By the time Abadie's (Gothic) restoration of the cathedral was dedicated, in 1869, the "profanations" of time at last been "effaced."[27]

The Effacement of Memory

Amidst the material restoration of the town, the figures of the long French Revolution in Angoulême were absorbed, for the most part, into the routines of bourgeois life. François Laplanche, the clerk in the affair of the tax office, survived the revolution, and died in Paris in 1802; his daughter, who was listed in the revolutionary register of 1791 as the owner of a house close to the church of St. Martial, married a trigonometrician, a "controller of direct taxation," and settled in a village to the north of Paris, where she was still living, in 1851, as a "pensioner of the state."[28]

Robin the American, who returned to Angoulême with his English wife after having been imprisoned in Martinique for stealing "forty or fifty slaves," retired to rural life during the revolution. He purchased the *bien national* in the center of Angoulême, but described himself, in 1793, as an "agriculteur."[29] He and his wife owned a property in the forest of Dirac, to the south of Angoulême, where she died in 1824, described as a "native of London."[30] Abraham François or François Abraham Robin then returned to Angoulême, and to the old "Rue de l'Evéché," now called the "Rue de la Préfecture." He was the neighbor, still, of the family of the widow who wrote the statement of women's rights in 1790.[31] He died in 1833, identified as a "former receiver of direct taxes."[32]

The municipal revolutionary Louis Félix, who was born in Saint-Domingue in 1765, and lived in the Place du Mûrier during the revolution, returned to his old profession. He was identified as a "merchant goldsmith," in 1820, in the record of the marriage of his son, also a goldsmith, to the daughter of another goldsmith; the family lived on the Rue de la Cloche Verte.[33] Louis Félix was a frequent signatory, still, of the records of domestic life: the marriage of his daughter, in 1821, to a printer; of two of his nieces, granddaughters of signatories of the marriage contract of 1764, to two brothers, booksellers on the Place du Mûrier; and of his granddaughter, in 1841, to a professor of music. In 1841, Louis Félix was again an employee of the prefecture.[34] He and his wife moved, eventually, to one of the new suburbs of the town, where he died in 1851, identified as a "rentier."[35]

Lecler-Raby, the inspector of prisons and suspicious schools, also retired into the amenities of restoration life. He was identified as a proprietor, when his wife died in 1812; in the first cadastral survey of Angoulême, in 1827, he and his sons were listed as the owners of eight separate properties in the small streets of the center of town.[36] In 1846, he was an "ex-merchant," living with his family and two domestic servants in a large house on the Rue du Minage. Jean Lecler-Raby died in Angoulême in 1848, at the age of eighty-two. He was recognized, in a new epoch of revolution, as "former merchant and former municipal administrator."[37]

Marguerite Aubert, the young girl who represented reason on the altar of the cathedral in 1793, became a respectable figure of commercial life in Angoulême. She was married in 1807 to an employee of the tax division of the Department of the Charente: an odd occasion, in which the bridegroom's mother refused to give her consent to the union, on the grounds that her husband "had just left the house."[38] Marguerite's godmother (and grandmother), a signatory of the marriage contract of 1764, was still living in Angoulême at the time.[39] Marguerite and her husband became shopkeepers under the restoration, and lived on the same street, near the Place du Mûrier, where Etienne Allemand had grown up half a century before. One of the malicious raconteurs of nineteenth-century Angoulême, an administrator in the municipal government, related that she was a draper, with no residual evidence of "the admiration of which she had once been the object, owing to the beauty of her face and of her sculptural form."[40] Marguerite died in 1842, at the age of sixty-seven, in a small town to the north of Angoulême, where she had settled with her daughter and son-in-law, a local notary.[41]

The Inheritance of Revolution

Marie Madeleine Virol and Léonard Robin, the two figures from Angoulême who became part of the large history of the revolution, returned home only in spirit, or in the imagination of their possible heirs. When Léonard Robin died in 1802, his father and two of his sisters were still living in Angoulême; three of his brothers also survived him. In the days after Léonard's death, his apartment on the Rue des Grands Augustins in Paris was the scene of an unseemly dispute over the inventory of his effects. Léonard's widow was present; there were several notaries, and two of Léonard's brothers, who identified themselves, together with their sisters in Angoulême and their other brother (a military *payeur* or paymaster, living at the time in the Department of the Indre) as the heirs to Léonard's estate. At this point there appeared another person— he was also living in the Indre—who identified himself as the "sole presumptive heir." He was called "Louis Léonard Robin," and he produced a certificate of his birth, in 1774, or many years before his father's marriage, registered as the son of Léonard Robin.[42]

Louis Léonard's uncles opposed his claims, and they invoked the restrictions that had been included in the reform of family law—the legislation to protect the "rights of natural children" that Léonard had helped to inspire—against the new heir, and the "species" to which he "belonged."[43] The parties agreed to an inventory, which unfolded over a period of sixteen days. Léonard's possessions were suited to the revolutionary times in which he lived. There were five pairs of black trousers and a black suit (which according to Léonard's widow might have to be returned to the constitutional tribunal), two small bronze busts of Voltaire and Rousseau, fifty-five volumes of the *Encyclopédie méthodique*, a copper medal with the inscription "Droits de l'homme, Constitution," and "two bad curtains" in "yellow taffeta." But it was the inventory of Léonard's papers that was most contested, and especially those related to the estate of his late Ottoman client Méhémet-Aly or Boullon Morange, and to the château in the Yonne that Léonard had bought as a *bien national*.[44] There was by now another claimant, called Amet-Mémis or

Canalès-Oglou, who described himself as the first cousin of Boullon Morange, and the son of the "Pasha of Smyrna" with a Catalonian captive, who appeared at the property in the Yonne in the days after Léonard's death; he too opposed the claims of Louis Léonard Robin, and of Léonard's widow (whom he accused of having impersonated a nurse at the deathbed of his late lamented cousin).[45]

The dispute involving Léonard's brothers and sisters—and the aging patriarch in Angoulême—became the subject of a notorious legal case over the rights of natural children. Léonard's son, by then, had the support of his stepmother, Léonard's widow, and the case was described in Sirey's legal dictionary as a "singular spectacle": a "completely strange case [in which] the *father* of the deceased rejects the child of his son, while the *widow* of the deceased welcomes the child, and protects him with all her force." Louis Léonard produced his birth certificate, and claimed that he had always been treated as Léonard's son; his uncles claimed that Léonard had never been married to Louis Léonard's mother, and that he had not been treated—at least by his grandfather— as Léonard's son. They invoked the jurisprudence of 1566, 1579, and 1667 in this repudiation of Léonard's entire revolutionary oeuvre; Léonard's father, Abraham François Robin, the author of the secret history of the financial crisis of 1769, died in Angoulême in 1804, at the age of eighty-eight, while the case was still under appeal.[46]

The court of appeal decided, eventually, in favor of Louis Léonard, who retired, together with his stepmother, to the family property in the Yonne.[47] But the litigious family in Angoulême won in the end. Louis Léonard died in 1825, and the property reverted to his uncles and one surviving aunt, who sold it later the same year. Léonard's widow remained in the property for five more years; she died in Paris in 1843. Marie Robin, the last of Léonard's brothers and sisters, who had been the godmother of the son of the absconding slave owner from St. Vincent many years before, died in Angoulême in 1837, at the age of eighty-eight.[48]

Marie Madeleine Virol, the heroine of the counterrevolution, had no estate. Even her clothes were the subject of contention in the summer of 1794. The day after she died on the guillotine, a prisoner in one of the other places of confinement of revolutionary Paris (the Picpus prison, where the Marquis de Sade was confined at the time) wrote to the public prosecutor to claim that she had been his servant, and to demand the right of inspecting her effects. "I have just learned from the newspaper that the citizen Virol has fallen to the sword of the law," he wrote, and "she undoubtedly deserved her fate." He "knew absolutely nothing of her conduct" over the past five months, but was convinced, "despite my astonishment, that this was the same girl who was in my service."[49]

"This girl lived in my house, where she had a room that must be filled with her things," the prisoner wrote, and they "now belong to the Republic"; he demanded to be taken home, in order to sort through her possessions. Two weeks later, he wrote again with further, peremptory details: "The person named Virol has been punished with death. She was in service with me. Her clothes are in a room that is part of my apartment. I demand to be released for twenty-four hours to return them to whoever has a right to them, given that someone else would not be able to recognize the underwear of this girl, which could be mixed up with my own. Greetings and Fraternity."[50]

But Marie Madeleine also had an afterlife, of sorts, in the property relationships or expectations of Angoulême. The widow of her uncle Noel Virol, who jumped out of the window in the prison of the Carmes in July 1794, died in Paris in 1810, and her estate, too, was the subject of a legal procedure. Marie Madeleine's younger brother Hypolite, a tailor living in a small town in the Deux-Sèvres, declared himself to be "the sole and unique heir" of his uncle's widow, whom he identified as either his mother or his sister ("mother" was crossed out, in the notarial record, and replaced with "sister").[51]

Noel Virol's widow had been living in a rented room in the house of a carpet-maker on the Rue St. Honoré, and her possessions were modest; they included the death certificate of Marie Madeleine's mother, and were valued at 189 francs, after the payment of 903 francs in medical costs.[52] But the uncertainty of the family relationships lived on in the parish registers of Angoulême. Hypolite's name, in the record of his baptism in 1775, was annotated with the "rectification" of a spelling mistake ("Virole" for "Virol"), by a "judgment of the tribunal of the first instance of the Department of the Seine, dated April 5, 1811"; so were the baptism records of Noel Virol, from 1736, of one of his sisters, and of his half brother, the father of Marie Madeleine and Hypolite.[53]

The Posterity of Gabriel

The Allemands and the Ferrands were part of the nineteenth-century history of Angoulême until 1841 (in the male lineage) and until the end of the century (in the lineage of Marie Aymard's daughters and grand-daughters). Gabriel Ferrand, who was the only one of Marie Aymard's children to have lived all his life amidst registers and receipts, and who became the archivist of the department, died in Angoulême in 1816.[54] He is the only person in the eighteenth-century family of whom an image exists (or once existed). A laconic note in the *Bulletins et mémoires de la société archéologique et historique de la Charente* for 1910 records that M. Biais, the nineteenth-century archivist of the municipality of Angoulême, "communicated a watercolor representing M. Ferrand, archivist of the Charente, painted from a portrait by M. Paillé."[55] But the watercolor is no longer there, or the portrait, and there is nothing left in Angoulême, even, of the paintings of "M. Paillé."[56]

Of Gabriel's six sons, at least three were married: the younger Gabriel in Les Sables d'Olonne; Etienne, the former priest; and the unfortunate invalid captain Pierre Alexandre, who died in Angoulême in 1841.[57] Only the younger Gabriel had children of his own (or children that I have so far been able to find). His son, (Vincent) Gabriel, died at the age of twenty-eight, leaving an only child, Pierre, who lived with his widowed mother in Paris, where she kept a reading room, a "cabinet de lecture," on the Rue du Cherche Midi. Pierre Ferrand, who was Marie Aymard's grandson's grandson, became a traveling salesman or *commis voyageur*, and married a seamstress, whose mother and father were both basketmakers.[58] (Pierre's own son, [Louis] Gabriel Ferrand, was a "garçon de magasin" in Paris, and married a laundress.[59] The last in the lineage of the Gabriel Ferrands, Louis Gabriel's son, [Eugène] Gabriel Ferrand, was killed in 1916 at Verdun, in the battle of the Mort-Homme, or Toter Mann, or Dead Man's Hill.)[60]

It was the younger Gabriel Ferrand's daughter, Stéphanie Ferrand, born in Les Sables d'Olonne in 1799—the granddaughter of the archivist, and Marie Aymard's great-granddaughter—who appeared, fleetingly, in the literary history of the nineteenth century. She was married in 1820 to a grocer from the Loir-et-Cher.[61] They too moved to Paris, and in 1854 she was listed in the commercial directory for Paris, the *Almanach-Bottin*, as the "veuve Dinochau," proprietor of a retail wineshop at 16, Rue Bréda, in the modern ninth arrondissement.[62] The Rue Bréda was in the romantic, or artistic, neighborhood of the city—a "bréda," at the time, was a lady of low renown—and Stéphanie Ferrand's shop became a rendezvous for painters, photographers, and lyric poets.[63] The diarist Edmond de Goncourt recalled dining there in 1856: a "bourgeois dinner" for thirty-five sous, of "soup and boiled meat." Many years later he recounted that a rococo painter who was working as a decorator nearby, and had gone into the shop to drink absinthe, noticed an aroma of cabbage soup, and asked if he could stay to dinner; this was the origin of the celebrated literary cabaret of the Rue Bréda.[64]

Manet and Baudelaire were customers, with Courbet and Alphonse Daudet; the photographers Nadar and Carjat; the journalists of the newly flourishing *Le Figaro*; Henri Murger, the author of *Scènes de la vie de bohème*; and the young Léon Gambetta.[65] The "Grande Fête du Réalisme" of 1859, in Courbet's studio, was accompanied by festivities in Stéphanie Ferrand's cabaret.[66] There was an entry for "Dinauchau" in the Larousse dictionary of 1870: "establishment celebrated in the literary history of these times," frequented by "men of letters, semibohemians, semijournalists, millionaires of the mind"; "ladies are admitted."[67] Stéphanie Ferrand kept the accounts, cooked, and maintained an intermittently "austere" order. She managed the shop with her two sons, and Edouard Dinochau—Marie Aymard's grandson's grandson—became known as the "restaurateur des lettres."[68] Stéphanie was also one of the very few individuals in the entire extended family of whom there is at least a glimpse of a visual description. She had "large protruding eyes, like the *buffers of a locomotive*," in the Goncourts' recollection.[69] Edouard "seemed to have inherited the eyes of his mother," with abundant wavy hair and "eyes like lotto balls"; there is a caricature of him in a white shirt and black waistcoat, opening a bottle of wine.[70]

Stéphanie Ferrand died in Paris in August 1870, as the French forces retreated in the early battles of the Franco-Prussian War.[71] Edouard and his younger brother Alfred Charles were by then deep in debt, after having provided extensive credit, over many years, to their impecunious customers. In June 1871, Edouard was arrested in the aftermath of the defeat of the Paris Commune, charged with "having been useful to the insurgents who were defending the barricade of the Place Pigalle." He was released after interrogation: "It was recognized that all he had done was to pour the wine that had been requisitioned."[72] In November 1871, the brothers' business failed.[73] Edouard Dinochau died unmarried on December 9, 1871, in the old cholera hospital of the tenth arrondissement, the Hôpital Lariboisière.[74]

The "Dinochau bankruptcy" was one of the literary spectacles of 1872. Alfred Charles was identified as "having lived at Rue Bréda 16, and presently of no known abode."[75] The brothers' only asset, as it transpired, consisted of the debts that were owed to them: balances in the names of 282 of their customers, evaluated in October 1872 at 107,548 francs. The identity of the customers, listed by the bankruptcy adjudicators, became the object of frenetic interest, and the "Dinochau debts" were put up for public auction, in the office of a notary on the Boulevard de Sébastopol.[76] The list was described as a "sort of kaleidoscope" of "forgotten artists and famous poets," journalists and clerks and women of the world.[77] Most of the debtors were neighbors in Pigalle: "Blanche" and "Juliette" and "Mlle Henriette"; there was an artist at the French theater in St. Petersburg and a laundress in the fifteenth arrondissement.[78] The purchaser of the balances, in the end—all 282 of them, for the sum of 4,350 francs—was the publisher of *Le Figaro*, as a "duty" to his friends; the accounts were put away to gather dust in a "cardboard box," or a "tomb of memories."[79] Alfred Charles Dinochau died unmarried in 1901, in the public hospital of the Kremlin-Bicêtre.[80]

The Posterity of Jean-Baptiste

Jean-Baptiste Ferrand, Marie Aymard's youngest son, and his wife, Elizabeth Boutoute, the refugees from Saint-Domingue, had left Angoulême by 1805. They lived in Paris for more than a quarter of a century; Elizabeth died there in 1830, and Jean-Baptiste died the following year, at the age of eighty-two.[81] His petitions for relief were a sequence of misery, as he moved from one rented lodgings to another. He had been living "in indigence" in the Rue de la Ferronnerie in 1805; he lived on the Rue du Faubourg St. Martin in 1822, on the Rue du Temple in 1824, and on the Rue des Billettes in 1831, "dying every day of deprivation." He thought of himself as a Creole, as he wrote in 1822. But he was removed from the list of proprietors eligible for compensation, by the "committee of notable colonists" who oversaw the distribution of entitlements, on the grounds, he wrote, that "the loss of a considerable shop, fifteen Negroes, a son dead in the service of the colony, fifteen years of residence in Cap François were no longer worthy titles to receive relief"; he was something less than a plantation owner, unable to prove the "possession of a corner of land."[82]

His and Elizabeth's daughter Françoise Ferrand, who was born in Angoulême in 1777 and gave birth to a daughter in New York, lived in Paris until her death. She was recognized, unlike her father, as an eligible refugee, the widow of a military officer. But she, too, moved from rented accommodation to rented accommodation, usually in and around the Rue de Rochechouart, a short walk from the restaurant of her first cousin once removed on the Rue Bréda; she was a virtuoso of petitions to the officials in charge of relief for the colonists of Saint-Domingue. By 1848, she was in a "deplorable position," living with her daughter, who was seriously ill and herself a widow, and supporting her two orphaned granddaughters; she was "losing her sight, day by day, as a consequence of excessive application to the work of embroidery, her only resource"; in 1859, she was in "indescribable distress."[83] When she died in 1860, at the age of eighty-two, she was living on the Rue Myrha in what had become the eighteenth arrondissement of Paris: the scene, a few years later, of Zola's tragedy of deprivation, L'assommoir.[84]

The last letter in the dossier of Françoise's petitions was from her daughter Clara Brébion Collet, after her mother's death. It was for money to buy clothes, having sold "the little she possessed": "I do not know how to present myself in order to get work without clothes I do not inspire confidence."[85] Over the next nineteen years, Clara had a dossier of her own, and her own sequence of petitions; she was described as having been born in New York in 1804, and she received "extraordinary" relief payments from the Ministry of the Interior, as the "daughter of a colonist." The petitions, like her mother's and her grandfather's, were a chronicle of deepening distress. She was in "the greatest misery without clothes"; she was unable to work because of her failing eyesight; she was "tormented" by her landlord; the winter of 1875 was "very hard"; "I cannot tell you all that I have suffered this winter lacking everything." One letter was marked in pencil by an official of the ministry, "very unhappy."[86]

Clara Brébion Collet died in 1889 at the age of eighty-five, still in the eighteenth arrondissement.[87] Her own daughters belonged to the generation of Marie Aymard's grandchildren's grandchildren; they were the third cousins of Louise Lavigerie Kiener and Cardinal Lavigerie. Rosalie Collet was a seamstress, like her mother and grandmother, and married a neighbor in the eighteenth arrondissement, a skilled worker in the building trade.[88] She had ten children, of whom nine died in infancy or childhood; she died in 1890.[89] Her surviving son was a lithographer, who married a laundress, and lived nearby on the Rue de la Goutte d'Or, where Zola's antiheroine Nana grew up in her mother's laundry shop, in L'assommoir.[90] Rosalie's sister, Louise Collet, was married to a carpenter, like her great-great-grandmother, Marie Aymard; when she died in 1899, in the Broca hospital for women, she was described as a street seller, a "marchande ambulante."[91]

A Lineage of Daughters and Sisters

Only Françoise Ferrand's five unmarried daughters, of her ten surviving children, became the owners of property in restoration Angoulême. The first cadastral register of the town, in 1827, lists the "soeurs Lavigerie maîtresses de pension" as owners of a substantial house on the Rempart du Midi. If one leaves the Place du Mûrier by the Rue de Beaulieu—past the house of the late printer Abraham François Robin on the right, and the (imagined) printing works of *Les illusions perdues* on the left—and continues to the end of the street, the sisters' house was the second on the left on the Rempart du Midi, bathed in sunlight in the evenings, and facing south across the ramparts toward Bordeaux and the sea.[92]

This has been a matrilineal history, in the sense that it has been the daughter of Marie Aymard, Françoise Ferrand (Allemand Lavigerie), who has been a central figure in the story so far; her own daughter, Jeanne Lavigerie (who married Silvestre Topin), and her granddaughter, Françoise Topin (Lavigerie), are the matriarchs of the nineteenth-century history. But the story is also a lineage of sisters, more than of mothers, in that it was the "soeurs Lavigerie," who never married and had no posterity, who were at the center of the extended, dispersed family—the field of attraction to which the generations of the Lavigeries returned. The fortune of Martial Allemand Lavigerie was founded, in his marriage contract of 1790, on the capital or savings of his two cousins, the seamstresses Jeanne and Marguerite Faure. The savings of the five unmarried sisters, from the 1810s to the 1860s, were the foundation, in turn, of the financial history—in subsequent marriage contracts, and in successive, elaborate wills—of an entire lineage of nieces, aunts, and sisters.

The marriage contract of 1764 was the point of departure for this family history, and the sisters on the ramparts presided over four more marriage contracts, of their nieces and great-nieces, signed in Angoulême in 1836, 1851, 1855, and 1858. Françoise Ferrand's grandsons found employment, for a time, in two of the most expansive "industries" of mid-nineteenth-century France—the administration of government revenue and banking—and her great-grandsons in the military and the church. One of her great-granddaughters was an occasional sojourner in Algeria, and another was the proprietor, in 1902, of "Brazilian," "Chinese," "Hellenic," and "Ottoman" obligations, and of a house, still, on the Rempart du Midi in Angoulême. The history of economic life in the nineteenth century, from the point of view of this single, extended, matrilineal family, is a story of private exchanges (within the household, or the family), and of the private-public economy: of public service, the military, banking, and the church.

The Pension on the Rempart du Midi

Françoise Ferrand died in Angoulême in 1805. Her widower, Etienne Allemand Lavigerie, who was living with his daughters in the house that he had acquired as a "national good," came to a melancholy agreement, in March 1811, with his ten surviving children. He was seventy-one, and he described himself as a "former professor of latinity." He was "of an advanced age," in the words of the agreement, and he "wished to live a quiet life"; his children, in turn, wished to "procure him an honest subsistence." After Françoise's death—which had taken place "subsequent to the promulgation of the Code Napoléon," by which the inheritance rights of children were regulated—there had been "no inventory, settlement, or distribution." The time had now come, the children determined, to settle the estate that had been outlined more than half a century before, in the marriage contract of 1764.[93]

The house in the former ecclesiastical property—it was described as being opposite the garden of the prefect of the department—was valued at 6,000 francs. Françoise and Etienne's furniture and effects were worth 1,139 francs. The most valuable possessions were eight beds and thirty-two sheets. There was "a very ancient" cabinet and, much as in Marie Aymard's inventory of 1764, a dozen tin spoons and "a dozen bad chairs," valued together at 5 francs. There were also fleeting glimpses of the color of the family's life. Three of the beds were garnished with green ribbons, and one had a yellow ribbon as well; there was a bedcover in Indian cotton.[94]

Etienne Allemand Lavigerie signed the agreement, together with five of his daughters, Jeanne *ainée*, Jeanne Julie, Jeanne Henriette, Françoise, and Louise Mélanie. The other five surviving children—Martial, Pierre, Joséphine, and Etienne, who were all in Bayonne, and Jeanne (Topin), who was at the time in Bar-le-Duc, near the Belgian frontier—had sent powers of attorney, and were represented by two local merchants.[95] By the terms of the contract, Etienne made an irrevocable gift of half of the house, and all the furniture, to his five unmarried daughters. So did the other, absent children, ceding their rights to their sisters. The sisters, in turn, indemnified them against any future debts in relation to their parents' estate, and agreed to make no "claims against them, under any pretext whatsoever." In respect of their father, the sisters promised to provide him with lodging, clothing, shoes, heating, lighting, food, and care, "in sickness and in health, until his death," or, if he preferred, with a pension of 700 francs per year. "After this," in the final words of the contract, "they find themselves the sole proprietors of the said house and effects," to be used or disposed of as they wish, "from this day forward."[96]

Some days later, the sisters entered into by far the largest capital transaction in the family's history. In 1799, when Jeanne *ainée* appeared in the sumptuary register of Angoulême, she was a "marchande," with a shop or boutique.[97] By 1811, she and her sisters were described as schoolteachers, and on March 26, 1811, they bought the house that became the pension on the Rempart du Midi. It was a vast property, listed in the register of 1791 as amounting to more than a thousand square meters.[98] The seller was a local proprietor (and later the mayor of Angoulême, from 1813 to 1816, and again from 1830 to 1833), who had acquired it, in turn, in an exchange with a former émigré (later a deputy for the Charente, in the restoration monarchy of Charles X). The sale contract was signed in the "house of the purchasers," the sisters. They agreed to pay the sum of 20,000 francs, in six installments, and to pay interest on the balance at 5 percent per year; the payments of principal and interest were all to be made in "gold or silver."[99]

This was the property on the ramparts that was at the center of the lives of the extended family, over so many years. Jeanne *ainée* was registered, two days after the sale, as the holder of a mortgage on the new house; for 22,000 francs, in the name of the five sisters.[100] The sisters' other house, or the property they had acquired from their father, was mortgaged to the seller of the house on the ramparts; they took out an additional mortgage of 3,450 francs, in 1817.[101] These were very large sums—the mortgages entered into by their parents, in the 1790s, were for 952 francs and 660 francs—and the sisters had become wealthy proprietors.[102]

The origins of the sisters' capital were obscured in the turmoil of postrevolutionary Angoulême. But they had evidently been industrious, in the management of Jeanne aînée's shop, and later of their school, and enterprising in their investments in urban property. They prospered in the "dark" economy of notarial credit, amidst the multiplicity of new opportunities that followed the revolutionary liberalization of financial markets.[103] They also perpetuated, until their deaths, the family tradition—as in Martial's marriage settlement of 1790—of reliance on the capital of aunts, nieces, and cousins. Their own estates were severely, and even startlingly, restricted to their female relations. Jeanne Julie was the first of the five sisters to die, in 1838, at the age of sixty-seven, and she left her property to three of her nieces. The house on the ramparts was at that point owned in fifteen shares, all held by Marie Aymard's granddaughters and great-granddaughters.[104] Jeanne aînée herself died in 1860, at the age of ninety-two; she left, as her universal heiress, her niece, Françoise Méloé Topin, with reversion to her great-niece, Françoise Méloé's daughter.[105]

The house on the ramparts was soon an attraction within the family in an immediate, material sense. The sisters' house was property no. 1314 in the Napoleonic cadaster, and in 1827 their neighbor to the left was an abbé; their neighbor to the right, around the corner on the Rue de Beaulieu, was a baker.[106] A few years later, their sister Jeanne moved into the house of the baker, together with her husband, the architect and military cartographer Laurent Silvestre Topin.[107] In 1844, Camille Allemand Lavigerie, the son of their brother Pierre in the Sarthe, bought the house of the abbé immediately next door, no. 1315.[108] A few years after that, yet another nephew came to live on the Rempart du Midi: the widower of their niece, Martial's daughter, who bought property no. 1347, four houses away from the sisters, and lived there with his children and grandchildren.[109] The pension itself was a success; in 1849, the municipality listed "les Dames Lavigerie" as the proprietors of a school providing superior or secondary instruction to thirty-six girls, all living on the premises.[110]

The pension was an attraction in a sentimental sense, as well. Martial, who had moved to Bayonne, returned, in retirement, to the pension on the Rempart du Midi. His wife Bonnite died in Bayonne in 1813, and their two surviving daughters came to live with their aunts in Angoulême; their youngest daughter, born in Bayonne, was married from the house on the ramparts in 1836. Martial's granddaughter was later a teacher in the pension. Jeanne Lavigerie Topin's granddaughter also lived in the pension; Pierre Allemand Lavigerie's granddaughter was married from the Rempart du Midi.[111] Laurent Silvestre Topin, after all his travels, died in 1860, in the house on the Rue de Beaulieu.[112]

The five sisters who owned the pension were figures of the ancien régime, born in Angoulême between 1768 and 1783. The oldest Jeanne, "Lavigerie *ainée*," was twenty-two when her grandmother, Marie Aymard, died in 1790. The history of private memory is evanescent, and it is impossible to know what she remembered of the anxieties of her grandmother, or of the events of the French Revolution, as they unfolded outside her window on the Place du Mûrier. It is impossible, too, to know what she and her sisters told their nieces and great-nieces, or their great-nephew the future cardinal, about the early lives of the family. But there were multiple occasions for storytelling, in the pension on the ramparts, and for family reunion. The marriage contracts that Jeanne *ainée* signed in Angoulême in 1836, 1851, 1855, and 1858, of her niece and three great-nieces, were all, as in 1764, occasions for the exchange of information; they were episodes in the history of private and public memory.

The Consanguine Marriage outside the Prison Gates

The family history of the Allemands, or the Allemand Lavigeries, as they were known by the 1830s, is an intricate story of connections across generations, including the sorts of relationships—between unmarried sisters and their first cousin once removed, or between the sisters in the pension and their nieces and great-nieces—that are almost invisible in the patrilineal (and matrilineal) histories of ancestry, genealogy, and descent. It is made even more involuted by the pronounced tendency within the family to give the same first names to so many of their daughters. There were the five daughters of Françoise Ferrand who were christened "Jeanne"; three of Martial's daughters were given (or eventually chose) the name "Françoise," and so was the daughter of his sister, Jeanne (Mariette).[113]

But there was one marriage, amidst all these intricacies, that turned out to be a founding moment in the nineteenth-century history of the family. It involved two of the grandchildren of Françoise Ferrand, and it took place—although nothing should be surprising, in the postrevolutionary journeys of the Allemands and the Ferrands—outside the gates of a maximum-security prison, in a desolate village in the Aube, six hundred kilometers to the northeast of Angoulême.

The period of the First Empire was turbulent for Jeanne (Mariette) Allemand Lavigerie (Topin) and her husband, Laurent Silvestre Topin, the former pupil of David, who lost his position as professor of design in Angoulême in the educational reforms of 1802–1804. Silvestre was employed, for a time, in the Department of the Charente; he "directed the decorations placed in the assembly rooms of the secondary schools," on the occasion of the coronation of Napoléon as emperor, consecrated in Paris in December 1804, and celebrated in Angoulême in February 1805.[114] He found lasting security—like his successor in Angoulême, Paul Abadie—only in the new architecture of order of the restoration.

In 1810, when Jeanne and Silvestre signed the power of attorney that made it possible for Jeanne's sisters to buy the house on the ramparts in March 1811, they were identified as living in Bar-sur-Ornain, later and earlier Bar-le-Duc, in the Department of the Meuse. (The signatures of Jeanne's husband and of her sister Joséphine's husband, in Bayonne, were required to authorize the transaction, under the restrictions of the Napoleonic legal code on the rights of married women.) Silvestre was described, by then, as "architect of the Department of the Meuse and of the *dépôt de mendicité* of the said department."[115] In a decree called "On the Extirpation of Begging," in 1808, the emperor had determined that "begging will be forbidden across the territory of the empire," and that arrangements would be initiated, within a month—as they were in

Angoulême—for places of confinement in each of the departments of France.[116] In the ensuing frenzy of construction, Silvestre was able to begin a new professional life in the Meuse.

By 1817, Silvestre was established in a lasting position, in the nearby Department of the Aube. He had become the architect of one of the most famous prisons in France; in the expression on his letterhead, he was "Architect of the Government, Director of the Works of the Public Establishments of Clairvaux." The *maison centrale de Clairvaux* was a high-security prison in the village of Ville-sous-la-Ferté, amidst the forests of the east of France. It was built on the site of a Cistercian abbey, and rebuilt, starting in 1808, in the pale neoclassical style of the times. Silvestre and Jeanne lived in the prison from 1817 to 1832, when he was replaced by his twenty-five-year-old son Charles, by then an architect (and a student, ten years before, at the transient Royal Naval College in Angoulême).[117] There are hundreds of Silvestre's plans in the archives of the prison, drawings of walls and grilles, leafy glades and workshops and new cells for the women prisoners. He signed contracts and planned the details of prison administration: how to provide better ventilation for the hospital, how to construct a prison within the prison for "turbulent" subjects, how to bathe new inmates or "entrants."[118]

There were inspiring moments, over the fifteen years that Silvestre and Jeanne spent in Clairvaux. When Silvestre and other officials of the prison were supervising the construction of a new workshop in 1820—the prisoners were to be employed in making Italian straw hats—they came upon the tomb of a twelfth-century archbishop, adorned with a gilded cross, a gold pin, and a pastoral ring (belonging to "someone with very big fingers").[119] But Clairvaux was most of all a scene of horror. The civil register of Ville-sous-la-Ferté was the record of a terrible succession of deaths within the prison walls: 143 prisoners in 1830 alone—the oldest was an eighty-year-old woman from Dijon and the youngest an eighteen-year-old boy from the Vosges—with the register signed in each case by the director of the prison.[120] Silvestre was a bystander, even, in the prison drama that became the basis for Victor Hugo's short story of prison conditions, "Claude Gueux."[121] The real Claude Gueux was admitted to the maison de Clairvaux in 1830, and the prison guard whom he killed died in 1831. The condition of the cells had been greatly exaggerated, the director wrote in April 1830, and "I support with all my forces the project [of renovation] presented by M. Silvestre."[122]

It was in this desolate scene that the marriage of Françoise Ferrand's grandchildren was celebrated in October 1830. The bride was the daughter of Jeanne Allemand Lavigerie Topin and Laurent Silvestre Topin, Françoise Méloé, who was described as living in Angoulême. The groom was Camille Alexandre Allemand Lavigerie, a clerk or *commis négotiant*, living in Lille, who was the son of Pierre Allemand Lavigerie and Adelaide Charlotte Maslin. This was a "consanguine marriage in the fourth degree," between first cousins. All four parents were there; the four witnesses were the director of the prison, the prison inspector, the registrar of the prison, and the building contractor for the neoclassical reconstruction.[123]

The autumnal marriage of 1830—the consanguine union in the shadow of the prison—was the foundation, eventually, of the nineteenth-century fortunes of the Allemand Lavigeries. The daughter of the young couple, Marie Louise Allemand Lavigerie, became the heiress of her five great-aunts in the pension on the ramparts. She was married in Angoulême in 1851, and her marriage contract, signed on the Rempart du Midi, was the basis for the ill-fated enterprise known as the "Banque Portet-Lavigerie"; her own daughter, in turn, married into the political elite of the Second Empire of Napoléon III, and into the family of Georges-Eugène, Baron Haussmann.

Chapter Eight

HISTORIES OF
ECONOMIC LIFE

Economic Time and Economic History

The Allemand Lavigeries are unlikely heroes and heroines in a history of economic transformation. Their lives in the 1790s were too uneventful or too obscure, at first sight, to enter into the political history of the French Revolution. Their nineteenth-century lives are too full of events, or too picaresque, to be a part of economic history. There is so much information about their marriages and their divergent destinies; they are difficult to think of as figures in a large historical story. Political time varies from moment to moment, in a familiar understanding of historical inquiry; economic time proceeds at a stately pace, over the long term of economic development, and the medium term of industrial (and agricultural) cycles.[1]

The economic lives of the Allemand Lavigeries were an anomaly, too, in the orderly history of the transition to modernity. The family prospered (or some of them prospered). But their advancement had very little to do with modern industry, or even with activities of an "economic character," in the austere definition of twentieth-century economic history. The sociologist and historian François Simiand, in his work on employment and social change using census data of 1866, identified those who worked in the "military, administrative public services, the liberal professions, and domestic service" as being "evidently not part of the population we wish to consider"—that is to say, as outside the "active population of an economic character."[2] It was in this supposedly uneconomic territory of the economy—in which some three million people out of a working population of fifteen million people were employed, in the middle decades of the nineteenth century—that the Allemand Lavigeries set out to improve their lives.[3]

The history of economic transformation is of necessity teleological. It is a story of change over time, from the perspective of the end of the story. It is an inspiring story, in respect of the economic expansion of the long nineteenth century, of spectacular (if unequal) improvements in living conditions and life expectancy. But it is also a story that has been written, many times, from the point of view of the industries that were themselves expanding: of the active or productive economy, in Simiand's sense. These were the industries, in turn, that were measured by contemporaries, or that measured themselves (as in the "public registers of which the records are sometimes published with so much parade," in Adam Smith's earlier description, and from which the activities of "the women" were so often excluded).[4]

The economic choices of the Allemand Lavigeries unfolded in the course of activities that were counted only approximately in the registers of the times, and that have counted for very little in the subsequent history of economic change. They saved and sought positions, made interest payments, and tried to do well out of public regulations. They imagined the future in their own economic lives, like Etienne, who promised in 1791 to pay for his house in twelve installments over twelve years, and his five daughters, with their many mortgages. This is the "microeconomic" time of individuals as (maximizing) subjects. But the history of their economic lives leads to unfamiliar territories of the nineteenth-century economy, as will be seen; it suggests unfamiliar questions about the economic history of modern times.

The perspective of this micro-medium-macro history has been to start with the most obvious and accessible evidence about individual lives, and to follow these lives wherever they lead. It has been an inquiry into different resolutions or scales of historical understanding, and also into different cadences of change over time.[5] In the history of the Allemand Lavigeries—the family of Marie Aymard in the matrilineal descent, and of the couple in the marriage contract of 1764—the inquiry has led to three branches or sectors of economic life, corresponding to the branches of the extended family. There is the administration of government revenues and the military, in which the children of Martial Allemand Lavigerie found more or less secure positions. There is banking and credit, from which the eighteenth-century Allemand Lavigeries and Ferrands had been so remote, and in which the children of Pierre Allemand Lavigerie, the former paymaster, sought their fortunes. There is the vast economy of the church, in which Charles Martial Allemand Lavigerie, Martial's grandson, became the most successful of all the children, grandchildren, and great-grandchildren.

The fixed point in all these activities, until the 1860s, was the family in Angoulême, and the house on the Rempart du Midi. The five unmarried sisters who remained in Angoulême were entrepreneurs, in their own way. They were teachers, like their father, their uncle, and their brother-in-law in Bayonne, and owners of property; they were surrounded, like their brother-in-law the architect (and their grandfather, so many years before), by the transactions of the construction industry. Their capital, or their savings, was of decisive importance in the marriage contract by which the Allemand Lavigeries entered into the bourgeoisie of Angoulême; they presided over the marriages, and the inheritance, of their nieces and great-nieces.

These are industries, or sectors of the economy, in which economic change is very difficult to measure, especially on the basis of national statistics of employment and output. But they were the industries in which millions of individuals were employed, in which there were histories of success as well as failure, and of which the economic consequences extended all across national life. The perspective of a history of economic life has led, in the case of the Allemand Lavigeries, to the supposedly uneconomic industries of the nineteenth century, and also to economic events that transgress the frontiers of the public and the private, of the household and the enterprise, of capital and income. It is complementary to economic history, in that it uses the same sorts of sources—mortgages and employment registers, records of births, marriages, and deaths (and occupations), inventories and credit notes, records of lawsuits—to ask a multiplicity of sorts of questions, in a multiplicity of historical idioms or methods. It is a history, too, of what really happened.

Histories of Economic Life: Administration

Martial Allemand Lavigerie, who was born in 1767, was the first of the family to become a government official, in the office of the collection of taxes, in the early months of the French Revolution.[6] By 1803, he and Bonnite, his wife from Saint-Domingue, were in Bayonne, and he was again a public official: "receveur de la loterie nationale," in the record of the birth of his daughter Adelaide, "receveur de la loterie impériale" in 1806, and an official of the lottery, in its successive iterations, until 1826.[7] He then became "secrétaire de l'intendance sanitaire," in this port town of frightening epidemics coming from the sea. He was identified as "secrétaire de l'intendance sanitaire," still, when his daughter Elisabeth died in Bayonne in 1838, and again, at the age of seventy-nine, when his brother-in-law died in 1847.[8]

Martial's associates were from the same milieu of public administration and imperial organization. The witnesses to the events in the life of the family—the births of Martial and Bonnite's children, Joséphine's mariage in 1807—were officials and merchants, neighbors in the old town of Bayonne: "controleur principal des droits reunis," "officier de l'administration de la marine impériale," "payeur de la marine impériale." One was Pierre Allemand Lavigerie, Martial's younger brother (and the father of Camille Alexandre, the bridegroom in the consanguine marriage), who also moved to Bayonne, in the expansive public economy of the First Empire; he was described as an employee of the treasury in 1809, an assistant in the office of the paymaster general of the war in 1810, and a counselor in the paymaster's office in 1813.[9]

This was a society, as in Martial's network of witnesses in revolutionary Angoulême, of the friends of political change. Martial and his family settled in the Rue Pont-Majour (now the Rue Victor-Hugo), which leads from the old town to the port, and where Frédéric Bastiat, the

ultraliberal economist, was born in 1801.[10] Pierre Jean Audouin, "controleur principal des droits réunis," who was a witness of the birth of
Martial's son Pierre in 1806, and of Joséphine's marriage in 1807, was also
a neighbor on the Rue Pont-Majour. He had a few years earlier been a
revolutionary journalist in Paris, and a "regicide" member of the Convention.[11] He had a period of exile as French vice-consul in Messina,
and then settled—like Martial—in what had been the old revolutionary
quarter of the town; the neighborhood of the earlier constitutional
societies of 1790–1793.[12]

Bayonne was a small provincial town, about the same size as
Angoulême in 1806.[13] But it was open to the world in ways that were
unimaginable in Angoulême: close to the sea, at the confluence of two
rivers, the Adour and the Nive, multilingual, with a vista of the Pyrénées, near the frontiers of France, by sea and by land.[14] It was a plural
society, in a way that the Angoulême of the restoration was not. The
new town hall, constructed while Martial was secretary of the sanitary
inspection, was situated on the waterfront, and had the multiple function of mayor's office, customs office, and theater.[15] Within a few years
of his arrival in the town, Martial had reconstituted his extended
family in the new setting. There were his two children by his first marriage, four children by his second marriage, his sister Joséphine and
her husband, his brother Pierre from the Sarthe, and his brother Etienne, the goldsmith: a new Angoulême, far from the old constraints
of home.

Martial himself played a part, eventually, in the politics of reform in
Bayonne. In 1829, he became the publisher and director of a new twice-
weekly newspaper, the *Courrier de Bayonne et de la péninsule: journal
politique, littéraire, commercial, maritime, d'annonces judiciaires et d'avis
divers*. The *Courrier* was printed in French and Spanish, and published
news and information about events in France, Spain, and Portugal. The
first words in the first issue, in October 1829, were a paean to the freedom of the press, amidst the last months of the conservative government of Charles X in France, and the suppression of opposition in Spain
and Portugal:

The first quality of a journalist, after the knowledge of foreign languages, so indispensable in the times in which we live, is truthfulness. Not to alter the facts with particular systems, not to seek to form public opinion but to express it, to be in accord with the well-recognized interests of society, to be always above personal fears when there is nothing but truth to proclaim, to defend and support our freedoms, to brave injustice, draw attention to abuses, provide help for the oppressed—this is, in politics, the course that a journalist should follow, and the one from which the editors of this newspaper will make it their duty never to diverge.[16]

The *Courrier* was a critic, in particular, of "these little inexpungable functionaries," especially local magistrates and country priests, and called for a "municipal administration" that would provide protection against "ignorance, the arbitrary, and stupid pride." One great cause, in March 1830, was to defend the peddlers who walked from village to village selling works of biography—such as "volumes in-18" of the abridged lives of Napoléon's generals—"poor merchants" who could differentiate between the volumes "only by their shape and color," and "struggled painfully against the sad destiny of the poor."[17] But Martial had by then retired. He resigned as director of the journal in December 1829, and handed over to another local official, Samuel Brutus Mendes. In May 1830, the journal was seized on grounds of "outrage to public and religious morality, and to the religion of the state"; in June 1830, Martial's successor as director was sentenced to three months of imprisonment, and publication ceased.[18] The *Courrier* had lasted for no more than seven months.

Amidst all his adventures, Martial became the founder of a small family industry of public administration: subordinate officials in the enterprise of the collection of direct and indirect taxes. All three of his sons followed him—with varying degrees of success—into the administration of public revenue, and the invigilation of France's frontiers. His daughter, Elisabeth, who was born in Angoulême in 1791, was the only exception; she was a music teacher in Bayonne, where she lived with her father until her death in 1838, listed in the *Annuaire des artistes français* as a "professor of music," and among the (few) luminaries of the arts in the Basses Pyrénées.[19]

Léon Philippe Allemand Lavigerie, Martial's oldest son, born in Angoulême in 1795, became a supernumerary clerk in the customs administration in Bayonne in 1817. He rose rapidly through the hierarchy of a vast national organization; he was "visitor" in Ustaritz, clerk or commis in Bayonne, "assistant verifier" in Vannes, near Lorient, and "verifier" in Libourne, near Bordeaux. By 1831, he was back in Bayonne as "principal clerk of navigation"; in 1842 he was "controller" of customs in Marseille, and in 1860 "principal receiver of customs" in Rochefort.[20] He married the daughter of another public official, the director of production in the Hôtel des Monnaies that manufactured gold, silver, and copper coins in Bayonne.[21] Léon Philippe and his wife, Louise Latrilhe, were the parents of Cardinal Charles Martial Allemand Lavigerie and of Louise Lavigerie Kiener, the last repository, and eventual nemesis, of the family's memory.

The administrative lives of Martial's younger sons—by his second marriage, with Bonnite, the once and future heiress from Saint-Domingue—were more troubled. Pierre Jules Edouard, of whose birth in Bayonne the old revolutionary Pierre Jean Audouin was a witness, joined the administration of indirect taxes, and was sent to Narbonne, in the Aude. He married in the Aude, had a child, and became a widower. He participated in none of the family occasions of the ensuing decades, and died in 1851 at the age of forty-five in the naval hospital in Rochefort, identified as a clerk in the tax administration who rode his horse around the Department of the Lozère.[22]

Victor Mamert, Martial's youngest son, had an even sadder destiny. He too joined the administration of indirect taxes. He never married, and retired to a village in the Landes where he died in 1885 at the age of seventy-eight. He was described in the register of deaths as "the son of an unknown father and mother"; the record was attested to by two of his neighbors, laborers who were unable to sign their names.[23] He was reported to have had a small concession to sell tobacco, and to have passed his time playing the flute.[24] On the day he died, his landlady wrote to his nephew—Charles Martial Allemand Lavigerie, by now archbishop of Algiers—to request instructions, as the "only relative." This was a matter of some "delicacy," she wrote, "given the precarious state of fortune of my tenant"; his friends had informed her that "his clothes, an armchair, and the modest sum of fifteen francs were, at this moment, his only possessions."[25]

Martial Allemand Lavigerie, the patriarch of these officials of the revenue, returned to Angoulême at some point after 1847 (when he signed the record of the death in Bayonne of his brother-in-law, Joséphine's husband), and to the pension on the Rempart du Midi. The census of the town in 1851 describes an imposing household of thirty-eight people. There were the four surviving sisters, the maîtresses de pension, Jeanne, Henriette, Françoise, and Louise Mélanie, aged from eighty-two to sixty; there was Martial, described as a "rentier," aged eighty-three; there was their nephew Camille Allemand Lavigerie (of the consanguine marriage), his wife, Françoise Méloé Topin, and their daughter Marie Louise, with her husband; there were also four servants and twenty-five schoolgirls (the "pensionnaires").[26] Martial Allemand died in 1856, at the age of eighty-eight, in the house on the Rempart du Midi.[27]

The Lost Inheritance

The lasting preoccupation of Martial's later years—in addition to municipal administration and magazine publishing—was the estate of his late wife, in the former colony of Saint-Domingue. Marie Louise Bonnite Raymond Saint Germain was born in the environs of Jérémie in Saint-Domingue, in or around 1776. Her mother, described as a "proprietor," died in Saint-Domingue when Bonnite was young, and her father died, like so many exiles, in Philadelphia. She made her way to Bordeaux, by 1797, and then to Angoulême. She died in Bayonne in 1813, in the aftermath of the birth of her sixth child.[28]

In the marriage contract she signed in Angoulême, Bonnite held out the promise, or the memory, of long-lost prosperity: the "other things generally whatsoever, of which her inheritance might be composed."[29] By 1813, Saint-Domingue had itself been lost to the French proprietors, with the proclamation of the Republic of Haiti in 1804. In 1825, the new

king Charles X of France issued the infamous ordinance—it was signed
in the palace of the Tuileries from which his brother Louis XVI had fled
in 1791, and of which Léonard Robin was fleetingly the commissioner—
that granted "independence" to "the present inhabitants of the French
part of the island of Saint-Domingue," in exchange for 150 million francs,
"destined to compensate the former colonists who claim an indemnity."[30] This was the "Haitian indemnity," imposed by a French fleet of
thirteen naval ships, under which the people of Haiti suffered for more
than 120 years.[31]

The ordinance of April 1825 inspired a compulsive spectacle among
the colonists—and "their heirs, legatees, donates, and assignees," in the
language of the eventual law—of claims, counterclaims, and inquiries
into the long-destroyed registers of long-vanished parishes.[32] A "proprietor" called "Lavigeris" was listed as signing one of the early manifestos
of the colonists, in 1819, and Martial Allemand Lavigerie, as Bonnite's
widower, was actively involved in the spectacle that began in 1825.[33]
There was a new commission established, charged with dividing up the
"indemnity available to the former colonists of Saint-Domingue"; there
were eventually six quarto volumes, over the period from 1828 to 1833,
detailing claims, settlements, notarized documents, disbursements, and
the correct spelling of names, in relation to more than ten thousand
proprietors and their families.[34]

Martial's evocation of the epistemology of public records—"In the
records of civil registration, where everything is grave, serious, and
important, it is rigorously required that all the enunciations they contain should be in conformity with the most exact truth"—came in the
same year. It was in the form of a marginal annotation to the register of
births in Bayonne for September 1826, inserted at Martial's request, and
reproducing the judgment of a Bayonne tribunal; the objective was to
rectify the transcription of his late wife's many Christian names, and to
amend five earlier records (the dates of her death and of the births of
four of her children).[35]

In the records, Martial and his lawyer explained, Bonnite had been
identified as "Marie Louise Philippine Aimée Bonne," when her real
name was "Marie Louise Bonnite." "It is easy to see where the error

came from," they noted; "Philippine" was the name of her mother; "Aimée" was a family name by which she had been known since her childhood; the name "Bonne" was given to her "only in order to render and translate into French the name of 'Bonnite,' which she had received in Saint-Domingue." Martial had in any case been obliged to record her names, he added, without being able to refer to their original marriage documents, which at the time were still in Angoulême. The rectification was permissible, the tribunal concluded, in the interest of truth and in order to avoid "inconvenience in the future" to the children concerned.[36]

But all Martial's efforts, in the end, amounted to very little. The family's claim to indemnity was settled in the last year of the long process. Pierre Jules Edouard and Victor Mamert, together with their two surviving sisters, Charlotte Ursule and Adelaide, were judged to be co-inheritors of their mother, the "former proprietor" of a cocoa plantation called Fond-Clement, in Cap Dame-Marie at the western extremity of Haiti. They were awarded 1,710 francs each, disbursed on July 1, 1832.[37] This was a modest outcome, even by the standards of the diaspora of Angoulême. One of the other inheritors recognized in 1832 was the daughter of the semiliterate surgeon who had corresponded in 1772 with his father, the dancing master in Angoulême, about another possible inheritance.[38] Marie Louise Lefort Latour, the granddaughter of the dancing master, was awarded 19,806 francs in the Haitian indemnity.[39]

The Marriage Contract of Charlotte Ursule

The prospect of the lost inheritance was long-lived in the family of the Allemand Lavigeries, and in the pension on the Rempart du Midi. Martial and Bonnite's daughter Charlotte Ursule, who was born in Bayonne in 1810, lived after her mother's death with her aunts in Angoulême. She met a young man called Pierre Auguste Henry Lacourade, who was the namesake and heir of her father's old friend from revolutionary times: Pierre Auguste Henry, paper manufacturer and friend of political change, who had signed the marriage records of Pierre Allemand Lavigerie in the Sarthe in 1796, of Martial Allemand Lavigerie in Angoulême in 1801, and

of Jeanne Lavigerie Topin in Angoulême, also in 1801.[40] The younger
Pierre Auguste was the great-nephew, too, of another figure in the revolutionary history of the town: Pierre-Matthieu Joubert, the constitutional bishop, who was his grandmother's brother.[41]

The younger Pierre Auguste Henry Lacourade was a paper manufacturer like his namesake, and he lived outside Angoulême, in the family
paper mill at La Courade, in the little papermaking town of La Couronne
from which Marie Aymard's grandfather had emigrated to Angoulême
as an apprentice shoemaker, in 1682. This was the mill that his great-
uncle had acquired as a *bien national*, from the Abbey of La Couronne.
Pierre Auguste and Charlotte Ursule were betrothed in the spring of
1836, agreed a marriage contract in June 1836—in the house of the five
aunts, the pension on the Rempart du Midi—and were married in
Angoulême four days later. The contract was signed, in the family tradition, by an imposing procession of friends and relations: fifty-four signatories, in all, including eleven Lavigeries, three Topins, and sixteen
girls with dutiful, childlike handwriting.[42]

In the contract, Charlotte Ursule, like her mother, Bonnite, in 1801
and her grandmother, Françoise Ferrand, in 1764, promised a fortune
yet to be found. She committed "her goods and rights of all kinds, already acquired and still to be acquired," from the inheritance of her
mother, "who was a native of Saint-Domingue, the district of Jérémie,"
and who "appeared to be the owner there of a fairly considerable fortune."[43] Even after the unimpressive indemnity settlement of 1832, there
was a fortune on the horizon, still, of family life.

But Charlotte Ursule's marriage contract was in the family tradition,
above all, in its confidence in the capital of cousins and aunts. The most
substantial part of the bride's property consisted in a different promise,
made by the five unmarried sisters in the pension. There were no fewer
than nine principals in the contract: the bride, the groom, the bride's
father, the groom's mother, and the bride's five aunts. Jeanne, Jeanne
Julie, Henriette, Françoise, and Louise Mélanie Lavigerie, "in order to
prove their attachment" to their niece, had made an "irrevocable" dona-
tion to her of one-third of the goods, furniture, and real property that
they might leave on their deaths, "thus constituting her their universal

heiress in this proportion."[44] Pierre Auguste was a wealthy manufacturer; it was with the promise of a missing inheritance, and the savings of five schoolmistresses, that Charlotte Ursule was constituted as a suitable bride.

Modern Times

Angoulême in the mid-nineteenth century was a prosperous and unindustrial town. In the extended family of the Allemand Lavigeries, it was only Pierre Auguste Henry Lacourade who was in any sense a figure of the Industrial Revolution. His uncles, with their patriotic antecedents, had been the first to introduce the new system of rotating cylindrical vats—and the mechanical paper about which the hero of *Les illusions perdues* discoursed to his wife at such inordinate length in the Place du Mûrier—to the paper industry of the Charente.[45] They won a bronze medal for industrial arts; they were sued by one neighbor for diverting water from his fountain, and for unfair labor practices by others, whom they in turn sued for defamation (in an odd case in which Pierre Auguste's uncle alleged that he had omitted to defend himself, because he happened to observe the presence of actual workers, in the public gallery of the court).[46]

Pierre Auguste moved with his young wife, Charlotte Ursule Allemand Lavigerie, to the Moulin de La Courade in 1836. It was a working paper mill, with mechanical vats, vast wooden wheels, and tenements for the paper workers. In the census of 1841, there were forty-one paper workers listed as living in the factory buildings.[47] But Charlotte Ursule died in 1840, and by 1846 Pierre Auguste had himself moved on, to another and less industrial way of life. The operation of the mill was contracted out; Pierre Auguste lived with his family in the Rue de l'Arsenal in the center of Angoulême, and described himself as a *négociant*.[48] In 1861, he had moved again, to the house he bought on the Rempart du Midi, a few steps away from the pension of the Lavigerie sisters.[49]

The old center of the town was a place, still, of services and small commerce. In the census of 1846, in which five of Marie Aymard's granddaughters were recorded as living on the corner of the Rempart du

Midi, there were 1,126 women listed as having a "profession" or "function"; 590 of them were either "servants" or "domestics." There were 112 seamstresses (like the granddaughters of the cousins once removed, in Paris and Vimoutiers); 72 tailors; 63 day laborers; 61 shopkeepers; 47 nuns; 11 teachers. There was a woman bookbinder, living on the Place du Mûrier, a tinmaker, and an (Italian) dentist, living on the ramparts, not far from the granddaughters' pension.[50]

Even the records of marriages in Angoulême were evocative of the occupations of the old regime. Of the 174 women who were married in the town over the course of 1846, there was no one for whom an occupation was listed. (It was a year of economic difficulty, in which there was a tendency for "the women" to "return to their parents," as Adam Smith wrote of the public registers of the eighteenth century.)[51] Among the 174 men, there were 15 shoemakers; the largest occupation, as in the parish records of 1764. There were 11 day laborers and 8 cultivators; and 38 men, in all, employed in the building industry: stonecutters, carpenters, joiners, plasterers, and house painters. There was a continuing flux of movement, as in eighteenth-century Angoulême, between the town and the surrounding countryside. Of the brides, 41 were the daughters of cultivators; 70 were born in villages and small towns elsewhere in the Department of the Charente. There were also brides born in Cap Haïtien, Ile Maurice, and Guadeloupe, and in Verona (the daughter of the dentist).[52]

The Allemand Lavigeries were surrounded, at the same time, by economic change. Less than twenty years later, in 1864, a century after the marriage contract of Françoise Ferrand and Etienne Allemand, there were many more women who declared their own occupations. Of the 188 women who were married in the town, 120 had occupations listed. Seamstresses or lingères were the largest group, once again; there were 24, as well as 20 cooks and 18 tailors. Ninety of the brides worked in the preparation of clothing, or food, or in domestic care. But there were also 10 paper workers, 6 day laborers, and two workers, or ouvrières. There was an artiste peintre, who married another artiste peintre; she was the daughter of a printer-lithographer. Among the 188 bridegrooms, there were 11 stonecutters (the largest occupation), 10 cultivators, and 7 carpenters; there were only 4 shoemakers, and 3 employees of the tax administration. There were also, in this town of industrial consumption, 4 employees of the railway, 3 photographers, a lithographer, an employee of the telegraph, and a "weaver of metallic cloth."[53]

The new industries were a condition, by then, of ordinary existence: a sight on the horizon, just as the new railway line from Angoulême to Bordeaux could be seen from the Rempart du Midi, and in the distance the vast royal explosives factory at La Poudrerie. The sisters on the ramparts lived amidst neighbors with occupations unimagined when they were growing up in Angoulême in the 1770s and 1780s. There was an "employee of the railways" listed in the 1846 census for the Rue du Marché, in the old Isle de la Cloche Verte; there was also an "employee of the telegraph" and an "employee of the gasworks." There was a lithographer on the Place du Mûrier in 1846, and a photographer in 1861.[54] The sisters' nephew, Camille, traveled from Le Mans to Paris, at the age of eighty-one, to visit the pavilion of posts and telegraphs in the Palais de l'Industrie, where he had the misfortune, reported as a "fait divers" in the journal *Le XIXe siècle*, to be jostled by a pickpocket, losing a wallet containing five banknotes, several letters, and his voter's identification.[55]

Histories of Economic Life: The Military

The vast nineteenth-century enterprise of military force was the next family industry, after the administration of public revenue, in which the Allemand Lavigeries sought their fortunes. Martial Allemand Lavigerie was a married man with a young family, and a collector of taxes, when the mass mobilization of the 1790s began in Angoulême. He was surrounded, like everyone else in France over the generation of the revolution and the First Empire, by the economic consequences of war: conscription, procurement, and the salaries, uniforms, and requisitions of universal mobilization. There was his brother in the battalion of the Charente, and his future brother-in-law with the army in Italy. Of his first cousins, there were three of Gabriel's sons in the army, including the unfortunate Pierre Alexandre, wounded at the Battle of the Mincio; there was Jean-Baptiste's surviving son, eventually a lancer in the

Imperial Guard, and his son-in-law from Saint-Domingue, the squadron leader.

It was Pierre Allemand Lavigerie, Martial's younger brother, who was most successful in the transition from military service to the administration of military finances (and eventually to financial administration in peacetime). He was a captain on active duty when he was married in the Sarthe in 1796, a "payeur" or paymaster when his first son, Jules Etienne Scipion, was born in 1797, and an "employee of the department," in the capital of the Sarthe, Le Mans, when Camille Alexandre was born in 1799.[56] In Bayonne, amidst the material and human consequences of the Peninsular Wars, Pierre was employed in the office of the military paymaster general, the "payeur de la guerre."[57] Like the rapacious brother of Léonard Robin in the Indre, and the family of Léonard's revolutionary colleague Jacques Pierre Brissot—whose brother was employed in the office of the "payeur de la guerre" in Bourges, and whose son worked for the imperial customs administration in Bayonne—he was part of the largest economic enterprise of the long revolutionary period, or the business of universal war.[58] There were 959,230 combatants in the armies of the republic in 1795, according to an estimate of 1842, and 879,416 in the imperial armies of 1812; soldiers to be paid, clothed, fed, listed, and moved around Europe and the world.[59]

The military economy was an enduring part of the family's life. Jeanne's husband Laurent Silvestre Topin, as a military cartographer, designed a black marble column to be constructed in Angoulême in 1800, in "honor of our brave armies"; it was destined for the terrace of Beaulieu, to which he retired so many years later.[60] His and Jeanne's son Charles, after his (short) naval education in Angoulême, became an itinerant architect in the Haute-Marne. He restored a stone bridge in 1836, built a (defective) water trough, and participated in the restoration of Romanesque churches; he named his daughter "Marie Antoinette."[61] Charles Silvestre Topin's oldest son, Louis, was in 1862 a subaltern officer in the lancers of the new Imperial Guard, in Fontainebleau (and later an inspector in an insurance company, the Progrès Agricole).[62] His younger son Henri was an employee of the Telegraph Administration of the French army, decorated for his service in the "army of Versailles" that suppressed the Paris Commune, in the "campaign of the interior of 1871."[63]

The sons of Léon Philippe Allemand Lavigerie, the official of the customs service, had the most adventurous military lives. The customs administration was itself a semimilitary—and in Libourne and Bayonne, a seminaval—institution, the largest public employer after the army, with its own elaborate uniforms.[64] When Léon Philippe and Louise Latrilhe were married in 1824, the witnesses included a retired employee of the navy and an employee in the food supplies of the army.[65] The couple's children grew up in the port cities of the Atlantic and the Mediterranean, and all three of their sons, including the future cardinal, were decorated with the Légion d'honneur for services overseas. But it was their younger sons, Pierre Félix and Léon Bernard, who traveled farthest from home, in the army and the navy.

Pierre Félix Allemand Lavigerie was born in Saint-Esprit (Bayonne) in 1828. He joined the tenth regiment of chasseurs as a soldier in 1846, became a sergeant in 1849, and a sublieutenant in 1859. In 1865 he joined the regiment of the Foreign Legion, where he served from 1865 to 1867 in the "Mexico campaign" (or the invasion that ended in the execution of the French-supported emperor Maximilian I), and from 1867 to 1873 in the "campaign of Africa" (or Algeria). Pierre Félix received the Mexican Order of Notre Dame de Guadalupe in 1867, and permission to wear a foreign decoration. He was a captain in the garrison town of Mascara, Algeria, when he was made chevalier of the Légion d'Honneur in 1872. In 1873 he retired to the vicinity of Angoulême; his address was the paper manufactory of his late aunt's husband, the "usine Lacourade."[66] He moved on, a few years later, to the seaside town of Capbreton in the Landes. Pierre Félix died in 1882, at the age of fifty-four, in the military hospital in Bayonne.[67]

The adventures of Léon Philippe's youngest son, Léon Bernard, were more elaborate. He was born in 1837, and joined the navy as a young man. By the age of twenty-three, he was a "pharmacist of the second class in the imperial navy," living with his father in the naval quarter of the arsenal of Rochefort, on the estuary of the Charente—the scene of the embarkation, a hundred years earlier, of the tragic expedition to

Cayenne in French Guyana. Léon Bernard was married in 1860 to a young woman from the maritime milieu of the estuary, the daughter of a "courtier des navires," or one of the officials who served as intermediaries between foreign ships and the formalities of the French customs. It was a dynastic marriage, within the naval economy of Rochefort; the witnesses, in addition to the bridegroom's father, principal receiver of customs, were another "courtier maritime" and two individuals described as "principal pharmacist of the navy," of whom one was the uncle of the bride.[68]

Léon Bernard and his wife had a daughter in 1861, and he left, shortly thereafter, for the other end of the world. He was sent as a naval pharmacist to the French protectorate of Tahiti, where he occupied himself with experiments on the color-giving properties of native plants. "Etude sur deux plantes tinctoriales de Taïti," by "M. L. Lavigerie, pharmacien de la marine"—it was the first and only scientific article in the family history of the Allemands, the Ferrands, and the Lavigeries—was published in 1862–1863, in two consecutive issues of the official journal of the French in Polynesia, the *Messager de Taïti*; it was reprinted in the *Archives de médecine navale*, between a note on poisonous fish and a report of the surgical treatment of osteomyelitis in naval recruits in Senegal. It is a lyrical evocation of the "beautiful blood-red color" of wool prepared with a solution of *Morinda citrifolia*, or beach mulberry, and of *Musa fehi*, a small banana, "red-currant red" at first sight, which in solution of ferrous sulfate produced blue silk "of beauty and solidity."[69]

A Canadian novelist who happened to be living in Tahiti at the time—she was en route from San Francisco to New Zealand—provided a more sociable description of Léon Bernard's Polynesian idyll. He was young, handsome, tall, and a good musician, she wrote in *Tahiti: The Garden of the Pacific*; he was also "a married man, whose wife, being an only child, had been prevented by her parents from accompanying her husband of a few months to a country so distant from France." But "happily for them, the young husband adored his wife," talked all the time about his wife and daughter, and was never seduced, like so many of his official friends, into living in a small hut on the beach with a "native wife." Léon Bernard rode around the island on a gray horse, played duets, and brought his piano with him on a sea excursion to Moorea, the volcanic island a few miles off the coast of Tahiti; "he was a fine young fellow," and "he was always ready for what he called a lark."[70]

Léon Bernard returned to Rochefort in 1865, and in 1866, he, too, became a chevalier of the Légion d'honneur.[71] His brilliant career then took another, unlikely turn. By the time his youngest child was born, the following year, Léon Bernard had left the navy and moved far inland to the spa town of Vichy, as a "consultant doctor."[72] He was thirty years old. One year later, in 1868, he published a 351-page book, *Guide médicale des eaux minerales de Vichy*, by "Le docteur Lavigerie, chevalier de la légion d'honneur, médecin-consultant aux eaux de Vichy, membre de plusieurs sociétés médicales."[73]

The work was in part a vindication of the "old reputation of Vichy"— based on "an experience of almost twenty centuries," and on the "grandiose and irreproachable installation of its thermal establishment"— and in part a lamentation about the new universe of medical publicity. "The ever-growing possibility of communication," together with the influence of "fashion" and "speculation," Léon Bernard wrote in 1868, had brought a multiplication of spas:

> Springs, perfectly unknown to this day, have been rescued from their obscurity by the advertisements, the prospectuses of all sorts, with which all of France has now been inundated. There is no trickle of water, more or less mineralized, that is not presumed to cure all human infirmities![74]

What was needed, he concluded, was not to show that the waters of Vichy did indeed cure, but "how they cured." In the same spirit of science that he had pursued in respect of the wild mulberries of Tahiti, he investigated the occasional, moral, and predisposing causes of digestive disease. He drew on the recent studies of Charcot and Claude Bernard, and invoked the experience of his own patients: a woman who could not permit herself "even the smallest fragment of potato," a young girl who could not "eat a single cherry without violent indigestion," so many "etiolated and languishing young girls" who had eventually "recovered their color, strength, and gaiety."[75]

Léon Bernard Lavigerie died in Vichy in October 1871, at the age of thirty-four.[76] Dora Hort, the restless friend from Tahiti, reported that when she met the cardinal, Léon's older brother, in Algiers some years later, she learned the "full particulars of his untimely death." In his medical practice, the cardinal reported, Léon Bernard "was deservedly popular and successful." But "unhappily he was not prudent about his own health, and succumbed to a violent cold contracted whilst out hunting."[77]

Léon Bernard's young widow returned to Rochefort, and to the old milieu of the naval economy. Their daughter, the little girl about whom Léon Bernard had talked so much in Tahiti, was married there ten years later. Her bridegroom was a serving military officer, and "medical assistant in the navy." The witnesses, once again, were from the world of maritime administration: a chief pharmacist of the navy, who was a cousin of the bride; a retired principal doctor of the navy, also a cousin of the bride; a chief doctor of the navy who was the cousin of the groom; and a frigate captain, the bride's uncle.[78] The family were living, still, on the Rue de l'Arsenal, on the estuary of the Charente.[79]

Chapter Nine

FAMILY CAPITAL

Histories of Economic Life: Banking and Packaging

The Allemand Lavigeries were established, by 1848, in their ventures into banking; they had become part of Simiand's "active population of an economic character," in respect of the branch of economic life described as "transport, credit, etc."[1] The financial turmoil of the revolutionary and Napoleonic decades, during which Jeanne *aînée* became the proprietor of a shop, and the five sisters accumulated enough capital, or credit, to buy the house on the ramparts, was the founding period of the nineteenth-century banking industry.[2] The credit crisis that had induced so much anxiety in eighteenth-century Angoulême was identified, in retrospect, as a turning point in the modern history of finance in France. The effect of Turgot's memorandum on the affair, and the freedom of financial markets that he proposed—and that was eventually enacted, like so much else in the history of economic liberalization in France, in the early months of the French Revolution—was "nothing less than triumphant," in the description of an Austrian minister of finance.[3] It was in this new economy of financial laissez-faire that Marie Aymard's family, or some of them, became proprietors and rentiers.

Banking was a success, at first, for the extended family. There was a natural progression from the military economy. Pierre Allemand Lavigerie, the second son of the couple in the marriage contract of 1764, proceeded from army service to the administration of military disbursements to commercial accounting. After the prosperity of the wartime years came to an end in Bayonne, he returned to Le Mans, and to his

238

wife's family in the Sarthe; one of his brothers-in-law was "controller of indirect taxes" in the town, and the other, "Décadi Montagnard Maslin," was a merchant in Le Mans.[4] Pierre found employment as a cashier in the commercial and banking house of the Sarthe, "Maison Thoré frères." He lived on the Rue Dorée in the center of Le Mans, and his two sons, Scipion and Camille, followed him into commercial life, as mercantile clerks and commercial travelers.[5] Pierre Allemand Lavigerie died in Le Mans in 1834, at the age of sixty-four, the cashier, still, of the Maison Thoré.[6]

It was Scipion Lavigerie, Pierre's older son, who founded the banking business of the family. Le Mans in the 1830s was at the outset of an enduring commercial and industrial expansion. "Thoré frères" identified themselves in 1841—the year in which Scipion appeared for the first time in the commercial directory *Firmin-Didot*, in the pages for Le Mans—as bankers, seed merchants with a special interest in clover, textile manufacturers, and specialists in washing semifinished cloth.[7] Scipion, who in 1832, at the age of thirty-five, was married to the orphaned daughter of a local draper—she was sixteen, and died only three years later—started out in business in packaging and debt collection, in Le Mans and the surrounding countryside.[8]

Scipion and his partner, called Allard, were listed in *Firmin-Didot* in 1841 as "bankers"; Allard was a manufacturer of the coarse cloth used for packaging, "toile d'emballage." It was in these sacks and bags, these "envelopes of commerce," that Scipion came to specialize.[9] In 1842, the firm was known as "Allard, Lavigerie et Demorieux," manufacturers of packing cloth "of all descriptions," and eventually of "all varieties of sacks"; they were also bankers, discounters, and collectors of debts. "Lavigerie et Demorieux," by 1849, were bankers in Le Mans, wholesale cloth merchants, and manufacturers of bags.[10] They had become a substantial partnership: the (unsuccessful) litigants, in 1850, in a case against the postmaster of Le Mans, for the nonarrival of "three recorded and registered letters, containing bills in the sum of fourteen thousand francs, addressed to three commercial houses in Nantes."[11]

Scipion Lavigerie was by then a public figure in the town. "M. Scipion Lavigerie, fabricant au Mans," provided statistical tables of the exorbitant duties charged on linen and hemp fibers, in 1840, to the republican journal *Revue du progrès*, founded by the utopian socialist Louis Blanc.[12] He was a signatory in 1842, together with his partners, of a petition in favor of free trade with Belgium, reprinted by the Chamber of Commerce of Bordeaux in one of innumerable eulogies to commerce without frontiers (and in opposition to the "prohibitionist industrialists," with their "army of customs officers").[13] Scipion lived with his widowed mother in the Place des Halles (now the Place de la République). He was a judge in the commercial tribunal of Le Mans, of which his father's old employer, Thoré, was the president; in 1849, Scipion was the adjunct mayor of the town.[14]

The journey of Pierre Allemand Lavigerie's younger son, Camille, to becoming a banker was more circuitous. He was a merchant's clerk in Lille when he was married in 1830 (outside the prison in the Aube), at a time of exuberant expansion in the textile industries of the north of France; one of the few continuing friendships of the nineteenth-century family, or relationships of patronage, was with the Fauchille family of textile manufacturers in Lille, who were signatories over three generations of the domestic ceremonies of the Allemand Lavigeries.[15] In 1833, when his twin daughters were born in Angoulême, Camille was a *commis voyageur* or traveling salesman.[16] He and his wife, Françoise Méloé, traveled between Angoulême and Le Mans over the course of some fifty years. He was in Le Mans for Scipion's marriage in 1833, and in the house on the Rempart du Midi for the marriage of his first cousin Charlotte Ursule in 1836; he was a merchant, or *négociant*, living in Angoulême, when he signed the civil record of her death in 1840; he started negotiations to buy the house on the ramparts, next door to his great-aunts, in 1844.[17]

It was the revolution of 1848 that launched Camille's public life. One of the earliest acts of the new, provisional government—between the declaration that there should be no slaves in French territory, leading to the legal abolition of slavery, in April 1848, and the establishment of savings banks ("of all property, the most inviolable and the most sacred is the savings of the poor")—was to establish a system of national discount banks, in Paris and all "industrial and commercial towns." The decree about discount banks called for a sequence of public-private partnerships, in light of the "considerable trouble that exists today in the means of private credit," or the severe financial crisis of the early months of 1848.[18] One month later, "by decree of the minister of finance of the provisional government of April 7, 1848," Camille Alexandre Allemand Lavigerie was appointed as the first director of the local branch of the new system, the "Comptoir National d'Escompte de la Ville d'Angoulême."[19]

Camille's elevation was warmly welcomed in Angoulême, according to one of the chroniclers of municipal life (the same raconteur who had been so disobliging about the young girl who had incarnated reason on the altar of the cathedral in 1793). There was a tree of liberty in the town in early 1848, according to the chronicle, but revolution was no longer imminent. In April 1848, there were 547 shareholders in the new comptoir national of Angoulême, by whom Camille's appointment as director was confirmed; "M. de Lavigerie, representative of commerce, enjoying a very honorable reputation and having recognized commercial aptitudes, is nominated with 278 votes . . . this nomination inspires great confidence for the success of the comptoir."[20] The office of the comptoir was established on the Place du Petit St. Cybard, a few steps from where Camille's grandparents' marriage contract had been signed in December 1764. Camille had become a wealthy man, or someone, at least, who had access to wealth; the director was required by the statutes of the comptoir to own least one hundred shares, which were valued at one hundred francs per share.[21]

The Marriage Contract of Marie Louise

The Rempart du Midi in Angoulême was the scene, in 1851, of a new ceremony of family signatures: a procession of uncles and cousins and schoolgirls with dutiful handwriting that became, like the christening in *Sleeping Beauty*, an omen of troubles to come. The occasion was the marriage of Marie Louise Allemand Lavigerie, the only child of Camille Allemand Lavigerie and Françoise Méloé Topin to survive infancy, to Jean Henri Portet, a clerk in the registry of the commercial tribunal of

Angoulême. Portet was born in a village to the west of Angoulême, and was described as the son of a "proprietor." He was the closest, in the extended nineteenth-century family, to the rural economy; one of his grandfathers was a farmer, and the other was a stonecutter.[22] The marriage contract was signed in the "Hôtel du Comptoir National d'Escompte," described as the "residence of M. and Mme. Lavigerie."[23]

The family in the pension on the ramparts had been sadly diminished, since the marriage of Charlotte Ursule in 1836. Jeanne Julie Allemand Lavigerie, the second of the five sisters who owned the pension, died in Angoulême in 1838, leaving her share of the property to her three nieces, Martial's daughters, Charlotte Ursule and Adelaide, and Jeanne's daughter Françoise Méloé. This was the inheritance by which the pension came to be owned in fifteen shares, all held by granddaughters and great-granddaughters of Marie Aymard.[24] But Adelaide died in 1839, at the age of thirty-five, and Charlotte Ursule died in 1840, at the age of twenty-nine, at her husband's paper mill at La Courade.[25] Françoise Méloé, the surviving niece, became the heiress to the pension.[26] In 1850, she was chosen by the oldest of the aunts, Jeanne *ainée*, as her own "universal heiress," with reversion to "my great-niece," the bride of 1851, Marie Louise Allemand Lavigerie.[27]

In the ceremony of the marriage contract, the bride's parents were there, and her maternal grandmother, Jeanne Lavigerie Topin, who lived round the corner on the Rue de Beaulieu. Her rich uncle Scipion Allemand Lavigerie had come from Le Mans. The four surviving Lavigerie sisters, the bride's great-aunts, were present, and her great-uncle Martial Allemand Lavigerie, together with his son-in-law, the paper manufacturer, and four of his grandchildren; these included Louise Lavigerie and Charles Martial, at the time the abbé Lavigerie, who was teaching theology in Paris, after having completed two doctoral dissertations on the history of early Christianity. There were cousins from the Sarthe, and Topin cousins from the family of the architects. There were also seventeen of the dutiful schoolgirls, as in the marriage contract of Charlotte Ursule, fifteen years earlier: sixty-two signatories in all.[28]

Marie Louise was clearly a rich heiress. Her contribution to the marriage consisted of personal property valued at 6,000 francs, and a dowry of 30,000 francs from her parents, an advance on her "future inheritance." The bridegroom's prospects were very different. He declared personal property valued at 6,000 francs ("furniture, paintings, engravings, his library"), and a life insurance policy worth 1,278 francs. He also declared debts of 20,000 francs. He valued his position of clerk in the commercial tribunal at 55,000 francs, "which brings the sum constituted to a net figure of 42,278 francs."[29]

It was a union of obligation and expectation, and the articles of the marriage contract were a history, in prospect, of present and future debts. The marriage was entered into under the regime of community property, with the exception of any "debts anterior to the union," which remained the separate responsibility of the respective spouses. The community was to consist of the "profits and economies" to be made by the spouses in the future, from "the revenue of their capital and the product of their industry." But Marie Louise and her eventual heirs were "guaranteed or indemnified," in turn, against debts yet to be contracted.[30] The marriage contract was invoked more than fifty years later, together with the house on the Rempart du Midi, in the settlement of the bridegroom's estate, in Paris in 1902.[31]

The Marriage Contract of Louise

Louise Lavigerie, the granddaughter of Martial Allemand Lavigerie, was married in Angoulême four years later, in 1855, on an occasion that was the last great gathering of the extended family. Her marriage contract was signed, once again, in the home of "M. and Mme. Camille Allemand Lavigerie"; Camille was described in the official record of the marriage as resident in Le Mans. Three of Marie Aymard's grandchildren were present: Martial Allemand Lavigerie, the grandfather of the bride, was eighty-eight, his sister, Jeanne *ainée*, was eighty-seven, and their youngest sister, Louise Mélanie, was seventy-two. Louise's father was there from Rochefort, and her brother, the abbé Lavigerie. There were thirty-one of the dutiful schoolgirls who signed: in all, fifty-five signatures.[32]

Louise was twenty-two, and a schoolteacher in Angoulême. She had lived for much of her childhood in Marseille, in a household near the old port, described by one of her parents' friends, a learned colleague in the customs administration, as a place of conversation about literature, evening parties, and the composition of poetry (by Louise's mother).[33] Louise's new husband, Gabriel Kiener, grew up in Paris in the Jardin des Plantes or botanical gardens, where his father was the head of the painting workshop; his uncle was the celebrated malacologist, or expert on molluscs, Louis Charles Kiener, author of a twelve-volume *Spécies général et iconographie des coquilles vivantes.*[34] Gabriel was twenty-four when he was married, and he had moved to Angoulême as an inspector of accounts for the Orléans Railway, whose vast headquarters in Paris was across the street from the Jardin des Plantes. In Angoulême, the Orléans Railway was installed in the neoclassical premises of the former naval college; the station had been inaugurated in October 1852 with a visit by the future emperor, "Prince-President" Louis Napoléon, followed by "sparkling" illuminations in the Place du Mûrier.[35]

The marriage contract of Louise and Gabriel was far more straightforward than the agreement signed by Marie Louise and Jean Henri Portet in 1851. Louise had a dowry of 10,000 francs in cash; Gabriel "declared that he did not at the moment have any assets to note, but that he constituted as a dowry all the goods and property that he might gather in the future, under any title whatsoever."[36] Five years later, the young couple were far from Angoulême, still in the service of the Orléans Railway. When Louise's younger brother, the aspiring naval pharmacist Léon Bernard Lavigerie, was married in Rochefort in 1860, Gabriel was a witness; he was identified as the station master of Villefranche, in the Aveyron.[37]

Gabriel was the only person in the extended family of the Allemand Lavigeries, in the end, who was an employee of the modern industries— railways, textiles, mining, machinery—that were at the heart of economic growth in the nineteenth century. The railway station of which he was the station master, in 1860, was one of the wonders of the Orléans company, the destination of a line that had been a triumph of railway engineering, amidst the ancient mines of the surrounding hills.[38] But within a few years, Gabriel left the railways, and returned to Angoulême, to a new vocation in the paper mill that was owned by his relatives by marriage, the Henry-Lacourade family. In 1872, there was a new household in the Moulin de Lacourade: Gabriel Kiener, "merchant and paper manufacturer," Louise, and "Augustin ab-del-Kader," described as a domestic servant aged nineteen, born in Algeria.[39]

The Marriage Contract of Marie Françoise

The last marriage contract on the Rempart du Midi, in September 1858, was a melancholy ceremony. Only two of Marie Aymard's grandchildren were still there: the oldest of the sisters in the pension, Jeanne *ainée*, and the youngest, Louise Mélanie. Martial Allemand Lavigerie, the bride's grandfather, had died two years before.[40] The abbé Lavigerie was present, and the Lavigerie-Portet family from Le Mans; there were two Topin/Silvestre cousins, no dutiful schoolgirls, and very few friends. There were forty signatories, in all: a small procession, by the standards of the extended family.[41]

The bride was Marie Françoise Henry Lacourade, daughter of the late Charlotte Ursule Allemand Lavigerie and her husband, the paper manufacturer, and the bridegroom was a twenty-four-year-old businessman from Angoulême, called Alexis-Henry-Evariste Brinboeuf-Dulary. The contract was essentially a list of assets. Alexis-Henry-Evariste declared the "sum of 40,000 francs that he had in his commercial balance, as he had justified to Mademoiselle Henry Lacourade and to her father." Marie Françoise declared assets of elaborate complexity, adding up to a value of 56,000 francs. They included a mortgage on a property on the Rue d'Assas in Paris; another property on the Avenue de Maine, also in Paris; and a cash gift of 5,000 francs from her father, for which she provided a receipt.[42]

There was also a vague allusion—as in the marriage contracts of Marie Françoise's mother in 1836, of her grandmother in 1801, and of her great-grandmother in 1764—to a distant fortune in the American islands: "the goods and rights, movable and immovable, that come to her from her mother, determined as they will be by a liquidation yet to come."[43] The bridegroom, Alexis-Henry-Evariste, was the heir, himself, of a family of merchants and slave traders in Saint-Domingue, and even of two of the most notorious contested inheritances in the late history of the colony, involving the families of his paternal grandfather (whose disputed inventories were part of the cargo of a slave ship seized by the British in 1780) and his paternal grandmother (whose family were sued in 1807 over a plantation in Saint-Domingue that was bought on credit in 1786, for a million livres, and never paid for).[44]

Marie Françoise and her husband had two children, and lived with her father on the Rempart du Midi. Alexis-Henry-Evariste died there in 1870, at the age of thirty-five; his death was registered by his brother-in-law and by his cousin by marriage Gabriel Kiener.[45] Marie Françoise never remarried, and retired to live in the Atlantic resort of Archachon; one of her children was a lieutenant in the infantry, and the other married a lieutenant in the cavalry.[46]

Angoulême in the 1860s

1860 was the end of an epoch for the Allemand Lavigeries. Jeanne *ainée*, the oldest of the sisters on the ramparts, died in Angoulême in July 1860; Silvestre Topin, Jeanne Mariette's widower, died in March of the same year. Of the other sisters, Jeanne Henriette and Jeanne Mariette had died in Angoulême in 1852, and Françoise in 1853; Joséphine died in Bayonne in 1855; Martial died in Angoulême in 1856.[47] By the end of the summer of 1860, Louise Mélanie, the youngest sister, and the youngest child of the couple in the marriage contract of 1764, was the only one left in the house on the Rempart du Midi.[48] A few weeks later, the railways were the scene of a new family tragedy. Léon Philippe, Martial's oldest son, who was born in Angoulême in 1795, retired after forty-three years in the customs administration, and soon after his (pharmacist) youngest son's marriage in Rochefort in June 1860.[49] He moved over the summer to the picturesque town of Saumur on the Loire, and died there, at the railway station, shortly before midnight on September 14, 1860. He was sixty-five. The witnesses of his death were two employees of the railway, neither of whom could sign their names.[50]

Angoulême in the 1860s was suffused, as it had been when Françoise Ferrand and Etienne Allemand were married a century earlier, with the institutions of the church and the state. In 1869, when the bishop of Angoulême blessed the new railway line from Angoulême to Rochefort, he eulogized the same three local industries that A.R.J. Turgot had identified at the time of the banking crisis of a century earlier: the manufacture of paper ("delivered white and immaculate to all the caprices of human thought"); the trade in brandy ("this precious liqueur"); and the forge industry for naval procurement, augmented, since 1819, by the *poudrerie nationale,* or royal factory for military explosives, in which Balzac had stayed during his sojourns in Angoulême.[51] There was also "the great enterprise" of construction, with its "indestructible cement"; the "maintenance of streets and public places"; the new churches of St. Jacques, St. Martial, and St. Ausone; and the revival of "municipal authority."[52]

The architecture of order—the "entrepreneurs" and enterprises of construction and demolition, of churches and "wide streets," and prison architects—was still, as in the early years of the restoration, at the center of the town's prosperity.[53] The architect Paul Abadie, in 1860, was still in Angoulême, and still the "inspector of diocesan buildings." His son, the younger Paul Abadie, had become the "diocesan architect" of the departments of the Charente, the Dordogne, and the Lot, and the municipal impresario of Angoulême.[54] The local building industry had been a flourishing business in 1753, when Louis Ferrand and his associate, a joiner and a carpenter, set out from Bordeaux to build a new plantation on the island of Grenada. Even the "expenses and works at the Temple of Reason," in 1793, required a substantial contract (for carpenters, stonemasons, and plasterers).[55] But the construction boom in nineteenth-century Angoulême was on a different and monumental scale.

The "magnificence of public things" was the enduring sign of successful towns, the bishop of Angoulême said at an earlier ceremony of secular consecration: the blessing of the first stone of the new town hall— the younger Abadie's neomedieval amalgamation of "nobility," "antiquity," "authority," and "memories"—to be built on the site of the old château. This was "serious luxury," suited to the restored society of the times.[56] The town hall, looming over the old Isle de la Cloche Verte and the abolished parish of St. Antonin, was a triumph of local industry. The "entrepreneur of public works" who was Abadie's contractor on the construction of the town hall was the grandson of a stonemason, one of the 4,089 individuals in the parish registers for 1764; he signed the register of St. Antonin on the occasion of the marriage of his sister to an invalid soldier, the son of an "entrepreneur of building works."[57]

The economic life of mid-nineteenth-century Angoulême was a spectacular instance of what David Todd has called "counter-revolutionary modernity."[58] It was also an instance of the fortunate concatenation of church, state, and business enterprise. Angoulême was a neo-Napoleonic town. Louis-Napoléon received 90 percent of votes in the first presidential election of December 1848, compared to 74 percent in the country as a whole.[59] The first blessing at the stone laying of the town hall, in 1858, was of "our glorious emperor," followed by the mayor and the "eminent architect, cherished child of this town"; the first stone of the neo-Gothic church of St. Ausone, paid for with a municipal loan of 1.5 million francs, was placed above "a gold piece with an effigy of Napoléon III of the vintage of 1864."[60] One of the odder festivities in connection with the consecration of the town hall was a 156-line ode composed by the municipal librarian of Angoulême: an evocation of the "luminous atmosphere" and "blond dawn" of the town, and also of ceremonies to come, in the thousand-year empire of the future "Napoléon XXX."[61]

The new imperial economy of Angoulême was pervaded, in these ceremonies, by military and overseas connections. The influence of the outside world was at the edge of the horizon in the provincial society of the town, as it had been in 1764, and in the lives of the Allemands and the Ferrands over the course of five generations. Universal peace was an "illusion of pride," the bishop of Angoulême said in a funeral oration for the soldiers killed in the Crimean War, and for other local sons, killed in Algeria, and in Paris—this was a reference to Etienne Ferrand's nephew by marriage, Jacques Martin de Bourgon, who died in the assault on the 1848 revolution—"for the defense of social order."[62] Even the municipal librarian included a few lines in his stone-laying ode about the "flood of bronze," transformed into a "hardened mass" in the local naval foundries, now on its way to "the Russian seas, to dismantle Sebastopol."[63]

Angoulême was a town, still, from which young men set off to make their fortunes far from home. The civil registers of deaths included transcriptions of the records of individuals from the town who had died elsewhere, and whose deaths had been notified to the registry of the town. In 1852, the year in which Jeanne Henriette and Jeanne Mariette died, there was a sailor who had died in Calcutta, and another sailor who died in Fort de France, Martinique; there were also a soldier who died in Corsica, and a tinsmith who died in Oran. A stonemason, or "entrepreneur" of masonry, died in San Francisco at the age of thirty-eight. There was another man from Angoulême who died in San Francisco (and whose brother had died in Guadeloupe); the witness to his death in San Francisco, who was himself born in Angoulême, was the grandson of a shopkeeper in the town, who had returned with a fortune from Guadeloupe.[64] In 1864, a century after the marriage contract of the sisters' parents, there was a soldier in the "light infantry of Africa," who died of dysentery in the maritime hospital of Shanghai; a fusilier in the "army of America" who died of yellow fever in Vera Cruz, in Mexico; and a "sailor, third class," who was a prisoner of war in the fortress of Ulúa, and died in the maritime hospital of Vera Cruz.[65]

Martial Allemand Lavigerie, who died in Angoulême in 1856, had been engaged throughout his life with news from overseas, and the family expectations continued after his death. There was his grandson in the army in Mexico, and the other grandson in the navy in Tahiti. His daughter died without inheriting the missing fortune in Saint-Domingue; his granddaughter, Marie Françoise, was married in 1858 into a dynasty of slave traders, also from Saint-Domingue. The only one of his grandsons who stayed in Angoulême, Marie Françoise's brother and the heir to the paper mill at La Courade, also married into a family of soldiers and plantation owners. Georges Henry Lacourade's father-in-law was a retired colonel; his wife was the great-granddaughter of Elizabeth Stubbs and Abraham François Robin, the absconding slave owners who had returned to Angoulême in the 1780s, from the island of St. Vincent.[66]

Maria Alida

Even the younger Paul Abadie, the architect of so much of nineteenth-century Angoulême, was connected to the islands of the French Empire. The lives of the Abadies were contiguous, over three generations, to the existence of the Allemand Lavigeries. Their existence, like that of Marie Aymard's grandchildren, was transformed by the turmoil of the revolutionary decades. Silvestre Topin aspired to the position of departmental architect, which the older Abadie held for thirty-five years; Abadie owned a house on the same street as Camille Allemand Lavigerie and Pierre Auguste Henry Lacourade.[67] The younger Paul Abadie was a witness, many years later, at the marriage of the son of Marie Louise Allemand Lavigerie and Jean Henri Portet, the bride and bridegroom in the ill-fated marriage contract of 1851.[68] He was the "cherished child of this town," for the bishop of Angoulême, and he was also a striking illustration of the changing conventions of the times.

Paul Abadie the younger was born in Paris in 1812; his parents were never married.[69] In 1846, described as "inspector of the restoration works of the cathedral church of Paris," he was married in Angoulême to a sixteen-year-old girl from Guadeloupe, Maria Alida Camia. Maria Alida was living in Angoulême, on the Rempart du Midi, in the home of a retired professor; the house was three doors away from the pension of the Allemand Lavigerie sisters. In the civil record of the marriage, she was described as having been born in Point-à-Pitre, the "minor daughter of an unknown father and mother."[70] The retired professor, an inventor of cosmographical instruments, was identified as Maria Alida's court-authorized guardian; his wife, in one of the coincidences with which the history of Angoulême is so replete, was the niece of the late revolutionary Léonard Robin, and the daughter of the most rapacious of the brothers who had presided over the inventory of Léonard's chattels, and over the dispossession of his "natural" son.[71]

Maria Alida Camia was born into slavery in Guadeloupe, in or around 1830. She appeared in the civil records of the island for the first time in 1834, when the overseer of a plantation in Sainte-Rose registered her emancipation, as a child of four.[72] Maria Alida was also an heiress, of sorts. The owner of the plantation in Sainte-Rose, by then living in the Gironde, recognized her as his child—"in terms that were in no way equivocal," according to a later court judgment—in a handwritten will of 1843.[73] The plantation overseer who had registered her emancipation in Guadeloupe, and who was by then also living in the Gironde, was one of the witnesses of the record of her marriage in Angoulême.[74]

Paul Abadie and Maria Alida Camia, like so many others in this history, signed a marriage contract in a house on the Rempart du Midi in Angoulême: the home of the professor with whom she was living. Paul brought to the marriage money and property to the value of 10,000 francs; his father, the older Paul Abadie, gave him a house in Angoulême. Maria Alida brought 80,000 francs, of which 10,000 francs were paid "immediately" to Paul, with interest to be paid annually, and the balance paid on the death of the plantation owner, Maria Alida's father. The contract was signed by an imposing array of local figures, in addition to the overseer of the plantation, Paul's parents, and Maria Alida's guardian, the cosmographer; there was a retired captain in the Napoleonic corps of engineers, who was the son of one of the signatories of the marriage contract of 1764; a furniture merchant; and the secretary of the municipal administration who had transcribed the revolutionary journals of the mayors of Angoulême.[75]

Paul Abadie, after the marriage, returned with Maria Alida to Paris, and to his work on the restoration of Notre Dame. Their son was born there in 1847, and in 1849 Paul was appointed diocesan architect of Angoulême, Périgueux, and Cahors.[76] Maria Alida's father died in 1860, and in 1862 Paul and Maria Alida were the losing parties in a lawsuit over her father's will: a case that denied the recognition of illegitimate children on the evidence of a handwritten will alone, uncertified by public authorities. But the sums due under the terms of the marriage contract were paid in full by 1869, and an additional sum of 40,000 francs, left to Maria Alida in another handwritten will, was settled in 1870.[77] Paul Abadie was selected, in 1874, as the architect of the new basilica of the Sacré-Coeur; he was described as a "convinced Catholic," whose sequence of past works—the cathedrals he had restored, and the "fourteen churches" he had built—were a promise of future success.[78]

Paul and Maria Alida lived on the Rue de Berlin, in Paris, and in a country house in the idyllic suburb of Chatou, on the Seine to the northwest of Paris. It was there that Paul Abadie died in 1884, in another family tragedy of the railway age. He was at the railway station on a summer evening, waiting for friends to arrive from Paris, when he died suddenly, of "apoplexy."[79] The inventory after his death showed an established and prosperous family. Paul Abadie owed 1,095 francs to the new department store, the Bon Marché; in the greenhouse of their country house, there were two thousand flower pots.[80] Maria Alida Camia died in 1903, in Neuilly-sur-Seine. She was described as having been born in Guadeloupe, the daughter of a mother and a father whose names were unknown.[81]

Histories of Economic Life: Banking and Inexactitude

The subsequent history of the Allemand Lavigeries in banking—to return to the economic lives of the family, and to the bridegroom of 1851— was a mixed success. Scipion Allemand Lavigerie, the founder of the banking house of "Lavigerie et Demorieux," died in his mansion in the center of Le Mans in 1853, at the age of fifty-six. He was a widower with no children, and his heir was his brother in Angoulême, Camille Allemand Lavigerie. Scipion was a wealthy man, with property in Le Mans and in the nearby commune of Saint-Pavace; his furniture and immediate possessions were valued at 154,356 francs.[82]

Camille moved to Le Mans with his wife, daughter, son-in-law, and young grandson, where they lived with his widowed mother in the house that Scipion had bought on the Place des Halles.[83] Henri Portet, Camille's son-in-law, was the protagonist in the last, turbulent period of the family's banking history. When the family returned to Le Mans, in 1854, the old partnership was still there: "Banquiers: Lavigerie et Demorieux."[84] By 1855, everything had changed. The mercantile listing in the *Firmin-Didot* directory had vanished, transposed into "Lemarchand, successeur de Lavigerie et Demorieux" (and a specialist, still, in the manufacture of sacks). The listing for bankers in *Firmin-Didot* was "Portet-Lavigerie et cie."[85]

It was an epoch of "limitless expansion," the linen merchants of Le Mans had written in the petition of 1842 that was signed by Scipion, in opposition to the "supposed protective rights" of the prohibitionists, identified, in the merchants' view, with the "industrial and commercial barbarism of the Middle Ages."[86] Le Mans was itself, by the 1850s, an industrial town, of "mechanical saws," starch produced with "steam engines," zinc foundries, and "hydraulic mills." (There were also the "voitures," weighing machines for "voitures," and "voitures of all sorts" that became the foundation, eventually, of the town's enduring destiny— including *L'Obéissante*, the first private automobile in France, produced by an inventor whose father was a caster of church bells in a suburb of Le Mans.)[87]

The Portet-Lavigerie bank, in these propitious times, was an immediate success. The "Maison Portet-Lavigerie" was the correspondent in Le Mans for some of the most grandiose investment projects of the Second Empire of Napoléon III: marble quarries, in 1856; the Galveston-to-Houston railway, in 1857; the Panama Canal.[88] The company specialized in arbitrage in the London markets, as described in a case they brought against a client for the nonpayment of 85,679 francs in commissions (and eventually lost on appeal, in a judgment that earned a modest place in the emerging commercial jurisprudence of foreign exchange; in the decision of the court, "the banker [must] inform the remitter of the profits arising from the exchange of pounds sterling for French values [and must not substitute] an average that he has established arbitrarily over the totality of the operation").[89]

Henri Portet started to use the name of his wife, and her successful uncle; he called himself "Portet-Lavigerie" in his public life. He gave expert testimony about the agricultural exports of the Department of the Sarthe, on the basis, he said, of his own "personal knowledge" and information gathered from "recognized and serious merchants."[90] He had an honorary position as an "administrator," and later as "Censeur," of the Le Mans branch of the Banque de France, the incipient central bank; a report to the central secretariat of the bank, in 1871, described him as "the principal banker of the town."[91] The family home, in Scipion's old residence on the Place des Halles, was identified in a travel guide as "the beautiful mansion now occupied by M. Portet-Lavigerie."[92] Henri also took on a younger partner from an established colonial family in Nantes, who had himself been the director of the Le Mans office of the Banque de France. The new banking house was called "Portet-Lavigerie et Talvande."[93]

The country residence of the Portet-Lavigeries in Bougeance, Saint-Pavace, became a home away from home for the extended family from Angoulême.[94] Louise Mélanie Allemand Lavigerie, the last of the five sisters in the pension on the Rempart du Midi, and the youngest of the thirteen children of the couple in the marriage contract of 1764, died there in 1865; she was eighty-three, and was said to have been visiting her nephew when she died in "his country house."[95] Her niece, Marie Théonie Topin, the daughter of Silvestre, the late revolutionary architect, also died in Saint-Pavace, at the age of sixty-seven, in 1868; she was described as "domiciled in Le Mans, Place des Halles," having died in "her country house in Bougeance."[96]

The worldly success of the Allemand Lavigeries reached its apogee in 1876, with the marriage of yet another daughter. Julie Marie Valentine Portet was the direct descendant—in the matrilineal line that has been a red thread in the lives of this sociable family—of Marie Aymard, the illiterate and inquisitive widow in Angoulême in 1764. Françoise Ferrand (who married Etienne Allemand in 1764) was Marie Aymard's daughter; Jeanne Allemand Lavigerie (who married Silvestre Topin in 1801) was Françoise's daughter; Françoise Méloé Topin (who married Camille Allemand Lavigerie in 1830) was Jeanne's daughter; Marie Louise Allemand Lavigerie (who married Henri Portet in 1851) was Françoise Méloé's daughter; Valentine Portet was Marie Louise's daughter, and by the time of her marriage in Le Mans in 1876, she had come a very long distance from her great-great-great-grandmother's social connections.

Valentine, like her mother, Marie Louise, in 1851, was a rich heiress, and she married into the political elite of the recently expired Second Empire. Olivier Boittelle, her husband, was described in the record of the marriage as the operations manager of a branch railway in the Sarthe. He was also the son of one of the most powerful and feared figures of the 1860s, Symphor Casimir Joseph Boittelle, prefect of police of Paris, and senator of Napoléon III. Olivier's mother, Guillaumine Haussmann, had died some years before. He was depicted with his father in a famous early photograph of family life, now in the Musée d'Orsay, amidst the portraits of the notables of the empire: a gray-haired figure, gazing fondly at an awkward young boy, "M. Boittelle et son fils Olivier."[97]

The record of Valentine's marriage was signed by her parents and her grandparents, Camille Alexandre Allemand Lavigerie and Françoise Méloé Topin, the couple in the consanguine marriage of 1830. There were no other Lavigeries; several Boittelles signed, and Portet-Lavigerie's new associate, Talvande. The bride's witness was her cousin Georges Henry Lacourade, from the paper mill in La Couronne. The bridegroom's witness, too, was his cousin: "Georges Eugène Baron Haussmann," distant relative of Olivier's late mother, prefect of the Seine, senator, and the demolitionist visionary of modern Paris.[98]

The young couple were ornaments, very soon, of the provincial society of the Sarthe. They went to live in another country estate outside Le Mans, the "Château de Mortrie," and devoted themselves to the existence of the landed gentry; Olivier Boittelle bred horses and bulls, established a stud farm, and became known as a "sportsman."[99] Valentine's brother René, who was born in Angoulême in 1852, studied law, and wrote two doctoral dissertations, which he dedicated to his grandparents. One, in Roman law, was on the juridical condition of freed slaves who were not citizens ("Latins Juniens"), and the other, in French law, was on naturalization and the juridical condition of foreigners in France.[100] René Portet was married in Paris in 1883—Paul Abadie, by then the architect of the neo-Byzantine, neo-Ottoman basilica of the

Sacré-Coeur in Paris, was a witness—and he returned some years later to Angoulême, as an official prosecutor of the Third Republic, in the Palais de Justice on the Place du Mûrier.[101]

In the economic history of the family, meanwhile, and in the banking business of the Portet-Allemand-Lavigeries, there were omens that all was not well. One of the early inspections of the Banque de France into the partnership between Henri Portet-Lavigerie and Talvande, in 1872, described it as "a bit eager, but well led by M. Portet who is very capable—Talvande very ardent but considered to be not very serious." In 1874, there was an account of "the somewhat adventurous manner in which they work." In 1876, the report was more positive—"in sum, in a good situation"—and in 1877 the bank was said to "inspire confidence." In 1880, they were described as "extending fairly numerous loans, but for amounts that could not compromise them."[102]

The "Banque Portet-Lavigerie et Talvande" ceased operations in 1881, and was succeeded by a new company, "Talvande et Cie," with a capital of six million francs, managed by Félix Talvande alone; the Banque de France inspection described it as having an "exceptionally good position." "M. Portet-Lavigerie," according to the reassuring circulars sent to clients, continued to provide "the support of his capital and the benefit of his experience."[103] Camille Allemand Lavigerie, the last surviving grandchild of the couple in the marriage contract of 1764, died in November 1881, at the age of eighty-one.[104] The formal liquidation of the Banque Portet-Lavigerie took place the following week; Henri Portet-Lavigerie became chairman of the supervisory board of Talvande et Cie.[105]

Some years later, a personal and economic drama unfolded in Le Mans, to scenes of what a local newspaper described as intense "emotion."[106] The inspection report of the Banque de France, in 1884, had noted—in red ink—that the operations of Talvande et Cie "are to be followed carefully," and, in 1885, that they "could be criticized." The bank's capital was said to have increased to ten million francs in 1887, and in 1888 they made loans to a value of twenty-two million francs.[107] In March 1889, "Talvande et Cie" went into judicial liquidation, and Félix Talvande declared personal bankruptcy. He was arrested and taken to the courthouse, and then to prison, in a carriage that was waiting in

the courtyard of his residence. His wife relinquished her "personal fortune." A shoe manufacturer in the town, who owed a million francs to
Talvande et Cie, and employed two hundred workers, was arrested the
same day; "further bad news was expected."[108]

The litigation that followed, over five years of judgments and appeals,
was unrelenting for Henri Portet-Lavigerie. The shareholders in the
Talvande bank, who lost six million francs, and the bank's creditors sued
Henri and other members of the supervisory board, in a widely attended legal case in 1890, in the commercial tribunal in Le Mans (in
which Scipion Allemand Lavigerie, Henri's uncle by marriage, and the
founder of the family bank, had earlier been a judge). Henri was convicted by the tribunal of having committed "serious faults," and ordered
to pay five hundred thousand francs in damages, together with interest
accrued and the costs of the legal action. A court in Angers, in 1891, reduced the damages payable by the other defendants, and maintained
the judgment against Henri.[109]

The details were devastating. The supervisory board never "undertook the verification required by the statutes of the company, and by
law," in the judgment of the court; if they had done so, they would have
easily recognized the multiple "inexactitudes of the accounts," and the
"excessive credits" that had been issued; they were responsible for a
reputation of "prosperity" that endured "until the final catastrophe."
Henri Portet-Lavigerie, in particular, was responsible as chairman for
providing reports to shareholders; he had personal knowledge of the
financial circumstances of the customers of the old bank and the new
bank; he was experienced in banking, and if he had even looked at the
portfolio and inventories, he would have "easily discovered the fraudu-
lent and lying character of the accounts"; he had received "large sums"
of money as his share in the profits of the bank.[110]

The eventual judgment of the Cour de Cassation, the highest civil
court, was implacable, in a decision in 1894 that became an important
monument of the jurisprudence of fiduciary responsibility of directors
of financial companies, and of the allocation of damages as between
creditors and shareholders. The obligation of the lower court had been
to divide the responsibilities of the members of the board "in proportion

to the gravity of the faults committed," the court wrote; "as regards Portet-Lavigerie," he was chairman of the board, with special responsibility for reports, and particular knowledge of the company's clients, and "at the time when the company was created, with the purpose of continuing his own banking affairs, he promised the company the benefits of his experience and his own special aptitudes." These were findings of fact, and not matters that could be reviewed by the higher court; the judgment of the lower courts was sustained.[111]

Henri had retired to Paris before the litigation made its way to the high court, and the intricacy of his involvement with the "Banque Talvande" began to unfold. Other judicial procedures followed. He, Félix Talvande, and the bank were coproprietors, as it turned out, of a slate-manufacturing enterprise in the wooded hills of the Ardennes; in Le Mans even the horticultural society of the prefecture was obliged to reduce its expenditures on the "embellishment" of the public gardens, "as a consequence of the failure of Banque Talvande."[112]

But the Portets were still a rich, respectable family. They owned a villa in Arcachon, which they called Valentine, after their daughter.[113] In Paris, they lived on the Rue Gluck, just behind the Opera, in the heart of the metropolis of Georges Eugène Haussmann, and then on the Rue Mogador, behind the Boulevard Haussmann.[114] The world of the Second Empire endured, in the lives of the family. Valentine lived nearby, on the Faubourg St. Honoré, and in the château (and stud farm) in the Sarthe.[115] Her husband, the son of the former prefect of police, was a loyalist of the lesser Napoléons; he was reported in *Le Figaro*, in July 1891, to have "embarked today on *Le Tigre*, of the Messageries Maritimes. He is taking three magnificent horses, which he will deliver to Prince Louis Napoléon in Tbilisi" (the younger brother of the pretender "Napoléon V," and at the time a colonel in the Russian Imperial Guards).[116]

The provincial family of the Allemand-Lavigeries had arrived, at last, in Paris. They were even almost neighbors—in a denouement of mobility and immobility, a tale of two cities—of their distant cousins from Angoulême, the family of the other Françoise Ferrand. The five unmarried sisters on the Rempart de Midi, who presided over so many of the family marriages, were first cousins of Françoise Ferrand, the daughter of Jean-Baptiste, who moved to Paris in the early years of the nineteenth century, and died in misery in 1860 on the Rue Myrha in Montmartre. The cousins knew each other, in the way that first cousins do; they had been neighbors as children, before Françoise emigrated to Saint-Domingue with her parents, and again when she returned to Angoulême as a refugee; their mother was the younger Françoise Ferrand's godmother.

By the 1890s, the two families were living a little over two kilometers apart, in two different universes. Rosalie and Louise Collet, Françoise Ferrand Brébion's two granddaughters, a seamstress and a street seller in Montmartre, were the third cousins of Marie Louise Portet-Lavigerie. But who knows, now or then, the addresses of their third cousins? In Montmartre, Rosalie and Louise lived in the shadow of the immense construction site of the church of the Sacré-Coeur: a representation of moral rebirth after the last struggle of the Second Empire (and of the Paris Commune, which the sisters survived in 1871), and under construction, still, when its architect, Paul Abadie, was a witness at the marriage of Marie Louise's son in 1883. These were divergent destinies, over the course of three generations, or in the economic history of inequality in nineteenth-century France. Louise Collet's husband, who was a carpenter, died in the public hospital of the Kremlin-Bicêtre, in 1901; Marie Louise Portet-Lavigerie's husband died in 1902, in his residence on the Rue Mogador, described as "a former banker."[117] His estate was a bonanza of public and private obligations, from the "crédit foncier egyptien," the "rente chinoise," the "chemins de fer ottomans," and the "hypothécaires" of the island of Cuba, to shares in Le Figaro and in "The Channel Tunnel Company Limited" ("the shares are worthless"). It was valued at 1,202,818 francs, with, written on the verso, "insufficient funds." He and Marie Louise were the owners, still, of the house on the Rempart du Midi in Angoulême.[118]

Economic and Uneconomic Lives

This inquiry into the history of economic life in the nineteenth century has followed a small number of individuals—the family of the couple in the marriage contract of 1764—over their journeys in space, time, and economic condition. It has led to mortgage records, employment registers, and the jurisprudence of foreign exchange; to Tahiti, Mexico, and a desolate village in the Landes. It has also led to parts of the economy that have been peripheral, for the most part, to the economic history of nineteenth-century France. The Allemand Lavigeries sought their fortunes in the subaltern administration of government revenues and military service; in eventually unsuccessful ventures in banking, including in the (changing) norms of financial regulation; and in the vast economy of the church, which will be the subject of the last part of the inquiry. The stable point, in all these journeys, has been a small, unindustrial town, and the investments of five unmarried schoolmistresses, founded on a property that had once belonged to the chapter of canons of the diocese of Angoulême.

The inquiry has led, along the way, to large questions about economic transformation and economic modernity. There is a now-old-fashioned view of economic history—as in Simiand's observation about "economic character"—as being mostly concerned with the production and consumption of material goods. The "individual number," or the individual destiny, was in a related view out of place, or even indecorous, in histories of economic change.[119] This inquiry is by contrast concerned with economic lives in multiple settings. It is economic, and even hypereconomic (or microeconomic), in its preoccupation with individuals, like Jeanne *ainée* and her great-nephew in Le Mans, who were maximizing their opportunities, making deductions from their taxes, and seeking advancement in the world.

One of the innovations of modern economic history has been to see the French countryside as a place of advancement, credit, and "peasants [who were] deeply involved in markets." There was no unique transition to industrialization, no dualism of the "economic" life of modern industry and the "uneconomic" conditions of agricultural existence.[120] About half of the population of France was employed in agriculture in the 1870s. Less than a third were "industrial," including those employed in construction, and the others—like Marie Aymard's family, for the most part—were employed in "services."[121]

Over the next century, the share of services increased to more than half of all employment.[122] But the individuals who worked in these disparate activities have been seen, still, as only incompletely economic. They have been thought of—like peasants in the presumption of an older economic and social history—as preoccupied with their own security, and confined in "rigid institutions"; they were unproductive, or productive only of impediments to advancement ("soldiers and tax gatherers").[123] There is an asymmetry, thereby, in the history of the modern economy, as divided, conventionally, into the primary (or agricultural), industrial, and service sectors (including public services). The primary sector, which is becoming less important over time, has come to be seen as inventive and modern; the service sector, which is increasing over time, and which is all around us, is diverse, difficult to count, and an anomaly in the long term of economic transformation.

The history of the Allemand Lavigeries has led, over the course of two centuries, to this unexplored continent of the semipublic, semiprivate, ever-expanding "service economy": the economy in which most of us are now employed, and the large majority of individuals in the richest countries.[124] The promise of the history of economic life, at its most general, is of thinking with history: of asking new questions, inspired by historical evidence, about the present and the past.[125] Economic history has been concerned, more than other kinds of history, with large, causal, important stories, of relevance for present choices (such as the story of how nations become rich). But there are other important stories, and other ways of thinking with historical evidence; one of these stories is about what it is like to be where we are now.

The Allemand Lavigeries were employed, or sought employment, in the most "public" of the services of the times. These were places of endless exchange, across the frontiers of the market and the state, or the public and the private. The pension of the five sisters was a private school, supervised by public inspection. The state was a source of contracts for wax tapers and uniforms, prisons and water troughs and neo-Gothic churches. The army and navy were labor markets, with their own networks of contacts and information, like the tax and customs officials

amidst whom Martial lived in Bayonne, or the extended family by marriage of his grandson, the naval veterinarian: maritime officials and sea
captains in Rochefort. Even the "political" and the "economic" were
difficult to disentangle, in this history of aspiration. It is evident, from
the history of the *biens nationaux* in the center of Angoulême, that political connections were a source of economic opportunity, as they were
for Etienne Allemand Lavigerie in 1791. The Abadies, father and son, and
Etienne's brother-in-law Silvestre Topin, with his own son and his
granddaughter named "Marie Antoinette," made their way as public architects in the ever-evolving circumstances of the restoration, the July
monarchy, and the empire.

The public or public-private services were archaic, in the sense that
the church, the military, and the collection of taxes were the enterprises that had been the source of so much employment—and so much
volatility—in eighteenth-century Angoulême. They were at the same
time modern in their relationship to new technologies. The Allemand
Lavigeries were at no point producers of new techniques, or employees,
like the weaver of metallic cloth who was married in Angoulême in 1864,
who produced commodities in new ways. But they were consumers of
the innovations of the times, and surrounded by new media of information and transportation; as in all those tragedies at railway stations. The
military—like the church, as will be seen in the history of Charles Martial in Algeria—was an imposing user of the newest technologies. Henri
Silvestre Topin was a "military engineer" before he was promoted to
lieutenant, in November 1870, for his services in the "telegraphic lines"
of the "army of Paris." Léon Bernard, who left the navy (and veterinary
medicine) for private medical practice in Vichy, was the closest in the
entire family to the modern science of the 1860s.

The "service economy" of the nineteenth century is a vast and vague
object of historical inquiry, and its constituent (unproductive) industries were studied at the time with very little parade. Its entrepreneurs
and employees were not exactly economic men and women; or they
were economic only in the unedifying sense of deviousness, rent seeking, and the continuous evaluation of norms and rules. But its history
is important, and it can be studied from below, or from within, just as

the history of agriculture and peasant production has been studied on the basis of legal records, credit transactions, and family life. The contiguous histories of the Allemand Lavigeries suggest some of the possibilities.

The inquiry into these family histories is complementary, too, to one of the other important innovations in the economic history of France, or the understanding of economic growth as the consequence, in multiple respects, of overseas exchanges.[126] This is a history, like the story of the Allemand Lavigeries—that began in the provincial society of Angoulême, and will now move, with Charles Martial and his sister Louise, into the French colonies—of influence as well as exchange. It began in the mid-eighteenth century, with the expansion in commerce and profits in the Atlantic slave-based economy, and continues into the boom in exports and overseas investments of the Second Empire and the Third Republic. It is an obscure history, still, in part because of the elusiveness of the distinction between "national" and "international" exchanges, within a multiterritorial state, multicontinental business enterprises, and informal as well as formal dominion. But it is a history—like the story of Marie Aymard's family over five generations—of networks of information, and even of a (social) contagion of overseas, in the deep interior of France.

There are other economic connections to pursue: other ways of thinking with the history of a small number of individuals, and of following their lives into larger or more important stories. The networks of the owners of urban *biens nationaux* in early nineteenth-century Angoulême, and especially the networks of market relationships—valuations, credit, registrations, repairs—that the new property required, suggest intriguing questions about the inheritance of revolution in the consolidation of market institutions in France. So do the vicissitudes of the registers of women's employment, and their changing relationship to other sources of information.

The history of inequality, too, has been intertwined with the entire nineteenth-century story of Marie Aymard's family. Inequality is a condition that can be measured in statistics of wealth, income, or quality of life, and it is a political circumstance, a part of people's lives. It has been more or less plausible, even in a family as inward-looking as their own, to assume that the third cousins in fin de siècle Paris—Louise Collet, the street seller, and Marie Louise Portet-Lavigerie—did not even know of each other's existence. But what of Jeanne *ainée*, in the pension on the Rempart du Midi, and her first cousin Françoise Ferrand, living with two destitute granddaughters on the Rue Myrha in Montmartre? Jeanne *ainée* and Françoise died a few weeks apart, in the early months of 1860. This is also part of the history of inequality, and of what it means, over the course of individual lives.

Chapter Ten

CHARLES MARTIAL
AND LOUISE

Histories of Economic Life: The Church

The last of the family enterprises was by far the most successful, and the only one in which the Allemand Lavigeries entered into world history. It was the enterprise, or industry, of a single individual, Charles Martial Allemand Lavigerie, the "abbé Lavigerie" of so many family events. It was an economic story, and also a story of political importance, with consequences for the lives of hundreds of thousands of people in Africa, Asia, and Europe; for the financial and institutional history of the Catholic Church and for the history of international philanthropy; for the material life of North Africa, in the epoch of a "builder of churches, schools, hospitals, monasteries, colleges, cathedrals"; and even for the future of Christianity in the twentieth century.[1] It was a story, eventually, that changed the lives of Charles Martial's own family.

Charles Martial has been an individual like any other, so far, in this history of a family and its social networks. He was one of the dependable cousins who made the journey to Angoulême, and to the pension on the Rempart du Midi, for the family ceremonies of the 1850s. He was the oldest grandson of Marie Aymard's oldest grandson, and he was in Angoulême with his grandfather, Martial Allemand Lavigerie, just as Martial had been there with his own grandmother, Marie Aymard, so many years before. Charles Martial was "our dear abbé," in the description of his mother's erudite customs officer friend in Marseille, and a convivial guest at dinner parties, the first to laugh at the recitation of comic verses.[2]

But Charles Martial Allemand Lavigerie is at the same time too imposing, or too dazzling, in relation to the family story. "He fills the world with his word, with his writings, with his person," in the summary of his first biographer, Louis Baunard, a hagiographer and historian (of "doubt") from Lille; for his enemies in the republican press, he was a "universal man," who "usurps everything and imposes himself everywhere."[3] In a history that started with an illiterate widow of whose existence there is almost no evidence, and in which almost everyone is obscure, Charles Martial is larger than life. He transforms the limits of the story, or turns it into a different kind of history. He is a historical figure: the object of histories and biographies, and even of a historiography of the histories, biographies, iconographies, and commemorations.[4]

There is an inequality of historical evidence, in particular, as between Charles Martial and everyone else in the story. This is so, most evidently, in the world of the printed word. There are 129 works by Charles Martial in the catalog of the Bibliothèque nationale de France, and almost nothing by anyone else: only the book on the medical properties of the spa waters of Vichy, by Charles Martial's younger brother, Léon Bernard Lavigerie, together with his earlier dissertation (on hepatitis); and a municipal announcement from the brief period, in 1849, when Scipion Lavigerie, their father's first cousin, was adjunct mayor of Le Mans.[5] The older Martial, Charles Martial's grandfather, was the publisher, for a few weeks in 1829, of the liberal *Courrier de Bayonne*. But the family were mentioned in newspapers and journals, for the most part, as no more than "faits divers," with the transient exception of the banker son-in-law's period of notoriety in Le Mans; and even he, when he died in 1902, was identified only as a former banker, and the father-in-law of his daughter's horse-loving husband.[6]

The disparity or inequality of evidence is even more striking in respect of archival sources. The Allemand Lavigeries were literate, for the most part, in the generation of Marie Aymard's children, born in Angoulême in the 1730s and 1740s, and fully literate in the generation of her grandchildren. They were even obsessively literate: schoolteachers, clerks in government bureaux, the archivist of the Department of the Charente. But they were not "paperassier," in the expression that the nineteenth-century schoolteacher in Angoulême used to describe the old paper merchant Abraham-François Robin, with his notebooks and scraps of paper and bundles of family letters.[7] They were not rich enough to be able to save their family papers, or they moved too often, or they had no children—in the case of the five sisters on the Rempart du Midi—to whom they could leave their archives of family memory. Everything in their history, to this point, has been in someone else's words, or in the stylized idiom of official exchanges: Etienne Allemand's letters asking for an increase in salary, and the piteous, iterative petitions for relief of Jean-Baptiste Ferrand, of his daughter on the Rue Myrha, and of his granddaughter in 1873.[8]

The papers of the cardinal are different—as "immense" and "universal" as his popularity was said to have been, in the years before his death in 1892.[9] There is an "Archives Lavigerie" on the Via Aurelia in Rome, opposite the Vatican—in the Archives of the Society of African Missionaries, or White Fathers, founded by Charles Martial in 1868—which holds the "correspondence, reports, diverse documents, and publications emanating from the founder."[10] There are drafts of lectures, family letters, reflections on indifference, descriptions of family illnesses, telegrams, letters dictated to secretaries, and 103 bound volumes of typescript transcriptions of Charles Martial's correspondence. There are also portraits of Charles Martial, drawings and photographs; extensive notes by successive biographers; and directions for walking tours of Rome, to visit the hotel in which the founder lived, and the churches in which he preached.[11] This has been a history, in large part, of women, and the only private letters of any of the women in the family are Louise's, conserved in the archive of her brother in Rome.

The most disconcerting inequality of evidence, as between Charles Martial and the rest of his family, is in this respect the most intimate. It is an inequality of knowing something, or anything, about what these individuals in the past were like. At the outset of his great sequence of novels, the *Rougon-Macquart*, which is the "natural and social history of a family under the Second Empire," Emile Zola wrote of the matriarch of the dynasty, a seller of cooking oil in a small provincial town, that she "looked far into the future," and "prepared herself to struggle against destiny, as though against a real individual who was trying to strangle her." Of Nana in *L'assommoir*, who lived, like the family of Françoise Ferrand Brébion, on the Rue de la Goutte d'Or in Paris, he wrote that she had a pink ribbon tied around her hair, and stopped in the street, "pale with desire," longing to have a room of her own.[12]

There has been nothing at all of this in the history of the Allemand Lavigeries. They are at the opposite extreme of historical imagination: figures in black and white, or in one dimension, of whom there is only the thinnest historical evidence. There is nothing of their vistas of the future, or of their pale desires and pink ribbons, their chance encounters in the streets of Paris. But Charles Martial is different, somewhere in between evidence and imagination. His biographers were drawn irresistibly to descriptions of his inner life. He was a man of "insatiable ambition," for one contemporary; "a sort of *conquistador*, a Napoléon of prayer and evangelization," for another; a "colossal figure of an athlete," who crushed and seduced; a "hurricane of thought and will," "egotistical, authoritarian, absolute, dominating, imperious to the point of despotism"; of "handsome presence and handsome being."[13]

There have been only the faintest glimpses, so far, of what the Allemand Lavigeries looked like. One cousin (the youngest grandson of Marie Aymard, who married the lemonade seller) was "one meter seventy-three centimeters" tall, with "a long oval face" and dark chestnut hair; the novelist in Tahiti described Léon Bernard as tall and handsome; there was the watercolor portrait of Gabriel Ferrand, the first archivist of the Charente, displayed in the historical society of Angoulême in 1910 and long since disappeared.[14] The evidence of the material existence of Charles Martial, once again, is very different. There are photographs of him as a young priest in Syria in 1860, with dark sunken eyes, dressed in a djellabah, and in Rome in an elaborate ecclesiastical-legal costume, with unruly black hair and extraordinarily long fingers. There are paintings of him as bishop of Nancy (with a strong resemblance to Napoléon I), and as a missionary in the robes of the White Fathers. There were statues in Biskra, Bayonne, Algiers, Tunis, and the African Pavilion in the Vatican, and a sepulchre in white marble, in which he is surrounded by "an Arab woman with her child," "converted Negroes carrying palms," and the kneeling figures of missionaries.[15]

In a portrait from 1888, more than twice as large as life, Charles Martial is dressed in scarlet satin and holding a pen, with his cardinal's hat resting on a map of Africa. He looks amused and massive, gazing at the painter; it was "Rabelais become a cardinal," in the description of the journal *La lanterne*.[16] Of the same portrait, now in Versailles, Charles Martial said himself, to the governor-general of Algeria, "[I was painted] sitting down, with a pen in my hand. I would rather he had painted me standing up, ready to fight the good fight."[17]

Charles Martial Allemand Lavigerie

Charles Martial's story is a part of the family history of the Allemand Lavigeries, at the same time, and a part of the history of economic life in nineteenth-century France. The point of this inquiry has been to start with individuals and their own connections, their families, neighbors, and friends, and to follow them into their different enterprises and industries. It has been a history from below, or from the micro to the macro, that has led to interstices of the economy that are obscure, for the most part, in large histories of economic growth. The nineteenth-century Allemand Lavigeries sought to make their fortunes in the administration of taxes and customs duties, in the military, and in the intermediate services of provincial banking. Charles Martial found fame (and fortune) in the least modern of all industries, which was also—at least in the view of its nineteenth-century enemies—at the center of economic power.

The advancement of Charles Martial started, in the chronology of his early biographers, with an act of adolescent rebellion against the influence of his family. He grew up, in these accounts, in a household in which religion was of less than central importance, amidst the "restless skepticism" of the end of the restoration and the "facile liberalism of the July monarchy." His parents, Léon Philippe, the receiver of customs, and the poetic Louise Latrilhe, were described as living in a sociable milieu of "very nuanced opinions," and "even, or so it appears, of fairly diverse beliefs," since "certain Jewish families" were "not excluded."[18] To become a priest, for Charles Martial, was in these accounts to reject the enduring influence of the Enlightenment, the French Revolution, and the control of the state over the rituals of birth, marriage, and deaths.

In 1841, at the age of sixteen, Charles Martial moved to Paris. He studied in the "Ecole des Carmes," or the college of religious instruction established in 1845 in the buildings of the old prison in which Léonard Robin had been held with the future Empress Joséphine during the French Revolution, and where Noel Virol, the counterrevolutionary surgeon from Angoulême, had leapt to his death in 1794.[19] Charles Martial was ordained as subdeacon in 1847, as deacon in 1848, and as a priest in 1849.[20]

In Paris, Charles Martial became a historian. The first of his two doctoral dissertations, in 1850, was on the early historian of Christianity Hegesippus, an almost unknown figure who came from Palestine and wrote in Greek; it is a study, in part, of the process of writing history on the basis of fragments.[21] (One of the fragments was about the devotion of St. James, who knelt so much that his knees were like those of camels: "instar cameli occalluerint," in Charles Martial's translation.)[22] The other dissertation was a history of the Christian school of Edessa in northern Mesopotamia, now the provincial capital of Urfa, in southeast Turkey. It is the portrait of a lost city on a hill, and an evocation of economic life: of a metropolis "on the route to India and Persia," where the "riches of the East were united with those of the Roman world." There was an upper town and a lower town, a port on the river Scirtus, a tributary of the Euphrates; it was a place of "artisans," "merchants," and Greek money changers, in which "men of all countries, in the clothing of their homelands, meet, engage with one another, and leave again," bringing brass from Persia, and loading textiles onto boats bound for "the Persian Gulf and the Eritrean Sea."[23]

There is a sense in the dissertation of longing and melancholy. Edessa was once a city of archives, of twelve Christian churches, and of an ancient library, "one of the richest of the East." It was the home for thirty years of the great Syriac poet St. Ephrem, orator of the "nothingness of human things." The school of Edessa was itself "entirely historical," believing in the "historical truth of the Bible"; it transformed the "religious destiny of the East," bringing Christian doctrine even to "India and China," and introducing the "philosophy of Aristotle to the Arabs." But on one terrible night, the waters of the Scirtus rose suddenly in the darkness, destroying the lower town. Edessa was ravaged by famine; the Christian school was expelled, in 489, by the Byzantine emperor Zeno.[24]

Charles Martial turned to the study of theology after his historical investigations, and was appointed in 1854, at the age of twenty-eight, to the chair of ecclesiastical history at the Sorbonne.[25] He visited his family on many occasions over these years, the divergence of political destinies notwithstanding. On his vacations, he stayed with his parents in Marseille, according to his mother's old friend, the book-loving customs official, who even published two little verses in Charles Martial's honor, "Stances à Monsieur l'Abbé L.***" and "Epître à Monsieur l'abbé L***."[26] He was in Angoulême for each of the elaborate marriage contracts of the 1850s: of his second cousin, Marie Louise, when she married the future banker Henri Portet-Lavigerie; for the marriage of his sister Louise and Gabriel Kiener; and for Marie Françoise, his first cousin once removed. He was part of the milieu of the elderly sisters on the Rempart du Midi, who were the repository of family memories, or the continuity, at least, between the eighteenth-century family in Angoulême and the nineteenth-century family dispersed around France and the world.

At the Sorbonne, Charles Martial lectured on the history of Protestantism and Jansenism in France. He published a bilingual edition of the *Oedipus* of Sophocles, and an "expurgated" edition of the third book of Cicero's *De officiis*, on utility and the state.[27] He was denounced for "rationalist and heretical instruction"—in his support for the doctrine of papal infallibility—and supported himself by collaborating on a series of small (18°) volumes for schools on geography and history, "from the Gauls to our own times."[28] But he was bored by his life in Paris. "I was teaching the history of Jansenism to twenty-five students," he recalled, in a reminiscence quoted by his biographer; "I had the sense that I was suffocating."[29]

The Syrian Crisis

In 1856, Charles Martial's destiny changed again. He was invited into an office at the center of French overseas power—the Depository of the Maps and Plans of the Navy, then on the Rue de l'Université—and informed that he had been appointed director of the newly established Oeuvre des Ecoles d'Orient, founded in the aftermath of the Crimean War to raise money for Catholic communities in the Ottoman Empire. It was a Catholic association or *opus*; a "civil society organization" or "nongovernmental organization," supported by the dignitaries of the new, expansive state of the Second Empire. The first honorary president of the Oeuvre was the general who had commanded the French army in Crimea. The second, who selected Charles Martial, was an admiral, at the time the director of the Depository of Naval Maps, who had been the last, reformist governor of Martinique before the abolition of slavery in 1848; "I have visited the plantations. I have listened to the masters and spoken to the slaves," he said in a speech in 1847; "I can attest that the slaves are enjoying the ameliorations that the law brings them, while retaining the mildnesses [*adoucissements*] that they owe to the will of the masters."[30]

The Oeuvre des Ecoles d'Orient was a return, for Charles Martial, to the lost world of Eastern Christianity. It was also the introduction to a new enterprise in which he was engaged for the rest of his life, and which he helped to invent, in France and around the world. This was the enterprise, or industry, of overseas philanthropy. Over the next three years, he preached and raised money in every part of France, from Nantes and Nancy to Marseille, Bordeaux, and Bayonne. There were new committees, a new "Bulletin," and letters of support from Pope Pius IX. The Oeuvre supported Christian schools in Smyrna, Damascus, and Jerusalem, provided funds for an Arabic printing press for Christian books in Ghazir, and purchased a "lithographic press" for the Dominicans in Mosul.[31]

The "Syrian massacres" of 1860—the terrible killings of Maronite Christians that became one of the first "humanitarian crises" of the modern times of lithographic and telegraphic news—changed Charles

Martial's life yet again. The news of the killings of Christian villagers by Druze militias in Mount Lebanon, within a long civil conflict in Lebanon, reached Europe in June 1860, and in July the tragedy had spread to Damascus. "The corpses of nearly twenty thousand victims" were covered by "bloody ruins," Charles Martial wrote later of the events of the summer of 1860; "nearly two hundred thousand Christians, of all denominations, of all rites, were wandering without shelter, without clothing, without food"; "three hundred thousand more were awaiting, anxiously, a similar fate."[32]

Over the course of 1860, the Oeuvre des Ecoles d'Orient became the essential relief organization in the crisis. There was a "centralization of assistance," and the Oeuvre was the fiduciary recipient for funds raised in campaigns by sixteen French newspapers. It was a liaison with the French expeditionary force that was sent as a "mission of humanity" to the eastern Mediterranean, and with the consular officials of the French Empire, protectors of Eastern Christians following the Treaty of Paris that ended the Crimean War.[33] The organization received donations from France, Belgium, Brazil, and Senegal, from Edinburgh and Bologna and Buffalo, New York. There were donations in kind, piles of clothes and church ornaments; it was estimated that 360 villages had been destroyed, and 560 churches. The Oeuvre had raised 16,000 francs in 1857, and 60,391 francs in 1859. In 1860–1861, over the nine months of the Syrian crisis, the receipts increased more than thirtyfold, to 2,136,701 francs.[34]

The year 1860 was a time of endings for the Allemand Lavigeries. Charles Martial himself was on medical leave early in the year; the oldest of his great-aunts, Jeanne *ainée*, died in Angoulême in July 1860; his father retired from the service of the customs administration.[35] But when the news from the East started to arrive in June 1860, Charles Martial returned to a period of intense activity. By early September, he was preparing to travel to Lebanon. He had a premonition of his own death. "I was convinced that I would not return from this voyage, and that I would die in this land of the East, where I was going to provide relief," he wrote in his report to the subscribers to the Oeuvre; "I said farewell, within myself, to my country, my family, and my studies," with "a secret joy that I was going to die, if God so wished, in assisting my brothers."[36]

Charles Martial's father, Léon Philippe, died on September 14: the death just before midnight in the railway station of Saumur, reported by the two employees of the railway.[37] Charles Martial was at the time on the way to Saumur, according to his biographer Baunard, who quoted a letter in which Charles Martial wrote that he was planning to pass through Tours on the way to visit his father in Saumur. Baunard surmised that he found his father dying: "M. Allemand-Lavigerie expired in a Christian manner, on September 15, 1860, in the arms and with the blessing of his son."[38] So Charles Martial was there, in this account, at the station of the Chemin de Fer d'Orléans in Saumur; or he arrived too late: these were tumultuous days in his life. He returned to Paris, in any case, left again on September 27, and embarked from Marseille on September 30, on a ship called the *Indus*, a small steamship of the Messageries Impériales, bound for Alexandria.[39]

"It was a spectacle of desolation and barbarism," Charles Martial wrote of the East to which he had come at last. Beirut was a city of horror, filled with "refugees, wandering like ghosts in the streets"; he saw "blood everywhere," and piles of ashes "filled with human bones." He traveled to the villages in Mount Lebanon where the killing had begun, and was greeted by 350 children singing, "Vive la France! Vive le directeur de l'Oeuvre des Ecoles d'Orient!" He was seriously injured when his horse fell on a stony mountain track near Hammana, on the road to Damascus.[40] He also visited Bethlehem, Jerusalem, and Nazareth. In Damascus, he met the emir 'Abd al-Qādir, the former leader of resistance to the French occupation of Algeria, later prisoner of the French, and the protector, depicted in orientalist painting, of Christians during the massacres.[41] In December 1860, Charles Martial returned to France, pausing on the way to visit Pope Pius IX in Rome.[42]

Charles Martial's account of his months in the East was an outline of the future destiny of French overseas power, as well as a report to the subscribers of the Oeuvre. The expedition of the French navy to Syria in the summer of 1860 had been a "mission of humanity," in the description of Napoléon III; "humanity demands a swift intervention."[43]

Charles Martial was full of praise for the French officers and diplomats, as well as for the French silk manufacturers in Mount Lebanon.[44] But he saw little hope, in the end, without a "vigorously constituted Christian government" of Lebanon, under the "official protectorate" of France. The Druze militias were for him no more than "instruments," and not the "truly guilty." There were many evil forces, including the Ottoman administration and the self-interested English (defenders of the Druze, and avid, like the "Prussians" and the "Anglo-Americans," for the souls of Catholic orphans). The true enemy was much larger, and it inhered, in Charles Martial's description, in a "general disposition of minds within Islam": in "Muslim fanaticism."[45]

The Bishop of Nancy

On his return to France, Charles Martial was awarded the Légion d'honneur for his work in raising money for Syria and his conduct in Lebanon; he was welcomed, at once, into the religious elite of the Second Empire.[46] In August 1861, he was appointed, on the nomination of the emperor, as a judge or auditor in the high Vatican court, the Rota.[47] He lived in Rome for less than two years, in a "modest" palazzo on the Piazza degli Santi Apostoli; this was the period when he was photographed in his ecclesiastical-legal costume.[48] He had a salon on Monday evenings, where he received the French community, "general officers, the embassy staff."[49] In March 1863, he was promoted once again, at the age of thirty-seven, to become bishop of Nancy, in Lorraine.[50] He chose the church of San Luigi dei Francesi in Rome—where Frédéric Bastiat, his grandfather's neighbor from Bayonne, had been buried in 1850—for his consecration as bishop, in the course of which he carried an imposing neo-Gothic miter, commissioned for the occasion.[51]

Charles Martial devoted himself, as bishop of Nancy—then a rich industrial town of small manufacturing enterprises, at the outset of a mining and metalworking boom—to the grandiose renovation of the eighteenth-century cathedral.[52] There were "literary and intellectual festivals," including a performance by local schoolboys, in Greek, of the *Electra* of Sophocles.[53] Charles Martial received permission from

Pius IX to wear a special kind of ornament called a "surhumeral" or "rationale": a "large stole, decorated with a fringe that dangles over the shoulders," and "covered with precious stones."[54] He had his own coat of arms, of which there is a watercolor draft in the Archives Lavigerie in Rome. It is a pelican, against a brilliant blue shield, piercing her own breast to feed three little birds, with the device *Caritas*, or charity, surmounted by the cross of Lorraine and the dangling, fringed stole.[55]

In July 1866, Charles Martial entertained the empress Eugénie and her unfortunate ten-year-old son, who later became the pretender "Napoléon IV," and died in the Anglo-Zulu War. The festivities of the imperial visit—which were the subject of a 178-page brochure published in Nancy—involved a further redecoration of the cathedral, with a "splendid gilded dome" and draperies of "deep red velvet, fringed in gold braid"; there was also a procession of schoolchildren, including a group from a local boys' school carrying "a sky-blue banner that bore the arms of M. Lavigérie."[56] Before returning to Paris, Eugénie invested Charles Martial with a new imperial distinction: a more elevated rank in the Légion d'honneur.[57] In November 1866, he was nominated as archbishop of Algiers, and left Nancy forever.[58]

"My Beloved Africa"

Charles Martial had arrived, at the age of forty-one, in the continent that he considered to be his destiny. He moved into the episcopal palace on the Place du Gouvernement in Algiers, a former residence of the bey or Ottoman governor—he described it, later that year, as "sordid," "absolutely lacking in air and space," "uninhabitable for a European," and with furnishings in a "state of dilapidation, disrepair and disorder"—in May 1867.[59] His responsibilities were extended, the following year, to a "vast territory" of "the Sahara and the Sudan." There was for the first time an "apostolic delegation"—with Charles Martial as the first delegate—for Saharan and sub-Saharan Africa, bounded to the west by the Atlantic Ocean, to the east by the "Egyptian desert," and to the south by "Senegal and Guinea."[60] Charles Martial became religious administrator of Tunis in 1881, a cardinal in 1882, and "primate of Africa" in 1884. He died in another palace in Algiers in 1892, after having written a "spiritual testament": "It is to you that I now come, oh my beloved Africa."[61]

The French colony in North Africa, when Charles Martial arrived in Algiers, was in the early months of the sequence of calamities that became the great Algerian famine of 1868, in which an estimated 150,000 people died, or almost 10 percent of the population.[62] His period in Africa started, as in the Syrian crisis of 1860, with a humanitarian emergency. He was depicted—in an inversion of the scene of 'Abd al-Qādir in Damascus—as saving Muslim children, held out by their mothers to his embrace. The first use he made in Algiers of his enduring literary powers—and his powers of fund-raising—was in heartbreaking descriptions of the famine: "I can see them still, these poor little children," "their great eyes" shining with "the sinister fever of hunger."[63] The palace on the Place du Gouvernement became a shelter for victims of the famine; there is a lithograph, published in *L'illustration*, of the archbishop receiving emaciated children.[64] Charles Martial asked the bishops of France for their assistance in a national campaign for the "Arab orphans," and established three different orphanages, in an estate rented from the Jesuits, followed by eight more nearby; in eight months, he wrote, he had "gathered 1,753 orphans."[65]

The Society of African Missionaries, which Charles Martial founded in 1868, was known as the society of the "White Fathers" because of their distinctive robes; they wore "Arab dress," ate the same food as "the natives," spoke only Arabic, and provided medical care to all.[66] They traveled into the Great Lakes region of sub-Saharan Africa, and promoted agricultural enterprises across the French colonies of North Africa; they had a monumental white stone residence, in the former Ottoman barracks of El-Harrach, now a northern suburb of Algiers. It was on "one of our beautiful spring evenings," Charles Martial wrote, that he was first taken to see an undeveloped property of six hundred hectares, extending south from El-Harrach, which the French called "La Maison-Carrée." It had "one of the most beautiful views in the world," and Charles Martial decided, like the rural potentate he had become, that this was where "my little children" would clear away the undergrowth, and build a new Africa for themselves and the future.[67]

Charles Martial was surrounded, for the rest of his life, by the children whom he described as "my adoptive family." There were children with him on his journeys in search of funds for relief, and children at his feet in photographs and statues. He published a pamphlet with the resounding title *Les orphelins arabes d'Alger, leur passé, leur avenir, leur adoption.* He even had two "young Arabs" brought to him in Rome, whom he presented to Pius IX. They recited the Ten Commandments, and were baptized in the church of the Trinità dei Monti by "Cardinal Bonaparte" (one of the great-nephews of Napoléon I). As recounted in the newspaper *L'univers,* "they were almost savages only a few years earlier, from Muslim Africa," and had been "saved from death by the archbishop of Algiers"; they "came to Europe to live there," and were called "Abd-el-Kader-ben-Mohamed and Hamed-ben-Aicha."[68]

Where Is Africa?

In his first pastoral letter as archbishop of 1867, even before he left France, Charles Martial outlined a vast project of restoring the "African church," and extending it to the "center of this immense continent." As in his early, melancholy study of the history of Eastern Christianity, the letter was an evocation of the lost Christian past in Africa, of St. Cyprian, bishop of Carthage, and St. Augustine, bishop of Hippo.[69] It was a description of an "early Christian world" that was unfamiliar then (as now); a society that "floats over the modern map of Europe, Africa and the Middle East," in Peter Brown's description, "like the gigantic cloud of a once-vibrant galaxy," "hesitant" in Western Europe and "thriving throughout northern Africa as far south as Ethiopia, and in the Middle East as far east as Iran and Central Asia."[70]

"Where is Africa, which was for the whole world a garden of delights?" asked Quodvultdeus—"what God wishes"—who was the last bishop of Carthage at the time of the Vandal conquest in 439, and whom Charles Martial invoked in welcoming a delegation of visiting nuns in 1872.[71] The old Africa had been a place of "opulent towns" and "fertile plains," in Charles Martial's description, and these, too, could rise from the dead.[72] This was the epoch of environmental optimism in French

North Africa, of the trans-Saharan railway, and of the "inland sea in Algeria," projected by a military cartographer in the oasis of Biskra and the promoter of the Suez Canal.[73] Charles Martial's eventual enterprise was of capacious historical scope. It was to find the Africa that had been lost—to turn back time, climate change, and the decline of the Roman Empire.

In 1867, in the initial pastoral letter, Charles Martial had cited his patron, Napoléon III, and the aspiration that "the glory of France," based "not on conquest but on the love of humanity and progress," should "resound from Tunis to the Euphrates."[74] But church and state and conquest—or humanity, commerce, and empire—were impossible to disentangle in his projects. There were armed missionaries in the oasis of Biskra to protect the settlements of the White Fathers: "armed brothers."[75] Charles Martial was a visionary of military victory, and a powerful auxiliary of the new and eventually republican imperialism of the times. For one of his early biographers, Charles Martial was "a sort of *conquistador*, a Napoléon of prayer and evangelization."[76] In the neo-revolutionary journal *La lanterne*, he was "a military autocrat, the Fernando Cortés of the Sahara."[77]

In Algiers, from his arrival in 1867 to his death in 1892, Charles Martial was a continuing exponent of armed expansion in Africa, over the course of dizzying changes in French public life, and in his own political positions. He was there, or going to and fro, on steamship journeys between North Africa, France, and Rome, in the last years of the Second Empire; in the Franco-Prussian War that ended the empire, and the Paris Commune of 1871; over the republican and monarchist governments of the early Third Republic, from 1871 to 1880. He was there, still, in the period of imperial conquest that started in 1881, with the military invasion of Tunis, and the republican imperialism of Léon Gambetta (prime minister in 1881–1882) and Jules Ferry, the "true creators of colonial policy," in the view of a contemporary.[78] Lavigerie and his missionaries, in Tunis, had "provided more services to France than an army corps," Gambetta told one of Charles Martial's emissaries; "anticlericalism is not a commodity for export."[79]

The ultimate enemy for Charles Martial in Africa, as in Syria, was the Muslim religion. His reason for accepting the position in Algiers, he wrote in a private letter quoted by his biographer Baunard, was that "I felt most intensely the shame of the French nation, in having been for almost forty years in proximity to a Muslim people, who were their subjects, not only without having tried to convert them, but even having prevented any attempts to do so by the Catholic clergy."[80] "How could the error of Islamism have extinguished the brilliant flame of the faith?" he asked in his report to donors in 1861 (in words he attributed to an "elegy on the ruins of Damascus," by students in the Christian college of Ghazir).[81] It was in a vast conflict with Islam, eight years later, that the new society of African missionaries found its enduring purpose. "Since the beginning of this century, more than forty million men have embraced Islamism" in sub-Saharan Africa, Charles Martial wrote in 1869; the eventual objective of his "little society" was "the conversion of all Muslim peoples," in the "entirety of Africa."[82]

Outside Angoulême

Charles Martial was by the 1870s a worldwide celebrity. An article by the travel writer Elizabeth Herbert about "his great and really superhuman work," reprinted in the American press, described him dressed in "full pontificals" to receive a procession of generals, under a "canopy borne by natives in white burnouses and scarlet sashes"; he was "'the great marabout,'" she wrote, and "the English Consul exclaimed: 'We have seen another St. Augustine!'"[83] Charles Martial was also an object of limitless satire in the republican press. He was never in Africa, according to the newspaper *La justice*, and always in Rome or Paris.[84] His elevation to the biretta of a cardinal in 1882, in the presidential palace of the Elysée in Paris, was like the ceremony of a lobster in boiling water, for *Le rappel*, to be celebrated by music to the tune of "Leaving for Syria / The handsome Lavigerie . . ."[85] For *La justice*, it was a "burlesque" of red robes, red caps, and a red hat on a crimson pillow, in which Charles Martial arrived in a violet robe, retired into an inner room, and emerged in a scarlet robe: a travesty of the separation of church and state.[86]

Over the quarter of a century of his life in North Africa, Charles Martial returned frequently to France. He took his summer holidays in Biarritz, and was sent by his doctors to the thermal spa of Cambo-les-Bains, near the Spanish frontier. He thought of buying a retirement home in the foothills of the Pyrénées. The bishop of Angoulême (and friend of the younger Paul Abadie) entrusted his letter of resignation, addressed to Pius IX, into the hands of "my venerable friend, the archbishop of Algiers."[87] Charles Martial went often to Angoulême, or at least passed through the town, on his way to visit his sister Louise, who had settled with her husband, Gabriel Kiener, in their own house in the paper mill at Lacourade, outside Angoulême, at the end of a row of workers' cottages, and opposite the entrance to the elegant residence of the Henry-Lacourade family.

Lacourade was the venue, even, of another of the deathbed scenes with which Baunard's biography of Charles Martial is so adorned; it was there that he "received the last breath of M. Keiner [*sic*], his brother-in-law."[88] Gabriel Kiener, "paper manufacturer, living in the factory at Lacourade," died in July 1875, at the age of forty-five. The witnesses were his cousin by marriage, Georges Henry-Lacourade, and another skilled employee in the mill, a "manufacturer of vegetable-based glue."[89] "Augustin ab-del-Kader," who was listed in the census of 1872 as the domestic servant of Louise Lavigerie and Gabriel Kiener, was the namesake of the "young Arab" baptized in Rome in 1870: "Abd-el-Kader-ben-Mohamed" (who "came to Europe to live there").[90] By 1876, Augustin ab-del-Kader was no longer there, in Lacourade; "Augustin Charles Abd-el-Kader," described as a domestic servant living in the fourteenth arrondissement in Paris, died in the hospital of the Kremlin-Bicêtre in 1898.[91]

Charles Martial corresponded with Louise throughout his years in Africa. She visited him in Algeria, and traveled to the oasis of Biskra, home of the armed missionaries; he met her in Paris, where she made elaborate arrangements for a hotel room that would be not too noisy, facing the Rue de Rivoli or the Opera (and not too surrounded, in another echo of Zola's sequence of family histories, by the new department stores that had "absorbed" ever more space).[92] Some of Louise's letters are formal; she addresses Charles Martial as "vous," and recommends the son of an old friend, an artillery officer in Tunis, or a pastry-maker in

Bona (Annaba), the son of the postman in La Couronne.[93] In others, there is the sense of a continuing, intimate conversation, about politics, money, and family relationships.

"Life is so sad, when one is feeling ill," Louise wrote from the Pyrénées, and, addressing him as "tu," "you really have no excuse for overworking in the way you are"; "I have placed the order in Angoulême to send you twelve bottles of brandy."[94] She reports on her own illnesses, and sends advice about his. She describes villas that he could rent for his summer holidays; there is a misunderstanding with a cousin on their mother's side over one of the properties, and a dubious character called "M. L——," of whom the cousin assures Louise that he is "only a republican in the sense that my father is, or my husband, or our Uncle Félix, and what is more he is perfectly Catholic, unlike them."[95] Louise is anxious about her own financial security, and the economic life of Angoulême. She asks Charles Martial's advice about whether she can afford to buy a house of which the price has recently been reduced, and place "my capital"—or the small inheritance from their mother's family—in a life tenancy. There has been a "local financial catastrophe," she writes from Lacourade; she is worried about the price of paper, "foreign competition" in the paper industry, and the possibility that she might no longer be able to live in the paper mill. Of Charlotte-Ursule's son, their first cousin and the heir to Lacourade, she writes that "his character is such that it is impossible to have a rational explanation with him."[96]

There are intricacies of family news, from time to time. "Have you seen the Portets?" Louise asks, as though with an ironic smile, of the rich second cousins from Le Mans. "They have been moving heaven and earth for the past ten days to try and reach you, in order to ask you to be kind enough to bless the marriage of their son, and to fix the date." This was the marriage of René, the law student with an interest in the Roman law of slavery, who was engaged to a "charming" young woman with "no fortune." "Everyone in the family loves and appreciates her," Louise wrote, except for "that unhappy Berthe" (one of the Topin cousins, who had earlier lived in the pension on the Rempart du Midi). Berthe had "once again had the clumsiness to take a violent dislike" to the new daughter-in-law, and would never be forgiven; "after her affairs with Val-

CHARLES MARTIAL AND LOUISE   283

entine, this was all that was needed to make her fully out of favor with them! It is jealousy that has made her lose her brain!"[97]

Lavigerie's Architecture

Louise was a connection between home and the empire even in respect of Charles Martial's largest conceptions. The old church in Africa was a land of "innumerable temples" and "seven hundred bishops," he wrote in his inaugural pastoral letter, and his enduring preoccupation was with the infrastructure of religion: the construction of churches, monasteries, and cathedrals, "provisional" and enduring. Under the debris of modern African cities, "below the temples of Islamism," there were still the "sacred remains of old basilicas," Charles Martial wrote in 1867, and it was amidst these ruins that the new church was to rise again.[98] He was eventually bishop of Carthage, himself, and he saw his own destiny, ever more explicitly, as the successor not only of Cyprian of Carthage and Quodvultdeus, but also of Augustine, "genius of our Africa," "writer, philosopher, theologian," and "my immortal predecessor."[99]

The Allemand Lavigeries had been at the margins, in France, of the economy of material restoration after the revolution: the economic life of the diocesan architect amidst which the Abadies flourished in Angoulême, of prison architects, and of the small churches in Champagne and Ardennes in which Charles-Silvestre Topin found intermittent employment.[100] In North Africa, Charles Martial was a master builder, or a pharaoh—like a "pyramid," in the image of another early biographer.[101] He was also strikingly engaged in the details of improvement, even from his earliest administrative letters, following his arrival in 1867. "The prelate appears to need to ask for the construction of a new palace," one of the officials in Paris wrote in a notation on his letter about the "state of dilapidation" of the old archepiscopal palace; a few weeks later, Charles Martial demanded that the land of the "present cavalry barracks" be sold, and used for a palace. "My creditors are asking for payment for the furniture provided," he wrote the following year, and the "situation is embarrassing and painful"; "the building contractor is very rich and can wait. But it is not the same with the founder of church bells."[102]

There was already a cathedral in the center of Algiers when Charles Martial arrived: once the Ketchaoua mosque, as it is now again. It was augmented, over the course of two generations, with a Romanesque pulpit, neo-Roman mosaics, and a "vault covered in arabesques."[103] It was inadequate, Charles Martial wrote to Paris, and "in the presence of our mosques, our temples, and our synagogues, it remains in a wounding condition of inferiority"; "wants credit of 100,000 f. for ornaments and furniture," another official noted on the letter.[104] There was later a new "Romano-Byzantine" Basilica of Notre-Dame d'Afrique; there were chapels, convents, and new buildings in the property extending south from El-Harrach.[105] But it was with the extension of French power to the east, toward Carthage, that the distinctive idiom of "Lavigerie's architecture," in the expression of a modern architectural historian, became evident. It was eclectic and impetuous, "early Gothic," "neo-Gothic," "heraldic," "Punic," and "Gallic."[106]

In Paris, the construction of the church of the Sacré-Coeur of which the younger Paul Abadie was the principal architect—described by its critics as the "mosquée Abadie"—began in 1875, and lasted for thirty-seven years.[107] In North Africa, French troops occupied Tunis in October 1881, and in November 1881 Charles Martial laid the first stone of a "provisional cathedral."[108] The construction was completed in eighty-two days, held "twelve hundred to fifteen hundred people," and was inaugurated on Easter Day 1882, with a sermon on the health of Queen Victoria.[109]

Charles Martial began raising funds, at once, for a permanent cathedral in Tunis, and for an even vaster cathedral to be built in Carthage, in the ruins of the Punic acropolis, above an old temple of Aesculapius, and on the site of an existing chapel to Louis IX of France, who had died in 1270 in North Africa, having paused to (try to) capture Carthage on the way to the Eighth Crusade.[110] The new campaign was directed explicitly to the "nobility of France." There was to be recognition of the donors, including the legitimist pretender to the French throne; the descendants of crusaders could have their heraldic arms inscribed in marble on the church walls, for gifts of one thousand livres or more.[111]

As archbishop of Algiers, Charles Martial was an enthusiastic patron of archaeology, preoccupied with the antiquity that was all around him. "Interrogate the ruins that cover your land," he urged his new parishioners in 1867.[112] In Rome, on his visits to the pope, he stayed in the Hotel Minerva, near the church that inspired Sigmund Freud in his celebrated simile of the historical levels of the human mind.[113] In North Africa, Charles Martial laid the foundation stone of the eventual Cathedral of St. Louis of Carthage, pale, "Romanesque" or "romane," in his own version of what he described elsewhere (in Jerusalem) as an "act of vandalism": the stone was taken from the ruins of the early Christian Basilica of Damous El Karita, where Augustine preached on his visits to Carthage.[114]

Louise, in one of her discursive letters from home, took a close interest in the business of religious architecture. "If it is really a question of appointing a diocesan architect for Tunis," she wrote to Charles Martial from Lacourade in July 1884, "I think you would make an excellent acquisition" in one of her acquaintances from the Dordogne. He was the uncle of "René's wife" (the charming and fortuneless young woman at whose marriage in 1883 Paul Abadie had been a witness), and a man of "unquestioned talent." He had worked with Abadie on the "restoration of Saint Front," Louise wrote—the eleventh-century cathedral in Périgueux, embellished with eight Kremlinesque domes—and the project was "much more his work than that of M. Abadie."[115]

The uncle was unmarried and lived with his elderly mother, and even his family history was seemly; his father had bought property "at a very low price, as a national good," Louise wrote, and returned it to its legitimate owners "when the torment had passed." (This was not the case in respect of the church property that their own great-grandparents had acquired in the same period, and that formed the basis of the fortune of their great-aunts on the Rempart du Midi.) The architect from the Dordogne was "excessively intelligent," "very erudite," and "had only one fault, if fault it be," which consisted in "not being a slave to worldly ways"; "he wears an overcoat instead of a suit, from time to time, and a woolen beret on social occasions." "This aside," Louise concluded, there was no one more upright or loyal, and "I would be very happy if it would suit you to have someone close to you who would be a marvelous support for your large conceptions."[116] But the uncle stayed in the Dordogne, in the end, and was still, in 1905, diocesan architect of Périgueux, organizing the "debris of medieval monuments," under the porch of the cathedral.[117]

A Millionaire, a Multimillionaire

Charles Martial was a worldly figure, in innumerable recollections. He was "a doer, a man of boldness and nerve, who loved noise and agitation"; with "his large face of a fighter, his inquiring and defiant eyes," he was "always in arms."[118] He was also a "marvelously adroit businessman," according to the newspaper *La lanterne*, and it was his economic activities in North Africa, above all, that made him such an object of fascination for the republican press in France. "He has made superb speculations, in Tunis, and a magnificent fortune," *La lanterne* wrote in 1886, and then, in 1888, "he is the most powerful person in Algeria or Tunisia."[119]

The prodigious success of Charles Martial's campaigns to raise money for charitable causes—the relief of refugees in Syria and Lebanon, the orphans in Algeria, the projects of the missionaries, the victims of famine, the Cathedral of St. Louis of Carthage—was only the beginning. He needed five hundred thousand francs in donations each year to support the society of missionaries (the White Fathers), and he was never in debt, he told his clergy in 1874.[120] There was an imposing network of benefactors, with newsletters, annual reports, and correspondents around the world. There were also the official subventions of the government in Paris. Charles Martial was a "mendicant millionaire," for the anticlerical press, and successful, time after time, with parliamentary committees and the politics of budgetary allocations.[121]

"He has a taste for building, modern building," *La justice* wrote in 1886, and the construction of cathedrals and villages—"your large conceptions," in Louise's expression—was itself a vast economic enterprise.[122] A Society for Social Economy, in Paris, listed some of his completed projects, in a tribute to "the fullest life, the most active apostolate, and most French heart of our times": in Algeria alone, there were "sixty-nine churches," two colleges, a seminary, and three hospitals.[123] In Tunis, in the first few months of the French occupation, Charles Martial "received and spent" 1,913,000 francs.[124] The institutions were even self-supporting: "The college of St.-Charles, like the hospital, is a private enterprise. M. le Cardinal de Lavigerie sells soup at St.-Charles, and tisane at the hospital. One does not enter there for free; the hospital costs two francs a day, even for the poor."[125]

Charles Martial's agricultural enterprises, too, were immense. There were vineyards in the new estate of El-Harrach, with irrigation ditches and reed hedges.[126] In the Biskra oasis, he wrote, "I started by buying arid land . . . I looked for underground water. It was found." The "marvelous" discovery was that even the garden vegetables of France could be grown there: "potatoes, cabbages, lettuce, peas, broad beans, artichokes."[127] There were new possibilities of exports, and artichokes were a particular success. Charles Martial was said to own "immense fields of artichokes"; "it appears that a large part of the artichokes we eat in Paris, in winter, come from the farms of M. Lavigerie," according to *La justice*.[128] In Tunis, his vineyards produced a celebrated sweet Muscat, for which he won a Grand Prize at the 1889 Universal Exhibition: awarded "to his eminence Cardinal Lavigerie," "proprietor of the famous vineyards planted on the very ruins of ancient Carthage."[129]

"This Lavigerie, it appears, is the cleverest and most successful business tycoon one could meet, in Tunisia or even in Algeria," *La lanterne* wrote in 1885.[130] He had "vast property holdings"; he bought land along the line of the projected railway, and seafront property near the naval base; he built holiday villas for the winter rental season. He lived like a rich man, in the episcopal palaces, "amidst an entirely oriental luxury."[131] "I was accused [of] being a millionaire, a multimillionaire," Charles Martial wrote in the only semiautobiographical biography that he authorized in his lifetime. Once, when his brother Félix had stopped to buy tobacco in a shop in Algiers, Charles Martial happened to pass by in a carriage, and the shopkeeper pointed him out as "the richest man in Algeria": "He is the proprietor of all the steamships in the port."[132]

"There are neither millions nor mine," Charles Martial wrote, and "I am poor." He rejected the "calumny of money and riches," of which his authorized biographer wrote that "envy, natural everywhere, is most particularly so in a colony where everyone has come out of the desire to make a fortune."[133] One of his old friends from his college days in Paris, who became the governor-general of Algeria, wrote that Charles Martial "loved magnificence" in religion and the "exterior life," and lived "in his personal life like a poor man"; "it is difficult to imagine anything more naked and more sad than his house and the room in which he lived."[134] His economic empire, like his "immense riches in Africa," was philanthropic, or humanitarian: a fortune made and expended every year, a practicality.[135]

Universal Slavery

Charles Martial's last cause was the one for which he was most famous at the time, and for which he was longest remembered. It had been at the edge of his vision since he arrived in North Africa. "Slavery still reigns" in the center of Africa, he wrote in one of his letters about the orphans of the 1868 famine; he invited the French army in Algeria, in 1875, to lift their sights beyond the limits of "our horizon," to the "universal slavery" of "this immense continent."[136] In the 1880s, with "the stories of the recent explorers," "Belgian, English-American"—and above all with the reports of the missionaries of his own order, who went south to the Great Lakes, starting in 1878—the trans-Saharan slave trade became a consuming cause.[137] There was an Oeuvre, again, and a commission from Pope Leo XIII: the "Oeuvre antiesclavagiste," or the Antislavery Mission.[138]

The history of slavery in the American colonies, Charles Martial said in July 1888, had "shamed the world for three centuries by its cruelty." Eventually, with the "crusade" of French and English writers, American slavery began to decline. Slavery ended in Cuba, and in Brazil (in May 1888). But "after having done away with slavery in America, and having established cruisers in the Red Sea and the Indian Ocean, which were to prevent the transport of slaves into Asia," the "zeal of the Christian nations grew cold." "The generous indignation died out," and "men seemed to have forgotten that slavery still existed upon earth." Yet slavery and the terrestrial slave trade were "still flourishing, with untold horrors, in the heart of Africa." It was indeed "a hundred times more horrible" than colonial slavery, Charles Martial said in a speech to launch the new mission, delivered in London, sponsored by the Antislavery Society, and advertised as "The Crusade against the Slave Trade." "African slavery," in Cardinal Manning's words, "was a thousand times worse than anything known in the west."[139]

"I have not slept in my own home or eaten at my own table" since the beginning of the mission, Charles Martial wrote in January 1889. The "crusade against the hideous exploitation of man by man" continued at an intense pace until 1891, with the signature of the Brussels Convention of 1890 that sought to "put an end to Negro Slave Trade by land as well as by sea."[140] As in his earliest writings in Africa, Charles Martial invoked "my immortal predecessor, St. Augustine"; he was in his own self-description, in an address in the cathedral of Milan, an "old African bishop," the "poor successor of St. Augustine."[141] As in Syria in 1860 and in Algeria in 1868, the antislavery mission was identified as part of a universal struggle against the "mahométisme" that had now invaded "half of Africa": an "esclavagisme" that was condoned only by Islam, and an "islamisme esclavagiste."[142]

The new campaign was the culmination, above all, of Charles Martial's inventiveness in "nongovernmental" or "humanitarian" organization. He gave speeches and press conferences in London, Rome, Naples, and Brussels; he corresponded with Bismarck, King Leopold of the Belgians, and the ten-year-old Queen Wilhelmina of Holland; there were corresponding societies in Haiti and Brazil; he was described as "the great liberator of Africa." The campaign for the abolition of "colonial slavery" was taken as an explicit model: the "story of infamous scenes," the intensity with which "news to do with slave ships" was "reported, commented, discussed," the treatises, apologias, and novels of which the outcome, eventually, was to transform "European opinion."[143] Even at the time of the Algerian famine of 1868, Charles Martial had been "a master in the mobilization of the different forms of media," in the description of a recent historian; he "used the new political spaces opened up by the international media" in a "popular culture of horror."[144] In the new media of the 1880s, and with a cause of cosmic horror, the culture of humanity was now literally worldwide.[145]

Charles Martial was a virtuoso, amidst all his eloquence, of visual persuasion. The "pilgrimage to Rome" of May 1888, in the course of which he was invested with the new Oeuvre, was described as the most grandiose ceremony since the adoration of the Magi; the future liberator was surrounded by "twelve Negro Christians from the interior of Africa," "twelve Arabs or Kabylians from Algeria," twelve priests from the twelve Algerian dioceses, and twelve White Fathers.[146] There were photographs, engravings, paintings, lithographs. The hyperbole of an early biographer, in 1905—"his image is familiar to all"—was the outcome of these campaigns.[147] Even in his letters from supporters, the represented and the remembered were jumbled together: "One of our stained glass windows represents the Mass in Kabylia of Horace Vernet, at which I was present as an ordinance officer," a retired general wrote to Charles Martial from the Marne in 1889, of the French military in Algeria in 1853, as depicted by the orientalist Horace Vernet.[148]

The 724 pages of documents on the Oeuvre antiesclavagiste that Charles Martial published in 1889 are a recitation of gifts, and a report, as in the aftermath of the Syrian crisis, to donors. He raised funds and distributed funds to the Afrikaverein Deutscher Katholiken and the British Anti-Slavery Society.[149] There was money from Leo XIII, money given by individuals in Holland to the campaign in Belgium, twenty-five hundred francs for the "printing and distribution" of Charles Martial's speech on the Belgian Congo, and twenty thousand francs for a prize to be awarded to "the work most capable of arousing emotion in Europe on the question of African slavery." There was also the sum of "seven francs" that missionaries from Algeria had spent to buy "eleven children," almost "reduced to skeletons," near Ujiji in modern Tanzania.[150]

Charles Martial's correspondence with the supporters of the cause was a history of terrible memories. "He had a horror of slavery," the widow of a French explorer (and promoter of the trans-Saharan railway) wrote of her late husband in 1890; the explorer had been in a village in the desert, in 1878, when he had come upon "a caravan of slaves that filled him with a great emotion, at the sight of these poor unhappy people."[151] The administrator of a bank in Haiti wrote to Charles Martial from the Place Vendôme in Paris, in 1889, enclosing a check for ten thousand francs; "this money being a tithe on profits made very fast, in a foreign country populated entirely by black people, it is to causes concerned with individuals of this race, I believed, that it should naturally return."[152]

The Brussels conference of 1889–1890 brought the passage of important measures against slavery in Africa. It was invoked as one of the promising omens of the "international leagues" to come; slavery was abolished in Egypt in 1895, in Madagascar in 1896, and in Zanzibar in 1897.[153] Charles Martial was not there (and he was the organizer of a competing conference of antislavery organizations that was held, eventually, in Paris).[154] But he was a notional, virtual presence. The Belgian foreign minister described the origins of the conference in the "touching and persevering eloquence of Cardinal Lavigerie [that] had moved the world for several years"; the British delegate spoke of the "ravages so powerfully depicted by Cardinal Lavigerie"; a memorandum from the Portuguese Ministry of the Navy referred to an "agreement" about missionaries on Lake Nyasa, "between the government of Portugal and Cardinal Lavigerie."[155]

Modern Humanity

Charles Martial Allemand Lavigerie was a great prose stylist and a great orator, a person with a sense of evil, and one whose descriptions of slavery are moving still. "It is an imposing figure who has died," his critics in *La lanterne* wrote after his death: someone who relied on "realities" more than "abstractions," "brilliant and complex, more than vast and profound."[156] He was a "state within the state," and a theorist of the French republican empire.[157] When Jules Ferry, the anticlerical visionary of secular education, traveled to Algeria in 1892, he was taken to visit Charles Martial in his episcopal palace of St.-Eugène. "I will always remember the encounter," the governor-general wrote later; "these two men had never met; they had no ideas in common; everything seemed to divide them; but they were united in love of country, and they fell into each others' arms."[158]

The enemy, for Charles Martial, was an ill-defined force of "Islamism," of which he was one of the first and most militant theorists, from his early mission in Syria to the struggle against the slave traders of Zanzibar. To the secretary of the British Anti-Slavery Society, in 1888, he said that "he had no intention of instituting a war against the Arabs," and "denie[d] that he has ever attacked in any way the Mahommedan religion, many Mussulmans in Africa having long been his firmest friends."[159] But he saw an enduring association of Islam, "Islamism," and "fanaticism."[160] "The Muslim religion is truly the masterpiece of evil," he wrote in 1879, in a letter reprinted in the biography he authorized; "how are we to tear souls from its empire?"[161]

Charles Martial's prospect of a Catholic Church that was ever more African, extending south in peaceful conquest, can be seen as a vision of twentieth-century religion. He was the first apostolic delegate for "the Sahara and the Sudan," and two hundred million Africans, now, are Catholic. His prospect of humanitarian compassion, too, and of lasting agricultural development, with schools for all children, was an anticipation of the future commitments of religious charity.

It was as a visionary of worldwide information, above all, that Charles Martial was a figure of the future, or of modern times. The relief organizations that he invented, almost from nothing, starting in 1856, were immense, efficient business enterprises. He was a prodigious fundraiser, and an irresistible attraction for subsidies from the French (imperial and republican) state, and from the Vatican. He had a worldwide network of correspondents, donors, and newspaper reporters. He installed an "electric telegraph" in the oasis in Biskra, and in the residence of the missionaries in Carthage.[162] He flourished in the early decades of photographic and lithographic diffusion, and he imagined a world of humanitarianism organized around children in Africa.

Charles Martial's admirers, like his critics, saw him as a virtuoso of the media of the times. "There has been scarcely a day over the past twenty-five years," in the account of his first biographer, when the newspapers of France (and Europe) "have not carried his name," with the "announcement of some initiative, usually in the form of his own notification to the public, in a letter, a demand, or a report"; "there are few others in our century who have made use of the press as much as he has, and have manipulated and exploited it as he has done."[163] For his critics, he was the "greatest entrepreneur of Christian propaganda of the epoch."[164]

This is a history that started with an illiterate woman in a small provincial town, Charles Martial's grandfather's grandmother, and the unrecorded, unremembered sources of information by which she was surrounded. Charles Martial made his way in the world in the early decades of the new information technologies of modern times. The telegraph was new; foreign correspondents were new; illustrated newspapers were new; lithographic printing was new. Charles Martial made brilliant use of the new technologies, as so many contemporaries observed. He also invented a new and even more modern way of being: a continuous self-expression, a relationship to hundreds of thousands of people; a universal network of humanitarian enterprise.

The Destiny of the Republic

"Rationalism, naturalism, pantheism, atheism": these were the errors that "covered the face of the world, in this moment," Charles Martial wrote in 1885.[165] His own political involvements, over the course of thirty years of public life, were eclectic to the point of extravagance. "Is it possible that at a certain period in our lives, we might have thought that there was good to be found in liberalism?" he reminisced in 1874, to one of his oldest friends from his student days in Paris.[166] He was an enthusiast of the Second Empire in the 1860s, welcoming the empress Eugénie to Nancy with her son in his black velvet suit, "the future heir of so much power and so much glory!"[167] "There is a gaping abyss on the brink of which we stand," he wrote in 1870, and "it is only the Empire that now separates us from this abyss."[168]

In 1871, Charles Martial was a candidate from the Department of the Landes in the parliamentary elections called in the immediate aftermath of the Franco-Prussian War, identified with the so-called liberal-conservative party, a transient formation devoted to "stability" with "monarchist nuances," according to its friends; for its opponents, it was a "confusing and suspicious anonymity," with no program other than "hatred of the republic" and "devotion to the wishes of Rome."[169] Charles Martial's own manifesto was less than resounding. He wanted to reduce regulations on hunting and fishing; he was not in favor of restoring tithes (to support the church), or the feudal obligation to build roads, or the old regime: "In a word, I think that the law should reduce your taxes and increase your well-being."[170] He came in sixth out of six candidates.[171]

In the 1870s, Charles Martial turned to the monarchist cause of his eventual donors in the cathedral in Carthage. He visited the pretender "Henry V" (the Comte de Chambord) in Bohemia in the summer of 1874, where they were being treated in neighboring spa towns, Carlsbad and Marienbad; the Algerian newspaper *L'akhbar*, in which Charles Martial was reported to have "succeeded in buying the majority of shares," was directed toward "conservative ideas."[172] These were the ideas with which he was now identified, long after Chambord's own retirement from political life. "Family connections united our family to that of your eminence," a descendant of the Dereix family of Angoulême wrote to him in 1891; she asked his help for her nephew, whose father had been "brusquely dismissed from his position, for his conservative and religious opinions."[173]

Charles Martial's last political adventure was another departure. On November 12, 1890, he was giving a banquet in his residence in St.-Eugène in honor of the general staff of the French Mediterranean fleet, then at anchor in the port: a day like any other in the life of the "primate of Africa." He had recently returned from a visit to the new pope Leo XIII, of whom the "Christian politics" had turned, by then, to a recognition that the future of the French church lay in reconciliation with the republican form of government. At the end of the banquet, in his toast to the visiting navy, Charles Martial referred to the "union" that existed between church and state in the overseas territories—surrounded as they were by the "foreign"—and expressed the hope, which he described as "authorized," that such union could be restored to France itself. The "will of the people had been clearly affirmed," and the republic that had existed in France since 1870 was not itself inconsistent with Christianity or civilization; the moment had come, therefore, for "adherence, without hesitation, to this form of government."[174] As the dignitaries left, Charles Martial ordered the apostolic band to play the "Marseillaise."[175]

The "Toast d'Alger" at the banquet was an immediate sensation, and became the first ceremonial event in a political process by which the French church "rallied" to the republic. It brought gratitude to Charles Martial from the pope, and abuse unlike anything in his earlier life; his biographer described a sort of flaming or trolling of the new age of information of the 1890s, with the news of the banquet reported by the telegraphic agencies within hours, followed by "mountains of insolence," anonymous letters, caricatures, and "disgusting" envelopes from Marseille.[176] Two years later, Leo XIII published the encyclical about church and state *Au milieu des sollicitudes*, which eventually vindicated Charles Martial: "In the changeable ocean of human affairs," and amidst the long violence of French history, there was a "social need" for "constituted power."[177]

A Red Tide

Charles Martial Allemand Lavigerie died on November 25, 1892, in his palace at St.-Eugène (the modern Bologhine in the suburbs of Algiers, overlooking the sea). He had been unwell for some time. "I cannot conceive the idea of no longer having you close to me," he wrote to his longtime servant Jean-Baptiste, who had retired to the Pyrénées, and then, when Jean-Baptiste wrote in response to say that he would return, "I will wait for you with impatience. Send me a telegram . . . and there will be someone to meet you at the port, as usual."[178] In death, Charles Martial, or his corpse, was moved from the state rooms in his palace to the Basilica of Notre-Dame d'Afrique, and thence to the cathedral in Algiers. There was a funeral service in the cathedral—"the obsequies were a triumph," in the hagiographer Baunard's awed description—and the cortege proceeded to the admiralty ramp, to the sound of cannons and military music. Charles Martial's coffin was then loaded on a naval cruiser, surrounded by whaling boats, each with twelve rowers, and sent to Tunis, to the (provisional) cathedral. It continued, eventually, by train to Carthage, where Charles Martial was buried in the Cathedral of St. Louis of Carthage that he had consecrated two years before.[179]

Louise, Charles Martial's sister, was there, with her two nephews, their brother Léon Bernard's surviving son, Louis Lavigerie, and the widower of his daughter. They were placed amidst the dignitaries of the church at the admiralty ramp; two of the whaling boats were reserved "for the family" and the "authorities."[180] Charles Martial left his papers and personal effects to Louise. She was the legal heir to half his property, which she renounced; his executors gave her 150,000 francs as a pension (of which 145,000 francs were left when she died).[181] For some years, there ensued an unseemly conflict with Louis Lavigerie, who was an actor and playwright. He later published a description of the executors assembled in Charles Martial's private library, valuing his religious ornaments with "burning eyes," in a "red tide" of "scarlet silk and deep red velvet"; Louis too came to an eventual settlement with his uncle's estate.[182]

Louise

The last family ceremony of the Allemand Lavigeries was not the signing of a marriage contract, but the announcement of a death. "Madame Kiener-Lavigerie" was listed as the principal mourner, in the *faire part* or written notification of Charles Martial's death in 1892; there were Léon Bernard's son and grandchildren; the children and grandchildren of Charlotte Ursule Lavigerie, the family from the paper mill in Lacourade; the envious Mademoiselle Berthe Topin of the family of the architects; the Portet-Lavigeries from Le Mans. There were also the Latrilhes, Charles Martial and Louise's relations on their mother's side, and ten other families listed as "cousins." It was a partial listing, as always: an inventory of the surviving respectable members of a large and disparate family.[183]

Charles Martial in his will expressed his "confidence" in Louise, and instructed that in the event of any litigation over his estate, the disputed "goods or values" would revert to her, to dispose of as she wished; she was to be "absolutely free and mistress" of his posterity.[184] He left all his personal papers to her, and the disposition of the papers, together with the relationship between his two families—the religious family in Africa and the private family in France—was the difficult task of the rest of her life. Her nephew Louis Lavigerie settled with the estate only in 1907; there is a note in the Archives Lavigerie from one of the executors (of whom Louis had described the "burning eyes"), annotated as "the conclusion of the affair."[185] When the sculpture in white marble with the "converted Negroes" was exhibited in Paris in 1898—it was destined to be Charles Martial's sarcophagus, and was en route for Carthage—Le Figaro reported that the guests included the banker, or former banker, from Le Mans, "M. Portet-Lavigerie."[186] On the occasion of the marriage of Charlotte Ursule's two grandsons to the daughters of a Paris notary, in 1901, the bridegrooms were described as the great-nephews of the late lamented cardinal, from "one of the oldest families in the Charente."[187]

This has been a family history that has been concerned, at every point, with the women in the extended lives of the Ferrands, the Allemands, and the Lavigeries. It began with an inquisitive widow in Angoulême, Marie Aymard; forty-three out of the eighty-three signatories of the marriage contract of Marie Aymard's daughter, in 1764, were women or girls; the five unmarried sisters on the Rempart du Midi, Marie Aymard's granddaughters, have been at the heart of the nineteenth-century history.

The generations of sisters and daughters have been invisible, at the same time, in the sense that there is so little of their own words, or their own handwriting. There is Jeanne ainée's confident entry about the imputed rental value of her shop, in the register of property in Angoulême in 1798; there are the younger Françoise Ferrand's petitions for relief as a refugee from Saint-Domingue, and the petitions of her daughter and granddaughter; there are the hundreds of signatures on marriage contracts and the registers of marriages. Louise Lavigerie Kiener is the only individual, over these five generations of women, of whom there are any letters at all that have survived (or any that I have been able to find): the letters that survive in the archive, in Rome, of the religious order founded by her world-famous brother.

Louise is invisible, too, in the sense that even her likeness is lost. There is a photograph in the Lavigerie Archive of Charles Martial in 1890, in the oasis settlement of Biskra, to the southeast of Algiers, seated in a garden with four young priests and his servant Jean-Baptiste; it is identified as a "photograph taken by Madame Kiener."[188] But there are no photographs of her that survive (or none, again, that I have been able to find). There is only a blur: a part of a panorama of Charles Martial's obsequies, as the cortege arrives at the admiralty ramp in the port of Algiers, with, to the right, the "bishops and officiants," and, "in their midst," "Madame Kiener-Lavigerie."[189] There is almost nothing, even, that describes what she looked like—only a few words, in Louis Lavigerie's evocation of the postmortem in the library: "I can still see my aunt, in the midst of the circle, pale and aloof in her mourning veil."[190]

In 1892, when Charles-Martial died, Louise was living in the foothills of the Pyrénées, and she stayed there for the rest of her life. She moved, eventually, to a house called "Monplaisir," in the village of Bénéjacq, 140 kilometers to the east of Bayonne, with a view to the south of the snow-capped peaks of the Pyrénées. She lived there with her niece, Jeanne Suberbie Byasson, known as Julie; the Suberbies and the Byassons appeared in the list of other families, in the announcement of Charles Martial's death. Julie Byasson, who was born in Pau in 1867, in a family of the same milieu of collectors of taxes as the Allemand Lavigeries, was Louise's niece in only an extended sense. She was the widow of a colonial administrator in Madagascar and former naval ensign, with whom she had four young children; her husband died on a crossing of the Red Sea in September 1903—he was on the way home on leave—and was buried at sea.[191]

Louise Lavigerie Kiener died on August 21, 1906, in the Villa Monplaisir in Bénéjacq, at the age of seventy-four.[192] It had been a terrible winter for the Catholic Church in France, after the adoption, on December 9, 1905, of the "law concerning the separation of churches and the state." France was now a secular state, and the early months of the year brought a sequence of violent conflicts over the valuation of church property: the "quarrel of inventories." "I am at last feeling better," Louise wrote to Charles Martial's executors in January 1906, but "it does not seem probable that we will be able to stop at the edge of the abyss"; her last letter, in June, was about a pectoral cross that was said to have belonged to her brother, and that had been offered for sale in Bayonne.[193] In September, Julie Byasson wrote to the executors about the death of her "second mother," "my intimate and faithful companion, my only support."[194] "There are very few papers left," she wrote; "for my poor aunt wished us to spend our long evenings of this winter in reading them, and for the most part, destroying them."[195]

Chapter Eleven

THE END OF
THE STORY

A History of Two Centuries

Marie Aymard was born in Angoulême in 1713; Louise Lavigerie Kiener, her great-great-granddaughter, died in the foothills of the Pyrénées in 1906. They lived in intersecting times. Martial Allemand Lavigerie, Marie Aymard's grandson and Louise Kiener's grandfather, the prophet of "truth" and "truthfulness," grew up in Angoulême a few steps away from his grandmother; she was there when he was married in 1790. He was there again, also a few steps away, when Louise, his granddaughter, was married to an employee of the railways in 1855. They knew each other; they belonged to the same history.

The story of the Allemands and the Ferrands started with the sources of information of Marie Aymard, who was illiterate, or the letters that had been written for her, and the things that she had been told by "persons in the town." It ends with Louise Kiener, who traveled to Algeria, and took photographs, and was photographed herself (at a great distance) in an image that was published around the world. Her occupation, in the long winter evenings of 1906, was to curate, and destroy, the historical record of her brother, Charles Martial Allemand Lavigerie. Charles Martial lived, like Louise, into the modern epoch of information technology, and he also helped to invent it, as a visionary of multimedia and multinational humanitarianism, and the "greatest entrepreneur of Christian propaganda of the epoch."

The Modern Novel

The Allemands and the Ferrands were tellers of stories, over the five generations of their history. Marie Aymard's power of attorney of 1764 was a story: the narrative, with sources of evidence, of a journey in space, time, and economic condition. Her son Gabriel told the story of his furniture, and of the plans that he had formed to become an instructor of youth. Her daughter Françoise's husband told the story of how his son Pierre had fallen in love in the Department of the Sarthe, and been accused of stealing a uniform, and how the uniform had been found in a trunk, somewhere between Nantes and Angoulême. They were surrounded, in the streets around the Place du Mûrier and the Minage, by the interminable "informations" of public life, from the stories of the witnesses in the case of the lady with the little dog, in 1769, to the clerk in the tax office, in 1778, and the riot outside the Café des Electeurs, in 1797.

Jean-Baptiste, Marie Aymard's youngest child, was a virtuoso of historical memory, in his petitions for relief as a destitute refugee from Saint-Domingue. So was his daughter Françoise Ferrand Brébion in 1859, and her daughter Clara Brébion Collet, in 1876: "I cannot tell you all that I have suffered this winter lacking everything." Charles Martial, the historian of early Christianity, told the story of the terrible night when the waters of the Scirtus rose suddenly, destroying the lower town of the city of Edessa. He spoke in the narratives of humanitarian crisis, and he recounted his own life in stories: "I was convinced that I would not return from this voyage," of his journey to Syria, and then, in Algeria, of "one of our beautiful spring evenings," when he found the site of his future orphanages. Louise, in turn, wrote to him with the stories of local life, in her letters from the paper mill outside Angoulême: the diocesan architect with the honorable father, who wore an overcoat instead of a suit.

This has been a history of stories, from the outset, and it has also been an encounter, at almost every turn, with the novels of modern times. The Place du Mûrier in Angoulême, which is the scene of so much sorrow in *Les illusions perdues*, was at the center of the lives of Marie Aymard's extended family. "I would like to know the name of the street by which you get to the Place du Mûrier and where your tinsmith's shop was," Balzac wrote in 1836 to his friend in Angoulême, about the Rue de Beaulieu, where Marie Aymard's granddaughter Jeanne was living in retirement at the time, with her husband, the romantic architect.[1] The little spotted dog that was stolen in 1769 belonged to the daughter of Laurence Sterne, who was also living on the Rue de Beaulieu, then called the Rue des Cordeliers, in the house of the aunt of the employer of Marie Aymard's husband. The only intimate description of anyone in the extended family, over the course of two centuries, was in a memoir by a visiting novelist, Dora Hort, about Léon Bernard Lavigerie in Tahiti.

In the nineteenth-century history, the lives of the real Allemand Lavigeries and Ferrands were a replica of the imagined lives of Zola's novels of the Second Empire. The novelist "tends to conceal the imaginary within the real," Zola wrote of Balzac, and of the "naturalist novel, the novel of observation and analysis."[2] The real, in this history, has been a semblance of the imagined. The grandchildren and great-grandchildren of Marie Aymard set out from an isolated provincial town, like the children of the matriarch in *La fortune des Rougon*, and made their way to the distant corners of France. Two of the great-grandsons, Scipion and Camille Allemand Lavigerie, reinvented themselves as bankers in the aftermath of the 1848 revolution, as in *La curée* and *L'argent*. Camille's daughter lived in a building near the Paris Opera, and was related by marriage to the family of Baron Haussmann. Her third cousin was a seamstress living in poverty, as in *L'assommoir*, on the Rue Myrha in Montmartre. The financial scandal in *L'argent* was precipitated by investment opportunities in Syria and Lebanon, following the humanitarian crisis of the 1860s. Louise Kiener and Charles Martial Allemand Lavigerie were driven to distraction, on their visits to Paris, by the expansion of the department stores, as in *Au bonheur des dames*; Charles Martial denounced "rationalism" and "naturalism" in 1885, the year of *Germinal*.

The history of the Allemands and the Ferrands has been a sequence of stories or episodes of ordinary life, and it is inspired, in this sense, by the "literature of ideas" of Sterne and Diderot (which was opposed, in *Les illusions perdues*, to the "literature of images" of the "modern novel" of the nineteenth century, or the historicism of Sir Walter Scott).[3] It is an encounter, in turn, with the naturalism of the (late) nineteenth-century novel, of which the eighteenth-century novelists were the "true ancestor," in Zola's description: an "exact study of facts and things," a compilation of circumstances, or a "positivism of art." Naturalism in history, for Zola, was "the reasoned study of facts and people, the research into sources, the resurrection of societies and their environments." Naturalism in the novel was "the continual compilation of human documents."[4]

But history, or this history, is also the opposite of the novel. For the circumstances to be compiled are all there is. The stories are exact, nothing more. There is no creation: no "entire world" or "complete society" that rises out of the earth, as in Zola's description of Balzac's *Comédie humaine*. There is no mise-en-scène, in the sense of the description of the sequence of novels that Zola attributes to the novelist Sandoz in *L'oeuvre*: "I am going to take a family, and I will study its members, one by one, where they have come from, where they go, how they react to each other . . . I will place my people in a determinate historical period, which will give me the milieu and the circumstances, a piece of history."[5]

There is no personality, even, in the sense of the individuality of the men, women, and children in the story, or of their "despairs and hopes."[6] There is nothing of what they are like, and almost nothing of what they look like. The family in Zola's novels are linked by an obscure medical-psychological malady, and there is nothing, in this history, of the illnesses of the Allemand Lavigeries and Ferrands—or no more than Louise's rheumatism ("I am at last feeling better") and Charles Martial's digestion. Jean-Baptiste, his daughter, and his granddaughter all suffered from "weakness of sight." The Allemand Lavigeries were beautiful, or some of them were beautiful; they were domineering, at least in the partial description of Charles Martial's biographers: that is all there is.

The history of the Allemand Lavigeries and the Ferrands is filled, too, with the possibility of the unexpected. It is a positivist history in the sense that everything is true—or at least it is identified in relation to "research into sources"—and also in the sense that everything is falsifiable. It started with a true statement—"this is a story—or ninety-eight stories"—and ends with a statement about truth: "Everything is true." So it ends, of necessity, in counting the stories (although what is a story, and what is part of a story?) and revisiting the sources (the endnotes). Some of the sources are more reliable than others; some of the missing persons are more important in the story.

It is possible that the missing brothers and sisters will be there, one day, in the websites of family history that change continuously over time (and in the bad infinity of iterated searching). Louise Kiener destroyed the family papers she had inherited, in 1906 in the Pyrénées. The family papers of her great-aunts, if they ever existed, are no longer to be found (or I have not been able to find them). When Jeanne *aînée* died in Angoulême in 1860, at the age of ninety-one, only Louise Mélanie was still alive, among her twelve brothers and sisters, who were the children of the couple in the marriage contract of 1764; when Louise Mélanie died in 1865, she was away from home, on a visit to her cousins in the Sarthe. The matriarch, at the end of the last novel in Zola's great sequence, succeeds, at last, in burning all the dossiers, in the blue paper files, of all the five generations of the extended family.[7] But it is possible that the granddaughters of Marie Aymard saved their own family papers in boxes or trunks, and that the papers were not destroyed; that someone, in the end, will be able to find out what happened to the cousins who have vanished without trace in this family history; and that it would then be a different sort of history.

Infinite Possibilities

This is, in the end, a circumstantial history within an infinity of possible evidence. It is a "flattened" history, in the expression of the Zola figure in *L'oeuvre*. There are more and more events, more and more episodes, more and more circumstances. The micro is connected to the medium, and the medium to the macro, by the individuals' own connections. The circumstances, which are true, constitute the historical story. The story started with the information society of Marie Aymard, and it became an inquiry into the multiple sources of information of hundreds of other people, even in the deep interior of France. It is a history by contiguity—in the social space of networks, the neighborhood space of the center of Angoulême, and the generations of family history—and it has become a political history, seen from below. It is a history of the long French Revolution, from the perspective not of the revolution, but of twenty or thirty individuals, connected to each other and to the small town of Angoulême, who lived through the revolutionary years.

The circumstantial history became a history, too, of the new economic times of the nineteenth century. It is a history not of the economy, but of the economic lives of Marie Aymard's grandchildren, and of the unmodern industries in which they made their ways. In following their idiosyncratic journeys, it became a sequence of microhistories of public administration, the military, banking, and the church. These were all industries in which the boundaries of the economy were changing over time, and in which the market was difficult to distinguish from the state, the "national" from the "overseas," and the self-interest of economic life from the norms of public society. The economic lives of the Allemand Lavigeries and the Ferrands were scenes of visible, immediate inequality. The only one of Marie Aymard's descendants who was a success, and a visionary of the modern multinational economy, was Charles Martial Allemand Lavigerie.

The influence of overseas was everywhere. Marie Aymard was informed, or misinformed, about events overseas, and so were her acquaintances and neighbors. She knew how much slaves were paid per day, on the island of Grenada, and the question of slavery has been at the edge of the horizon from the beginning to the end of this history of provincial life. There was her husband's employer, who owned fifty slaves; her daughter's cousin by marriage, with his runaway pregnant slave who spoke French and Spanish; her son, the watchmaker, with his memories of having once been rich, "with fifteen slaves," and his daughter and granddaughter, with their entitlements to relief, from 1814 to 1873.

There was Louis Félix, "commissioner of the directory to the municipal administration" in Angoulême, who was born into slavery in Saint-Domingue in 1765. There was Marie Aymard's grandson Martial Allemand Lavigerie, who claimed compensation for a share of a cocoa plantation. There was Martial's granddaughter, who married into the family of a slave-trading dynasty from Bordeaux. There was Paul Abadie, who married Maria Alida Camia, born into slavery in Guadeloupe. There was the great-great-grandson who wrote his thesis about the Roman law of slavery, and there was Charles Martial, who may or may not have known about the history of his family in Grenada and Saint-Domingue, and who was the most famous opponent of slavery of his own times.

These are all, in the end, fairly large stories. But there are always more stories to be told, and more individuals to be found. This is not a map of the world as large as the world, or a history as long as history. It is a story, most of all, about the infinite possibilities of history, even of flat, positivistic history. Martial Allemand Lavigerie, who was halfway between Marie Aymard and Louise Lavigerie Kiener, in the generational time of family history, evoked truth, in Bayonne in 1826, in order to claim an indemnity from the new republic of Haiti for his late wife's plantation. He evoked truthfulness, in 1829, in the *Courrier de Bayonne*, as "indispensable in the times in which we live": "There is nothing but truth to proclaim."

ACKNOWLEDGMENTS

I am deeply grateful to the staff of the Archives municipales d'Angoulême, and especially M. Florent Gaillard, Mme. Stine Krause, and Mme. Catherine Portelli, and of the Archives départementales de la Charente, especially M. Dominique Guirignon and M. Jean-Philippe Pichardie; to the staff of the Archives de la Société des Missionnaires d'Afrique, Via Aurelia, Rome; to M. David Richard of the Archives diocésaines d'Angoulême; to the curators of the Musée d'Angoulême; to the staff of the Archives nationales de France, in Paris and Pierrefitte, and of the Archives nationales d'outre-mer, in Aix-en-Provence; to M. Fabrice Reuzé of the Archives de la Banque de France; to the staff of the Archives de Paris, of the Bibliothèque nationale, and of the Bibliothèque historique de la Ville de Paris; to the staff of the National Archives in Kew and of the British Library; and to the Mairie d'Angoulême for the invitation to present the story of Marie Aymard at the Hôtel de Ville.

Victoria Gray, Ian Kumekawa, David Todd, Francesca Trivellato, and Mary-Rose Cheadle read the manuscript, and I am more grateful than I can say for their comments, and for conversations throughout this long journey.

There are many conversations that have contributed to this book, particularly with Amartya Sen, and with Indrani Sen, Sunil Amrith, Armando Antinori, Bernard Bailyn, Keith Baker, Abhijit Banerjee, Shane Bobrycki, Niko Bowie, Sidney Chalhoub, Arun Chandrasekhar, Robert Darnton, Rohit De, Tracy Dennison, Rowan Dorin, Esther Duflo, Dan Edelstein, Iris Goldsmith, Ben Golub, Tim Harper, Hendrik Hartog, Lynn Hunt, Penny Janeway, Maya Jasanoff, Mary Kaldor, Diana Kim, Claire Lemercier, Noah Millstone, Renaud Morieux, Julian Perry Robinson, Tatiana Petruzelli, Gilles Postel-Vinay, Amy Price, Jacques Revel, Carol Richards, Daniel Roche, Paul-André Rosental, Eric de Rothschild, Rebecca Scott, Gareth Stedman Jones, Julia Stephens, Barry

Supple, Melissa Teixeira, Brandon Terry, Fei-Hsien Wang, Paul Warde, Tony Wrigley, and Alexia Yates.

The Visualizing Historical Networks project began at the Joint Center for History and Economics in 2012, and Ian Kumekawa, Amy Price, and I have worked since then with Madeleine Schwartz, Jessica Crown, Paul Talma, Fanny Louvier, Nicolas Todd, Ye Seul Byeon, Lux Zhao, and Oliver Riskin-Kutz.

Mary-Rose Cheadle and Hannah Weaver provided exceptionally helpful comments on the manuscript. Emily Gauthier, Jennifer Nickerson, Mary-Rose Cheadle, Inga Huld Markan, and Amy Price have created an inspiring environment at the Joint Center for History and Economics, as have Asha Patel and Noala Skinner, with whom I first went to Angoulême in 1995.

Brigitta van Rheinberg has been a great editor since the beginning of the project, and I am very grateful to Lauren Lepow for her perceptive editing.

This book was written in Palo Alto, Cambridge (England), Angoulême, Santineketan, Cambridge (Massachusetts), Sabaudia, and Rome. I am grateful, most of all, for kindness and friendship along the way.

Appendix One

CHILDREN AND GRANDCHILDREN

Name	Birth	Death	Father	Mother	Spouse
Marie Aymard	1713	1790			*Louis Ferrand* (1735)
Ferrand, Gabriel	1738	1816	LF	MA	*Marie Adelaide Devuailly* (1763)
Ferrand, Françoise	1740	1805	LF	MA	*Etienne Allemand Lavigerie* (1764)
Ferrand, François	1742	>1766	LF	MA	
Ferrand, Mathurin	1743	>1764	LF	MA	
Ferrand, Marguerite	1744	>1768	LF	MA	
Ferrand, Jean-Baptiste	1749	1831	LF	MA	*Elizabeth Boutoute* (1774)
Ferrand, Gabriel	1764	1816	GF	MAV	*Florence Borgnet* (1796)
Allemand, Marie	1765	?	EA	FF	

Continued on next page

Name	Birth	Death	Father	Mother	Spouse
Ferrand, Etienne	1766	>1794	GF	MAV	*Marie Chausse Lunesse* (1794)
Ferrand, Jean	1766	?	GF	MAV	
Allemand, Martial	1767	1856	EA	FF	*Louise Vaslin/Bonnite Raymond St Germain* (1790/1801)
Ferrand, Jean François	1768	?	GF	MAV	
Allemand, Jeanne	1768	1860	EA	FF	
Allemand Lavigerie, Pierre	1769	1834	EA	FF	*Adelaide Maslin* (1796)
Ferrand, Joseph Marie	1770	1793	GF	MAV	
Allemand, Jeanne	1770	1838	EA	FF	
Allemand, Jeanne Henriette	1771	1852	EA	FF	
Allemand, Jeanne	1773	1852	EA	FF	*Laurent Sylvestre Topin* (1801)
Allemand, Antoine	1774	>1801 <1811	EA	FF	
Ferrand, Pierre Alexandre	1775	1841	GF	MAV	*Auguste Siva de Villeneuve Solard* (?)
Ferrand, Martial	1775	1793	JBF	EB	
Ferrand, Françoise	1777	1860	JBF	EB	*Joseph Brébion* (1800)
Allemand, Marie Françoise	1778	1853	EA	FF	
Allemand, Josephe	1779	1855	EA	FF	*Joseph Alexandre César Ponsard* (1807)
Allemand, Etienne	1781	>1837	EA	FF	*Marie Montesquieu* (1807)

Name	Birth	Death	Father	Mother	Spouse
Allemand Lavigerie, Louise Mélanie	1783	1865	EA	FF	
Ferrand, Jean-Baptiste	1796	1873	JBF	EB	*Elisa Collet/Anne Thiriot*(?/1839)
Allemand Lavigerie, Elisabeth	1791	1838	MAL	LV	
Allemand Lavigerie, Léon-Philippe	1795	1860	MAL	LV	*Louise Latrilhe* (1824)
Ferrand, Vincent Gabriel	1796	1825	GF	FB	*Susanne Coureaux* (1821)
Allemand Lavigerie, Jules Etienne Scipion	1797	1853	PA	AM	*Louise Marguerite Poirier* (1832)
Ferrand, Stéphanie	1799	1870	GF	FB	*Jean Dinochau* (1820)
Allemand Lavigerie, Alexandre Camille	1799	1881	PA	AM	*Françoise Méloé Topin* (1830)
Topin, Marie Théonie	1801	1868	LST	JA	
Topin, Françoise Méloé	1803	1878	LST	JA	*Alexandre Camille Allemand Lavigerie* (1830)
Lavigerie, Adelaide	1803	1839	MAL	BR	
Topin, François	1804	?	LST	JA	

Continued on next page

Name	Birth	Death	Father	Mother	Spouse
Brébion, Clara	1804	1889	JB	FF	*Pierre Rose Collet* (1826)
Brébion, Jean Baptiste Adolphe	1805	>1829	JB	FF	*Monique Vicaire* (1829)
Lavigerie, Pierre Jules Edouard	1806	1851	MAL	BR	*Eugénie Cassan* (1838)
Topin, Charles	1807	1886	LST	JA	*Aglaée Doré/Pauline Elisa Mairet* (1833/1862)
Lavigerie, Mamert Victor	1808	1885	MAL	BR	
Ponsard, Alexandre Etienne	1809	?	JACP	JA	
Brébion, Josephine Louisa	1809	>1814	JB	FF	
Lavigerie, Charlotte Ursule	1810	1840	MAL	BR	*Pierre Auguste Henry Lacourade* (1836)
Topin, Marie Louise	1813	?	LST	JA	
Ferrand, Rose Calista	1833	1891	JBF	EC	*Ferdinand Amedée Esnault* (1864)
Dinochau, Mélanie	1822	1893	JD	SF	*Eugène Célestin Rabier* (1842)
Ferrand, Pierre Lucien Eugene	1823	1881	VGF	SC	*Eugénie Clémentine Lormeau* (1852)
Dinochau, Edouard	1823	1871	JD	SF	
Lavigerie, Charles Martial Allemand	1825	1892	LPAL	LL	

Name	Birth	Death	Father	Mother	Spouse
Dinochau, Alfred Charles	1827	1901	JD	SF	
Lavigerie, Pierre Félix	1828	1882	LPAL	LL	
Lavigerie, Louise	1832	1906	LPAL	LL	*Charles Gabriel Kiener* (1855)
Allemand Lavigerie, Marie Louise	1833	1909	ACAL	FMT	*Jean Henri Portet* (1851)
Topin, Louis Sylvestre	1834	1870	CT	AD	
Topin, Louise Marie Antoinette	1835	?	CT	AD	
Lavigerie, Léon Bernard	1837	1871	LPAL	LL	*Amélie Chesse* (1860)
Henry Lacourade, Marie	1837	1907	PAHL	CUL	*Alexis-Henry-Evariste Brinboeuf-Dulary* (1858)
Collet, Rosalie Marie	1837	1890	PRC	CB	*Raphael Victor Bossard* (1861)
Lavigerie, Joseph Victor	1839	?	PJEL	EC	
Henry Lacourade, Georges	1839	1907	PAHL	CUL	*Jeanne Angélique Adèle Daniel de Colhoe* (1868)
Collet, Louise Jeanne	1840	1889	PRC	CB	*Jérôme Lerouge* (1887)
Topin, Henri Sylvestre	1846	1902	CST	AD	*Marie Lucie Levaux* (1893)
Esnault, Isabelle Marthe Calista	1865	1891	FAE	RCF	

Appendix Two

THE EIGHTY-THREE
SIGNATORIES

Albert was *Michel Albert*. He was born in 1732 in St. Ausone, Angoulême, and was the son of *M. Albert*. He was a hatmaker. He
was married in 1751 to *Marie Tilhard*. Archives municipales
d'Angoulême [hereafter AM-A], GG59/41, GG61/9.

M. Albert was *Michel Albert*, the father of the younger *Michel Albert*.
He was also a hatmaker. He was born around 1704 and died in
1768. He was married to Françoise Bellet, who was the first cousin
of Marie Aymard's mother. He lived in the Isle St. Pierre/Quartier
des Bacheliers. AM-A, GG59/34, GG61/132; CC42/3/3, CC62/
49/1909.

Etienne Allemand was the bridegroom. He was born in St. Antonin,
Angoulême, in 1740 and died in 1821. He was a teacher. He was
married in 1765 to *Françoise Ferrand*, and was the son of *Marc
Allemand*. AM-A, GG53/12, GG14/36, 1E63/64.

Allemand Père was *Marc Allemand*. He was born in 1698 in St. Paul,
Angoulême, and died in 1781. He was the father of *Etienne
Allemand* and *Marie Allemand*. He was a tailor. He was married
to Elisabeth Lecler, who died in 1731, and to Marie Giraud, who
died in 1745. He lived in the Isle Chabrefy/Cloche Verte. AM-A,
GG88/79, GG39/158, GG73/50, GG53/45, GG14/61; CC42/1/11,
CC62/9/328.

Marie Allemand was the half sister of *Etienne Allemand* and the
daughter of *Marc Allemand*. She was born in St. André, Angoulême, in 1730 and died in 1797. She was unmarried. AM-A,
GG39/133, 1E12/67.

Marguerite Barathe was the step-grandmother of *Etienne Allemand*. She was born in 1699 in St. Jean, Angoulême, and died in 1766. Her father was a tailor. She was married in 1721 to *Jean Giraud*. AM-A, GG72/128–129, GG72/223, GG9/9.

Marie Bonnard was born in St. André, Angoulême, in 1743 and died in 1770. Her mother and father were bakers. She was married at the age of thirteen, in 1756, to *Jean Godinaud*, who was a baker and a second cousin of the groom. She lived in the Isle Presbytère St. André. AM-A, GG40/139, GG42/63, GG45/5; CC42/1/23, CC62/20/767.

Catherine Bonvallet was born in St. Paul, Angoulême, in 1710 and died in 1781. She was a tobacconist. She was the widow of Martial Hay, and was a neighbor of *Gabriel Ferrand*. AM-A, GG88/119, GG90/123; CC42/2/12.

A-M Bouhier was *Anne-Marguerite Bouhier*. She was born in St. Antonin, Angoulême, in 1702, and was the sister of *Catherine Bouhier* and the aunt of *Marguerite Faveraud*. Her father was a commissioner of police. She was a neighbor of *Marc Allemand*. AM-A, GG52/62; CC42/1/11; CC62/9/330.

Catherine Bouhier was the sister of *Anne-Marguerite Bouhier*. She was born in St. Antonin, Angoulême, in 1717 and died in 1795 in La Rochefoucauld. She was married to Jean Joseph Faveraud, a merchant from La Rochefoucauld, and was the mother of *Marguerite Faveraud*. AM-A, GG52/109, GG53/16; AD Charente, La Rochefoucauld, 1793–1794, 3E304/10, 212/224.

Elizabeth Bourdage was born in St. André, Angoulême, in 1705 and died in 1785. She was married to Jean Tabourin, dit Charas, who was a shoemaker when they married, and later a cloth merchant. She was the mother of *Catherine Charas*, *Marie Charas*, and *Anne Tabourin*. She was the immediate neighbor of *Marc Allemand* in the Isle Chabrefy/Cloche Verte. AM-A, GG38/27, GG39/25, GG55/43; CC42/1/11, CC62/9/327.

Philippe Briand was a schoolboy. He also signed the marriage record of *Etienne Allemand* and *Françoise Ferrand*, and the baptism record of the son of *Gabriel Ferrand* and *Marie Adelaide Devuailly.* AM-A, GG14/36.

Brillet was *Marie Brillet.* She lived in the Isle du Maître Ecole. AM-A, GG42/2/9, GG62/30/1166. [low confidence]

Brillet was *Jean-Baptiste Brillet.* He was born around 1717 in Compiègne and died in Angoulême in 1799. He was the receiver of the *aides* imposition. He was married in 1751 to *Elisabeth Yver Brillet.* He lived in the Isle de la Grande Maison des Carmélites. AM-A, GG54/3; AD Charente, Angoulême, 1798–1799, 3E16/67, 89/176; AM-A, CC42/1/7, CC62/6/219.

Yver Brillet was *Elisabeth Yver Brillet.* She was born in St. Paul, Angoulême, in 1707 and died in 1780. Her father was a watch-maker. She was married in 1751 to *Jean-Baptiste Brillet.* She lived in the Isle de la Grande Maison des Carmélites. AM-A, GG88/112, GG54/3, GG90/117; CC42/1/7, CC62/6/219.

Catherine Chabot was born in Notre Dame de Beaulieu, Angoulême, in 1724 and died in 1803. She was a merchant and lived in the Isle des Carmélites. She was the sister of *Jeanne Chabot.* AM-A, GG7/120, 1E34/96; CC42/2/4, CC62/25/950.

Jeanne Chabot was born in Notre Dame de Beaulieu, Angoulême, in 1725, and died in 1800. She was a merchant, selling cooking fat and pottery, and lived in the Isle des Carmélites. She was the sister of *Jeanne Chabot.* She was married in 1756 to *Jean Yrvoix*, a second cousin of the groom. AM-A, GG7/125, GG8/114, 1E21/181; CC42/2/4, CC62/25/950.

Chatherine Charas was *Catherine Tabourin dit Charas.* She was born in St. Antonin, Angoulême, in 1743 and died in 1801. She was a neighbor of *Marc Allemand.* She was the daughter of *Elizabeth Bourdage* and Jean Tabourin, and the sister of *Marie Charas* and *Anne Tabourin.* She was married in 1777 to Barthélemy Rullier, a surgeon. AM-A, GG53/32, GG55/19, 1E24/144; CC42/1/11, CC62/9/327.

Marie Charas was *Marie Tabourin dit Charas.* She was born in St. Antonin, Angoulême, in 1737 and died in 1812. She was a neighbor of *Marc Allemand*. She was the daughter of *Elizabeth Bourdage* and Jean Tabourin, and the sister of *Catherine Charas* and *Anne Tabourin*. She was married in 1772 to François Nadaud, a watchmaker. AM-A, GG52/184, GG54/72; CC42/1/11, CC62/9/327; AD Charente, Roullet Saint-Estèphe, 1802–1812, 3E311/5, 310/323.

Marie Anne Josephe Geneviève Chaumont veuve Gautier was born in Notre Dame de Beaulieu, Angoulême, in 1732 and died in Gurat, Charente, in 1805. She was the immediate neighbor of *Gabriel Ferrand* in the Isle de Marvaud/Place du Collège. She was married in 1747 to Jean Gautier, a lawyer. AM-A, GG7/166, GG41/52; AD Charente, Gurat, 1802–1812, 3E171/5, 51/190; AM-A, CC42/2/11, CC62/32/1233.

Marie Claude was the first cousin of the groom. *Marc Allemand* was her uncle, and *Daufinete* was her brother. She was born in St. André, Angoulême, in 1745, and died in 1814. She was unmarried. Her father was a tailor. AM-A, GG41/7, 1E50/77.

St. Mexant De Crevecoeur was François St. Mexant De Crevecoeur Boisnier. He was born around 1752 in Aigre, Charente, and died there in 1839. He was married to Augustine Chedaneau, and was a tax collector in Aigre and in Civray, Vienne. AD Charente, Aigre, 1763–1792, 3E5/1, 63/322, 1828–1842, 3E5/5, 260/341; AD Vienne, Civray, 1780–1782, 9E92/3, 29/102.

Daufinete was *Pierre Claude*. He was the first cousin of the groom. *Marc Allemand* was his uncle and *Marie Claude* was his sister. He was born in St. André, Angoulême, in 1743. His father was a tailor. AM-A, GG40/114.

Elizabeth Demiere was a seamstress. She was born in St. Martial, Angoulême, in 1725, and died in 1779. She was the daughter of a blacksmith. She was unmarried. She lived in the Isle des bouchers près de celle de Genève. AM-A, GG104/6, GG90/111; CC62/12/447.

M. Devuailly Ferrand was *Marie Adelaide Devuailly*. She was married in 1763 to *Gabriel Ferrand*. She was born around 1741, and died in Angoulême in 1819. She was the sister of *Dorothée Devuailly*, and the sister-in-law of *Françoise Ferrand, Jean-Baptiste Ferrand,* and *Gabriel Lemaitre.* AM-A, GG8/143, 1E57/92.

Jean Dumergue was the second cousin of the groom. He was born in St. André, Angoulême, in 1725 and died in 1792. He was a saddler and was married in 1754 to *Marguerite Monnaud.* His brother, François Dumergue, was a merchant in Saint-Domingue, and his daughter, Marthe, was married to Louis Félix, who was born in slavery in Saint-Domingue. He lived in the Isle Cheval Blanc/ Prieuré de Navarre. AM-A, GG39/54, GG39/186, GG42/24, GG25/25, 1E14/114–115; CC42/1/19, CC62/16/622.

Magdelaine Dumergue was married in 1728 to *Pierre Marchais,* an innkeeper and pastry-maker. She lived in the Isle Cheval Blanc/ Prieuré de Navarre. She was the sister-in-law of *Jean-Baptiste Marchais de la Chapelle.* AM-A, GG66/28; CC42/1/19, CC62/ 16/622.

Louis Dupard was the first cousin once removed of the groom. He was born in 1729 and died in Angoulême in 1782. He was a button-maker, and was married to Marie Guimard, a seller of used clothes. He was the brother-in-law of *Guillaume Guimard,* and lived in the Isle de M. Arnaud/Point du Jour. AM-A, GG41/96, GG42/89, GG46/70; CC42/1/18, GG62/15/587.

Marie Durand was married in 1752 to Jean-Baptiste Marchais, a brandy merchant. She was the daughter-in-law of *Jean-Baptiste Marchais de la Chapelle* and the mother of *Jean-Baptiste Marchais.* AD Charente, Saint-Simon, 1737–1798, 3E387/1 178/298.

Rosse Duriou was *Françoise Rose Duriou.* She was born in St. André, Angoulême, in 1750. She was married in 1794 to a soldier from Dijon, Claude Mathey. AM-A, GG41/124, 1E2/141.

Marguerite Durousot was born in Montbron, Charente, around 1726, and died in Angoulême in 1809. She was married in 1753 to *Jean Joubert,* who was a second cousin of the groom. She was the daughter of a wigmaker, and her husband was a draper. Her granddaughter and goddaughter, Marguerite Aubert, represented Reason in 1793. She lived in the Isle de M. Arnaud/Point du Jour. AM-A, GG74/56, 1E42/208; CC42/1/17, CC62/15/557.

Faure was *Jean Faure*. He was born around 1690 and died in St. André, Angoulême, in 1765. He was a musician. He was married in 1718 to Anne Allemand, and was the brother-in-law of *Marc Allemand*. He was the father of *Jeanne Faure* and *Marguerite Faure*, the father-in-law of *Anne Faure*, and the uncle of *Etienne Allemand* and *Marie Allemand*. He lived in the Isle des Tiercelettes. AM-A, GG38/186, GG42/109, GG43/12; CC42/1/24.

Anne Faure was born in St. André, Angoulême, in 1739. She was married in 1757 to Antoine Faure, the first cousin of the groom. She was the daughter of a shoemaker, the daughter-in-law of *Jean Faure*, and the sister-in-law of *Jeanne Faure* and *Marguerite Faure*. In 1775 she signed the baptism record of "Jean L'Accajou," aged fifteen, who had been brought to France on the slaving ship *La Cicogne*. AM-A, GG39/246, GG42/90, GG68/58.

Jeanne Faure was the first cousin of the groom. She was a seamstress. She was born in St. André, Angoulême, in 1729 and died in 1797. She was the daughter of *Jean Faure*, the sister of *Marguerite Faure*, and the sister-in-law of *Anne Faure*. She lived in the Isle des Tiercelettes. AM-A, GG39/117, 1E12/108; CC42/1/24, CC62/821.

Marguerite Faure was the first cousin of the groom. She was a seamstress. She was born in St. André, Angoulême, in 1721 and died in 1809. She was the daughter of *Jean Faure*, the sister of *Jeanne Faure*, and the sister-in-law of *Anne Faure*. She lived in the Isle des Tiercelettes. AM-A, GG39/1, 1E42/350; CC42/1/24, CC62/821.

M. Faveraud was *Marguerite Faveraud*. She was born in La Rochefoucauld in 1742 and died there in 1819. She was the daughter of *Catherine Bouhier* and the niece of *Anne-Marguerite Bouhier*. She was married in 1771 to a surgeon, Louis Fouchier. AD Charente, La Rochefoucauld-Saint Cybard, 1737–1756, 3E304/4, 64–65/188, 1757–1785, 3E304/5, 193/438; La Rochefoucauld, 1818–1822, 3E304/15, 157/425.

Françoise Ferrand was the bride. She was born in St. Martial, Angoulême, in 1740, and died in 1805. She was the sister of *Gabriel Ferrand* and *Jean-Baptiste Ferrand*, and the sister-in-law of *Marie Adelaide Devuailly*. AM-A, GG106/151, GG14/36, 1E38/212.

Ferrand was *Gabriel Ferrand*, the brother of the bride. He was born in St. Paul, Angoulême, in 1738, and died in 1816. He was married in 1763 to *Marie Adelaide Devuailly*. He was a master writer, teacher, and archivist. He was the brother of *Jean-Baptiste Ferrand*, and the brother-in-law of *Dorothée Devuailly Lemaitre* and *Gabriel Lemaitre*. He lived in the Isle de Marvaud/Place du Collège. AM-A, GG89/36r (undigitized); GG8/143, 1E52/426; CC42/2/11, CC62/32/1234.

J. Ferrand was *Jean-Baptiste Ferrand*, the brother of the bride. He was born in St. André, Angoulême, in 1749, and died in Paris in 1831. He was the brother of *Gabriel Ferrand*. He was married in 1774 to Elizabeth Boutoute, and they emigrated to Saint-Domingue. He was a watchmaker. AM-A, GG41/108, GG45/64; Archives de Paris, V3E/D552, 10/37.

Fonchaudière was *Jean-Baptiste Chaigneau Fonchaudière*. He was born in St. Paul, Angoulême, in 1732 and died in 1774. He was a lawyer and director of the post in Angoulême. He was married to *Anne Magdeleine Gralhat Fonchaudière*. He lived near *Gabriel Ferrand* in the Isle du Collège. AM-A, GG89/2, GG14/20, GG45/61; CC42/2/12, CC62/32/1264.

Gralhat Fonchaudière was *Anne Magdeleine Gralhat Fonchaudière*. She was born around 1736, and died in 1779. She was director of the post in Angoulême after 1774. She was married to *Jean-Baptiste Chaigneau Fonchaudière* and was the daughter of *Jacques Gralhat*. She lived near *Gabriel Ferrand* in the Isle du Collège. AM-A, GG14/20, GG45/178; CC42/2/12, CC62/32/1264.

Marie Iandron was *Marie Gendron*. She was born in St. Jacques, Angoulême, in 1712, and died in 1792. She was the daughter of a cooper. She was married to *Jean Glaumont*, who was the first

cousin once removed of the bridegroom. She was the mother
of *Magdelaine Glaumont, Jean Glaumont fils ainé* and *Antoine
Glaumont*, and the mother-in-law of *Catherine Lecler*. AM-A,
GG123/65, GG125/91, GG39/215, GG39/234, GG126/2,
GG129/5–6, GG134/150.

Giraud was *Jean Giraud*. He was the grandfather of the groom. He
was born in St. André, Angoulême, in 1685 and died in 1766. He
was married to Susanne Dufort in 1708 and to *Marguerite Barathe*
in 1721. He was a tailor. He had sixteen children, and was the
father of *Françoise Giraud, Pierre Giraud*, and *Pierre André
Giraud*. AM-A, GG35/231, GG72/174, GG72/223, GG9/10.

François[e] Giraud was the groom's aunt. She was born in St. Jean,
Angoulême, in 1724, and died in 1798. She was the daughter of
Jean Giraud and *Marguerite Barathe*, and the sister of *Pierre
Giraud* and *Pierre André Giraud*. AM-A, GG72/238, 1E15/140–141.

P. Giraud was *Pierre André Giraud*. He was the groom's uncle. He
was born in St. Jean, Angoulême, in 1727 and died in 1816. He was
a master writer. He was married to Louise Grelier in 1767. He was
the son of *Jean Giraud* and *Marguerite Barathe*, and the brother of
Françoise Giraud and *Pierre Giraud*. AM-A, GG73/10, GG90/19,
1E52/310.

Giraud fils was *Pierre Giraud*, also known as Pierre André Giraud.
He was the groom's uncle. He was born in St. Jean, Angoulême,
in 1739. He was a tailor. He was married to Magdelaine Richin in
1756 and to Françoise Fetis in 1761. He was the son of *Jean Giraud*
and *Marguerite Barathe*, and the brother of *Françoise Giraud* and
Pierre André Giraud. He lived in the Isle St. François. AM-A,
GG73/59, GG74/69, GG74/94; CC62/2/904.

Antoine Glaumont was the groom's second cousin. He was born in
St. Jacques, Angoulême, in 1742 and died unmarried in 1817. He
was a merchant. He was the son of *Jean Glaumont* and *Marie
Gendron*, the nephew of *Elizabeth Glaumont*, the brother of *Jean
Glaumont fils* and *Magdelaine Glaumont*, and the brother-in-law
of *Catherine Lecler*. AM-A, GG126/2, 1E53/361.

Elizabeth Glaumont was the groom's first cousin once removed. She
was born in St. André, Angoulême, in 1715 and died in St. Paul,
Angoulême, in 1777. She was married in 1746 to Louis Merceron,
a butcher. She was the sister of *Jean Glaumont*, the sister-in-law of
Marie Gendron and *Gilles Yrvoix*, and the aunt of *Antoine Glaumont*,
Jean Glaumont fils, *Magdelaine Glaumont*, and *Jean Yrvoix*. She lived
in the Isle Cambois de Chenausac/Place des Bouchers. AM-A,
GG38/139, GG89/55, GG90/39; CC42/1/9, CC62/7/267.

Glaumont was *Jean Glaumont*. He was the groom's first cousin once
removed. He was born in St. André, Angoulême, in 1713. He was
a saddler. He was married in 1733 to *Marie Gendron*. He was the
brother of *Elizabeth Glaumont*, the father of *Antoine Glaumont*,
Jean Glaumont fils, and *Magdelaine Glaumont*, the father-in-law of
Catherine Lecler, the brother-in-law of *Gilles Yrvoix*, and the
uncle of *Jean Yrvoix*. AM-A, GG38/96, GG125/91.

Glaumont fils ainé was *Jean Glaumont fils*. He was the groom's
second cousin. He was born in St. André, Angoulême, in 1735,
and died in 1810. He was a registry clerk and later a merchant. He
was married in 1770 to *Catherine Lecler*. He was the son of *Jean
Glaumont* and *Marie Gendron*, the nephew of *Elizabeth Glaumont*,
and the brother of *Antoine Glaumont* and *Magdelaine Glaumont*.
AM-A, GG39/234, GG129/5–6, 1E43/24.

Magdelaine Glaumont was the groom's second cousin. She was born
in St. André, Angoulême, in 1734. She was the daughter of *Jean
Glaumont* and *Marie Gendron*, the niece of *Elizabeth Glaumont*,
the sister of *Antoine Glaumont* and *Jean Glaumont fils*, and the
sister-in-law of *Catherine Lecler*. AM-A, GG39/215.

J. *Godinaud* was *Jean Godinaud*. He was the groom's second cousin.
He was born in St. André, Angoulême, in 1731, and died in 1818.
He was a baker. He was married in 1756 to *Marie Bonnard*, and
in 1781 to Jeanne Elizabeth Nouveau. He was the brother of
Marguerite Godinaud and *Pierre Godinaud*. He lived in the Isle
Presbytère St. André. AM-A, GG39/163, GG42/63, GG46/48,
1E54/95; CC42/1/23, CC62/20/767.

Marguerite Godinaud was the groom's second cousin. She was born in St. André, Angoulême, in 1740, and died in the aftermath of childbirth in 1769. She was married in 1764 to Joseph Farbos, a merchant from the Landes. She was the sister of *Jean Godinaud* and *Pierre Godinaud*, and the sister-in-law of *Marie Bonnard*. She lived in the Isle du Point du Jour. AM-A, GG40/72, GG42/226, GG44/28; CC62/15/589.

Pierre Godinaud was the groom's second cousin. He was born in St. André, Angoulême, in 1727, and died in 1801. He was a baker. He was married in 1751 to Jeanne St. Amant and in 1758 to Elizabeth Grelier. He was the brother of *Jean Godinaud* and *Marguerite Godinaud*. He lived in the Isle des Tiercelettes. AM-A, GG39/93, GG41/146, GG82/178, 1E24/89; CC42/1/23, CC62/22/831.

Gralhat was *Jacques Gralhat*. He was the director of the post. He was the father of *Anne Magdeleine Gralhat Fonchaudière* and the father-in-law of *Jean-Baptiste Chaigneau Fonchaudière*. He lived near *Gabriel Ferrand* in the Isle du Collège. AM-A, GG14/20; CC42/2/12, CC62/32/1264.

Guimard was *Guillaume Guimard*. He was born in St. André, Angoulême, in 1719, and was married in 1749 to Marie Garnier. He was a shopkeeper and was the brother-in-law of *Louis Dupard*. AM-A, GG38/206, GG41/113.

Jean Guiton was a schoolboy in a boarding school. He also signed the marriage record of *Etienne Allemand* and *Françoise Ferrand*. AM-A, GG14/36.

J. Joubert was *Jean Joubert*. He was the second cousin of the groom. He was born in St. André, Angoulême, in 1725 and died in 1768. He was married in 1753 to *Marguerite Durousot*. He was a draper, and lived in the Isle de M. Arnaud/Point du Jour. AM-A, GG39/51, GG74/56, GG44/13; CC42/1/17, CC62/15/557.

Antoine Laforet was a grocer and seller of cooking fat. He was a neighbor of *Marc Allemand* in the Isle Chabrefy/Cloche Verte. AM-A, CC42/1/10, CC62/8/323.

Catherine Lecler was born in St. André, Angoulême, in 1743 and died in 1803. She was the daughter of a tanner. She was married in 1759 to the younger *Jean Glaumont*, the second cousin of the groom. She was the daughter-in-law of *Jean Glaumont* and *Marie Gendron*, and the sister-in-law of *Antoine Glaumont* and *Magdelaine Glaumont*. She was the aunt and godmother of the revolutionary official Jean Lecler-Raby. AM-A, GG40/131, GG129/5–6, GG43/29–30, 1E34/54.

D. Lemaitre was *Dorothée Devuailly Lemaitre*. She was the sister of *Marie Adelaide Devuailly*, and the sister-in-law of *Gabriel Ferrand*. She was married in 1764 to *Gabriel Lemaitre*. AM-A, GG8/147–148.

Gabriel Lemaitre was born in 1741 in Notre Dame de Beaulieu, Angoulême. He was a painter. He was married in 1764 to Dorothée Devuailly. He was the brother-in-law of *Marie Adelaide Devuailly* and *Gabriel Ferrand*. AM-A, GG8/38, GG8/147–148.

Marchais de la Chapelle was *Jean-Baptiste Marchais de la Chapelle*. He was born in St. André, Angoulême, in 1695 and died in 1765. He was a goldsmith and merchant. He was married in 1723 to Rose Jussé. He was the brother of *Pierre Marchais*, the brother-in-law of *Magdelaine Dumergue*, the uncle of *Marguerite Marchais*, the father-in-law of *Marie Durand*, and the grandfather of *Jean-Baptiste Marchais*. He lived in the Isle de M. Pechillon. AM-A, GG37/58, GG58/149, G43/6; CC42/1/13.

Jean-Baptiste Marchais was born around 1754 and died in Saint-Simon, Charente, in 1824. He became a merchant, and was married in 1792 to Marie David. He was the son of *Marie Durand* and the grandson of *Jean-Baptiste Marchais de la Chapelle*. AM-A, GG109/187; AD Charente, Angoulême, St. Martial, 3E16/21, 350/522; AD Charente, Saint-Simon, 1737–1798, 178/298; Saint-Simon, 1821–1836, 48/308. [medium confidence]

Marguerite Marchais was born in St. Antonin, Angoulême, in 1729. Her father was a wigmaker. She was the niece of *Jean-Baptiste Marchais de la Chapelle*, *Pierre Marchais*, and *Magdelaine Dumergue*. AM-A, GG52/155.

P. Marchais jeune was *Pierre Marchais*. He was born in St. André, Angoulême, in 1700 and died in 1776. He was a pastry chef, caterer, and innkeeper. He was married in 1728 to *Magdelaine Dumergue*. He was the brother of *Jean-Baptiste Marchais de la Chapelle* and the uncle of *Marguerite Marchais*. He lived in the Isle Cheval Blanc/Prieuré de Navarre. AM-A, GG37/138, GG66/28, GG45/100; CC42/1/19, CC62/16/619.

Marin was *François Marin*. He was born in St. André, Angoulême, in 1718 and died in 1794. He was a trinket seller. He was married in 1741 to Marguerite Boilevin and in 1744 to Rose Rezé. He was the father of *Rose Marin* and *Rosemarin,* and the brother-in-law of the older *Rose Rezé.* He was a neighbor of *Marc Allemand* in the Isle Chabrefy/Cloche Verte. AM-A, GG38/189, GG40/90, GG53/38, 1E6/19; CC42/1/11, CC62/9/332.

Rose Marin was born in St. Antonin, Angoulême, in 1748 and died in 1824. She was married in 1767 to Claude Rezé and in 1793 to Pierre Corliet Coursac. She was the daughter of *François Marin* and the sister of *Rosemarin.* She was a neighbor of *Marc Allemand* in the Isle Chabrefy/Cloche Verte. AM-A, GG53/66, GG54/54–55, 1E2/2, 1E74/43; CC42/1/11, CC62/9/332.

Rosemarin was born in St. Antonin, Angoulême, in 1754. She was the daughter of *François Marin* and the sister of *Rose Marin.* She was a neighbor of *Marc Allemand* in the Isle Chabrefy/Cloche Verte. AM-A, GG54/14; CC42/1/11, CC62/9/332.

Mazaud was a teacher and a master of arts. He was a neighbor of *Marc Allemand* in the Isle Chabrefy/Cloche Verte. AM-A, CC42/1/11, CC62/9/333.

M. Monaud was *Marguerite Monnaud.* She was born in St. André, Angoulême, in 1732 and died in 1812. Her father was a tailor. She was married in 1754 to *Jean Dumergue,* who was the second cousin of the groom. In 1798 she signed the marriage record of her daughter, Marthe, and the revolutionary Louis Félix, who was born in slavery in Saint-Domingue. She lived in the Isle Cheval Blanc/Prieuré de Navarre. AM-A, GG39/175, GG42/24, 1E14/114–115, 1E45/395; CC42/1/19, CC62/16/622.

Racom is unknown.

Rose Rezé was born in St. Antonin, Angoulême, in 1703 and died in 1781. She was a trinket seller. She was unmarried. She was the sister-in-law of *François Marin*, and the aunt of *Rose Marin* and *Rosemarin*. She was the immediate neighbor of Marc Allemand in the Isle de la Cloche Verte. AM-A, GG52/67, GG55/29; CC62/9/329.

Jean Roy is unknown.

Anne Tabourin was born in St. Antonin, Angoulême, in 1741 and died in 1793. She was unmarried. She was the daughter of *Elizabeth Bourdage* and Jean Tabourin, and the sister of *Marie Charas* and *Catherine Tabourin*. She was a neighbor of *Marc Allemand* in the Isle Chabrefy/Cloche Verte. AM-A, GG53/17, 1E6/9; CC42/1/11, CC62/9/327.

Antoinette Thibaud was born in St. Antonin, Angoulême, in 1716 and died in 1773. Her father was a joiner. She was unmarried. She was the sister of *Mathieu Thibaud* and the aunt of *Barthélemi Thibaud*. AM-A, GG52/108, GG54/74.

Barthélemi Thibaud was born in St. Antonin, Angoulême, in 1753 and died in 1832. He became a lawyer. He was the son of *Mathieu Thibaud* and the nephew of *Antoinette Thibaud*. He was a neighbor of *Marc Allemand* in the Isle Chabrefy/Cloche Verte. AM-A, GG54/9, 1E98/75; CC42/1/10, CC62/8/322.

Thibaud was *Mathieu Thibaud*. He was born in St. Antonin, Angoulême, in 1709 and died in 1796. He was a registry clerk. He was married in 1746 to Françoise Chabaribeire. He was the father of *Barthélemi Thibaud* and the brother of *Antoinette Thibaud*. He was a neighbor of *Marc Allemand* in the Isle Chabrefy/Cloche Verte. AM-A, GG52/87, GG107/114, 1E9/71; CC42/1/10, CC62/8/322.

Marie Tilhard was born in St. Ausone, Angoulême, in 1728. Her father was a hatmaker. She was married in 1751 to *Michel Albert*, and was the daughter-in-law of the older *Michel Albert*. AM-A, GG59/13, GG61/9.

Mauricette Vinsac was born in Notre Dame de la Peine, Angoulême, in 1732. Her father was a printer and binder. She was a neighbor of *Gabriel Ferrand* in the Isle du Collège. AM-A, GG13/113; CC42/2/12, CC62/33/1269.

Yrvoix was *Philippe Yrvoix*. He was born in St. André, Angoulême, in 1737 and died in 1818. He was a legal practitioner and merchant. He was married to Anne Mercier. AM-A, GG40/20, 1E54/307–308.

Gilles Yrvoix was born in 1700 in St. Paul, Angoulême, and died in 1766. He was the first cousin of *Marc Allemand*, and the father of *Jean Yrvoix*. He was a butcher. He was married in 1731 to Magdelaine Glaumont. He was the brother-in-law of *Elizabeth Glaumont* and *Jean Glaumont*. He lived in the Isle Cambois de Chenausac. AM-A, GG88/86, GG39/150, GG90/7; CC42/1/9.

J Yrvoix was *Jean Yrvoix*. He was born in 1734 in St. Paul, Angoulême. He was the second cousin of the groom, and the son of *Gilles Yrvoix*. He was a candle merchant. He was married in 1756 to *Jeanne Chabot*, and was the brother-in-law of *Catherine Chabot*. He was the nephew of *Elizabeth Glaumont* and *Jean Glaumont*. He lived in the Isle des Carmélites. AM-A, GG89/13, GG8/114; CC42/2/4, CC62/25/950.

NOTES

Introduction

1. This was the description of A.R.J. Turgot, the royal administrator of the province from 1761 to 1774; A.R.J. Turgot, "Mémoire sur les prêts d'argent" (1770), in *Oeuvres de Turgot et documents le concernant*, ed. Gustave Schelle, 5 vols. (Paris, 1913–1923), 3:155–157. On the affairs of the 1760s and 1770s, see below, chapter 4.

2. Honoré de Balzac, *Les illusions perdues* (1837–1843) (Paris, 1974), pp. 56, 176; Honoré de Balzac, "Avant-propos," in *Oeuvres complètes de M. de Balzac*, 17 vols. (Paris, 1842–1848), 1:7–32, 12, 14.

3. "Procuration par Marie Aymard," October 16, 1764, Archives départementales de la Charente [hereafter ADC], Bernard, notary, 2E153; "Contrat de marriage de Estienne Allemand et Françoize Ferrand," December 9, 1764, Bernard, 2E153.

4. The dates of birth and death of the children, grandchildren, great-grandchildren, and great-great-grandchildren of Marie Aymard, together with the names of their spouses, are given in appendix 1.

5. Gioachino Rossini, *La gazza ladra* (1817); Théodore Baudouin d'Aubigny and Louis-Charles Caigniez, *La pie voleuse* (Paris, 1815).

6. Carlo Ginzburg and Carlo Poni, "Il nome e i come: scambio ineguale e mercato storiografico," *Quaderni Storici* 40 (1979): 181–190.

7. Giacomo Leopardi, "L'infinito" (1819):

   ... Così tra questa
immensità s'annega il pensier mio:
e il naufragar m'è dolce in questo mare

In Jonathan Galassi's translation:

  So my mind sinks in this immensity:
  and foundering is sweet in such a sea.

Giacomo Leopardi, *Canti*, trans. Jonathan Galassi (New York, 2010), pp. 106–107.

8. See below, chapter 3.

9. Emile Zola, *L'oeuvre* (1886) (Paris, 1983), p. 403; "Les réalistes du salon," in Zola, *Oeuvres critiques* (*Oeuvres complètes*, vol. 32) (Paris, 1906), p. 86, and see below, chapter 11.

10. See Marc Bloch, *L'étrange défaite: témoignage écrit en 1940* (Paris, 1957), p. 22.

11. Adam Smith, *The Theory of Moral Sentiments* (1790), ed. D. D. Raphael and A. L. Macfie (Oxford, 1976), p. 234. As Edmund Burke wrote of the economists of "men in general," "they reduce men to loose counters, merely for the sake of simple telling, and not to figures whose power is to arise from their place in the table." Edmund Burke, *Reflections on the Revolution in France* (1790) (Harmondsworth, 1969), p. 168.

12. As in the famous opening credits of the soap opera *Peyton Place*, the camera hovers high above a small, quiet town, and then zooms in to the houses, and the families within. In a different vista, in the opening of Wang Anyi's novel *The Song of Everlasting Sorrow*, Shanghai's neighborhoods are "looked down upon from the highest point in the city," first as a "dark mass," and then, at dawn, as the "clothes hanging out to dry . . . hint at the private lives and loves that lie hidden beneath." Wang Anyi, *The Song of Everlasting Sorrow: A Novel of Shanghai* (1995), trans. Michael Nerry and Susan Chan Egan (New York, 2008), pp. 3, 6–7.

13. Transcription of the judgment of the tribunal civil de première instance of Bayonne on the request of Martial Allemand Lavigerie, Archives départementales des pyrénées atlantiques [hereafter ADPA], Bayonne, Naissances, 1826–1837, no. 351, September 7, 1826, 52–53/904. See below, chapter 7.

14. On the formality of the records of civil registration, and earlier of parish registers—of "poor data" or "données pauvres"—see Paul-André Rosental, *Les sentiers invisibles: espaces, familles et migrations dans la France du 19e siècle* (Paris, 1999), pp. 22–23. The registers are also "structurally numerical," in the sense that they can be counted or "dépouillés" (despoiled or skinned), reduced to numbers. François Furet, "Quantitative History," *Daedalus* 100, no. 1 (Winter 1971): 151–167, 158. In the family history of historical demographers, the names of individuals were a sort of intermediate resource, to be used and disposed of in a statistical history that was "interested only in groups; the elements of which they are constituted are not of interest in themselves." Louis Henry, "Problèmes de la recherche démographique moderne," *Population* 21, no. 6 (1966): 1093–1114, pp. 1096–1097; Michel Fleury, *Nouveau manuel de dépouillement et d'exploitation de l'État civil ancien* (Paris, 1985).

15. On the footnote, see Anthony Grafton, *The Footnote: A Curious History* (Cambridge, MA, 1999).

16. See "Historique des fonds de la série B," in ADC, *Répertoires numériques de la série A et la série B*, ed. Léo Imbert and Léon Burias (Angoulême, 1925), i–iii, p. i. On the definition of the "isle de maisons" in eighteenth-century town design—"an isolated space of streets, occupied by buildings"—which was the unit used in the tax rolls of Angoulême, see M. Buchotte, *Les règles du dessein et du lavis, pour les plans particuliers des ouvrages et des bâtiments* (Paris, 1754), pp. 36–37. The "cadastre" or register of landed property was established on a national scale in France in 1807; see Marcel Marion, *Dictionnaire des institutions de la France aux XVIIe et XVIIIe siècles* (Paris, 1923), pp. 64–65, and on the "cadastre napoléonien" in the Charente, https://archives .lacharente.fr/s/1/cadastre-napoleonien/?.

17. This is Mark Zuckerberg's description of the "core" of Facebook, January 11, 2018. https:// www.facebook.com/zuck/posts/10104413015393571.

18. On the sociology of influence, see Elihu Katz, "Lazarsfeld's Legacy: The Power of Limited Effects," in Elihu Katz and Paul F. Lazarsfeld, *Personal Influence: The Part Played by People in the Flow of Mass Communications* (Piscataway, NJ, 2006), xv–xxvii. On social networks of information, see Ronald S. Burt, "Social Contagion and Innovation: Cohesion versus Structural Equivalence," *American Journal of Sociology* 92, no. 6 (May 1987): 1287–1335, and on "developing micro-macro linkage with the help of network analysis," see Mark S. Granovetter, "The Strength of Weak Ties," *American Journal of Sociology* 78, no. 6 (May 1973): 1360–1380, p. 1378.

19. Abhijit Banerjee, Arun G. Chandrasekhar, Esther Duflo, and Matthew O. Jackson, "Gossip: Identifying Central Individuals in a Social Network," February 2016, https:// economics.mit.edu/faculty/banerjee/papers, NBER Working Paper No. 20422, National Bureau of Economic Research, August 2014, p. 2. On the data to be derived from 90,118 interviews with American adolescents in 1994–1995, see Ben Golub and Matthew O. Jackson, "Does Homophily Predict Consensus Times? Testing a Model of Network Structure via a Dynamic Process," *Review of Network Economics* 11, no. 3 (2012): 1–28. As Matthew Jackson wrote in 2014, the "main impetus" for the recent study of networks in economics is "that as economists endeavor to build better models of human behavior, they cannot ignore that humans are fundamentally a social species with interaction patterns that shape their behaviors. People's opinions, which products they buy, whether they invest in education, become criminals, and so forth, are all influenced by friends and acquaintances. Ultimately, the full network of relationships—how dense it is, whether some groups are segregated, who sits in central positions—impact how information spreads and how people behave." Matthew O. Jackson, "Networks in the Understanding of Economic Behaviors," *Journal of Economic Perspectives* 28, no. 4 (Fall 2014): 3–22, p. 3.

20. The single bookseller identified in the tax registers of the town in 1763–1766, Rezé, was listed as living near the formerly Jesuit college; Isle du Collège, in "Cahiers de l'état des classes faites pour la faction du role pour 1763," AM-A, CC42/2/12, "Répartition de la taille," 1766, CC62/32/1260, and see below, chapters 2 and 3. On Paris as an information society, see Robert Darnton, "An Early Information Society: News and the Media in Eighteenth-Century Paris," *American Historical Review* 105, no. 1 (February 2000), 1–35.

21. On the restaurant, see Firmin Maillard, "Les derniers bohèmes," *La Renaissance littéraire et artistique* 1, no. 31 (November 23, 1872): 245–246, and below, chapter 8.

22. Louis Henry, "La fécondité naturelle. Observation, théorie, résultats," *Population* 16, no. 4 (1961): 625–636, p. 626.

23. "Our Story," https://www.ancestry.com/corporate/about-ancestry/our-story, accessed on January 7, 2020.

24. The corporate histories of ancestry.com and geneanet.com identify 1996 as the outset of the contemporary story; see https://www.familysearch.org/wiki/en/Geneanet and https:// www.ancestry.com/corporate/about-ancestry/our-story. The industry is itself at least as old, in France, as the "general archives of the entire world" proposed by Napoléon in 1812, with a tariff of prices to be charged for inquiries on behalf of "families, or individuals, who might be interested." Henri Bordier, *Les Archives de la France* (Paris, 1855), p. 19, and "Arrêté du 6 mai 1812," p. 393. On the construction of the archive, which was not completed, see Emma Rothschild, "The Archives of Universal History," *Journal of World History* 19, no. 3 (September 2008): 375–401.

25. Archives départementales de Seine-et-Marne [hereafter ADSM], Montereau-Fault-Yonne, 1839–1841, marriage of Jean-Baptiste Ferrand and Anne Nicolas Thiriot, January 23, 1839, 47–48/356, and see below, chapters 7 and 8.

26. Baptism of Gabriel Ferrand, April 13, 1738, AM-A, St. Paul, GG89/36r; page omitted in the online record, between views 89/32 (34v–35r) and 89/33 (36v–37r.) It is missing, in turn, in the transcription of the register published by a public-spirited local historian, Hubert

Marchadier; https://en.geneanet.org/archives/releves/publi/hmarchadier/, accessed on January 9, 2020.

27. Marriage of Gabriel Ferrand and Marie Adelaide Devuailly, October 30, 1763, AM-A, Notre Dame de Beaulieu [hereafter NDB], GG8/143.

28. "Table alphabétique des successions collatérales payées," ADC, 2C2/39, p. 30, and see below, chapter 5. I am most grateful to Dominique Guirignon in the Archives départementales de la Charente for providing me with a copy of the missing page.

29. "Séance du mercredi 8 decembre 1909," *Bulletins et mémoires de la société archéologique et historique de la Charente* [hereafter *BSAHC*], ser. 8, 1 (1910): xliv, and see below, chapter 7.

30. On the seductions of "side-glancing" and "drive-by transnationalism," see Lara Putnam, "The Transnational and the Text-Searchable: Digitized Sources and the Shadows They Cast," *American Historical Review* 121, no. 2 (April 2016): 377–402. On historians of culture (or intellectual historians) and "l'élargissement brutal des corpus," see Antoine Lilti, "Le pouvoir du crédit au XVIIIe siècle: histoire intellectuelle et sciences sociales," *Annales. Histoire, Sciences Sociales* 70, no. 4 (2015): 957–978, p. 968.

31. William Wordsworth, *The Prelude*, bk. 4, lines 62–63.

32. Georges Lefebvre, "L'oeuvre historique d'Albert Mathiez," *Annales historiques de la révolution française* 51 (May–June 1932): 193–210.

33. "Prologue," in Luis González y González, *San José de Gracia: Mexican Village in Transition*, trans. John Upton (Austin, TX, 1974), xv–xxviii, pp. xviii, xxii, xxv.

34. On the realism of nineteenth-century Paris, see below, chapters 7 and 11, and on the lives of industrious women in twentieth-century Shanghai, see Anyi, *The Song of Everlasting Sorrow*, and Wang Anyi, *Fu Ping: A Novel*, trans. Howard Goldblatt (New York, 2019).

35. "I have thus decided that no papers or registers, whether emanating from offices or archives, can be suppressed or sold without my prior approval," another minister wrote, ten years later. Circulars of July 17, 1829, and August 8, 1839, in ADC, Archives, 1 TPROV 1. There was an abundance of parish registers and notarial acts in France in 1789, and there has been a prodigious, sustained enterprise of the production, classification, and conservation of archives that started with the French Revolution, and has continued ever since. On the history of French and British archives, see François-Joseph Ruggiu, "Autres sources, autre histoire? Faire l'histoire des individus des XVIIe et XVIIIe siècles en Angleterre et en France," *Revue de Synthèse* 125, no. 1 (2004): 111–152, pp. 116, 139, and on notarial archives and social history, see Scarlett Beauvalet-Boutouyrie, Vincent Gourdon, and François-Joseph Ruggiu, "L'acte notarié d'ancien regime au service d'une histoire sociale des individus," in *Liens sociaux et actes notariés dans le monde urbain en France et en Europe*, ed. Beauvalet-Boutouyrie, Gourdon, and Ruggiu (Paris, 2004), 7–13. On the notaries practicing in Angoulême in 1764, typescript list of notaries by residence and name, ADC, February 6, 2015. There is more than a linear kilometer of notarial acts, starting in 1395, in the departmental archives of the Charente; Francine Ducluzeau, *Guide des archives de la Charente* (Angoulême, 1983), pp. 66–68. On the royal edict of 1765, see "Les notaires de l'Angoumois et le dépôt général de leurs minutes," in ADC, *Répertoire numérique de minutes notariales (série E) dressé par MM. de la Martinière et Imbert* (Angoulême, n.d.), iv–lxiii, pp. xvi–xxxv.

36. Alain Corbin, *Le monde retrouvé de Louis-François Pinagot* (1998) (Paris, 2016), pp. 7, 9. Louis-François Pinagot, an unexceptional man, or a man without a destiny, was born in 1798 in

lower Normandy, and was a maker of wooden shoes, like Marie Aymard's father-in-law, two generations earlier.

37. Rosental, *Les sentiers invisibles*, p. 166, and Paul-André Rosental, "Pour une analyse mésoscopique des migrations," *Annales de démographie historique* 104, no. 2 (2002): 145–160. On scales and timescales, see Les Annales, "Tentons l'expérience," *Annales: Economies, Sociétés, Civilisations* 44, no. 6 (1989): 1317–1323; *Les formes de l'expérience: une autre histoire sociale*, ed. Bernard Lepetit (Paris, 1995); and *Jeux d'échelles: la micro-analyse à l'expérience*, ed. Jacques Revel (Paris, 1996). On histories that sought "to employ the micro-scale of analysis in order to test the validity of macro-scale explanatory paradigms," see Francesca Trivellato, "Is There a Future for Italian Microhistory in the Age of Global History?" *California Italian Studies* 2, no. 1 (2011), http://escholarship.org/uc/item/0z94n9hq.

38. On the social history of individuals, and on the possibility of a "nominal history" that proceeds by the "accumulation of pieces of information, often of a disparate nature," see François-Joseph Ruggiu, *L'individu et la famille dans les sociétés urbaines anglaise et française (1720–1780)* (Paris, 2007), and Ruggiu, "Autres sources, autre histoire?" p. 139.

39. On social networks and "bridging the micro-macro link," see Claire Lemercier, "Formal Network Methods in History: Why and How?" https://halshs.archives-ouvertes.fr/halshs-00521527v2, and "Formal Network Methods in History: Why and How?" in *Social Networks, Political Institutions, and Rural Societies*, ed. George Fertig (Turnhout, 2015), 281–310. The metaphor of the social network exploded, in history as elsewhere, in the 2000s. "The word 'network' is everywhere today, including in history," Claire Lemercier wrote in 2005. See Claire Lemercier, "Analyse de réseaux et histoire," *Revue d'histoire moderne et contemporaine* 52, no. 2 (April–June 2005): 88–112; Claire Lemercier, "Analyse de réseaux et histoire de la famille: une rencontre encore à venir?" *Annales de démographie historique* 109, no. 1 (2005): 7–31; Michel Bertrand, Sandro Guzzi-Heeb, and Claire Lemercier, "Introduction: où en est l'analyse de réseaux en histoire?" *Revista hispana para el análisis de redes sociales* 21, no. 1 (December 2011): 1–12, http://revista-redes.rediris.es/html-vol21/vol21_1f.htm. On "connecting micro- and macro-histories by the history of the individuals' own connections," see Emma Rothschild, *The Inner Life of Empires: An Eighteenth-Century History* (Princeton, NJ, 2011).

40. Marc Bloch, *Apologie pour l'histoire, ou métier d'historien* (Paris, 2007), pp. 73–74, 132; and on Bloch's interest in "the reactions of human beings in the presence of economic facts, their sentiments of insecurity or of confidence, of anger or of satisfaction," see Georges Lefebvre, "Le mouvement des prix et les origines de la Révolution française," *Annales d'histoire économique et sociale* 9, no. 4 (1937): 138–170, p. 153, citing Bloch's description of the documents that were missing in the work of the economic historian François Simiand.

41. Bloch, *Apologie pour l'histoire*, p. 79. On the microeconomics of development, which starts with "the economic lives of the poor," and is open to "many . . . kinds of evidence," qualitative and quantitative, see Abhijit Banerjee and Esther Duflo, *Poor Economics: A Radical Rethinking of the Way to Fight Global Poverty* (New York, 2011), pp. x, 15. Among recent economic histories and histories of life that draw on diverse kinds of evidence, in relation to different times and places, see Sheilagh Ogilvie, "Servage et marchés: l'univers économique des serfs de Bohême dans le domaine de Friedland (1583–1692)," *Histoire & Sociétés Rurales*, no. 14 (2000): 90–125; Hans-Joachim Voth, *Time and Work in England 1750–1830* (Oxford, 2000); Claire Zalc, *Melting*

Shops: une histoire des commerçants étrangers en France (Paris, 2010); Tracy Dennison, *The Institutional Framework of Russian Serfdom* (Cambridge, 2011); Janet Y. Chen, *Guilty of Indigence: The Urban Poor in China, 1900–1953* (Princeton, NJ, 2012); Francesca Trivellato, *The Familiarity of Strangers: The Sephardic Diaspora, Livorno, and Cross-cultural Trade in the Early Modern Period* (New Haven, CT, 2012); Sunil Amrith, *Crossing the Bay of Bengal: The Furies of Nature and the Fortunes of Migrants* (Cambridge, MA, 2013); Rohit De, *A People's Constitution: The Everyday Life of Law in the Indian Republic* (Princeton, NJ, 2018); Philip T. Hoffman, Gilles Postel-Vinay, and Jean-Laurent Rosenthal, *Dark Matter Credit: The Development of Peer-to-Peer Lending and Banking in France* (Princeton, NJ, 2019).

42. The "distorting effect" of the "why approach," as Christopher Clark wrote in his study of the origins of the First World War, is that "it creates the illusion of a steadily building causal pressure; the factors pile up on top of each other pushing down on the events; political actors become mere executors of forces long established and beyond their control." Christopher Clark, *The Sleepwalkers: How Europe Went to War in 1914* (London, 2013), p. xxvii.

43. Bloch, *Apologie pour l'histoire*, p. 131.

44. On the presumption of economic disquiet that preceded the French Revolution, see below, chapters 4 and 6. On the change in mentalities that Tocqueville observed in the mid-eighteenth century as a "cultural revolution (or a moral or intellectual revolution, if one prefers)," see Alexis de Tocqueville, *L'ancien régime et la révolution*, ed. J.-P. Mayer (Paris, 1967), and François Furet, *Penser la révolution française* (Paris, 1978), p. 248. On the debates over cultural explanations of economic growth, see François Crouzet, "The Historiography of French Economic Growth in the Nineteenth Century," *Economic History Review* 56, no. 2 (2003): 215–242, and for a recent view of cultural origins, see Joel Mokyr, *A Culture of Growth: The Origins of the Modern Economy* (Princeton, NJ, 2016).

45. On the multiple, contested meanings of the industrial modernity of nineteenth-century France, see Emmanuel Fureix and François Jarrige, *La modernité desenchantée: relire l'histoire du XIXe siècle français* (Paris, 2015).

46. A. C. Grussenmeyer, *Documents biographiques sur son éminence le cardinal Lavigerie*, 2 vols. (Algiers, 1888), 2:305–308; *La lanterne* 3448 (September 29, 1886), 4140 (August 21, 1888).

47. See Claire Lemercier and Claire Zalc, *Quantitative Methods in the Humanities: An Introduction*, trans. Arthur Goldhammer (Charlottesville, VA, 2019), especially on numbers and sources (pp. 26–27), on completeness and the longing for exhaustiveness (pp. 3, 37), and on the pleasures of *"input"* (pp. 51–52).

Chapter One. The World of Marie Aymard

1. Baptism of Marie Aymard, February 8, 1713, AM-A, St. Antonin, GG52/97; burial of Marie Aymard, April 22, 1790, Petit St. Cybard [hereafter PSC], GG68/117.

2. The word *marchand*, which was used frequently in the parish registers of eighteenth-century Angoulême, can be translated both as "merchant" and as "shopkeeper." I have in general, and with some hesitation, used the English word "shopkeeper." On the difficulties of translating *marchand*, see Edmond Huguet, *L'évolution du sens des mots depuis le XVIe siècle* (Geneva, 1967), pp. 63–64, and Francesca Trivellato, *The Promise and Peril of Credit: What a Forgotten Legend*

about Jews and Finance Tells Us about the Making of European Commercial Society (Princeton, NJ, 2019), p. 100; see also Michael B. Katz, "Occupational Classification in History," *Journal of Interdisciplinary History* 3, no. 1 (Summer 1972): 63–88. Marriage of Pierre Aymard and Anne Queil, November 11, 1711, AM-A, St. Antonin, GG52/94. On Anne Queil's parents, see baptism of Françoise Dorbe, February 8, 1661, marriage of Pierre Cueil and Françoise Dorbe, April 6, 1676, baptism of Claude Queil, January 4, 1682, and baptism of Anne Queil, August 8, 1689, St. Antonin, GG51/6, 97, 113, GG52/28.

3. Marriage of Gabriel Boisdon and Anne Queil, June 22, 1718, AM-A, St. Antonin, GG52/111.

4. Marriage of Marie Aymard and Louis Ferrand, November 21, 1735, St. Paul GG 89/20. Louis Ferrand was born in "Toussigny" (Tauxigny) in the Loire, a village or "bourg" with an estimated 270 households. Baptism of Louis Ferrand, son of Claude Ferrand and Louise Douard, January 3, 1706, AD Indre-et-Loire, Tauxigny, 1706–1707, 2/23. Abbé Expilly, *Dictionnaire géographique, historique et politique des Gaules et de la France*, 6 vols. (Paris, 1762–1770), 4:340. Claude Ferrand was identified as a *sabotier* at the baptism of his older son, Claude, in 1696. AD Indre-et-Loire, Tauxigny, 1696, 7/13.

5. Baptism of Anne Ferrand, August 17, 1736, AM-A, St. Paul, GG89/25; death of Anne Ferrand, March 28, 1738, St. Paul, GG89, 36r (page missing in the online record); baptism of Gabriel Ferrand, April 13, 1738, St. Paul, GG89, 36r; baptism of Léonard Ferrand, August 27, 1739, St. Martial, GG106/116; baptism of Françoise Ferrand, November 1, 1740, St. Martial, GG106/151; death of Léonard Ferrand, September 24, 1741, PSC, GG67/14; baptism of François Ferrand, May 6, 1742, PSC, GG67/18; baptism of Mathurin Ferrand, September 23, 1743, St. André, GG40/150; baptism of Marguerite Ferrand, December 27, 1744, St. André, GG40/176; baptism of Jean Ferrand, June 13, 1749, St. André, GG41/108.

6. Baptism of Jean Ferrand, June 13, 1749, AM-A, St. André, GG41/108.

7. Communautés, Menuisiers, AM-A, HH5, 1744–1745. Louis Ferrand's father-in-law, Gabriel Boisdon, who was identified as a "master carpenter," had also been a *sindic* of the community of joiners. The rankings within these little communities were represented only approximately in the parish registers. In the register of his marriage, in 1735, Louis Ferrand was identified as "garçon menuisier," with a line through the word "garçon" (apprentice). At the baptism in 1736 of their first child, Anne, who died in infancy, he was a "maître menuisier," and at the baptism of Gabriel, in 1738, he was again a "garçon menuisier;" by the baptism in 1739 of Léonard, who also died in infancy, he was a "maître menuisier." AM-A, St. Paul GG 89/20, 25, 36, St. Martial, GG106/116. The words *menuisier*—carpenter specializing in furniture, or joiner—and *charpentier*, or carpenter, are difficult to distinguish in contemporary English. On the two crafts, see Prosper Boissonnade, *Essai sur l'organisation du travail en Poitou depuis le XIe siècle jusqu'à la Révolution*, 2 vols. (Paris, 1900), 1:343–346.

8. AM-A, St. Paul, GG89/25; St. Paul, GG89, 36r; St. Martial, GG106/116; St. Martial, GG106/151; PSC, GG67/18; St. André, GG40/150; St. André, GG40/176; St. André, GG41/108; and on the profession of Léonard Marechal, the godfather of Léonard, St. Jean, GG74/98.

9. "Registre des ordinations remis aux archives de l'Evêché en septembre 1912," 24 June 1753, Archives diocésaines d'Angoulême. Marie Aymard's name was spelled as "Amard" in the register, and corrected in the margin to "Aimard." On the free instruction provided by the college, see Prosper Boissonnade and Jean-Marie-Jules Bernard, *Histoire du collège et du lycée d'Angoulême (1516–1895)* (Angoulême, 1895), pp. 126–127, 210.

10. "Marché d'engagement de Ferrand et Delorière à M. Cazeau de Roumillac," December 15, 1753, ADC, Caillaud, notary, 2E259. On the "revolution" of 1769, see below, chapter 4.

11. When Delorière's son was married in September 1757, he was described as the son of the late Hugues Delorière. Marriage of Jacques Delorière and Marie Boilevin, September 6, 1757, AM-A, St. Martial, GG108/185.

12. "Acte entre Aymard Ve Ferrand et Ferrand son fils," May 6, 1760, ADC, Jeheu, notary, 2E850. The number of notaries in Angoulême was "so excessive," according to the royal decree of 1765, as to have led to abuses, indolence, and "activities incompatible with their functions." *Edit du roi, contenant règlement pour les Notaires de la ville, faubourgs et banlieue d'Angoulême* (Compiègne, 1765), p. 1; and see "Les notaires de l'Angoumois et le dépôt général de leurs minutes," pp. xvi–xxxv. The "bad character" of Guillaume Jeheu was considered to have been one of the causes of the crisis over the excessive supply of notarial activity; "Les notaires de l'Angoumois," p. xii.

13. "Acte entre Aymard Ve Ferrand et Ferrand son fils," May 6, 1760, ADC, 2E850.

14. "Acte entre Aymard Ve Ferrand et Ferrand son fils," May 6, 1760, ADC, 2E850. The fee for the notarial act was two livres and ten sols, and the event was so unimportant that it was not included in the inventory of notarial records drawn up, in the late nineteenth century, by the archivists of the Charente; inventory of acts passed by Guillaume Jeheu in 1760 in *Inventaire sommaire des archives départementales antérieures à 1789, Charente, Archives civiles—série E (967–1385)*, ed. M. P. de Fleury (Angoulême, 1887), pp. 185–186.

15. "Mariage de Sr. Gabriel Ferrand avec Dlle. Marie Adelaide Devuailly," October 15, 1763, ADC, Sicard, notary, 2E6662. Marie Adelaide's grandfather, two uncles, and a cousin were cloth-dyers in Amiens. See "Depost d'actes et jugement par les Srs. Lemaitre et Ferrand," October 10, 1769, ADC, Caillaud, 2E290. Her father and mother took a nine-year lease of a house in Angoulême, in 1760, from the principal local landlady in the neighborhood where Gabriel was living, "la dame abbesse de Ste Ausone." "Contrôle des actes des notaires et actes sous seing privé," April 24–October 4, 1760, ADC, 2C2/162, 20/153.

16. "Vente de meubles par Marie Aymard à Gabriel Ferrand son fils," January 10, 1764, ADC, 2E153. Gabriel's signature, which had been large and confident in the record of a parish assembly in 1757, and something of a scrawl in the melancholy declaration following his father's death, was now an extraordinary apparition of curlicues and flourishes: the hand of a public writer. AM-A, "Assemblée de paroisse," April 1, 1757, NDP, GG14/23–24; "Acte entre Aymard Ve Ferrand et Ferrand son fils," May 6, 1760, ADC, 2E850.

17. "Vente de meubles par Marie Aymard à Gabriel Ferrand son fils," January 10, 1764, ADC, 2E153.

18. "Vente de meubles par Marie Aymard à Gabriel Ferrand son fils," January 10, 1764, ADC, 2E153.

19. "Quittance par Marie Aimard à M. Cazau," January 11, 1764, ADC, Sicard, 2E6663.

20. "Procuration par Marie Aymard," October 16, 1764, ADC, 2E153.

21. "Procuration par Marie Aymard," October 16, 1764, ADC, 2E153.

22. "Procuration par Marie Aymard," October 16, 1764, ADC, 2E153. The language of "personnes publiques" was a standard idiom of notaries; so was the menacing expression about obligating and mortgaging "tous et chacuns ses biens." See, for example, "Chetel pour Marguerite Labonne et Pierre Bruchier son fils à Mr. François Laforet," December 9, 1770, ADC, Ber-

nard, 2E164; "Procuration pour agir donnée par Coignet à Blanloeil sa femme," March 29, 1768, ADC, Caillaud, 2E287; and see Claude-Joseph de Ferrière, *La science parfaite des notaires, ou le moyen de faire un parfait notaire*, rev. ed. (Paris, 1752), 2 vols.

23. "Procuration par Marie Aymard," October 16, 1764, ADC, 2E153.

24. *Mémoire pour Jean-Alexandre James, nègre, Intimé. Contre le Sieur CAZEAU, Appellant de la Sentence de l'Amirauté* (Paris, [1779]), pp. 3–4, 11.

25. Burial of Marie Aymard, April 22, 1790, AM-A, PSC, GG68/117.

26. Baptism of Anne Ferrand, August 17, 1736, AM-A, St. Paul, GG89/25; death of Anne Ferrand, March 28, 1738, St. Paul, GG89/36r.

27. Baptism of Gabriel Ferrand, April 13, 1738, AM-A, St. Paul, GG89/36r, following a preliminary blessing, "given the danger of death," on April 10, 1738; page missing in the online record.

28. Baptism of Pierre Alexandre Ferrand, March 16, 1775, AM-A, NDP, GG14/53; death of Gabriel Ferrand, December 19, 1816, 1E52/426–427.

29. Baptism of Léonard Ferrand, August 27, 1739, AM-A, St. Martial, GG106/116; death of Léonard Ferrand, September 24, 1741, PSC, GG67/14.

30. Baptism of Françoise Ferrand, November 1, 1740, AM-A, St. Martial, GG106/151.

31. Baptism of Françoise Lafont, February 16, 1756, AM-A, St. Martial, GG108/143.

32. Marriage of Martial Allemand Lavigerie and Louise Vaslin, April 13, 1790, AM-A, St. André, GG47/64–65; divorce of Martial Allemand Lavigerie and Louise Vaslin, 2 brum. 5 (October 23, 1796), 1E11/4; marriage of Martial Allemand Lavigerie and Marie Louise Bonnite Raymond Saint Germain, 28 prair. 9 (June 17, 1801), 1E23/69–70; marriage contract of Martial Allemand Lavigerie and Marie Louise Bonnite Raymond Saint Germain, 20 prair. 9 (June 9, 1801), ADC, Duval, notary, 2E6272.

33. Baptism of François Ferrand, May 6, 1742, AM-A, PSC, GG67/18; "Marriage de Gabriel Ferrand avec Marie Adelaide Devuailly," October 15, 1763, ADC, 2E6662.

34. Baptism of Jean Ferrand, December 26, 1766, AM-A, NDP, GG 14/38.

35. Isle des Jacobins, in "Cahiers de l'état des classes faites pour la faction du role pour 1763," AM-A, CC42/1/11, and Isle des Jacobins, "Répartition de la taille pour la classe au dessus de 10s. de subsistance," 1766, CC62/9/346. In 1765, the François Ferrand who was a domestic servant, two years earlier, was listed as a day laborer, and married; there is no record of his marriage in the twelve parish registers for Angoulême in 1763–1765.

36. www.geneanet.com, www.filae.com, and www.ancestry.com, accessed on October 20, 2019.

37. Baptism of Mathurin Ferrand, September 23, 1743, AM-A, St. André, GG40/150.

38. Baptism of François Ferrand, AM-A, May 6, 1742, PSC, GG67/18; "Marriage de Gabriel Ferrand avec Marie Adelaide Devuailly," October 15, 1763, ADC, 2E6662.

39. "Etat des garsons fugitifs de la milice," October 4, 1758, AM-A, EE5. "Tourangeau garson de Raby" was listed as coming from the parish of St. Martial in one of the lists, and from "Beaulieu" in the other list, with the same date. On the confusing entries in the militia lists, see below, chapter 2.

40. Baptism of Marguerite Ferrand, December 27, 1744, AM-A, St. André, GG40/176; "Procuration par Marie Aymard," October 16, 1764, ADC, 2E153.

41. Burial of Jeanne Allemand, September 20, 1767, AM-A, St. Martial, GG110/87; baptism of Martial Allemand, October 22, 1767, St. Antonin, GG54/56; baptism of Jean François Ferrand, February 28, 1768, NDP, GG 14/41; ADC, St. Martial, 3E16/21, 438/522.

42. Bloch, *Apologie pour l'histoire*, p. 74.

43. Baptism of Jean Ferrand, June 13, 1749, AM-A, St. André, GG41/108.

44. Marriage of Jean Ferrand and Elizabeth Boutoute, May 14, 1774, AM-A, St. André, GG45/64.

45. Baptism of Martial Ferrand, March 30, 1775, of Etienne Ferrand, June 3, 1776, of Françoise Ferrand, June 12, 1777, death of Etienne Ferrand, November 19, 1777, birth of Jean-Baptiste Ferrand, 8 pluv. 4 (January 28, 1796), AM-A, PSC, GG68/56, St. André, GG45/100, GG45/124, GG45/133, 1E7/40. Jean-Baptiste was called "Jean" in the records of the baptisms of his three older children, as he was in his own baptism, and "Jean-Baptiste" in the record of the birth of his youngest child.

46. *Supplément aux Affiches Américaines*, no. 90 (December 19, 1789): 1100; Dossiers "Ferrand" and "Ferrand (Jn. Bte.)," Archives Nationales [hereafter AN], Secours aux réfugiés et colons spoliés, F/12/2795.

47. "Etat des Refugiés, Déportés, et Propriétaires Colons," ADC, L152. Petition to the minister of the interior, received February 24, 1831, in dossier "Ferrand," AN, Secours aux réfugiés et colons spoliés, F/12/2795. Death of Jean-Baptiste Ferrand, 9e arr., November 16, 1831, Archives de Paris [hereafter AdP], Fichiers de l'état civil reconstitué, V3E/D552, 10/37.

48. It is also awkward and even invasive, in respect of the possibility, for example, that Louis Ferrand was still alive in 1764, living with his slaves and a new companion, in Grenada under British dominion.

49. Baptism of Jean-François Cazaud, April 21, 1756, AM-A, St. Jean, GG74/70.

50. "Recensement général de l'isle de la Grenade," May 25, 1755, Archives Nationales d'Outre-Mer [hereafter ANOM], Dépôt des papiers publics des colonies, G/1/498. The other categories of white male inhabitants were "boys bearing arms," "boys below twelve," and "men who were excessively old and infirm."

51. "Etat général, année 1742," Grenada, ANOM, C/10a/2/2; "Recensement général de l'isle de la Grenade," 1755, ANOM, G/1/498; "Isle de la Grenade et dépendances, resultats des états dressés pour l'année 1782," ANOM, C/10a/4. The number of whites fell from 1,187 in 1742 to 1,077 in 1755, and increased to 1,189 in 1782.

52. Letter of July 7, 1758, from M. de Rochemore, in ANOM, Grenada, Correspondance à l'arrivée, C/10a/2; letter of March 20, 1758, to Antoine Lefebvre de Givry, in ANOM, Colonies B107/43r–44v, duplicata, fonds ministeriels, Isles du Vent 1758.

53. Census of Grenada, 1763, in The National Archives, Kew [hereafter TNA], CO 101/1/part 1/22v, 25r.

54. Adelaide Herbert du Jardin was born in Martinique in January 1763, in the short-lived legal no-man's-land of British occupation, between the signature of the preliminary and the final versions of the Treaty of Paris that ended the Seven Years' War. The case involved her right to inherit the property of her uncle, Joseph Herbert, who had died in Grenada, intestate and unmarried, in the course of another short-lived no-man's-land, or the period of eighteen months following the signature of the definitive version of the Treaty of Paris, on February 10, 1763, during which French subjects retained entire rights of emigration—to "retire with all safety and freedom"—from the new British dominions of Canada and Grenada. Joseph, when he died in January 1765, was in the midst of trying to sell two large plantations on Grenada, for 2,400,000 livres. Adelaide's inheritance was contested between her aunt in Martinique and her mother,

the widow of Louis Ferrand's acquaintance, who had moved to Grenada, married her English lawyer, and sent Adelaide away to London, "to be raised in the Anglican religion." "Herbert Du Jardin, Léon Marie, négociant à la Martinique," 1781, ANOM, COL E 220.

55. ANOM, Martinique, St. Pierre le Mouillage, parish register for 1771, death of Marie Chambert, wife of Pierre Vanda, 5/37; 1772, marriage of Pierre Vvanda and Marie Macary, 12/29; 1774, birth of Anne Marie Vanda, 15/18; 1775, burial of Pierre Vandas, aged sixty-six, 6/23; 1776, burial of Bernard Vandas, aged "around seventy," 6/7. Registers of the parish of La Madeleine, Mont-de-Marsan, available at Archives départementales des Landes [hereafter AD Landes]; 1707, E192/GG24, 4/26; 1709, E192/GG26, 13/29. Pierre Vanda was one of the major creditors of the Jesuit Fathers in Martinique. *Ordre général et définitif de tous les créanciers des ci-devant soi-disans jésuites, soit en France que dans les colonies* (Paris, 1772), p. 118.

56. Baptism of Jean Pascal Yrvoix Chauvin, son of Philippe Yrvoix Chauvin and Françoise Durand, April 6, 1738, AM-A, St. André, GG40/30. Gabriel Ferrand was baptized in the parish of St. Paul the following week.

57. "Chauvin, Jean Yrvoix, négociant, lieutenant d'artillerie et capitaine de milice bourgeoise à Sainte-Lucie, sa succession 1786," ANOM, COL E 77.

58. "Missions religieuses, administration des hopitaux" (1771), ANOM, COL F5a/16/3; "Hopitaux de la Martinique," "Hopitaux des frères de la charité."

59. On the "Punic conduct" of the British in 1759, the fire of 1759, and the hurricane of 1780, see Sidney Daney de Marcillac, *Histoire de la Martinique, depuis la colonization jusqu'en 1815*, 6 vols. (Fort Royal, 1846), 3:255–274, and F.-R. Roux, "Guide des ouragans," *Revue maritime et coloniale* 31 (1871): 619–754, pp. 729–730. On the eruption of Mount Pelée in 1902, see Philippe Deschamps, *Deuil national: les cataclysmes de la Martinique, Saint-Pierre et Saint-Vincent, 8 mai–30 août 1902* (Paris, 1903).

60. Baptism of Jean Alexandre, son of Jean-François Cazeau du Brueil and Marthe de Bologne, September 19, 1727, ANOM, parish register of Basse-Terre, Guadeloupe, 1727, 4/15.

61. Letter of September 27, 1729, from Champigny de Noroy and Pannier d'Orgeville, ANOM, Martinique, Correspondance à l'arrivée, C8a/40/97v–98r.

62. Baptism of Jean-François-Auguste, July 19, 1733, AM-A, St. André, GG39/205.

63. Baptism of George Alexandre de Bologne, March 16, 1748, AM-A, St. Jean, GG74/4; baptism of Jean François Cazaud, April 21, 1752, St. Jean, GG74/70; baptism of Marie Marthe Cazaud, June 16, 1757, GG74/76; "Scellé après le décès de madame la marquise de Cazot" [hereafter "Scellé Cazot"], May 22, 1781, AN, Y//13802. Cazaud described himself as having been in the regiment of the Marquis de Surgère, which during the War of the Austrian Succession of 1740–1748 participated in the relief of the Siege of Prague in 1742; GG74/4. Jean-François Cazaud, the father of Jean-Alexandre, was buried in Angoulême in 1734, and his wife, Marthe de Bologne, died there in 1744. Burial of Jean-François Cazaud, January 16, 1734, AM-A, St. Jean, GG73/32; burial of Marthe de Bologne, October 26, 1744, ADC, NDB, 3E16/1, 55/176.

64. Baptism of Silvie Calixte Benoit, May 7, 1735, AM-A, St. André, GG39/231; marriage of Jean Alexandre Cazaud and Silvie Calixte Benoit des Essarts, September 19, 1752, St. André, GG41/181. The marriage took place five months after the baptism of their "natural and legitimate son," Jean François, as noted in the margin of the parish register of St. Jean; baptism of Jean François Cazaud, April 21, 1752, St. Jean, GG74/70. Cazaud was earlier present in Angoulême in 1743, 1744, 1745, and 1748; GG73/80, 86, 93, GG74/4.

65. "Marché d'engagement de Ferrand et Delorière à M. Cazeau de Roumillac," December 15, 1753, ADC, Caillaud, 2E259.

66. Baptism of Jean François Cazaud, April 21, 1752, AM-A, St. Jean, GG74/70.

67. "Cause entre le sieur de Cazeaux, Français, naturalisé Anglais, domicilié à l'Isle de la Grenade; M. Delpech de Montreau, Et la Dlle. Lucie," *Gazette de Tribunaux* 18, no. 50 (1784): 369–373, p. 370.

68. Census of Grenada, 1763, TNA, CO 101/1/part 1/22v, 25r.

69. Baptism of Mélanie Gabriele Sophie Cazaud, September 20, 1764, AM-A, St. André, GG42/230.

70. "Cause entre le sieur de Cazeaux et la Dlle. Lucie," pp. 370, 373.

71. Letter from Dugout de Casaud, enclosed in a letter of July 9, 1811, from Mr. W. Manning to Mr. Richard Ryder, TNA, HO/1/6/6.

72. "Cazaud de Roumillac habitant de la Grenade 1780–1782," ANOM, Secrétariat d'Etat à la Marine—Personnel colonial ancien, COL E 66; letter of Cazaud de Roumillac to the Comte de Durat, November 12, 1781, "Raport, Le Sieur de Cazaud, François, habitant de la Grenade," undated.

73. "Copy of a Memorial of the Proprietors of Land in the Island of Grenada," enclosed in the complaint of Colonel Alexander Johnstone of December 1, 1769, TNA, Privy Council Papers, PC1/60/7, and Rothschild, *The Inner Life of Empires*. One year later, Cazaud was among the five neighboring proprietors who "viewed and examined" Colonel Johnstone's plantation, called "Bacaye," and estimated its value to be £95,017.1s.8d., including 266 slaves, listed by name and category—"31 Children @ £30," "16 Infirm & Superanuate @£10"—of whom the value was estimated to be £18,372. "Inventory & Valuation of Bacaye Estate," December 1, 1770, University of Bristol, West Indies Papers, Westerhall Estate, DM41/32/1.

74. "Report presented to the Committee on February 20 1770," TNA, PC1/60/7; [Anon.], *A Narrative of the Proceedings upon the Complaint against Governor Melvill* (London, 1770), pp. 105–116.

75. *Narrative of the Proceedings*, pp. 2, 92, 116.

76. "Cause entre le sieur de Cazeaux et la Dlle. Lucie," p. 370.

77. *Mémoire pour Jean-Alexandre James*, pp. 2–3; petition of Jean-Alexandre Gintz, June 9, 1779, in AN, Amirauté, Minutes, 1779, Z/1d/135. The "Kingdom of Timor" was identified in the printed pamphlet as being on the Gold Coast in Africa; Jean-Alexandre was called "Gintz" in the first petition, and "James" in subsequent petitions.

78. *Mémoire pour Jean-Alexandre James*, pp. 2–3. Petition of Jean-Alexandre Gintz, June 9, 1779, judgment by default, Jean-Alexandre James plaintiff versus Decazeaux defendant, July 7, 1779; petition of Jean-Alexandre James plaintiff versus Decazeaux defendant, September 6, 1779, in AN, Amirauté, Minutes, 1779, Z/1d/135.

79. Slavery, in the argument of Jean-Alexandre's lawyers, had been abolished first in France and then in England. It subsisted in the European colonies as no more than "a practice sustained by the sole authority of the magistrates who had been established in these conquered lands." By the English "jurisprudence of Negroes," every African who had claimed his freedom in Britain was declared free, and by current jurisprudence in France, as in the "well-known decrees of Francisque, Pampy, and Juliette," slavery was no more than a practice "maintained by public authority in the [French] colonies"; Jean-Alexandre, who had been brought to Grenada when

it was under British law, and who had lived in England and France, could not be deemed a slave under the law, or the practice, of the French colonies. *Mémoire pour Jean-Alexandre James*, pp. 4–8.

80. *Mémoire pour Jean-Alexandre James*, pp. 3–4, 9, 12.

81. Mr Cazaud, *Account of a New Method of Cultivating the Sugar Cane. Read at the Royal Society, Feb. 25, 1779* (London, 1779), p. 70.

82. Election of Mr Cazaud, https://royalsociety.org/about-us/fellowship/fellows/.

83. Marquis de Casaux, *Considérations sur quelques parties du méchanisme des sociétés* (London, 1785), p. 207.

84. "Cause entre le sieur de Cazeaux et la Dlle. Lucie," p. 372.

85. The household of "M. Casaud, à la guadeloupe en amerique," was listed in the Isle de M. de Chabrefy, later the Isle de la Cloche Verte, in the tax register for 1763; "Cahiers pour 1763," AM-A, CC42/1/10. In the 1766 tax register, "La Dame Cazaud, fille du Sr. Benoist, som mari aux Isles" was listed in the Isle des Tiercelettes; "Répartition de la taille," 1766, AM-A, CC62/22/815.

Chapter Two. The Marriage Contract

1. "Contrat de marriage de Estienne Allemand et Françoize Ferrand," December 9, 1764, ADC, 2E153. Emma Rothschild, "Isolation and Economic Life in Eighteenth-Century France," *American Historical Review* 119, no. 4 (October 2014): 1055–1082.

2. The cost of constructing a bourgeois house in the town was twelve to fifteen thousand livres, and the price was about a third less than the cost of construction. E. Munier, *Essai d'une méthode générale propre à étendre les connoissances des voyageurs*, 2 vols. (Paris, 1779), 1:93; Etienne Munier's son was baptized in the parish of St. Antonin in September 1766, and the daughter of Etienne Allemand and Françoise Ferrand a few weeks later; baptism of Jean Munier, September 14, 1766, and of Jeanne Allemand, October 22, 1766, AM-A, GG54/52.

3. "Contrat de marriage de Estienne Allemand et Françoize Ferrand," December 9, 1764, ADC, 2E153. The expression that Françoise Ferrand used to describe the source of the money— "pour provenir de son péculle"—was derived from *peculium*, the term used in Roman law to denote the small savings of a slave (or son) dependent on the power of a master. The contemporary meaning was "that which someone who is in the power of another has acquired by his industry and his savings, and of which he is permitted to dispose." *Le Grand vocabulaire françois, par une société de gens de lettres*, 30 vols., 1767–1774 (Paris, 1772), 21:323.

4. The marriage contract of Gabriel Ferrand's sister-in-law, in the late summer of 1764, was signed by twenty-five people. Gabriel's own marriage contract, in October 1763, was signed by twenty-nine people, and Jean-Baptiste Ferrand's, in 1774, by eleven. "Mariage du sieur Lemaitre et demoiselle Vuailly," August 26, 1764, Caillaud notary, ADC, 2E280; "Mariage de Gabriel Ferrand avec Marie Adelaide Devuailly," October 15, 1763, ADC, 2E6662; "Mariage de Jean Ferrand avec Elizabeth Boutoute," May 1, 1774, ADC, Sicard, 2E6673. In the seventy marriage contracts studied by Ruggiu in Amiens and Charleville—among more prosperous families—there were fewer than nine signatories per contract; Ruggiu, *L'individu et la famille*, pp. 130–136.

5. See marriage of Marie Aymard and Louis Ferrand, November 21, 1735, AM-A, St. Paul GG 89/20; "Acte entre Aymard Ve Ferrand et Ferrand son fils," May 6, 1760, ADC, 2E850; "Vente de

meubles par Marie Aymard à Gabriel Ferrand son fils," January 10, 1764, ADC, 2E153; "Procuration par Marie Aymard," October 16, 1764, ADC, 2E153; baptism of Gabriel Ferrand, November 7, 1764, NDP, GG14/36.

6. See Claire Lemercier, "Analyse de réseaux et histoire de la famille." As Vincent Gourdon has written, the number of signatures on a marriage contract drawn up by a notary was not restricted, which "leads certain families to use the signing to display the breadth of their social network." Vincent Gourdon, "Aux cœurs de la sociabilité villageoise: une analyse de réseau à partir du choix des conjoints et des témoins au mariage dans un village d'Île-de-France au XIXe siècle," *Annales de démographie historique*, no. 109 (2005): 61–94, p. 62.

7. "Rosemarin," or Rose Marin, was baptized on July 3, 1754, AM-A, St. Antonin, GG54/14; Jean Giraud was baptized on July 17, 1685, St. André, GG35/231.

8. See appendix 2.

9. Death of Jean-Baptiste Marchais, April 9, 1765, AM-A, St. André, GG43/6; death of François Boisnier, April 10, 1839, ADC, Aigre 1828–1842, 260/341.

10. Decision of 2 niv. 2 (December 22, 1793) and marginal note of "representative of the people" Guimberteau, letter sent to the minister of police on 10 flor. 6 (April 29, 1798), in "Marin, Rose," AN, "Police générale—Emigrés: demandes de radiation de la liste," Charente, F/7/4990, dossier 32, 10/56, 32/56. On the travails of Rosemarin and on Jean Guimberteau, one of the representatives of Angoulême in the revolutionary Convention, see below, chapter 5.

11. "Racom" may be a name, or part of another name. I am most grateful to the staff of the Archives départmentales de la Charente for help in trying to read these characters. The signatures can be seen at http://histecon.fas.harvard.edu/visualizing/angouleme/aymard-files/adc _19712_2E153_5.JPG and http://histecon.fas.harvard.edu/visualizing/angouleme/aymard-files /adc_19712_2E153_6.JPG.

12. "Contrat de marriage de Estienne Allemand et Françoize Ferrand," p. [2r]. The contract is a single folio, folded to form four (unpaginated) pages. The signatures begin at the foot of the third page, [2r], and cover the whole of the fourth page, [2v].

13. Etienne Allemand was baptized on February 29, 1740; on January 29, 1752, he signed the baptism record of Jeanne Longeau, the daughter of Jean Longeau, a master locksmith, and Jeanne Giraud; AM-A, GG53/12, GG54/5.

14. "Contrat de marriage de Estienne Allemand et Françoize Ferrand," p. [1r]; marriage of Etienne Allemand and Françoise Ferrand, January 7, 1765; baptism of Marie Allemand, December 1, 1765; AM-A, NDP, GG14/36, St. Antonin, GG54/50.

15. Burial of Guillaume Allemand dit Lavigerie, aged fifty-five, November 6, 1687, AM-A, St. Paul, GG88/42.

16. Death of Marguerite Allemand, daughter of Guillaume Allemand, September 16, 1808, ADC, Saint-Saturnin, deaths, 1802–1812, 148/248; Pierre Allemand, living in Lavigerie, ADC, Saint-Saturnin, Recensement, 1841, 8/39 and 1846, 16/34.

17. "Cahiers pour 1763," AM-A, CC42/1/11. Marc Allemand signed the records of the corporation or guild of "tailleurs" in multiple years, sometimes as "Lavigerie" and sometimes as "Allemand"; AM-A, HH5, Tailleurs, 1745, 1747, 1748, 1752, 1753, 1755, 1760.

18. Marc Allemand was married to Elisabeth Lecler, who died in 1731, and then, in 1736, to Etienne's mother, Marie Giraud; AM-A, St. André, GG39/158, St. Jean, GG73/50. His children

were baptized in 1727, 1730, 1731, 1739, 1740, 1741, 1743, and 1744; St. André, GG39/91, 133, 158, and St. Antonin, GG53/5–6, 12, 19, 31, 39.

19. Jean Giraud was married to Susanne Dufort in the parish of St. Jean on December 1, 1708, and to Marguerite Barathe, also in St. Jean, on January 29, 1721. His sixteen children were baptized in the same parish. AM-A, GG72/174, 177, 188, 206, 209, 218, 223, 233, 238 (the baptism of twins); GG73/4, 10, 18, 24, 31, 47, 59, 67. On Guillaume Dufort and Jean Barathe, tailors, see GG72/128–129, 177.

20. Marriage of Madeleine Allemand and Roch Godinaud, January 21, 1685, AM-A, St. Paul, GG88/26; marriage of Madeleine Allemand and Jean Glaumont, October 30, 1700, St. André, GG37/138; marriage of Elisabeth Glaumont and Jean Dumergue, July 1, 1721, St. André, GG38/232; marriage of Madeleine Glaumont and Gilles Yrvoix, January 9, 1731, St. André, GG39/150; baptism of Jeanne Joubert, daughter of Marguerite Allemand and Pierre Joubert, January 27, 1681, St. Paul, GG88/2.

21. "Cahiers pour 1763," AM-A, CC42, "Répartition de la taille," 1766, AM-A, CC62. The 1763 roll extends over sixty-four pages, in three "cahiers," and the 1766 roll over seventy pages, listing 2,548 households. Both reach beyond the central parishes of Angoulême, to the largely rural suburbs. On the tax reforms and categories of the 1760s, see Mireille Touzery, L'invention de l'impôt sur le revenu (Paris, 1994), chapter 4, available at https://books.openedition.org/igpde/2079. A.R.J. Turgot, as intendant of the generality, was involved to a bizarre extent in the details of the tax rolls: "I think it would be suitable to allocate a square piece of paper to each house," with each "isle de maisons" to be surveyed by walking round the island assigning numbers to all the houses, and with the pieces of paper to be divided into two or more columns. Turgot also circulated a "fictive" model of a tax roll, for a house occupied in 1763 by a wigmaker, and in 1766 by a merchant with seven children, a valet, and a servant, whose wife died in the course of the year. "Lettre circulaire aux officiers municipaux sur les rôles des tailles dans les villes," August 31, 1762, in Oeuvres de Mr. Turgot, ministre d'Etat, ed. Dupont de Nemours, 9 vols. (Paris, 1808–1811), 9:433–437.

22. "Contributions, matrices foncières," 1791, AM-A, unclassified, 11B47, and see below, chapter 5.

23. Boissonnade and Bernard, Histoire du collège d'Angoulême (1516–1895).

24. Emile Biais, "Notes sur les anciennes paroisses d'Angoulême," BSAHC, ser. 5, 4 (1881): 171–215, and 5 (1882): 247–284, pp. 249–251.

25. They were Marie Anne Chaumont Gautier, the widow of a lawyer; Anne Marie Gralhat Fonchaudière, the daughter of the director of the post; her husband, who was a lawyer; her father; and Mauricette Vinsac, the daughter of a printer. In 1763, Mme. Chaumont Vve. Gautier was listed as living in the same small island, of only nine households—it was then called "Isle du Sr. Marvaud"—as Gabriel; Anne Marie Gralhat Fonchaudière and her husband, and Mauricette Vinsac, lived in the immediately adjoining Isle du Collège St. Louis; AM-A, CC42/2/11–12. In 1765, Gabriel and Mme. Chaumont Gautier were listed as immediate neighbors in the Isle de la Place du Collège—their numbers in the register were 1233 and 1234—and the Fonchaudières and Mauricette Vinsac lived in the Isle du Collège; CC62/16–17/1233, 1234, 1264, 1269.

26. AM-A, CC42/1/10–11; CC62/8–9. The island was known in 1763 as the "Isle de M. de Chabrefy."

27. They were Philippe Briand and Jean Guiton, identified as "pensionnaires écoliers in this parish" in the record of the marriage of Etienne Allemand and Françoise Ferrand, on January 7, 1765; AM-A, NDP, GG14/36.

28. The signatories were Jean-Baptiste Marchais de la Chapelle; his younger brother Pierre Marchais, an innkeeper; Marguerite Dumergue (Marchais), the sociable wife of Pierre; his daughter-in-law, Marie Durand; his grandson, also Jean-Baptiste Marchais; and his niece, Marguerite Marchais, who was the daughter of another brother, a wigmaker. All except the grandson had some years earlier signed the marriage contract of Marie Durand and the younger Jean-Baptiste Marchais; Mariage du Sr. Marchais de la Chapelle et Dlle. Durand, Caillaud, September 22, 1752, ADC, 2E257. The signature of Jean-Baptiste Marchais, who signed the marriage contract of December 1764 near Briand and Guiton, the schoolboys, is not that of the younger Jean-Baptiste, husband of Marie Durand. The only family signature it resembles is that of the oldest son of Jean-Baptiste and Marie Durand, also Jean-Baptiste Marchais, and grandson of the patriarch; see baptism of Jean Clement Marchais, Jean-Baptiste Marchais de la Chapelle fils aîné, godfather, November 23, 1764, AM-A, St. Martial, GG109/187. Jean-Baptiste Marchais was ten at the time; see the record of his death, ADC, Saint-Simon 1821–1836, April 26, 1824, 48/308.

29. Catherine Bonvallet was baptized in 1710, the daughter of the "concierge of the royal prisons"; AM-A, October 29, 1710, St. Paul, GG88/119. Marie Aymard's maternal grandfather, Pierre Queil, and her maternal uncle, Louis Queil, were described as (among other occupations), "concierge of the prisons of the château," and "concierge of the château;" AM-A, St. Antonin, GG52/20, 45, 62, 82, 86.

30. They were Jean-Baptiste Brillet, his wife, Elisabeth Yver Brillet, and "Brillet" (Marie Brillet). The "aides" were a tax or "droit" imposed largely on the sale of merchandise and beverages, of which the incidence was diverse and unpopular. See Marcel Marion, *Dictionnaire des institutions de la France*, pp. 8–12.

31. "Marriage de Gabriel Ferrand avec Marie Adelaide Devuailly," October 15, 1763, ADC, 2E6662. In the 1764 marriage contract, the signature of "St Mexant de Crevecoeur" is located near the signatures of the two schoolboys, and of the younger Jean-Baptiste Marchais. It is very similar to that of "F. Crevecoeur," who signed Gabriel's marriage contract, in 1763. The signatures are similar, too, to that of "François St Mexant De Crevecoeur Boisnier," who signed the parish register of Aigre in 1770; ADC, Aigre 1763–1792, 63/322. By 1780, he was the controller of the "vingtième" imposition in Civray, and signed his name "François Boisnier de St Maixent." AD Vienne, Civray 1780–1782, 28/95. His father, Jean-César Boisnier, was the director of the post in Aigre, and described himself as "Sieur de Crèvecoeur"; his mother's family had purchased the property of St. Maixent. The older brother of François Boisnier, Louis Boisnier de Crevecoeur de la Richardière, was an army officer in Guadeloupe, who died in Aigre in 1830; Aigre 1828–1842, 52–53/341; "Boisnier de Crevecoeur, Louis, 1753–1786," ANOM, COL E 36.

32. Benjamin Golub and Matthew O. Jackson, "Naïve Learning in Social Networks and the Wisdom of Crowds," *American Economic Journal: Microeconomics* 2, no. 1 (2010): 112–149, 112. On the language of relatives and friends, see AM-A, St. André, GG45/128.

33. Closeness is defined here, restrictively, as the relationship of being a parent, a child, a sibling, a spouse, or a "godparent-relation" (godparent of, godchild of, godparent to the child of). Families in Angoulême tended to follow the traditional practice, in the eighteenth century, of nominating a maternal and a paternal grandparent as the godparents of the first child. The

godparents of subsequent children were a somewhat closer approximation to the identity of godparents, or "godparent-relations," as social connections: friends or potential patrons. On godparents and witnesses, see Guido Alfani, Vincent Gourdon, Cyril Grange, and Marion Trévisi, "La mesure du lien familial: développement et diversification d'un champ de recherches," *Annales de démographie historique*, no. 129 (2015): 277–320; Gourdon, "Aux cœurs de la sociabilité villageoise"; and, on friendship and family networks in the nineteenth century, Corbin, *Le monde retrouvé de Louis-François Pinagot*, pp. 87–91.

34. On the "Erdös number," which measures the proximity of other mathematicians to the Hungarian mathematician Paul Erdös, with proximity defined as the coauthorship of scientific papers, see M.E.J. Newman, "The Structure of Scientific Collaboration Networks," *Proceedings of the National Academy of Sciences of the United States of America* 98, no. 2 (January 16, 2001): 404–409.

35. Social networks are "not a paradigm that, by some mystical virtue, rehabilitates the individual within social sciences that are still traumatized by two decades of excessive structuralism." Claire Lemercier and Paul-André Rosental, "'Pays' ruraux et découpage de l'espace: les réseaux migratoires dans la région lilloise au milieu du XIXe siècle," *Population* 55, no. 4 (2000): 691–726, p. 707; Lemercier, "Formal Network Methods in History: Why and How?" https://halshs.archives-ouvertes.fr/halshs-00521527v2.

36. See Granovetter, "The Strength of Weak Ties," p. 1378.

37. Bloch, *Apologie pour l'histoire*, p. 131.

38. Adam Smith, *An Inquiry into the Nature and Causes of the Wealth of Nations*, ed. R. H. Campbell and A. S. Skinner (Oxford, 1976), p. 768.

39. Banerjee et al., "Gossip: Identifying Central Individuals in a Social Network," p. 3.

40. Complaint of Rose Rezé against Bussac, [March 17, 1769], ADC, 1B1090/2.

41. These were the parishes of Notre Dame de Beaulieu, Notre Dame de la Peine, Petit St. Cybard, St. André, St. Antonin, St. Jacques, St. Jean, St. Martin, and St. Paul. See GG38/138 (September 5, 1715); GG39/1; GG39/85; GG66/27; GG39/91; GG39/97; GG39/102; GG39/117; GG39/130; GG39/133; GG39/158; GG39/163; GG39/165; GG125/91; GG39/191; GG81/205; GG39/196; GG7/173; GG73/31; GG89/28; GG8/3; GG8/12; GG73/50; GG53/5–6; GG53/16; GG53/31; GG53/38; GG53/39; GG53/48; GG89/55; GG8/51; GG42/31; GG42/38; GG74/67; GG74/69; GG8/114; GG42/89; GG74/87; GG74/95; GG14/36; GG54/50; GG43/49; GG44/8; GG14/44 (September 11, 1770). Marc Allemand was the godfather of one signatory, Marguerite Faure, and of the children of four other signatories; he signed the baptism records of four of the signatories, and the marriage records of twelve signatories.

42. Etienne had two surviving half siblings, Marie or Emerie, who signed the marriage contract, and Martial, who did not. He also had three full siblings, Marguerite, Jeanne, and Jean, who did not sign. See AM-A, GG39/133, 158, GG53/5–6, 19, 39, GG43/49, 1E3/140. Of Françoise's five living siblings, only Gabriel and Jean (later Jean-Baptiste) signed.

43. See AM-A, "Faure musicien ses filles et sa belle soeur lingères," "Cahiers pour 1763," "Répartition de la taille," 1766, AM-A, CC42/1/24, CC62/22/821; "Rose Rezé fille marchande clincaillerie," CC42/2/13 and "Rose Rezé fille majeure," CC62/9/329. The "taille" was a tax imposed on persons and property, from which the nobility and the clergy were exempt. See Marion, *Dictionnaire des institutions de la France*, pp. 526–532, and below, chapters 4 and 5.

44. "Répartition de la taille," 1766, AM-A, CC62/8–9.

45. "Cahiers pour 1763," "Répartition de la taille," 1766, AM-A, CC42/1/7; CC62/33.

46. Death of Jean-Baptiste Marchais de la Chapelle, April 9, 1765, AM-A, St. André, GG43/6. On the purchase of the office of mayor, see Jean Jézéquel, *La révolution française 1789–1799 à Angoulême* (Poitiers, 1988), p. 13; M. J. Dupin, "Notices sur Abraham François Robin, premier échevin de la ville d'Angoulême et Léonard Robin son fils, membre du tribunat," *BSAHC*, ser. 4, vol. 6, pt. 2 (1868–1869): 825–906, pp. 847–848.

47. Burial of Marie Bonnard, aged twenty-nine, May 12, 1770, AM-A, St. André, GG 45/5; burial of Marguerite Godinaud, aged twenty-nine, December 23, 1769, St. André, GG 44/28. The other young married women among the signatories were Marie Adelaide Devuailly, Françoise's sister-in-law, who died in 1819, aged seventy-seven; her sister, Dorothée Devuailly Lemaitre; and Catherine Lecler, who died in 1803 at the age of sixty. AM-A, 1E34/54; 1E57/92.

48. She signed records in five different parishes, St. Jean, Petit St. Cybard, St. André, St. Martial, and St. Jacques, over the period from 1719 to 1768; see AM-A, GG72/216; GG66/13; GG72/237; GG66/23; GG66/27; GG66/32; GG73/20; GG39/228; GG67/31–32; GG42/197; GG109/132; GG130/71; GG43/39–40; GG44/8.

49. Pierre Marchais and Marguerite Dumergue were married on January 27, 1728, AM-A, PSC, GG66/28. On the baptisms and burials of their children, see AM-A, GG7/139, 149; GG7/144, GG41/37; GG7/156; GG39/182, 199, GG41/15; GG39/203, 242; GG39/236; GG39/256; GG40/25, 79; GG40/53; GG40/92, 123; GG40/120; GG40/149, GG41/21; GG41/124.

50. Burials of Marie Godinaud and Philippe Dumergue, August 6, 1740, of Jean-Louis Dumergue, August 22, 1740, and of Pierre Marchais, August 29, 1740; AM-A, St. André, GG 40/76–79.

51. "Inventaire reqt. le Sr. Ferrand," October 27, 1763, "Mariage de Gabriel Ferrand avec Marie Adelaide Devuailly," October 15, 1763, ADC, 2E6662.

52. The "generalities" were the financial divisions or provinces of France, each administered by a royal "intendant." See Marion, *Dictionnaire des institutions de la France*, p. 257. Angoulême was at the time a part of the generality of Limoges, of which Turgot was the intendant. A.R.J. Turgot, "Edit de suppression" (1776), in *Oeuvres de Turgot*, 5:238–255. Marc Allemand signed the records of the "Tailleurs" in multiple years; Louis Ferrand signed the record of the "Menuisiers"—the account of a "contravention," as so often—as late as 1752, the year before he left for Grenada; Pierre Godinaud, a signatory, signed the record of the "Boulangers" in 1762. AM-A, HH5, Tailleurs, 1745–760; Menuisiers, 1745, 1752; Boulangers, 1762.

53. "Mémoire en forme d'observations pour servir à toutes fins de doléances et plaintes de la ville d'Angoulême," in Prosper Boissonnade, *Cahiers de doléances de la sénéchaussée d'Angoulême* (Paris, 1907) [hereafter Boissonnade, *Doléances*], 96–153, p. 120.

54. On Anne Magdelaine Gralhat Fonchaudière as director of the post between the death of her husband in 1774 and her own death in 1779, see communication of M. Dujarric-Descombes, "Séance du mercredi 9 mai 1917," in *BSAHC*, ser. 8, 8 (1917): l.

55. On patrons and other "hierarchical superiors" as witnesses of nineteenth-century marriages, see Vincent Gourdon, "Réseaux des femmes, réseaux de femmes. Le cas du témoignage au mariage civil au xixe siècle dans les pays héritiers du Code Napoléon (France, Pays-Bas, Belgique)," *Annales de démographie historique*, no. 112 (2006): 33–55, p. 37.

56. All but two of the sixty-two were baptized in the inner parishes of Notre Dame de Beaulieu, Notre Dame de la Peine, St. André, St. Antonin, St. Jean, St. Martial, and St. Paul; Michel Albert, the hatmaker, and his wife, Marie Tilhard, were born in St. Ausone. See appendix 2. On mobility within France, and on "*commerce* in its old sense—commerce of men, commerce of ideas," see Daniel Roche, *Humeurs vagabondes: de la circulation des hommes et de l'utilité des voyages* (Paris, 2003), p. 10, and two special issues of *French Historical Studies*, on mobility (vol. 29, no. 3, Summer 2006) and on the work of Daniel Roche (vol. 27, no. 4, Fall 2004).

57. I am extremely grateful to M. David Richard, the archivist of the diocese of Angoulême, for his kindness in helping me with the records of ordination, and in showing me the archives of the diocese.

58. There were two Alberts (the family of the hatmakers), Gabriel himself, a Dexmier, a Giraud (Etienne's uncle Jacques, the ninth child of his maternal grandfather), a Glaumont, a Godinaud, a Guimard, a Laforet, a Lemaitre, a Jean-Baptiste Marchais, a Rezé, a Jean Roy, a Vinsac, two Yrvoix, and an Yver. See J. Nanglard, *Deux registres d'ordinations du diocèse d'Angoulême, 1587–1603 et 1741–1769* (Angoulême, 1912).

59. Baptism of Matthieu Thibaud, September 19, 1709, AM-A, St. Antonin, GG52/87; baptism of Françoise Chabaribeire, July 18, 1728, St. Martial, GG104/67; marriage of Françoise Chabaribeire, April 24, 1746, St. Martial, GG107/114.

60. Baptism of Françoise Dorbe, February 8, 1661, marriage of Pierre Cueil and Françoise Dorbe, April 6, 1676, AM-A, St. Antonin, GG51/6, 97; on Pierre Queil's successive identifications, see GG51/113, GG52/20, 25, 45, 47, 50, 55.

61. AM-A, St. Antonin, GG52/61–63.

62. AM-A, St. Antonin, GG52/82, 86, 92, 95, 108, 112.

63. Baptism of Rose Marthe Jussé, June 2, 1695, marriage of Jean Marchais and Rose Jussé, November 16, 1723, AM-A, St. Ausone, GG58/24, 149; on Jacques Jussé, see Paul Mourier, "Recherches sur la fabrication des cartes à jouer à Angoulême," *BSAHC*, ser. 7, 3 (1902–1903): 179–232, pp. 189, 212.

64. Abraham-François Robin, "Recueil Secret des pièces utiles et intéressantes concernant la Révolution Arrivée dans le Commerce de Banque de la Ville d'Angoulême, et les Persécutions Suscitées aux Banquiers en 1769," ADC, Fonds Mazière, item J607. A transcription of the "Recueil" was published in 1919, and all references are to the published version, except as noted. Robin, "Recueil Secret," ed. Abbé Mazière, *BSAHC*, ser. 8, 9 (1918): 3–76, p. 42. Jean-Baptiste Marchais came to a tentative settlement with his creditors, for debts of more than sixty-seven thousand livres, in July 1765; "Concordat entre le Sr. Marchais de la Chapelle et ses créanciers," July 27, 1765, Caillaud, ADC, 2E282.

65. This was the description of the nineteenth-century historian of the parishes of Angoulême; Biais, "Notes sur les anciennes paroisses d'Angoulême," pt. 2, p. 251.

66. Paul de Fleury, *Recherches sur les origines et le développement de l'imprimerie à Angoulême* (Angoulême, 1901), pp. 44–50; see Bibliothèque nationale de France [hereafter BNF], catalog references FRBNF30479086, FRBNF33251218, FRBNF33986736. Ode 1, in the volume of poems, was about the tropical storm in Guadeloupe in 1738: "temples, palaces" were reduced to dust, on the "happy shores, beloved land," in which "almost without expense and without cultivation, we see nature lavishing her gifts twice every year"; "there, on the shores of a pure wave," "Liberty"

reigns. Pierre de Bologne, *Odes sacrées, Dédiées à Monseigneur le Dauphin, Par M. de Bologne de l'Amérique*, rev. ed. (Paris, 1758), pp. 1–5.

67. See the records of Simon Rezé, marchand cartier, 1725, St. André, GG39/69. The older Pierre Rezé was described as a pastry-maker on his marriage in 1747; AM-A, GG73/99. The other Pierre Rezé was described as a musician at the baptism of his daughter Rose in 1735, and at his second marriage, in 1745; at the baptism of Rose's first child, in 1762, he was described as a "marchand de draps." AM-A, GG73/38, GG41/16, GG42/188.

68. Undated memorandum from Rezé, AM-A, Milice, carton EE5.

69. Rose Rezé (1), the signatory of the marriage contract, was baptized on May 18, 1703, and [Luce] Rose Rezé (2) was baptized on January 10, 1715, both daughters of Simon Rezé and Luce Jussé: AM-A, St. Antonin, GG52/67, 103. Rose Rezé (2) was married to the signatory François Marin; St. Antonin, GG53/38. Rose Rezé (3), the daughter of Jacques Rezé and Marguerite Desboeufs, was baptized on March 13, 1730, St. André, GG39/134; [Jeanne] Rose Rezé (4), daughter of Pierre Rezé and Françoise Barraud, was baptized on February 24, 1735, St. Jean, GG73/38. Rose Rezé (4), the niece and goddaughter of the Rose Rezé who was a signatory, was married to Louis Bignon, described variously as "controller of the intendancy of the navy in Rochefort," "writer for the navy," and "commissioner of the classes of the navy." AM-A, St. André, GG42/188, 207; death of Louis Bignon, AD Gironde, La Teste de Buch, 1783–1791, April 26, 1786, 101/252. Rose Rezé (1) died in Angoulême, unmarried, on May 24, 1781, and Rose Rezé (2) on 19 germ. 3 (April 4, 1795), AM-A, GG55/29, 1E6/79; Rose Rezé (3) died in Angoulême, unmarried, on 30 fruct. 13 (September 17, 1805), 1E38/344–345; Rose Rezé (4) died in Angoulême on July 15, 1816, 1E52/232–233.

70. See the records of Simon Rezé, "cy devant maréchal des logis du régiment de la reine, 1769, St. Jacques, GG130/159; Simon Rezé, marchand de modes, 1780, PSC, GG68/125.

71. "Sommation respectueuse à la requete de Claude Rezé à Jacques Rezé et Marguerite Desboeufs son epouse," August 6, 1767, ADC, Bernard, 2E158; "Contrat de mariage de Claude Rezé, et de Rose Marin," August 9, 1767, ADC, Bernard, 2E158; marriage of Claude Rezé and Rose Marin, AM-A, August 11, 1767, GG54/54–55.

72. Complaint of André de Bussac against Claude Rezé, March 25, 1769, ADC, 1B1090/1.

73. She was Rose Rezé (3). Complaint of Rose Rezé against Bussac, [March 17, 1769], ADC, 1B1090/2; complaint of Claude Rezé and Rose Marin against Bussac, March 25, 1769, ADC, 1B1090/1; evidence of Pierre Naudon, April 1, 1769, ADC, 1B1090/1.

74. On the influence of external commerce in eighteenth-century France, see François Crouzet, "Angleterre et France au XVIIIe siècle: essai d'analyse comparée de deux croissances économiques," *Annales: Economies, Sociétés, Civilisations* 21, no. 2 (March–April 1966): 254–291; Guillaume Daudin, *Commerce et prosperité: la France au XVIIIe siècle* (Paris, 2005). On the origins of the new global history, see Caroline Douki and Philippe Minard, "Histoire globale, histoires connectées: un changement d'échelle historiographique? Introduction," *Revue d'histoire moderne et contemporaine* 54, no. 4bis (2007): 7–22, and *The French Revolution in Global Perspective*, ed. Suzanne Desan, Lynn Hunt, and William Max Nelson (Ithaca, NY, 2013); see also Emma Rothschild, "A Horrible Tragedy in the French Atlantic," *Past and Present* 192 (August 2006): 67–108.

75. "Patrik Cremen," captured on the *King of Prussia*, died in St. Antonin in 1757, and "Cornoille Mollony," "confessor of the English prisoners, Irish priest," was buried in the vault of the

parish church. Burial of Patrik Cremen, September 11, 1757, burial of Cornoille Mollony, November 24, 1757, AM-A, St. Antonin, GG54/24.

76. "Procès verbal et visitte de pain," October 26, 1757, ADC, Caillaud, 2E266.

77. There was an expert on the essential maritime business of storing merchandise on ships (an *arimeur de navire*) in the parish of St. Antonin: an unlikely figure described as "a native of "Chatel" in England, who had recently moved to Angoulême from Bordeaux. Burial of Thomas Pressis, July 27, 1762; AM-A, St. Antonin, GG54/39.

78. "Acte contenant déclarations et protestations," January 16, 1765, ADC, Caillaud, 2E281. Louis Marchais was a brandy merchant and former wigmaker, the younger brother of the signatory Jean-Baptiste Marchais de la Chapelle.

79. ADC, "Procès-verbal de deux cabriolets," July 22, 1766, Bernard, 2E156.

80. Turgot himself oversaw the lottery as administrator of the generality of Limoges, a few years later. See "Lettre au ministre de la guerre," January 8, 1773, and "Lettre au Chancelier," January 30, 1774, in *Oeuvres de Turgot*, 3:597–612, 655–660.

81. Undated memorandum from Claude Rezé requesting an "augmentation of wages" from the mayor on the grounds of increased costs in connection with "public ceremonies." AM-A, Milice, carton EE5.

82. Memoranda of Claude Tremeau, mayor, February 24, 1758, and October 4, 1758. "Etat des miliciens," "Etat des garçons fugitifs," February 24, February 26, October 4, October 9, 1758, AM-A, EE5.

83. "Se faire donner main forte." Memorandum of Claude Tremeau, February 24, 1758, AM-A, EE5; Turgot, "Lettre au ministre de la guerre," January 8, 1773, p. 611.

84. Turgot, "Lettre au ministre de la guerre," January 8, 1773, p. 605.

85. André Corvisier, *L'armée française de la fin du XVIIe siècle au ministère de Choiseul: le soldat*, 2 vols. (Paris, 1964), 1:197–258; Boissonnade and Bernard, *Histoire du collège d'Angoulême*, p. 185.

86. "Relevé des états fournis à M. l'Intendant des garçons sujets à la milice dans la ville d'Angoulême," October 4, 1758; "Milice 4: 8re 1758," memorandum of Claude Tremeau. AM-A, EE5.

87. "Relevé des états fournis," October 4, 1758; "Etat des garçons fugitifs de la milice," October 4, 1758; "Etat des habitants de la paroisse de St Paul qui doivent contribuer à la conduite des miliciens d'Angoulême à Limoges," October 4, 1758. AM-A, EE5. A marginal note to the left of the entry for "Lavigerie" reads, "To verify—find out how long the one has been in service, and if the other has not interrupted his studies since at least the past six months." The note in the right margin reads, "Given the certificate of the teacher, exempt." Etienne Allemand (Lavigerie) was eighteen at the time.

88. "Milice 4: 8re 1758," AM-A, EE5. Gabriel Merceron, a butcher, was the nephew of Elisabeth Glaumont's husband, Louis Merceron, also a butcher; GG7/169, GG7/175, GG89/55.

89. "Nom des presens sur qui le sort a été tiré, Nom des absens"; "Généralité de Limoges, Milice 175—," AM-A, EE5.

90. "Etat des garçons fugitifs de la milice," October 4, 1758, "Etat des garçons fugitifs de la milice de la ville d'Angoulême," October 4, 1758. AM-A, EE5.

91. "Procuration par Marie Aymard," October 16, 1764, ADC, 2E153; "Marché d'engagement de Ferrand et Delorière à M. Cazeau de Roumillac," December 15, 1753, 2E259.

92. "Relevé des états fournis à M. l'Intendant des garçons sujets à la milice dans la ville d'Angoulême," October 4, 1758, "Milice d'octobre 1758." AM-A, EE5. Gabriel, the oldest of Marie Aymard's four sons was twenty in 1758; François was sixteen, Mathurin was fifteen, and Jean or Jean-Baptiste was nine. In one of the February 1758 lists, there is a note of "the son of the widow Ferrand," identified as "too short." "Etat des garsons qui doivent tirer au sort pour la milice le 24 fevrier 1758," AM-A, EE5.

93. See Jan de Vries, *The Industrious Revolution: Consumer Demand and the Household Economy, 1650 to the Present* (Cambridge, 2008), Michael Kwass, *Contraband: Louis Mandrin and the Making of a Global Underground* (Cambridge, MA, 2014), and Pierre Force, *Wealth and Disaster: Atlantic Migrations from a Pyrenean Town in the Eighteenth and Nineteenth Centuries* (Baltimore, 2016). Pierre Léon's study of two families from the French interior and their exports "d'indiennes, des mouchoirs, de 'limoges', de mousselines, de siamoises," provides a vivid account of the connections of the interior and the colonial economies; Pierre Léon, *Les Dolle et les Raby* (Grenoble, 1963).

94. "Acte en forme de déclaration requérant Nevers," December 30, 1768, ADC, Caillaud, 2E288.

95. "Cahiers pour 1763," AM-A, CC42/2/12.

96. Paul Faveraud, who was born in La Rochefoucauld in 1743, married Marie Hypolite Delafond in 1775. He was the son of Catherine Bouhier, and the nephew of A. M. Bouhier and M. Faveraud. Baptism of Paul Faveraud, March 11, 1743, ADC, La Rochefoucauld-St. Cybard, 1737–1756, 3E304/4, 74/188; marriage of Paul Faveraud and Marie Hypolite Delafond, February 28, 1775, AM-A, NDP, GG14/52. On the inventory included in the marriage contract, see Albertine Cadet, "Les apothicaires du temps passé à Angoulême," *BSAHC* (1981–1982): 47–60, p. 57.

97. On African traders as a market for French producers of counterfeit Indian and English textiles, see Edgard Depitre, *La toile peinte en France au XVIIe et au XVIIIe siècles: industrie, commerce, prohibitions* (Paris, 1912), pp. 242–258; and Pierre H. Boulle, "Marchandises de traite et développement industriel dans la France et l'Angleterre du XVIIIe siècle," *Revue française d'histoire d'Outre-Mer* 62 (1975): 309–330.

98. "Verbal contenant depost reqt. les Dlles. Roger et Desbrandes," May 31, 1760, ADC, Jeheu, 2E850.

99. "La grande et capitale révolution a été l'indienne . . . Tout ce peuple de femmes qui présente sur nos promenades une éblouissante iris de mille couleurs, naguère etait en deuil. Ces changements, qu'on croit futiles, ont une portée immense. Ce ne sont pas là de simples améliorations materielles, c'est un progrès du peuple dans l'extérieur et l'apparence, sur lesquels les hommes se jugent entre eux; c'est, pour ainsi parler, l'*égalité visible*." Jules Michelet, *Le peuple*, 2 vols. (Brussels, 1846), 1:34.

100. "Recollement de l'inventaire des meubles et effets de feues M. et Mme. Robuste de Frédilly," May 24, 1745, ADC, Bernard, 2E134; "Inventaire des meubles, effets, titres et papiers de la communauté de M. Trémeau et de déffunte dame Gonnet son épouse," December 5–7, 1768, ADC, Caillaud, 2E288. The demoiselles Robuste were neighbors of the signatory Jean-Baptiste Brillet; "Déclaration par M. Brillet," September 5, 1764, ADC, Bernard, 2E153.

101. "Acte entre Aymard Ve Ferrand et Ferrand son fils," May 6, 1760, ADC, 2E850. "Mariage de Jean Ferrand avec Elizabeth Boutoute," May 1, 1774, ADC, 2E6673.

102. "Inventaire reqt. le Sr. Ferrand," October 27, 1763, ADC, 2E6662. The eight beds and fifty-eight sheets accounted for 1,598 livres out of a total property valued at 2,268 livres; there

was in addition 300 livres owed "by his *pensionnaires* and others." At two points in the proceedings, the bookseller making the inventory opened a cupboard and found underclothing, or *hardes*, belonging to the "Dlle Ferrand, his sister."

103. In 1763, he was listed as paying no taxes, because he was in Guadeloupe; in 1766, Silvie, his by then estranged wife, was listed as having "nothing," and living in the Isle des Tiercelettes. "Cahiers pour 1763," AM-A, CC42/1/10; "Répartition de la taille," 1766, CC62/22/815.

104. Baptism of Claude, September 3, 1758, AM-A, St. André, GG42/113.

105. "Cahiers pour 1763," AM-A, CC42/1/23-24-2/1; "Répartition de la taille," 1766, CC62/20–22. Marriage of Claude Benoit des Essarts and Marguerite Tremeau, October 18, 1757, AM-A, PSC, GG67/84.

106. Baptism of François Martin Aliquain, AM-A, St. Jean, October 1, 1775, GG75/46; on the Martin de Bourgon family, see below, chapter 6.

107. Baptism of Catherine Bracher Toussaint, November 10, 1773, AM-A, PSC, GG68/47, and of Yves Louis Thomas Toussaint Brachier, February 2, 1775, PSC, GG68/54. Catherine's godmother, who could not sign, was "Catherine Dauphinet," and her godfather was Jean Letourneau.

108. Baptism of Jean L'Accajou, September 3, 1775, AM-A, PSC, GG68/58. He was described as having been declared at the Admiralty in La Rochelle on January 26, 1773.

109. The journey that ended in 1772 was voyage 32267 in the Trans-Atlantic Slave Trade Database, http://www.slavevoyages.org/voyage/32267/variables, and the voyage on which Michel Delage died was voyage 32279; see Jean Mettas, *Répertoire des expéditions négrières françaises au XVIIIe siècle: ports autres que Nantes* (Paris, 1984), p. 322. Delage had started his career as a slave-ship captain in 1754. *La Cigogne* was owned by Daniel Garesché, a rich slave trader and proprietor in Saint-Domingue, who was later the revolutionary mayor of La Rochelle. It was an ill-fated vessel, for its crew as well as its captives; an earlier captain had also died while trading on the west coast of Africa, in 1769, and the ship was later captured by the English in 1778. Daniel Garesché then outfitted two further ships, also called *La Cigogne*, which traded until September 1792; he was the owner of thirty-three slave expeditions, in eighteen different ships, over the period from 1769 to 1793.

110. Baptism of Elizabeth Boutoute, September 16, 1755, AM-A, St. André, GG42/54; marriage of Elizabeth Boutoute and Jean Ferrand, May 14, 1774, AM-A, St. André, GG45/64.

111. On the expedition to Cayenne, in which an estimated nine thousand out of fourteen thousand emigrants died, see Rothschild, "A Horrible Tragedy in the French Atlantic."

112. "Ferme de privillege de perruquier," June 16, 1772, ADC, Caillaud, 2E295.

113. Jean Dumergue, and his eleven brothers and two sisters, were the children of the older Jean Dumergue and of Elizabeth Glaumont; Elizabeth Glaumont was the daughter of Jean Glaumont and Madeleine Allemand, Etienne Allemand's great-aunt. AM-A, St. Paul, GG87/52, GG88/5, GG88/79; St. André, GG37/138, GG38/232, GG39/54; St. Antonin, GG53/12.

114. Baptism of François Dumergue, November 27, 1732, AM-A, St. André, GG39/186.

115. Letter of February 2, 1769, from François Dumergue in Fort Dauphin, "Depost d'une lettre missive par le Sr. Dumergue aîné," May 31, 1770, ADC, Caillaud, 2E291. On the "American revolution" of the French colonists in Saint-Domingue in 1768–1769, a movement for independence in the view of the rebels, and antimonarchist sedition in the view of the administration, see Charles Frostin, *Les révoltes blanches à Saint-Domingue aux XVIIe et XVIIIe siècles (Haïti avant 1789)* (Paris, 1975), pp. 297–388.

116. *Supplément aux Affiches Américaines*, no. 35 (September 4, 1769): 316.

117. *Supplément aux Affiches Américaines*, no. 17 (April 28, 1770): n.p. Nannette was aged "25–27 years," and was believed to be in Cap-Français, with a "free Negro."

118. *Supplément aux Affiches Américaines*, no. 29 (July 11, 1770): 299; there were further announcements of the procedure in issues no. 34 (August 15, 1770): 336–337, no. 35 (August 22, 1770): 347, and no. 36 (August 29, 1770): 353.

119. Jean Joubert was the second cousin of Etienne Allemand; his grandmother, Marguerite Allemand, was Etienne's great-aunt. Jean Joubert married Marguerite Durousot or Durousseau on November 21, 1753. Marc-René Lefort Latour was the godfather of Jean Joubert and Marguerite Durousot's son, Marc-René Joubert, and of Jean Joubert's brother, also called Marc-René Joubert. AM-A, St. André, GG39/51, 124–125, GG42/199; St. Jean, GG72/149, GG74/56.

120. Power of attorney of August 5, 1771, Berlin, and August 23, 1771, ADC, Caillaud, 2E296.

121. Letter from Louis Gabriel Latour in Saint-Domingue to Marc-René Lefort Latour in Angoulême, August 8, 1772, ADC, Caillaud, 2E296.

122. Letter from Louis Gabriel Latour, August 8, 1772.

123. "Quittance de 150 livres donnee par le sieur Lefort de la Tour pour ses enfants," September 18, 1772, ADC, Caillaud, 2E296.

124. See Crouzet, "Angleterre et France au XVIIIe siècle"; Daudin, *Commerce et prosperité*.

Chapter Three. A Bird's-Eye View

1. The project that led to the visualization of individuals in the parish registers of 1764 in Angoulême began in 2012, and has been coordinated, throughout, by Ian Kumekawa. It is described in detail at http://histecon.fas.harvard.edu/visualizing/angouleme/index.html. Ian Kumekawa and I are particularly grateful to Amy Price, the web designer for the website; to Jessica Crown for transcriptions; and to Madeleine Schwartz, Paul Talma, Nicolas Todd, Fanny Louvier, Ye Seul Byeon, Lux Zhao, and Oliver Riskin-Kutz.

2. The parish records used are those available on the website of the Archives municipales, for the twelve parishes into which Angoulême was divided in 1764, together with the parish of the Hôtel-Dieu hospital. The earliest records are from 1583, and the records of civil registration are available from 1793 to 1900; there are complementary records for the town available on the website of the Archives départementales de la Charente. As the author of the only extensive study of the parish registers of Angoulême wrote in 1992, "we are confronted with a prodigious and immense source that remains sadly unexploited." Laurent Raynaud, "La population d'Angoulême au XVIIIe siècle (1700–1791): essai démographique" (master's thesis, University of Poitiers, 1992), chap. 1, unpag.

3. The abbé Expilly estimated the population of Angoulême to consist of 2,240 households in 1763, with around 11,200 people. Expilly, *Dictionnaire géographique*, 1:188. A survey of Angoulême published in Limoges in 1765, based on a "Dénombrement fait dans cette Ville au commencement de Juin 1764"—which can no longer be found—gave the population as 12,174 people; *Éphémérides de la généralité de Limoges pour l'année 1765* (Limoges, 1765), p. 103. Jacques Necker estimated the population to be around 13,000, a few years later; Necker, *De l'administration des finances de la France* (1784), in *Oeuvres complètes de M. Necker*, ed. A.L. de Staël-Holstein, 15 vols. (Paris, 1820–1821), 4:327.

4. AM-A, GG52/164–165, 178–179. Jean Calvin lived in Angoulême in 1534—in a house on the Rue de Genève, in the center of the old town—before he settled in Geneva. On Jean Calvin's period in Angoulême, writing and rewriting his *Psychopannychia*, "the sleep of the soul," see Bruce Gordon, *Calvin* (New Haven, CT, 2011), pp. 38–40. There are anecdotes of the visit of the "heretic" in Louis Fourgeaud, *Origine et introduction du protestantisme en Angoumois: séjour de Calvin à Angoulême, son influence et ses résultats, ravages des protestants* (Angoulême, 1909).

5. Burial of Dame Marie Jullie de Vassoigne, August 18, 1764, AM-A, St. Antonin, GG54/46.

6. Corbin, *Le monde retrouvé de Louis-François Pinagot*, pp. 7–9.

7. Transcription of the judgment of the tribunal civil de première instance of Bayonne on the request of Martial Allemand Lavigerie, ADPA, Bayonne, Naissances, 1826–1837, no. 351, September 7, 1826, 52–53/904.

8. Rosental, *Les sentiers invisibles*, pp. 22–23.

9. In a single page of the 1763 tax roll for the crowded tax island in St. André where the former musician and cloth merchant Pierre Rezé was listed, toward the end of the first "cahier," there are thirty-nine entries, with twenty-three errors corrected, in three different clerical hands. AM-A, CC42/1/22.

10. A relative of one of the signatories was described as "five foot two inches, chestnut hair, blue eyes, a big nose"; a fugitive who had already been arrested had "a scar above the left eye, blue eyes that are slightly sticky, a well-made mouth which is a bit crooked, a round chin." AM-A, "Milice," EE5, Memorandum of Claude Tremeau, February 24, 1758; Memorandum of Tremeau, October 4, 1758.

11. *Esquisse d'un tableau historique des progrès de l'esprit humain* (1793–1794), in M.J.A.N. Condorcet, *Oeuvres de Condorcet*, ed. A. Condorcet O'Connor and M. F. Arago, 12 vols. (Paris, 1847–1849), 6:233–234.

12. Pierre Goubert, "Une richesse historique en cours d'exploitation: Les registres paroissiaux," *Annales. Histoire, Sciences Sociales* 9, no. 1 (1954): 83–93, p. 85.

13. Necker's estimate, published in 1784, was based on a ratio of births to population of 1:27, which would yield, for a population of around 13,000, around 491 births. Necker, *De l'administration des finances de la France*, p. 327.

14. Baptism of Marie [Charpentier], July 18, 1764, AM-A, St. Martin, GG83/58.

15. Baptism of Pierre, son of Jean Epagnon Desisles and Marie Yrvoix Chauvin, January 6, 1764, AM-A, St. André, GG42/218; baptism of Pierre, son of Jean Epagnon Desisles and Marie Yrvoix Chauvin, December 6, 1764, GG42/234. Baptisms of Jean Pascal Yrvoix Chauvin and Marie Yrvoix Chauvin, GG40/30, GG40/142; marriage of Jean Epagnon Desisles and Marie Yrvoix Chauvin, January 13, 1761, GG42/162.

16. This is likely to have been an underestimate of the number of deaths, since the curés of the different parishes seem to have followed different practices in respect of registering the deaths of infants and young children. See Goubert, "Une richesse historique en cours d'exploitation: les registres paroissiaux," p. 86.

17. This rate includes deaths in 1765 of children born in 1764, but less than one year old at the time of death: six girls and nine boys. The infant mortality rate is the number of deaths of children aged less than 1, as a proportion of live births, or the "probability of dying between birth and exactly 1 year of age, expressed per 1,000 live births." https://data.unicef.org/topic /child-survival/under-five-mortality/. The overall infant mortality rate of 121 per 1,000 for

children born in 1764 in Angoulême was considerably lower than the estimated rate of 164 per 1,000 for the (rural) southwest of France in the eighteenth century, and of more than 200 per 1,000 elsewhere in France; see Jacques Houdaille, "La mortalité des enfants dans la France rurale de 1690 à 1779," *Population* 30, no. 1 (1984): 77–106; and Pierre Goubert, "Legitimate Fecundity and Infant Mortality in France during the Eighteenth Century: A Comparison," *Daedalus* 97, no. 2 (Spring 1968): 593–603.

18. There were 263 burials in 1764 in Raynaud's overview, compared to 351 per year over the decade of the 1760s, and 288 per year over the entire period from 1700 to 1791. "Table Annuelle," in Raynaud, "La population d'Angoulême," conclusion. The numbers derived for this inquiry differ slightly from Raynaud's numbers for 1764. We estimate 327 burials; this includes 63 recorded in two registers of the hospital, the "parish" of the Hôtel-Dieu, AM-A, GG22 and GG23. We also estimate 505 rather than 502 births, and 122 rather than 119 marriages.

19. "Chetel pour Marguerite Labonne et Pierre Bruchier son fils à Mr. François Laforet," December 9, 1770, ADC, Bernard, 2E164.

20. Twenty children died in St. Martial in these months in 1764, and sixty-eight in the corresponding months in 1765; AM-A, GG109/176–185, GG110/18–30. Over the entire century, a quarter of all burials occurred in September and October alone. "Des mouvements saisonniers 1700–1791," in Raynaud, "La population d'Angoulême," chapter 2.

21. Marriage of Joseph La Chapelle and Anne Alary, November 30, 1764, AM-A, St. Antonin, GG54/47; marriage of Louis Roy and Anne Bergeasson, March 6, 1764, St. Jacques, GG130/7; baptism of Louis Roy, September 8, 1751, St. Jacques, GG127/93. When he died in 1816, Louis Roy, widower of Anne Bergeasson, was described as aged sixty-five; death of Louis Roy, March 10, 1816, 1E52/102.

22. Burial of Marguerite Cassaud, AM-A, NDB, October 6, 1764, GG8/149.

23. Marriage of Jacques Hazard and Jeanne Nouel, January 16, 1764, burial of Louis Hazard, February 15, 1764, baptism of Gabrielle Hazard, October 20, 1764; AM-A, St. Martin, GG83/54, 55, 60.

24. "Acte de delliberation des habitants de la parroisse St. Martial de la ville d'Angoulême," September 1, 1782, ADC, Bernard, 2E188. Raynaud estimated that more than 30 percent of the population of St. Martial, other than those living within the town walls, were "rural," mostly agricultural day laborers. Raynaud, "La population d'Angoulême," chap. 4.

25. On the "sycophantic prosperity" of "sterile" expenditures, see Victor de Riqueti, Marquis de Mirabeau, and François Quesnay, *Philosophie rurale, ou Economie générale et politique de l'agriculture* (Amsterdam, 1763), p. 277. On Adam Smith's view of productive and unproductive activities, see Smith, *The Wealth of Nations*, pp. 330–336.

26. AM-A, GG68/2, GG14/35, GG130/17, GG89/107, GG42/230.

27. AM-A, CC42/1/24; CC62/20/803.

28. AM-A, CC42/1/4.

29. "Vente de meubles par Marie Aymard à Gabriel Ferrand son fils," January 10, 1764, ADC, 2E153.

30. AM-A, CC42/1/12, CC62/10/386; CC42/1/21, CC62/18/690; CC42/1/10; CC42/1/24.

31. AM-A, CC42/1/4.

32. AM-A, CC42/1/14–15.

33. Jeanne Mercier and her husband, whose son was born in September 1764 in Notre Dame de la Peine, were the same people as "Maingaud perruquier et sa femme lingère," in the tax roll for 1766; AM-A, CC62/32/1257; GG14/35. There were four different individuals called "Marguerite Sibilotte" in the parish records, and two individuals called "Marguerite Sibilotte" in the tax records, one a tailor and one a hide merchant. Geneviève Tardat, who was the godmother of three children born in St. André in the course of 1764, was "Geneviève Tardat boulangère." CC42/1/20, CC42/1/21; CC62/17/648, CC62/749; GG42/221, 223, 224, 230, 232, GG68/3. Anne Rezé, who signed a baptism record in St. Martial in August, was "Anne Rezé veuve Merceron marchande." CC42/1/17; baptism of Rose L'Homme, August 19, 1764, GG109/178; marriage of Anne Rezé and Pierre Merceron, June 5, 1721, GG52/119. Rose Rezé, who was the godmother of a baby born in St. Jean in November, was the niece of the seller of trinkets and signatory of the marriage contract. Baptism of Rose Chataignon, November 3, 1764, GG74/122. She was Rose Rezé (3); see above, chapter 2.

34. Marriage of Gabriel Lemaitre and Dorothée Devuailly, September 4, 1764, AM-A, NDB, GG8/147–148.

35. Marriage of Joseph Farbos and Marguerite Godinaud, June 27, 1764, AM-A, St. André, GG42/226.

36. Burial of Marguerite Godinaud, December 23, 1769, AM-A, St. André, GG44/28; marriage of Joseph Farbos and Madeleine Courteau, July 24, 1770, St. Paul, GG90/43; burial of Joseph Farbos, July 23, 1771, St. André, GG45/19; baptism of Jean Abraham Rodriguez Sarzedas, June 9, 1773, St. Jean, GG75/25–26; marriage of Jean Marie Abraham Sarzedas and Madeleine Courteau, December 21, 1774., St. André, GG45/73; burial of Madeleine Courteau, June 11, 1776, GG45/100; marriage of Jean Marie Abraham Sarzedas and Cecile Labrue, April 8, 1777, PSC, GG68/66; burial of Cecile Labrue, January 4, 1778, GG45/136; burial of Jean Marie Abraham Sarzedas, October 22, 1783, St. André, GG46/102.

37. Baptism of Gabriel Ferrand, November 7, 1764, AM-A, NDP, GG14/36.

38. Marriage of Antoine Duvignaud and Marguerite David, January 10, 1764, marriage of Jacques Forgeron and Marguerite Rougnac, March 5, 1764, baptism of Magdelaine Forgeron, October 31, 1764, AM-A, St. André, GG42/219, 222, 231.

39. Baptism of François Joseph Varache, July 7, 1764, AM-A, NDP, GG14/35.

40. Baptism of Rose Campot, November 17, 1764, AM-A, St. André, GG42/233. Rose Marin's father, François Marin, and her neighbor, the son of the registry clerk, were signatories of the same baptism.

41. The Dupard family lived in the Isle de M Arnaud/Point du Jour, CC42/1/18, CC62/15/587; the Faure family in the Isle des Tiercelettes, CC42/1/24, CC62/22/821; and the Yrvoix family in the Isle de Carmélites, CC42/2/4, CC62/25/950.

42. Marriage of Magdelaine Faure and Jean Roy, AM-A, October 29, 1764, St. Jacques, GG130/25; "Mariage de Jean Roy et Magdeleine Faure," October 28, 1764, ADC, Mallat, notary, 2E908.

43. Signatures of Magdelaine Faure, September 21, 1764, St. Jacques, GG130/22, October 23, 1764, St. Paul, GG89/108, November 18, 1764, St. Martial, GG109/186.

44. Baptism of Magdelaine Faure, AM-A, August 21, 1743, St. Jacques, GG126/48; signatures of Magdelaine Faure, GG129/9, 109, 158, GG130/22, 39, GG89/90, 108, GG109/186; signatures

of Luce Faure, GG129/9, 52, 109, 158, GG130/22, 39, 44, GG89/90. On the occupations of her sister and her brother-in-law, see GG89/90, GG129/109, 157–158, GG130/9, 44.

45. "Faubourg de l'Houmeau, Platte forme du Palet," "Isle du Château-Gaillard," AM-A, CC42/2/14, 42/2/17; "Faubourg de l'Houmeau," "Isle du Château-Gaillard," CC62/34/1332, 62/37/1461.

46. "I sent some books to my binder, among others the *Système de la Nature*," Madame La Baronne writes at the outset of the abbé Barruel's antiphilosophical novel *Les Helviennes*, published shortly before the revolution. The binder's apprentice "spent the night leafing through these books, and took some liberties with his master's daughter," to whom he said confidently "that there was no hell, and he had just read it in one of Madame La Baronne's books." [Abbé Barruel], *Les Helviennes, ou Lettres Provinciales Philosophiques*, 4th ed., 3 vols. (Paris, 1789), 1:5.

47. Marriage of Jean Roy and Marie Doraud, January 13, 1767, AM-A, GG43/39; marriages of Jean-Jacques Roy (son of Jean Roy) and Jean-Baptiste Durand (grandson of Jean Roy), 1E33/36, 1E76/69–70, and see http://elec.enc.sorbonne.fr/imprimeurs/node/23542 and http://elec.enc.sorbonne.fr/imprimeurs/node/23543.

48. Of the 122 couples, 74 had marriage contracts drawn up, in 1764, by notaries listed in the bureau of Angoulême; it is likely that others had contracts drawn up elsewhere. Enregistrement des actes notariés, Table des contrats de mariages, 1760–1767, ADC, 2C2/29.

49. Repertory of acts by Jean Bernard, ADC, 2E130; marriages celebrated on February 4, 1764, July 17, 1764, October 30, 1764, St. Martial, AM-A, GG109/164, 175, 185; February 28, 1764, October 1, 1764, St. Martin, GG83/55, 59. On Bernard, see J. de la Martinière, "Avant-Propos," in *Inventaire sommaire des archives départementales antérieures à 1789, Charente, Archives civiles— série E (1736–3040)*, ed. P. de Fleury and J. de la Martinière (Angoulême, 1906), i–iii, p. ii. Bernard had a particular affinity for the transient. He drew up a marriage contract, a few years later, for a peddler from the diocese of Albi, who had "for the past two years been frequenting the tavern" of an innkeeper in the parish of St. Martial in Angoulême, and the daughter of another peddler, from the diocese of Cahors, who had been frequenting the same tavern. The witness was the innkeeper, who "certified that he knew the said parties because he had seen them very often and almost habitually in his said tavern, over the past two years." The couple agreed to share all their goods "half and half, without being concerned about whether one of them has or will have more than the other." Marriage of Jean Bourgnol and Françoise Delbreil, St. Martial, January 21, 1772, GG111/31; "Contrat de marriage de Jean Bougnol and Françoise Delbrel," November 19, 1771, ADC, Bernard, 2E166.

50. Marriage of Jacques Thinon and Marie Leger, July 17, 1764, AM-A, St. Martial, GG109/175; "Contrat de marriage de Jacques Thinon et de Marie Leger," May 21, 1764, ADC, Bernard, 2E153.

51. Expilly, *Dictionnaire géographique*, 2:494.

52. "Contrat de marriage de Jacques Thinon et de Marie Leger," May 21, 1764, ADC, 2E153.

53. Baptism of Jean Thinon, June 4, 1767, Marie Thinon, August 4, 1768, Guillaume and Antoine Thinon, October 24, 1771, Simon Thinon, May 16, 1774, François Thinon, May 7, 1777, and Marie Thinon, August 23, 1780; AM-A, St. Jacques, GG130/92, 126, GG131/25, 110, 231, GG132/93.

54. Expilly, *Dictionnaire géographique*, 1:440.

55. "Vente par Jacques Thinon, Marie Leger son epouse, Marie et autre Marie Godinaud à Jean Marchesson," February 3, 1776, ADC, Bernard, 2E175.

56. "Vente par Jacques Thinon," February 3, 1776, ADC, 2E175.

57. Baptism of Marie Thinon, August 23, 1780; burial of Marie Leger, November 29, 1780; marriage of Jean Thinon and Françoise Brunet, February 20, 1781; baptism of Cecile Thinon, April 21, 1783; AM-A, St. Jacques, GG132/93, 107, 120–121; GG133/8.

58. Marriage of Nicholas Gendron and Marie Thinon, July 6, 1790, St. Jacques, AM-A, GG134/101; death of Nicholas Gendron, November 17, 1848, 1E142/97, and of Marie Thinon, May 8, 1850, 1E154/39.

59. Burial of Marie Jarton, May 14, 1764, AM-A, St. Jean, GG74/119; baptism of Françoise Durand, daughter of Cybard Durand and Marie Jarton, June 1, 1717, marriage of Philippe Yrvoix Chauvin and Françoise Durand, January 20, 1734, St. Jean, GG72/208, GG73/37.

60. "La veuve Yrvoix Chauvin, marchande de graisserie et Jean Desisles son gendre"; AM-A, CC42/1/14.

61. See GG42/162, 218, 234; GG43/20, 50, and on Desisles's debts, see below, chapter 4.

62. "Chauvin, Jean Yrvoix, négociant, lieutenant d'artillerie et capitaine de milice bourgeoise à Sainte-Lucie, sa succession 1786," ANOM, COL E 77. There was another, apparently unrelated, Jean Chauvin who did settle in Martinique, and became a "practical" or "coastal" pilot; a "superior subject," in the description of the naval officers whose protection he sought. He even precipitated a minor crisis in the course of the French-American naval conflict of 1776–1778, when he threatened to "go and seek his fortune elsewhere," if he was not given a government stipend. He did not see "his daily bread being secure in the service of the king," the naval officers reported, and despite "all sorts of efforts" by the local fort commander—who was the father of the future empress Joséphine—he "would go and place himself at the service of the merchants." Letters from the Chevalier de Beausset of March 28, 1777, and April 6, 1777, and of December 28, [1776] from the Chevalier d'Orves—who was an intermediary in cruises involving the "New Englanders," which he described as "a dog's life"—in "Chauvin, Jean, pilote côtier à la Martinique 1777/1778," ANOM, COL E 77. Jean Chauvin was finally offered a royal salary in January 1778; "Chauvin, Jean," and letter of June 29, 1777, from the Marquis de Bouillé, governor of Martinique, in ANOM, Martinique, Correspondance à l'arrivée, C8a/76/65.

63. Baptism of Nicolas Picard, August 25, 1764, AM-A, St. Martial, GG109/178.

64. Baptism of Jeanne Boutoute, January 6, 1764, AM-A, St. André, GG42/218.

65. Signature of Rose Civadier, May 1, 1764, AM-A, GG89/106; marriage contract of Antoine Pissiez and Rose Civadier, December 12, 1765, ADC, Caillaud, 2E283; marriage of Antoine Pissiez and Rose Civadier, January 28, 1766, ADC, Balzac 1737–1792, 201/461.

66. Supplement to the baptism of Radegonde Françoise Bareau, April 10, 1764, AM-A, NDP, GG14/34.

67. See the Trans-Atlantic Slave Trade Database, http://www.slavevoyages.org/voyage /32242/variables.

68. Baptism of Marc Bodet, November 4, 1764, AM-A, St. Yrieix, GG117/24; marriage contract of Marc Gestraud and Mathurine Rippe, September 16, 1764, ADC, Caillaud, 2E27185.

69. "Opposition par Thereze Grellier au mariage de Marc Gestraud son fils," September 22, 1764, ADC, Bernard, 2E153.

70. Consent of August 28, 1764, Coulomb, notary, Toulon, in "Mariage de Gestraud et Rippe," September 16, 1764, ADC, Caillaud, 2E27185; [M. Choquet], "Bagne," *Nouveau Dictionnaire pour*

servir de supplément aux dictionnaires des sciences, des arts et des métiers, ed. Jean d'Alembert and Denis Diderot, 4 vols. (Paris, 1776), 1:744–747.

71. Marriage of Marc Gestraud and Mathurine Rippe, February 11, 1765, AM-A, St. Yrieix, GG117/27. The family were reconciled the following year, when Marc and Mathurine named their daughter "Thérèse," and Thérèse Grellier was godmother; November 22, 1766, AM-A, St. Yrieix, GG117/48.

72. Marriage of Guillaume Nouel and Jeanne Tabuteau, June 13, 1764, AM-A, St. Jean, GG74/120; marriage of Gabriel Lemaitre and Dorothée Devuailly, September 4, 1764, NDB, GG8/148.

73. Baptism of Gabriel Lemaitre, son of Charles Lemaitre and Marie Anne Klotz, August 20, 1741, AM-A, NDB, GG8/38; burial of Marie Anne Klotz, November 4, 1748, NDB, GG8/76.

74. Marriage of Johann Georg Klotz and Moricette Bourdage, November 3, 1717, AM-A, NDB, GG7/91; baptism of Marie Anne Klotz, March 29, 1718, NDB, GG7/94.

75. On Abraham Janssen and the paper industry, see Jules Mathorez, *Les étrangers en France sous l'ancien régime: histoire de la formation de la population française,* 2 vols. (Paris, 1919–1921), 2:243–245, and on Theodore Janssen, http://www.historyofparliamentonline.org/volume/1715 -1754/member/janssen-sir-Theodore-1654-1748.

76. See AM-A, NDB, GG7/91, 94, GG8/2, 38, 76; St. Jean, GG72/216, 221, 229, 234, 237, 239.

77. Death of Marie Rose Klotz, January 6, 1813, aged around eighty-one, born Larochebeau-court, Dordogne, AM-A, 1E49/8–9; NDB, GG8/147–148, St. Jean, GG74/120. The sister-in-law of Marie Anne Janssen, Marie Rose de la Place, was married to Charles Galard de Béarn of Larochebeaucourt.

78. Marriage of Marie Anne Klotz and Charles Lemaitre, May 7, 1737, AM-A, GG8/2; marriage of Marie Anne Klotz and Jean Louis Nouel, June 15, 1751, GG8/89–90.

79. Marriage of Jacques Klotz and Edmée Victoire Dupuis, November 6, 1755, Dampierre-en-Yvelines, St. Pierre, AD Yvelines, 1751–1775, 82–84/379; baptism of Rose Aglaée Klotz, July 2, 1756, 95–96/379.

80. http://www2.assemblee-nationale.fr/sycomore/fiche/(num_dept)/13631. Record of house number 706, Section A, Beaulieu, in "Contributions, matrices foncières," 1791, AM-A.

81. Baptism of Mélanie Gabriele Sophie Cazaud, September 20, 1764, AM-A, St. André, GG42/230.

82. "Scellé Cazot," May 22, 1781, AN, Y//13802.

83. Madeleine Very, "Scellé Cazot," AN, Y//13802.

84. "Scellé Cazot," AN, Y//13802. Clement Tiffon was the brother of Catherine Tiffon, the mother of "Rosse," or Françoise Rose Duriou, who was baptized in the parish of St. André in 1750; AM-A, St. André, GG41/32–35, 124, GG42/21.

85. Me François, "Scellé Cazot," AN, Y//13802.

86. Pierre Aubry, "Scellé Cazot," AN, Y//13802.

87. The will was made on August 28, 1780, and registered with a Paris notary, Pierre Collet. It was referred to in the matter of the seals, in Cazaud's lawsuit, and in the repertory or list of Collet's acts for 1780; Me Delamotte, November 28, 1781, "Scellé Cazot," AN, Y//13802; "Cause entre le sieur de Cazeaux et la Dlle. Lucie," p. 371; repertory, MC/RE/X/14.

88. "Cause entre le sieur de Cazeaux et la Dlle. Lucie," p. 370.

89. "Cause entre le sieur de Cazeaux et la Dlle. Lucie," pp. 369, 372; Article IV of the Treaty of Paris of February 10, 1763, https://avalon.law.yale.edu/18th_century/paris763.asp.

90. "Cause entre le sieur de Cazeaux et la Dlle. Lucie," pp. 372–373.

91. Baptism of Marie Marthe Cazaud, June 16, 1757, AM-A, St. Jean, GG74/76.

92. *Mémoire justificatif du Marquis de Casaux, de la Société Royale de Londres* (London, 1784), pp. 18–22, 37, 104.

93. Marriage of Elizabeth Bénédictine de Bologne and Etienne Clairefontaine, March 13, 1776, AD Lot et Garonne, Agen, St. Etienne, marriages, 1771–1781, 106–107/199; Elizabeth Bénédictine was the daughter of Georges de Bologne, the younger brother of Cazaud's mother.

94. *Mémoire justificatif*, p. 208.

95. *Mémoire justificatif*, p. 41.

96. *Mémoire justificatif*, p. 89, "Pièces justificatives," pp. xxii, xxiv; Smith, *The Wealth of Nations*, pp. 625–626.

97. "Thoughts on the Mechanism of Societies," *Critical Review* 62 (1786): 42–47, pp. 42–43.

98. "Observations sur la lettre monarchique de M. Casaux, imprimée dans la Gazette universelle, du 5 juillet 1791," in J. P. Brissot, *Recueil de quelques écrits, principalement extraits du "Patriote françois"* (Paris, 1791), 24–28, p. 25.

99. "Sur la grande question du veto," September 1, 1789, in *Oeuvres de Mirabeau,* ed. Mérilhou, 9 vols. (Paris, 1825–1827) 7:244n1.

100. Malouet was a former intendant of French Guyana, and minister of the navy and colonies in 1814; "M. Malouet has written to Monseigneur . . . that he has seen M. de Cazaud frequently for the past two years, and that he has always found him to have the tone and conduct of a man of honor, and a great deal of enlightened knowledge about the culture and the police of the colonies." "Cazaud de Roumillac habitant de la Grenade 1780–1782," ANOM, COL E 66; undated note of 1781 or 1782, "Raport, Le Sieur de Cazaud, François, habitant de la Grenade."

101. "DETOURNENT DE L'IDEE D'UNE LANTERNE." M. de Cazaux, *Argumens pour et contre le commerce des colonies* (Paris, 1791), pp. 1, 6.

102. Burial record for January 20, 1796, St. Mary the Virgin, Woodford; Woodford Register of Burials, 1766–1812, p. 57, available from Essex Records, www.seax.essexcc.gov.uk

103. "Cause entre le sieur de Cazeaux et la Dlle. Lucie," p. 371. The will itself is missing from the acts of the notary by whom it was drawn up; AN, Collet, notaire, MC/ET/X/688 (July–August 1780).

104. *Mémoire justificatif*, pp. 193–194, 197.

105. Baptism of Jean-François Cazaud, April 21, 1756, AM-A, St. Jean, GG74/70; letter of July 9, 1811, from Dugout de Casaud, enclosed in a letter of July 9, 1811, from Mr W. Manning to Mr Richard Ryder, TNA, HO/1/6/6.

106. Will of John Francis Dugout, Marquis de Casaux, proved March 10, 1832, TNA, PROB 11/1796; letter of July 9, 1811, from Dugout de Casaud.

107. Will of Henriette Dugout de Casaux, registered in Nantes on January 23, 1852, and proved in London on March 22, 1852, TNA, PROB 11/2148.

108. Marriage contract of Mr. de Bologne and Mlle. Husson, January 2, 1738, ADC, Caillaud, 2E27163; marriage of Pierre de Bologne and Bénédictine Husson, January 16, 1738, AM-A, St. Jean, GG73/52.

109. Robin, "Recueil," p. 59.

110. Complaint of Elizabeth Sterne, Information of October 9–11, 1769, ADC, 1B1090/2. "I wish I had a dog—my daughter will bring me one," Laurence Sterne wrote to a friend in 1767, and then, to his daughter, "Your lively French dog shall have his place on the other side of my fire." Letters of August 11, 1767, to J——H——S and of August 24, 1767, to Lydia Sterne, in *Letters of the late Lawrence Sterne* (London, 1794), pp. 211, 215.

111. Complaint of Elizabeth Sterne, ADC, 1B1090/2.

112. Complaint of Elizabeth Sterne, ADC, 1B1090/2.

113. Testimony of François Veillon, oven-keeper, and Jean Gimon, master wigmaker, Information, October 11, 1769, ADC, 1B1090/2.

114. Testimony of François Foucaud, master knife-maker, Nicolas Boissard, and Jacques Matard, merchant, Information, October 11, 1769, ADC, 1B1090/2.

115. Marriage of Alexandre Prevaut and Liberalle Langlade, St. André, June 13, 1769, AM-A, GG44/20; baptism of Jeanne Prevaut, St. Jean, October 28, 1769, AM-A, GG74/161.

116. The complaint of Elizabeth Sterne is marked on the verso of the final page, "sent to Paris 9 December 1769." ADC, 1B1090/2.

117. Laurence Sterne, *A sentimental journey through France and Italy* (London, 1768), p. 208.

118. Letter of March 2, 1770, from Lydia Sterne to Elizabeth Montagu, *Letters of Laurence Sterne*, ed. Lewis Perry Curtis (Oxford, 1935), pp. 454–455.

Chapter Four. The First Revolution

1. The onset of the inner changes was located, successively, in 1749–1759 ("about thirty or forty years before the revolution broke out"), 1769 (the government had become more active "since twenty years"), 1774 ("the reign of Louis XVI"), and 1774–1779 ("during the ten or fifteen years which preceded the French Revolution"). Tocqueville, *L'ancien régime*, pp. 47, 238, 269, 270, 280; *L'ancien régime et la révolution: fragments et notes inédites sur la révolution*, ed. André Jardin, in Tocqueville, *Oeuvres complètes*, ed. J.-P. Mayer (Paris, 1952), vol. 2, pt. 2, pp. 33, 37. On the influence of A.R.J. Turgot's provincial writings on Tocqueville, see Robert T. Gannett Jr., *Tocqueville Unveiled: The Historian and His Sources for The Old Regime and the Revolution* (Chicago, 2003), pp. 70, 87–107, and Robert M. Schwartz, "Tocqueville and Rural Politics in Eighteenth-Century France," in *Tocqueville and Beyond: Essays on the Old Regime in Honor of David D. Bien*, ed. Robert M. Schwartz and Robert A. Schneider (Newark, DE, 2003), 172–191.

2. "Pendant la Révolution, la Charente reçut le contrecoup des grands évènements se déroulant à Paris et aux frontières en évitant les abus et les dérèglements." See http://www.charente .gouv.fr/Services-de-l-Etat/Organisation-administrative-de-La-Charente/Presentation-du -departement/Son-histoire, accessed on July 14, 2019.

3. J.-P.-G. Blanchet, *Le clergé charentais pendant la révolution* (Angoulême, 1898), p. 450, and see below, chapter 6.

4. Tocqueville, *L'ancien régime*, pp. 270–271.

5. AM-A, marriage of Martial Allemand Lavigerie and Louise Vaslin, April 13, 1790, St. André, GG47/64–65. Louise Vaslin was the daughter of the late Jean Vaslin, apothecary, and Elisabeth Bouchet, the daughter of a master wigmaker; marriage of Jean Vaslin and Elisabeth Bouchet,

AM-A, July 5, 1768, PSC, GG68/21. Elisabeth Bouchet lived on the Rue de Genève in the center of Angoulême, near the corner of the street that led to Marc Allemand's home in the Petit Rue du Palais. Record of house number 403, Section A, Beaulieu, in AM-A, "Contributions, matrices foncières," 1791.

6. Baptism records, AM-A, St. Antonin, GG54/50, 52, 56, 60; NDP, GG14/36, 37, 38, 41, 43, 44, 45, 46, 48, 49, 53, 56, 58, 61, 65.

7. Baptism of Marie Françoise Allemand, August 7, 1778, NDP, GG14/56, and of Josephe Allemand, September 12, 1779, NDP, GG14/58. Marie Mandrou was the widow of Guillaume Berthoumieu, "habitant à la ravine de la cartier de la paroisse de notre dame de l'assumption des cayes du fonds isle avache cote St Domingue."

8. These were among the occupations of the godparents of Marie Aymard's and Louis Ferrand's children; AM-A, St. Paul GG 89/25, 36, St. Martial, GG106/116, 151, PSC, GG67/18, St. André, GG40/150, 176, GG41/108. The godparents of the five children of Marc Allemand and Marie Giraud included a seamstress, a shoemaker, and a tailor; St. Antonin, GG53/5–6, 12, 19, 31, 39.

9. Baptism of Jeanne Henriette Allemand Lavigerie, December 16, 1771, AM-A, NDP, GG14/46.

10. Of Gabriel's children, Joseph died in 1793, Gabriel in 1816, and Pierre in 1841; Etienne (Ferrand) married in 1794, and either Jean or Jean François received a certificate of "civisme" in 1793; "Certificats de civisme," ADC, L146, and see below, chapter 6. Six of Françoise's children died in Angoulême, between 1838 and 1860; Pierre died in Le Mans in 1834, Josephe in Bayonne in 1855, and Louise Mélanie in Saint-Pavace in 1865. Etienne was married in Pau in 1807, and Antoine signed the record of Martial's second marriage in 1801. Her second daughter, the oldest Jeanne, died in infancy and was buried in the parish of St. Martial; baptism of Jeanne Allemand, October 22, 1766, GG54/52, burial of Jeanne Allemand, September 9, 1767, GG110/87. There are one of Gabriel's children and one of Françoise's children, that is to say, of whom there is no evidence (at this point) other than the records of the initial baptism: Marie Allemand, born in 1765; and either Jean Ferrand, born in 1766 or Jean François Ferrand, born in 1768. The parish of Notre Dame de la Peine, in which the families lived, was one of those in which the burials of infants and children were recorded; there were 103 infants baptized, and 23 burials of infants and young children, over the period from 1764, when Gabriel's first child was born, to the birth of Françoise's youngest child in 1783; see AM-A, NDP, GG14/36–65. It is possible that Marie Allemand, like Jeanne, was sent away as an infant to a nearby or rural parish. On the variations in parish practices, see Goubert, "Une richesse historique en cours d'exploitation: les registres paroissiaux."

11. Death of Jeanne Allemand Lavigerie, AM-A, July 3, 1860, 1E185/57; death of Martial Allemand Lavigerie, August 18, 1856, 1E173/83–84; death of Louise Mélanie Allemand Lavigerie, October 10, 1865, AD Sarthe [hereafter ADSa], deaths, Saint-Pavace, 1853–1882, 182/275.

12. Death of Jean-Baptiste Ferrand, AD Orne, Vimoutiers, deaths, 1863–1873, August 12, 1873, 527–528/543.

13. Turgot, "Mémoire sur les prêts d'argent," p. 156.

14. See Turgot, "Mémoire sur les prêts d'argent," p. 157; Robin, "Recueil," pp. 27, 31; and see Emma Rothschild, "An Alarming Commercial Crisis in 18th Century Angoulême: Sentiments in Economic History," *Economic History Review* 51, no. 2 (May 1998): 268–293. Contemporary

accounts of the "affaire d'Angoulême" include [Mathieu François Pidanzat de Mairobert], *L'Observateur Anglois; ou, Correspondance secrète entre Milord All'Eye et Milord Alle'Ar*, 4 vols. (London, 1777–1778), 3:307–311; [M. de Bachaumont], *Mémoires secrets pour servir à l'histoire de la république de lettres en France, depuis MDCCLXII jusqu'à nos jours*, 36 vols. (London, 1777–1789), 9:143–144, 244–246.

15. Turgot, "Mémoire sur les prêts d'argent," pp. 155, 159–161; Robin, "Recueil," pp. 27, 31.

16. Turgot, "Mémoire sur les prêts d'argent," p. 156; M. Turgot, *Mémoires sur le prêt à intérêt et sur le commerce des fers* (Paris, 1789), p. 2. It was "the most complete and most perfect work ever written on the subject of lending money at interest," for the economist and minister of finance Léon Say; Léon Say, *Turgot* (1887), trans. G. Masson (London, 1888), pp. 74–76, 83.

17. "I very much urge" my children to keep the history secret, Robin wrote, because in it he named persons "whom it is still very dangerous to offend." Robin, "Recueil," pp. 18, 23.

18. P.-J.-L. Nouel, l'ainé & fils, & Drou, *Au roi, et à nosseigneurs de son conseil* (Paris, 1776), pp. 2, 54; *Arrest du Conseil d' Etat du Roi, Qui ordonne la suppression d'une Requête imprimée, signée P.J.L. Nouel père & fils, & Drou Avocat. Du 9 Septembre 1776* (Paris, 1776), p. 3.

19. Robin, "Recueil," pp. 19–20; Turgot, "Mémoire sur les prêts d'argent," pp. 160, 197, 199. The word "capitaliste," well before the use of the later word "capitalisme," denoted owners of liquid or "mobile"—as distinct from landed—assets. See Marc Bloch, Lucien Febvre and Henri Hauser, "Capitalisme et capitaliste," *Annales d'histoire sociale* 1, no. 4 (October 1939): 401–406, p. 406n1.

20. Robin, "Recueil," pp. 45–46. "Il faisait un peu de banque avec ses propres fonds"; Dupin, "Notices sur Abraham François Robin et Léonard Robin," p. 828.

21. Baptism of Mélanie Gabriele Sophie Cazaud, September 20, 1764, AM-A, St. André, GG42/230.

22. Turgot, "Mémoire sur les prêts d'argent," pp. 159–166; Robin, "Recueil," pp. 21, 26, 31–34.

23. Turgot, "Mémoire sur les prêts d'argent," p. 158.

24. Robin, "Recueil," pp. 20–27, 49.

25. The older Pierre Nouel signed the record of the marriage of his son Guillaume Nouel to Jeanne Tabuteau, June 13, 1764, AM-A, St. Jean, GG74/120; his grandson, Pierre Nouel, the son of Jean-Louis Nouel and Marie Anne Klotz, was baptized on February 15, 1764; NDB, GG8/145.

26. Robin, "Recueil," p. 26.

27. Nouel and Drou, *Au roi, et à nosseigneurs de son conseil*, pp. 11, 25, 31, 45; Conseil d'Etat, in Robin, "Recueil," p. 49.

28. Baptism of Rose Chatagnon, November 5, 1764, AM-A, St. Jean, GG74/122; baptism of Pierre and Marie David, AM-A, St. Antonin, GG54/67, 73; record of house no. 999, Section C, Château, "Contributions, matrices foncières," AM-A, 1791; *Au roi, et à nosseigneurs de son conseil*, p. 19.

29. Turgot, "Mémoire sur les prêts d'argent," p. 155.

30. Robin, "Recueil," p. 26; "Sommation faite par M. Marot, receveur des tailles," November 23, 1771, ADC, Caillaud, 2E294.

31. Robin, "Recueil," pp. 25–26.

32. Baptism of Pierre Joseph Audry, November 26, 1764, AM-A, St. André, GG42/233; Robin, "Recueil," p. 24.

33. There was a shoemaker, who had taken over the rights of another shoemaker, and who was represented by a lawyer, to whom Marie Aymard owed 72 livres 19 sols; a seller of potash or washing powder, to whom she owed 74 livres; a seller of cooking fat, to whom she owed 94 livres; and a clothmaker and his wife, also represented by a lawyer, to whom she owed 49 livres 11 sols. "Vente de meubles par Marie Aymard à Gabriel Ferrand son fils," January 10, 1764, ADC, 2E153. None of these eight individuals, with their elaborate arrangements, appeared in the competing enumerations of the crisis. *Au roi, et à nosseigneurs de son conseil*, pp. 10–12, 25–26, 31, 45–48; Robin, "Recueil," pp. 41–44.

34. Robin, "Recueil," p. 42.

35. His creditors, in an earlier bankruptcy, included his brother, his first cousin, the Nouels (father and son), and the brother-in-law of Pascal Chauvin, the itinerant sailor. Robin. "Recueil," p. 42; "Concordat entre le Sr. Marchais de la Chapelle et ses creanciers," July 27, 1765, ADC, 2E282.

36. AM-A, CC42/1/9, 42/1/23, 42/2/1; CC62/9/324, 62/20/776, 62/22/835.

37. Gabriel Ferrand's tax number was 1234, in the Isle de la Place du Collège, in the roll for 1766, and the tax number for Faunier Duplessis, the brother-in-law of the forgemaster Lapouge, was 1240, in the Isle du Collège; AM-A, CC62,/32/1234, 32/1240.

38. Robin, "Recueil," p. 29.

39. Complaint of Lapouge, October 28, 1769, "Information faitte en la chambre criminelle," October 28, 1769, ADC, 1B1090/2.

40. "Acte entre Aymard Ve Ferrand et Ferrand son fils," May 6, 1760, ADC, 2E850.

41. Boissonnade and Bernard, *Histoire du collège d'Angoulême*, pp. 97–120; and see Albert de Massougnes, *Les Jésuites à Angoulême, leur expulsion et ses conséquences (1516–1792): étude historique* (Angoulême, 1880).

42. Boissonnade and Bernard, *Histoire du collège d'Angoulême*, pp. 97–120.

43. In 1764, "Dorliet étudiant" and "Viger étudiant" were witnesses in Notre Dame de la Peine to the burial of Jeanne Sauvet, a single woman aged around eighty-four; September 9, 1764, AM-A, NDP, GG14/35. "Charles Menut étudiant" was a witness, some years later, at the burial of Jean Naigrier, who had died at the age of twenty-two, in his room in the house of Sr Matard, a wax-maker, where he was a boarder; August 22, 1776, AM-A, NDB, GG9/111.

44. Boissonnade and Bernard, *Histoire du collège d'Angoulême*, pp. 142, 153, 167, 169, 177, 180; petitions of February 14 and February 15, 1766, cited p. 179.

45. Jean Rollet, "me de pention," AM-A, CC42/1/24; Jean Rolet, "cy devt homme d'affaires," CC62/21/813; and see Boissonnade and Bernard, *Histoire du collège d'Angoulême*, pp. 150, 159. The tax rolls list teachers at CC62/4, 62/6, 62/9, 62/12, 62/20, 62/21, 62/24, 62/31, 62/32 (three), 62/35, 62/44, 62/57; see also CC42/1/10, 1/11, 1/14, 1/22, 1/24, 2/11 (two), 2/12.

46. Collège d'Angoulême, deliberations du bureau, entries for January 21, June 3, September 2, and November 25, 1774, ADC, D29, pp. 153–154; death of Roch Letourneau, November 11, 1774, AM-A, St. Paul, GG90/82.

47. Boissonnade and Bernard, *Histoire du collège d'Angoulême*, p. 223.

48. "Registre des ordinations remis aux archives de l'Evêché en septembre 1912," Archives diocésaines d'Angoulême.

49. Letter to the administration of the collège d'Angoulême from Coulon and Lavigerie, dated "Angoulême 26—de l'an 1786," ADC, D30.

50. Letter to the administration of the collège d'Angoulême from Lavigerie, April 23, 1790, ADC, D30.

51. Boissonnade and Bernard, *Histoire du collège d'Angoulême*, p. 212.

52. "Mémoire historique sur le séminaire d'Angoulême par un prêtre de la mission," *BSAHC*, ser. 4, 6 (1868–1869): 293–387, p. 307.

53. Boissonnade and Bernard, *Histoire du collège d'Angoulême*, pp. 145, 200, 409; Collège d'Angoulême, deliberations du bureau, ADC, D29

54. Robin, "Recueil," pp. 20–23, 27; Boissonnade and Bernard, *Histoire du collège d'Angoulême*, p. 408.

55. Boissonnade and Bernard, *Histoire du collège d'Angoulême*, pp. 163, 200–203; Bernard Destutt de Tracy, *Remarques sur l'établissement des Théatins en France* (n.p., 1755), pp. 137–138.

56. On the edict of March 1768 concerning religious establishments, described as the "model" for the revolutionary reform of October 1790, see Edme Champion, "La première atteinte à l'empire du catholicisme en France," in *La Révolution française: revue historique* 45 (1903): 97–104; "Etablissements religieux," in *Jurisprudence générale du royaume en matière civile, commerciale et criminelle*, ed. Dalloz (Paris, 1849), Cour de Cassation, pp. 161–162.

57. "Mémoire historique sur le séminaire d'Angoulême," pp. 329–330, 350.

58. "Mémoire historique sur le séminaire d'Angoulême," pp. 332–336; Abbé A. Mazière, *L'affaire Mioulle et le séminaire d'Angoulême en 1779* (Angoulême, 1916).

59. Jean-Baptiste Mioulle was baptized on July 30, 1757; AM-A, St. Antonin, GG54/23.

60. Mazière, *L'affaire Mioulle*, pp. 7–12, and map opposite p. 4.

61. Mazière, *L'affaire Mioulle*, pp. 10, 16, 20–26, 30–31, 34, 37.

62. "Mémoire historique sur le séminaire d'Angoulême," p. 336.

63. *Histoire du collège d'Angoulême*, pp. 195–196; "Mémoire historique sur le séminaire d'Angoulême," p. 336; Mazière, *L'affaire Mioulle*, p. 24.

64. AM-A, EE1, Affaires militaires, "Expédition de délibération pour l'établissement provisoire d'un guet de nuit," August 13, 1779, approved by the intendant, November 11, 1779.

65. AM-A, EE1, Affaires militaires, "Procès verbal des capitaine et premier sergent," December 4, 1779.

66. AM-A, EE1, Affaires militaires, "Procès verbal des capitaine et premier sergent," December 4, 1779; "Procès verbal des blessures reçues par M. le maire," December 4, 1779.

67. AM-A, EE1, Affaires militaires, "Procès verbal des capitaine et premier sergent," December 4, 1779. Burial of Jean Yrvoix, identified as having died on December 3, December 4, 1779, AM-A, St. André, GG45/181. His parents were Jean Yrvoix and Thérèse Tabuteau. He was the nephew of Philippe Yrvoix, who signed the marriage contract. Baptism of Jean Yrvoix, son of Jean Yrvoix and Thérèse Tabuteau, November 28, 1749, NDB, GG8/83; baptism of Jean Yrvoix and Philippe Yrvoix, sons of Jean Yrvoix and Marie Mesnard, November 6, 1733, and November 7, 1737, St. André, GG39/206, GG40/20.

68. Jean Tarrade, "De l'apogée économique à l'effondrement du domaine colonial (1763–1830)," in Jean Meyer et al., *Histoire de la France coloniale: Des origines à 1914* (Paris, 1991), p. 199.

69. Victor Malouet, "Les quatre parties du jour à la mer" (1785), in *Mélanges de littérature*, ed. J.B.A. Suard, 3 vols. (Paris, 1806), 2:341–383, 370.

70. The Trans-Atlantic Slave Trade Database; see http://www.slavevoyages.org/assessment /estimates, accessed on December 31, 2018. The total population of Saint-Domingue at the time

of the French Revolution was estimated at 520,000, including (at least) 452,000 enslaved Africans. M.L.E. Moreau de Saint-Méry, *Description topographique, physique, civile, politique et historique de la partie Française de l'isle Saint-Domingue*, 2 vols. (Philadelphia, 1797), 1:5.

71. Marriage of Jean Ferrand and Elizabeth Boutoute, May 14, 1774, AM-A, St. André, GG45/64.

72. Dossier "Ferrand (Jn. Bte.)," AN, Secours aux réfugiés et colons spoliés, F/12/2795, petition of October 16, 1824; dossier "Ferrand," AN, F/12/2795, petition of December 18, 1822. Jean-Baptiste and Elizabeth were still in Angoulême in 1777; baptism of Françoise Ferrand, June 12, 1777, burial of Etienne Ferrand, November 19, 1777, AM-A, St. André, GG45/124, 133. The family lived in Cap-Français for "fifteen years," until 1793 or 1794; dossier "Ferrand (Jn. Bte.)," petition of October 16, 1824.

73. *Supplément aux Affiches Américaines*, no. 91 (December 23, 1789): 1101; *Supplément aux Affiches Américaines*, no. 4 (January 26, 1788): 710; *Supplément aux Affiches Américaines*, no. 10 (May 17, 1788): 822. The shop was on the corner of the Rue Vaudreuil and the Rue Saint Joseph, near the Place de Clugny and the quayside. It was a landmark in the town: a recently arrived maker of (comfortable) whalebone corsets, in the "latest taste," advertised in 1789 that she was lodging "next to M. Ferrand horloger," and a musician offering instruction in opera arias advertised that he was living between "M. Ferrand, horloger" and the "hatmakers." *Supplément aux Affiches Américaines*, nos. 52, 64 (August 8, 1789, September 19, 1789): 969, 1017. On the streets around the Rue de Vaudreuil, see Moreau de Saint-Méry, *Description topographique*, 1:383, 410–412.

74. *Supplément aux Affiches Américaines*, no. 24 (May 2, 1789): 850. The impresario, Daniel Bowen, subsequently moved his exhibition to Boston, as the "Columbian Museum." Samuel Adams Drake, *Old Landmarks and Historic Personages of Boston* (Boston, 1873), p. 41.

75. Robin, "Recueil," pp. 26, 42, 54.

76. Robin, "Recueil," p. 42; "Procuration donnée par le sieur Pechillon de la Bordrie," May 1, 1773, "Vente faitte à la demoiselle Marchais, épouse dudit Sr Pechillon," June 13, 1773, ADC, Caillaud, 2E297.

77. Letter of October 22, 1770, from Blanchard de Sainte-Catherine, ADC, J563.

78. AM-A, CC42/2/11–12, CC62/32–33.

79. Baptism of Marie Bellat, January 19, 1662, marriage of Pierre Tremeau and Marie Bellat, February 4, 1674; AM-A, St. Ausone, GG56/224, 257.

80. "Acte de notoriété justificatif du nombre des héritiers du sieur Tremeau du Pignon," August 24, 1769, ADC, Caillaud, 2E290.

81. "Depost de testament de M. Tremeau," March 14, 1761, ADC, Caillaud, 2E273.

82. "Règlements et partage de partie des biens de la succession de feu Monsieur Trémeau Dupignon fait entre ses héritiers," May 10, 1768, p. [7]. ADC, Caillaud, 2E287.

83. Baptism of Noel Virol, son of Guillaume Virol, wigmaker, and Marie Brandt, November 22, 1736, AM-A, NDP, GG13/119; "Brevet d'apprentissage du Sr. Virol chez le Sr. Sirier maître chirurgien," January 26, 1760, ADC, Caillaud, 2E271. In the summary prepared for the lottery for the militia in 1758, Virol, wigmaker, was listed as having two (male) children, "one in the navy and one in America." AM-A, EE5, "Relevé des états fournis à M. l'Intendant des garçons sujets à la milice dans la ville d'Angoulême," October 4, 1758.

84. "Règlements et partage," May 10, 1768, pp. [17, 18, 19, 24, 25, 26–27, 35, 41, 42, 47]; ADC, Caillaud, 2E287. "Depost de testament de M. Tremeau," March 14, 1761, ADC, Caillaud, 2E273.

85. Letters of August 17 and 19, 1783, from Aretas Akers, in "Akers, Aretas, habitant de l'isle Saint-Vincent, et Robins, chirurgien Français, 1783," ANOM, COL E 2. The younger Abraham François Robin was born on March 23, 1750, and died on January 13, 1833. He was described as former surgeon major of the island of St. Vincent in the baptism record of his daughter, on July 21, 1788. His older daughter was baptized on March 19, 1785, and was described as having had a preliminary baptism in St. Vincent on December 21, 1782. AM-A, St. André, GG41/125, GG46/149; PSC, GG68/95; 1E102/7. In 1791 Robin was listed as living in house number 1014, close to the (former) church of Notre Dame de la Peine. Section C, Château, "Contributions, matrices foncières," AM-A, 1791. He was the first cousin once removed of the secret historian. Abraham François Robin, the historian (son of Félix Robin), and his cousin, a surgeon called Félix Robin (son of François Abraham Robin), between them had five sons who were baptized "Abraham François" or "François Abraham" in Angoulême over the period from 1740 to 1757; St. André, GG40/79, 41/76, 41/125; PSC, 67/49, 67/79; 1E66/49, 1E89/8, 1E95/53, 1E102/7.

86. "Quittance de 4542 l. Donné par M. et Mad. Delaplace Delatourgarnier à M. Delaval-lière," September 6, 1765, ADC, Caillaud, 2E282; "Avis des parents du fils mineur," November 23, 1766, Caillaud, 2E285.

87. Marriage of Charles Henri David de Lastour and Marie Louise Jeanne de Mons, AM-A, St. André, April 1, 1765, GG43/5–6; marriage of François Dumontet and Françoise Abelard, NDB, October 21, 1765, GG8/159.

88. "Traité entre Dognon et M. Heritier," April 29, 1766, ADC, Jeheu, 2E851.

89. "Procuration donnée par madame Le Fleche de Grandpré à M. de Conan son mari," March 7, 1772, ADC, Caillaud, 2E295.

90. *Affiches Américaines*, no. 7 (February 13, 1771): 53.

91. "Quittance ou descharge donnée par madame Le Fleche de Grandpré au Sr. de Conan son mari," August 16, 1772, ADC, Caillaud, 2E296.

92. "Obligation de la somme de soixante dix mille livres par dame Marie Magdelaine Veyrier de Montaugé à M. Emery Chaloupin," November 4, 1780, ADC, Bernard, 2E184. *Supplément aux Affiches Américaines*, no. 25 (May 25, 1779): 176. Within the complex social relationships of the exiles, Marie Magdelaine Veyrier and Emery Chaloupin were co-godparents, in 1781, in the parish of St. Jacques in Angoulême; in 1784, Marie Magdelaine Veyrier, described as "presently in France," was the godmother, in Fort Dauphin, Saint-Domingue of the daughter of Jean-Baptiste Chaloupin; in 1791, Emery Chaloupin was the godfather of the son of Jean-Baptiste Chaloupin, who had by then moved to Angoulême. AM-A, St. Jacques, GG132/151, St. Antonin, GG55/69; baptism of Marie Françoise Chaloupin, March 29, 1784, ANOM, Fort Dauphin, 4/25.

93. Burial of Thomas Sutton, Comte de Clonard, September 15, 1782, AM-A, St. Paul, GG90/131; Louis M. Cullen, "Irish Businessman and French Courtier: The Career of Thomas Sutton, Comte de Clonard, c. 1722–1782," in *The Early Modern Atlantic Economy*, ed. John J. McCusker and Kenneth Morgan (Cambridge, 2000), 86–104.

94. Burial of Marie Lenoir, October 12, 1786, AM-A, St. Paul, GG90/155.

95. "Procuration donnée par la dlle Chauvineau au sr Civadier son fils," April 11, 1772, ADC, Caillaud, 2E295; baptism of Louis Michel Civadier, September 17, 1741, AM-A, St. Paul, GG89/43. On the Civadier and Chauvineau families, see GG89/4, 38, 60.

96.. *Affiches Américaines*, no. 6 (February 7, 1776): 66; *Supplément aux Affiches Américaines*, no. 50 (November 25, 1786): 585–586.

97. Marriage of Louis Michel Civadier and Marie Charlotte Pissiez, February 9, 1790, ADC, Balzac, 1737–1792, 427–428/461.

98. Burial of Marie Charlotte Pissiez, July 25, 1790, ANOM, Saint-Domingue, Jacmel 1790, 16/24; marriage of Louis Michel Civadier and Anne Rose Pissiez, 14 pluv. 4 (February 3, 1796), Jacmel 1796, 21–22/30. The record of the second marriage invoked the revolutionary law of September 20, 1792, whereby a prospective spouse could present "seven friends," in place of absent parents. Marie Charlotte was twenty-three when she married, and her uncle was forty-eight; when he married Anne Rose, she was eighteen, and he was fifty-four. Baptism of Louis Michel Civadier, September 17, 1741, AM-A, St. Paul, GG89/43; baptisms of Marie Charlotte and Anne Rose Pissiez, November 30, 1766, and May 23, 1777, ADC, Balzac, 1737–1792, 207, 291/461.

99. Ogerdias bought the office in April 1773 for forty thousand livres, from one of the protagonists—the chief prosecutor—in the affairs of the capitalists and cabalists. He was described as a "bourgeois de Paris." "Vente de l'état et office de conseiller du roi maître particulier des eaux et forêts d'angoumois, " April 12, 1773, ADC, Caillaud, 2E297; and see petition of July 9, 1773, AD Vienne, maîtrise des eaux et forêts de Poitiers, B68.

100. Role du *Duc de la Vrillière*, 1772, Role de l'*Hector*, 1771–1772, in Rôles d'équipages, available at http://www.memoiredeshommes.sga.defense.gouv.fr/. Michel Guesnois was accompanied by her mother, sister, and niece, in addition to her two children and her three "black servants," Antoine Julie, a cook, Suzanne Marie, a nurse, Jean Poupe, Flore, and Marine.

101. "Contrat de mariage de Sr. Ogerdias et demoiselle Michel Guenois," May 19, 1762, ANOM, INDE, serie O, carton no. 26, 1762–1766; marriage of Ogerdias and Guesnois, June 12, 1762, ANOM, Chandernagor, 1762. Claude Ogerdias's career in the service of the Dutch East India Company is described in F. Lequin, *Het Personeel van de Verenigde Oost-Indische Compagnie in Azie in de Achttiende Eeuw* (Leiden, 1982), pp. 105, 137, 283. I am most grateful to Professor Diana Kim for help in locating the marriage contracts for Chandernagor. The dowry of Michel Guenois was complex, and included 2,333 rupees "of which the payment is mortgaged on that of a bill on the Council of Chandernagor in favor of [the bride's mother] dated February 1, 1757," as well 10,000 rupees in the form of "presents" to the bride on the occasion of her marriage, the "donors of which have expressed the desire not to make themselves known."

102. Baptism of Jean-Baptiste Ogerdias, who was born in 1765, April 10, 1768; ANOM, Chandernagor, 1768. The godfather was Jean-Baptiste Chevalier, the governor of the colony; see Jean Deloche, *Jean-Baptiste Chevalier, 1729–1789: le dernier champion de la cause française en Inde* (Paris, 2003).

103. "Complaint of Claude Ogerdias," listing the "adventures" in which he had been "concerned together" with Chevalier, whom he accused of subsequently "combining and confederating" with the English officials; July 16, 1774, TNA, C 12/1041/9.

104. The description of the pursuit by officers on horseback is in a letter of August 18, 1772, in the personnel file of Ogerdias; "Ogerdias, Habitant de Chandernagor 1772," ANOM, COL E325. Ogerdias was described as "very opulent, the only man whom Chevalier trusts"; letter of July 27, 1772.

105. "Vente de l'état et office," April 12, 1773, ADC, 2E297; Registres des audiences de la maitrise des eaux et forêts, ADC, B 140 58. Ogerdias presided over such causes as a dispute over the payment of twenty livres for the sale and delivery of four hundred bundles of oak twigs

(July 19, 1773). The previous owner of the office was the prosecutor's father-in-law, described by Robin in his secret history as "this insatiable man," who died with an estate valued at six hundred thousand livres; "this fortune is the fruit of the vexations and extortions he has always practiced in the exercise of his office," and of the "doubly usurious rates of interest that he charged on his different loans." Robin, "Recueil," p. 31.

106. "Bail amphitéotique par les dames Carmélites a M. Ogerdias," April 17, 1775, ADC, Crassac, notary, 2E10145. Record of house number 185, occupied by the widow of Ogerdias, Section B, St. Martial, in AM-A, "Contributions, matrices foncières," 1791. Rose Civadier, whose two daughters married her brother in Saint-Domingue, was a near neighbor in house number 188.

107. Death of Michel Beatrix Guesnoy, January 3, 1830, AM-A, 1E92/3; baptism of Michel Beatrix Guenois, February 12, 1744, ANOM, Chandernagor, 1744.

108. Marriage of Martial Allemand Lavigerie and Louise Vaslin, April 13, 1790, St. André, AM-A, GG47/64–65; baptism of Elisabeth Allemand Lavigerie, February 5, 1791, St. André, GG47/82.

109. Record of house number 243, Section B, St. Martial, in AM-A, "Contributions, matrices foncières," 1791; baptism of Françoise Philippine Lavigerie, May 27, 1792, St. Pierre, GG25/26. On the final months of the *taille*, see Mireille Touzery, "La dernière taille: abolition des privilèges et technique fiscale d'après le rôle de Janvry pour les derniers mois de 1789 et pour 1790," *Histoire & Mesure* 12, nos. 1–2 (1997): 93–142.

110. Birth of Léon Philippe Allemand Lavigerie, 13 prair. 3 (June 18, 1795), AM-A, 1E4/94.

111. Tocqueville, *L'ancien régime*, p. 182.

112. Decrees of April 1, 1776, and September 9, 1776, in Robin, "Recueil," pp. 66–69; Nouel and Drou, *Au roi, et à nosseigneurs de son conseil*, p. 71.

113. Letter of February 22, 1777, from Léonard Robin to Abraham-François Robin, ADC, J700.

114. Baptism of Claude, September 3, 1758, AM-A, St. André, GG42/113.

115. The family historian of the Robins, Dupin, wrote that Robin's third son, Félix-Léonard, was a lawyer for the sovereign council of Port-au-Prince, Saint-Domingue. Dupin, "Notices sur Abraham François Robin, et Léonard Robin," p. 901.

116. [Chupin], *Précis pour messire Elie-Joseph de Miomandre marquis de Châteauneuf. . . . contre les sieurs Marot, père et fils* (Paris, 1785), p. 6; [Riffé de Caubray], *Mémoire pour un homme condamné deux fois à la mort* (Paris, 1788), p. 58.

117. Baptism of Jean-Pierre Marot, November 29, 1749, AM-A, St. Paul, GG89/62. When he was married in Cognac the year before, he described himself as a cashier, "caissier à la recette des tailles," from the village of Guimps. Marriage of Pierre Marot and Marie Chabot, November 4, 1748, ADC, register of Cognac, Saint-Leger, 1744–1751, 3E108/15, 115/182.

118. "Sommation faitte par M. Marot, receveur des tailles," November 23, 1771, ADC, 2E294.

119. The lawyer to whom he complained was the father of the "abbé Mioulle." "Sommation faitte par M. Marot," November 23, 1771, ADC, 2E294.

120. [François Laplanche], *Doutes, réflexions et résultats sur l'accusation en crime de vol intentée par le sieur Marot* (Paris, 1785), p. 7; *Précis pour messire Elie-Joseph de Miomandre*, pp. 6–7.

121. Caubray, *Mémoire*, p. 58. Nouel and Drou, *Au roi, et à nosseigneurs de son conseil*, pp. 10–15.

122. Marriage of François Laplanche and Susanne Basque, January 24, 1775, AM-A, St. Martial, GG111/139–140.

123. Baptism of François Laplanche, August 15, 1751, AM-A, St. Jacques, GG127/93.

124. Baptism of Anne Tournier, July 23, 1764, AM-A, St. Jacques, GG130/15.

125. Caubray, *Mémoire*, p. 3n1.

126. *Mémoire à consulter et consultation pour les Sieurs Marot* (Paris, 1784), p. 2; baptism of Marguerite Tardat, November 22, 1772, AM-A, St. Paul, GG90/65.

127. Marriage of François Laplanche and Susanne Basque, January 21, 1775, AM-A, St. Martial, GG111/139–140; baptism of Jeanne Julie Laplanche, April 29, 1775, St. Martial, GG111/146; baptism of Susanne Basque, February 20, 1751, St. Martial, GG108/6.

128. *Mémoire à consulter*, pp. 2–5.

129. *Mémoire à consulter*, pp. 5–12.

130. *Gazette des tribunaux* 27, no. 8 (1789): 116; *Doutes, réflexions et résultats*, pp. 5–6, 34, 47, 55–56; *Mémoire pour un homme condamné deux fois à la mort*, pp. 9–10.

131. *Mémoire à consulter*, p. 54n1.

132. "Une marchande fripière d'Angoulême, nommée Dupart," according to the memoir, made an "arbitary estimation" of the furniture, clothes, and underclothing of Laplanche and his wife; she was Marie Guimard, who was married in 1749 to Louis Dupard. *Mémoire pour un homme condamné deux fois à la mort*, p. 6; AM-A, CC42/1/18, CC62/15/587, GG41/96.

133. Caubray, *Mémoire*, p. 77. The contents of the house were the subject, a few weeks later, of a public sale. *Doutes, réflexions et résultats*, p. 56; *Points essentiels à saisir dans l'affaire des sieurs Marot, contre Laplanche* (Paris, 1789), p. 16.

134. *Mémoire à consulter*, p. 55; *Doutes, réflexions et résultats*, p. 38n1.

135. *Doutes, réflexions et résultats*, p. 19.

136. Caubray, *Mémoire*, p. 18; *Mémoire à consulter*, p. 16.

137. Entry for February 3, 1785, in *Correspondance secrète, politique & littéraire*, 18 vols., 1787–1790 (London, 1789), 17:311–312, p. 312.

138. Cahiers Laplanche, November 17, 1778, ADC, 1B1099/2.

139. Entries for May 15, 1783, and May 30, 1783, in *Mémoires historiques, politiques et littéraires*, 2 vols. (London, 1783), 6:48–59, 65–78, p. 71; entry for February 8, 1785, in *Mémoires secrets*, 28:116–122, p. 116. As late as 1789, it was described as "this extraordinary affair"; *Mercure de France*, no. 19 (May 9, 1789): 90–96, p. 91.

140. Jules Simon, *La liberté politique*, 4th ed. (Paris, 1871), p. 131.

141. *Doutes, réflexions et résultats*, pp. 41, 102.

142. *Mémoire à consulter*, p. 4.

143. *Doutes, réflexions et résultats*, pp. 65–71.

144. *Précis pour messire Elie-Joseph de Miomandre, marquis de Châteauneuf*, pp. 2–4; *Consultation pour messire Elie-Joseph de Miomandre marquis de Châteauneuf* (Paris, 1784), pp. 1–2.

145. Entry for May 15, 1783, in *Mémoires historiques, politique et littéraires*, 6:55–56; entry for February 8, 1785, in *Mémoires secrets*, 28:117. In Paris, Laplanche found a powerful friend, the Cardinal de Rohan, who visited him in prison, admired his sense of security, and observed an "inner sentiment that only innocence could produce." Letter of August 17, 1784, from the cardinal de Rohan, quoted in *Doutes, réflexions et résultats*, p. 84n1. The copy in the Bibliothèque nationale de France of the 1788 publication in support of Laplanche is inscribed

"Monsieur Lenoir Conseiller d'Etat à la Bibliothèque du Roy de la part de madame La Princesse de Rochefort"; the Princesse de Rochefort was the goddaughter and later the heiress of the cardinal de Rohan. *Mémoire pour un homme condamné deux fois à la mort*, p. 1; BNF 4-FM-17558.

146. Caubray, *Mémoire*, p. 6n1.

147. *Mémoire à consulter*, pp. 2, 4; *Précis pour messire Elie-Joseph de Miomandre*, pp. 6–7.

148. The text of 1788 on his behalf was identified as a "Mémoire pour François Laplanche, ci-devant commis aux écritures dans l'un des deux bureaux de la recette des tailles d'Angoulême." *Mémoire pour un homme condamné deux fois à la mort*, p. 1.

149. Caubray, *Mémoire*, pp. 48, 50, 52, 55; *Doutes, réflexions et résultats*, pp. 74–77, 127.

150. Caubray, *Mémoire*, pp. 31, 66; *Mémoire à consulter*, pp. 3, 24, 32, 40; *Doutes, réflexions et résultats*, pp. 72–73, 105, 134.

151. Caubray, *Mémoire*, pp. 31, 66; *Mémoire à consulter*, pp. 3, 24, 32, 40; *Doutes, réflexions et résultats*, pp. 72–73, 105, 134.

152. Caubray, *Mémoire*, p. 29.

153. *Doutes, réflexions et résultats*, pp. 90–91n1, 134.

154. *Doutes, réflexions et résultats*, p. 8; testimony of Jean Gaudichaud, Information, November 17, 1778, ADC, 1B1099/2.

155. *Précis pour messire Elie-Joseph de Miomandre*, p. 1; *Doutes, réflexions et résultats*, p. 90.

156. Caubray, *Mémoire*, pp. 83–84.

157. Tocqueville, *L'ancien régime*, pp. 213, 290.

158. Nouel and Drou, *Au roi, et à nosseigneurs de son conseil*, pp. 2, 54.

159. See François Furet, "Tocqueville est-il un historien de la Révolution française?" *Annales. Economies, Sociétés, Civilisations* 25, no. 2 (1970): 434–451; Furet, *Penser la révolution française* (Paris, 1978), especially pp. 36–37, 229–250; Keith Michael Baker, *Inventing the French Revolution: Essays on French Political Culture in the Eighteenth Century* (Cambridge, 1990.)

160. "It is a dimension of the life of men that never interested him except in its social or intellectual effects, and never for itself or as a fundamental mechanism of change"; Furet, *Penser la révolution française*, pp. 238–239.

161. C.-E. Labrousse, *La crise de l'économie française à la fin de l'ancien régime et au début de la révolution* (Paris, 1944), "Plan de l'ouvrage," unpag., p. xxxii.

162. Tocqueville, *L'ancien régime*, pp. 270–271.

163. Hoffman, Postel-Vinay, and Rosenthal, *Dark Matter Credit*, chapter 2. I am most grateful to Professor Postel-Vinay for providing me with access to the authors' Charente files.

164. Tocqueville, *L'ancien régime*, pp. 271, 273. Daudin, *Commerce et prosperité*, and see Jean Tarrade, *Le commerce colonial de la France à la fin de l'ancien régime: l'évolution du régime de l'Exclusif de 1763 à 1789* (Paris, 1972), Jean-Pierre Poussou, "Le dynamisme de l'économie française sous Louis XVI," *Revue économique* 40, no. 6 (November 1989): 965–984, and Loïc Charles and Guillaume Daudin, "La collecte du chiffre au xviiie siècle: Le Bureau de la Balance du Commerce et la production de données sur le commerce extérieur de la France," *Revue d'Histoire Moderne et Contemporaine* 58, no. 1 (2011): 128–155.

165. Philip T. Hoffman and Jean-Laurent Rosenthal, "New Work in French Economic History," *French Historical Studies* 23, no. 3 (2000): 439–453, pp. 442–443, and see *The French Revolution in Global Perspective*, especially Lynn Hunt, "The Global Financial Origins of 1789," and

Michael Kwass, "The Global Underground: Smuggling, Rebellion, and the Origins of the French Revolution."

166. "Cahiers des doléances et remontrances de la communauté de Châlus," in Archives révolutionnaires de la Haute-Vienne, *Doléances paroissiales de 1789* (Limoges, 1889), p. 3.

Chapter Five. The French Revolution in Angoulême

1. Jézéquel, *La révolution française à Angoulême*, pp. 7, 167; Jean Jézéquel, "Charente," in *Grands notables du premier empire*, ed. Louis Bergeron and Guy Chaussinand-Nogaret (Paris, 1986), p. 1.

2. "History is made up of the ordinary life of individuals, and it is in extraordinary moments that one should also observe the behavior of ordinary people"; Jézéquel, *La révolution française à Angoulême*, p. 7.

3. On the cahiers de doléances, see *1789, les Français ont la parole: cahiers de doléances des Etats généraux: suivi d'un glossaire pratique de la langue de quatre-vingt-neuf*, ed. Pierre Goubert and Michel Denis (Paris, 2013), and Timothy Tackett, "Use of the Cahiers de Doléances of 1789 for the Analysis of Regional Attitudes," *Mélanges de l'école française de Rome* 103, no. 1 (1991): 27–46.

4. Procès-verbal d'assemblée de la ville et commune d'Angoulême, February 26, 1789, ADC, 142B6; and see Boissonnade, *Doléances*, pp. 28–31.

5. Cahier de doléances, maîtres selliers et charrons d'Angoulême, February 24, 1789, ADC, 142B8; Boissonnade, *Doléances*, pp. 50–52.

6. Cahier de doléances, maîtres serruriers, maréchaux, taillandiers et forgerons grossiers d'Angoulême, February 24, 1789, ADC, 142B8; Boissonnade, *Doléances*, pp. 52–54.

7. Cahier de doléances, maîtres tailleurs d'Angoulême, February 24, 1789, ADC, 142B8; Boissonnade, *Doléances*, p. 41. Jean Chauvignon, who signed the procès-verbal, was married to Jeanne Allemand, the daughter of Marc Allemand and Marie Giraud; AM-A, NDP, GG14/44.

8. Cahier de doléances, maîtres cordonniers d'Angoulême, February 25, 1789, ADC, 142B8; Boissonnade, *Doléances*, pp. 44–45. On the shoemaker Pierre Basque, see AM-A, St. Martial, GG110/106, 165, GG111/184, 221.

9. Boissonnade, *Doléances*, pp. 72–74, 108–109; Mémoire en forme d'observations pour servir à toutes fins de doléance et plaintes de la ville d'angoulême, que les députés du tiers Etat de la dite ville adressent au ministre des finances, n.d. [1789], ADC, 142B6.

10. Boissonnade, *Doléances*: Angoulême, cordonniers, p. 43, serruriers, p. 53, communes, pp. 62–63; Courlac, p. 197, Orival, p. 212, Ruffec, p. 368, Villegast, p. 457.

11. Boissonnade, *Doléances*: Angoulême, tailleurs, p. 42, cordonniers, pp. 44–45, selliers, p. 52, ville d'Angoulême, pp. 145, 152–153; Bon-de-Montmoreau, p. 193, Palluaud, p. 215, La Valette, p. 347.

12. "Cahier des doléances et réclamations des femmes du département de la Charente," in Léonce Grasilier, "Le féminisme en 1790," *Nouvelle revue rétrospective* 11 (July–December 1899): 87–102, pp. 89, 91, 94, 102; Léon Burias, "Un cahier des doléances des femmes en 1790," *BSAHC* (1957): 37–46; *Cahier des doléances et réclamations des femmes par Madame B*** B**** (n.p., 1789),

pp. 1, 5, 8. On the cahiers des femmes, see Christine Fauré, "Doléances, déclarations et pétitions, trois formes de la parole publique des femmes sous la Révolution," *Annales historiques de la Révolution française* 344 (2006): 5–25. Marie Sauvo was born in the Dordogne and married at eighteen to a much older lawyer from Angoulême, Pierre Decescaud, later known as Decescaud de Vignerias. They lived in Angoulême and in Vignerias, in the canton of Marthon, near Charras to the west of Angoulême. See AD Dordogne, Bussière-Badil, baptism of Anne Marie Sauvo, October 3, 1757, 275/771, and marriage of Marie Sauvo and Pierre Decescaud, February 15, 1776, 515–516/771. Pierre Decescaud was buried in Charras on January 21, 1790; ADC, Charras, 3E88/3, 82/127.

13. "Cahier des doléances des femmes de la Charente," p. 90 (emphasis added); *Cahier des doléances des femmes par Madame B****, p. 3. Robin lived in house number 1012 on Rue de l'Evêché in the Château section; the Sauvo family lived in house number 1013, and Marie Sauvo Vignerias in house number 1014; her neighbors on the other side were the Sazerac family of the affair of the hatmaker's grandchildren and the inheritance in Martinique. Records of house numbers 1012, 1013, 1014, 1011, 1010, Section C, Château, in AM-A, "Contributions, matrices foncières," 1791.

14. "Cahier des doléances des femmes de la Charente," pp. 101–102; *Cahier des doléances par Madame B****, p. 18. Marie Sauvo was remarried in 1792, to Léonard Bargeiron, and they had a son the following year; marriage of Marie Sauvo and Léonard Bargeiron, October 22, 1792, AM- A, GG25/44, birth of Jean Bargeron, April 28, 1793, ADC, Charras, 1793–1801, 4/196. She died in Souffrignac, near Charras, at the age of eighty-two; July 7, 1840, ADC, Souffrignac, 1823–1842, 240–241/268.

15. Letter of May 11, 1788, from Léonard Robin to Abraham-François Robin, and earlier letter of February 22, 1777, ADC, J700.

16. M. D. Massiou, *Histoire politique, civile et religieuse de la Saintonge et de l'Aunis*, 2nd ed., 6 vols. (Saintes, 1846), 6:43–44. The Department of the Charente of which Angoulême was the capital was also known as the Haute Charente; Saintes was the initial capital of the Department of the Charente Inférieure, now the Charente Maritime.

17. The numbers in the registers correspond to the house numbering system established in 1769, and to the "Plan Directeur" of 1792, now hanging on the wall of the Archives municipales d'Angoulême. See J. George, *Topographie historique d'Angoulême* (Angoulême, 1899), pp. 2, 4.

18. "Contributions, matrices foncières," 1791, AM-A. On the procès-verbal of streets and houses of 1792, see George, *Topographie historique d'Angoulême*, p. 2.

19. The census was described in one of the most intriguing sources for the history of revolutionary and early imperial Angoulême, the "Journal" of successive mayors of the town, transcribed by the secretary of the mayoralty in the mid-nineteenth century. See the entry for 9 brum. 3, in *Journal des maires d'Angoulême, 1790–1808*, ed. Vincent Mercier (Angoulême, 1989), p. 45. On Mercier, see below, chapter 9.

20. Entry for 11 vent. 8, in *Journal des maires d'Angoulême*, p. 161.

21. "Etat sommaire des registres et papiers," in "Inventaire des papiers du district d'Angoulême au moment de sa suppression," 22 brum. 4, ADC, L238.

22. "Registre pour recevoir les déclarations des citoyens domiciliés dans cette commune," AM-A, Contributions/Contributions personelles 1798/1799.

23. March 3, 1793, *Archives parlementaires de 1787 à 1860: recueil complet des débats législatifs et politiques des chambres françaises*, ed. J. Mavidal and E. Laurent (Paris, 1867–) [hereafter *AP*], 60:108.

24. Entry for 26 vent. 3, in *Journal des maires d'Angoulême*, p. 51.

25. Undated and heavily annotated draft of the organization of correspondence in the Department of the Charente, in "Archives. Récépissés d'objets et de documents," ADC, L131. The annotations have to do, in particular, with the role of the "secretary-general"; "letters and packages sent to the directory will be placed on the bureau, opened by the president, read to the assembled directory, registered *by the secretary-general*, and distributed *by him* without delay to the offices."

26. "Registre destiné à constater la présence des employés," 12 germ. 7 to 21 mess. 7, ADC, L121.

27. September 8, 1793, *AP*, 73:521. On the revolutionary festivals, see Mona Ozouf, *La fête révolutionnaire: 1789–1799* (Paris, 1976).

28. December 20, 1793, *AP*, 82:20–23.

29. Entries for 19 vent. 7, 9–10 therm. 7, in *Journal des maires d'Angoulême*, pp. 121–122, 138.

30. The new calendar, in the expression of its principal visionary—Gilbert Romme, who was also a representative of the revolutionary Convention in Angoulême, in charge of the requisition of beans and forges—"opens a new book to history," and "must engrave with a new blade the annals of France regenerated." See Michel Froeschlé, "À propos du calendrier républicain: Romme et l'astronomie," *Annales historiques de la Révolution française*, no. 304 (1996): 303–325, p. 308. On Romme in Angoulême, described by Mercier in one of his asides as a "bloodthirsty proconsul," see *Journal des maires d'Angoulême*, pp. 29–41, 55.

31. "Baptism" of Marie Andrée Marguerite Tessier—the old expression was still used in the margin of the register—in AM-A, 1E1/106–107; baptism of Pierre Nouel, February 15, 1764, NDB, GG8/145. The first use of the new revolutionary names came a few days later, on the 27 brum. 2 (November 17, 1793); 1E1/116.

32. On the construction of the "état civil," see Gérard Noiriel, "L'identification des citoyens: Naissance de l'état civil républicain," *Genèses*, no. 13 (1993): 3–28.

33. There were three remaining parishes: a new parish of St. Pierre, with the cathedral as its church, St. Jacques, and St. Martial. In the parish of St. Pierre, the transition from parochial to civil registration took place on November 5, 1792, and in St. Martial on November 15, 1792; St. Pierre, AM-A, GG25/47, and St. Martial, ADC, 1791–1792, 3E16/23, 452/465. In St. Jacques, one volume ends on October 27, 1792, and a new volume begins, in the new republican form, on November 18, 1792; AM-A, GG134/186 and GG135/1.

34. The father of the new bishop, Pierre-Mathieu Joubert, was a doctor in Angoulême, and his mother died young; when he was seven, his father married the sister of the dancing master. AM-A, baptism of Pierre-Matthieu Joubert, November 18, 1748, marriage of Roch Joubert and Jeanne Lefort Latour, December 23, 1755, St. André, GG41/93, GG42/60; and see Jean Jézéquel, *La Charente révolutionnaire 1789–1799* (Poitiers, 1992), pp. 188–191. In December 1792, Pierre-Mathieu resigned as bishop; the occasion, according to the historian of the clergy of the Charente, was a dispute over his travel expenses, or the extension of a leave of absence, or both. He was married in Versailles in 1793, and died in Paris in 1815, after a long and tranquil career in the imperial administration of the Department of the Seine. Blanchet, *Le clergé charentais pendant*

la révolution, pp. 134–140, 604–606. On Joubert's efforts to have his name removed from the list of émigrés, his reasons for resigning, and his "crowd of enemies," see "Joubert, Pierre-Mathieu," AN, Police générale, Charente, F/7/490, dossier 12, 56/56.

35. Baptism of Marie Anne Guimberteau, November 5, 1792, birth of Pierre Tournier and death of Magdeleine Brun, November 6, 1792; AM-A, St. Pierre, GG25/47.

36. AM-A, divorce of Catherine Dorisse and Nicholas Valteau, November 14, 1792, St. Pierre, GG25/51–52. The witness was Jacques Rezé, the son of the Pierre Rezé who was first a musician and then a draper; see GG45/3–4.

37. The first use of the new revolutionary names in the record of a birth was on 27 brum. 2 (November 17, 1793); of a marriage, on 6 frim. 2 (November 26, 1793), and a divorce on 13 frim. 2 (December 3, 1793); and of a death on 20 brum. 2 (November 10, 1793). AM-A, 1E1/116, 1E2/52, 54, 1E3/105.

38. See AM-A, 1E3/102, 105.

39. Divorce of Jean Proullaud and Rose L'Homme, February 14, 1793, AM-A 1E2/10; arbitration of December 18–22, 1792, ADC, Sentences arbitrales, L2158; baptism of Jean Proullaud, January 24, 1764, St. André, GG42/220; baptism of Rose L'Homme, August 19, 1764, St. Martial, GG109/178.

40. The first divorce recorded in the civil registers of the town was on November 14, 1792, and the last—until 1884—on April 23, 1814; AM-A, GG25/51, 1E50/130–131; 1E260/121. All the 24 divorces on grounds of emigration were between November 1793 and June 1794. Of the divorces unrelated to emigration, 30 were in the early period of the law, from 1792 to 1795; 13 plaintiffs were male and 16 were female. As the law and practice of divorce became more restrictive, from 1796 to 1814, there were 42 divorces; 5 plaintiffs were male and 28 were female. There were also 9 divorces by mutual consent. A study of the "dissolute" life of married couples in the Charente estimated, on the basis of a partial study, that there were around 258 divorces in the department over the period; Xavier Cottet, "La vie dissolue des époux charentais, de la Révolution au début de la Restauration: impact sociologique de l'introduction de la divorce en Charente, 1792–1816," *Revue de la Saintonge et de l'Aunis: bulletin de la Société des archives historiques* 28 (2002): 77–110, p. 78n5.

41. Marriage of Marie Fougere and Pierre Michel Rigaud, February 7, 1780, AM-A, St. André, GG46/3; divorce of Marie Fougere and Pierre Michel Rigaud, September 25, 1793, 1E2/44; marriage of Marie Fougere and François Pasturaud, October 14, 1793, 1E2/48.

42. Marriage of Guillaume Roch Letourneau and Anne Morin, AM-A, May 2, 1775, GG68/56; divorce, June 29, 1793, 1E2/24–25.

43. On the two sisters, both called Françoise Coupeau, their first husbands, Marc and François Andraud, and their second husbands, both called Jean Clochard, see AM-A, GG109/167; 1E2/72, 73; 1E23/17–18, 19, 25–26, 60–61; 1E25/138.

44. Baptism of Jeanne David, February 19, 1761, AM-A, St. Ausone, GG62/65; marriage of Bartélemi Ramond and Jeanne David, 13 vend. 4 (October 5, 1796), 1E8/2.

45. Preliminary act in the divorce of Jeanne David and Bartélemi Ramond, 10 niv. 5 (December 30, 1796), 1E11/19–20; "it is by error" that the preliminary act "has been inscribed in the present register," according to a marginal note (in the same hand as the report of the act). Divorce of Jeanne David and Bartélemi Ramond, 23 prair. 5 (June 11, 1797), 1E11/76; the record cites three preliminary acts, of 10 niv. 5, 10 vent. 5, and 10 prair. 5, and a convocation of 19 prair. 5.

46. Death of Jeanne David, 6 vend. 6 (September 27, 1797), 1E15/4.

47. See, for example, AM-A, 1E3/121.

48. "Baptism" of Catherine, illegitimate girl, March 1, 1793, AM-A, 1E1/23–24.

49. Baptism of Guillaume Verliac, May 16, 1789, marriage of Guillaume Verliac and Catherine Mesnard, May 19, 1789, petition of Guillaume Verliac, AM-A, St. Martin, GG84/139–143. Guillaume Verliac founded a dynasty of carpenters, joiners, and ebony craftsmen in Angoulême; his grandson, who died in 1900, was "head of division" in the prefecture of the town. Death of Laurent Verliac, March 22, 1900, AM-A, 1E310/34.

50. Calculated on the basis of AM-A, 1E31, ten-year table of deaths.

51. AM-A, civil register for the year 13, 1E38/9–22. The descriptions of the ribbons were sometimes extraordinarily precise. "Denis" was "marked with a piece of silk cloth, bronze with little yellow stripes, bordered at one end by a piece of finely striped fabric [*milleraies*, written as "milleret"] of the same color, the said piece of cloth of fifteen centimeters long by four centimeters wide, attached to the right wrist of the said infant."

52. AM-A, 1E45/405, 407, 409 (1812), 1E49/413 (1813), 1E50/350 (1814), 1E51/384 (1815), 1E52/448, 449 (1816).

53. George, *Topographie historique d'Angoulême*, pp. 84, 112–116; James Forgeaud, "La Place du Mûrier et ses environs," *BSAHC* 143 (1987): 37–70; Forgeaud, "L'Ouest de la ville et le groupe épiscopal d'Angoulême," *BSAHC* 144 (1988): 98–112.

54. "Bail amphitéotique de 29 années par les dames relligieuses du tiers ordre de St. François à Me Jean Bernard notaire royal," August 5, 1770, ADC, Caillaud, 2E292.

55. AM-A, CC42/1/23–24, CC42/2/1, CC62/20–22. George, *Topographie historique d'Angoulême*, pp. 76–77; James Forgeaud, "Le Château, le Chatelet, la Petite Halle et la Porte Chandos," *BSAHC* 143 (1987): 174–200.

56. "Titres et effets," May 20, 1790, in ADC, 1QPROV 1/164–167 (Q VI 6). Of the ninety-six nuns within Angoulême, many of whom had lived in the communities since they were young girls, ninety-four declared that they wished to remain. Blanchet, *Le clergé charentais pendant la révolution*, pp. 38–39, 420–428.

57. "Chapelles," July 6, 1791, in ADC, 1QPROV 1/164–167 (Q VI 9).

58. Blanchet, *Le clergé charentais pendant la révolution*, pp. 151–152, 194–200; Jézéquel, *La révolution française à Angoulême*, pp. 59–69.

59. "Vente de mobilier d'église," January 23–February 10, 1793, in ADC, 1QPROV 2 24.

60. Blanchet, *Le clergé charentais pendant la révolution*, pp. 151–152, 194–200; Jézéquel, *La révolution française à Angoulême*, pp. 59–69.

61. "Procès verbal des cy-devant Dominiquains," January 13, 1791, in ADC, 1QPROV 1/164–167 (Q VI 6).

62. Forgeaud, "La Place du Mûrier et ses environs," p. 41; Jézéquel, *La révolution française à Angoulême*, p. 68.

63. Jean Théodore Henry, known as "Henry l'aîné," was the oldest son of Jacques David Henry and Marie Lesueur; his brother, Joseph Frédéric Henry, was married to Marie Joubert, the daughter of Roch Joubert and sister of Pierre-Matthieu Joubert. Marriage of Joseph Frédéric Henry and Marie Joubert, September 8, 1772, St. André, GG45/182. "Le seminaire d'Angoulême," March 17, 1792, in "Décompte pour acquisition de domaines nationaux," no. 2062, in ADC, 1QPROV 2 41 (Q XVIII 40). In the record of plot number 127 in the "Plan Directeur," "le séminaire"

is crossed out and replaced with "Henry l'aîné"; Section B, St. Martial, in AM-A, "Contributions, matrices foncières," 1791.

64. On the obligation to swear loyalty to the new order, see Timothy Tackett, *Religion, Revolution, and Regional Culture in Eighteenth-Century France: The Ecclesiastical Oath of 1791* (Princeton, NJ, 1986).

65. Report of citizens Mignot, Menault, and Gerbaud, quoted in Blanchet, *Le clergé charentais pendant la révolution*, p. 218n2; Forgeaud, "La Place du Mûrier et ses environs," p. 41.

66. The immense literature on the *biens nationaux* is summarized in Bernard Bodinier and Eric Teyssier, *L'événement le plus important de la Révolution: la vente des biens nationaux (1789–1867) en France et dans les territoires annexés* (Paris, 2000). The circumstances of the sales of church property in Bordeaux, with substantial urban holdings—as in Angoulême—were described by Marcel Marion, and, in the district of Caen, by Alain Corbin. Marcel Marion, *La vente des biens nationaux pendant la Révolution: étude spéciale des ventes dans les départements de la Gironde et du Cher* (Paris, 1908); Alain Corbin, "Les biens nationaux de première origine dans le district de Caen," *Annales de Normandie* 39, no. 1 (1989): 91–119.

67. For a remarkable demonstration of the potential of plans and maps for historical understanding—in this case of the market for slaves in nineteenth-century Rio de Janeiro—see Zephyr Frank and Whitney Berry, "The Slave Market in Rio de Janeiro circa 1869: Context, Movement and Social Experience," *Journal of Latin American Geography* 9, no. 3 (2010): 85–110.

68. "Décompte," no. 2020, in ADC, 1QPROV 2 41 (Q XVIII 40).

69. "Décompte," no. 2152, in ADC, 1QPROV 2 41 (Q XVIII 40).

70. "Vente de biens nationaux," 25 therm. 3, in ADC, 1QPROV 2 1 (Q XVIII 1).

71. "Vente de biens nationaux," 25 therm. 3, in ADC, 1QPROV 2 1 (Q XVIII 1); record of house number 8C, Section C, Château, in "Contributions, matrices foncières," 1791, AM-A; lifetime tenancy of Catherine de Saint-Mesmy, May 31, 1785, ADC, 2C2/239, 70/102; death of Catherine Saint-Mesmy, January 1, 1827, AM-A, 1E83/8.

72. Record of house number 988, acquired by Thibaud, Section C, Château, in "Contributions, matrices foncières," 1791, AM-A; "Décompte," no. 2259, in ADC, 1QPROV 2 41 (Q XVIII 40).

73. "Décompte," adjudications of March 5, 1791, and 9 niv. 2 (no. 2169), in ADC, 1QPROV 2 41 (Q XVIII 40). The house in the Rue de Genève was owned by the "émigré Viville"; and see "Information faitte en la chambre criminelle," Louis Arnauld de Viville, November 17, 1778, ADC, 1B1099/2.

74. "Décompte," no. 349, in ADC, 1QPROV 2 41 (Q XVIII 40).

75. Record of house number 1014, in Section C, Château, in "Contributions, matrices foncières," 1791, AM-A; "Décompte," no. 315, in ADC, 1QPROV 2 41 (Q XVIII 40).

76. Submission no. 1, July 1, 1790, in Enregistrement des soumissions, ADC, 1QPROV 1 27.

77. Submission no. 158, August 2, 1790, in Enregistrement des soumissions, ADC, 1QPROV 1 27.

78. "Vente de biens nationaux," 21 fruct. 3, in ADC, 1QPROV 2 1 (Q XVIII 1); "Table alphabétique des successions collatérales payées," 1765–year 7, ADC, 2C2/39, 6/29.

79. "Tableau des baux des biens et revenus nationaux," ADC, 1QPROV 1/343 (Q XIV 1); and, for the third lease, in 1794 (10 vent. 2), "Table alphabétique des successions collatérales payées," ADC, 2C2/39, 2/29.

80. "Table alphabétique des successions collatérales payées," ADC, 2C2/39. This is a list of revolutionary-era transactions, using an earlier paper form, with the names of the "ci-devant propriétaires" replacing the names of the deceased, and the names of the "fermiers" replacing the names of the heirs. The pages listing the property of the Tiercelettes—including Gabriel's church—were omitted in the online version of the document, and I am exceptionally grateful to Dominique Guirignon in the Archives départementales de la Charente for providing me with copies of the missing pages (pp. 29–32, between images 27/29 and 28/29 in the online document).

81. Baptism of Marguerite Aubert, December 27, 1774, AM-A, St. André, GG45/73–74; her grandmother was Marguerite Durousot and her grandfather was Jean Joubert; *AP*, December 20, 1793, 82:20–23.

82. December 20, 1793, *AP*, 82:20–23.

83. Marriage of Marguerite Aubert and Jean Noel Bonniceau, April 5, 1807, AM-A, 1E40/80–81. J.-B. Quignon, "Notices historiques et anecdotiques," 8 vols., 8:334, ADC, J75.

84. "Fête de la Raison," ADC, L144, (19)-(40); and see Ozouf, *La fête révolutionnaire*.

85. Jean Glaumont was Lecler-Raby's maternal uncle, and Catherine Lecler was his paternal aunt; his maternal grandparents were Jean Glaumont and Marie Gendron. Marriage of François Lecler and Françoise Glaumont, April 30, 1759, AM-A, St. Jacques, GG129/5–6; baptism of Jean Lecler, June 29, 1766, St. André, GG43/29–30; marriage of Jean Lecler and Catherine Raby, May 12, 1789, NDB, GG10/72.

86. See AM-A, 1E1/166, 1E2/97, 1E3/148.

87. Report of citizens Chancel, Blandeau, and Lecler-Raby, 5 prair. 7, quoted in *Journal des maires d'Angoulême*, pp. 128–130.

88. *Journal des maires d'Angoulême*, pp. 168, 199; death of Jean Lecler, August 22, 1848, AM-A, 1E148/69.

89. Burial record for January 20, 1796, St. Mary the Virgin, Woodford; see above, chapter 3.

90. Bénédictine Bologne was baptized on September. 3, 1753, and died on March 13, 1841; she was described as living on the Rue de la Cloche Verte. AM-A, St. Jean, GG74/55, 1E126/25. When Bénédictine was given the keys to the house, she discovered that it was dilapidated, and returned with a notary to provide an inventory of its condition. "Procès-verbal de maison pour Bénédictine Bologne," 13 flor. 3 (May 2, 1795), ADC, Bourguet, notary, 2E10192; déclaration 86, "Registre pour recevoir les déclarations des citoyens domiciliés dans cette commune," AM-A, Contributions/Contributions personelles 1798/1799; AM-A, 1F1, Recensement [1801], p. 15.

91. Marriage of Jean-Baptiste Marchais and Marie David, May 8, 1792, ADC, Saint-Simon, 1737–1798, 3E387/1, 178/298. The location of the house was noted in the record of the baptism of Marie David's brother; March 10, 1771, St. Antonin, GG54/67.

92. Death of Marie Billard, 24 germ. 3 (April 13, 1795), AM-A, 1E6/82.

93. The note, about the events of July 29, 1789, was quoted in a collection published in 1902; A. Lecler, "La grande peur en Limousin," *Bulletin de la société archéologique et historique du Limousin* 51 (1902): 17–62, p. 39. The fear, in Lefebvre's great study *La grande peur*, moved from Ruffec south to Angoulême and east to Limoges; it was carried by, among others, an official from the Treasury who was looking for brigands, an architect specializing in the repair of churches, and four or five men who said they were collecting money for captive Christians. It is interesting that Lecler's description of the Limousin, which was Lefebvre's principal source

for his account of the generality, contained even more references to outside enemies. The architect reported that he had been staying with someone who had received a letter announcing that *"forty thousand Spaniards* had ravaged the Languedoc"; there was a "cannoneer," "surrounded by the brave companions who had gone through the Seven Years' War with him"; "in Brive, it was the English who were coming from Bordeaux. In Tulle, it was the Austrians who were arriving by the Lyon road"; in Aubusson, there were "two cannons which had been given by a sovereign of Morocco." Georges Lefebvre, *La grande peur de 1789* (Paris, 1988), pp. 171–179, 168, 189, 213–215, 227, "Notes bibliographiques," 237; Lecler, "La grande peur en Limousin," pp. 27, 37, 39, 43, 47, 50, 59.

94. Jérôme Bujeaud, "Le conventionnel Jean-Antoine Dubois de Bellegarde," *Bulletin de la Société charentaise des études locales* 41 (May 1924): 118–179, pp. 120–124.

95. Bujeaud, "Dubois de Bellegarde," pp. 124–126, 138–140, 150.

96. Letter of October 31, 1791, from Mte Allemand in Angoulême to "Monsieur Baignoux l'aîné" in Bordeaux; AD Gironde, Fonds des négociants, Baignoux et Quesnel, Correspondance commerciale, 7B1007. On the *Jeune-Créole* owned by Baignoux and Quesnel, which left Bordeaux for the Île de France in 1789, see Eric Saugera, *Bordeaux, port négrier: chronologie, économie, idéologie, XVIIe-XIXe siècles* (Paris, 2002), p. 360.

97. They were Dubois de Bellegarde, Jean Guimberteau, Pierre Maulde de l'Oisellerie, and Jean Brun; see http://www2.assemblee-nationale.fr/sycomore/recherche.

98. Entries for Dubois de Bellegarde, Guimberteau, and Maulde, *AP*, 51:310, 421, 560; "Dons patriotiques," April 25, 1792, *AP*, 51:380–381. Dubois de Bellegarde was listed in 1763 as living in the same tax island, the Isle de la Grande Maison de Carmélites, as Marot, the tax collector, and Brillet, the signatory of the marriage contract; AM-A, CC42/1/7, CC62/6/221. His immediate neighbors, in 1791–1792, were his parliamentary colleague Guimberteau and the printer Rézé; records of house numbers 327–330, Section B, St. Martial, in AM-A, "Contributions, matrices foncières," 1791.

99. Opinion of Dubois de Bellegarde, January 7, 1793, *AP*, 56:383–384; "I will speak only from my heart . . . hasten to cut off this criminal head" ("hâtez-vous donc de faire sauter cette tête criminelle"). Guimberteau, Dubois's neighbor, also voted for death, as did Jean Brun, a lawyer from Angoulême and a new member of the Convention, of whom Reveillaud, the parliamentary historian of the region, wrote that "he played no more than the most modest of roles." The fourth member, Maulde de l'Oisellerie, voted first for death and then for life imprisonment; see http://www2.assemblee-nationale.fr/sycomore/recherche and Eugène Reveillaud, *Histoire politique et parlementaire des départements de la Charente et de la Charente-Inférieure: de 1789 à 1830* (Saint-Jean-d'Angély, 1911), pp. 275–276, 292n2.

100. Letter of Jean Guimberteau, 27 brum. 2 (November 17, 1793), read to the Convention on November 21, 1793; *AP*, 79:566.

101. Prosper Boissonnade, *Histoire des volontaires de la Charente pendant la Révolution (1791–1794)* (Angoulême, 1890); entries for 14 brum. 2, 8 vent. 2, 13 germ. 2, 26 prair. 2, and 14 flor. 3, in *Journal des maires d'Angoulême*, pp. 26, 30, 31, 35, 54.

102. "An de J.C. 1795," in Louis Desbrandes, "Chronique de la province d'Angoumois," AM-A, fol. 380: "After having stayed for nearly a year at the port, the administration judged that it was more suitable for the bell to be hauled back to town by cart, and replaced in the bell tower of St. André, which was done, at great expense and with much effort."

103. "An de J.C. 1794," in Desbrandes, "Chronique d'Angoumois," fol. 379.

104. Entry for July 19, 1792, in *Journal des maires d'Angoulême*, p. 18.

105. Jézéquel, *La révolution française à Angoulême*, p. 107.

106. AM-A, 28 pluviôse 3, 1E6/59.

107. Entries for 14 flor. 3, 10 nivôse 14, and May 22, 1807, in *Journal des maires d'Angoulême*, pp. 54, 203–204, 209.

108. Letters of 17 mess., 19 therm., 5 fruct., and 7 fruct. 2, in "Prisonniers de guerre," ADC, L745.

109. Letter of 7 fruct. 2, in ADC, L745.

110. Report of Blandeau and Lecler-Raby, 1 germ. 8, quoted in *Journal des maires d'Angoulême*, pp. 162–163.

111. Boissonnade, *Histoire des volontaires de la Charente*, p. 148.

112. "Observations impartiales sur une procédure instruite dans la commune d'Angoulême relativement aux troubles qui y ont éclaté dans les journées des 13 et 14 mess. an 5," "Copie du cahier de l'information," AN, Correspondance générale de la Division criminelle du ministère de la Justice (An IV-1816), BB/18/218.

113. Declaration of Catherine Callaud, femme Labonne, 28 mess. 5, "Copie du cahier de l'information," AN, BB/18/218.

114. "Copie du cahier de l'information," AN, BB/18/218.

115. House number S, in Section D, St. Pierre, in AM-A, "Contributions, matrices foncières," 1791; and see "Extrait du registre des certificats de résidence," 25 brum. 6, in "Marin, Rose," AN, Charente, F/7/4990, dossier 32, 15/56. The new quarter consisted of houses built subsequent to the numbering system of 1769; Rosemarin's house was very close to the "salle de spectacle," house number U—where her cousin Rose Rezé was living at the time—near the modern theater, on the Place New York. The army officer who acquired Rosemarin's house, later a general in the *gendarmes*, was (Cybard) Florimond Gouguet.

116. Letter of "15 vantos lan 5" from Rose Marin to Guimberteau, in "Marin, Rose," AN, Police générale, Charente, F/7/4990, dossier 32, 53/56.

117. Decision of 2 niv. 2 (December 22, 1793) and marginal note of "representative of the people" Guimberteau, letter sent to the minister of police on 10 flor. 6 (April 29, 1798), in "Marin, Rose," AN, F/7/4990, dossier 32, 10/56, 32/56; signatures, 10, 17, 45, 51/56.

118. "Marin, Rose," AN, F/7/4990, dossier 32, 10, 11, 12, 27, 28, 33, 36, 43/56.

119. Letter of "15 vantos lan 5" in "Marin, Rose," AN, F/7/4990, dossier 32, 2/56.

120. Marginal note of 10 flor. 6, in "Marin, Rose," AN, F/7/4990, dossier 32, 10/56.

121. Letters of "15 nivos lan 5" and "15 vantos lan 5" in "Marin, Rose," AN, F/7/4990, dossier 32, 50–51/56, 53/56.

122. Letters from Guimberteau in Tours of 3 pluv. 2 (January 22, 1794) and 16 pluv. 2 (February 4, 1794), in "Conseil provisoire et convention: comité de salut public," AN, AF/II/172.

123. Letter of 24 frim. 2 (December 14, 1793) from Guimberteau in Tours, marginal note of 10 flor. 6, in "Marin, Rose," AN, Charente, F/7/4990, dossier 32, 10/56, 46/56.

124. Decision of the municipal bureau of Angoulême, 2 niv. 2 (December 22, 1793), "Radiation," 2 therm. 6, letter of 10 flor. 6, in "Marin, Rose," AN, Charente, F/7/4990, dossier 32, 5/56, 10/56, 32/56. Guimberteau's comment in the letter of 1793 was more circumspect than as summarized; he wrote that "I have been assured by citizens whose patriotism is known," that Rose Marin had not left Tours, and had not emigrated; 46/56.

125. Baptism of "Louis Mulatre fils naturel d'un père inconnu et d'Elizabeth negresse esclave," November 1, 1765, ANOM, parish register of Saint-Marc, Saint-Domingue, 13/15, available at http://anom.archivesnationales.culture.gouv.fr/caomec2. On Louis Félix in the revolution, see Jézéquel, *La Charente révolutionnaire*, pp. 173–174.

126. Confirmation of Louis Félix, April 16, 1780, AM-A, PSC, GG68/81.

127. Baptism of Françoise-Louise Javotte, natural daughter of Anne Mathieu and Louis Félix, October 2, 1785, AM-A, NDB, GG10/42.

128. Marriage of Louis Félix and Anne Mathieu, November 17, 1789, AM-A, St. Martial, GG113/153–154.

129. Death of Anne Mathieu, 15 pluv. 6 (February 1, 1798), AM-A, 1E15/41; marriage of Louis Félix and Marthe Dumergue, 29 fruct. 6 (September 15, 1798), AM-A, 1E14/114–115.

130. See, for example, AM-A, 1E7/29, 1E8/11–12, 1E9/35.

131. Testimony of Jean Rippe, "Copie du cahier de l'information." AN, BB/18/218. Blandeau, an apothecary and later mayor of the town, and Latreille, a librarian and a former priest, were two of the prominent figures of the revolutionary Terror of 1793; see Jézéquel, *La Charente révolutionnaire*, pp. 141–143, 194–195.

132. Entry for 25 fruct. 5, in *Journal des maires d'Angoulême*, p. 83. The president of the new administration was Blandeau, the apothecary.

133. Entries for 14 niv. 6, 16 pluv. 6, and 8 germ. 8, in *Journal des maires d'Angoulême*, pp. 93, 97, 165.

134. Jézéquel, *La révolution française à Angoulême*, pp. 152–154, 167; entry for 4 vend. 8, in *Journal des maires d'Angoulême*, pp. 147–148.

135. Marriage of Pierre Félix and Françoise Mallat, July 27, 1820, AM-A, 1E59/79–80.

136. Death of Louis Félix, October 3, 1851, AM-A, 1E157/89–90; his age was given incorrectly as eighty-two. He was described as the widower of "Jeanne Chasteigner," rather than Anne Mathieu, by his first marriage, and of Marthe Dumergue by his second marriage. Jeanne and Anne Chatainer were his sisters-in-law, the spouses of Marthe's brothers Pierre and Jean. Marriages of Pierre Dumergue and Jeanne Chatainer, February 1, 1790, and of Jean Dumergue and Anne Chatainer, October 3, 1791, AD Puy-de-Dome, Clermont-Ferrand, St. Pierre, 1787–1791, 98–99/223 and 157–158/223.

137. Léonard Robin was baptized on June 23, 1745; AM-A, PSC, GG67/31. Abraham-François Robin and Anne Puisnege had four daughters and nine sons, according to Dupin, of whom three daughters and seven sons survived infancy; Dupin, "Notices sur Abraham François Robin et Léonard Robin," pp. 900–901. Six of the sons were called "Léonard." On political history and history seen from on high, see Lefebvre, "L'oeuvre historique d'Albert Mathiez," pp. 196, 209.

138. Abraham-François Robin, "Notes historiques," ADC, J700; this is an eleven-page obituary written by Robin after his son's death in 1802.

139. On the "affaire d'Angoulême," see letters of February 22, 1777, and March 28, 1778, from Léonard Robin in Paris to Abraham-François Robin in Angoulême, ADC, J700. On the jurisprudence of "terrains vains et vagues," see M. Baudrillart, *Traité général des eaux et forêts, chasses et pêches*, 5 vols. (Paris, 1825), 2:871; on Léonard's memoranda in the case of the communes of Marquenterre—a large marshland in Picardy, near the mouth of the Somme—in which he argued successfully for the future Charles X against the local communities, see "Jugemens relatifs à la propriété des communes," in Jean Baptiste Denisart, *Collection de décisions nouvelles et de notions relatives à la jurisprudence*, 9 vols. (Paris, 1786), 4:754–755.

140. Letters of January 3, 1788 [1787], May 11, 1788, and December 29, 1788, from Léonard Robin to Abraham-François Robin, ADC, J700.

141. Letters of May 11, 1788, and August 9, 1788, from Léonard Robin to Abraham-François Robin, ADC, J700; on Méhémet-Aly, who converted to Christianity in 1751 under the name Jean-Marie-Alix Boullon Morange, see *Réclamations pour le sieur Charles-Marie Canalès-Oglou* (Paris, 1806), pp. 11–12, 21–22, 49–60, 66.

142. Letter of January 3, 1788, from Léonard Robin to Abraham-François Robin, ADC, J700.

143. Letters of January 3, 1788, December 29, 1788, and January 24, 1789, from Léonard Robin to Abraham-François Robin, ADC, J700.

144. Letter of August 30, 1789, from Léonard Robin to Abraham-François Robin, ADC, J700.

145. Letter of August 30, 1789, from Léonard Robin to Abraham-François Robin, ADC, J700.

146. Letter of September 15, 1789, from Léonard Robin to Abraham-François Robin, ADC, J700.

147. Letter of September 15, 1789, from Léonard Robin to Abraham-François Robin, ADC, J700. Léonard Robin's address was Rue Beaubourg, Hôtel de Fer, or Hôtel de la Fere; see the list of the names and home addresses of the three hundred "deputies" or representatives of the commune elected on September 18, 1789, in *Exposé des travaux de l'Assemblée-Générale des Représentans de la Commune de Paris*, ed. Jacques Godard (Paris, 1790), p. 244; *Almanach général du département de Paris pour l'année 1791* (Paris, 1791), p. 19. On the copper plate factory at the same address, established in 1770, see *Dictionnaire raisonné universel des arts et metiers*, new ed., ed. Abbé Jaubert, 5 vols. (Paris, 1793), 3:475. The Féline bankers, Léonard's clients in the Rouen fraud case, were also tenants in the same building; *Almanach du voyageur à Paris* (Paris, 1787), p. 115.

148. *Actes de la Commune de Paris pendant la révolution*, ed. Sigismond Lacroix, 19 vols. (Paris, 1894–1955), 1st ser., 1:383–384; the more celebrated *Déclaration des droits des communes*, drafted by J.-P. Brissot, came two weeks later.

149. Statement of January 30, 1790, in *Actes de la Commune de Paris*, 1st ser., 3:645–647; *AP*, 10:761.

150. Letter of November 3, 1789, from Léonard Robin to Anne Puisnege (Robin), ADC, J700.

151. Sigismond Lacroix, "Ce qu'on pensait des juifs à Paris en 1790," *Revue Bleu*, 4th ser., 9, no. 14 (April 2, 1898): 417–424, p. 424; *Actes de la Commune de Paris*, 1st ser., 5:498, 593–596; Robert Badinter, *Libres et Egaux . . . L'émancipation des Juifs sous la révolution française (1789–1791)* (Paris, 1989), p. 203, and, on the earlier declaration, pp. 186–190.

152. Léonard Robin, *Rapport et projet de réglement général sur les concours, pour tous les monumens et ouvrages publics de la ville de Paris* (Paris, 1791), p. 5. Léonard Robin, *Rapport fait au nom des commissaires nommés pour l'examen du Mémoire de M. de Vauvilliers, sur l'administration et la juridiction pour les transports par eau des approvisionnemens de Paris* (Paris, 1790), p. 11.

153. Jacques Godard and Léonard Robin, *Rapport de messieurs J. Godard and L. Robin, commissaires civils, envoyés par le roi, dans le département du Lot* (Paris, 1791).

154. Léonard made public speeches in Nîmes and Alès, and the emissaries returned to Paris; the camps of Jalès remained. Robin, Mulot prêtre, Bigot, Robin jeune, Durouzeau, *Proclamation des commissaires civils, envoyés par le roi dans le département du Gard, et autres départemens voisins* (Nîmes, 1791). The abbé Mulot was president of the Paris Commune at the time of Godard's and Robin's petitions in favor of the Jews of Paris, of whom he declared, in a speech drafted by

Godard, that "all of them, everywhere, have been irreproachable in their conduct," recounting "the social qualities of the Jews, their patriotic virtues, [and] their lively love of liberty." Speech of February 25, 1790, quoted in Lacroix, "Ce qu'on pensait des juifs," p. 423. Bigot de Préameneu, a lawyer from Rennes, was a member, together with Mulot and Robin, of the general council of the Paris Commune in 1791; he was later minister of religion in 1808. François Rouvière, *Histoire de la révolution Française dans le département du Gard: la constitutante, 1788–1791,* 4 vols. (Nîmes, 1887), 1:323–324; François de Jouvenel, "Les camps de Jalès (1790–1792), épisodes contre-revolutionnaires?" *Annales historiques de la révolution française* 337 (2004): 1–20.

155. *Actes de la Commune de Paris,* 2nd ser., 5:10, 127–128.

156. *Actes de la Commune de Paris,* 2nd ser., 5:127–137, 161–177.

157. P.-J.-B. Buchez and P.-C. Roux, *Histoire parlementaire de la révolution française,* 40 vols. (Paris, 1834–1838), 12:481–482. Bigot, Mulot, and Godard, Léonard's co-commissioners in his expeditions to the Lot and the Gard, were, respectively, fifth, sixteenth, and seventeenth on the list. Léonard became the pure expression, for Condorcet and his friends, of the reign of obscurity and self-promotion. The Paris vote was a subject of heavy irony, as in the reflections, in the *Chronique du mois* in May 1792, on the relative merits of elections by lottery and elections by ballot: "If you want *places* only for people who need to do nothing, or to use them to achieve some *superiority,* some degree of tyranny, everything is marvelously well-arranged for that; I admit that it is still possible, in the present order of things, although I think it would nevertheless be difficult, to think of a Rousseau, a Mably, a Bernardin de Saint Pierre. Who knows? Chance! Who would think, I beg you, of M. Léonard? Of Robin Léonard or Léonard Robin, deputy from Paris! On the ballot with Condorcet, and who won! Happily that in a third ballot Condorcet finally won over other intrigues, like J. P. Brissot, who was on the ballot fourteen times." *La chronique du mois,* May 1792, p. 30n1.

158. *AP,* vol. 34, October 10, 1791, pp. 163–164, October 28, 1791, 461; vol. 43, May 11, 1792, p. 250; vol. 44, May 25, 1792, pp. 99–100, June 1, 1792, pp. 443–444. The priests who were nonjuring, or "insermentés," had refused to swear the oath of obedience to the law establishing the civil constitution of the clergy that went into effect on December 26, 1790. On the registration of foreigners, see the report of the session of May 18, 1792, *Gazette nationale ou le Moniteur universel,* no. 141 (May 20, 1792): 582.

159. Abraham-François Robin, "Notes historiques," ADC, J700. Léonard Robin died in 1802 at the age of fifty-seven, shortly before his father's eighty-sixth birthday.

160. Speech of Léonard Robin of September 7, 1792, *AP,* 49:432–433, reprinted as *Rapport et projet de décret sur le divorce, par M. Robin* (Paris, n.d. [1792]); speeches of September 6, September 7, September 13, September 14, September 15, 49:400, 432–436, 608–613, 643–644, 678; September 18, September 19, September 20, 50:112–113, 149, 188–191.

161. *AP,* vol. 50, September 20, 1972, pp. 179–184 (état civil), 188–191 (divorce).

162. *AP,* vol. 50, September 20, 1972, p. 194. The text of the report and draft law was published as Léonard Robin, *Opinion et projet de decret sur les enfants naturels* (Paris, n.d. [1792]); and see *AP,* 50:194–199. The Legislative Assembly was concluded the following day, and at the end of the morning session of September 21, 1792, the deputies proceeded to the Tuileries, to welcome the revolutionary Convention; *AP,* 50:201.

163. Léonard Robin, *Instruction sur la loi, qui détermine les causes, le mode et les effets du divorce* (Paris, 1793), pp. 3–4, 25. The disputes were over whether couples who had divorced could be

remarried, immediately, to each other; a provision in the legislation that "many people" had taken to be a "typographical error in the printed versions of the law," Léonard wrote, was instead a last-minute revision of the original draft, introduced on the floor of the assembly.

164. Printed list of members, dated December 21, 1790, in F.-A. Aulard, *La Société des Jacobins, 1789–1790* (Paris, 1889), p. lxxi; Abraham-François Robin, "Notes historiques," ADC, J700.

165. Abraham-François Robin, "Notes historiques," ADC, J700; Huguet, *Discours prononcé par Huguet, sur la mort du citoyen Robin, membre du Tribunat, séance extraordinaire du 26 Thermidor an 10* (Paris, 1802), p. 5 (in ADC, J700); Abbé Mulot, *À la mémoire de Léonard Robin, tribun et membre de l'Académie de législation, discours prononcé à la séance publique du 1er Germinal an 11 par le cit. Mulot, ex-législateur* (Paris, 1802), p. 14.

166. Narrative of the actor Coittant, in [Riouffe], *Mémoires sur les prisons*, 2 vols. (Paris, 1823), 2:30; Robin, "Recueil," p. 37. Malesherbes, who was then seventy-two, was taken from the Port-Libre to the much more ominous prison of the Conciergerie and died by the guillotine on April 22, 1794; his granddaughter, Louise Le Peletier de Rosanbo, and her husband, Hervé Clérel de Tocqueville, the parents of Alexis de Tocqueville, were also imprisoned, and escaped execution.

167. Letter of August 9, 1788, from Léonard Robin to Abraham-François Robin, ADC, J700.

168. Letter of August 30, 1789, from Léonard Robin to Abraham-François Robin, ADC, J700.

169. Letter of September 24, 1788, from Léonard Robin to Abraham-François Robin, ADC, J700.

170. On the confiscation and sale of the property of Guillaume-Alexandre de Polignac, over the period from December 16, 1792, to October 26, 1795, see H. Monceaux, "La révolution dans le département de l'Yonne: essai bibliographique 1788–1800," in *Bulletin de la Société des Sciences Historiques et Naturelles de l'Yonne* 43 (1889): 45–586, pp. 390–392, 460–470, 530–533, 539, 578.

171. Letter of 20 nivôse 9 (January 10, 1801) from Léonard Robin to Canalès-Oglou, quoted in *Réclamations pour le sieur Charles-Marie Canalès-Oglou*, p. 98.

172. Maurice Roy, "Léonard Robin," *Bulletin de la société archéologique de Sens* 29 (1915): 95–119, pp. 96–98, 101n1; marriage of Léonard Robin and Marie Elisabeth Emilie Aubourg, 2 nivôse 5 (December 22, 1796), ADSM, Fontainebleau, 1796–1797, 97/199; on Léonard's new life, "dans un pays charmant, un peu eloigné de Paris avec un fort joli château pour logement, et des servitudes très convenables," see Abraham-François Robin, "Notes historiques," p. 7, ADC, J700.

173. On the position of "conservateur des hypothèques," see Honoré de Balzac, *La vieille fille* (1836) (Paris, 1978), pp. 111–112.

174. Abraham-François Robin, "Notes historiques," pp. 8–10.

175. Letter of 19 therm. 9 (August 7, 1801) from Léonard Robin to "la citoyenne Robin," Bibliothèque Historique de la Ville de Paris, Révolution française, collection Etienne Charavay, ms. 814, fol. 479.

176. Death of Léonard Robin, 18 mess. 10 (July 7, 1802), AD Yonne, 2E288/9, Paron, year 10–1825, 6/134.

177. The period from 1792 to 1816 when divorce was legal in France was the subject of little attention in the historiography of the revolution, and Léonard Robin's own role in the events of 1792 was obscured, as it was for his family in Angoulême, in the retrospect of the restoration. As the author of the first detailed study wrote more than a century later, in 1897, it was "a little-known phase in the history of divorce in France." Pierre Damas, *Les origines du divorce en France,*

étude historique sur la loi du 20 septembre 1792 (Bordeaux, 1897), p. 7; Léonard's role is discussed on pp. 106–117.

178. Baptism of Marie Madeleine Virol, October 25, 1768, AM-A, St. Martial, GG110/116.

179. Baptism of Noel Virol, November 22, 1736, AM-A, NDP, GG13/119; "Brevet d'apprentissage du Sr. Virol chez le Sr. Sirier maître chirurgien," January 26, 1760, ADC, Caillaud, 2E271. François Tremeau, merchant on the island of Martinique, and at the time in Angoulême, agreed to take Noel Virol "under his protection, by procuring for him an advantageous and suitable condition for gaining his living."

180. Guillaume Virol was buried on December 22, 1763; AM-A, St. Antonin, GG54/44. He was listed in the tax roll for 1763 as living in the Isle des Jacobins, and in the lowest income class; his immediate neighbor was François Ferrand, the domestic servant of Pierre Marchais. AM-A, CC42/1/11. On his death, his son Antoine, Marie Madeleine's father, requested an inventory of his possessions, which were valued at sixty livres; they included two shirts, a bad pair of shoes, his wigmaker's sign, a hat, and a "bad wig." "Inventaire des meubles de Guillaume Virol," December 28, 1763, ADC, Bernard, 2E152. Antoine Virol had himself leased the rights of the wigmaker Louis Deschamps, when he left on his ill-fated journey to Cayenne, the rights that were sold by the family of Jean-Baptiste Ferrand's wife Elizabeth Boutoute. ADC, 2C2/172, 175/203.

181. Noel Virol married in Paris, and he and his wife were the godparents of Marie Madeleine's younger sister. Baptism of Marie Brigitte Scholastique Virol, May 8, 1774, AM-A, St. Paul, GG90/81.

182. Interrogatoire de Marie Madeleine Virolle, 14 flor. 2, "Comité révolutionnaire de la section des tuileries, contre Félicité Mélanie Ennouf et Marie Madeleine Virolle," in "Affaire filles Virolle, Eunouf, Loisieller et autres," AN, W//359/759. In Marie Madeleine's account, she had worked for the "Comte de Culla" until "two years earlier," and then for the "Marquise Cheverlai." Claude Gigon, who included Marie Madeleine in his mid-nineteenth-century study of the victims of the Terror in the Charente, surmised that "Culla" was the Comte de Culant, an army officer and son of a former military official in Martinique, who was a representative of the nobility of the Charente in the Etats généraux of 1789; the "Marquise Cheverlai" was the wife of the Marquis de Chauveron, a former governor of the château of Angoulême. Claude Gigon, *Les victimes de la terreur du département de la Charente: récits historiques*, 2nd ed. (Angoulême, 1866), p. 197; and on the Comte de Culant, http://www2.assemblee-nationale.fr/sycomore/fiche/%28num_dept%29/11708.

183. Interrogatoire de Marie Madeleine Virolle, 14 flor. 2, AN, W//359/759; Audience du 16 flor., *Bulletin du tribunal révolutionnaire*, no. 71 (Paris, 1794), p. 283.

184. "Voisi ma carte de citoiyen," in "Affaire filles Virolle, Eunouf, Loisieller et autres," AN, W//359/759. *Bulletin du tribunal révolutionnaire*, no. 71, pp. 283–284; Henri Wallon, *Histoire du tribunal révolutionnaire de Paris*, 6 vols. (Paris, 1880–1882), 3:382–392. On the expression *pla bougre*, see "Curiositez françoises," in La Curne de Sainte-Palaye, *Dictionnaire historique de l'ancien langage françois*, 10 vols. (Paris, 1875–1882), 10:333.

185. "Voisi ma carte de citoiyen," AN, W//359/759.

186. "Félicité Mélanie," in "Affaire filles Virolle, Eunouf, Loisieller et autres," AN, W//359/759.

187. Wallon, *Histoire du tribunal révolutionnaire de Paris*, p. 385.

188. "Mandat d'arret," in "Affaire filles Virolle, Eunouf, Loisieller et autres," AN, W//359/759.

189. "Mandat d'arret," Interrogatoire de Félicité Mélanie Ennouf, in "Affaire filles Virolle, Eunouf, Loisieller et autres," AN, W//359/759.

190. Interrogatoire de Marie Madeleine Virolle, 14 flor. 2, AN, W//359/759.

191. This was the expression used on the masthead of the court record: see *Bulletin du tribunal révolutionnaire, établi au Palais, à Paris, par la Loi du 10 Mars 1793, pour juger sans appel les CONSPIRATEURS*, no. 72, p. 284.

192. *Bulletin du tribunal révolutionnaire*, no. 72, pp. 284–285.

193. *Bulletin du tribunal révolutionnaire*, no. 72, p. 285.

194. "Liste des guillotinés," in *Liste générale et très-exacte des noms, âges, qualités et demeures de tous les Conspirateurs qui ont été condamnés à mort par le Tribunal révolutionnaire*, no. 4 (Paris, year 2), p. 22.

195. Charbonnier, commissaire de police, in "Affaire filles Virolle, Eunouf, Loisieller et autres," AN, W//359/759.

196. Alexandre Sorel, *Le Couvent des Carmes et le séminaire de Saint-Sulpice pendant la Terreur* (Paris, 1863), pp. 436–437.

197. Interrogation of Noel Virol or Virolle, 30 mess. 2, "Sur la prétendue conspiration des Carmes," in Saladin, *Rapport au nom de la commission des vingt-un* (Paris, year 3), pp. 173–184.

198. Saladin, *Rapport au nom de la commission des vingt-un*, pp. 178–179.

199. Saladin, *Rapport au nom de la commission des vingt-un*, pp. 173–174; and, on the two ropes, pp. 175, 180–182.

200. Testimony of Belavoine, in Saladin, *Rapport au nom de la commission des vingt-un*, p. 174.

201. Testimony of Jean-Baptiste Cacaut, in Saladin, *Rapport au nom de la commission des vingt-un*, pp. 174–175. Jean-Baptiste Cacaut was imprisoned in the Carmes on 11 niv. 2 (December 31, 1793), on the charge of being suspicious, and released on 1 fruct. 2 (August 18, 1794). See Sorel, *Le Couvent des Carmes*, pp. 380–381. A Jean-Baptiste Cacaud, living in the suburb of St. Denis, had earlier received a police card in Paris; he was described as thirty-eight years old, having come to Paris from Angoulême in 1777. AN, Police générale, F/7/4787, available at http://www.geneanet.org/archives/registres/view/?idcollection=19949&page=336. Jean Cacaud, son of Antoine Cacaud and Jeanne Bonnin, was baptized in St. Martial on January 13, 1754; AM-A, St. Martial, GG108/85. His parents and younger brother were among the 4,089 individuals in the parish records for 1764.

202. Testimony of Claude-Gabriel Chavard and Jean-Anne-Michel Manuel, in Saladin, *Rapport au nom de la commission des vingt-un*, pp. 178–180. Chavard and Manuel, like Cacaut/Cacaud, were released in August 1794; Sorel, *Le Couvent des Carmes*, pp. 384–385, 416–417.

203. Testimony of Noel Virolle, in Saladin, *Rapport au nom de la commission des vingt-un*, pp. 176–177. The deputy from Angoulême was Dubois de Bellegarde, the intemperate army officer with the patriotic sons.

204. "*Virol*, s'est jeté par la fenêtre, au moment où nous venions de l'interroger." Saladin, *Rapport au nom de la commission des vingt-un*, p. 173.

205. "Liste des guillotinés," in *Liste générale et très-exacte*, no. 9, pp. 26–29; list of prisoners in Sorel, *Le Couvent des Carmes*, pp. 371–437.

Chapter Six. A Family in Changing Times

1. "Certificats de civisme," ADC, L146; listings for Gabriel Ferrand, 28 brum. 2 (November 18, 1793), Ferrand père, Pierre Alexandre Ferrand and Etienne Ferrand, 1 niv. 2 (December 21, 1793), and "Ferrand jeune instituteur," 26 prair. 2 (June 14, 1794.) Death of Joseph Marie Ferrand, in his house near the Place de Beaulieu, at the age of twenty-three, AM-A, August 17, 1793, 1E3/61.

2. Record of house number 913, Section C, Château, in "Contributions, matrices foncières," 1791, AM-A. In the annotations to the register, which can be dated by references to transactions in the years 6 and 7, the house is described as having been "rebuilt" and "reconstructed."

3. See above, chapter 5.

4. "Actes civils," 1792–year 2, in "Justices de paix," Angoulême, *intra muros*, ADC, L2780.

5. Entries for 25 brum. and 19 frim. 7, in Mercier, *Journal des maires d'Angoulême*, pp. 116–118. The administrator in charge of the procedure was Lecler-Raby, Etienne Allemand's second cousin once removed.

6. Undated draft of the organization of correspondence in the Department of the Charente, ADC, L131, and see above, chapter 5.

7. See note of 22 frim. 5, in "Archives. Correspondance passive," ADC, L2026: "I request citizen Ducluzeau to show citizenness Dubousquet the bell that has been deposited in the departmental archives."

8. Notes of 2 niv. 6, 27 germ. 6, 8 frim. 8, and 28 brum. 8, ADC, L131.

9. Note of 7 fruct. 2, in ADC, L745.

10. Notes of 2 niv. 6, 27 germ. 6, 8 frim. 8, and 28 brum. 8, ADC, L131.

11. "Registre destiné à constater la présence des employés," 12 germ. 7 to 21 mess. 7, ADC, L121. The other employee of the division of archives signed "Dupuy"; "Ducluzeau" was also described as an archivist in 1796 and 1797. Receipt of 9 prair. 4, note of 22 frim. 5, ADC, L2026; note of 22 fruct. 5, ADC, L131.

12. Declaration of Gabriel Ferrand, entry 309, 21 mess. 7 (July 9, 1799), "Registre pour recevoir les déclarations des citoyens domiciliés dans cette commune," AM-A, Contributions/Contributions personelles 1798/1799.

13. Death of Gabriel Ferrand, December 20, 1816, AM-A, 1E52/426.

14. Records for July 1790 to April 1791; parish register of Jauldes, 1737–1792, ADC, 3E178/1, 357–364/376. The diocesan records of Angoulême show "Ferrand Gabriel alias Etienne," with Etienne's date of birth, January 2, 1766, as having become vicar of Jauldes in 1789; his first signature in the parish register of Jauldes was on July 11, 1790. "Registre des ordinations remis aux archives de l'Evêché en septembre 1912," Archives diocésaines d'Angoulême.

15. Percentage of juring priests calculated on the basis of Blanchet, *Le clergé charentais pendant la révolution*, pp. 449–464; Tackett, *Religion, Revolution, and Regional Culture in Eighteenth-Century France*, p. 367.

16. By a decree adopted by the National Assembly on April 29, 1791, the cathedral parish (St. Pierre) was delineated in an extremely elaborate plan—"suivant ledit mur à gauche passant sur la porte du Palais, prenant les deux maisons qui y sont construites"—and St. Martial was assigned "le surplus de la ville, laissé par les confrontations de celles de St. Pierre." *Procès-verbal de l'assemblée nationale, imprimé par son ordre*, vol. 54 (Paris, [1791]), pp. 8–9. On the events of

March and April 1791 in Angoulême, see Blanchet, *Le clergé charentais pendant la révolution,* pp. 64–92.

17. Several of the others later retracted, or swore conditional, restricted oaths, and four were deported. Blanchet, *Le clergé charentais pendant la révolution,* pp. 57, 449–453; "Mémoire historique sur le séminaire d'Angoulême," pp. 342–344.

18. Baptism of Marguerite Rouhier, June 12, 1791, St. Martial, AM-A, GG113/209; ADC, register of St. Martial, 1781–1792, 391/465.

19. "Mémoire historique sur le séminaire d'Angoulême," pp. 344; Blanchet, *Le clergé charentais pendant la révolution,* p. 450.

20. Etienne signed every entry in the parish register from June 12, 1791, to August 13, 1791; ADC, St. Martial, 1781–1792, 391–398/465.

21. ADC, St. Martial, 1781–1792, 452/465.

22. Dossier "Ferrand (Jn. Bte.)," AN, F/12/2795; petition of October 16, 1824.

23. *Plan de la ville du Cap Français sur lequel sont marqués en teinte noire les ravages du premier incendie, et en rouge les islets, parties d'islets, édifices, etc. qui existent encore le 21 juin 1793,* BNF, available at http://gallica.bnf.fr/ark:/12148/btv1b55005281x/f1.item.zoom. On the fire, see Convention nationale, *Relation détaillée des événements malheureux qui se sont passés au Cap depuis l'arrivée du ci-devant général Galbaud jusqu'au moment où il a fait brûler cette ville et a pris la fuite* (Paris, year 2), pp. 52–62.

24. Dossier "Ferrand (Jn. Bte.)," AN, F/12/2795; petition of October 16, 1824; Dossier "Ferrand," AN, F/12/2795, petition of December 18, 1822; "I lost an eighteen-year-old son in the defense of the colony." Martial Ferrand was baptized in Angoulême on March 30, 1775. His godfather was his seven-year-old cousin, Martial Allemand; AM-A, PSC, GG 68/56.

25. "Etat des Refugiés, Déportés, et Propriétaires Colons," ADC, L152.

26. "Etat des Refugiés," ADC, L152; birth of Jean-Baptiste Ferrand, 8 pluv. 4 (January 28, 1796), AM-A, 1E7/40. On the English, Spanish, Portuguese, and Austrian prisoners in the college, see Boissonnade and Bernard, *Histoire du collège d'Angoulême,* p. 257.

27. "Etat des Refugiés," ADC, L152. The refugees were admitted to assistance between January and December 1795; the certificates of indigence were issued in the summer and autumn of 1798.

28. "Registre destiné à constater la présence des employés," ADC, L121. The signature of "Ferrand jeune," in the register for 19 mess. 7 (July 7, 1799) was the same as the signature of Jean-Baptiste Ferrand in the record of the birth of the younger Jean-Baptiste Ferrand on 8 pluv. 4, AM-A, 1E7/40. On the responsibilities of the Third Bureau, see Jules de la Martinière and Léo Imbert, *Répertoire numérique de la série L administration de 1789 à l'an VIII* (Angoulême, 1911), p. L3.

29. Entry 308, 21 mess. 7, "Registre pour recevoir les déclarations des citoyens domiciliés dans cette commune," AM-A, Contributions/Contributions personelles 1798/1799.

30. Dossier "Ferrand (Jn. Bte.)," AN, F/12/2795; certification of 4 vend. 14 (September 26, 1805). Antoine-Guillaume Chéreau, who signed the certification, was the author, the following year, of two apparently demented works about squares, crosses, revenge, and metempsychosis, *Explication de la croix philosophique* (Paris, 1806) and *Explication de la pierre cubique* (Paris, 1806).

31. AM-A, 1E12/67, 1E23/70, 1E25/31. There were far more men than women as witnesses in the civil registers of Angoulême, even before the national legislation of 1803 that required four

male witnesses for the registration of civil marriages; see Gourdon, "Réseaux des femmes, réseaux de femmes," p. 35 and n2.

32. Déclarations 704, 714, 750, "Offrandes volontaires: dons patriotiques pour la contribution des habitants d'Angoulême," 1790, AM-A, CC58; déclaration 375, "Déclarations à fournir pour ceux dont le revenu est inférieur à 400 livres," 1790, AM-A, CC59.

33. "Certificats de civisme," Allemand Lavigerie, May 31, 1793, and 26 prair. 2 (June 14, 1794); Martial Allemand Lavigerie, October 8, 1793, and 21 fruct. 2 (September 7, 1794); Antoine Allemand Lavigerie, June 15, 1793; "Lavigerie fils volontaire," 26 prair. 2 (June 14, 1794.) ADC, L146.

34. Record of house number 935, Section C, Château, in AM-A, "Contributions, matrices foncières," 1791, and see "Par devant Duval notaire," agreement between Etienne Allemand and his children, March 16, 1811, ADC, Duval, notary, 2E8751.

35. Undated letter from Coulon, Lavigerie, and Richein, in "Collège d'Angoulême," year 2–year 5, ADC, L422.

36. Letter of 16 germ. 3 (April 5, 1795) from the "Commission exécutif de l'instruction publique" to the administrators of the Department of the Charente, objecting to their order of the preceding month, in which they had authorized an increase in the pension accorded to the "scholars entrusted to citizen Lavigerie." Instruction publique, "Réponse des municipalités cantonales," ADC, L420. On Etienne's students, see Boissonnade and Bernard, *Histoire du collège d'Angoulême*, p. 212n2.

37. Of the three professors who wrote the letter about their contradictory orders, one died soon after, and another died a few years later, "in a state of total deprivation." Etienne, "who was responsible for twelve children," received his pension only until 1797; in order to survive, he "was compelled, even though he was in his sixties, to accept the position of a copy clerk in the bureaux of the department." Boissonnade and Bernard, *Histoire du collège d'Angoulême*, p. 220.

38. "Paiement des traitements," in "Compabilité générale du département," ADC, L206, and "Personnel," "Pièces diverses relatives au traitement du personnel des bureaux," ADC, L120.

39. "Indemnité aux employés du bureau des domaines," years 3–4, in ADC, 1QPROV 1/234–236.

40. Petition of citizens Rullier, Henry, and Lavigerie, 12 pluv. 4 (February 1, 1796), ADC, Personnel, L120.

41. Extrait des registres des délibérations du directoire, 3 brum. 4 (October 25, 1795) and 15 niv. 4 (January 5, 1796), ADC, Personnel, L120.

42. Letter of 26 frim. 4 (December 17, 1795) from Etienne Allemand Lavigerie to Aubert Dubayet, transcription in the Archives Lavigerie, Archives de la Société des Missionnaires d'Afrique, Via Aurelia, Rome [hereafter AL-R], A2-216 (51), fol. 1. Of the thirteen children of Etienne and Françoise, the oldest of their daughters called Jeanne, baptized in 1766, died in infancy, and it is likely that their first child, Marie, also died in infancy; she appears in none of the copious parish records of the family in Angoulême after her baptism.

43. See above, chapter 2.

44. Letter of 26 frim. 4 from Etienne Allemand Lavigerie to Albert Dubayet, AL-R, A2-216 (51), fpl. 3; Jules Pelisson, "Fondation de l'église de Gondeville 1683–1703," *Archives historiques de la Saintonge et de l'Aunis* 8 (1880): 17–27, p. 25.

45. Marriage of Pierre Allemand Lavigerie and Adelaide Charlotte Maslin, Sillé-le-Guillaume, 12 pluv. 4 (February 1, 1796), ADSa, 1793–year 10, 58–59/398.

46. Declaration of Etienne Allemand, entry 372, undated (23 or 24 mess. 7), AM-A, "Registre pour recevoir les déclarations des citoyens domiciliés dans cette commune."

47. Declarations of Abraham-François Robin, entry 114, Louis Felix, entry 160, Pierre Marchais Delaberge, entry 371, and Michel Guenois, veuve Ogerdias, entry 383, AM-A, "Registre pour recevoir les déclarations des citoyens domiciliés dans cette commune." In an earlier declaration, Michel Guenois stated she had now rented out a part of the house, because she could no longer afford the rent that was stipulated in the original agreement. "Contribution personelle," no. 332, 17 brum. 6; AM-A, "Contributions/Contributions personelles," 1798–1799.

48. Record of house number 995, Section C, Château, in AM-A, "Contributions, matrices foncières," 1791.

49. Declaration of Jeanne Lavigerie *aînée*, entry 493, 29 mess. 7, AM-A, "Registre pour recevoir les déclarations des citoyens domiciliés dans cette commune." Jeanne Lavigerie was then thirty; she was baptized on November 10, 1768, in the parish of St. Antonin. AM-A, GG54/60.

50. Jean-Baptiste and Elizabeth were "admitted to assistance" in Angoulême on 3 flor. 3, or April 27, 1795; their son Jean-Baptiste Ferrand was born on 8 pluv. 4, or January 28, 1796. "Etat des Refugiés, Déportés, et Propriétaires Colons," ADC, L152; AM-A, 1E7/40.

51. Balzac, *La vieille fille*, pp. 84–86; "de 1789 à 1799, les circonstances furent très défavorables à ses prétentions."

52. Marriage of Martial Allemand Lavigerie and Louise Vaslin, April 13, 1790, AM-A, St. André, GG47/64–65; burial of Marie Aymard, April 22, 1790, PSC, GG 68/117.

53. Baptism of Martial Allemand, October 22, 1767, AM-A, St. Antonin, GG54/56; baptism of Louise Vaslin, May 5, 1769, St. Jean, GG74/159.

54. Françoise's mother, Marie Aymard, lived in the Isle de la Place du Collège, when they married in 1765, and Etienne's father in the Isle de la Cloche Verte, a few minutes' walk away; the parents of Gabriel's wife, Marie Adelaide, lived a few minutes farther along the Rue des Cordeliers (the modern Rue de Beaulieu) in the Isle des Dames de Beaulieu, and the mother of Jean-Baptiste's wife, Elizabeth Boutoute, in St. André. AM-A, CC42/1/11, 42/2/7, 42/2/11; GG45/64.

55. Louise Vaslin's mother, Elisabeth Boucher, lived with her other daughter and son-in-law on the Rue de Genève, a few steps away from the house of Martial and Louise on the corner of the Petit Rue du Palais, where his father and grandfather had lived in 1764; records of house number 403, Section A, Beaulieu, and house number 243, Section B, St. Martial, in AM-A, "Contributions, matrices foncières," 1791. Louise's grandmother, described as "la veuve de Louis Bouché et Gimon son gendre perruquier," earlier lived with her daughter and son-in-law, a wigmaker, in the Isle des Tiercelettes, AM-A, CC42/1/24 and CC62/21/809; baptism of Louis Deschamps, AM-A, St. Martial, September 1, 1738, GG106/73.

56. "Mariage de Sr Lavigerie et Dlle Vaslin," March 19, 1790, ADC, Callandreau notaire, 2E9754. Martial was described as the clerk of "M. Barbier," who signed the contract, together with his wife.

57. "Mariage de Sr Lavigerie et Dlle Vaslin," March 19, 1790, ADC, Callandreau notaire, 2E9754.

58. Administration general des domaines, Contrôle des actes des notaires et sous signature-privée, bureau d'Angoulême, no. 1, March 19, 1790, ADC, 3QPROV 12608.

59. Marriage of Etienne Ferrand and Marie Chausse Lunesse, 4 mess. 2 (June 22, 1794), AM-A, 1E2/124. Marie Chausse Lunesse was born in Marsac, her mother's home, on July 1, 1764;

ADC, Marsac, 1737–1787, 117/275. Four of her brothers and sisters were baptized in the parish of St. Martial, and her sister Françoise was married there, by Etienne's immediate predecessor, on January 25, 1790. AM-A, January 25, 1790, GG113/159–160; GG110/100, 133, GG111/47, 196.

60. Marriage of Etienne Ferrand and Marie Chausse Lunesse, 4 mess. 2 (June 22, 1794), AM-A, 1E2/124. On Guillaume Roch Letourneau, described as "officier municipal révolution-naire," see AM-A, 1E2/91; and on his earlier career, see Blanchet, *Le clergé charentais*, pp. 107–108.

61. Marriage of Françoise Chausse Lunesse and Joseph Martin de Bourgon, January 25, 1790. AM-A, GG113/159.

62. H. Beauchet-Filleau and Paul Beauchet-Filleau, *Dictionnaire historique et généalogique des familles du Poitou*, 4 vols. (Poitiers, 1895), 2:332–333. Alcide Gauguié, *La Charente com-munale illustrée: histoire et géographie pittoresque de la Charente* (Angoulême, 1868), pp. 104–105.

63. "Décompte," no. 302, in ADC, 1QPROV 2 34 (Q XVIII 33).

64. Letter received, 24 germ. 9, "certificat de résidence," 25 brum. 13, summary of petition of 4 pluv. 4, petition for a visa to citoyen Fouché, 14 frim. 9, in "Chausse Lunesse, Jean," AN, Cha-rente, F/7/4988, dossier 8, 6–7, 14, 16, 18/25.

65. Marriage of Françoise Chausse Lunesse and Joseph Martin de Bourgon, January 25, 1790. AM-A, St. Martial, GG113/159–160.

66. AM-A, St. André, September 3, 1758, GG42/113; baptism of François Martin Aliquain, St. Jean, October 1, 1775, GG75/46.

67. Letters of February 28, 1790, April 8, 1790, August 8, 1790, and August 16, 1791, in "Bour-gon, Jacques Martin de, maréchal de camp, gouverneur de la Guyane," ANOM, COL E 48. Jacques Martin de Bourgon then retired to Angoulême, where he lived in rented accommoda-tion near the fish market (and the Place du Mûrier); record of house number 692, Section A, Beaulieu, in AM-A, "Contributions, matrices foncières," 1791. His certificates of residence, non-emigration, and nondetention were signed by Louis Félix and Lecler-Raby. In 1802, he wrote to the ministry, and to Napoléon, asking to be exempted, as a sexagenarian, from the obligation of having to return to his property in Guadeloupe, which was being administered by "Citizen Salager, *white* merchant in the said island" (emphasis in original); he died in Angoulême in 1820. Letters of 30 vend. 11 and 17 brum. 11, certificates of 29 pluv. 4, 4 jour compl. 5, 9 frim. 6, 14 flor. 7, and 2 flor. 8, in "Bourgon, Jacques Martin de"; death of Jacques Martin de Bourgon, Octo-ber 23, 1820, AM-A, 1E60/121–122.

68. The sentence was described as having been signed by eleven judges, and was presented by one of the signatories of the marriage contract of Etienne Allemand and Françoise Ferrand, Thibaud, *commis du greffe*. Baptism of Jacques de Bourgon, October 30, 1787, AM-A, GG90/159.

69. The child "est de leurs faits et oeuvres." Marriage of Françoise Chausse Lunesse and Joseph Martin de Bourgon, AM-A, GG113/159–160.

70. Jacques de Bourgon, born in 1787, became a naval officer; François, born in 1792, was a general serving in Algeria; and Jacques Alfred, born in 1794, was a general who was killed on the barricades of Paris Saint-Denis in June, 1848. AM-A, GG90/159, GG25/50, 1E4/26; Départe-ment de la Charente, *Procès-verbal des délibérations du conseil general, 1847* (Angouleme, 1847), p. 121; AN, Légion d'honneur, LEONORE, LH/1766/43; Leonard Gallois, *Histoire de la révolu-tion de 1848*, 4 vols. (Paris, 1849–1850), 3:52–54.

71. Letter of 26 frim. 4 from Etienne Allemand Lavigerie to Aubert Dubayet, AL-R, A2-216 (51), fol. 1.

72. Birth of Décadi Montagnard Maslin, 21 vent. 2 (March 11, 1794), ADSa, Sillé-le-Guillaume, births, 1793–1802, 29/273.

73. Marriage of Pierre Allemand Lavigerie and Adelaide Charlotte Maslin, 12 pluv. 4 (February 1, 1796), ADSa, Sillé-le-Guillaume, marriages and divorces, 1793–year 10, 58–59/398. Etienne enclosed a copy of a letter from Charlotte's mother, Charlotte Sevin, written in Lille on 28 brum. 4 (November 19, 1795) in his letter to Aubert Dubayet.

74. Pierre Auguste Henry "fils ainé," who signed Pierre Allemand Lavigerie's marriage record in the Sarthe, was the son of Jean Théodore Henry, the owner of the seminary; he was the nephew of Jean Théodore's brother, also called Pierre Auguste Henry. Baptism of Pierre Auguste Henry, March 11, 1770, AM-A, St. Jacques, GG130/173–174; and see Jézéquel, *La révolution française à Angoulême*, pp. 90, 127, 162–163, and Jézéquel, "Charente," in *Grands notables du premier empire*, pp. 58–59.

75. Marriage of Pierre Allemand Lavigerie and Adelaide Charlotte Maslin, 12 pluv. 4, ADSa, Sillé-le-Guillaume, 58–59/398; marriage of Etienne Ferrand and Marie Chausse Lunesse, 4 mess. 2 (June 22, 1794), AM-A, 1E2/124. The witness was Antoine Brun.

76. "Registre tenu pour le service des gardes nationales," September 13, 1790, AM-A, EE11; ADC, "Certificats de civisme," L146.

77. See Boissonnade, *Histoire des volontaires de la Charente*, pp. 159–160, 210, 221–224; and the commissioner Pierrat's description of horrible butchery, p. 167. Boissonnade refers in passing to a "company under the orders of Captain Ferrand," p. 188.

78. Expilly, *Dictionnaire géographique*, 5:299.

79. AD Vendée, Les Sables d'Olonne, AC194, Table alphabétique des sépultures et des déces, 1701–1802. There were 18 individuals whose names began with a B who died in the town in 1789, and 213 in the year 2 (1793–1794): 101 from among the population and 112 "military and refugees." See 17–19/118, and, 18/118, "les suppliciés sont indiqués par une x."

80. AD Vendée, Les Sables d'Olonne, AC194, births and marriages, year 4, 24 flor. (May 4, 1796), 182–183/216. The late father of Gabriel's wife, Florence Scholastique Borgnet, was a pulley-maker (*poulieur*); for other relatives, see AD Vendée, Les Sables d'Olonne, 6M309, liste nominative 1799, 20/121. Gabriel's witnesses were figures from the military world of the town; an adjutant major in the "place" of Les Sables, and a functionary in the "subsistence" of the army.

81. AD Vendée, Les Sables d'Olonne, AC194, birth of Vincent Gabriel Ferrand, 11 fruct. 4 (August 28, 1796), births and marriages, year 4, 54–55/216; birth of Stéphanie Ferrand, 24 niv. 7 (January 13, 1799), 11 fruct. 4, 182–183/216.

82. Death of Gabriel Ferrand, September 19, 1816, AD Loiret, Beaugency, deaths, 1811–1820, 180/284.

83. Divorce of Martial Allemand Lavigerie and Louise Vaslin, 2 brum. 5 (October 23, 1796), AM-A, 1E11/4.

84. Speech of Léonard Robin of September 7, 1792, *AP*, 49:432–433.

85. On the ninety-six divorces in Angoulême, see above, chapter 5.

86. Birth of Léon-Philippe Allemand Lavigerie, 13 prair. 3 (June 18, 1795), AM-A, 1E4/94.

87. Marriage of Martial Allemand Lavigerie and Marie Louise Bonnite Raymond Saint Germain, 28 prair. 9 (June 17, 1801), AM-A, 1E23/69–70.

88. Marriage of Martial Allemand Lavigerie and Bonnite Saint Germain, AM-A, 1E23/69–70.

89. Marriage contract of Martial Allemand Lavigerie and Marie Louise Bonnite Raymond Saint Germain, Duval, 20 prair. 9 (June 19, 1801), ADC, 2E6272.

90. Marriage contract of Martial Allemand Lavigerie and Bonnite Saint Germain, ADC, 2E6272. "Marchais de Laberge fils ainé," who signed the marriage contract, was "Jean-Baptiste Marchais de Laberge," who together with his father, the former mayor Pierre Marchais de Laberge, employed Etienne Allemand as farm manager on their country estate, and were the landlords of the "citoyennes Lavigerie" on the Place du Mûrier; marriage of Jean-Baptiste Marchais de Laberge and Catherine Brun, July 27, 1784, AM-A, GG46/128.

91. Birth of Françoise Sylvia Allemand Lavigerie, 12 frim. 10 (December 3, 1801), AM-A, 1E25/31.

92. Births of Adelaide Allemand Lavigerie, 19 mess. 11 (July 8, 1803); Pierre Jules Edouard Allemand Lavigerie, December 30, 1806; Mamert Victor Allemand Lavigerie, May 11, 1808; Charlotte Ursule Allemand Lavigerie, October 23, 1810; Adelaide Théonie Allemand Lavigerie, March 8, 1813; ADPA, Bayonne, births, years 6–11, 775/875; births, years 12–1813, 224, 336, 548, 754/820.

93. Baptism of Françoise Ferrand, June 12, 1777, AM-A, St. André, GG45/124; "Etat des Refugiés," ADC, L152.

94. Marriage of Joseph Brébion and Françoise Ferrand, Paris, 4e arr., 10 flor. 8 (April 30, 1800), Table des mariages et des divorces célébrés à Paris de 1793 à 1802, AdP, V10E/2, available at https://www.geneanet.org/archives/registres/view/32378/235; Dossier "Ferrand, Françoise, Ve. Brébion," AN, F/12/2795. In 1872, Françoise's daughter Clara provided a certificate stating that she had been born in New York on January 29, 1804; "Certificat de vie," March 11, 1873, in "Brébion Collet (veuve)," AN, F/12/2757.

95. Statement of the mayor of the seventh arrondissement of Paris, August 24, 1814, in dossier "Ferrand, Françoise, Ve. Brébion," AN, F/12/2795. The statement, on the attestation of two neighbors, Gunther, an organist, and Garnier, a baker, gave the ages of Françoise's children as nine and a half, seven and a half, and five, suggesting that they were born in early 1805, early 1807, and 1809. Françoise was living in the Rue Grenier St. Lazare, in the modern third arrondissement.

96. Letter of August 19, 1814, from Lareintz of the Bureau de Secours, Ministry of the Navy and Colonies, in "Ferrand, Françoise, Ve. Brébion," AN, Secours aux réfugiés et colons spoliés, F/12/2795.

97. Letter of August 10, 1860, from the director of foreign commerce to the minister of agriculture, in "Ferrand, Françoise, Ve. Brébion," AN, F/12/2795.

98. C.M.F. Puthod, Coup d'oeil sur les moyens les plus praticables de procéder à la liquidation de l'indemnité affectée aux colons français (Paris, 1825), pp. 4, 15.

99. Death of Auguste Siva de Villeneuve Solard, June 4, 1839, AM-A, 1E120/36. Her address was given as Rue François 1er in the center of the town, not far from the Place du Mûrier.

100. "Certificats de civisme," ADC, L146; listing for Pierre Alexandre Ferrand, 1 niv. 2 (December 21, 1793).

101. Stéphane Calvet, Dictionnaire Biographique des Officiers Charentais de la Grande Armée (Paris, 2010), pp. 116–117.

102. Calvet, *Dictionnaire Biographique*, pp. 116–117.

103. Death of Pierre Alexandre Ferrand, December 4, 1841, AM-A, 1E126/97. His address was given as Rue de Périgueux.

104. Death of Auguste Siva de Villeneuve Solard, June 4, 1839, AM-A, 1E120/36.

105. Court of Chancery, London, Complaint of Clara Sophia Augusta de Ceve de Villeneuve Solar, January 23, 1786, Response of Sir Richard Worsley, December 8, 1786, TNA, C/12/149/6. On Sir Richard Worsley, and his earlier litigation with his wife, see Hallie Rubenhold, *The Lady in Red: An Eighteenth-Century Tale of Sex, Scandal, and Divorce* (New York, 2009).

106. Session of August 13, 1792, in Henry Lemonnier, *L'académie royale d'architecture 1671–1793*, 10 vols. (Paris, 1911–1929), 9:330.

107. Lemonnier, *L'académie royale d'architecture*, 9:332, 348–350. "Salon de 1795," in *Collection des livrets des anciennes expositions depuis 1763 jusqu'en 1800* (Paris, 1871), p. 80. On Silvestre Topin as a "remarkable student" and protégé of Jacques Louis David, see Boissonnade and Bernard, *Histoire du collège d'Angoulême*, p. 250.

108. Letter from the minister of the interior, 21 pluv. 5 (February 9, 1797), "Collège d'Angoulême," ADC, L422; payment for travel expenses, "Etat des dépenses de l'an 5 de l'école centrale," undated, "Ecole centrale d'Angoulême," ADC, L423; Boissonnade and Bernard, *Histoire du collège d'Angoulême*, pp. 249–250n1.

109. "Etat des dépenses," ADC, L423; Boissonnade and Bernard, *Histoire du collège d'Angoulême*, pp. 266, 290–291.

110. Letter from the minister of the interior to the administrators of the Department of the Charente, 23 prair. 6 (June 11, 1798), ADC, L422. General Leclerc, the brother-in-law of Napoléon Bonaparte, died in Saint-Domingue in 1802.

111. Letter of 26 flor. 7 (May 15, 1799) from Silvestre announcing that he had returned to Angoulême, that he intended to resume his duties on 1 prair. (May 20), and that his temporary replacement should stop work "tomorrow"; letter of the same date informing him that he had to provide evidence of his release from the army; letters of 18 frim. 6 and 2 niv. 6 describing Silvestre as "ex professeur de dessein et réquisitionnaire," and proposing a new competition to find his permanent replacement, ADC L423; letters to the administrators of the department from the minister of war, on 3 mess. 7 (June 21, 1799) and from the minister of the interior on 10 mess. 7 (June 28, 1799), ADC, L422.

112. Letter of 7 germ. 7 (March 27, 1799) from Silvestre in Lyon, ADC L423.

113. Silvestre Topin, Receipt for the reimbursement of the cost of "objects" ordered from Paris "for the distribution of prizes," 28 fruct. 7, ADC L423.

114. Payment to Valleteau, menuisier, "Etat des dépenses de l'an 5 de l'école centrale," undated, ADC, L423; Boissonnade and Bernard, *Histoire du collège d'Angoulême*, pp. 266, 290–291. Nicolas Valleteau or Valteau, the carpenter, had earlier become the first man to be divorced in Angoulême; AM-A, November 14, 1792, St. Pierre, GG25/51.

115. Marriage of Laurent Silvestre Topin and Jeanne Lavigerie, 4 therm. 9 (July 23, 1801), AM-A, 1E23/82–83. On the printer and former priest François Tremeau, see Boissonnade and Bernard, *Histoire du collège d'Angoulême*, p. 235; baptism of François Tremeau, January 19, 1765, AM-A, NDP, GG14/36. He was the great-nephew of the merchant who made a fortune in Martinique, and the nephew of Jean Brun, the member of the revolutionary Convention. His second

cousin, also called François Tremeau, died in Martinique in 1802; see Jézéquel, *La Charente révolutionnaire*, pp. 224–226.

116. Agreement between Nicolas Topin and Jeanne Lorin in respect of the manufacture and sale of helmets (*calottes*), December 3, 1756, AN, MC/ET/XLI/537; David Harris Cohen, "The 'Chambre des Portraits' Designed by Victor Louis for the King of Poland," *J. Paul Getty Museum Journal* 19 (1991): 75–98, pp. 83, 91–92, 96. Silvestre Topin was born in Paris on June 22, 1771, as reported in the record of his marriage; AM-A, 1E23/83. Nicolas Topin left Paris in 1773, according to a declaration by Marie Catherine Lacorne in 1790, and she had not heard from him since then. "Marriage de Topin," December 11, 1790, in connection with the marriage of Silvestre's older brother; AN, Y//5197/A, available at https://www.geneanet.org/archives/registres/view/?idcollection=3914&page=409.

117. Marie Catherine's late father, Jacques Lacorne, was described in his daughter's marriage contract, in 1762, as "maître d'académie pour la danse des pages de S.A.S. le duc d'Orléans." Marriage contract of May 7, 1762, AN, Denis, notary, MC/ET/LX/345. *Déclaration de la citoyenne Topin, sous-gouvernante de Louise-Eugénie-Adelaide d'Orléans* (Paris, 1793); Stéphanie Félicité de Genlis, *Mémoires inédits de madame la comtesse de Genlis*, 10 vols. (Paris, 1825), 4:74.

118. *Déclaration de la citoyenne Topin*, pp. 1–4. *Vie politique de Louis-Philippe-Joseph, dernier duc d'Orléans* (Paris, 1802), pp. 164–172.

119. "Madame Topin hastened voluntarily to that execrable inquisition the *Commune* of Paris, and denounced the emigration of her benefactors, and endeavoured to make their conduct still more odious by malignantly adding" that she had overheard irreligious remarks on the part of Madame de Genlis. "Personal History of Louis Philippe," *Quarterly Review* 52 (1834): 519–572, p. 534.

120. Births of Marie Théonie Topin, October 15, 1801 (23 vend. 10), Françoise Méloé Topin, January 14, 1803 (29 niv. 11), and François Topin, August 12, 1804 (24 therm. 12), AM-A, 1E25/12, 1E32/50, 1E35/133.

121. Boissonnade and Bernard, *Histoire du collège d'Angoulême*, pp. 313–316.

122. AdP, état civil reconstitué, births of Charles Silvestre Topin, June 16, 1807, 9e arr., and of Marie Louise Topin, September 17, 1813.

123. "Inventaire Veuve Topin," November 14, 1810, AN, Trubert, notary, MC/ET/XLII/748. The declaration was made by Silvestre Merys, peintre. The "musée des artistes" was a creation of the consulate; a retirement home and sales space for visual artists, created in a part of the former Sorbonne as a lodging for the crowd of artists who had been living in the Louvre, and were displaced when the government decided in 1801 that the books from the Bibliothèque nationale should be relocated to the Louvre. Louis-Pierre Baltard, *Paris et ses monuments, mesurés, dessinés et gravés par Baltard* (Paris, 1803), p. 40.

124. AM-A, marriage of Martial Allemand Lavigerie and Louise Vaslin, April 13, 1790, St. André, GG47/65.

125. ADPA, marriage of Etienne Allemand Lavigerie and Marie Montesquieu, January 1, 1807, Pau, marriages, 1807–1812, 2/272. Marie's father, Jean Montesquieu, was described as a shopkeeper; her mother, Marie Barrère, was identified on her death as a *marchande epicière*. Death of Marie Barrère, May 22, 1832, Pau, deaths, 1823–1832, 621/654.

126. Statement of November 16, 1810, Duhalde, notary in Bayonne, enclosed in "Par devant Duval notaire," March 16, 1811, ADC, 2E8751.

127. ADPA, death of Marie Montesquieu, wife of Etienne Allemand Lavigerie, March 3, 1837, Pau, deaths, 1833–1842, 311/667.

128. The dates of birth, marriage, and death of the grandchildren are given in appendix 1. The two grandsons of whom so little is known are Jean and Jean François Ferrand, two of the six sons of Gabriel Ferrand and Marie Adelaide Devuailly. Antoine Allemand Lavigerie, the former clerk, was a witness of the marriages of his brother and sister in Angoulême in the summer of 1801; by March 1811, when his father signed an agreement for maintenance with his surviving children, he was no longer alive. Marriages of Martial Allemand Lavigerie and Jeanne Lavigerie, AM-A, 1E23/69–70 and 82–83; "Par devant Duval notaire," March 16, 1811, ADC, 2E8751, and see below, chapter 7.

129. Baptism of Josephe Allemand Lavigerie, September 12, 1779, AMA, NDP, GG14/58.

130. ADPA, Bayonne, marriage of Joséphine Allemand Lavigerie and Joseph Alexandre César Ponsard, September 23, 1807, marriages, 1807–1823, 28/857; birth of Alexandre Etienne Marcellin Ponsard, April 20, 1809, births, year 12–1813, 427/820; and see birth of Camille Alexandre Allemand Lavigerie, 21 frim. 8 (December 12, 1799), ADSa, Le Mans, births, year 8, 59/122.

131. In 1813, they were witnesses to the birth of another daughter; Alexandre was identified, again, as "instituteur," and Pierre was "counselor of the paymaster of war." ADPA, Bayonne, births of Charlotte Ursule Allemand Lavigerie, October 23, 1810, and Adelaide Théonie Allemand Lavigerie, March 8, 1813, births, year 12–1813, 548/820 and 754/820.

132. ADPA, Bayonne-Saint Esprit (Landes), marriage of Léon Philippe Allemand Lavigerie and Hermine Louise Laure Latrilhe, November 3, 1824, marriages, 1814–1831, 248/1460.

133. ADPA, Bayonne, deaths of Joseph Alexandre César Ponsard, February 24, 1847, and Joséphine Allemand Lavigerie, April 29, 1855, deaths, 1842–1857, 237/884 and 646/884.

134. "Registres matricules des sous-officiers et hommes de troupe de l'infanterie de ligne (1802–1815)"; "Vélites placés à la suite du 2e régiment de chevau-légers lanciers de la garde impériale, 21 août 1811–29 mars 1814." SHD/GR YC 163/94/114, at http://www.memoiredeshommes .sga.defense.gouv.fr/.

135. Birth of Rose Calista Ferrand, 5e arr., September 12, 1833, death of Elisa Collet, 9e arr., April 5, 1836, AdP. ADSM, Montereau-Fault-Yonne, 1839–1841, marriage of Jean-Baptiste Ferrand and Anne Nicolas Thiriot, January 23, 1839, 47–48/356. Jean-Baptiste described himself as the widower of Elisa Collet; the record of her death, in the hôpital de l'Hôtel Dieu, describes her as single. AdP, DQ8, 785/2225, third bureau.

136. Death of Anne Nicolas Thiriot, October 21, 1861, ADSM, Montereau-Fault-Yonne, 1860–1862, 274/422; marriage of Rose Calista Ferrand and Ferdinand Amédée Esnault, a tinmaker, June 7, 1864, Montereau-Fault-Yonne, 1863–1865, 185–186/380. Jean-Baptiste was described as an artist and painter; Rose Calista's witnesses were a bookseller-compositor and an engraver.

137. AD Orne, Vimoutiers, deaths, 1863–1873, August 12, 1873, 527–528/543. Rose Calista Ferrand had a daughter, Isabelle Marthe Calista Esnault. Isabelle died at the age of twenty-five, in April 1891; she was described as a seamstress, living with her parents. Her mother, the last of Marie Aymard's great-grandchildren, died six days later. Vimoutiers, births, 1864–1873, April 24, 1865, 56/325; deaths, 1885–1892, April 14, 1891, 277/480, and April 20, 1891, 278/480. Vimoutiers, Table de successions et absences, 1882–1893, 58/176.

138. Etienne Ferrand was not unusual in his trajectory; of the 169 of the priests in the diocese who took the oath, 60 were eventually married. Blanchet, *Le clergé charentais pendant la révolution*, pp. 510, 555.

139. Record of house number 935, Section C, Château, in AM-A, "Contributions, matrices foncières," 1791.

140. See Jézéquel, *La révolution française à Angoulême*, pp. 90, 127, 162–163, and Jézéquel, "Charente," in *Grands notables du premier empire*, pp. 58–59.

141. Letter of August 30, 1789, from Léonard Robin to Abraham-François Robin, ADC, J700.

142. Clark, *The Sleepwalkers: How Europe Went to War in 1914*, p. xxvii.

143. Tocqueville, *L'ancien régime*, pp. 107, 291.

144. Louis de Bonald, "Sur les éloges historiques de MM. Séguier et de Malesherbes," in *Mélanges littéraires, politiques et philosophiques; par M. de Bonald*, 2 vols. (Paris, 1819), 1:217–241, p. 225; Jean-Etienne-Marie Portalis, *Eloge d'Antoine-Louis Séguier, Avocat-Général au Parlement de Paris* (Paris, 1806), pp. 66–67, 80, 82. See also Felicité de Lamennais, *Réflexions sur l'état de l'église en France pendant le dix-huitième siècle, et sur sa situation actuelle* (Paris, 1814), pp. 45–46, 78; and Emma Rothschild, *Economic Sentiments: Smith, Condorcet, and the Enlightenment* (Cambridge, MA, 2001).

145. Bonald, "Sur les éloges historiques de MM. Séguier et de Malesherbes," p. 224.

146. Tocqueville, *L'ancien régime*, p. 182.

147. Georges Lefebvre, introduction to Tocqueville, *L'ancien régime et la révolution* (Paris, 1952), 9–30, p. 21.

148. See Georges Lefebvre, "Les foules révolutionnaires" (1934), repr. in Lefebvre, *La grande peur*, 241–264, pp. 245–246; and Jacques Revel, "Présentation," in *La grande peur*, 7–23. On Marc Bloch's interest in the collective representations of social groups, and in the relationship between collective and individual consciousness, see Charles-Edmond Perrin, "L'oeuvre historique de Marc Bloch," *Revue Historique* 199, no. 2 (1948): 161–188, 184–187. On the ways in which the "mechanisms" of future change can be identified in the "configurations" of a particular historical time, see "Tentons l'experience," p. 1318; Jean-Yves Grenier and Bernard Lepetit, "L'expérience historique: à propos de C.-E. Labrousse," *Annales: Economies, Sociétés, Civilisations* 44, no. 6 (1989): 1337–1360; Jacques Revel, "Présentation," in Revel, *Un parcours critique: douze exercises d'histoire sociale* (Paris, 2006), 9–27, pp. 23–24, 26; and Revel, "L'institution et le social," in Lepetit, *Les formes de l'expérience*, 63–84.

149. The apothecary's shop on the Place du Mûrier, which was so rich in colonial commodities, changed owners three times, over the course of 1769–1775. It passed to Marguerite Delafond, the daughter of a master surgeon, on the death of her first husband, a master apothecary; to her second husband, also a master apothecary; to her, once again, on the death of her second husband; and then to her third husband—Paul Faveraud, the son, nephew, and brother of signatories of the marriage contract of 1764—who was himself admitted as a master apothecary in the town, following the wedding. Paul Faveraud was the son of Catherine Bouhier, the nephew of A. M. Bouhier, and the brother of M. Faveraud. Baptism of Marguerite Favereau, March 19, 1742, baptism of Paul Favereau, March 12, 1743, ADC, Larochefoucauld—Saint Cybard, 1737–1756, 64–65, 74/188. Marguerite Delafond was twenty-three when she married her first husband; thirty-eight when she married her second husband, who was aged twenty, and the former apprentice of her first husband; and forty-three when she married Paul Faveraud. ADC,

Montmoreau-Saint Cybard 1651–1792, 3E247/1, 103/244; AM-A, NDP, GG14/42, 43, 48, 52; "Receptions d'apothicaires de 1765 à 1787," *BSAHC*, ser. 2, 3 (1861): 174–175; and see Albertine Cadet, "Les apothicaires du temps passé à Angoulême," p. 55.

150. Giacomo Leopardi, "Dialogo di Tristano e di un amico" (1832), in Leopardi, *Tutte le opere*, ed. Walter Binni, 2 vols. (Milan, 1993), 1:184.

151. Tocqueville, *L'ancien régime*, p. 43.

152. Letter of May 11, 1788, from Léonard Robin to Abraham-François Robin, ADC, J700.

153. See above, chapter 5.

154. On historical experience, the choice of economic indicators, and historical causation, see Grenier and Lepetit, "L'expérience historique: A propos de C.-E. Labrousse."

155. Balzac, *Les illusions perdues*, pp. 30, 34. The father, in the novel, was a printing worker who was able to buy the printing press from the widow of the former owner. He received the contract to print the decrees of the revolutionary government, and, although himself illiterate, employed as his compositors first a nobleman from Marseille, in hiding in the town—"he composed, read, and corrected the decrees that imposed the penalty of death against citizens who hid the nobility"—and then a refractory clergyman. By 1802, the older Séchard was a rich man; in 1819 he owned the only newspaper publishing judicial announcements, and, like Abraham-François Robin before the revolution, had the printing business of the diocese.

156. Records of house numbers 632–639 (Beaulieu), on the north side of the Place du Mûrier, and house numbers 1002–995 (Château), on the south side, in "Contributions, matrices foncières," 1791, AM-A.

157. Entry for 10 therm. year 4, in Mercier, *Journal des maires d'Angoulême*, pp. 73–74.

158. Letter from Angoulême of the representative Roux-Fazillac, October 18, 1793, *AP*, 76:691. On executions in the Place du Mûrier, see George, *Topographie historique d'Angoulême*, p. 111.

159. Report of citizens Mignot, Menault, and Gerbaud, quoted in Blanchet, *Le clergé charentais pendant la révolution*, p. 218n2; Forgeaud, "La Place du Mûrier et ses environs," p. 41.

160. In the register of 1791, there are six substantial properties in the immediate vicinity of the Place du Mûrier listed as belonging to the Tiercelettes, and fifteen belonging to the Jacobins or Dominicans, whose "convent" formed the eastern end of the place. The Jacobins were the proprietors, too, of much of the Isle de la Cloche Verte, where so many of the signatories of the marriage contract lived in 1764. One of their properties, on the Place, appears in the annotated register as belonging to the nation (which is crossed out), as having been acquired (also crossed out), and eventually as the acquisition of the historian of the credit crisis of 1769, Léonard Robin's father; "M. Robin the former printer has become the proprietor." Records of house numbers 614, 615, 629, 630, 635 (Beaulieu) and 276–290 (St. Martial), in "Contributions, matrices foncières," 1791, AM-A.

161. Record of house number 1000 (Château) in "Contributions, matrices foncières," 1791, AM-A.

162. "Since property is an inviolable and sacred right, no one shall be deprived thereof except where public necessity, legally determined, shall clearly demand it." "Procès-verbal fixative des alignements des rues de la ville d'Angoulême," July 11, 1792 (manuscript copy), pp. 1, 12, 20, 25, 26, references to houses numbered 632, 761, and 1014; ADC, J112.

163. Declaration no. 332 of Citoyenne Veuve Ogerdias, 17 brum. 6, AM-A, Contributions personelles, 1798–1799. Baptism of Jeanne Françoise Ogerdias, who was born on April 2, 1767,

ANOM, Chandernagor, 1768, April 10, 1768; Blanchet, *Le clergé charentais pendant la révolution*, p. 425.

Chapter Seven. Modern Lives

1. "Brillat-Savarin," in *Oeuvres complètes de H. de Balzac*, 22 vols. (Paris, 1870–1879), 22: 231–238, p. 238. Brillat-Savarin was born in Belley, in the Ain, in 1755, and died in Paris in 1826.

2. Maurice Lévy-Leboyer, "La croissance économique en France au XIXe siècle," *Annales. Economies, Sociétés, Civilisations* 23, no. 4 (1968): 788–807. On continuity in the economic history of nineteenth-century France, see Patrick Verley, *Nouvelle histoire économique de la France contemporaine: l'industrialisation 1830–1914* (Paris, 2003); Fureix and Jarrige, *La modernité desenchantée*, chapter 2; and David Todd, *A Velvet Empire: French Informal Imperialism in the Nineteenth Century* (Princeton, NJ, 2021).

3. On the "uniform, constant, and uninterrupted," or "universal, continual, and uninterrupted" desire of bettering one's condition, see Smith, *The Wealth of Nations*, pp. 341–345.

4. On the "bad infinity" of "uninterrupted flitting over limits which it is powerless to sublate"—in this case, the information in genealogy websites that change over time—see Georg Wilhelm Friedrich Hegel, *The Science of Logic*, ed. and trans. George Di Giovanni (Cambridge, 2010), pp. 192–193, and Rothschild, *The Inner Life of Empires*.

5. On the "juxtaposition of generations within a limited space," in respect of the "evocation of distant memories," see Corbin, *Le monde retrouvé de Louis-François Pinagot*, p. 87. The pension of the five sisters on the Rempart du Midi was a place of juxtaposition in this sense; the sisters lived there, at one time or another, with three nieces, a nephew, four great-nieces, a great-nephew, and a great-great-nephew. In ending with the generation of the grandchildren's grandchildren, the inquiry ends substantially before the birth of any subsequent generation whose own children could be alive in the twenty-first century. On the privacy of the dead and their descendants, see Julia Stephens, "Picking the Pockets of the Dead: A Reflection on the Ethical Dilemmas of Writing Legal Lives" (Writing Legal Lives workshop, Harvard University, September 21, 2019).

6. Guyot de Fère, *Annuaire des artistes français* (Paris, 1832), p. 377; Firmin-Didot, *Annuaire générale du commerce et de l'industrie, de la magistrature et l'administration, ou almanach des 500,000 adresses* (Paris, 1842), pp. 1229–1230; *Annuaire générale du commerce* (1857), p. 1483.

7. *Almanach-Bottin du commerce de Paris* (Paris, 1854), pp. 193, 459, 1008.

8. Condorcet, *Esquisse d'un tableau historique des progres de l'esprit humain*, pp. 233–234, and see above, chapter 2.

9. Louis Baunard, *Le cardinal Lavigerie*, 2 vols. (Paris, 1896), 1:xii; Vicomte de Colleville, *Le cardinal Lavigerie* (Paris, 1905), p. 203.

10. The figure of the prefect, as the historian Alphonse Aulard wrote of the actions of the early prefects of the Charente, in 1800–1814, was of "a prudent and exact executor of ministerial orders, but no zealot of obedience. He never took any initiative, except in opposition to individual freedom." Aulard, "La centralisation napoléonienne: Les préfets," *La révolution française* 61 (July–December 1911): 322–342, pp. 324–325. On the building of the préfecture, and the new building on the modern Rue de la Préfecture, see "La préfecture au fil des siècles" (2015),

http://www.charente.gouv.fr/Services-de-l-Etat/Prefecture-et-sous-prefectures/Prefecture
-de-la-Charente/La-prefecture-au-fil-des-siecles.

11. On the reconstruction of the college, see "Le lycée Guez de Balzac d'hier et d'aujourd'hui: quelques repères historiques" (2009), http://etab.ac-poitiers.fr/lycee-guez-de-balzac/.

12. "Délibérations du conseil général de la commune, 1804–1815," AM-A, fols. 84v–85r. On the "effacement" of the "profanations" of the sixteenth and eighteenth centuries, see "Discours sur l'église cathédrale d'Angoulême" (January 17, 1869), in Antoine-Charles Cousseau, *Oeuvres historiques et archéologiques de Mgr Cousseau, ancien évêque d'Angoulême*, 2 vols. [vols. 1 and 3] (Angoulême, 1891–1892), 3:87, and see below, chapter 9.

13. The monument is described at http://www.culture.gouv.fr/public/mistral/merimee_fr ?ACTION=CHERCHER&FIELD_1=REF&VALUE_1=PA00104206; Odette Hamard, "Autour d'une Visite de Madame Royale Duchesse d'Angoulême," *BSAHC* (1970): 131–138.

14. See below, chapter 9, and, on the Abadies, *Entre archéologie et modernité: Paul Abadie architecte 1812–1884*, ed. Claude Laroche (Angoulême, 1984), and *Répertoire des architectes diocésains du XIXe siècle*, edited by Jean-Michel Leniaud, http://elec.enc.sorbonne.fr/architectes/.

15. "Abadie (Paul)," in Alexandre Du Bois and Charles Lucas, *Biographie universelle des architectes célèbres* (Paris, 1868), 14–21, p. 17.

16. AN, Prisons-Charente, F/16/997.

17. AM-A, "Prisons." Drawing dated 1816, no. 43; reports about Abadie's successive projects dated April 22, 1822, May 20, 1828, and February 7, 1832, nos. 43, 50, 55, and unnumbered. There were at least eleven different buildings used as prisons in Angoulême in the revolutionary period. Abadie's first proposal for a renovated prison, on the site of the present food hall, was made in June 1819, and the work was undertaken in 1821–1823, with multiple repairs in subsequent years. See Monique Bussac, "Brève histoire des prisons d'Angoulême," in Jean-François Buisson et al., *Châtelet-Les Halles: 1,000 ans d'histoire urbaine à Angoulême (Charente)* (Angoulême, 2005), pp. 34–39.

18. *Paul Abadie architecte 1812–1884*, pp. 36–37; on the modest cost of the (grandiose) Palais de Justice, see "Abadie (Paul)," *Biographie universelle*, pp. 18–19n5.

19. On the new prefecture, see http://www2.culture.gouv.fr/public/mistral/mersri_fr ?ACTION=CHERCHER&FIELD_1=REF&VALUE_1=PA00104226.

20. "Chronique," *L'écho du soir*, no. 128 (October 22, 1826): 4. *Ordonnance du roi portant création d'un collège royal de marine* (Brest, 1816); the new college was placed under the protection of the "admiral of France," who was the Duc d'Angoulême.

21. "Procès-verbal de prise de possession de l'apanage du comte d'Artois à Angoulême" (1774), ed. Léon Burias, *BSAHC*, ser. 8, 15 (1924): 133–146, p. 137; AM-A, Plan Directeur.

22. *Histoire d'Angoulême et de ses alentours*, ed. Pierre Dubourg-Noves (Toulouse, 1989), p. 292.

23. "Discours de M. L'évêque," July 4, 1852, in Cousseau, *Oeuvres*, 3:150.

24. Notice no PA16000017, base Mérimée; http://www2.culture.gouv.fr/public/mistral /mersri_fr?ACTION=CHERCHER&FIELD_1=REF&VALUE_1=PA16000017.

25. "Eglise St Martial," available at www.culture.gouv.fr/Wave/image/merimee/PROT /PA16000018_DOC.pdf.

On the white exterior of the new church, see Louis-Edouard May, *Consécration de l'église St-Martial, 1853*, Musée des Beaux-Arts d'Angoulême.

26. "When God effaces, it is to write anew." "Discours pour la bénédiction de la première pierre de l'église de St Ausone," December 4, 1864, in Cousseau, *Oeuvres*, 3:184.

27. "Discours sur l'église cathédrale d'Angoulême," January 17, 1869, letter to Prince Louis-Napoléon, 1852, in Cousseau, *Oeuvres*, 3:87, 417.

28. The date of death of François Laplanche was given as 3 prair. 10 (May 23, 1802), in Paris, in the marriage record of his daughter; marriage of Aristide Louis Marthe Soulas and Jeanne Julie Laplanche, 16 frim. 11 (December 7, 1802), AD Val de Marne, Villeneuve-Saint-Georges, 1802–1803, 32–33/75. Record of house number 51, Section D, St. Pierre, in "Contributions, matrices foncières," 1791, AM-A. Aristide Soulas died in 1850 in the village of Arnouville, described as a former controller of direct contributions; AD Val d'Oise, Arnouville, 1844–1853, 52/83. Jeanne Julie was still there, described as a "pensioner of the state," "aged fifty-nine," in 1851; she was seventy-six. AD Val d'Oise, Arnouville, recensement de population, 1851: 2/14. A. L. Soulas, "contrôleur des contributions directes," was the author of a volume published in 1820, *La levée des plans et l'arpentage rendus faciles; précédés de notions élémentaires de trigonométrie rectiligne, à l'usage des employés au cadastre de la France* (Paris, 1820). Their son, Achille Elie Joseph Soulas, who was born in 1800 and recognized on the occasion of their marriage, in 1802, was an inventor, who received a patent, in London in 1841, for "improvements in apparatus for regulating the flow of fluids": a feedback control device. AD Val de Marne, Villeneuve-Saint-Georges, 1799–1801, 36/140; *The Repertory of Patent Inventions*, vol. 15, January–June, 1841 (London, 1841), p. 256.

29. Birth of Adelaide Henriette Robin, February 16, 1793, AM-A, 1E1/19; Robin was described as an "agriculteur," and signed his name, "Robin Américain."

30. Death of Elizabeth Stubbs, December 28, 1824, ADC, Dirac, 1823–1832, 3E128/6, 35/260.

31. Angoulême, Etats des sections, 1827, ADC, 3 PPROV 16 3, properties 1094 and 1095, 297–298/336.

32. Death of François Abraham Robin, January 13, 1833, AM-A, 1E102/7.

33. Marriage of Pierre Félix and Françoise Mallat, July 27, 1820, AM-A, 1E59/79–80; Matrice des propriétés bâties et non bâties, Angoulême-Ville, 1835–1911, ADC, 3 PPROV 16 5, 66/183.

34. Marriages of Françoise Louise Javote Félix and Louis Emery, September 13, 1821; Louise Charlotte Léontine Emery and Michel Guichard, June 30, 1841; Marie Marthe Dumergue and Joseph Bargeas, December 16, 1820; and Thérèse Dumergue and Jean-Baptiste Bargeas, December 16, 1820; AM-A, 1E62/99–100, 1E125/62, 1E59/128–130.

35. Dénombrement de la population, Etat nominatif, Angoulême 1846, ADC, 6M84, 283/646; death of Louis Félix, October 3, 1851, AM-A, 1E157/89; his age was given incorrectly as eighty-two.

36. Death of Catherine Raby, June 1, 1812, AM-A, 1E45/156; Etats des sections, Angoulême, 1827, ADC, 3 PPROV 16 3, properties 17, 20, 80, 85, 86, 87, 219, and 306; 185, 262, 264, 265, 269, 272/336.

37. Death of Jean Lecler, August 21, 1848, AM-A, 1E148/69.

38. Marriage of Marguerite Aubert and Jean Noel Bonniceau, April 5, 1807, AM-A, 1E40/80–81.

39. Death of Marguerite Durousseau, widow of Jean Joubert, July 6, 1809, AM-A, 1E42/208.

40. Blanchet, the historian of the church in revolutionary Charente, gave her address as "sise Rue du Palais," which was the address of a house belonging to Marguerite's brother Théodore Aubert, by then a merchant in Paris. Blanchet, *Le clergé charentais pendant la Révolution*, p. 157n1;

ADC, Etats des sections, Angoulême, 1827, 3 PPROV 16 3, 288/336; Matrice des propriétés bâties et non bâties, 1835–1911, 3 PPROV 16 5, 73/183; Quignon, "Notices historiques et anecdotiques," 8:334, ADC, J75.

41. Death of Marguerite Aubert, April 1, 1842, ADC, Rouillac 1833–1845, 3E310/8, 413/541.

42. Léonard Robin died in Burgundy on 17 mess. 10 (July 6, 1802); AD Yonne, Paron, 2E288/9, year 10–1825, 6/134. "Inventaire après le décès du citoyen Robin, 21 thermidor an 10," Jean Petit, notary, AN, MC/ET/CX/586.

43. "The condition of the rights of children born out of wedlock whose fathers were still alive at the time of the law of 12 brumaire 2, the species to which the said citizen Louis Léonard Robin belongs, being indeterminate, they oppose the pretensions of the latter," the brothers declared; the parties agreed to proceed to an inventory. "Inventaire apres le décès du citoyen Robin," AN, MC/ET/CX/586. On the inheritance of natural children, see Jean-Louis Halpérin, "Le droit privé de la Révolution: héritage législatif et héritage idéologique," *Annales historiques de la Révolution française*, no. 328 (2002): 135–151.

44. "Inventaire apres le décès du citoyen Robin," AN, MC/ET/CX/586.

45. *Réclamations pour le sieur Charles-Marie Canalès-Oglou*, pp. 11–12, 42–43.

46. J.-B. Sirey, *Jurisprudence de la cour de cassation, an XIV–1806* (Paris, n.d.), 307–312, p. 308.

47. Sirey, *Jurisprudence de la cour de cassation*, pp. 311–312.

48. Death of Louis Léonard Robin, January 18, 1825, AD Yonne, Paron, 2E288/9, year 10–1825, 129–130/134; Roy, "Léonard Robin," pp. 104–105. Death of Marie Elisabeth Emelie Aubourg, May 24, 1843, 12e arr.; AdP, état civil reconstitué. Death of Marie Robin, Angoulême, March 27, 1837; AM-A, 1E114/31. Baptism of Jean Abraham François Robin, St. André, March 19, 1785, GG46/149–150; Marie Robin was identified as a paternal cousin.

49. Letter of 17 flor. 2 (May 6, 1794) from Citoyen Muron to the prosecutor Fouquier Tinville, AN, Tribunaux révolutionnaires et hautes cours du XIXe siècle, W//132, no. 70; Neil Schaeffer, *The Marquis de Sade: A Life* (Cambridge, MA, 2000), pp. 447–450.

50. Letters of 17 flor. 2 and 3 prair. 2 (May 22, 1794) from Muron to Fouquier Tinville, AN, W//132, no. 70, W//152, no. 157.

51. Marie-Brigitte-Scholastique Virol, Acte de notoriété, October 18 and October 25, 1810, and "Inventaire," October 22, 1810, Louis Athanaze Rendu, notary, AN, MC/ET/CVIII/731.

52. "Inventaire," October 22, 1810, AN, MC/ET/CVIII/731.

53. AM-A, baptisms of Antoine, Noel, and Marie Marguerite Virol, January 15, 1732, November 22, 1736, and May 24, 1740, NDP, GG13/111, 119, 125, and of Thibault Hypolite Virol, August 23, 1775, St. Paul, GG90/89.

54. Death of Gabriel Ferrand, December 20, 1816, AM-A, 1E52/426.

55. "Séance du mercredi 8 decembre 1909," *BSAHC*, ser. 8, 1 (1910): xliv.

56. I am most grateful to M. Florent Gaillard for his search for the portrait in the holdings of the Société archéologique et historique de la Charente. Gustave Paillé was one of the successors of Silvestre Topin as professor of design in the college of Angoulême, and his son, Maurice, was "a very distinguished artist"; "it is regrettable," Emile Biais wrote in the catalog of the Angoulême museum, "that there should be no works at all by these intelligent and well-appreciated painters." Emile Biais, *Catalogue du musée d'Angoulême: peintures, sculptures, estampes* (Angoulême, 1884), p. 20n1.

57. See above, chapter 6.

58. Death of Vincent Gabriel Ferrand, February 14, 1825, AD Loiret, Beaugency, deaths, 1821–1832, 131/414; birth of Pierre Lucien Eugène Ferrand, January 6, 1823, AD Loiret, Beaugency, births, 1821–1826, 88/252; marriage of Pierre Lucien Eugène Ferrand and Eugénie Clementine Lormeau, May 22, 1852, AD Hauts de Seine, Montrouge, marriages, 1852, 19–20/57; death of Pierre Lucien Eugène Ferrand, May 28, 1881, AdP, 3e. arr., act no. 838; and on the "cabinet de lecture" of "Mme. Veuve Ferrand," *La presse*, no. 5057, May 9, 1850.

59. Birth of Eugène Gabriel Ferrand, August 24, 1884, AdP, 4e arr., act no. 2183; birth of Juliette Marie Ferrand, February 25, 1886, 10e arr., act no. 980; marriage of Louis Gabriel Ferrand and Marie Emma Mélanie Manchuette, June 2, 1888, 3e arr., act no. 413; death of Louis Gabriel Ferrand, April 23, 1907, 10e arr., act no. 2169.

60. Mort pour la France, Eugène Gabriel Ferrand, May 5, 1916, https://www .memoiredeshommes.sga.defense.gouv.fr.

61. Marriage of Jean Dinochau and Stéphanie Ferrand, December 9, 1820, AD Loiret, Beaugency, marriages, 1810–1820, 290–291/302.

62. *Almanach-Bottin du commerce de Paris* (Paris, 1854), pp. 193, 459, 1008.

63. In the critic Louis Etienne's description of Manet's *Déjeuner sur l'herbe* in 1863, "a bréda of some sort, as naked as can be, lounges brazenly between two dandies, also as clothed as can be." Louis Etienne, *Le jury et les exposants: salon des refusés* (Paris, 1863), p. 30; and see Pierre Bourdieu, *Manet: une révolution symbolique* (Paris, 2013), p. 629.

64. Edmond de Goncourt, *Journal des Goncourt: mémoires de la vie littéraire*, 9 vols. (Paris, 1851–1896), 1:126, 7:256.

65. Among the many reminiscences of the restaurant on the corner of the Rue Bréda and the Rue Navarin, see Etienne Carjat, "Le Saint-Charles, ou une soirée chez Dinochau," *Le Figaro*, no. 423 (March 6, 1859): 3–5; "Un diner chez Dinochau," in Louis Lemercier de Neuville, *Les tourniquets: revue de l'année 1861* (Paris, 1862), pp. 41–50; Alfred Delvau, "Le cabaret Dinochau," in *Histoire anecdotique des cafés et cabarets de Paris* (Paris, 1862), pp. 15–21; "Courrier de Paris," *Le monde illustré*, no. 766 (December 16, 1871): 37; "Chronique de Paris," *Le voleur illustré: cabinet de lecture universel*, December 22, 1871, pp. 1069–1070; Firmin Maillard, "Les derniers bohèmes, I" in *La Renaissance littéraire et artistique*, year 1, no. 31 (November 23, 1872): 245–246; Firmin Maillard, *La cité des intellectuels: scènes cruelles et plaisantes de la vie littéraire des gens de lettres au XIXe siècle* (Paris, 1905), pp. 286–289; "L'entresol de Dinochau: La Bohème en 1860," in Louis Lemercier de Neuville, *Souvenirs d'un montreur de marionnettes* (Paris, 1911), pp. 119–169; Pierre Dufay, "Jean-Edouard Dinochau restaurateur des lettres," *Mercure de France* 281, no. 951 (February 1, 1938): 489–514. On the literary cabarets of Paris, see Joëlle Bonnin-Ponnier, "Les lieux de sociabilité de la bohème," *Cahiers Edmond et Jules de Goncourt*, no. 14 (2007): 103–124, Gilbert Beaugé, "L'autopsie d'un acte manqué: l'hommage à Delacroix d'Henri Fantin-Latour," https://halshs .archives-ouvertes.fr/halshs-00356960, Bourdieu, *Manet: une révolution symbolique*, p. 669.

66. Firmin Maillard, "Les derniers bohèmes," p. 246.

67. "Dinochau," in Pierre Larousse, *Grand dictionnaire universel du XIXe siècle*, vol. 6 (Paris, 1870), p. 870.

68. On Edouard Dinochau as "restaurateur des lettres," see Delvau, *Histoire anecdotique*, p. 20; on Stéphanie as "austere," *Journal des Goncourt*, 7:257; on her cooking, "Chronique de Paris," *Le voleur illustré*, December 22, 1871, p. 1069; and on the account books, Lemercier de Neuville, *Souvenirs*, p. 122.

69. *Journal des Goncourt*, 7:256, 257.

70. Lemercier de Neuville, *Souvenirs*, p. 124, Dufay, "Jean-Edouard Dinochau restaurateur des lettres," p. 494, "J.-E. Dinochau," in Lemercier de Neuville, *Souvenirs*, p. [121]. There is another caricature of him, also in white voluminous shirtsleeves and a black waistcoat, carrying a bottle of champagne, against the background of the extremely crowded dining room, in the "Diner chez Dinochau" of 1862; Lemercier de Neuville, *Les tourniquets*, p. 48.

71. Death of Stéphanie Ferrand, August 14, 1870, AdP, 9e arr., act no. 1250.

72. *La liberté*, June 9, 1871.

73. Tribunal de commerce de la Seine, "Dissolutions," *Journal officiel de la République française*, November 7, 1871, p. 4344.

74. Death of Edouard Dinochau, December 9, 1871, AdP, 10e arr., act no. 8530.

75. Tribunal de commerce de la Seine, "Qualifications de faillite," *La liberté*, July 16, 1872.

76. Cahier de charges, requête de M. Normand, syndic de la faillite Dinochau, October 19, 1872, Paul Rigault, notary, AN, MC/ET/LXXXVI/1220.

77. *La liberté*, October 21, 1872; *Le Figaro*, October 20, 1872.

78. "Etat des créances," in Cahier de charges, Rigault, AN, MC/ET/LXXXVI/1220.

79. *Le Figaro*, October 21, 1872; "Adjudication au profit de M. de Villemessant," in Cahier de charges, AN, MC/ET/LXXXVI/1220.

80. Death of Alfred Charles Dinochau, AD Val de Marne, Le Kremlin-Bicêtre, February 22, 1901, 32/179.

81. Death of Elizabeth Boutoute, 5e arr., June 13, 1830; death of Jean-Baptiste Ferrand, 9e arr., November 16, 1831; AdP, état civil reconstitué. The old fifth arrondissement corresponded to the modern second and tenth, and the ninth to the modern fourth and first. The date and location of Jean-Baptiste's death was confirmed in the record of his youngest son's second marriage; ADSM, Montereau-Fault-Yonne, 1839–1841, marriage of Jean-Baptiste Ferrand and Anne Nicolas Thiriot, January 23, 1839, 47–48/356.

82. Dossier "Ferrand (Jn. Bte.)," AN, F/12/2795; certification of 4 vend. 14 (September 26, 1805); letters of December 12, 1822, and October 10, 1824, and petition received February 24, 1831.

83. Dossier "Ferrand, Françoise, Ve. Brébion," AN, F/12/2795; letter of September 26, 1848, from Françoise Ferrand; letter of November 9, 1859, from Françoise Ferrand; letter of April 5, 1860, from C. Brébion Ve. Collet; letter of August 10, 1860, providing a grant of five hundred livres to Mme. Ve. Collet. There is no evidence in the dossier, after 1814, of Françoise's other two children, Jean-Baptiste Adolphe and Joséphine Louisa.

84. Death of Françoise Ferrand, aged eighty-three, living Rue Myrha, no. 17, March 26, 1860, AdP, 18e arr., act no. 594.

85. Dossier "Ferrand, Françoise, Ve. Brébion," AN, F/12/2795; letter of April 5, 1860, from C. Brébion Ve. Collet.

86. Dossier "Brébion Collet (veuve)," AN, F/12/2757; letters of March 12, 1866, March 12, 1870, January 16, 1873, September 17, 1774, March 9, 1875, March 8, 1876, and December 23, 1876.

87. AdP, death of Marie Thérèse Clara Brébion, aged eighty-two, living Rue Labat, 49, April 23, 1889, 18e arr., act no. 1454. Clara's date of birth was given as January 29, 1804, in her dossier for extraordinary relief; dossier "Brébion Collet (veuve)," AN, F/12/2757. Clara

Brébion's husband, Pierre Rose Collet, died on October 25, 1843, in the (old) seventh arrondissement (the modern third and fourth.) AdP, état civil reconstitué, notice 1220.

88. Marriage of Rosalie Marie Collet, couturière, and Raphael Victor Bossard, métreur, September 21, 1861, AfP, 18e arr., act no. 678.

89. This was an extraordinarily high mortality rate, in a city where average infant mortality at the time was around one in five; Etienne van der Walle and Samuel H. Preston, "Mortalité de l'enfance au XIXe siècle à Paris et dans le département de la Seine," *Population* 29, no. 1 (1974): 89–102. The Bossards were a family of the center of Paris, and all the births and deaths were within the city. Birth of Louis Victor Bossard, March 3, 1861, AdP, 18e arr., act no. 650; death of Louis Victor Bossard, April 22, 1861, AdP, 18e arr., act no. 802; birth of Jeanne Bossard, January 25, 1862, 18e arr., act no. 198; death of Jeanne Bossard, May 13, 1866, 18e arr., act no. 1131; birth of Augustine Clara Bossard, October 11, 1865, 18e arr., act no. 3275; death of Augustine Clara Bossard, November 13, 1865, 18e arr., act no. 3390; birth of Francisque Joseph Victor Bossard, May 23, 1868, 18e arr., act no. 1727; birth of Jeanne Bossard, October 29, 1869, 18e arr., act no. 3638; death of Jeanne Bossard, December 19, 1869, 18e arr., act no. 3005; birth of Joséphine Fernande Bossard, July 1, 1871, 18e arr., act no. 2184; death of Joséphine Bossard, May 16, 1878, 7e arr., act no. 1071; birth of Berthe and Charles Bossard, January 10, 1876, 18e arr., acts no. 103 and 104; death of Berthe Bossard, January 15, 1876, 18e arr., act no. 138; death of Charles Bossard, February 2, 1876, 18e arr., act no. 286; birth of Henri Léon Bossard, August 31, 1877, 7e arr., act no. 1203; death of Henri Léon Bossard, August 1, 1885, 18e arr., act no. 2710; birth of Charles Albert Bossard, July 27, 1880, 18e arr., act no. 2658; death of Charles Albert Bossard, August 24, 1880, 18e arr., act no. 2891; death of Rosalie Marie Collet, October 8, 1890, 18e arr., act no. 3617. Francisque Joseph Victor Bossard, Rosalie's fourth child, and the only one to survive childhood, died in the ninth arrondissement of Paris on April 15, 1925; 9e arr., act no. 520.

90. Marriage of Francisque Joseph Victor Bossard, lithographer, and Marie Madeleine Andres, laundress, April 25, 1891, AdP, 18e arr., act no. 578; the family were listed as living at 42, Rue de la Goutte d'Or when their daughter Germaine Marguerite was born in 1894, and at 50, Rue de la Goutte d'Or when their son Louis Roger Henri was born in 1904; AdP, 18e arr., 1894, act no. 5098; 1904, act no. 3368.

91. Marriage of Louise Jeanne Collet and Jérôme Lerouge, February 12, 1887, AdP, 11e arr., act no. 221; death of Louise Jeanne Collet, August 3, 1899, 13e arr., act no. 1850; death of Françoise Marie Rosalie Collet, October 8, 1890, 18e arr., act no. 3617. Louise Jeanne Collet died in the Broca hospital; Jérôme Lerouge died in 1901 in the Bicêtre hospital, described as the widower of Jeanne Louise Collet; AD Val de Marne, Le Kremlin-Bicêtre, November 20, 1901, 153/179. On the regulation of *marchands ambulants* over the period before and after Louise's death, see Claire Zalc, *Melting Shops: une histoire des commerçants étrangers en France* (Paris, 2010), pp. 42–47.

92. Property 1314, Rempart du Midi, ADC, Etats des sections, Angoulême, 1827–1961, 3 PPROV 16 3, 305/336.

93. Agreement between Etienne Allemand Lavigerie, Jeanne, Jeanne Julie, Jeanne Henriette, Françoise, and Louise Allemand Lavigerie, Jean Théodore Henry l'aîné, and Isaac Damade, "Par devant Duval notaire," March 16, 1811, ADC, 2E8751.

94. "Etat estimatif des meubles et effets," March 16, 1811, enclosed in agreement between Etienne Allemand Lavigerie and his children, March 16, 1811, ADC, 2E8751; Record of house number 935, Section C, Château, in AM-A, "Contributions, matrices foncières," 1791.

95. Procuration to Jean-Théodore Henry l'aîné, November 16, 1810, Duhalde notary, Bayonne, and procuration to Isaac Damade, December 15, 1810, Jean Louis Pierre, notary, Bar-sur-Ornain, enclosed in agreement between Etienne Allemand Lavigerie and his children, March 16, 1811, ADC, Duval notary, 2E8751. Jean-Théodore Henry was seventy-six at the time, and was the father of Pierre Auguste Henry, the witness at both Pierre's and Martial Allemand Lavigerie's marriages. Baptism of Pierre Auguste Henry, March 11, 1770, St. Jacques, AM-A, GG130/173–174; death of Jean-Théodore Henry, November 2, 1818, 1E54/354–355. Isaac Damade, described as a proprietor, was seventy at the time. Death of Isaac Damade, January 16, 1823, 1E71/5.

96. Agreement between Etienne Allemand Lavigerie and his children, March 16, 1811, ADC, 2E8751.

97. Declaration of Jeanne Lavigerie *aînée*, entry 493, 29 mess. 7, AM-A, "Registre pour recevoir les déclarations des citoyens domiciliés dans cette commune."

98. Record of house number 856, Section C, Château, in AM-A, "Contributions, matrices foncières," 1791. The taxable value of the house was estimated as 450 francs, and the area as 266 "toises carrées," or 1,010 square meters. The family house in the same section, was estimated, by contrast, at 100 francs, and 25 toises carrées. House number 935, Section C, Château.

99. Contract for the sale of a house on the Rempart du Midi by Philippe Pierre Lambert to Jeanne, Jeanne Julie, Jeanne Henriette, Françoise, and Louise Mélanie, March 26, 1811, Duval, ADC, 2E8751. Lambert appeared in the same sumptuary register for 1799 as Jeanne *aînée*, and declared a female servant, having been "without a domestic since the revolution"; entry 387, 26 mess. 7, AM-A, "Registre pour recevoir les déclarations des citoyens domiciliés dans cette commune." On Lambert's periods as mayor, see https://maam.angouleme.fr/archives-municipales /histoire-dangouleme/les-maires-dangouleme/. Lambert had acquired the house by an "act of exchange" of 10 pluv. 13 (January 13, 1805), with Alexandre René Gabriel Terrasson Montleau. On Terrasson as a deputy under the restoration, see http://www2.assemblee-nationale.fr /sycomore/fiche/(num_dept)/17218, and on his efforts to be removed from the list of émigrés, on the grounds that he had left France only in order to pursue his business studies in a commercial house in Hamburg, see his extensive file in the records of the "Police générale: les émigrés de la révolution," AN, F/7/4991/2/dossier 20.

100. ADC, Archives de l'enregistrement, Case no. 390, "Allemand Lavigerie, Jeanne, institutrice à Angoulême," March 28, 1811, 4QPROV 1/7777.

101. ADC, Case no. 390, "Allemand Lavigerie, Jeanne, institutrice à Angoulême," September 24, 1817, 4QPROV 1/7777; sale contract of March 26, 1811, Duval, ADC, 8751.

102. ADC, Case no. 320, "Allemand Lavigerie, Etienne and Françoise Ferrand," 4QPROV 1/7705.

103. Hoffman, Postel-Vinay, and Rosenthal, *Dark Matter Credit*, chapter 3. There was a recovery in the quantity of credit, and a change in the composition of credit, toward new and different financial instruments, and also toward different borrowers, especially those, like the sisters' father, who bought the urban property of expropriated landlords.

104. Transcription of agreement between Jeanne, Jeanne Henriette, Françoise, and Louise Mélanie Allemand Lavigerie, Charlotte-Ursule Allemand Lavigerie, and Françoise Méloé Silvestre Topin, November 13, 1839, in ADC, 4QPROV 1/2932.

105. Will of Jeanne Allemand Lavigerie, dated June 12, 1850, and registered on July 9, 1860, ADC, Goyaud, notary, 2E10292.

106. Properties 1311 and 1315, Rempart du Midi, ADC, Etats des sections, Angoulême, 1827–1961, 3 PPROV 16 3, 305/336.

107. Property no. 1311, ADC, Matrice des propriétés bâties et non bâties, 1835–1911, 3 PPROV 16 5, 81/183.

108. Property no. 1315, ADC, Matrice des propriétés bâties et non bâties, 1835–1911, 3 PPROV 16 5, 87/183. Camille also owned a house on the Rue de l'Arsenal, no. 837, 124/183.

109. Property no. 1347, ADC, Matrice des propriétés bâties et non bâties, 1874–1892, 3 PPROV 16 8, fol. 1165, 14/314. Pierre Auguste Henry-Lacourade was listed as living on the Rempart du Midi in 1861; ADC, état nominatif, Angoulême, 1861, 194/765.

110. AM-A, "Ecoles Privées," 1849.

111. Charlotte-Ursule Lavigerie was described as living in Angoulême on her marriage in 1836; Françoise Méloé Allemand Lavigerie, described as a native of Bayonne, was living on the Rempart du Midi when she died in 1839; Françoise Topin, too, was described as living in Angoulême when she married in the Aube in 1830. Louise Lavigerie, the daughter of Martial's son Léon Philippe, was living with her great-aunts on the Rempart du Midi when she was married in 1855; Marie Lacourade, the daughter of Charlotte-Ursule, was living with her father in his own house on the ramparts (no. 1347) when she was married in 1858; Marie Françoise, the daughter of Camille and Françoise, was living with her parents in their house next to the pension (no. 1315) when she was married in 1851. Berthe Louise Topin/Taupin was listed as living in the pension on the Rempart du Midi in the census of 1861. AM-A, 1E110/73–74, 1E120/26, 1E156/16, 1E169/31–32, 1E178/109; marriage of Camille Alexandre Allemand Lavigerie and Françoise Méloé Topin, October 4, 1830, AD Aube [hereafter ADAu], Ville-sous-la-Ferté, marriages, 1825–1860, 4E426/10, 53–54/289; ADC, état nominatif, Angoulême, 1861, 192/765.

112. Death of Laurent Silvestre Topin, March 29, 1850, AM-A, 1E185/28.

113. The iteration of names and variations was perplexing, in turn, for the clerks of the civil registers of Angoulême. AM-A, GG25/26, 1E25/31, and see below, on the successive records of (Françoise) Adelaide (Méloé) Allemand Lavigerie and Charlotte (Alida) Ursule (Adelaide) Allemand Lavigerie.

114. Entry for 21 pluv. 13, *Journal des maires d'Angoulême*, pp. 197–198.

115. "Procuration," December 15, 1810, Jean Louis Pierre, Bar-sur-Ornain, enclosed in agreement between Etienne Allemand Lavigerie and his children, March 16, 1811, ADC, 2E8751.

116. "Sur l'extirpation de la mendicité," July 5, 1808, in *Corps du droit français, ou Recueil complet des lois, décrets, ordonnances*, ed. C.-M. Galisset, 14 vols. (Paris, 1828–1853), 2:819–820.

117. ADAu, Fonds de la maison centrale de Clairvaux, 2Y1–2Y10. Silvestre prepared an estimate of the costs of the building work as early as January 1817, and his expenses in moving to Clairvaux were covered later that year; memoranda of January 26, 1817, and December 1817, 2Y3, 289/475, 310/275. Charles-Silvestre Topin was nominated as a student pensioner of the Royal Naval College in Angoulême on March 6, 1822; M. Bajot, *Annales maritimes et coloniales*, 1822, pt. 1 (Paris, 1822), p. 294. "Silvestre fils" appears in the records of the Clairvaux prison from April 1833; 2Y10, 575, 578/642. When he was married, also in April 1833, his parents were described as living in Angoulême; ADAu, Brienne-le-Château, 4E06420, 3–5/227.

118. Memorandum of August 16, 1823, about the "bains des entrans," and of June 5, 1831, about the "prison des turbulens," ADAu, Fonds Clairvaux, 2Y5, 149/764, 2Y9, 488–490/527.

119. Letter from Jean-Baptiste Gaide, director of the prison, to the Prefect of the Aube, August 17, 1820, ADAu, Fonds Clairvaux, 2Y4, 88–91/764, and see Laurent Veyssière, "La tombe découverte à l'abbaye de Clairvaux 1820 est-elle celle de Guillaume de Joinville archevêque de Reims († 1226)?" *Bibliothèque de l'Ecole des chartes* 164, no. 1 (2006): 5–41, pp. 15–17.

120. ADAu, Ville-sous-la-Ferté, deaths, 1830–1837, 4E42614, 2–32/248. Of the 173 deaths recorded in the village in 1830, 143 were of prisoners: 24 women and 119 men.

121. Victor Hugo, *Claude Gueux* (Paris, 1834), and see http://www.victorhugo2002.culture .fr/culture/celebrations/hugo/fr/index1.html.

122. In the story, it is the director who is killed. Letter from Jean-Baptiste Gaide to the prefect of the Aube, April 16, 1830, ADAu, Fonds Clairvaux, 2Y8, 623–628/698; death of Pierre Etienne Delaselle, November 9, 1831, ADAu, Ville-sous-la-Ferté, deaths, 1830–1837, 4E426/14, 59/248.

123. Marriage of Camille Alexandre Allemand Lavigerie and Françoise Méloé Topin, October 4, 1830, ADAu, Ville-sous-la-Ferté, marriages, 1825–1860, 4E426/10, 53–54/289. The witnesses were Jean-Baptiste Gaide, the director of the prison and the signatory of so many records of the deaths of prisoners; Ferdinand Jolain, the contractor; Marc-Antoine Ragon, the registrar; and Nicholas Thevenin, the inspector.

Chapter Eight. Histories of Economic Life

1. On the fluctuations that are left out of so much of the history of long-term economic growth, and the long-term and the "median" as exactly the conditions about which individuals never have information, and can never know, see Grenier and Lepetit, "L'expérience historique: à propos de C.-E. Labrousse."

2. François Simiand, *Le salaire, l'évolution sociale et la monnaie*, 3 vols. (Paris, 1932), 2:117.

3. The "liberal professions"—which included soldiers, sailors, government employees, teachers, doctors, pharmacists, and the clergy—accounted for about one million of the employed population of France in the mid-nineteenth century, according to contemporary estimates, and domestic service for about two million. See Maurice Block, *Statistique de la France*, 2nd ed., 2 vols. (Paris, 1875), 1:55–57. The classification of occupations changed from one census to the next, as Block pointed out, and the census of 1872, in particular, left much to be desired; "hotel keepers, gravediggers, and acrobats" could have been included in "industry," in his view, rather than in "miscellaneous professions," and porters need not have been included with rentiers and proprietors in the category of "persons living exclusively from their revenues"; p. 57.

4. These were public registers of manufactures, and in particular of textile manufacturing. Smith, *The Wealth of Nations*, p. 103.

5. On scales and timescales, see *Jeux d'échelles*, ed. Revel. Among the studies of micro-macro history since the 1990s, Rosental's *Les sentiers invisibles* is a contribution, among other things, to the economic history of the nineteenth century; Dennison's *The Institutional Framework of Russian Serfdom* uses the individual scale of economic lives in the (medium) scale of a particular serf estate to illuminate the insitutional basis of serfdom in Russia, and how it changed over time; Zalc's *Melting Shops* combines a (micro)history of the individual lives of shopkeepers with the (medium-scale) history of a trade, and the large-scale history of citizens and noncitizens in twentieth-century France.

6. Marriage of Martial Allemand Lavigerie and Louise Vaslin, April 13, 1790, St. André, AM-A, GG47/64–65; baptism of Françoise Philippine Lavigerie, May 27, 1792, St. Pierre, GG25/26.

7. ADPA, Bayonne, births, years 6–12, 775/875; year 12–1813, 224/820; 1826–1837, 52–53/904.

8. Death of Elisabeth Allemand Lavigerie, May 4, 1838, ADPA, Bayonne, 1826–1841, 620/818; death of Joseph Alexandre César Ponsard, February 24, 1847, Bayonne, 1842–1857, 237/883.

9. Birth of Alexandre Etienne Marcellin Ponsard, April 20, 1809, ADPA, Bayonne, year 12–1813, 427/820; births of Charlotte Ursule Allemand Lavigerie, October 23, 1810, and Adelaide Théonie Allemand Lavigerie, March 8, 1813, 548/820 and 754/820.

10. Birth of Claude Frédéric Bastiat, 11 mess. 9 (June 30, 1801), ADPA, Bayonne, years 6–12, 518/875; death of Marie Julie Frechou, Bastiat's mother, May 27, 1808, year 9–1810, 592/854. The Bastiat family lived at 27, Rue Pont-Majour, and the Allemand Lavigerie family at 16, Rue Pont-Majour. Births of Pierre Jules, Victor Mamert, Charlotte Ursule, and Adelaide Théonie Allemand Lavigerie, year 12–1813, 224, 336, 548, 754/820.

11. Death of Pierre Jean Audouin, May 11, 1808; ADPA, Bayonne, year 9–1810, 589/854; "Je persiste à croire que je mériterais moi-même la mort, si je ne la demandais pour le tyran. Je vote pour la mort." January 16–17, 1793, *AP*, 57:374; http://www2.assemblee-nationale.fr/sycomore /fiche/(num_dept)/12891. Birth of Pierre Jules Edouard, November 11, 1806, year 12–1813, 224/820; marriage of Joséphine Allemand Lavigerie and Joseph Alexandre César Ponsard, September 23, 1807, 1807–1823, 28/857.

12. Josette Pontet, "La Société des Amis de la Constitution de Bayonne (juillet 1790–juillet 1793)," *Annales du Midi* 106, no. 208 (1994): 425–449. The three streets where the society was particularly well represented were the Rue des Basques, Rue Pont-Majour (where Martial lived for most of his years in Bayonne), and Rue Bourgneuf, where he was living with his daughter Elisabeth when she died in 1838 (p. 431). Pierre Jean Audouin also lived on the Rue Pont-Majour, as did the two signatories of the record of his death in 1808—Jean Duverdier and Louis Peche—who were signatories of the record of the birth of Martial's son Victor in the same year; ADPA, Bayonne, births, year 12–1813, 336/820, deaths, year 9–1810, 589/854. Audouin's activities as vice-consul, conferring in Rome with his colleagues from Malta, Tripoli, Constantinople, and Corfu, are noted in *Journal politique de l'Europe*, no. 330 (November 22, 1798): [3].

13. The population of Angoulême was around fifteen thousand in 1806, and the population of Bayonne around fourteen thousand. See http://cassini.ehess.fr/cassini/fr/html/fiche.php?select _resultat=853 and http://cassini.ehess.fr/cassini/fr/html/fiche.php?select_resultat=2448.

14. As Martial's grandson Charles Martial Allemand Lavigerie told a Spanish naval officer, many years later, "my entire childhood was spent near the frontiers of Spain, in the shadows of the mountains and by the shores of the waves that separate our two countries." Baunard, *Lavigerie*, 2:467–468.

15. The Hôtel de Ville of Bayonne, built in 1838–1843, has a plaque identifying its original function as "mairie, hôtel de douanes et théatre."

16. *Courrier de Bayonne et de la peninsule: journal politique, commercial, litteraire et maritime* 1829, no. 1 (October 8, 1829): 1, facsimile reprint in J.-B. Daranatz, *Le centenaire du « Courrier de Bayonne »* (Bayonne, 1930), p. 33; and see Jean Crouzet, *Bayonne entre l'équerre et le compas, 1815–1852* (Bayonne, 1986), p. 92.

17. *Courrier de Bayonne et de la peninsule* 1830, no. 48 (March 16, 1830): 3–4; BNF, FRBNF32750179.

18. Crouzet, *Bayonne entre l'équerre et le compas, 1815–1852*, p. 94.

19. Guyot de Fère, *Annuaire des artistes français*, p. 377; Guyot de Fère, *Annuaire des artistes français, statistique des beaux-arts en France* (Paris, 1833), p. 295. The Department of the Basses Pyrénées corresponds to the modern Pyrénées-Atlantiques. Elisabeth Allemand Lavigerie was listed in 1837 in a register of musicians; she died in Bayonne on May 4, 1838. Planque, *Agenda musical ou indicateur des amateurs, artistes et commerçants en musique de Paris, de la province et de l'étranger* (Paris, 1837) p. 231; ADPA, Bayonne, deaths, 1826–1841, 620/818.

20. "Lavigerie (Léon-Philippe), Details des services depuis l'entrée en fonctions," undated, in AL-R, A2.216; marriage of Léon Bernard Lavigerie, June 12, 1860, AD Charente Maritime [hereafter ADCM], Rochefort, marriages, 52/134.

21. Marriage of Léon-Philippe Lavigerie and Louise Latrilhe, November 3, 1824, ADPA, Bayonne-Saint Esprit (Landes), 1814–1831, 248/1460; *Almanach royal et national pour l'an 1831* (Paris, 1831), p. 202. Léon-Philippe's father-in-law was listed, like his sister, as a local figure of the arts; Guyot de Fère, *Annuaire des artistes français*, p. 377.

22. Marriage of Pierre Jules Edouard Allemand Lavigerie and Eugénie Cassan, May 6, 1838, AD Aude, Lezignan, 1837–1840, 81/253. Birth of Joseph Victor Lavigerie, February 9, 1839, AD Aude, Narbonne; 29/172. Pierre Jules Edouard was identified in the record of his marriage as "employé aux contributions directes," and in the record of Joseph Victor's birth as "employé des contributions indirectes." Death of Pierre Jules Edouard Allemand Lavigerie, widower of Eugénie Cassan, living in Mende in the Lozère, December 23, 1851; ADCM, Rochefort, deaths, 1851, 184/200.

23. Death of Victor Lavigerie, May 16, 1885, AD Landes, Pouillon, deaths, 1880–1894, 439/595.

24. Emile Daru, "Un grand Landais: S.E. le cardinal Lavigerie (1825–1892)," *Bulletin de la Société de Borda* 50 (1926): 33–39, p. 35. Daru, who was unable in 1926 to establish "the exact family connection existing between Victor and Charles Lavigerie," described Victor Lavigerie as having moved to Pouillon in 1870, and "living as an old bachelor, on a modest pension and the product of a tobacconist's shop that had been conceded to him."

25. Letter of May 16, 1885, from Veuve Dufor in Pouillon to Cardinal Lavigerie, AL-R, A2.128.

26. AM-A, "Dénombrement 1851," Rempart du Midi, unpag.

27. Death of Martial Allemand Lavigerie, August 18, 1856, AM-A, 1E173/83–84.

28. Death of Marie Louise Aimée Philippine Bonne de Raymond Saint-Germain, aged thirty-six, April 9, 1813, ADPA, Bayonne, deaths, 1811–1825, 203/861. The youngest daughter of Bonnite and Martial, Adelaide Théonie, was born on March 8, 1813; ADPA, Bayonne, births, year 12–1813, 754/820. She was sent to be looked after by a wet nurse, the wife of a fisherman, in the village of Urt, a few kilometers to the east of Bayonne, and died there at the age of four months, in July 1813. Death of Adelaide Théonie Lavigerie, July 21, 1813, ADPA, Urt, deaths, 1813–1822, 5/83.

29. Marriage contract of Martial Allemand Lavigerie and Bonnite Saint Germain, ADC, 2E6272.

30. *Loi et ordonnances relatives à la République d'Haïti et aux indemnités stipulées en faveur des anciens colons de Saint-Domingue* (Paris, 1826), pp. [3]–4.

31. *Le télégraphe, gazette officielle* (Port-au-Prince), no. 29 (July 17, 1825). On the consequences of the indemnity for Haiti, see Frédéric Marcelin, *Haïti et l'indemnité française* (Paris,

1897); François Blancpain, *Un siècle de relations financières entre Haïti et la France (1825–1922)* (Paris, 2001), pp. 62–79.

32. Law of April 30, 1826, in *Loi et ordonnances relatives à la République d'Haïti*, p. 5.

33. "Liste des colons propriétaires à Saint-Domingue," meeting of October 15, 1819, in *Droits de souveraineté de la France sur St-Domingue, contrat qui l'établit, violation de ce contrat, principes de compensations invoqués par les colons* (Paris, 1821), p. 53. There is no known colonist by the name of "Lavigeris," and of the eleven instances of the word in Gallica, the online collection of the BNF, as of September 14, 2020, one is in the 1821 memorandum, and all the others are misrecognitions or misspellings of the name of Martial's grandson Cardinal Lavigerie.

34. *Etat détaillé des liquidations opérées par la commission chargée de répartir l'indemnité attribuée aux anciens colons de Saint-Domingue*, 6 vols. (Paris, 1828–1833), and on the documents produced or requested, see Paul Roussier, "Le dépôt des papiers publics des colonies," *Revue d'histoire moderne* 4, no. 22 (1929): 241–262, pp. 251–252.

35. Transcription of the judgment of the "tribunal civil de première instance" of Bayonne at the request of Martial Allemand Lavigerie, ADPA, Bayonne, births, 1826–1837, no. 351, September 7, 1826, 52–53/904.

36. ADPA, Bayonne, births, 1826–1837, September 7, 1826, 52–53/904.

37. *Etat détaillé des liquidations*, vol. 6, claim number 4506, payments numbers 8854 and 8857, pp. 596–597. Bonnite's name was wrongly spelled: "Raymond Saint-Cermain." There were two different settlements, one on January 1, 1832, in favor of Pierre Jules Edouard, Victor Mamert, and Charlotte Ursule (born in Bayonne in 1806, 1808, and 1810), for three-quarters of the cocoa plantation, and one on May 22, 1832, in favor of Adelaide (born in Bayonne in 1803), for one-quarter of the plantation.

38. Letter from Louis Gabriel Latour in Saint-Domingue to Marc-René Lefort Latour in Angoulême, August 8, 1772, ADC, 2E296.

39. *Etat détaillé des liquidations*, vol. 5, claim number 6077, p. 240. Louis Gabriel Lefort Latour had married in Saint-Domingue; his daughter was recognized as the heiress of her maternal grandmother and her father, "former proprietors."

40. Pierre Auguste Henry Lacourade (iii) was born on March 8, 1811, and was the son of Jean Théodore Henry Lacourade (ii) and Marie Françoise Lambert; the witnesses of his birth record were Pierre Auguste Henry Lacourade (ii), "oncle breton," the first cousin of his father—and the old friend of Martial, Pierre, and Jeanne Allemand Lavigerie—and Jean-Baptiste Georgeon, his uncle by marriage. AM-A, 1E44/102–103. Marriage of Pierre Allemand Lavigerie and Adelaide Charlotte Maslin, 12 pluv. 4 (February 1, 1796), ADSa, Sillé-le-Guillaume, 1793–year 10, 58–59/398; marriage of Martial Allemand Lavigerie and Bonnite Saint Germain, AM-A, 1E23/69–70; marriage of Laurent Silvestre Topin and Jeanne Lavigerie, 4 therm. 9 (July 23, 1801), 1E23/82–83. The naming practices of the Henry family were as obscure as those of the Allemand Lavigeries. Jean Théodore Henry (i)—or "Henry l'aîné," who was the purchaser of the seminary and the representative of Martial, Pierre, Etienne, and Joséphine in the matter of the sale of their parents' house—had two brothers, Pierre Auguste Henry (i), born in 1738, and Joseph Frédéric Henry, born in 1741. He had a son, Pierre Auguste Henry (ii), born in 1770. Joseph Frédéric Henry Lacourade, who died in 1790, had a son, Jean Théodore Henry Lacourade (ii), born in 1776, who became the heir of Pierre Auguste Henry (i); Pierre Auguste Henry Lacourade (iii) was the son of Jean Théodore Henry Lacourade (ii). AM-A, St. Jacques,

GG124/120, 187, GG130/173–174, GG131/187, GG134/112; Jézéquel, "Charente," in *Grands notables du premier empire*, p. 29.

41. Pierre Auguste Henry (iii)'s father, Jean Théodore Henry (ii), was the son of Joseph Frédéric Henry and of Marie Joubert, the daughter of Roch Joubert and sister of Pierre-Matthieu Joubert. Marriage of Joseph Frédéric Henry and Marie Joubert, September 8, 1772, AM-A, St. André, GG45/35; baptism of Jean Théodore Henry, St. Jacques, April 16, 1776, GG131/187.

42. Marriage contract of Pierre Auguste Henry Lacourade and Charlotte Ursule Allemand Lavigerie, June 18, 1836, Simeon Mathé-Dumaine, notary, ADC, 2E6622; marriage of Pierre Auguste Henry Lacourade and Charlotte Ursule Allemand Lavigerie, June 22, 1836, AM-A, 1E110/73–74.

43. Marriage contract, June 18, 1836, ADC, 2E6622.

44. Marriage contract, June 18, 1836, ADC, 2E6622.

45. Auguste Lacroix, *Historique de la papeterie d'Angoulême* (Paris, 1863), p. 60. Séchard's disquisition on the scientific history of Chinese, Turkish, and Dutch paper lasts for five pages, in "one of these limpid conversations in which two lovers can say anything to each other"; it was supposed to have taken place at midnight, while the villainous competitor Cointet lurked outside the printing house on the Place du Mûrier, "gazing at the shadows of the wife and husband on the muslin curtains." *Les illusions perdues*, pp. 507, 510.

46. Cour royal de Bordeaux, "Lacourade, C. Laroche-Lacour et autres," January 6, 1829, in Roger, Garnier, and Roger, *Annales universelles de la législation et de la jurisprudence commerciales*, 7 vols. (Paris, 1824–1830), 6:148–151.

47. ADC, état nominatif, La Couronne, 1841, 6M75, Moulin de Lacourade, 21–24/86.

48. ADC, état nominatif, La Couronne, 1846, 6M87, Moulin de Lacourade, 47–51/81; état nominatif, Angoulême, 1846, 37/646; Lacroix, *Historique de la papeterie d'Angoulême*, pp. 78, 81.

49. ADC, état nominatif, Angoulême, 1861, 194/765.

50. Dénombrement de la population, Etat nominatif, Angoulême 1846, ADC, 6M84, 92/646. The summary statistics for women's employment are for the central part of the town, 2–241/646.

51. Smith, *The Wealth of Nations*, p. 103.

52. AM-A, 1E141/2–134; for the brides born in Cap-Haïtien, Ile Maurice, Verona, and Point-à-Pitre, see 1E141/11–12, 19, 115, 127.

53. AM-A, 1E197/2–94.

54. ADC, état nominatif, Angoulême, 1846, 54, 57, 61/646.

55. "Faits divers," *Le XIXe siècle*, no. 3526 (August 25, 1881): [3].

56. Marriage of Pierre Allemand Lavigerie and Adelaide Charlotte Maslin, 12 pluv. 4 (February 1, 1796), ADSa, Sillé-le-Guillaume, 58–59/398; birth of Jules Etienne Scipion Allemand Lavigerie, 4 fruct. 5 (August 21, 1797), ADSa, Sillé-le-Guillaume, births, 1793–year 10, 128–129/274; birth of Camille Alexandre Allemand Lavigerie, 21 frim. 8 (December 12, 1799), ADSa, Le Mans, births, year 8, 59/122.

57. Births of Charlotte Ursule Allemand Lavigerie, October 23, 1810, and Adelaide Théonie Allemand Lavigerie, March 8, 1813, ADPA, Bayonne, births, year 12–1813, 548/820 and 754/820.

58. Abbé Boudet, "Jacques-Pierre Brissot," *Procès-verbaux de la Société archéologique d'Eure-et-Loir*, vol. 14 (Chartres, 1936), 461–467, pp. 465–466.

59. Capitaine Sicard, "Tableau statistique des armées mises sur pied par la France," *Journal des travaux de la société française de statistique universelle* 12 (1842): 207–224, cols. 217, 222.

60. Emile Biais, quoted in "Procès-verbaux, January 9, 1895," *BSAHC*, ser. 6, 5 (1895): xxiii–xxiv.

61. There was a stone bridge over the Traire that Charles built not long after leaving the prison service; he was sued by the commune of Perusses for defective work on the construction of an *abreuvoir* and a *lavoir*, in a case that he eventually won on appeal, on the grounds that the expert witness about the construction had failed to testify under oath. "Travaux publics, experts, serment," August 25, 1849, *Journal du palais: jurisprudence administrative* 11 (1849–1851): 125–126; the bridge is described at http://www.culture.gouv.fr/public/mistral/merimee_fr?ACTION =CHERCHER&FIELD_1=REF&VALUE_1=PA52000011. Charles Silvestre Topin was married on April 15, 1833, to Aglaée Doré, in Brienne-le-Château, about forty kilometers from the prison. His son Louis Silvestre and daughter Louise Marie Antoinette were born there in 1834 and 1835; ADAu, Brienne-le-Château, marriages, 1833–1846, 3–5/227, and births, 1834–1847, 12, 51/299.

62. Louis Silvestre was the witness at his father's second marriage, to Pauline Elisa Mairet, on June 19, 1862; AdP, 10e arr., act 519. Death of Louis Silvestre Topin, March 9, 1870, ADAu, Brienne-le-Château, deaths, 1861–1874, 180/298. Brienne-le-Château was known for a time as Brienne-Napoléon—according to the register of deaths, from December 28, 1849, to December 31, 1879—in honor of Napoléon I's having attended the military school there. ADAu, Brienne-le-Château, deaths, 1847–1860, 52/251, deaths, 1875–1889, 123/399.

63. Henri Silvestre Topin was born in Chaumont on October 2, 1846; AD Haute-Marne, Chaumont, births, 1843, 38–39/52. His service in the army of Versailles is described in his dossier as a recipient of the Légion d'honneur; AN, LEONORE, LH/2613/24.

64. David Todd, *L'identité économique de la France: libre-échange et protectionnisme, 1814–1851* (Paris, 2008), chapters 3 and 8; "Ordonnance du roi relative à l'uniforme des directeurs, inspecteurs, sous-inspecteurs et employés du service active des douanes," June 30–July 6, 1835, in *Jurisprudence générale du royaume en matière civile, commerciale et criminelle, 1835*, ed. Dalloz (Paris, 1835), p. 86.

65. Marriage of Léon-Philippe Lavigerie and Louise Latrilhe, ADPA, Bayonne-Saint Esprit (Landes), November 3, 1824, marriages, 1814–1854, 248/1460.

66. AN, LEONORE, LH/1507/29.

67. Death of Pierre Félix Allemand Lavigerie, July 10, 1882, ADPA, Bayonne, deaths, 1880–1891, 166/806.

68. Marriage of Léon Bernard Lavigerie and Augustine Marie Joséphine Amélie Chesse, June 12, 1860, ADCM, Rochefort, marriages, 52/134. Léon Philippe Allemand Lavigerie lived at Rue de l'Arsenal 4, and the address of the young couple was Rue de l'Arsenal 44; Rochefort, 1854, deaths, 80/236, and Rochefort, 1861, births, 66/157.

69. L. Lavigerie, "Etude sur deux plantes tinctoriales de Taïti," in *Archives de médecine navale*, ed. A. Le Roy de Méricourt, vol. 3 (Paris, 1865), 147–156.

70. Dora Hort, *Tahiti: The Garden of the Pacific* (London, 1891), pp. 141–142, 198, 203, 219, 229.

71. Birth of Léon Louis Adolphe Gabriel Lavigerie, January 17, 1866, ADCM, Rochefort, births, 11/165.

72. Birth of Emile Léon Gabriel Lavigerie, August 22, 1867, AD Allier, Vichy, births, 1863–1871, 162/300.

73. L. Lavigerie, *Guide médicale aux eaux minérales de Vichy* (Paris, 1868).

74. Lavigerie, *Guide médicale*, pp. iii–iv.

75. Lavigerie, *Guide médicale*, pp. iv, vi, 58, 149, 219–224, 239, 244, 248, 284. On the procedures of scientific inquiry, see Lavigerie, "Etude sur deux plantes tinctoriales de Taïti," p. 148; "before even thinking of fixing a colorant matter, it is indispensable to understand its properties; here, as in other sciences, one must go from the simple to the composite, and proceed by induction."

76. Death of Léon Bernard Lavigerie, October 3, 1871, AD Allier, Vichy, deaths, 1863–1882, 2E311 14, 312/751.

77. Hort, *Tahiti: The Garden of the Pacific*, p. 230.

78. Marriage of Paul Marie Emmanuel Pouvreau and Alice Laure Augustine Amélie Lavigerie, October 19, 1881, ADCM, Rochefort, marriages, 96/123.

79. Birth of Henri Marie Léon Pouvreau, July 3, 1884, ADCM, Rochefort, births, 2E311/389*, 107/220; the address was Rue de l'Arsenal 46, a few steps away from where his grandfather and great-grandfather had lived thirty years before.

Chapter Nine. Family Capital

1. Block, *Statistique de la France*, 1:56; Simiand, *Le salaire, l'évolution sociale et la monnaie*, 2:117.

2. See Alain Plessis, "La Révolution et les banques en France: de la Caisse d'escompte à la Banque de France," *Revue économique* 40, no. 6 (1989): 1001–1014; Bertrand Gille, *La banque et le crédit en France de 1815 à 1848* (Paris, 1959). On the transformation in property markets associated with the *biens nationaux*, see Bodinier and Teyssier, *L'événement le plus important de la Révolution*, and for a detailed study of the lasting effects in the east of the Napoleonic Empire, Gabriele B. Clemens, "Vieilles familles et propriété neuve—spéculations sur les biens nationaux dans les départements rhénans," *La Révolution française* 15 (2018), http://journals.openedition.org/lrf/2251.

3. E. v. Böhm-Bawerk, *Capital and Interest, a Critical History of Economical Theory* (1884), trans. W. Smart (London, 1890), p. 55; Turgot, *Mémoires sur le prêt à intérêt et sur le commerce des fers*.

4. The brothers-in-law were witnesses of the registration of the death of their nephew, Jules Etienne Scipion Allemand Lavigerie, on July 23, 1853; ADSa, Le Mans, deaths, 1853–1855, 60/463.

5. See marriage of Camille Alexandre Allemand Lavigerie, ADAu, Ville-sous-la-Ferté, 53–54/289; marriage of Jules Etienne Scipion Allemand Lavigerie, ADSa, Le Mans, 246/338.

6. Death of Pierre Allemand Lavigerie, April 26, 1834, ADSa, Le Mans, deaths, 1833–1834, 461/524.

7. Firmin-Didot, *Annuaire générale du commerce* (1841), pp. 1338–1339.

8. Marriage of Jules Etienne Scipion Allemand Lavigerie and Louise Marguerite Poirier, December 26, 1832, ADSa, Le Mans, marriages, 1831–1832, 246/338.

9. On the envelopes of commerce, see Tariq Ali's study of the jute packaging industry of Bengal, *A Local History of Global Capital: Jute and Peasant Life in the Bengal Delta* (Princeton, NJ, 2018).

10. Firmin-Didot, *Annuaire générale du commerce* (1842), pp. 1299–1300; 1849, pp. 1229–1230; 1850, pp. 1710–1711.

11. "Lavigerie et Demorieux C. Fourché et l'administration des postes," in *Recueil Dalloz Sirey de doctrine de jurisprudence et de législation* (Paris, 1850), pt. 3, p. 66.

12. B. Houreau, "Question des fils de chanvre et de lin," in *Revue du progrès*, 2nd ser., 4 (August 1840): 38–52, pp. 47–50. On the *Revue du progrès*, see Cyrille Ferraton, "Organiser le travail. La *Revue du progrès* de Blanc," in *Quand les socialistes inventaient l'avenir*, ed. Thomas Bouchet et al. (Paris, 2015), 151–157.

13. Chambre de Commerce de Bordeaux, *De l'union douanière de la France avec la Belgique* (Bordeaux, 1845), pp. 108, 157, and see Todd, *L'identité économique de la France*, chapter 14.

14. Firmin-Didot, *Annuaire générale du commerce* (1849), p. 1229; 1852, p. 1710; Scipion Lavigerie, *Arrêté du 26 avril 1849 concernant le jour du marché de la ville du Mans, Signé: l'adjoint, Scipion Lavigerie* (Le Mans, 1850).

15. "M. Fauchille" signed the record of Camille's marriage outside the prison in 1830, "Jean-Baptiste Fauchille" and "B. Fauchille" signed the marriage record of Camille's daughter Marie Louise in Angoulême in 1851, and "Edouard Victor Fauchille" signed the marriage record of Marie Louise's son René, in Paris in 1883. Marriage of Camille Alexandre Allemand Lavigerie and Françoise Méloé Topin, ADAu, Ville-sous-la-Ferté, 53–54/289; marriage contract of Jean Henri Portet and Marie Louise Allemand Lavigerie, ADC, Raynal-Rouby, notary, 2E10262; marriage of Jean Henri Portet and Marie Louise Allemand Lavigerie, AM-A, 1E156/16; marriage of Etienne Henry Marie René Portet and Jeanne Anne Parot, AdP, 1e. arr., act no. 385. On the long history of the Fauchilles, see Paule Danes-Fauchille, *Sayetterie et bourgetterie lilloises ou l'industrie drapière à Lille* (Nanterre, 1991).

16. Births of Silvestre Allemand Lavigerie, June 27, 1831, and of Marie Louise and Françoise Julia Allemand Lavigerie, January 9, 1833, AM-A, 1E93/71, 1E100/4. On the figure of the *commis voyageur*, see Claire Lemercier, "Un litige entre un commis voyageur et sa maison de commerce en 1827," *Entreprises et histoire*, no. 66 (2012): 228–231, and Arnaud Bartolomei, Claire Lemercier, and Silvia Marzagalli, "Les commis voyageurs, acteurs et témoins de la grande transformation," *Entreprises et histoire*, no. 66 (2012): 7–21.

17. Marriage of Jules Etienne Scipion Allemand Lavigerie, ADSa, Le Mans, 246/338; record of the death of (Charlotte) Ursule (Adelaide) Allemand Lavigerie, August 5, 1840, ADC, La Couronne, 1833–1842, 3E120/7, 425/561; Property no. 1315, ADC, Matrice des propriétés bâties et non bâties, 1835–1911, 3 PPROV 16 5, 87/183.

18. *Recueil général des lois, décrets et arrêtés depuis le 24 février*, vol. 1 (Paris, 1848), articles 67 (March 6, slavery), 75 (March 7, *comptoir national*), 77 (March 8, savings banks) and 306 (April 27, abolition of slavery), pp. 17–19, 107. On the short history of the *comptoirs nationaux d'escompte*, established for the benefit of "small commerce," see Alphonse Courtois, *Histoire de la Banque de France et des principales institutions françaises de crédit depuis 1716* (Paris, 1875), pp. 172–179.

19. "Statuts du comptoir national d'escompte de la ville d'Angoulême May 5, 1848," *Bulletin des lois de la République française*, 1848, ser. 10, suppl., part 2 (Paris, 1849), 228–233, p. 228.

20. Quignon, "Notices historiques et anecdotiques," 3:194–199, ADC, J70.

21. "Statuts du comptoir national d'escompte," pp. 230, 232.

22. Birth of Jean Henri Portet, June 3, 1823, ADC Sireuil 1823–1832, 8/198; marriage of Jean Portet and Julie Besson, daughter of Jean Besson, "tailleur de pierre," July 8, 1822, ADC Saint-

Simon 1821–1836, 20/308; birth of Jean Portet, son of Jean Portet, "cultivateur," from the hamlet of Patureau, 24 pluv. 7, ADC Sireuil 1793–1802, 101/170.

23. Marriage contract of Jean Henri Portet and Marie Louise Allemand Lavigerie, February 3, 1851, ADC, 2E10262; marriage of Jean Henri Portet and Marie Louise Allemand Lavigerie, February 4, 1851, AM-A, 1E156/16. Marie Louise was the older of the twin girls born on January 9, 1833. Her sister Françoise Julia died the following day, and their older brother, Silvestre Allemand Lavigerie, died after only a few days of life, in 1831; AM-A, 1E93/71, 1E95/65, 1E100/4, 1E102/4.

24. Death of Jeanne Julie Allemand Lavigerie, May 19, 1838, AM-A, 1E117/34; transcription of agreement of November 13, 1839, in ADC, 4QPROV 1/2932.

25. Adelaide Lavigerie was born in Bayonne on 19 mess. 11 (July 8, 1803); ADPA, 775/875. She signed her name "Adelaide Méloé Lavigerie" in the marriage contract of her sister, Charlotte Ursule, and was identified as "Françoise Méloé Allemand Lavigerie" in the record of her death; in the agreement about the property on the ramparts following her death, she was identified as "Françoise Adelaide Méloé Allemand Lavigerie." Charlotte Ursule signed her name as "Charlotte Ursule" in her marriage contract, and as "Alida Henry-Lacourade, nee Allemand Lavigerie" in the agreement of November 1839; in the record of her death, she was identified as "Ursule Adelaide Allemand Lavigerie." Marriage contract, June 18, 1836, ADC, 2E6622; AM-A, 1E120/26; ADC, La Couronne, 1833–1842, 425/561; transcription of agreement, November 13, 1839, in ADC, 4QPROV 1/2932.

26. The agreement of November 1839, signed following the death of (Françoise) Adelaide, but prior to the death of Charlotte Ursule, provided for the four surviving sisters to give their share of the property of the Rempart du Midi to Charlotte Ursule and Françoise Méloé in equal parts, reserving the right to live in the property until the death of the last surviving sister. The sisters in fact owned thirteen-fifteenths of the property at the time, and their nieces owned one-fifteenth each, by the terms of Jeanne Julie's will. The fifteenth share, which had been left to the late Adelaide, was purchased by the sisters from their brother, Martial Allemand Lavigerie (Adelaide's father); Adelaide's own estate, in a digression from the family propensity for female inheritance, had devolved to her father and her three brothers, the collectors of taxes and duties. Transcription of agreement, November 13, 1839, in ADC, 4QPROV 1/2932.

27. Will of Jeanne Allemand Lavigerie, signed on June 12, 1850, deposited on January 10, 1851, and registered on July 9, 1860, ADC, 2E10292.

28. Marriage contract of Jean Henri Portet and Marie Louise Allemand Lavigerie, February 3, 1851, ADC, 2E10262.

29. Marriage contract, February 3, 1851, ADC, 2E10262.

30. Marriage contract, February 3, 1851, ADC, 2E10262.

31. Succession of Jean Henri Portet, AdP, December 17, 1902, DQ32554.

32. Marriage contract of Charles Gabriel Kiener and Louise Allemand Lavigerie, March 21, 1855, ADC, De Jarnac, notary, 2E14663; marriage of Charles Gabriel Kiener and Louise Allemand Lavigerie, March 22, 1855, AM-A, 1E169/31–32.

33. This is the description by the author, book collector, and customs official Lambert Ferdinand Joseph Van Den Zande, who was the neighbor of the Lavigeries in Marseille; letter of September 28, 1852, from Van Den Zande to François Grille, in Grille, *Miettes littéraires,*

biographiques et morales, 3 vols. (Paris, 1853), 3:63–66, in which he mentions that Louise had become a teacher in Angoulême; "Notice sur Van Den Zande," in *Catalogue de la bibliothèque de feu M. Van Den Zande* (Paris, 1853), pp. v–x.

34. Death of Etienne Marie Kiener, December 27, 1871, AdP, 5e arr., 25/31.

35. Marriage of Charles Gabriel Kiener and Louise Allemand Lavigerie, March 21, 1855, AM- A, 1E169/31–32. On Louis-Napoléon's visit to Angoulême, see F. Laurent, *Voyage de Sa Majesté Napoléon III, empereur des Français, dans les départements de l'est, du centre et du midi de la France* (Paris, 1853), pp. 439–448.

36. Marriage contract of Charles Gabriel Kiener and Louise Allemand Lavigerie, March 21, 1855, ADC, 2E14663.

37. Marriage of Léon Bernard Lavigerie, ADCM, Rochefort, marriages, 52/134.

38. *Notice historique et descriptif du chemin de fer de Montauban à Rodez* (Villefranche, 1859).

39. ADC, état nominatif, La Couronne, 1872, Moulin de Lacourade, 10/85.

40. Death of Martial Allemand Lavigerie, August 18, 1856, 1E173/83–84.

41. Marriage contract of Alexis-Henry-Evariste Brinboeuf-Dulary and Marie Françoise Henry Lacourade, September 25, 1858, ADC, De Jarnac, 2E14677.

42. Marriage of Alexis-Henry-Evariste Brinboeuf-Dulary and Marie Françoise Henry Lacourade, September 29, 1858, AM-A, 1E178/109; marriage contract, September 25, 1858.

43. Marriage contract, September 25, 1858, ADC.

44. Alexis-Henry-Evariste Brinboeuf-Dulary was born in Angoulême on February 11, 1834, and was the son of Alexis-Eugène Brinboeuf-Dulary—who was the son of Henri Brinboeuf-Dulary and Therese (Mimi) Demontis—and Pauline Neuiller-Noguera. AM-A, 1E103/17, 1E43/10–11. His grandfather, Joseph Dulary, lived in Artibonite, Saint-Domingue, and died in Cap-Français; marriage of Henri Brinboeuf-Dulary and Therese Demontis, ADC, Barbezieux-Saint-Hilaire, 1805–1809, 127/273. On the slave trade of the Brinboeuf-Dulary family see TNA, HCA30/304, *Amitié de Nantes*, intercepted mails and papers. On the many legal troubles of the Demontis family, including over the debt for the plantation, see "Houdaigné C. les heritiers Demontis," July 30, 1811, in J.-B. Sirey, *Recueil général des lois: Jurisprudence de la cour de cassation* (Paris, 1811), vol. 11, pt. 1, pp. 345–346, and "Réplique pour le sieur Frichou-Lamorine, contre le sieur Roy d'Angeac, tuteur de la veuve Demontis," in *Annales du barreau Français*, 13 vols., 1822–1847 (Paris, 1841), 11:223–288.

45. Birth of Marie Alexis Robert Brinboeuf-Dulary, January 3, 1863, birth of Louise Marie Germaine Brinboeuf-Dulary, June 18, 1869; death of Alexis-Henry-Evariste Brinboeuf-Dulary, October 11, 1870; AM-A, 1E193/2, 1E211/53, 1E216/178. The family of Alexis-Henry-Evariste were short-lived; his father had died in Angoulême at the age of twenty-five, and his grandfather at the age of forty-one. Death of Henri Brinboeuf-Dulary, December 15, 1830, AM-A, 1E92/126; death of Alexis-Eugène Brinboeuf-Dulary, November 26, 1835, 1E108/116.

46. Marriage of Marie Alexis Robert Brinboeuf-Dulary and Louise Anne Elisa Plantevigne, October 21, 1895, ADC, Marcillac-Lanville 1893–1902, 72/273; marriage of Louise Marie Germaine Brinboeuf-Dulary and Marie Aimée Poute de Puybaudet, May 16, 1889, AD Gironde, Arcachon, 23–24/63.

47. Deaths of Jeanne Allemand Lavigerie, wife of Laurent Silvestre Topin, March 26, 1852, and of Jeanne Henriette Allemand Lavigerie, July 27, 1852, AM-A, 1E160/35, 79; of Joséphine

Allemand Lavigerie, April 29, 1855, ADPA, Bayonne, deaths, 1842–1857, 646/884; of Laurent Silvestre Topin, March 29, 1860, AM-A, 1E185/28; and of Jeanne Allemand Lavigerie, July 3, 1860, 1E185/57.

48. ADC, état nominatif, Angoulême, 1861, 192/765.

49. Marriage of Léon Bernard Lavigerie, ADCM, Rochefort, 52/134.

50. Death of Léon Philippe Allemand Lavigerie, September 15, 1860, AD Maine et Loire, Saumur, deaths, 1856–1860, 273/287; "Etat civil," *L'echo saumurois*, no. 118 (October 2, 1860): unpag., p. [3]. The witnesses were Stanislas Chantoiseau and Jean Bougron.

51. "Discours pour la bénédiction du chemin de fer de Cognac," October 15, 1867, in Cousseau, *Oeuvres*, 3:365–367; http://www.musee-du-papier.fr/projet-memoires-de-la-poudrerie/. On Balzac's stays at the poudrerie, of which his friend Zulma Carraud's husband was the director, see Honoré de Balzac, *Correspondance avec Zulma Carraud*, ed. Marcel Bouteron (Paris, 1951).

52. "Discours pour la bénédiction de la première pierre de l'église de St Ausone," December 4, 1864, "Discours prononcé pour la bénédiction de la première pierre de l'Hôtel de ville," August 15, 1858, in Cousseau, *Oeuvres*, 3:184, 348–349. On Cousseau's friendship with the younger Paul Abadie, see the exchanges of letters in Cousseau, *Oeuvres*, 3:418–432, and with Charles Martial Allemand Lavigerie, the letter of August 12, 1872, pp. 393–394.

53. François Caron, *Histoire économique de la France, XIXe–XXe siècles* (Paris, 1981), pp. 50–64; on entrepreneurs, see Hélène Vérin, *Entrepreneurs, entreprise. Histoire d'une idée* (Paris, 2011).

54. "Abadie, Paul, père," http://elec.enc.sorbonne.fr/architectes/o; "Abadie, Paul," http://elec.enc.sorbonne.fr/architectes/1.

55. "Fête de la Raison," ADC, L144(19).

56. "Un certain luxe grave"; "Discours prononcé pour la bénédiction de la première pierre de l'Hôtel de ville," August 15, 1858, in Cousseau, *Oeuvres*, 3:348–349.

57. Signature of Antoine Laurent, marriage of Albert La Goutte, dit La Feuillade and Antoinette Laurent, May 8, 1764, AM-A, St. Antonin, GG54/46; baptism of Pierre Laurent (Lorant), son of Antoine Laurent, stonemason, and Catherine Piffre, April 10, 1768, St. Martial, GG110/102; birth of Etienne Laurent, son of Pierre Laurent, stonemason, and Anne Varache, December 5, 1811, 1E44/346; marriage of Etienne Laurent, "entrepreneur des travaux publics," and Geneviève Tardieu, November 9, 1835, 1E107/124; birth of Jeanne Marie Laurent, daughter of Etienne Victor Laurent, "entrepreneur," and Geneviève Tardieu, January 20, 1845, IE137/11. On Laurent's role in Abadie's projects, see *Paul Abadie architecte 1812–1884*, pp. 19, 156. Etienne Victor Laurent was present at the stone laying of the church of St. Ausone in 1864, and his fine execution of the cathedral restoration was noted by the bishop in 1869; "Discours sur L'église cathédrale d'Angoulême," January 17, 1869, Procès-verbal, December 4, 1864, in Cousseau, *Oeuvres*, 3:87, 449.

58. See Todd, *Velvet Empire*.

59. Dubourg-Noves, *Histoire d'Angoulême*, p. 225.

60. There was also a small silver effigy of Pius IX. "Discours prononcé pour la bénédiction de la première pierre de l'Hôtel de ville," August 15, 1858, Procès-verbal, December 4, 1864, in Cousseau, *Oeuvres*, 3:350, 447.

61. No! After a thousand years
Proud of our destinies
A mayor in future ages

Presenting the keys of Angoulême

To Napoléon the Thirtieth

Shall say to him: 'Enter, Sire, within our walls.'

Jean-François Eusèbe Castaigne, *Ode lue à la pose de la première pierre de l'hôtel de ville d'Angoulême le 15 août 1858* (Angoulême, 1858), pp. 6, 9, 12.

62. "Oraison funèbre du général de Pontevès et des Français morts devant Sebastopol," in Cousseau, *Oeuvres*, 3:305, 306, 326.

63. Castaigne, *Ode*, p. 11.

64. Deaths of Jean Thibaud in Calcutta, Jean Viand in Fort de France, Louis Mouchère in Bastia, and Noel Merceron in Oran; death of Louis Queille in San Francisco; death of Jean Juzeaud in San Francisco. AM-A, 1E160/143–145. Pierre Hector Juzeaud was born in Angoulême in 1810; his brother André, born in 1808, died in Basse-Terre, Guadeloupe, in 1849. 1E41/60, 1E43/65, 1E154/103–104. The witness of Juzeaud's death was Emmanuel Guiot Desvarennes, a former postmaster in Angoulême, and the grandson of Guillaume Guiot Desvarennes and Françoise Bresdon, who married in Guadeloupe. AM-A, 1E50/132, 1E131/13, 1E198/95.

65. Deaths of Andre Fondrat in Shanghai, Philippe Pingeon in Tejeria, Vera Cruz, and Pierre Huchet in Vera Cruz; AM-A, 1E198/6, 17, 107.

66. Marriage of Georges Henry Lacourade and Jeanne Angelique Adele Daniel de Colhoe, May 16, 1868, AM-A, 1E209/44. His wife was the granddaughter of Adelaide Henriette Robin, daughter of Abraham François Robin and Elizabeth Stubbs, and of Pierre Denis Robin, son of Jean Abraham François Robin and Catherine Henriette Audouin. Marriage of Adelaide Henriette Robin and Pierre Denis Robin, another consanguine union in the fourth degree, July 7, 1813, 1E49/236–237; death of Adelaide Henriette Robin, February 16, 1873, AM-A, 1E226/18. In an indication of the complexity of the Robins' naming practices, Adelaide Henriette was identified in the marriage record as the daughter of Abraham François Robin, and Pierre Denis, who was her first cousin, as the son of Jean Abraham François Robin; the principal witness to the marriage was identified as Abraham François Robin, "paternal uncle of the said spouses." The record of Adelaide's own birth, on February 16, 1793, noted that "the citizen Adelaide Henriette, sister of the child, gave her the name 'Adelaide Henriette.'" Adelaide had two sisters, one called Françoise Angelique Aimée, who was born on November 11, 1782, in Saint-Vincent, and baptized in Angoulême on March 19, 1785; and one called Adelaide Françoise Angelique, who was baptized in Angoulême on July 21, 1788; AM-A, GG46/149, GG68/95.

67. See "Abadie, Paul, père," http://elec.enc.sorbonne.fr/architectes/0. Camille Allemand Lavigerie's house was at plot no. 837 on the Rue de l'Arsenal, and Paul Abadie's at plot no. 854; ADC, Matrice, Angoulême, 1835–1911, 3 PPROV 16 5, 124/183 and 3 PPROV 16 6, 91/211. Martial Allemand Lavigerie's widowed son-in-law, Pierre Auguste Henry Lacourade, was living on the Rue de l'Arsenal with his two children in 1846; ADC, Etat nominatif, 1846, 37/646. The older Abadie also bought a property in St. Jacques de l'Houmeau, from the family of the Henry Lacourade. ADC, Matrice, Angoulême, 1834–1887, 3 PPROV 16 6, 49/211.

68. Marriage of Etienne Henry Marie René Portet and Jeanne Anne Parot, June 18, 1883, AdP, 1e. arr., act no. 385.

69. AdP, état civil reconstitué, birth of Paul Mallard, November 9, 1812, (old) 4e arr., 9/51. The younger Abadie's record as an officer of the Légion d'honneur, LH/1/36, gives only the place of birth. The older Paul Abadie was listed in the census of 1846 as a single man, living on

the Rue d'Austerlitz in Angoulême. ADC, Etat nominatif, 1846, 48/646. He was the father, too, of a daughter born in Angoulême in 1826, whom he recognized in 1857; AM-A, August 4, 1826, 1E78/96, annotation, March 4, 1857. The older Abadie was by then the "inspector of diocesan buildings," in a provincial society in which the designation of *enfant naturel* was apparently indelible—more than half a century after Léonard Robin's plea for the rights of all children—as it was, in the same census of 1846, for "Marguerite," aged forty and a pickle seller, and "Jacques," aged seventy, together with his wife, also aged seventy, "femme Jacques." Marguerite, Rue de Sully, and Jacques, Rue à la Hart, in ADC, Etat nominatif, 1846, 173, 208/646.

70. November 25, 1846, AM-A, 1E141/127–128; marriage contract of Paul Abadie and Maria-Alida Camia, November 25, 1846, ADC, André Saint-Marc, notary, 2E19907. Paul Abadie was married under his legal name, "Paul Mallard," or "Paul Mallard surnommé Abadie," and described as having been born in the fifth arrondissement of Paris in 1812; both of his parents signed the record of his marriage.

71. Louis Tourneur, Maria Alida's guardian, was married in 1832 to Anne Adelaide Robin, daughter of Félix-Michel Robin. They lived at 15, Rempart du Midi; AM-A, July 7, 1832, 1E97/65–66; ADC, état nominatif, Angoulême, 1846, 93/646. On Louis's five-year patent, issued in 1836, for an instrument to be used in teaching cosmography that he described as "uranographique" and "amphéligéographe," see *Bulletin des lois du royaume de France*, 9th ser., 12 (Paris, 1836): 326–327.

72. Statement of Simon Vieilh, "géreur de l'habitation de monsieur Martin Subercasaux," April 16, 1834, ANOM, Sainte-Rose, Guadeloupe, état civil, 14/35, and Sainte-Rose, affranchissements, 8/15. The emancipation was "as prescribed by article 5 of the royal ordinance of July 12, 1832"; this was the administrative ordinance of Louis-Philippe that provided "facilities," or procedures, for persons who wished to emancipate their slaves.

73. Abadie C. Subercaseaux, "Un enfant naturel ne peut etre reconnu par testament olographique, un tel acte n'ayant pas le caractère d'un acte authentique." Judgment of the cour de cassation, March 18, 1862, in *Jurisprudence générale du royaume en matière civile, commerciale et criminelle, cour de cassation*, ed. Dalloz (Paris, 1862), pp. 284–285.

74. François Simon Vieilh, identified as a "rentier," living in La Sauve, Gironde, was one of the signatories of the record of Maria Alida's marriage in 1846; AM-A, 1E141/127–128.

75. Marriage contract of Paul Abadie and Maria-Alida Camia, November 25, 1846, ADC, 2E19907. Jacques Nadaud, the retired engineer, was born in Angoulême in 1774, the son of François Nadaud and Marie Tabourin (Marie Charas), and died there in 1854; AM-A, NDP, GG 14/48, 1E167/104, and see AN, LEONORE, LH/1972/55. Nicolas Veillon or Vellion, the furniture merchant, was the father-in-law of Vincent Mercier, the secretary of the *mairie*, and editor of the revolutionary-era *Journal des maires d'Angoulême*. Marriage of Vincent Mercier and Marie Anne Veillon, March 15, 1832, AM-A, 1E97/23–24; the older Paul Abadie signed the record. Paul Abadie was living at the time with Vincent Mercier, his wife, and his two brothers-in-law. Rue d'Austerlitz, ADC, Etat nominatif, 1846, 47–48/646.

76. "Abadie, Paul," http://elec.enc.sorbonne.fr/architectes/1.

77. Abadie C. Subercaseaux, March 18, 1862, in Dalloz, *Jurisprudence générale*, pp. 284–288. The additional sum of forty thousand francs was secured by Maria Alida's father against contestation "by my heirs, for whatever motive." "Déclaration et acceptation d'emploi par Madame Abadie," August 20, 1870, AN, Panhard, notary, Paris, MC/ET/XIV/906.

78. Alfred Van den Brule, *Hubert Rohault de Fleury, secrétaire général du Voeu national: le Sacré-Coeur de Montmartre* (Paris, 1928), pp. 343, 366; and see "Le Sacré-Coeur de Montmartre," in *Paul Abadie architecte 1812–1884*, pp. 129–145.

79. Death of Paul Abadie, August 3, 1884, AD Yvelines, Chatou, 1882–1884, 223–224/271; *Le Figaro*, August 3, 1884. Paul's mother, Louise Joséphine Mallard, had died in Chatou sixteen years before, at the age of eighty; October 1, 1868, Chatou, 1867–1872, 273/553.

80. "Inventaire apres le decès de M. Abadie," August 29, 1884, AN, Georges Magne, notary, Paris, MC/ET/LXXVI/1047.

81. Death of Alida Camia, widow of Paul Abadie, June 24, 1903. AD Hauts de Seine, Neuilly-sur-Seine, deaths, 1903, 142/297. Her death was declared by her son, who lived in Rue St. Honoré in Paris, and a local official, "in the absence of any other relative or neighbor." The names of her late mother and father were said to be "unknown to the declarants."

82. Table des successions et absences, Le Mans, Jules Etienne Scipion Allemand Lavigerie, died July 22, 1853, succession declared January 19, 1854; ADSa, 1853–1854, no. 21, 2/200. Death of Jules Etienne Scipion Allemand Lavigerie, banker, in his domicile on the Place des Halles, ADSa, Le Mans, deaths, 1853–1855, 60/463.

83. Marie Louise Allemand, her infant son, her mother, and her husband were among the (relatively fortunate) victims of a terrible railway accident in September 1853, when the night train from Paris to Bordeaux collided with a goods train coming from Angoulême to Paris, killing six employees of the railway, and wounding more than thirty passengers; in one report, she was described as "Mme Porté from Angoulême," who broke her collarbone, and in another as "a young mother who was weeping and crying out for her child." The infant was found safe and sound, "playing in the sand underneath the wreckage"; "Mme Lavigerie" and Jean Henri Portet, "greffier du tribunal de commerce d'Angoulême," were slightly injured, and the family were able to continue their journey. *Journal des débats*, September 21, 1853, *La presse*, September 24, 1853, *Le pays*, September 25, 1853. Birth of Etienne Henry Marie René Portet, February 2, 1852, AM-A 1E158/16; the family were living on the Rempart du Midi at the time, and Martial Allemand Lavigerie, aged eighty-four and described as the child's grandfather—he was in fact his great-great-uncle—was a witness. Their second child, known as Valentine, was born in Le Mans. Birth of Julie Marie Valentine Portet, October 21, 1856, ADSa, Le Mans, births, 185–1857, 275/532. The family were now living at 33, Place des Halles, and Camille Alexandre, the grandfather, was a witness. Death of Adelaide Charlotte Maslin, aged eighty, widow of Pierre Allemand Lavigerie, living Place des Halles, January 18, 1858; ADSa, Le Mans, deaths, 1856–1858, 437–438/647. René Maslin, Adelaide Charlotte's brother, who had been a constant feature of the recorded lives of the Allemand Lavigeries in different departments of France—he signed the records of Adelaide Charlotte's wedding, in 1796, of Scipion's birth in 1797 and Camille's birth in 1799, of Camille's marriage (in the Aube) in 1831 and Scipion's marriage in 1832, of Pierre's death in 1833, of Marie Louise's wedding (in Angoulême) in 1851, and of Scipion's death in 1853—died two days later, on January 20, 1858; ADSa, Le Mans, deaths, 1856–1858, 438/647.

84. Firmin-Didot, *Annuaire générale du commerce* (1854), p. 1934.

85. Firmin-Didot, *Annuaire générale du commerce* (1855), pp. 1934, 1936; *Annuaire générale du commerce* (1856), p. 1937, at which point Lemarchand had a new associate in the mercantile business, "Lemarchand et Ravase, successeurs de Lavigerie et Demorieux, *fabr. de sacs.*"

86. *De l'union douanière de la France avec la Belgique*, pp. 93, 153–154.

87. Firmin-Didot, *Annuaire générale du commerce* (1852), pp. 1710–1711; on *L'Obéissante*, see Pierre Souvestre, *Histoire de l'automobile* (Paris, 1907). Ernest Bollée, the father of the "father" of the first French automobile, Amédée Bollée, appears in the 1852 *Annuaire* as a founder of church bells, in the village of Ste-Croix-Lez-Le-Mans; p. 1712.

88. *Le Canal des deux mers: journal du commerce universel* 1, no. 38 (September 21, 1872): 655. *Bulletin du canal interocéanique* 2, no. 42 (May 15, 1881): 371. On the banking expansion of the Second Empire, see Alain Plessis, *The Rise and Fall of the Second Empire, 1852–1871*, trans. Jonathan Mandelbaum (Cambridge, 1979), pp. 71–83.

89. Cour de cassation, no. 8824, November 15, 1875, in *Journal des tribunaux de commerce* 25 (1876): 382–387; "Banquiers, comptes," in Dalloz, *Jurisprudence générale du royaume en matière civile, commerciale et criminelle* (1876), pp. 212–214; summarized in "Change," *Journal du droit international privé* 4 (1877): 143.

90. Oral testimony of "M. Portet-Lavigerie, banquier au Mans," Ministère de l'Agriculture, *Enquête agricole: enquêtes départementales. IIe série, 2e circonscription, Orne, Mayenne, Sarthe, Maine-et-Loire* (Paris, 1867), p. 206.

91. Report of December 29, 1871, in Archives de la Banque de France [hereafter ABF], Secrétariat du Conseil Général, MA.AO.15.B.5, Correspondance et propositions, 1862–1959. Portet-Lavigerie was an administrator and member of the local council on discount rates from 1856 to 1872, when he was promoted to the position of Censeur.

92. F. Legeay, *Le guide du voyageur au Mans* (Le Mans, 1879), p. 85; the house, built by the merchant Le Prince around 1760, was adjacent to the prison; it is now the office of the Crédit Lyonnais, in the Place de la République.

93. Félix Talvande was himself the son of the director of the Nantes office of the Banque de France; marriage of Félix Talvande and Marguerite Adelaide Louise Froger de Mauny, June 8, 1862, ADSa, marriages, 1861–1862, 260–261/518; *Journal officiel de la République française*, September 16, 1879, p. 9176.

94. The estate was listed later as the property of "M. et Mme. Henri Portet-Lavigerie." *Annuaire des châteaux et des départements, 1897–1898: 40,000 noms & adresses de tous les propriétaires des châteaux de France, manoirs, castels, villas, etc. etc.* (Paris, 1897), p. 688.

95. Death of Louise Mélanie Allemand Lavigerie, October 10, 1865, ADSa, deaths, Saint-Pavace, 1853–1882, 182/275.

96. Death of Marie Théonie Topin, September 3, 1868, ADSa, deaths, Saint-Pavace, 1853–1882, 193/275; Marie Théonie Topin was born in Angoulême on 23 vend. 10 (October 15, 1801), AM-A, 1E25/12.

97. Eugène Adolphe Disdéri, "M. Boittelle et son fils Olivier," http://www.musee-orsay.fr /fr/collections/catalogue-des-oeuvres/notice.html?nnumid=69612.

98. Marriage of Olivier Boittelle and Julie Marie Valentine Portet, May 30, 1876, ADSa, Le Mans, marriages, 1875–1876, 316–317/446.

99. *Annuaire des châteaux et des départements* (1899–1900), p. 95; *Touring Club de France: revue mensuelle* 15 (1905): 396; *Le XIXe siècle: journal quotidien politique et littéraire*, February 10, 1890, p. 2 (on the award of a prize for a red and white bull).

100. René Portet, *Des latins juniens; De la condition juridique des étrangers en France et de la naturalisation* (Evreux, 1882).

101. Marriage of Etienne Henry Marie René Portet and Jeanne Anne Parot, June 18, 1883, AdP, 1e. arr., act no. 385. In the vertiginous mobility that was characteristic of the legal administration, René Portet began his judicial career in 1885 as a *juge suppléant* in Clermont (Oise) and then in Le Havre (Seine et Oise); he became a substitute prosecutor in Bernay (Eure) in 1886, and in Libourne (Gironde) in 1887, followed by Angoulême in 1889; he was named prosecutor in Marmande (Lot et Garonne) in 1891, in Apt (Vaucluse) in April 1894, and in Clermont, again, in August 1894. René Portet died in Clermont in December 1894, at the age of forty-two. *Journal officiel de la République française*, 1885–1894; AD Oise, Clermont, 1894–1896, December 21, 1894, 121/417.

102. Reports of July 7, 1872, June 9, 1874, October 10, 1876, May 24, 1877, and November 3, 1880, in ABF, Inspection Générale, PA.K.6.B.3.

103. Report of June 22–July 7, 1881, in ABF, Inspection Générale, PA.K.6.B.3 "Liquidateurs judiciaires de la Banque Talvande et Cie et consorts c. Porte-Lavigerie et consorts, cass. civ.," March 19, 1894, in *Journal des faillites et des liquidations judiciaires françaises et étrangères: revue de jurisprudence* 13 (1894): 193–214, pp. 194, 199.

104. Death of Camille Alexandre Allemand Lavigerie, November 7, 1881, ADSa, deaths, 1880–1881, 400/436.

105. The agreement between Talvande and Henri Portet-Lavigerie was finalized on November 15–16, 1881; "Liquidateurs judiciaires," p. 199 and "Soc. *Talvande et Cie.*," in *Revue des sociétés* (1894): 223–232, p. 229.

106. *Le gaulois*, no. 2395 (March 20, 1889): p. 3.

107. Reports of October 6–13, 1884, July 4, 1885, June 24, 1887, and June 1, 1889, in ABF, Inspection Générale, PA.K.6.B.3.

108. *Le gaulois*, no. 2395 (March 20, 1889): 3; "Liquidateurs judiciaires," p. 194.

109. "Liquidateurs judiciaires," pp. 194, 196.

110. "Liquidateurs judiciaires," pp. 197–201.

111. "Soc. *Talvande et Cie.*," p. 231.

112. Vente par licitation, in *Le petit ardennais*, no. 3078 (July 13, 1889): [4]. *Rapport du préfet, conseil général de la Sarthe* (Le Mans, 1889), p. 405. Henri retired only in December 1890 from his position as "Censeur" of the Banque de France, responsible for the "surveillance" of local banks; the director of the Le Mans branch noted that in 1888 he had been present at three out of twelve meetings of the bank's council. Letters of January 1, 1889, from the director to the governor, and of December 25, 1890, from Henri Portet to the governor, in ABF, Secrétariat du Conseil Général, MA.AO.15.B.5.

113. Propriétaires des villas, in *L'avenir d'Arcachon*, no. 544 (May 7, 1887): unpag.

114. The address on Rue Gluck is given in the marriage record of René Portet, in 1883, and in the notice of the liquidation of the slate factory in 1889; Jean Henri Portet died on June 18, 1902, in his house on the Rue Mogador. AdP, 9e. arr., act no. 898.

115. *Annuaire des châteaux et des départements* (1887–1888), p. 688; (1899), pp. 96, 1196; *Le petit ardennais*, July 13, 1889, p. [4].

116. *Le Figaro*, July 26, 1891. Louis Napoléon was the younger brother of "Napoléon IV," the pretender at the time to the French throne.

117. Death of Jérôme Lerouge, November 20, 1901, AD Val de Marne, deaths, 1901, Le Kremlin-Bicêtre, 153/179; death of Jean Henri Portet, AdP, 9e. arr., act no. 898.

118. "Succession de M. Jean Henri Portet," AdP, DQ7/32554, December 17, 1902.

119. One of the early aspirations of modern social science was to turn away from the "unique" to the "regular," as in Simiand's manifesto of 1902: "to eliminate the individual in order to study the social." François Simiand, "Méthode historique et science sociale," *Revue de synthèse historique* 5 (1902), no. 1, 1–22, and no. 2, 129–157, pp. 17, 21, 154–155. The "singular number, considered individually"—the price of a donkey, "the number of abandoned children in a parish"—was for C.-E. Labrousse, following Simiand, no more than the detritus of a "profane" history. Labrousse, *La crise de l'économie française*, p. 122.

120. Hoffman and Rosenthal, "New Work in French Economic History," p. 449. On the similarly implausible dualism of financialization, measured in the published statistics of banking, as the condition for economic development, versus the multiplicity of financial instruments in small towns, see Hoffman, Postel-Vinay, and Rosenthal, *Dark Matter Credit*. On formal and informal social networks as "an important source of credit, insurance, information, advice, and other economic and non-economic benefits," see Abhijit Banerjee, Arun G. Chandrasekhar, Esther Duflo, and Matthew O. Jackson, "Changes in Social Network Structure in Response to Exposure to Formal Credit Markets" (MIT, 2019).

121. Block, *Statistique de la France*, 1:55; Olivier Marchand and Claude Thélot, *Deux siècles de travail en France: population active et structure sociale, durée et productivité du travail* (INSEE, Paris, 1991), table 3t, p. 175; and on some of the difficulties of long-term estimates, Alain Blum, "Bibliographie critique," *Population* 4 (1991): 1009–1011.

122. Block, *Statistique de la France*, 1:55; Marchand and Thélot, *Deux siècles de travail en France*, p. 175.

123. It was peasants, in an older economic and social history, who were imprisoned in institutions, including their own desires for security, and impeded by transaction costs, including those perpetrated by soldiers and tax collectors. Hoffman and Rosenthal, "New Work in French Economic History," pp. 446, 449–450. On the difficulties of accounting for services in French national accounts, see François Fourquet, *Histoire des services collectifs dans la comptabilité nationale* (Paris, 1976).

124. World Bank, "Employment in services (% of total employment)," https://data .worldbank.org/indicator/sl.srv.empl.zs, accessed on August 30, 2019. The statistics used show an increase in service-sector employment—"defined as persons of working age who were engaged in any activity . . . for pay or profit . . . [in] wholesale and retail trade and restaurants and hotels; transport, storage, and communications; financing, insurance, real estate, and business services; and community, social, and personal services"—from around 35 percent in 1991 to around 49 percent in 2018. With the addition of even a modest estimate of unpaid household labor, the majority of everyone in the world can be seen as working in services. The most recent value given for France was 77 percent, for Germany 72 percent, for Sweden 80 percent, for the United Kingdom 81 percent, and for the United States 79 percent.

125. Carl E. Schorske, *Thinking with History: Explorations in the Passage to Modernism* (Princeton, NJ: Princeton University Press, 1998).

126. See Daudin, *Commerce et prosperité*; Todd, *Velvet Empire*.

Chapter Ten. Charles Martial and Louise

1. Baunard, *Lavigerie*, 1:vi.

2. There was a "monster capon stuffed with truffles" and "Champagne Moët," at one small dinner; "at dessert, I permitted myself to read to my little verses ("versiculets"), *faits en omnibus*. All the guests laughed at them, and M. l'abbé was the first to laugh." Letters of September 28, 1852, and January 6, 1853, from Joseph Van Den Zande to François Grille, in Grille, *Miettes littéraires, biographiques et morales*, 3:63, 95.

3. Baunard, *Lavigerie*, 1:vi, ix, xii, 19; Louis Baunard, *Le doute et ses victimes dans le siècle présent* (Paris, 1866); *La lanterne* 2940 (May 9, 1885), 5098 (April 6, 1891).

4. Claude Thiébaut, "Les manifestations pour le centenaire de la naissance du cardinal Lavigerie (Rome, Alger, Tunis, et Paris, 1925)," *Revue historique* 291, no. 2 (April–June, 1994), 361–399.

5. Léon Lavigerie, *De l'hépatite et des abcès du foie (cand. Léon Lavigerie)* (Paris, 1866); Scipion Lavigerie, *Arrêté du 26 avril 1849*.

6. *La presse*, June 19, 1902, p. 2.

7. "M. Robin était paperassier"; J. Dupin, "Notices sur Abraham François Robin et Léonard Robin," p. 829.

8. Letter of January 16, 1873, from Clara Collet, Rue des Quatres Frères, Paris 18, in "Brébion Collet (veuve)," AN, F/12/2757; this was the letter marked in pencil, "très malheureuse."

9. Colleville, *Le cardinal Lavigerie*, p. 203.

10. Société des Missionnaires d'Afrique, Accueil, at http://www.mafrome-archivio.org /index_fr.html.

11. See "Rome: In the footsteps of Lavigerie," http://peresblancs.org/lavigerie_vie_romegb .htm, and "Le cardinal Charles-Martial Lavigerie: Photos Archives," http://peresblancs.org /photoslavigeriegb.htm.

12. Emile Zola, *La fortune des Rougon* (1871) (Paris, 1981), pp. 28, 99, 101; *L'assommoir* (1876) (Paris, 1978), pp. 159, 415, 434.

13. Colleville, *Le cardinal Lavigerie*, pp. 8, 18–19; Baunard, *Lavigerie*, 1:v, xi.

14. Registres matricules des sous-officiers et hommes de troupe de l'infanterie de ligne (1802–1815), and see above, chapter 6; Hort, *Tahiti: The Garden of the Pacific*, p. 241; "M. Biais communique une aquarelle représentant M. Ferrand, archiviste de la Charente, peinte d'apres un portrait de M. Paille." *BSAHC*, ser. 8, 1 (1910): xliv.

15. Sculpture by Gustave Crauk of Cardinal Lavigerie, *Le Figaro*, February 11, 1898; Thiébaut, "Les manifestations pour le centenaire de la naissance du cardinal Lavigerie," pp. 370–374, 396.

16. *La lanterne* 4140 (August 21, 1888): 3; https://commons.wikimedia.org/wiki/File:Bonnat _-_Le_cardinal_Charles_Lavigerie,_archev%C3%AAque_d%27Alger_(1825-1892).jpg. The painter, Léon Bonnat, was born in Bayonne in 1833; his parents lived on the Rue Pont-Majour, like Martial Allemand Lavigerie, Frederic Bastiat, and the revolutionary Pierre Jean Audouin. June 22, 1833, ADPA, births, 1826–1837, 577/904.

17. Jules Cambon, "Souvenirs sur le cardinal Lavigerie," *Revue des deux mondes* 32 (1926): 277–289, p. 279.

18. Baunard, *Lavigerie*, 1:4.

19. Baunard, *Lavigerie*, 1:4. On the Ecole des Carmes, or the Ecole ecclésiastique des hautes études, see Brigitte Waché, "L'École des Carmes, 1845–1875," *Revue d'histoire de l'Église de France* 81, no. 206 (1995): 237–253.

20. Baunard, *Lavigerie*, 1:24–26; Denys Affre, archbishop of Paris and founder of the Ecole des Carmes, by whom Charles Martial was ordained as subdeacon, was killed by a stray bullet on June 25, 1848, while trying to intercede on the barricades of the Faubourg-Saint-Antoine; see Louis Girard, *Nouvelle histoire de Paris: la deuxième République et le Second Empire, 1848–1870* (Paris, 1981), pp. 34–43.

21. C. Allemand-Lavigerie, *De Hegesippo: disquisitionem proponebat Facultati litterarum Parisiensi* (Paris, 1850), pp. 2–12, 43–44.

22. Allemand-Lavigerie, *De Hegesippo*, p. 29.

23. Ch. Allemand-Lavigerie, *Essai historique sur l'école chrétienne d'Edesse: thèse presentée à la faculté des lettres de Paris* (Paris, 1850), pp. 7–8, 16.

24. Allemand-Lavigerie, *Essai historique sur l'école chrétienne d' Edesse*, pp. 12, 14, 41, 68–69, 71, 112, 117.

25. Baunard, *Lavigerie*, 1:43.

26. J. R. [Ferdinand Van Den Zande], *Stances à Monsieur l'Abbé L.**** (Paris, 1852) and *Epître à Monsieur l'abbé L**** (Paris, 1852).

27. *Oedipe à Colone, de Sophocle. Edition nouvelle, par l'abbé Lavigerie* (Paris, 1850); *M. T. Ciceronis ad M. filium de Officiis libri tres. Edition classique, revue, expurgée et annotée par M. l'abbé Lavigerie* (Paris, 1853).

28. P. Clausolles and Charles-Martial Allemand Lavigerie, *Cours complet d'histoire et de géographie de M. l'abbé Lavigerie et de M. P. Clausolles: histoire de France élémentaire. Depuis les Gaulois jusqu'à nos jours* (Lyon, 1853); http://ife.ens-lyon.fr/ife. The denunciation for rationalism was in the Gallican journal *L'observateur catholique*, exponent of the cause of an autonomous church in France; Baunard, *Lavigerie*, 1:48.

29. Baunard, *Lavigerie*, 1:52.

30. "Discours prononcé par M. le contre-amiral Aimé Mathieu, gouverneur de la Martinique, à l'ouverture de la session coloniale de 1847, le 17 juin" (Martinique, 1847), available on the website of the Bibliothèque Schoelcher; http://www.patrimoines-martinique.org/ark:/35569/a011416928915afUxwv. Mathieu was president of the Oeuvre des Ecoles d'Orient from 1858 to 1861; his predecessor was Pierre François Joseph Bosquet, marshal of France, who was a particularly brutal general in Algeria before commanding a division of "zouaves," or Kabylian soldiers in the French army, at the Battle of the Alma in the Crimean War. See "Directeurs généraux et présidents successifs de l'Oeuvre d'Orient," *Oeuvre d'Orient*, no. 552 (1966): 350.

31. Baunard, *Lavigerie*, 1:55–57.

32. Oeuvre des Ecoles d'Orient, *Souscription recueillie en faveur des chrétiens de Syrie: rapport de M. l'abbé Lavigerie* (Paris, 1861), p. 2. On the civil war in Lebanon, see Leila Tarazi Fawaz, *An Occasion for War: Civil Conflict in Lebanon and Damascus in 1860* (Berkeley, 1994.) On the history of humanitarian intervention, see Davide Rodogno, *Against Massacre: Humanitarian Interventions in the Ottoman Empire, 1815–1914* (Princeton, NJ, 2011), and Gary J. Bass, *Freedom's Battle: The Origins of Humanitarian Intervention* (New York, 2008).

33. *Souscription recueillie*, pp. 1, 9; and see Bernard Heyberger, "La France et la protection des chrétiens maronites: généalogie d'une représentation," *Relations internationales*, no. 173 (2018): 13–30.

34. *Souscription recueillie*, p. 66, and on the geographical origins of the donations, pp. 10–11. The estimate of the number of villages and churches destroyed was from the *Bulletin* of the Oeuvre, quoted in Baunard, *Lavigerie*, 1:61.

35. Death of Laurent Silvestre Topin, March 29, 1850, AM-A, 1E185/28, death of Jeanne Allemand Lavigerie, July 3, 1860, 1E185/57.

36. *Souscription recueillie*, p. 18.

37. AD Maine et Loire, Saumur, deaths, 1856–1860, September 15, 1860, 273/287.

38. Baunard, *Lavigerie*, 1:64.

39. *Souscription recueillie*, pp. 18–19; *Indicateur marseillais* (Marseille, 1860), pp. 98–99.

40. *Souscription recueillie*, pp. 30, 33. The 350 children, "among whom there were a multitude of orphans," were described by the French orientalist historian Baptistin Poujoulat, who was in Lebanon at the time; Baptistin Poujoulat, *La vérité sur la Syrie et l'expédition française* (Paris, 1861), pp. 297–300.

41. This was the scene depicted in the Flemish orientalist Huysmans's painting of 1861, *Mon salut d'amitié et de respect à tous ceux qui vous parleront de moi*, which depicts the emir saving Christian women and children, against a background of fire, smoke, scimitars, and the French flag, and of which the title was taken from one of the chroniclers of Charles Martial's own journey. *Souscription recueillie*, pp. 41, 50–52; Poujoulat, *La vérité sur la Syrie*, p. 445; https://en .wikipedia.org/wiki/Emir_Abdelkader#/media/File:Jean-Baptiste_Huysmans_1.jpg. On the episode involving 'Abd al-Qādir, see Leila Fawaz, "Amīr 'abd al-Qādir and the Damascus 'Incident' in 1860," in *Études sur les villes du Proche- Orient XVIe–XIXe siècles: hommage à André Raymond*, ed. Brigitte Marino (Damascus, 2001), available at http://books.openedition.org /ifpo/3351.

42. Baunard, *Lavigerie*, 1:89.

43. Decision of Napoléon III, quoted in a letter of July 7, 1860, from the minister of foreign affairs, Thouvenel, to the minister of the navy; "Humanity demands a swift intervention and urgent dispositions," Thouvenel wrote the previous day, in a letter to the French ambassador in Constantinople; letters of July 6, 1860, and July 7, 1860, in Ministère des affaires étrangères, *Documents diplomatiques, 1860* (Paris, 1861), pp. 196, 197.

44. On the silk merchant and manufacturer Fortuné Portalis, who was the president of Charles Martial's local committee, and whose silk factory in "Pteter" (Btater) provided shelter for Christian refugees, see *Souscription recueillie*, pp. 32–34.

45. *Souscription recueillie*, pp. 48, 56–57, 62, 71–78.

46. Charles Martial "devoted himself with as great zeal as success" to raising the relief required following the news of the "massacres of Syria," and his "conduct" in the "desolate territories of Lebanon" did "honor to our country." *Le constitutionnel*, 46th year, no. 44 (February 13, 1861): [3].

47. *Le constitutionnel*, no. 240 (August 28, 1861): [1].

48. See "Rome: In the footsteps of Lavigerie," http://peresblancs.org/lavigerie_vie_romegb .htm, and "Le cardinal Charles-Martial Lavigerie: Photos Archives," http://peresblancs.org /photoslavigeriegb.htm; Baunard, *Lavigerie*, 1:101.

49. V. de Maumigny, *Les voix de Rome: impressions et souvenirs de 1862* (Paris, 1863), pp. xvii–xviii.

50. Decree of March 5, 1863, in *Collection complète des lois, décrets, ordonnances, réglements, et avis du conseil d'état*, vol. 63 (Paris, 1863), p. 213.

51. On the controversy over the miter, see Bernard Berthod, "Retrouver la foi par la beauté: réalité et utopie du mouvement néogothique dans l'Europe du XIXe siècle," *Revue de l'histoire des religions*, no. 227 (2010): 75–92. On the burial of Bastiat, see Pierre Ronce, *Frédéric Bastiat: sa vie, son oeuvre* (Paris, 1905), pp. 266–267.

52. On the economic history of the region, and the expansion that followed the German annexation of Alsace in 1870, see Louis Laffitte, "L'évolution économique de la Lorraine," *Annales de géographie* 21, no. 120 (1912): 393–417. On the dispiriting environment of Nancy thirty years earlier, see Stendhal, *Lucien Leuwen* (1837) (Paris, 2002), pt. 1.

53. "The bishop was delighted" by this (unusual) occasion, Baunard wrote, and by the "ardent and passionate performance of these young actors, into whom the souls of Electra, Orestes, Aegisthus, and Clytemnestra had migrated." Baunard, *Lavigerie*, 1:139.

54. The stole was associated with the diocese of Toul, of which Charles Martial was also bishop. Authorization of March 16, 1865, in Abbé Pierre-Etienne Guillaume, *Le surhuméral: prérogative séculaire des seuls évêques de Toul, chez les Latins, en raison de l'antiquité de leur église* (Nancy, 1865), pp. 5–6.

55. AL-R, Casier A2–280.

56. *Relation des fêtes qui ont eu lieu à Nancy les 14, 15, 16 et 17 juillet 1866* (Nancy, 1866), pp. 83–84, 117, 134. The theme of velvet was everywhere; young workers in blue velvet hats, the prince in black velvet, the deep red velvet of the draperies and the green velvet banners fringed with gold of the municipalities, bouquets wrapped in red velvet for the empress and in green velvet for the prince; even in the empress's bedroom there was a portrait of "a personality dressed in red velvet"; pp. 96–97, 100, 119, 128, 141, 168.

57. *Relation des fêtes*, pp. 133–134.

58. Baunard cites a letter of November 17, 1866, from the governor of Algeria to Charles Martial, offering him the position, and his response on November 19; he left Nancy in April 1867. Baunard, *Lavigerie*, 1:149–150, 156. The appointment was reported late in December 1866; *La presse*, December 31, 1866, p. [2].

59. Letters of October 31, November 6, November 23, and December 22, 1867, from Charles Martial in Algiers to the "Administration des Cultes" in Paris; AN, F/19/7595, dossier 15. His predecessor had abandoned the palace, he wrote, and "after some days of struggle," he had been forced to do the same; he used the palace only for "official receptions," "his secretariat," and as a "pied à terre." Charles Martial conveyed a sense of being imprisoned in an enclosed space, "under the African sky," and without a garden "where the bishop can take the exercise that is necessary to him"; "a bishop, in particular," cannot "go out for a walk in the streets and the squares."

60. *Annales de la propagation de la foi* 40 (Lyon, 1868): 485–486; Baunard, *Lavigerie*, 1:266–269.

61. Baunard, *Lavigerie*, 2:672.

62. Bertrand Taithe, "La famine de 1866–1868: anatomie d'une catastrophe et construction médiatique d'un événement," *Revue d'histoire du XIXe siècle*, no. 41 (2010): 113–127, p. 119.

63. *Les orphelins arabes d'Alger, leur passé, leur avenir, leur adoption en France et en Belgique: lettre de Monseigneur d'archevêque d'Alger* (Paris, 1870), p. 6.

64. *L'illustration, journal universel*, no. 1299 (January 18, 1868); see https://www.gettyimages .com/detail/news-photo/starvation-inalgeria-in-1868-orphans-are-taken-in-by-chruch-news -photo/89866327?adppopup=true. Charles Martial evoked the famine, a few months later, in his continuing exchanges with the administration in Paris over his effort to get a walled garden; "the wall is essential for us because of the scarcity that is returning, and fills the streets with Arab vagabonds of the worst sort." Letter of December 19, 1868, in AN, F/19/7595, dossier 15.

65. *Recueil de lettres publiées par Mgr l'archevêque d'Alger, délégué apostolique du Sahara et du Soudan, sur les oeuvres et missions africaines* (Paris, 1869), pp. 29, 65; Baunard, *Lavigerie*, 1:211.

66. *Recueil de lettres*, pp. 5, 91.

67. Baunard, *Lavigerie*, 1:279–280, quoting a letter to an unnamed friend, and pp. 462–463.

68. The article was reproduced as a long footnote in *Les orphelins arabes d'Alger*, in the self-referential way that was so characteristic, by then, of Charles Martial's public writing. *Recueil de lettres*, p. 65; *L'univers*, no. 989 (January 19, 1870): [2], reproduced in *Les orphelins arabes d'Alger* as footnote 1, pp. 2–4. The "two new Christians," as in Angoulême so many years before, were given "two symbolic wax tapers."

69. "Lettre pastorale pour la prise de possession du diocèse d'Alger," May 5, 1867, in *Recueil de lettres*, 7–25, pp. 9, 13.

70. Peter Brown, "A World Winking with Messages," *New York Review of Books*, December 20, 2018, 52–54, p. 52.

71. Quoted in Peter Brown, *Through the Eye of a Needle: Wealth, the Fall of Rome, and the Making of Christianity in the West, 350–550 AD* (Princeton, NJ, 2012), p. 452. On the nuns, who were from Oloron in the Pyrénées, see Baunard, *Lavigerie*, 1:385–386.

72. *Recueil de lettres*, p. 9.

73. On François Elie Roudaire in Algeria in the 1870s, see Philipp Nicolas Lehmann, "Changing Climates: Deserts, Desiccation, and the Rise of Climate Engineering, 1870–1950" (PhD diss., Harvard University, 2014); on the trans-Saharan railway, see T. W. Roberts, "The Trans-Saharan Railway and the Politics of Imperial Expansion, 1890–1900," *Journal of Imperial and Commonwealth History* 43 (2015): 438–462.

74. *Recueil de lettres*, pp. 14, 15, 21.

75. On the "frères armés," see Baunard, *Lavigerie*, 2:663–666; Colleville, *Le cardinal Lavigerie*, pp. 178–179, 212–213.

76. Colleville, *Le cardinal Lavigerie*, p. 8.

77. *La lanterne* 5098 (April 6, 1891).

78. Eugène Etienne, born in Oran in 1844, and the leader of the colonial party, quoted in Charles-Robert Ageron, "Gambetta et la reprise de l'expansion coloniale," *Revue française d'histoire d'outre-mer* 59, no. 215 (1972): 165–204, pp. 165–166. Jules Ferry, the exponent of secular education as well as colonial policy, was prime minister in 1880–1881 and 1883–1885.

79. Paul Deschanel, *Gambetta* (Paris, 1919), p. 261.

80. Undated letter, quoted in Baunard, *Lavigerie*, 1:150–151. On the conflict between Charles Martial and the governor-general of Algeria over conversion, see Marcel Emerit, "Le problème de la conversion des musulmans d'Algérie sous le Second Empire: le conflit entre MacMahon et Lavigerie," *Revue historique* 223 (1960): 63–84.

81. *Souscription recueillie*, p. 88.

82. Letter of May 10, 1869, in *Recueil de lettres*, pp. 89–90, 93.

83. This was an account by the English traveler Lady Herbert; Lady Herbert, "The Arab Christian Villages in Algeria," reprinted in *Littell's Living Age*, no. 1693 (November 25, 1876): 500–504.

84. *La justice* 256 (September 27, 1880).

85. "Confection d'un Cardinal," *Le rappel* 4454 (May 21, 1882).

86. "Gazette du jour," *La justice* 858 (May 22, 1882), "Mamamouchi," *La justice* 859 (May 23, 1882).

87. Letter of August 12, 1872, in Cousseau, *Oeuvres*, p. 393–394.

88. This was in 1875, and Baunard also places Charles Martial in Lacourade for his holidays in 1873; Baunard, *Lavigerie*, 1:413, 494. Louise Lavigerie Kiener, whom Baunard refers to throughout as "Keiner," is otherwise almost invisible in the biography.

89. Death of Charles Gabriel Kiener, July 10, 1875, ADC, La Couronne, 1873–1877, 2E120/14, 205/394. The registrar added a personal note: Gabriel "died in a house that he had occupied for only a few days."

90. Charles Martial had gone to Paris after the baptism ceremony; he was in Lyon the following month, and in Marseille in July. *La presse*, February 1, 1870; *Le gaulois* 590 (February 15, 1870); *L'univers* 1172 (July 24, 1870).

91. ADC, état nominatif, La Couronne, 1876, Lacourade (Village, Usine), 57–60/93. AD Val de Marne, Le Kremlin-Bicêtre, January 31, 1898, 17/172.

92. Letter dated "Dimanche," from Louise to Charles Martial, AL-R, A2/147. "The Hôtel du Louvre is no longer habitable, since the department stores have absorbed most of it," she wrote of the building that was at the center of the property speculation in Zola's novel of commerce, *Au bonheur des dames*, and the venue of a particularly inauspicious marriage banquet in *Pot-bouille*.

93. Letters dated "November 5" and September 15, 1882, from Louise to Charles Martial, AL-R, A2/148, A2/150.

94. Letter dated "Nay, December 5," from Louise to Charles Martial, AL-R, A2/146.

95. Letter dated "Lacourade, July 8 [1883]," from Louise to Charles Martial, AL-R, A2/154.

96. Letter dated "Lacourade, February 28," from Louise to Charles Martial, AL-R, A2/157.

97. Letter dated "Lacourade, May 28 [1883]," from Louise to Charles Martial, AL-R, A2/153. René and Jeanne Anne Parot were married in Paris on June 18, 1883. AdP, 1e. arr., act no. 385.

98. Pastoral letter of May 1867, in *Recueil de lettres*, pp. 8, 11.

99. *Documents sur la fondation de l'Oeuvre antiesclavagiste, par S. Em. le cardinal Lavigerie* (Saint-Cloud, 1889), pp. 388, 566.

100. There was a "diocesan architect" in Nancy, when Charles Martial was bishop: a former prison architect like Charles Martial's great-uncle, Silvestre Topin, and a minor figure, in 1866, in the festivities of the empress Eugénie. On Charles-François Chatelain, see the *Répertoire des architectes diocésains du XIXe siècle*, http://elec.enc.sorbonne.fr/architectes/.

101. Colleville, *Le cardinal Lavigerie*, p. 1.

102. Letters of October 31 and November 6, 1867, and September 16, and December 19, 1868, from Charles Martial in Algiers to the Administration des Cultes in Paris; AN, F/19/7595. Charles Martial had already formed a distinctive view of the society in which he had settled:

"We are living, here, in a country where everything is judged hierarchically and in a military fashion, and an archbishop necessarily loses all his authority and all his prestige when he is seen as living in worse accommodation than a lieutenant in the Arab Bureau" (letter of October 31, 1867).

103. Félix-Augustin Leclerc de Pulligny, *Six semaines en Algérie: notes de voyage d'un membre du Congrès scientifique tenu à Alger (avril 1881)* (Paris, 1884), pp. 159–163.

104. Letter of October 31, 1867; AN, F/19/7595.

105. Baunard, *Lavigerie*, 1:379–381, 404, 462.

106. Daniel E. Coslett, "(Re)Creating a Christian Image Abroad: The Catholic Cathedrals of Protectorate-Era Tunis," in *Sacred Precincts: The Religious Architecture of Non-Muslim Communities across the Islamic World*, ed. Gharipour Mohammad (Leiden, 2014), 353–375, pp. 356–362.

107. Message of the archbishop of Paris, January 18, 1872, in *Oeuvre du voeu national au Sacré-Coeur de Jésus* (Paris, 1872), pp. 42, 44; http://www.sacre-coeur-montmartre.com/francais/histoire-et-visite/article/histoire. Charles Martial sent a personal contribution of one thousand francs; see Coslett, "(Re)Creating a Christian Image Abroad," p. 368n61. On the "mosquée Abadie," see *L'église du Sacré-Coeur à Montmartre: sera-t-elle de notre style national, ou sera-t-elle d'un style etranger? Par un comité d'archéologues* (Paris, 1875), pp. 11, 12, 18, 44.

108. Charles Martial was by then the apostolic administrator. Baunard, *Lavigerie*, 2:158, 166, 172, 209.

109. Victor Guérin, *La France catholique en Tunisie, à Malte et en Tripolitaine* (Tours, 1892), pp. 48–53. It was Charles Martial's own estimate that the cathedral was built in eighty-two days; see Coslett, "(Re)Creating a Christian Image Abroad," p. 358. The occasion for Charles Martial's celebration of Queen Victoria—"bless England for having conserved its social virtues"—was her having escaped assassination at Windsor railway station. *L'univers*, no. 5270 (April 15, 1882): [2].

110. Jacques Legoff, *Saint Louis* (Paris, 1996), pp. 295–297.

111. In the first year, 250 signed up; the most prominent was the legitimist pretender to the French throne, the Comte de Chambord, grandson of Charles X, who left an additional one hundred thousand livres when he died in 1883. Baunard, *Lavigerie*, 2:236–237, 245–246.

112. *Recueil de lettres*, p. 8; *De l'utilité d'une mission archéologique permanente à Carthage, par l'archevêque d'Alger* (Algiers, 1881).

113. The past continued to exist, in Freud's description, much as the same ground bore "the Church of Santa Maria Sopra Minerva and the old temple over which it was built." Sigmund Freud, *Civilization and Its Discontents*, trans. Joan Riviere (New York, 1958), p. 9. The guide *Rome: In the Footsteps of Lavigerie*, by the late Father Jacques Casier, recounts that Charles Martial, in August 1872, and on the occasion of the name day of Saint Augustine, was "staying in Rome in the Hotel Minerva, Piazza della Minerva 69, a good hotel with three hundred beds. Meals for 6, 22, and 27 lire. The nineteenth-century guide says it caters for ecclesiastics." http://peresblancs.org/lavigerie_vie_romegb.htm.

114. The earlier act of vandalism that Charles Martial described was the removal of part of the wall of the already-dilapidated twelfth-century church of Saint Anne of Jerusalem, to provide stones for the construction of an Ottoman barracks (on the site of the former palace of Pontius Pilate); the restored church was then administered by the "White Fathers." *Sainte Anne de Jérusalem*

et Sainte Anne d'Auray, lettre à Mgr l'évêque de Vannes par l'archevêque d'Alger (Saint-Cloud, 1879), p. 74. The cathedral was consecrated in May 1890, and is now a concert venue, the "Acropolium." The nonprovisional cathedral in Tunis was the subject of an architectural competition, and was constructed under the direction of a diocesan architect from Smyrna in the "Romano-Byzantine" style, on the site of an old Christian cemetery. See the description on the Halimede architecture website, http://halimede.huma-num.fr/node/1154, and Coslett, "(Re)Creating a Christian Image Abroad," p. 365.

115. Letter of July 11, 1884, from Louise in Lacourade to Charles Martial, AL-R, A2/159. On the Cathedral of Saint-Front, see *Paul Abadie architecte 1812–1884*, pp. 87–101.

116. Letter of July 11, 1884, from Louise in Lacourade to Charles Martial, AL-R, A2/159.

117. Session of September 7, 1905, in *Bulletin de la Société historique et archéologique du Périgord* 32 (1905): 374; *Annuaire du tout Sud-Ouest illustré* (Paris, 1906), p. 1231; and see http://elec.enc.sorbonne.fr/architectes/305?q=Lambert.

118. *La justice* 4703 (November 29, 1892).

119. *La lanterne* 3448 (September 29, 1886), 4140 (August 21, 1888).

120. Baunard, *Lavigerie*, 1:452.

121. *La lanterne* 2940 (May 9, 1885).

122. *La justice* 2443 (September 22, 1886).

123. Georges Picot, *Le cardinal Lavigerie et ses oeuvres dans le bassin de la Méditerranée et en Afrique* (Paris, 1889), pp. 1, 8.

124. Picot, *Le cardinal Lavigerie*, p. 14.

125. *La lanterne* 3448 (September 29, 1886).

126. Baunard, *Lavigerie*, 1:319.

127. "Extrait de la lettre de son éminence le cardinal Lavigerie à M. Keller, sur le Sahara et le Soudan," in *Allocution prononcée le 21 septembre 1890 par son éminence le cardinal Lavigerie* (Paris, 1890), 91–100, pp. 95–96.

128. *La justice* 4703 (November 29, 1892).

129. *Journal officiel de la République française* 264 (September 9, 1889); *Tunis journal* 624 (August 15–17, 1889), 640 (October 1, 1889).

130. *La lanterne* 2940 (May 9, 1885).

131. *La lanterne* 2940 (May 9, 1885), 5700 (November 28, 1892).

132. Grussenmeyer, *Documents biographiques*, 2:305–308.

133. Grussenmeyer, *Documents biographiques*, 2:292–315.

134. Cambon, "Souvenirs sur le cardinal Lavigerie," p. 288.

135. Grussenmeyer, *Documents biographiques*, 2:301.

136. Letter of April 15, 1869, in *Recueil de lettres*, p. 68; *L'armée et la mission de la France en Afrique: discours prononcé dans le cathédrale d'Alger par Mgr. l'archevêque d'Alger* (Algiers, 1875), p. 63.

137. *L'esclavage africain: conférence faite dans l'église de Saint-Sulpice à Paris par le cardinal Lavigerie* (Paris, 1888), pp. 5–6; *Documents sur la fondation*, p. 50.

138. *Documents sur la fondation*, p. 49; Baunard, *Lavigerie*, 2:444–447.

139. "Discours prononcé par son éminence le cardinal Lavigerie," July 31, 1888, in *Documents sur la fondation*, pp. 83–117; *Times* 32451 (July 30, 1888), 32453 (August 1, 1888).

140. *Documents sur la fondation*, pp. 430, 623.

141. *Documents sur la fondation*, pp. 427–428, 566.

142. *Documents sur la fondation*, pp. 86, 161, 296–297..

143. *Documents sur la fondation*, pp. 289, 308–309.

144. Taithe, "La famine de 1866–1868," pp. 122, 125.

145. *Documents sur la fondation*, p. 86.

146. Baunard, *Lavigerie*, 2:444.

147. Colleville, *Le cardinal Lavigerie*, p. 203.

148. Letter of November 20, 1889, to Charles Martial from General Count Dampierre, AL-R, D1/920. The *Première messe en Kabylie* by Horace Vernet, painted in 1854, depicted a mass celebrated in eastern Algeria during the military campaign of 1853.

149. The message was to Cardinal Manning: "Hand to the Antislavery Society my order on Paris for 50,000 francs (£1,975)." *Times*, no. 32547 (November 11, 1888), no. 32536 (November 6, 1788).

150. *Documents sur la fondation*, pp. xl, xli, 165, 170, 687.

151. Letter of August 30, 1890, to Charles Martial from the widow of the explorer Paul Soleillet, AL-R, D1/923. Soleillet was the author of a project for the trans-Saharan railway published in 1881, and the associate of Arthur Rimbaud in African arms deals; he died in Aden in 1886. *Les voyages et découvertes de Paul Soleillet dans le Sahara et dans le Soudan en vue d'un projet d'un chemin de fer transsaharien*, ed. Jules Gros (Paris, 1881); Henri Dehérain, "La carrière africaine d'Arthur Rimbaud," *Revue de l'histoire des colonies françaises* 4 (1916): 419–450.

152. Letter of February 2, 1889, to Charles Martial from Charles de Montferrand, AL-R, D1/874. Montferrand was listed in 1894 as the "administrator" of a commercial bank, the Banque nationale de Haïti, with its principal office in Port-au-Prince, and a capital of ten million francs. Advertisement in Ottomar Haupt, *Traité des opérations de banque contenant les usages commerciaux*, 8th ed. (Paris, 1894), unpag. On the history of the bank, see Frédéric Marcelin, *La Banque nationale d' Haïti; une page d'histoire* (Paris, 1890); Blancpain, *Un siècle de relations financières entre Haïti et la France*, pp. 91–110.

153. Ministère des affaires etrangeres, *Conférence internationale de Bruxelles: 18 novembre 1889–2 juillet 1890, protocoles et acte finale* (Paris, 1891); W. R. Bisschop, "International Leagues," in British Institute of International and Comparative Law, *Problems of the War*, 3 vols. (Cambridge, 1915–1917), 2:117–133.

154. On the proposed conference of Luzerne, canceled by Charles Martial at the last moment because of the French elections, and the eventual Paris conference, see Baunard, *Lavigerie*, 2:496–509, 544–550.

155. *Conférence internationale de Bruxelles*, pp. 12, 16, 30; Alfred Le Ghait, "The Anti-Slavery Conference," *North American Review* 154, no. 424 (March 1892): 287–296, p. 288.

156. *La lanterne* 5700 (November 28, 1892).

157. *La lanterne* 5098 (April 6, 1891).

158. Cambon, "Souvenirs sur le cardinal Lavigerie," p. 286; François Furet, *La Révolution de Turgot à Jules Ferry, 1770–1870* (Paris, 1988).

159. *Times*, no. 32507 (October 3, 1888).

160. On "mahométisme," "islamisme," and "fanaticisme," see *Recueil de lettres*, pp. 10–17, 76–90.

161. The Muslim faith, Charles Martial wrote in 1879, "provides a sort of satisfaction to the deepest needs of the human heart, to religious needs, by the component of truth that it retains,

and at the same time it opens all the barriers to the passions, it legitimizes all the disorders of the senses, it deifies brutal force"; it "can die only of its own force." Report of Msgr. Lavigerie to the Oeuvre de la propagation de la foi, in *Oeuvre de Saint Augustin et de Sainte Monique* 29 (January 1879): 370; quoted in Grussenmeyer, *Documents biographiques*, 1:539.

162. Baunard, *Lavigerie*, 2:423, 532. On the new media in North Africa in Charles Martial's period, see Arthur Asseraf, *Electric News in Colonial Algeria* (Oxford, 2019), and especially the introduction and chapter 1, about the news of the Tunisian invasion in the Place du Gouvernement in Algiers, where Charles Martial lived in the early, constraining days of his life in Africa.

163. Baunard, *Lavigerie*, 2:627–628.

164. *La lanterne* 5700 (November 28, 1892).

165. Grussenmeyer, *Documents biographiques*, 2:349.

166. Letter of January 3, 1874, to Monseigneur de Rodez, quoted in Baunard, *Lavigerie*, 1:422.

167. *Relation des fêtes qui ont eu lieu à Nancy*, pp. 82–83. The "prince imperial" was described as holding his mother by the hand, and wearing a "black velvet suit, with red silk stockings."

168. This was in relation to the plebiscite on constitutional reform of May 1870, soon transcended by the Franco-Prussian War. *Le constitutionnel* 128 (May 8, 1870).

169. *Annales de l'Assemblée nationale* 4 (1871), session of July 12, 1871, pp. 7–8, and on the liberal-conservative party, "La semaine politique," in *La revue politique et littéraire*, no. 53 (July–December 1871): 1245–1247, p. 1246.

170. Charles Martial's election statement is quoted in Daru, "Un grand Landais," pp. 37–38; and see J. Tournier, *Le cardinal Lavigerie et son action politique (1863–1892)* (Paris, 1913).

171. *Annales de l'Assemblée nationale*, session of July 12, 1871, p. 7; F. Laudet, "Le cardinal Lavigerie et la Gascogne," *Revue de Gascogne*, n.s., 21 (1926): 5–21.

172. Tournier, *Le cardinal Lavigerie et son action politique*, pp. 36–40. On the press in colonial Algeria, see Asseraf, *Electric News*.

173. Letter of February 13, 1891, to Charles Martial from Claire Boissart de Lagrave, née Dereix, AL-R, D1/927.

174. On Leo XIII and France, see Mgr de T'Serclaes, *Le pape Léon XIII: sa vie, son action religieuse, politique et sociale*, 3 vols. (Paris, 1894–1906), 2:310–509; Baunard, *Lavigerie*, 2:557–567.

175. Xavier de Montclos, *Le Toast d'Alger: documents 1890–1891* (Paris, 1966); Baunard, *Lavigerie*, 2:564.

176. Baunard, *Lavigerie*, 2:563–567.

177. *Au milieu des sollicitudes*, February 16, 1892, http://w2.vatican.va/content/leo-xiii/en/encyclicals/documents/hf_l-xiii_enc_16021892_au-milieu-des-sollicitudes.html; Tournier, *Le cardinal Lavigerie et son action politique*, pp. 390–401.

178. Copy of an undated letter and letter of September 1, 1890, from Charles Martial to Jean-Baptiste Etchevery, AL-R, D8/21, 23.

179. Félix Klein, "La mort et les funérailles du cardinal Lavigerie," *La semaine des familles* 51 (March 18, 1893): 810–813 and 52 (March 25, 1893): 820–822; Baunard, *Lavigerie*, 2:674–678, and http://peresblancs.org/lavigerie_deces1892gb.htm.

180. Klein, "La mort et les funérailles du cardinal Lavigerie," p. 813; A. Joseph Rance-Bourrey, *Les obsèques du cardinal Lavigerie (Alger, Tunis, Carthage): journal d'un témoin* (Paris, 1893).

181. Will of Charles Martial, AL-R, D-20-1; the 145,000 francs that Louise had in Tunis in 1906 are mentioned in a letter of September 12, 1906, from Mme. Byasson, AL-R, D20/137.

182. Louis Lavigerie, "L'héritage du cardinal Lavigerie: Le Diamant," in *Les temps nouveaux: supplément littéraire* 4, no. 47 (undated): 486–488, p. 487.

183. "Faire Part," in AL-R, A2–216. The family members mentioned, in addition to Louise and Léon's widow, with her son, son-in-law, and two grandchildren, were Charles Martial's first and second cousins, at different removes: all descendants of Françoise Ferrand and Etienne Allemand, the couple in the marriage contract of 1764. There was his first cousin, who was the widow of Brinboeuf-Dulary, the merchant from the family of slave traders; her son, an army officer, her daughter and her son-in-law, also an army officer; her brother, who had married the great-granddaughter of Elizabeth Stubbs and Abraham François Robin, the absconding slave owners of the 1780s; and Berthe Topin, whom Louise described as "that unhappy Berthe."

184. Will of Charles Martial, AL-R, D-20-1.

185. Note of February 27, 1907, AL-R, D20/6(2); Lavigerie, "L'héritage du cardinal Lavigerie," p. 487. AL-R, D20/6(2); Lavigerie, "L'héritage du cardinal Lavigerie," p. 487.

186. Sculpture by Gustave Crauk of Cardinal Lavigerie, *Le Figaro*, February 11, 1898.

187. *Le Figaro*, July 23, 1901.

188. http://peresblancs.org/lavigerie_alger2.htm, Photos Archives, 1882–1892, 1890 à Biskra, "Photo prise par sa soeur, Vve Kiener"; http://peresblancs.org/archives/2Cardinal_90Biskra2 .jpg.

189. http://peresblancs.org/lavigerie_deces1892.htm; http://peresblancs.org/archives /cardinal_deces11.jpg.

190. Lavigerie, "L'héritage du cardinal Lavigerie," p. 487.

191. Birth of Marie Amanda Dominica Jeanne Suberbie, daughter of Jean Clotaire Suberbie, controller of indirect taxes, November 6, 1867, ADPA, Pau, Naissances, 1863–1872, 473/1078; marriage of Jeanne Suberbie and Jean Marcel Byasson, AdP, June 2, 1891, 16e. arr., act no. 366. Jean-Henri-Marcel Byasson was born in Paris in 1866, and served in the navy—on a ship called the *Sfax*, after the town in Tunisia, the scene of a violent bombardment by the French in 1881— until 1894, when he joined the colonial administration of Madagascar. He was an administrator in Ivongo and then in Farafangana; he was known for "experience, tact and administrative zeal." "Nécrologie," in *Journal officiel de Madagascar et dépendances*, no. 852 (November 11, 1903): 10235–10236. He died at sea, on his way home to Bénéjacq for a six months' leave. *Journal officiel de Madagascar*, no. 824 (August 5, 1903): 9812.

192. Death of Madame Louise Allemand-Lavigerie, August 21, 1906, ADPA, Bénéjacq, deaths, 1902–1908, 26/48.

193. Letters of January 3, 1906, and June 23, 1906, from Louise to Charles Martial's executor, AL-R, D20/133, 134. "I am a little tired and preoccupied with household work," she wrote in January, but "the enteritis from which I have been suffering for so long is calming down a little."

194. Letter of September 12, 1906, from Mme. Byasson, AL-R, D20/137. Julie Byasson was by the terms of Louise's will her "universal heir," and, like her brother, Louise determined that in the event of dispute over the estate, which was left in equal parts to Louis Lavigerie and the two children of his late sister, the property would revert to Julie. In respect of the "clothing and silver that came from the cardinal," Julie could keep whatever she wanted; she, too, was to be

"absolutely free and mistress" in her choice. She was directed to be "*alone* in going through the wardrobes, drawers, and papers." Julie was herself in great need, she wrote, with "three boys to be prepared for the struggle of life. This is going to be difficult for Catholics, in light of present times."

195. Letter of September 21, 1906, from Mme. Byasson, AL-R, D20/141. All Louise's papers had been left to her, she had written four days before, after receiving a letter from Louis Lavigerie, "so that they would not pass to him, and I could destroy them, for the most part." Copy of a letter of September 12, 1906, from Louis Lavigerie to Mme. Byasson, letter of September 17, 1906, from Mme. Byasson, AL-R, D20/138, 148. Louis Lavigerie was living at the time on the Rue Lepic in the eighteenth arrondissement of Paris, in the shadow, like his cousins, the granddaughters of Françoise Ferrand, of the new Sacré-Cœur.

Chapter Eleven. The End of the Story

1. Letter of June 26, 1836, from Balzac and reply of June 28, 1836, in Balzac, *Correspondance avec Zulma Carraud*, pp. 224–227.

2. Emile Zola, "Le sens du réel," in *Le roman expérimental*, 5th ed. (Paris, 1881), p. 206.

3. The critic Lousteau, in Paris, instructs Lucien Chardon de Rubempre in how to endorse, successively, the "substantial" and "incisive" novels of Diderot and Sterne, the "literature of ideas," as against the "literature of images," in the form of the excessively accessible and overly "dramatized" "modern novel" of Walter Scott; and the nineteenth-century literature of images, filled with passion and style, as against the "positivism" of the eighteenth-century "literature of ideas," "cold and mathematical," calling "everything into question." Balzac, *Les illusions perdues*, pp. 362, 378–379.

4. On the "exact study of facts and things," see Emile Zola, "Les réalistes du salon," in *Oeuvres critiques*, p. 86, and on naturalism in history and the novel, "Le naturalisme au théâtre," in Zola, *Théâtre* (*Oeuvres completes*, vol. 31) (Paris, 1906), p. 293. On the "positivism of art," see Emile Zola, *Le ventre de Paris*, p. [212], and on Diderot as a positivist, "Le naturalisme," in *Oeuvres critiques*, p. 520.

5. Emile Zola, *L'Oeuvre*, p. 192; *Mes haines*, in *Oeuvres critiques*, p. 54.

6. Emile Zola, *Mes haines*, in *Oeuvres critiques*, p. 55.

7. Emile Zola, *Le Docteur Pascal*.

INDEX